# A RUSSIAN JEW OF BLOOMSBURY

# A RUSSIAN JEW OF BLOOMSBURY

THE LIFE AND TIMES OF

## SAMUEL KOTELIANSKY

GALYA DIMENT

McGILL-QUEEN'S UNIVERSITY PRESS

Montreal & Kingston · London · Ithaca

ISBN 978-0-7735-3899-3

Legal deposit fourth quarter 2011
Bibliothèque nationale du Québec

Printed in United States on acid-free paper that is 100% ancient forest free,
processed chlorine free

McGill-Queen's University Press acknowledges the support of the Canada
Council for the Arts for our publishing program. We also acknowledge the
financial support of the Government of Canada through the Canada Book
Fund for our publishing activities.


Library and Archives Canada Cataloguing in Publication

Diment, Galya
A Russian Jew of Bloomsbury : the life and times
of Samuel Koteliansky / Galya Diment.

Includes bibliographical references and index.
ISBN 978-0-7735-3899-3

1. Koteliansky, S. S. (Samuel Solomonovitch), 1880-1955.
2. Translators–Great Britain–Biography. 3. Bloomsbury
group–Biography. I. Title.

PR478.B46D56 2011        418'.02092        C2011-903137-X

Designed and typeset by studio oneonone in Minion 10.3/14

Frontispiece: Kot in his study in the 1940s. Behind him, on the wall, is a portrait of
Mansfield, while on the mantle is a painting by Lady Glenavy (see 1.14). (CSA.)

To my father, Shleime Itzkhak Diment, and to the memory of his father, Mordekhai Diment, a Pale of Settlement rabbi

To my mother-in-law, Zdenka Bienenstock Grunbaum, a hidden child of the Holocaust, whose entire family perished at Auschwitz

# CONTENTS

# ACKNOWLEDGMENTS

This book would have not been possible without all the help and encouragement I received while I worked on it for almost ten years. My greatest debt is to two people: Catherine Stoye, who is in charge of Koteliansky's estate, and George Zytaruk, a prominent Lawrence scholar whose 1970 *The Quest for Rananim: D.H. Lawrence's Letters to S.S. Koteliansky* was also published by McGill-Queen's University Press. Catherine Stoye, granddaughter of H.G. Wells and daughter of Marjorie Wells, Koteliansky's extraordinary friend and confidante, shared with me her own memories of Koteliańsky, or "Koto," as she called him as a child, and gave me permission to quote from Koteliansky's letters and other materials related to him. In addition, she and her husband John kindly tolerated my presence in their house in Oxford for several summer weekends two years in a row, while I was going through the boxes in her private Koteliansky archive.

George Zytaruk, who at one time had planned to write his own biography of Koteliansky, generously shared with me all the materials he had accumulated. His archives contain interviews with people no longer alive by the time I started my book, as well as copies of pictures and letters which are still not in any archive. George also became my first expert reader of the manuscript, and his comments and encouragement were priceless. His *Quest for Rananim* continues to be a valuable source of Lawrence's letters to Koteliansky, even though it has been superceded by the eight-volume Cambridge edition of Lawrence letters. I found his volume more convenient and expedient to use for my purposes, which is reflected in my endnotes (the CUP edition pages are given there as well but in parentheses). I am also enormously thankful to George Zytaruk's daughter, Dr Maria Zytaruk, for her initiative and assistance, and to his wife JoAnn for all her help and support, as well as for willingly becoming herself one of my first readers and proofreaders.

In London, my heartfelt thanks go to Luke Gertler, who invited me to his house and provided copies of Koteliansky's letters to his father, Mark Gertler, as well as gave me permission to quote from his father's unpublished letters; to Nina (Salaman) Wedderburn, whom I interviewed several times and who sent me the originals of Koteliansky's letters to her parents, Esther and Myer Salaman, as well as photographs and her mother's books; to Nadia Slow, whose parents were friends with Grisha and Sonia Farbman as well as with Fanny Stepniak, and who has become my very dear friend and gracious host when I visit London; to Andrei Rogatchevski, who published a rare article on Koteliansky and has been very helpful and supportive of my efforts; to Katya Rogachevskaya, curator of Russian Collections at the British Library, who assisted me in my research there and was great lunch company; to Gertler's biographer, Sarah MacDougall, who was kind enough to meet with me and was always available for additional questions and assistance by email, both at the outset of this project and toward its end; to Ivor Powell, who allowed me to copy letters from Koteliansky to his aunt, Dilys Powell; to Barbara Sullivan, who volunteered to send me pictures of Kot she found among the papers of her late husband, Navin Sullivan, the son of J.W.N. Sullivan; to my friend and fellow Nabokovian Jenefer Coates, who gave me great suggestions as well as fed me homemade dinners; and to Seth Graham, another friend and former colleague, who now teaches at the University College, London, and helped with practical matters.

In Montreal, my book was greatly assisted by the enthusiastic cooperation of the families of Koteliansky's niece, Pauline Smith, and of his brother, Moishel Koteliansky. I owe special gratitude to Jackie Freedman, Pauline Smith's daughter, who is the keeper of the family's archive from where so many of Koteliansky's letters came into my book. I spent many hours in Jackie's kitchen looking at all the memorabilia and talking to her and her younger sister, Sharon Smith. Their brother, Marvin Smith, sent me his mother's pictures. Sonny Surkes, a grandson of Moishel, shared his family archive with me, and he and his wife Cheryl made copies of numerous photographs they had of the family, including some very rare ones. They also arranged for me to meet Judith Adamson, a professor of English at Dawson College, who edited the letters of Leonard Woolf to Trekkie Ritchie Parsons and whose insights on Leonard Woolf were very useful to me. I am further grateful to the Surkes and Freedman families for recommending Janie Respitz Ben-Shach as a translator of the Yiddish materials kept at the Hebrew University of Jerusalem. She did a superb job with rather difficult texts. Last but not least, my good friends Dana Dragunoiu and Andrew Wallace, who now both teach at Carleton University, were most gracious hosts during the time I stayed with them in Montreal.

My research in Ostropol was greatly facilitated by Petro Vlasenko, who was born and raised in Starokonstantinov. He met my husband and me in Kiev and arranged our car trip to to Ostropol, as well as our accommodations in Starokon-stantinov. Our driver, Viktor Vintskovsky, who lives in Starokonstantinov, turned out to be a wonderful guide as well. My information about Anatoly Polonsky, the only remaining Jew in Ostropol, came largely from Dean Echenberg, another descendant of the Ostropol clan living in Monreal, to whom I am very grateful. We spent several days with Anatoly and his wife Katya, eating, drinking, and talk-ing. It is because of Anatoly's efforts that many gravestones from the vandalized Jewish cemeteries in Ostropol have been saved and are now stored in his garden.

I would also like to thank Martin Packman, whose grandmother was Kotelian-sky's first cousin, for sharing the family lore with me; Natalie Wexler, who al-lowed me to use her unpublished interview with her uncle, Harry Wexler; Paul Wexler, who gave me information about his trip to Ostropol, as well as some of the pictures he took; my University of Washington colleagues Barbara Henry and Naomi Sokoloff for helping me with Yiddish and Hebrew; as well as very competent and helpful staff at numerous archives that I visited or contacted, and in particular that of the Manuscript Collections and Archives at the British Library, and Harry Ransom Humanities Research Center at The University of Texas at Austin, places where I spent many days doing my research. I am also very grateful to Trevor James Bond, Interim Head of Manuscripts, Archives, and Special Collections at the Washington State University, who opened the collec-tion for me during the weekend to accommodate me while I was in Pullman.

My research and travel were made possible through grants from the Ameri-can Philosophical Society (Franklin Research Grant, 2003); Memorial Founda-tion for Jewish Culture (2004); and *Modern Language Quarterly* (Library Research Grant, 2005). I would also like to thank the College of Arts and Sci-ences at the University of Washington and Robert Stacey, the dean for Human-ities and Arts, for their contribution to and assistance with this project. The final stages of copyediting the book took place amidst beauty and peace of the idyl-lic San Juan Island at the University of Washington's Helen Riaboff Whiteley Center in Friday Harbor. I am grateful to have been selected as one of the schol-ars in residence, and thankful to Kathy Cowell, the Center's coordinator, for making my stay so pleasant.

Mark Abley, my editor at McGill-Queen's University Press, was judicious in choosing excellent readers, whose comments and suggestions aided me enor-mously in revising the book. Mark's patience, good humour, and enthusiasm about my manuscript gratified me to no end. I was also very lucky to have Claude Lalumière as my exacting and astute copy editor.

Finally, my family – my husband, Rami, and daughters, Mara and Sasha – in addition to being the loves and lights of my life, helped with the manuscript as well. Rami and Mara, both more talented writers than I am and both absolutely topnotch copy editors, helped curb my wordiness and tendency to digress on peripheral topics that happen to catch my fancy, while Sasha lended her technological savvy and supreme calmness every time I panicked that my computer crashed.

# A RUSSIAN JEW OF BLOOMSBURY

Ah, what a man! … He would say something, and there were
depths that I have met nowhere else! What was it? A deep
suffering for humanity.
~ Esther Polianowsky Salaman, 1967 interview

# RIGHT PLACE, RIGHT TIME

Those years from 1915 onwards saw the real spread of Russian literature in England. Constance Garnett had been a forerunner; alongside
her Herculean labours on the great Russian writers, Koteliansky's
output was slight. But ... Koteliansky did as much by his influence
as by his work.
~ Oliver Edwards, "Talking of Books"

The most elementary remarks upon modern English fiction can
hardly avoid some mention of the Russian influence.
~ Virginia Woolf, *Common Reader*

One of Samuel Koteliansky's closest friends, the Irish poet and novelist James
Stephens, once said that "the greatest book never written about English literature
was by Koteliansky."[1] He did not mean that Koteliansky, a transplant from a small
Ukrainian shtetl who in England became a literary translator, was an exceptionally perceptive or sophisticated critic. Evidence suggests that he was not – he was
always more a man of ideas than a man of style and finesse. What Stephens meant
was that Koteliansky intimately knew so many people who were creating the
English literature of his era. This book is enriched by their personal voices for,
wherever possible, I tried to let their correspondence with him, both previously
published and not, resonate through the narrative.

It was his friendship with D.H. Lawrence that would prove to be Koteliansky's
most lasting legacy. As a personality and as a translator, Koteliansky had a substantial imprint on two of Lawrence's novels: *Kangaroo* and *Lady Chatterley's
Lover*. Lawrence wrote more letters to him than to anyone else outside of his family, and his letters to Koteliansky are crucial for our understanding of him as a
writer, a philosopher, and a person. Koteliansky was also an intimate friend of
Katherine Mansfield and shaped her awareness and knowledge of Chekhov, who

was the most influential presence in her art. In the 1930s, after he lost both Mansfield and D.H. Lawrence to tuberculosis, Koteliansky became very close to Ottoline Morrell, one of the most colourful personalities of the Bloomsbury set. Among the other friends with whom he frequently corresponded were H.G. Wells, Esther Polianowsky Salaman, Dorothy Richardson, and May Sarton, a rare American in his orbit.

Given that he was already in his thirties when he came to London, a seemingly provincial Russian Jew not at all known for any particular talents or achievements, it is truly stunning that he was able to befriend so many by now legendary people. Much of it had to do with the intense interest that Great Britain manifested toward Russia prior to the Russian revolution of 1917 and says more about England at the time and, in particular, Bloomsbury, one of the collective protagonists of this book, than it does about Koteliansky.

Vladimir Nabokov's uncle, Konstantin Nabokov, was appointed counsellor at the Russian Embassy in London in 1915, and he immediately took notice of how "Sympathy with Russia was manifested in every direction, in all classes of society. A long series of books appeared ... Anglo-Russian Societies were founded all over the country ... In several Universities chairs of the Russian language were established ... Broad circles of British educated society were beginning to realise that Russian literature was not limited to the works of Tolstoi, Dostoyevski and Tourgenev."[2]

London's literary and artistic circles were in particular abuzz about all things Russian. Frances Partridge, one of the second generation of the Bloomsbury artists, summed up her experience as a child catching the Russian "bug" as follows: "Everything Russian was fantastically moving to me. I was thrilled by the novels, translated by Constance Garnett, who was known to be the best ... And at the same sort of time I got taken to Diaghilev's ballet and we sat in a box and saw *La Boutique Fantasque* in the Coliseum ... and I remember someone brought a Russian Prince to our country house in Surrey, and of course he wasn't really very glamorous, but anything Russian was so marvellous ..."[3]

Bloomsbury's fascination with Russia indeed had two major components: the Ballets Russes and Russian literature. The Imperial Russian Ballet first came to London in 1911, the same year Samuel Koteliansky arrived there. The 1911–14 seasons of the Diaghilev Ballet were so influential that the bohemian crowd in London started decorating their houses in the bright colours they saw on stage, leading the famous cartoonist and art critic Osbert Lancaster to dub these years the "First Russian Ballet Period."[4] "[N]ight after night," Leonard Woolf would remember, "we flocked to Covent Garden, entranced by a new art, a revelation to us benighted British, the Russian Ballet in the greatest days of Diaghilev and

Nijinsky ... The Russian Ballet became for a time a curious centre of both fashionable and intellectual London ... In all my long life this is the only instance in which I can remember the intellectuals going night after night to a theatre, opera, concert or other performance."[5] Lydia Lopokova, a Diaghilev ballerina who became a permanent fixture in Bloomsbury after marrying John Maynard Keynes, astutely summarized some of the reasons for this remarkable success and staying power when she wrote in an obituary for Diaghilev in 1929 that he "had the cunning ... to combine the excellent with the fashionable, the beautiful with the chic, and revolutionary art with the atmosphere of the old regime."[6]

The blossoming of a fuller awareness of Russian literature was greatly nourished by recent translations by not only Constance Garnett but also Louise and Aylmer Maude. Prior to Garnett and the Maudes, translations from Russian were often bad renditions from French.[7] As a result of better translations, now directly from Russian, most members of Bloomsbury regarded Tolstoy and Dostoevsky more as contemporaries than writers from the previous era. Tolstoy, in particular, hit the spot. Virginia Woolf considered him simply "the greatest of all novelists." "Nothing seems to escape him," Woolf mused in her 1925 essay "The Russian Point of View." "Nothing glances off him unrecorded ... Even in a translation we feel that we have been set on a mountain-top and had a telescope put into our hands. Everything is astonishingly clear and absolutely sharp."[8] Woolf found solace in rereading *War and Peace* during the first dark months of the Second World War. "War and Peace is the greatest novel in the world," she informed Leonard's niece Philippa in 1939, "and if I'm not bombed I shall read that and Anna Karenina this winter."[9]

Ottoline Morrell remembered how she and Katherine Mansfield used to lose themselves "in scene after scene of *War and Peace* – especially [Katherine] loved the chapters where the young girls washed and dressed themselves with excitement for a ball, or went on masquerading expeditions in sledges, and then the scene where Natasha slipped off the slippers from her little feet and jumped into her mother's bed while her mother was reciting her evening prayer."[10] "Dear Madam," Mansfield wrote to Constance Garnett in 1921, "As I laid down my copy of War & Peace tonight I felt I could no longer refrain from thanking you for the whole other world that you have revealed to us through these marvellous translations from the Russian ... [M]y generation ... and the younger generation owe you more than we ourselves are able to realise. These books have changed our lives, no less. What would it be like to be without them!"[11]

The World War I era was, in short, a very opportune time to be *any* Russian in London. Therefore Samuel Koteliansky, neither glamorous nor a Russian prince, was seen as a true marvel by his new English friends. While Koteliansky had nothing to do with the Ballets Russes, since he had never seen any good ballet performances in Russia (having never been allowed to travel to Moscow or St Petersburg), like many in Bloomsbury he did worship Tolstoy. "In the hierarchy of creation," he liked to say, "there is God Almighty and Leo Tolstoy."[12] He also loved Chekhov, whom the English intelligentsia were just happily discovering. So, unsurprisingly, it was Tolstoy and, more specifically, Maxim Gorky's reminiscences of him that served as Koteliansky's entrée into the very heart of Bloomsbury: Virginia and Leonard Woolf's Hogarth Press; and it was Chekhov who kept him collaborating with them for several years to come. Translations from Russian classics would become a staple of the Woolfs' press. Richard Kennedy, who worked there in the early 1920s, echoed the sentiments of many Bloomsbury readers when he wrote in his diary: "I like the Russian books better than any others we publish."[13]

While he was born in Ukraine, then a part of the Russian Empire, Koteliansky always considered himself "a Russian Jew." He was not alone in that. Since living in the Pale of Settlement was not their choice, and Jews largely felt that they truly belonged nowhere, many in the turn-of-the-century better-educated and more secular younger generation usually strove to speak, in addition to Yiddish, fluent and educated Russian and devoured Russian literature.[14] Having escaped the worst of both Russian and Ukrainian anti-Semitism, Koteliansky came to England and might have hoped for a haven. The move most likely did save his life. Had he stayed, he would have probably been killed, either by Bolsheviks, like his brother-in-law, or by Nazis, like many other Jews who remained in Ukraine. Or, like his father and sister, he could have died during the devastating epidemics following the revolution. But in England he still had to contend with plenty of anti-Jewish prejudices. Even Lawrence – long after he and Koteliansky became close – often sounded virulently anti-Semitic.

Not surprisingly, Koteliansky would form one of his closest friendships with Mark Gertler, a young painter who had a very similar background and for whom Koteliansky became a stern but very loving surrogate older brother. Since one of the main themes I am pursuing is how it felt to be a Jew in Bloomsbury, Gertler, a fellow Jew from Eastern Europe who was even more of an integral part of the group than Koteliansky ever was, likewise receives a major share of attention in this book. When Koteliansky himself needed moral support, he would turn to yet another Bloomsbury Jew – Leonard Woolf. Koteliansky also befriended other prominent London Jews, among them David Eder, an early Zionist and an influential English psychoanalyst; Sydney Schiff, a novelist and a gracious social host; and Sidney Bernstein, an arts enterpreneur. In the 1930s, Koteliansky was given a job by another powerful English Jew: Dennis Cohen, a publisher and director of the Cresset Press. The discussion of their interactions with him, as well as their own experiences, allow me to further probe the position of Jews within the English cultural elite in the first half of the twentieth century.

In his attitude toward people Koteliansky was Dr Jekyll and Mr Hyde. People either mattered to him a lot, or not at all. With those he disliked, and they were legion, he could be quarrelsome, petulant, unjust, and insulting – "intransigence personified," as one of his friends described him.[15] Even his handshake hurt. "I always had a secret hope," Leonard Woolf remembered, "that this devastating handshake meant that Kot liked one … and so it was worthwhile enduring the pain."[16] To Virginia Woolf this handshake was truly emblematic of the man that Koteliansky was: "His clasp of the hand crushes the little bones: his hand though inches thick is hard as bone, & typifies that dense, solid, concentrated man."[17] Koteliansky often signed his letters with a typical Russian ending, "Krepko zhmu ruku," which he translated as "I grip your hand firmly," probably making his correspondents wince just imagining it.[18]

In his typically categorical way, Koteliansky once advised Esther Polianowsky Salaman – a writer and another transplanted Russian Jew who even hailed from the same province as Koteliansky – that "the most cardinal point" about writing was that "a writer always selects certain things only to write about, dismissing or ignoring all complexities and confusions, that life, the life of everyone, repre-sents."[19] In his own life complexities and confusions truly abounded, but I would be loath to take his advice and dismiss or ignore them for the sake of artificial clarity and cohesion.

I have to admit that while writing this book I often did not know whether I liked Koteliansky enough to wish I had known him personally. I found myself at times siding with people whom I thought he treated unfairly – like his niece Polly, whose early life was tragic beyond human endurance but who, despite it all, managed not only to survive but create a large loving family in Canada. She worshipped her uncle, sought his advice in everything, constantly sent him packages and money – while he, more often than not, berated her for placing too much value on material possessions, writing to him about things that he found meaningless, or not bringing up her four children properly. I also found him exceedingly harsh not just with his enemies but also with people who were very generous and kind to him, like Sydney Schiff.

And yet, when he truly loved someone, there was no friend more loyal, help-ful, or concerned. He was particularly generous with warmth and tenderness toward the younger women in his circle – Dilys Powell, Juliette Huxley, Marjorie Wells, and May Sarton. With them he played the role of a loving older brother or uncle, but then could also rely on their nurturing and compassionate natures when he was sick or growing old. One of them, Marjorie Wells, essentially took care of him, almost on a daily basis, for the last fifteen years of his life.

"Some people have a capacity for writing, painting," he wrote to Ottoline Morrell in 1936, "mine is a capacity for friendship. Were I to be found wanting in every other way, – there's one thing that should be counted as merit: my capacity of being a true friend."[20] "[Y]ou misunderstand my character," he once told Virginia Woolf when she was prodding him for gossip. "I do not find fault with the people I really like – I never discuss them."[21] In a society where rumours were routinely traded like valuable commodities, he was indeed a great person to confide in. "Entirely safe," according to Juliette Huxley. "You knew that nothing would pass his lips."[22] His "most precious gift of all," Dilys Powell wrote in the *Times* of London obituary, "was his personal friendship, at once fierce and incorruptible, demanding always the absolute honesty it offered. Of not many it is said 'I am proud that he liked me.'"[23] He did like her, and many of the letters he wrote to Powell in the 1930s, when she was an aspiring young writer, were so fatherly and warm, they bring tears to one's eyes. Koteliansky placed such an immense value on human relationships because he believed they alone could allow one not only to survive in the brutal century he lived in but also to remain, in the words and language of his father, a "mensch." That through it all he indeed managed to remain one is reflected even today in the unique fondness with which people who knew him well – like H.G. Wells's granddaughter and Marjorie Wells's daughter Catherine, and Esther Polianowsky Salaman's daughter Nina – remember him.

His English friends would invariably call him a "rabbi" or an "Old Testament prophet." For a secular Jew, Koteliansky was indeed interestingly rabbinical in the way he conducted his life in England. Bookish and authoritative, he paid little attention to anything that was not directly related to cerebral matters, spending most of his life worshipping "sacred" books – in his case Tolstoy and Chekhov, rather than the Old Testament.[24] Virginia Woolf saw it very clearly. "It struck me," she wrote once in her diary after a dinner in his company, "he lives in what he reads: makes it do instead of living. Then fabricates what he calls a theology."[25] He once suggested to Ottoline Morrell that the best thing for him, even in England, might have been "settling down as an obscure rabbi."[26] People who came to him for advice did so not because his knowledge of the society they lived in was great – it was not – but because they felt that his wisdom and honesty transcended that limitation. He functioned as their moral compass; they came to him for his pronouncements of what was right and what was wrong, and his approval somehow meant much more than almost anyone else's.

Toward the end of writing my book, as I traced Koteliansky becoming more feeble but also more humble and humane, I made my peace with him. I suspect a reader will also go through mixed emotions reading this book. This complexity of emotions is an understandable reaction to not only Koteliansky's personality but to the entire age he embodied as well as to the two cultures he inhabited – one that firmly shaped him in his youth and the other that he stubbornly helped to shape in his later years.

Beila Koteliansky (née Geller) (1852–1930), Koteliansky's mother, who financed his move to England in 1911 and whom he was not destined to see again, despite several attempts to obtain the necessary papers to go back to Russia (CSA).

The wooden synagogue in Ostropol as it appeared at the time Koteliansky was born. The synagogue, which may have been featured in the early twentieth-century play *The Dybbuk*, was destroyed soon after the 1917 Bolshevik revolution.

"Shmilik" Koteliansky at the age
of fourteen or fifteen (CSA).

The remnants of a flour mill in Ostropol that the Kotelianskys may have owned.

The river "Sluch," where Koteliansky's niece, Perl (Polly), almost drowned.

Koteliansky at the time he was leaving Ukraine in 1911. He made postcards of this photo and gave them to his English friends. The reverse side of this postcard says "To Sullivan from Kot." (Courtesy of Barbara Sullivan.)

Koteliansky standing between Grisha and Sonia Farbman, his housemates at
5 Acacia Road. Most likely taken in 1915, when Koteliansky and the Farbmans
were moving into the house they agreed to rent from Katherine Mansfield
and J. Middleton Murry. Koteliansky will stay there for the rest of his life.
(The identity of the man with a broom standing next to Sonia Farbman is
unknown.) (CSA.)

5 Acacia Road.

D.H. Lawrence in the late 1910s (National Portrait Gallery, London).

Katherine Mansfield in 1913, a year before
Koteliansky met her (National Portrait
Gallery, London).

Koteliansky circa 1918 (CSA).

*Katherine Mansfield and S.S. Kotelianskty in the Garden*, by Beatrice
Campbell. Early 1920s. Kot was very fond of this painting. Museum of
New Zealand Te Papa Tongarewa. (Courtesy of Hon. Bridget Campbell
and the Estate of William Holden.)

A very young-looking Mark Gertler in the early 1930s (courtesy of Luke Gertler).

Mark Gertler, *Rabbi and Rabbitzin* (1914). Watercolour and pencil on paper. Ben Uri Gallery. (Courtesy of Luke Gertler.)

Mark Gertler, *Artist's Mother* (1913). Oil on canvas. Glynn Vivian Art Gallery. (Courtesy of Luke Gertler.)

Mark Gertler, *Portrait of Koteliansky* (1921), as it appeared in his 1925 catalogue. Oil on canvas. The painting was owned by Lady Glenavy and her heirs until 1990. Current location unknown. (Courtesy of Luke Gertler.)

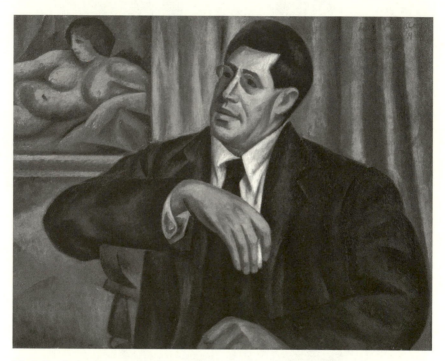

Mark Gertler's 1930 portrait of Koteliansky. Oil on canvas. Placing Kot, who was not known to have much interest in female bodies, next to a representation of a voluptuous nude must have struck Gertler as a fun idea. The painting in the background is somewhat reminiscent of Gertler's "Queen of Sheba" (1922). Anonymous owner. (Courtesy of Luke Gertler.)

Virginia and Leonard Woolf (with their dog, Sally) in the late 1930s. Kot's work for the Woolfs' Hogarth Press and his collaboration with the couple on several translations were the highlights of his career as a translator. Kot would seek Leonard out in the most trying moments of his life, including while on his deathbed. (Courtesy of Estate Gisèle Freund/IMEC Images.)

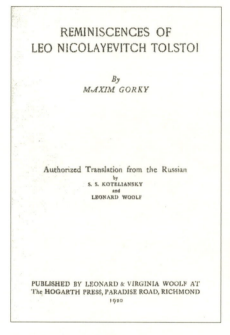

REMINISCENCES OF
LEO NICOLAYEVITCH TOLSTOI

*By*
*MAXIM GORKY*

Authorized Translation from the Russian
by
S. S. KOTELIANSKY
and
LEONARD WOOLF

PUBLISHED BY LEONARD & VIRGINIA WOOLF AT
The HOGARTH PRESS, PARADISE ROAD, RICHMOND
1920

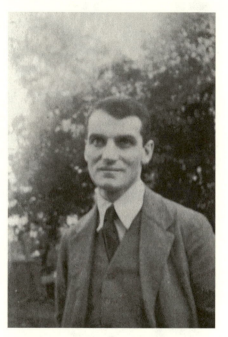

The title page of Gorky's reminiscences of Tolstoy. The book became the first bestseller of the fledging press.

J. Middleton Murry in 1917, in a photograph taken by Ottoline Morrell. Kot and Murry never had a smooth relationship despite occasionally collaborating on translations. It became irreparably broken in 1924, after they could not resolve their differences over the future of *The Adelphi*. (National Portrait Gallery, London.)

The first issue of *The Adelphi*.

A page from Kot's address book. The entries for Frieda and D.H. Lawrence are from 1923, when they split up and Frieda came to London while Lawrence went to Mexico. (CSA.)

"Kot … took a piece of paper out of a drawer, on which a few bars of music had been written by some musical friend. He asked me if I could sing it. I could not manage the Hebrew words but I sang the notes …" (Lady Glenavy). Inspiration for Lawrence's notion of utopian "Rananim." (CSA.)

D.H. Lawrence and Frieda Lawrence in 1928.
The picture was probably taken by Ottoline Morrell.
(National Portrait Gallery, London.)

PART 1

# FROM SHMILIK TO KOT

## 1880–1930

1

# "SHMILIK"

If you are too bitter, the world will spit you out. Too sweet,
and it will gobble you up.
~ Hershel of Ostropol

He often talked of you all, and of Ostropol and the horse
which took you to the station, and of the little synagogue and
so on, and the flour mill.
~ Marjorie Wells to Koteliansky's sister Rokhl, 28 April 1955

"Kot was not a comfortable man," Leonard Woolf wrote in Koteliansky's obituary in 1955.[1] He was definitely not, and his environment was not particularly comfortable either. In 1918, when Koteliansky was already in England, Russian-Jewish writer and historian Simon Dubnov wrote a story called *History of a Jewish Soldier: A Confession of One of Many*, in which the narrator lamented: "I was born in 1881. Later I understood the full symbolic meaning of this fateful date of my life, for it was the year when the era of pogroms began, and a pogrom in a variety of incarnations has accompanied me from my cradle to my grave, at the edge of which I now find myself."[2]

Koteliansky was born in 1880, a year before Dubnov's soldier, and he, too, felt that the pogroms, both literal and metaphorical, followed him everywhere. While he left the horrors of the anti-Jewish violence and discrimination physically behind him once he came to England, he could never shake off many of the consequences of this experience, including the effect it had on what he called his "black moods," long and painful bouts of severe depression when for weeks he would stay indoors and see no one. There are very few documents from his early years in Russia, and some of the unique elements of his childhood and youth are irrevocably lost, yet it still behooves us to start there because these were, for better or for worse, his truly formative years.

Samuel (Shmul) Koteliansky was born in the region where most Russian Jews of that period were born – the notorious Pale of Settlement, far away from the central parts of Russia from which Jews had been barred ever since Catherine the Great decreed it so in 1791. Koteliansky's family lived in the small Ukrainian town of Ostropol (now Starii Ostropil). Prior to the annexations at the end of the eighteenth century due to Catherine's successful wars, Ostropol and surrounding territory belonged to Poland. The town is believed to have been founded in 1576, but archaeological digs routinely find traces of much earlier habitation, as far back as the pre-Christian era (fourth to eighth centuries CE).[3] While the centre of the town was heavily Jewish, Ostropol's overall population was, according to the all-Russian Census of 1897, more mixed than that of many nearby towns, with only 37 percent of its 7,300 inhabitants being Jewish.[4] Ostropol was about 300 kilometres from Kiev, and in order to go there to study Koteliansky, as a Jew, would need to obtain a special permit.

The family name of Koteliansky is very rare and all Kotelianskys are believed to be direct relatives. The name itself most likely comes from a small town less than 30 kilometres from Ostropol called "Kotelianka," and it simply means that the bearers of that name were originally from there. Many Jews in this part of Ukraine shared their last names with the villages and towns their ancestors inhabited at one point or another.[5] In the 1880s a Russian historian who visited Starokonstantinov, a larger town 20 kilometres away, complained that the area was "full of yids ['polon zhidami'], wherever you go you see their houses, near which there are lakes of garbage."[6] Martin Packman, whose grandmother was Samuel Koteliansky's first cousin, remembers his parents telling him that Ostropol "was the classic shtetl, with all of the grubbiness and none of the romanticism."[7] Another former citizen of Ostropol, Harry Wexler, who lived there until he was twelve, told his grandniece that his most vivid memory of Ostropol were its dirt roads: "[T]he mud [was] about a foot deep, more than that. Sometimes the horses and the wagons couldn't get out … In winter it used to freeze. That was a blessing. You could use sleds."[8] These descriptions, however, do not do Ostropol full justice. Now reduced to a small village with fewer than 1,000 inhabitants (and virtually none of them Jews), Ostropol, carved out by the curly shores of a plentiful river and surrounded by luscious forests, can still conjure images of a very attractive place in its heyday.

The river Sluch is one of Ukraine's liveliest. It originates not very far from Ostropol and continues for almost 200 kilometres north. The river figured prominently in the lore of the Koteliansky family. Koteliansky told his friends in England that his earliest childhood memory was of "a night when a man had been drowned. The people of his village had no knowledge of present-day methods of artificial respiration. The drowned man was put on a horse, in front of a rider, then the horse was galloped as hard as possible; apparently breathing was sometimes restored by this process." He could see "the gleaming white face of the drowned man bobbing about and hear the wails of the people as the horse thundered past, going round and round the village. Each time it returned there was the white face and the wailing."[9] And then the Sluch almost claimed Koteliansky's niece, Perl, who would remember later how as a very little girl she went to the river with her father, who instructed her to hold onto a boat chain fastened to a rock while he took a swim. Feeling bored, after a short while she let go of the chain and was immediately swept away by the current. Fortunately, her father saw it and rescued her. She recalled that once she was saved, "there was a great celebration … in Ostropol, the kind of celebration where they threw money on the street."[10]

Celebrations were common in Ostropol. The town was, in fact, considered by residents and visitors alike to be a very joyful and vibrant place, and even, according to some, "the merriest of all shtetls."[11] Abe Koosis, who was born in Ostropol in 1904, remembered it, especially during summer time, with much fondness: "The air was perfumed with the fragrance of lilac. The woods and orchards around us were beautiful. We kids used to go in the woods and pick wild strawberries that grew in the tall grass beneath the trees … We'd go frolicking in the river which was behind the house, to the disgust of the people trying to fish."[12] As one of his friends tells us, Koteliansky, too, cherished the memories of the fragrance in the Ostropol air when winter would finally give way to spring: "It was marvelous to hear him tell of spring in Russia, how after the dark and terrible cold, suddenly the air was full of the scent of violets and people went literally mad with joy."[13]

Ostropol owed its reputation as a merry shtetl to a legendary character of Jewish folklore, Hershel ("Gershele") Ostropolier, a wandering beggar ("schnorrer") and local wit. Ben Richman, who lived there as a child at the turn of the last century, told his grandchildren that everyone in Ostropol felt an intimate connection with the mythical jester: "[He] clowned around for Hasidic Rabbis about 150 years before I was born. Legend gave him a site in the marketplace where he was buried. And the Jews were paying tribute to him …"[14] Often penniless and without food, the Hershel of Jewish lore never allowed cold, hunger, and social injustice to destroy his high spirits and keen sense of humour. Among the witty aphorisms attributed to him are such gems as "God must love poor people. Why else would He make so many of them?"; "How to get rid of someone for good: If he's rich, ask to borrow money. If he's poor, lend him some"; "Never wish the doctor or the undertaker a good year."

Hershel was esteemed as much for his integrity as for his jokes. "Better an honest slap than a false kiss" was one of his celebrated statements, something that Koteliansky would both say and, to the chagrin of many of his friends, ruthlessly practice during his years in England.[15] "He always speaks the truth," Virginia Woolf recorded in her diary in 1920, "& laying waste many a fair garden."[16] "Kot's condemnations were terrific," wrote Leonard Woolf. "[Y]ou felt that his vehemence had blown away all screens, disguises, veils, and uncovered the nakedness of some wretched sinner."[17] Not even his closest relatives were spared Koteliansky's denunciatory slaps, especially when it came to what he perceived as lack of honesty. Hershel was also credited with saying: "Better a whole lie than a half-truth," and that was another maxim Koteliansky definitely believed in.[18] "I told you on a number of occasions, throughout the years," he would characteristically berate his niece in Canada, "that I hate and abominate tricks, diplomacy, and lies. If one does not tell the complete truth, or is silent about matters that need an answer, this person can never be trusted by me, whatever happens ... In writing you either tell me the truth, or better not write at all."[19]

Koteliansky's parents were Avrum-Shloima Koteliansky and Beila Geller. One of Koteliansky's closest friends in England, Marjorie Wells, daughter-in-law of H.G. Wells, remembered being told by Koteliansky that his father "was a [wheat]-merchant, among other things, who collected wheat from various parts of Russia and sold it to the French firm of Dreyfus."[20] He also may have at some point owned the very mill that was in the town centre and whose ruins are still in evidence today.[21] Beila Koteliansky, who was considered the real business brains in the family, ran a very successful fabric store from their house.[22] The reason we know it was successful is because it was even listed in *The All-Russian Business Directory*.[23]

Beila hailed from Annopol, which was very close to Ostropol. We learn more about her early years than her husband's because of the autobiography she wrote at the request of her son when Koteliansky was already in England. Entitled "The Life of a Simple Woman" and written in Yiddish, the document provides an interesting glimpse of Beila's life prior to the marriage:

My father hired people to work in his factory and in his fields, only Jews. He was very good to his workers ... When a worker had a daughter, he didn't have to worry about having to find a spouse for her. My father would pay the dowry, and they would pay him back slowly after the wedding. If someone couldn't pay him back, my father would not ask for the money ... My father and brother travelled together to see the Rebbe. We kids were jealous of my brother. The people who couldn't travel, women, the infirm and children were not happy to be left home for the holidays. We asked those travelling to ask the Rebbe for a blessing … My father saw that the girls were jealous, but he couldn't do anything because you don't take girls to the Rebbe. Our mother cooked fish for Rosh Hashanah and Yom Kippur and we hoped that our father and brother would return home before Sukkoth.

She also left a nostalgic description of a Passover celebration in their household:

My father came home from prayers and wished everyone a Kosher Pesakh. My mother began to bake Matzahs. The baker had new tables. Everyone washed their hands. It took time to bake Matzah … We had a big room we only used for Pesakh. We all dressed up in new clothes and went into the Pesakh room. A big silver samovar stood on the table with delicious food kosher for Pesakh … My father and brother would lead the Seder. After they read the Hagaddah, we ate … The meal went on for a long time, even after the Haggadah. I remember I liked to stay up late, until after singing Khad Gadya.[24]

If the wedding of Beila and Avrum-Shloima took place in Ostropol, it was probably similar to the ones described by Ben Richman: "Weddings in Ostropol lasted a minimum of six days. The families each vied to have a day of celebrating in their houses – with food, drinks, and music and dancing. The last day of the wedding a parade went through town, music blaring and leading to the supposed grave of Hershel. The dancing there was particularly wild and all passersby joined in the festivities."[25] The Kotelianskys would have, all in all, three sons and two daughters.

Ostropol had a busy marketplace near the main road (which led to Starokonstantinov), a sizable wooden synagogue with several structures under separate roofs connected together (it now exists only in old photographs and drawings), and at least three water-powered flour mills, one right below the market square. Richman also left a description of "market Mondays," when "wagons with merchandise … gathered next to all centre highways and displayed their wares. Customers paraded back and forth among wagons looking, inspecting, bargaining …"[26] Koteliansky's parents must have been among the regular customers there, since, unlike the majority of the Jewish population in the Pale, they were quite prosperous. Their granddaughter Perl would remember that, while outside their house it was only mud, inside it was "pure Paris."[27]

Avrum-Shloima was twenty-seven and Beila twenty-eight when the son they lovingly called "Shmilik" was born.[28] The references to his parents in Koteliansky's letters are not frequent, but they do give a hint of their personalities. He wrote to his niece that Avrum-Shloima liked to say "Well, my son, be a mensch!" whenever Koteliansky found himself in a difficult situation, while his mother admonished him to be humble and always remember "that there actually are people so very much better than oneself."[29]

According to the Russian passport he brought to England with him, the date of Koteliansky's birth was 28 February. His English documents, however, including the passport he was issued upon his naturalization in 1929, list 1 April as his date of birth. The discrepancy is hard to account for, since the difference between the Russian old calendar and the Gregorian calendar is less than two weeks. One tends to believe the Russian passport more since it was presumably based on the original birth certificate, in which case 1 April would be Koteliansky's self-deprecatory joke. It allowed him to share his made-up birthday with, among others, Pushkin's Ivan Belkin, whose being born on April Fool's Day was meant to signal to the readers of *The Tales of Belkin* all they needed to know about Belkin's intellectual and narratorial abilities. Koteliansky apparently confessed to his English friends that he simply did not know when he was actually born because "around Kiev at that time they only remembered such things by the season," so one date was almost as good as any other.[30]

Self-depreciation aside, Koteliansky was quite proud of his heritage. He traced it back to a celebrated Talmudic scholar of the seventeenth century, Yom-Tov Lipman Heller (1578–1654), author of the famous *Tosafot yom tov* Mishnah commentary, and a disciple of the legendary Rabbi Judah Loew of Prague. Even among the most celebrated Jewish Talmudists and rabbis, Heller, whom Koteliansky once characterized to his niece as "not only a great scholar, but a fine man,"[31] was one of the truly distinguished. He was further acclaimed for his poem, written in Hebrew, about the Jewish massacres of 1648, which took place in Ukraine, Poland, and Lithuania, killing, according to some Jewish sources, more than 100,000 Jews while destroying more than 300 Jewish communities.[32] Little had changed more than two hundreds years later. Pogroms, indeed, accompanied Koteliansky from his cradle. A year after Koteliansky's birth, the region witnessed a series of particularly violent ones that were occasioned by the 1 March 1881 assassination of Alexander II. Some members of the terrorist wing of "Narodnaia volia" (People's Will) were Jewish, and as *The London Jewish Chronicle* reported on 6 May 1881, the role of Jews in the assassination became one of the foci of the investigation: "The Czar's assassination happened on a day that is kept up festively by the Jews in Russia [i.e., Purim], and after the event they were charged with having made merry in anticipation of what was going to happen."[33] The intensity of pogroms increased further toward the turn of the century. In April 1903, Russian Jews in Kishinev were subjected to one of the bloodiest massacres of all. *The New York Times* described it as "worse than the censor will permit to publish": "The mob was led by priests, and the general cry, 'Kill the Jews,' was taken up all over the city. The Jews were taken wholly unaware and were slaughtered like sheep. The dead number 120 and the injured about 500. The scenes of horror attending this massacre are beyond description. Babes were literally torn to pieces by the frenzied and bloodthirsty mob. The local police made no attempt to check the reign of terror. At sunset the streets were piled with their corpses and wounded. Those who could make their escape fled in terror, and the city is now practically deserted of Jews."[34]

In 1905 and 1906, according to a commission appointed by the Zionist relief fund in London, approximately 690 anti-Jewish pogroms took place, principally in the southern and southwestern provinces, and in Kiev and Odessa.[35] The 1905 pogroms in the southern provinces of Russia, which bordered on Volhynia, accounted for 62 percent of all Jewish deaths there that year.[36] By the end of 1906 more than 3,000 Jewish lives were lost. Ivan Bunin, whose famous story "The Gentleman from San Francisco" Koteliansky would later translate with the help of D.H. Lawrence, was in Odessa at the time. "At about three o'clock," he wrote in his diary on 22 October 1905, "I ran into an acquaintance who told me that … Ukrainian men and lads were going down the streets with scythes and daggers … They were beating the Jews mercilessly, savagely on Moldavanka … The Cossacks soon arrived but they passed by the scene with smiles on their faces." A nurse at a local hospital reported to Bunin that "on Romanov Square children's heads were being bashed against the wall, and that the soldiers and Cossacks stood idly by, shooting their guns in the air…."[37]

Koteliansky's English friend, Lady Glenavy (Beatrice Campbell), probably got the story of his early education somewhat wrong when she recorded in her memoirs that "At the age of nine years he told his parents that he no longer believed in the Jewish faith and he wished to learn Russian and go to a Russian school."[38] Sending him to a Russian school, in addition to a Hebrew one (a "heder"), was most likely his parents' idea; it was routinely done by well-off Jewish parents throughout the Pale in order to assure that their children spoke good Russian and could therefore succeed in the wider world. It was also a good preparation for gymnasium, where children of well-off Jews were expected by their parents to enroll later. Koteliansky probably attended the same Russian elementary school Ben Richman would attend fifteen years later. "The school I went to," writes Richman, "was a gov[ernment] school and Jews [unlike Russians] had to pay tuition.

My Grandmother wanted me to get a Russian education as well as Hebrew. I was in that school six days a week and enjoyed it very much – 8 AM to 2:30 PM. After that school I went to Hebrew school where I was instructed only in Hebrew and had to memorize various writings of the prophets. This school stressed Isaiah and Jeremiah." Richman further describes the Russian school in Ostropol as "a big white one-story building in a beautiful garden, fruit trees and grass."[39]

Another friend, Marjorie Wells, gleaned from Koteliansky's stories that his parents "belonged to the Chassidic sect; they were closely connected with a, so to speak, private – if this is the right word – synagogue in the village [while] Ostropol was … famous for its larger, beautiful wooden synagogue."[40] Smaller and much plainer Hasidic prayer houses – "shtiblakh" – were indeed common in that part of Ukraine, which was the very cradle of the Hasidic movement. The main Hebrew school may have been in one of the numerous structures of the wooden synagogue, but, if the Kotelianskys indeed belonged to a smaller Hasidic synagogue, he probably attended a heder there. Ostropol heders, both Hasidic and otherwise, were undoubtedly similar to Hebrew schools everywhere else in the Pale. Chaim Weizmann, who would become a British subject in 1910 and then the first President of Israel upon its formation, did not have fond memories of his. He was born in 1874 in the Grodno Province, which bordered Volhynia on the northwest, and his early Hebrew lessons took place in "a squalid, one-room school … If my cheder differed from the others, it was perhaps in the possession of a family goat, which took shelter with us in cold weather. And if my first Rebbi, or teacher, differed from the others it was in the degree of his pedagogical incompetence."[41]

Similarly, David Levinsky, a famous fictional character of Abraham Cahan (1860–1951), a Russian-American Yiddish writer and the founder of *The Jewish Daily Forward*, whose own father had been a Hebrew teacher – "melamed" – in the Pale, did not have much good to say about his time at the Hebrew schools:

[I]nstruction in these cheders was confined to the Hebrew Old Testament and rudiments of the Talmud, the exercises lasting practically all day and part of the evening. The class-room was at the same time the bedroom, living-room, and kitchen of the teacher's family. His wife and children were always around. These cheder teachers were usually a haggard-looking lot with full beards and voices hoarse with incessant shouting … Overworked, underfed, and goaded by the tongue-lashings of their wives, these enervated drudges were usually out of sorts. Bursts of ill temper, in the form of invective, hair-pulling, ear-pulling, pinching, caning, "nape-cracking," or "chin-smashing," were part of the routine…[42]

How important was this imperfect Jewish education for Koteliansky? Probably more than he thought at the time. Lady Glenavy would later remember his description of "how his father used to chant some plain-song or psalm every Saturday night while the children all sat around waiting for the stars to come out ... As Kot was telling me this he took a piece of paper out of a drawer, on which a few bars of music had been written by some musical friend. He asked me if I could sing it. I could not manage the Hebrew words but I sang the notes ... We sang it together over and over again. It was getting dusk, and we kept on singing and looking out of the window ... waiting for the stars to appear. Kot had a strange hypnotized look on his face."[43] Koteliansky would tell another friend that crocuses in his London garden "reminded him of the candles in the synagogue."[44]

Koteliansky's Hasidic anti-materialistic leanings (which at some point may have merged into his Socialist leanings) remained with him for the rest of his life as well. Perl, who was born the year Koteliansky left, remembered the stories she had heard from her older relatives about Samuel dressing up the family dog in Ostropol "with all the jewels found in the house and let[ting] the dog run through the streets of the town," much to the chagrin of his mother, whose jewelry the dog was scattering in the mud.[45] When Perl, already in Canada, suffered a breakdown later in life and was felled with a very severe depression – a condition Koteliansky should have readily related to – he would attribute even that to what he thought was her misguided preoccupation with material values: "It seems to me that you are obsessed by money; and that that is your chief trouble ... Money can become a most terrible obsession, almost a madness."[46]

Once he was older and done with both Russian and Hebrew elementary schools, Koteliansky went on to study in two gymnasiums, first in Ostropol and then in Zhitomir.[47] One of Koteliansky's closest friends in England, Esther Polianowsky Salaman, a student of Eistein and an early Zionist who would become a prolific English author, was born and raised in Zhitomir, which was in the same Volhynia province, halfway between Kiev and Ostropol. She felt that a Russian gymnasium there, which she also attended (an all-women gymnasium, in her case), was a rather democratic place at the time: "The children in Russian gymnasia came from every class except the poorest: the landed aristocrat's daughter and the kulak's; the judge's and his copying clerk's; the doctor and his apothecary's. The schools were truly comprehensive: besides children of all classes, races, religions, there were those of every kind of ability in the same form."[48]

Unlike Russian or Ukrainian students, however, Jewish students had to fit into a very small quota – Jews were allowed to be only 10 percent of the entire student body in schools within the Pale of Settlement, and 3-5 percent outside it. Even in gymnasiums of this "democratic" kind they were not guaranteed free admission and often had to pay full tuition.[49] Well-to-do families, like the Kotelianskys or Polianowskys, were usually not deterred by the costs and hired private tutors to make sure their children (more often sons than daughters) were well prepared for entrance exams. Quotas were not the only issue, though. The Jewish communities themselves often posed challenges to students who desired secular education. Harry Wexler remembered such a controversy surrounding the Ostropol gymnasium: "The religious Jews in our town refused to let the Jewish students attend the government … gymnasium because they had classes on Saturday. And they had picketing lines, picketing the Jewish students that did go to the school on Saturday. And most of them did go to school on Saturday."[50]

In seeking a good secular education, Koteliansky was not altogether an atypical Jewish adolescent in the Pale. Unlike their parents and grandparents, his generation was usually fluent in Russian as well as Yiddish and Hebrew, and some even acquired a decent knowledge of English, German, or French. In fact, despite both severe quotas and pressure from the Jewish Orthodox community, the 1897 Russian census revealed that while the overall percentage of literate males ten years and older was 38.7, among the Russian Jews it reached 64.6.[51] The same year Anton Chekhov, who was born and raised in the south of Russia, which had strong pockets of Jewish population, noted in his story "Ionych" that provincial libraries would have had to close "if it weren't … for young Jews."[52]

Having graduated from the Zhitomir gymnasium, Koteliansky went on to study in Odessa, where he apparently became engaged in political activities. According to what he told Marjorie Wells, when he was twenty, in 1900, "he was ordered to live in Ostropol under police surveillance and had to remain there until 1906 when the restrictions were relaxed, after which he went to study in Kiev."[53] His other close friend, Dilys Powell, included this episode – of which she had probably learned either directly from Koteliansky or indirectly from Wells – in her *Times* obituary of him, which went on to say that Koteliansky "felt acutely the restricted education available for children of his race, and he occupied himself in founding, with his brother, a library and a school."[54] Koteliansky provided more details of this enterprise for his niece in 1944. He described to her how "about 1902" he started an unofficial, and thus illegal, library in Ostropol to allow Jewish children to study Russian. He requested some books for the library in a letter to Maxim Gorky, who was highly esteemed by many Jews because of his strong condemnations of anti-Semitism, which he considered "of all … animosities … the most abominable."[55] To the young Koteliansky's "joy and surprise, Gorky replied that he would send us through his friends … a few roubles. In a few days I received … 335 roubles." Koteliansky further informed his niece that "Gorky's letter was kept for years by your father and mother, – as at any time our house might have been searched by the gendarmerie – but what subsequently happened to the letter, I do not know."[56]

In his autobiography, Leonard Woolf included one other tale, often echoed among Koteliansky's friends, wherein Koteliansky (presumably during that time of his forced stay in Ostropol) walked for miles late at night to see his girlfriend: "When a young man in the Ukraine he had fallen in love with a woman living in a village about five miles from his home. He used once a week to go and see her, and then had to walk back the five miles late at night. The darkness, loneliness, silence terrified him, and he taught himself to howl like a dog because then the dogs in distant villages howled back in answer to him, and he felt that at any rate he was not entirely alone in a dark and hostile world."[57] His London friends, and in particular Katherine Mansfield, would often beg him to reproduce the howling sounds.

Koteliansky's friends in London also circulated further, albeit conflicting, stories about the woman in question. According to one version, she was engaged to Koteliansky but "jilted him, leaving a permanent wound."[58] Another version attributed the permanent wound – his friends' convenient explanation for why he never seemed to develop romantic attachments to women during the English period of his life – to a later relationship, in Kiev. "Katherine [Mansfield] told me," writes Lady Glenavy, "that there had once been a 'Sonia' in Kot's life. They had been fellow students of Kiev University [*sic*]. Kot had said, 'Wherever Sonia was there was laughter and happiness.' The attachment lasted for three years, then another man took Kot's place. According to Katherine, 'One day Kot went to her house as usual, rolling his Russian cigarettes. She just shut the door in his face.' He liked her for ending it that way: no excuses, no apologies, no explanations. Sonia and her new friend were later arrested as revolutionaries and sent to Siberia. Kot never heard what became of them."[59] Esther Salaman remembered Koteliansky's story in much less romantic terms. He apparently told her that the young woman was a general's daughter and not Jewish. "I came one day and she was gone," she recalled Koteliansky saying during one of their frequent conversations comparing their pasts in Ukraine. He also assured Salaman that the wound had, in fact, quickly healed: "It was just an affair, not much more."[60]

In 1906, at the age of twenty six, Koteliansky was granted a permission to study at the Kiev Commercial Institute (not Kiev University, as Glenavy asserts). The choice of the Commercial Institute was a forced one: Koteliansky was never a very practical man and from early on he was interested in literature, history, and philosophy while detesting anything having to do with money. However, institutes of commerce (as opposed to universities) were among the very few higher education venues that a Jewish student could enter at the time. During the very same years, Koteliansky's now famous Russian-Jewish contemporary, Isaac Babel, who likewise could not care less about business or trade, was enrolled in the Nicholas I Commercial Institute in his native Odessa.[61] Koteliansky's transcripts reveal that he took courses in economics, statistics, bookkeeping, law, history, and geography, as well as in French, German, English, and, during his last year, Italian. The transcripts bear no grades; they just list the courses he took in 1906–10, and the names of the instructors who taught them. English, for example, was taught by someone whose last name was "Ferbern."[62]

In spring 1910, as Koteliansky was graduating from the Commercial Institute, twelve hundred Jewish families were expelled from the city because of their supposedly radical political activities,[63] and Koteliansky himself might have once again come close to feeling the wrath of the czarist police. Katherine Mansfield liked to tell a story of how, back in Kiev, he single-handedly "organized a revolution … against the Czarist regime": "On the day appointed for the rising, no one turned up at the meeting place except Kot; he was so shattered that he started walking, and never stopped till he got to the Tottenham Court Road."[64]

That Koteliansky was a revolutionary of some kind was a common assumption among many of his English friends, and revolutionaries were indeed not uncommon among the Ostropol Jewish population at the time. Harry Wexler remembers that at the turn of the century the town had "one of those revolutionary cells … a big group … consisting of the intelligentsia," including his own father.[65] The cell produced at least one famous Russian Jewish revolutionary, Moisei Volodarsky, who was arrested in 1911 and sent into exile.[66] It is hard to say, nevertheless, how radical Koteliansky's politics really were at the time. His niece would characterize his views as "though not at all extreme … progressive enough to attract the attention of the authorities,"[67] while May Sarton referred to him as her "Russian anarchist friend."[68] "Kot wanted a form of Socialism," Esther Salaman told George Zytaruk, "but not the destruction of human values." She also recalled him saying: "I'd rather be dead than Bolshevik."[69]

He was, most likely, typical in that too – angry and politicized but no bomb thrower, not unlike other young Jews of his generation whom Esther Salaman remembers seeing in Zhitomir when she was a child. They distributed leaflets and stood out in the way they were dressed and carried themselves, but most of them were by no means fearless professional agitators: "I was looking out of the window, with my eyes on two women running past, just underneath, each frightened in her own way. They had neither hats nor kerchiefs and their hair was bobbled. 'The Revolutionaries,' Mother said close behind me."[70] Many Russian Jews at the turn of the century also belonged to – or sympathized with – the General Jewish Workers' Bund (or simply BUND, Yiddish for "Union"), which originated in the Pale of Settlement and called for the end of discrimination against Jews. Formed in 1897, BUND functioned both as a political party and a trade union.[71] It would have not been at all surprising if Koteliansky did, indeed, join BUND at some point during his college years.

His friends' assumptions about Koteliansky's political leanings were also based on his friendship with Fanny Stepniak, the widow of Sergei (Kravchinsky) Stepniak, an anarchist revolutionary and, like Volodarsky, a terrorist, who was active in "People's Will." Stepniak fled Russia after successfully assassinating General N.V. Mezentsev, Alexander II's chief of police, by stabbing him with a dagger in 1878.[72] Even in England, where he kept company with people like William Morris and Constance Garnett and where he was intentionally vague about his participation in the assassination, Stepniak continued to be unabashed in his admiration of the typical Russian terrorist whom he described as "noble, terrible, irresistibly fascinating, for he combines in himself the two sublimities of human grandeur, the martyr and the hero."[73]

Like Koteliansky, Fanny Stepniak (Fanya Lichkus) came from the Pale of Settlement.[74] The Stepniaks settled in London in 1884, and soon thereafter Sergei founded two influential Russian émigré organizations, the Society of Friends of Russian Freedom and the Russian Free Press Fund. Although not Jewish himself, Stepniak was known for his progressive views toward Jews and cited their situation in Russia as one of the reasons for an immediate revolution. "Indignation that we feel when confronted with the persecution of the peaceful, law-abiding people whose only crime is the fact that they are Jews," he wrote in 1891, "is one more reason for us to wish that the liberation of Russia should take place as soon as possible."[75]

Koteliansky never met Sergei, who was killed by a train while crossing railway tracks in 1895. Twenty-five years older than Koteliansky, Fanny Stepniak was no longer a radical political activist by the time he befriended her, soon upon his arrival in England, so few definite conclusions can be drawn from their relationship.[76]

Whatever the nuances of Koteliansky's politics were, that he left Russia in 1911 was no coincidence. Volodarsky's arrest and exile that year most likely played a role in his decision, but of much more consequence at the time was a different event unfolding in Kiev, where he probably still resided in 1911. In March the mutilated body of twelve-year-old Andrei Yushchinsky was discovered in a cave in the outskirts of the city. Since it was around Passover and his body was drained of blood, rumours quickly spread that the boy was a victim of a ritual murder perpetrated by Jews. A typical leaflet at the time read: "Christians, protect your children. Jewish Passover has started on March 17."[77] Abe Koosis, a seven-year-old boy living in Ostropol in 1911, remembers that as a result of Yushchinsky's murder, his town "became steeped in gloom and fear – verging on panic. All one could hear was anguished talk, arguments, whispers about the latest development in Kiev … I could feel the agitation and gloom."[78] A new wave of harsh pogroms was widely expected.

Esther Salaman told George Zytaruk that "Kot was sent to England by his mother, and it was his mother who supported him during his first few months in England."[79] They probably chose England because the family had friends there, including, perhaps, people associated with Koteliansky's first job, at the Russian Law Bureau. Since the move was supposed to be temporary, just to wait until the political repressions and anti-Jewish violence calm down, it made sense for him to go to Europe, still in the close vicinity of Russia, rather than to the United States, a more common point of destination for Russian Jews at the time. The United States – or Canada – were also a bad fit for Koteliansky, who always viewed them as excessively materialistic.

His travel passport was issued in Kiev on 17 May 1911. Three passport stamps testify to his further progress: they show that Koteliansky began his journey on 23 June 1911, stayed overnight in Warsaw – which was still a part of the Russian Empire then – in a hotel called "Sport," and then arrived in England on 7 July. If the Warsaw-London leg of the trip looks unreasonably long, it is because once he left Russia, Koteliansky traded not just countries but also calendars. At the time Russia was still following the Julian calendar, which was thirteen days behind the Gregorian calendar. Translated into the Gregorian calendar Koteliansky's itinerary would have him leaving Kiev on 5 July, probably early in the morning, getting to Warsaw late at night of the same day, and then going the following morning straight to London, by trains and a boat, and arriving there on 7 July, probably also quite late.

On 22 July, two weeks after Koteliansky came to London, Mendel Beilis – a Kiev Jew, manager at a brick factory, former soldier, and father of five – was arrested on suspicion of having committed a ritual murder of a Christian boy. This was the beginning of the so-called "Beilis Affair" and subsequent "Beilis Trial," which would receive much attention throughout the world, including in England. Two months later, in early September 1911, Kiev also became the place where Russia's reactionary Prime Minister Pyotr Stolypin was assassinated, and once again Jews lived in fear of brutal pogroms. "The Jewish population of Kiev is in panic," wrote the liberal newspaper "Rech"("Speech"). "Many are leaving town."[80] Koteliansky had wisely left town – and Russia – ahead of them all.

2

# "KOT": THE JEW IN LONDON

He is very persistent – he endures hardships and faces opposition
with a conquering perseverance.
~ *The Jew in London* (1901)

Possibly, your being a Jew comes in also at this point. You seem
so foreign.
~ Virginia Stephen to Leonard Woolf, 1 May 1912

The England to which Koteliansky arrived in 1911 did not have pogroms and
smugly prided itself on its enlightened attitude toward Jews. In *The Jew in London,*
published in 1901 and described as "A Study of Racial Character and Present-
Day Conditions," C. Russell wrote: "[O]ne can dwell with unmixed satisfaction
upon the absence among ourselves of any recrudescence of mediaeval intolerance
toward a people whose peculiar defects are fairly chargeable upon what they have
been forced in the past to suffer, whose possession of some peculiar merits cannot be denied, and who have made within recent times extraordinary contributions to learning and philosophy, to science and to … art." The same author
proclaimed that because Jews were "better treated in England than anywhere else
in Europe," there was a strong possibility that the race soon would "dissolve like
a lump of salt in water."[1]

Many English Jews at the time probably took such pronouncements with if not
a lump then at least a huge grain of salt. England was, after all, not only the orig-
inator of the blood-libel accusations against Jews but also one of the few European countries to have, at one point, expelled them. In 1144 the Jews of Norwich,
in the first such recorded occurrence, were charged with torturing and then murdering a Christian child in order to use his blood in baking the Passover matzah.
The expulsion took place at the end of the thirteenth century, so by the time
Shakespeare and Marlowe produced their famous Jewish villains, Shylock and

Barabas, the real-life examples were quite scarce. A large-scale return of the Jews to England did not occur till 1656, when Oliver Cromwell allowed Sephardic Jews, who had been dispersed as a result of several waves of the Spanish Inquisition, to settle in London. Before that could happen, Rabbi Menasseh Ben Israel of Amsterdam had to convince Cromwell that Jews, in fact, did not practice any form of ritual murder of Christians, an assurance that had to be repeated as late as 1840 by Britain's then chief rabbi, Solomon Herschell: "I swear, without any deceit or fraud, by the most high God, the creator of heaven and earth … that I never yet to this day saw any such custom among the people of Israel."[2] Among the Spanish Jews allowed into the country by Cromwell were the forbears of Benjamin Disraeli (1804–1881), who would become one of England's most famous prime ministers. Ashkenazi Jews – German and, occasionally, Eastern European – started arriving toward the end of the same century. By 1700, there were roughly 1,000 Sephardic and 500 Ashkenazi Jews in the country.[3]

Jews gained full citizenship rights in 1829. In 1835, David Salomons became the first Jew to attain a high political office, when he was elected sheriff of the City of London; twenty years later he would be elected to the office of lord mayor of London.[4] After the Parliament passed the law in 1858 allowing Jews to serve in the legislature, other prominent Jewish politicians followed, with Lionel de Rothschild being admitted as a member of Parliament the same year. This political progress culminated, of course, in the career of Disraeli, who, as leader of the Tories, served as prime minister in 1867 and then again in 1874. Disraeli's success was made possible by the baptism that he had undergone at the age of thirteen, and yet, as Robert Winder points out in *Bloody Foreigners: The Story of Immigration to England*, he never ran away from the fact that he was born a Jew. When disparaged by his opponents for his roots (people used to shout "Shylock!" at him when disagreeing with his policies) Disraeli would refer to his superior heritage – what Ashkenazic Jews call "yikhes" (a Yiddish word derived from Hebrew) – suggesting that, when the ancestors of his opponent were still "brutal savages in an unknown island," his were "priests in the temple of Solomon."[5]

By the time Koteliansky arrived in England, there were around 250,000 Jews in the country, constituting 0.6 percent of the entire population. Many English Jews at the time – among them Leonard Woolf, whom Koteliansky would get to know well and work for – came from families that had already been in the country for several generations. Yet, even for them, the "lump-of-salt-in-water" effect was still but a dream. As Winder suggests, while anti-Semitism in England at the time might have been less "ferocious" than in the rest of Europe, it was still plenty "infuriating": "One German characterized it as 'exclusion from garden parties, refusing certain cherished intimacies, and occasional light-hearted sneers.'"[6]

Leonard Woolf, his Cambridge education notwithstanding, definitely felt the "exclusion": "I was an outsider … because although I and my father before me belonged to the professional middle class, we had only recently struggled up into it from the stratum of Jewish shopkeepers. We had no roots in it."[7]

Anti-Semitism often went beyond just social exclusion, however, and affected careers. A good case in point was Dr David Eder (1866-1936), a friend of the Stepniaks and a member of A.R. Orage's circle, whom Koteliansky, too, would later befriend. Eder was born in London to a middle-class Jewish family that was rather typical for the times, inasmuch as they considered themselves Jews and attended a synagogue but were also quite acculturated into British social life. Eder went on to become a successful physician and psychoanalyst – as well as an early English Zionist – but after obtaining his medical degree in 1895 he immediately knew that, because he was a Jew, "the number of salaried medical posts open to him in England of those days was limited."[8] He therefore spent the next ten years practicing in South Africa and South America before returning to London in 1905 to open a modest clinic.

Even the Bloomsbury Group, which prided itself on tolerance and open-mindedness, was far from immune to strong anti-Semitic sentiments. In 1909, in a brief narrative called "Jews," Virginia Woolf wrote about her well-heeled Jewish neighbour: "One wonders how Mrs Loeb became a rich woman. It seems an accident; she might be behind a counter … She is a fat Jewess … coarsely skinned, with drooping eyes, and tumbled hair … Her food, of course, swam in oil and was nasty."[9] "I do not like the Jewish voice, I do not like the Jewish laugh," Woolf wrote in her diary in 1915, three years after she married Leonard.[10] "How I hated marrying a Jew – how I hated their nasal voices, and their oriental jewellery, and their noses and their wattles," she confessed to a friend later.[11] "Jew" became Leonard's nickname, used freely both by Virginia and her friends, and often in his presence.

Quentin Bell, Virginia Woolf's nephew and biographer, felt that the notion of anti-Semitism within Bloomsbury and the English educated classes in general had been exaggerated. He believed in particular that since Leonard "was liked, accepted, elected to Apostles [at Cambridge] and became a central figure amongst the intellectuals of his generation" one should be able "to assess and to put in its proper perspective the assertion that the set in which he now found himself was anti-semitic."[12] Yet it is hard to overlook numerous instances that point in a different direction. Thus Maynard Keynes would happily inform Quentin's mother, Vanessa Bell, that, when he visited the Woolfs, her sister was there "but no Jew,"[13] while Lytton Strachey felt free to declare to Leonard that the Jewish playwright Alfred Sutro was as bad as he was because he possessed the "placid easy-flowing vulgarity of *your* race."[14] A Bloomsbury scholar, Peter F. Alexander, cites another telling example, this time of a typical exchange between the spouses themselves when there was company: "Someone asked a question and Virginia called out, 'Let the Jew answer.' 'I won't answer until you ask me properly,' said Leonard with restraint."[15]

"[N]early all Jews are both proud and ashamed of being Jewish," Leonard Woolf postulated in *Sowing*, the first volume of his autobiography.[16] His own feelings were no exception: in his autobiography Leonard described, with some apprehension, the "look of stern rabbinical orthodoxy" among his paternal male ancestors who had come from the "old country," and noted, with a sense of palpable relief, the much lighter, less religiously doctrinaire Jewishness of his mother's family, who had lived for generations in Holland. Woolf even went as far as to deduce that, judging by how "fair-haired and facially very unlike the 'typical' Jew" some of his maternal relatives looked, they must have had "a good deal of non-Jewish blood" in their ancestry.[17] At the same time Leonard was in awe of his father's family perseverance and desire for good education: he tells us with much pride that he was not the first in his family to receive excellent schooling; Leonard's father, Sidney, had been sent by his own "large, stern, black-haired, and black-whiskered, rabbinical" father to obtain higher education either at Kings College or University College (Leonard was not sure which).[18]

Leonard's mixture of anxiety and dignity about being Jewish is perhaps even better revealed in a short story entitled "Three Jews," which he wrote in 1917, more than fifty years prior to the autobiography. It takes place on a nice spring day in Kew Gardens where the narrator shares a table with another man and they immediately recognize each other as fellow Jews. They then strike up a very casual but highly meaningful conversation about what it feels like being a Jew in England:

"Fine day," he said, "wonderfully fine day, the finest day I ever remember. Nothing to beat a fine English spring day."

I saw the delicate apple-blossom and the pale blue sky behind his large dark head. I smiled. He saw the smile, flushed, and then smiled himself.

"You are amused," he said, still smiling, "I believe I know why."

"Yes," I said, "you knew me at once and I knew you. We show up, don't we, under the apple-blossom and this sky. It doesn't belong to us, do you wish it did?"

"Ah," he said seriously, "that's the question. Or rather we don't belong to it. We belong to Palestine still, but I am not sure that it doesn't belong to us for all that."

"Well, perhaps your version is truer than mine. I'll take it, but there's still the question, do you wish *you* belonged to *it*?"

… He didn't answer my question; he was thinking, and when he spoke, he asked another:

"Do you ever go to Synagogue?"

"No."

"Nor do I, except on Yom Kippur. I still go then every year – pure habit. I don't believe in it, of course; I believe in nothing – we're all sceptics. And yet we belong to Palestine still. Funny, ain't it? How it comes out! Under the apple-blossom and blue sky, as you say…"[19]

Throughout the story there is one other unposed but seemingly implied question which is equally, if not more, important – "Do you wish *they* thought you belonged to it?" If life was still hard for well-rooted, acculturated, and secular British Jews at the time, it was incomparably more difficult for recent immigrants from Russia and Eastern Europe, who fled the pogroms only to be contemptuously referred to by British conservative politicians as "the very scum of the unhealthiest of the Continental nations."[20] Between 1881 and 1914, close to 150,000 Jewish immigrants came to Britain. They were, for most part, poor and not well educated, and, as such, lacked support even from their better-established brethren. This became obvious when several Jewish politicians went on record as supporting the 1905 "Alien Act," which was aimed at "the absolute prevention of Alien Pauper immigration."[21] Among those "Alien Paupers" was the family of a young boy, Mark Gertler, one of the future Bloomsbury artists, with whom Koteliansky was to form a very close, almost brotherly, bond. His well-documented personal story helps to make one appreciate what many Jewish refugees were going through at the time.

Gertler's parents, Golda and Louis, first came to London in 1886 from Przemsyl, located in Poland's Galicia region, which bordered Ukraine. Mark was born in the slums of London's heavily Jewish East End in 1891. Soon after his birth the family, incapable of making a living in a new country, was forced by circumstances to go back to Poland. By the time they made a second attempt to settle in England Mark was six years old. They moved back into Whitechapel, in the East End, and resumed the ways of the old country, speaking the only language they knew, Yiddish, and sending their sons to a Hebrew school. In his unfinished memoirs, started several years before his suicide in 1939, Gertler remembered his early experience with both fondness and resentment: "I was sent to 'Maida,' a Hebrew class. I hadn't far to go, as this institution existed in the same square, only a few yards from our house. The teacher was an old Rabbi of about seventy with [a] long white beard which ended in two points. The class consisted of one room with a long narrow table, at the head of which the old Rabbi sat and we children all around the rest of it. The Rabbi used to read the Old Testament to us in Hebrew, translating each sentence, or sentences, each word into Yiddish, in a rapid, hardly intelligible monotone, and we had to drone on after him, repeating the parts we could catch, and filling up the rest with noises that meant nothing whatsoever. Only occasionally, when he felt like it, would he pull us up and, choosing a boy quite indiscriminately, thump him."[22]

One of Gertler's biographers, Sarah MacDougall, describes the general environment and atmosphere young Mark was exposed to as follows: "London's Jewish quarter had its own shops, baths, a hospital ... and its own newspapers. Both written and spoken, the language was Yiddish ... Despite the poverty and overcrowding, on Fridays – the eve of Sabbath – the Jewish community sprang to life, with the cobbled streets and dark alleys ablaze as candles were set in the front windows of the crowded tenements. The orthodox bathed on Fridays at Scveik's Russian Vapour Baths in Brick Lane, and after the evening service at the synagogue Kiddush wine would be drunk and bread broken, and fathers blessed their children."[23]

In short, it was most definitely a quasi-Eastern-European shtetl. As in most shtetls in the old country, in the East End Jews had to co-exist with the non-Jewish poor, and the hostility was often quite palpable. John Woodeson, another biographer of Mark Gertler, quotes a typical report that accused Jews of not adjusting to the customs of their adopted country: "A foreign Jew will take a house, and he moves in on a Sunday morning, which rather, of course, upsets all the British people there ... [I]n the evening the women and girls sit out on the pavement and make a joyful noise ... [and] on Sunday the place is very different to what the English are accustomed to."[24] One way to change the situation was, of course, for English missionaries to convert the new arrivals to Christianity. However, as Woodeson points out, "The London Society for Promoting Christianity among Jews" consistently underachieved, its hefty budget of £35,000 a year notwithstanding: "[I]n spite of tempting bribes – 'Board and lodging at a specially provided house ... free education and free maintenance of Jewish children brought up in the Christian faith' – out of forty thousand Jews who were estimated to be in want, only twelve were baptized in a typical year."[25]

The prejudice against the Eastern European newcomers was not limited to the lower classes or expedient politicians. A month after Koteliansky arrived in Great Britain, in a typical article in a respectable journal, a returning British exile lamented that he could not recognize Great Britain because parts of it were now "inhabited by the scum of Lithuania or Poland." He advocated that this "scum" should all be shipped to colonies like Canada, where the Jews could be used to cultivate Canadian "arable, arboricultural, and metalliferous lands."[26] Jane Ellen Harrison, a rare female scholar at Cambridge, who might have been expected to be sympathetic to the fate of other underdogs, complained that, when she applied for a new passport, she suffered the indignities of not only being deprived of lunch but also of having to "stand for hours in a queue of Polish Jews."[27] H.G. Wells, to whose family Koteliansky would become close in the 1920s, strongly objected to the Jewish immigrants' way of life on the grounds that Jews were "people who cluster close in families," in a way that the English found "antipathetic."[28]

Koteliansky's soon-to-be intimate friend and confidant, D.H. Lawrence, found especially chilling words to express his feelings about the changing fabric of English society. "If I had my way," he wrote to Blanche Jennings in 1908, "I would build a lethal chamber as big as the Crystal Palace, with a military band playing softly, and a Cinematograph working brightly; then I'd go out in the back streets and main streets and bring them all in, the sick, the halt, the maimed; I would lead them gently and they would smile a weary thanks; and the band would softly bubble out the 'Hallelujah Chorus.'"[29] While this sentiment did not necessarily apply just to Jews but to London undesirables in general, including the natives,[30] Lawrence's remarks specifically about Jews did tend to be virulently anti-Semitic. In 1912, during a spike in antagonism toward his New York publisher William Heinemann, Lawrence referred to him as "his Jew-ship" and "the rotten little Jew."[31] In summer 1913, a year before meeting Koteliansky, he wrote to friends from the sea resort of Kingsgate that he had nothing to do "with fat, fatherly Jews and their motor cars and their bathing tent," and that he felt "horribly out of place among these Jews' villas and the babies and papas."[32]

Some Lawrence biographers suggest that he merely "spoke with the casual anti-Semitism common to his day" and that his life-long friendship with Koteliansky proved that, "ugly as some of his remarks appear to later generations, his was in no sense a blind bigotry."[33] It is definitely true that one should always be cautious about accusations of bigotry without taking into account the prevailing sentiments of the era. Lawrence, furthermore, had several other close Jewish friends, who, like Koteliansky, cherished his companionship, appreciated his honesty and generosity, revered his talent, and were inspired by his idealism. And yet, as late as 1921, seven years into his intense friendship with Koteliansky, Lawrence could still write to a sympathetic correspondent: "I hate Jews and I want to learn to be more *wary* of them all,"[34] which comes dangerously close to a blind, even if rather common, prejudice. It is particularly startling in his case because in most other matters Lawrence was anything but simplistic or common.

Arriving in London in early July 1911, Koteliansky considered himself bilingual but, when he stopped someone to ask for directions, he understood nothing. "It was a real blow to him," his niece would tell an interviewer later.[35] A friend remembered Koteliansky telling her that he "used to go to churches to hear English spoken" since he "couldn't understand the spoken language when he arrived even though his theoretical English was good."[36] Koteliansky probably did not ever consider settling in the East End, despite the fact that both the cultural and linguistic atmosphere there would have been quite familiar to him. Instead, his earliest address, as gleaned from a press card issued to him in 1911, appears much more respectable – 5 Victoria Gardens, Notting Hill Gate – and this is probably the very address for which he sought the directions.[37] The press card enabled "Mr S. Coteliansky," representing the newspaper "*Post of Kieff*," to attend the First Universal Races Congress which was held at the University of London on 26–29 July 1911. Two other documents we have from the same time, issued in 1911 and valid for one year and five years respectively, state, in Russian and French, that Koteliansky was, indeed, a correspondent for *Kievskaia pochta*, or "Kiev Post," and also for a magazine called *Otechestvo* (Fatherland).

The Universal Races Congress was a great undertaking. Organized with the help of people such as W.E.B. DuBois, a writer, historian, and a prominent advocate for black equality who a year earlier had co-founded the NAACP in the United States, its purpose was "to discuss, in the light of science and the modern conscience, the general relations subsisting between the peoples of the West and those of the East, between so-called whites and so-called coloured peoples, with a view to encouraging between them a fuller understanding, the most friendly feelings, and a heartier co-operation."[38] It was attended by more than 3,000 people and featured many prominent scholars, among them Franz Boas, a German Jew who was living in the United States and who is considered by many to be the father of cultural anthropology. What drew Koteliansky to this particular congress is easy to deduce. It was widely publicized and attracted many Russian academics (mostly specialists in sociology, history, and international law), so if Koteliansky was serious about attempting a career as a foreign correspondent for the *Kiev Post* or any other paper, this was an important event for him to cover. In addition, the theme of the congress appealed to his liberal views, while some of the papers dealt with the position of Jews in the world and were thus of particular interest and relevance to him.[39]

One of those papers was given by Israel Zangwill (1864–1926), Eder's closest friend and the foremost British-Jewish writer at the time, whose 1908 play *Melting Pot*, about a Russian Jew adjusting to his life in the United States, gave the name to American immigrant assimilation processes in general. Zangwill was the founder of the Jewish Territorial Organization (ITO), their aim being to establish a Jewish homeland wherever possible. However unrealistic, the whole notion that one day Jews may "dissolve like a lump of salt in water" was something Zangwill was vociferously opposed to at the time. As he stated in his presentation to the congress, "While to the philosopher the absorption of the Jews may be as desirable as their regeneration, in practice the solution by dissolution presses most heavily upon the weakest. The dissolution invariably begins from above, leaving the lower classes denuded of a people's natural defences, the upper classes. Moreover, while ... the Jewish upper classes are, if anything, inferior to the classes into which they are absorbed, the marked superiority of the Jewish masses to their environment, especially in Russia, would render *their* absorption a tragic degeneration."[40]

Soon after the congress, Koteliansky visited Paris. We know that because of the letter he wrote to his niece in 1947 on the occasion of her sending him a new wallet from Canada. "I shall start using it," he assured her, "when my wallet, which I bought in Paris in the autumn of 1911, is no longer usable. I have had mine for 36 years and it was not at all an expensive one, but it is still good."[41] It is doubtful that he had much currency to put into that wallet during his first months in England, since he probably had to pay substantial rent in places he inhabited without having any steady income.

Koteliansky's first dwelling at 5 Victoria Gardens was a two-storied unit in a brown brick building on a very quiet and short street, just off much noisier Notting Hill Gate (and between the equally tiny Bulmer Place and Ladbroke Road). According to both the 1911-12 Polling Index for Pembridge District and the 1911 Kelly's Kensington, Notting Hill, Brompton & Knightsbridge Directory, the house belonged to Mr James Knowles, who, unlike almost all of his neighbours, did not officially rent it to lodgers but lived there by himself.[42] The contemporaneous Post Office London Directories further reveal that, of the two James Knowles listed there in the 1909-13 volumes, the one most likely to have been the owner of 5 Victoria Gardens is the James Knowles who worked in the "British Museum, Director & Principal Librarian's Office."[43]

Koteliansky's next recorded London address was 53 Whitehall Park, in Highgate. The house was a semi-detached three-storied red brick dwelling on a leafy residential street near Archway and Holloway Roads. He would later remember the Holloway Road as "terribly long and poor."[44] The dates of his residence there are not very clear, though. He lists it as his "Last previous place of residence" in his identity book (no. 118050), which gives his "present residence" – dating from "about September 1914" – as 212 High Holborn, WC. In his 1912 press ticket to the Latin-British Exhibit, however, the address given is already that of 212 High

Holborn, which, as we will see, was also the address of his first employment. According to the electoral roll for Whitehall Park, in 1911, 53 Whitehall Park belonged to someone named Peter Macpherson, but there are no official lodgers listed for that year. The list of owners and lodgers on the street in general bespeaks their largely English or Scottish ancestry ("Grant," "Watson," "Langley," "Scott," McCormick," "McKenzie," "Mackie," etc.); there appear to be virtually no foreigners among them, and almost definitely no Jews.[45] How Koteliansky ended up in such a neighbourhood is unclear.

In 1913 Koteliansky no doubt followed very closely the developments in the Beilis trial. There were protests in London. In her autobiography Russian revolutionary Alexandra Kollontai specifically noted that she came to London in 1913 "in order to take an active part in a protest action against the famous 'Beilis Trial' which had been instigated by the anti-semites in Russia."[46] The *Times* of London suggested, overly optimistically, as it turned out, that the trial signified "possibly a final fight for existence on the part of the innermost powers of reaction against all modern forces in Russia."[47] Beilis, who did not even know the murder victim, Andrei Yushchinsky (killed, most likely, by the mother of the boy's best friend), was acquitted after a forceful defense and vigorous campaign by several progressive Russian intellectuals. Beilis contemplated settling in London. As he would record in his 1926 autobiography, the Rothschild family offered him "a fully furnished home that would become my property as soon as I arrived in London."[48]

There were no Rothschilds in Koteliansky's life, so he was reduced to a more traditional way of making money: finding a job. Although rumour back in Ostropol had it that Koteliansky had become "assistant editor of the London Times,"[49] Koteliansky instead put his bilingual skills to work at the Russian Law Bureau, or "Ruslabu," as it was listed in the commercial section of the 1914 Post Office London Directory. Located at 212 High Holborn, the Bureau was run by a fellow Russian Jew, Ruvin (or Ruvim) Solomonovich Slatkowsky, who is listed in the same directory as "Russian advocate." The four-storied pale grey mansion near the corner of Southampton Row is described in the directory as both an office and a dwelling house, since the top floor was let out to lodgers, Koteliansky among them. Slatkowsky shared the space with Herbert Barley and John Marks, "auctioneers," while the top floor had at least one more dweller, identified elsewhere as George Henry Reynolds.[50]

Several of Koteliansky's friends who visited him at 212 High Holborn left descriptions of Ruslabu. Lady Glenavy's memoirs are less than utterly reliable, since she erroneously places the office in Whitechapel – which, rather than the respectable business locale at the crossroads of Holborn and Bloomsbury, would have, indeed, been a much more logical place for this practice with largely Russian clientele. The office itself she remembers as "hideous": "the darkness, the horsehair-covered furniture, a picture of kittens playing in a basket of pansies, and an even more incongruous picture for such a place, a Christ surrounded by little children."[51] Katherine Mansfield likewise left a record of the place. It comes in a nostalgic letter to Koteliansky she sent from Menton, France on 19 February 1921. Signed as "Kissinka" (Russian for "little kitten") the letter, in typical Mansfield fashion, is often missing question marks: "What has happened to the ink-stand with the elephants on it – mother-of-pearl, inlay – or was it ivory. Some of the inlay had begun to come off; I fancy one of the elephants had lost an eye. And that dim little picture of a snowy landscape hanging on the wall in your room. Where is it now? And where are the kittens and the children and Christ, who looked awfully like a kitten, too, who used to hang in the dining room. And that leather furniture with the tufts of horse-hair stuffing coming out. Where are all the hats from the hatstand … Then there was the statue on the stairs, smiling, the fair caretaker, always washing up, the little children always falling through her door. And your little room with the tiny mirror and the broken window and the piano sounding from outside … And then Slatkowsky – his *beard*, his 'glad eye' – his sister, who sat in front of the fire and took off her boot."[52]

Mansfield's much earlier 1915 letter gives us the best glimpse, perhaps, of how Koteliansky himself felt at the time about his job and the office in general: "As I write I hear your voice and I see you swing out in the hall of the bureau as though you were going to beat to death the person who had dared to come in."[53] Mark Gertler joked that his friend's sole job was to blacken Slatkowsky's beard,[54] and Slatkowsky's reputation with Koteliansky's friends in general was very poor – the result, most likely, of Koteliansky's own contempt for him. Frieda Lawrence remembered that Koteliansky's treatment of his boss was literally dismissive: "[Koteliansky] was a mystery because he was supposed to be in law office but he would take us there and bounce his boss out of the place and mix up sour herring and mashed potatoes for us on the spot."[55] Her husband, who likewise enjoyed "our sour, sour herrings, in the Russian Law Bureau," referred to Slatkowsky as "the obscene Slat."[56] "It will be a great boon if S. goes to Russia," Lawrence suggested to Kotelianky in 1916, "we might have a very free and simple time at 212. But I suppose the old landlord will *never* clear out. And he is impossible."[57] When Slatkowsky unexpectedly died in 1917, Lawrence refused to be charitable even to his memory: "Well, one blot is under the earth instead of upon it – which is a blessing!"[58]

Another person who was working at the Bureau at the time was an English barrister by the name of Horne. It was Horne who first introduced Koteliansky to D.H. Lawrence when he brought Koteliansky along for a walking tour in the Lake District at the end of July 1914, on the very eve of the war.[59] In addition to Horne, Koteliansky, and Lawrence, the walking party included an engineer named Lewis. Koteliansky would later tell Catherine Carswell that either Horne or Lewis had described Lawrence to him as "a writer chap with ideas about love" and that, on the second night of their walk, "they had to be put up in a cottage where there was only one bed … Lawrence, as the delicate one, was made to sleep in the bed, and Koteliansky as the visitor was urged to share it. He was very unwilling. Never in his life had such a thing befallen him. But Lawrence was so gay and easy that all shyness vanished."[60]

Lawrence remembered the occasion quite vividly more than ten years later, as he told Koteliansky: "I remember very well the famous walk in the Lake district, how you suffered having to sleep in the same bed – & how we got water-lilies – and came down to Lewis's unattractive home, & it was war, & you departed in a cloud."[61] Earlier, he had described the walk with fuller detail to Lady Cynthia Asquith: "The War finished me: it was the spear through the side of all sorrows and hopes. I had been walking in Westmorland, rather happy, with water-lilies twisted round my hat – big, heavy, white and gold water-lilies that we found in a pool high up – and girls who had come on a spree and who were having tea in the upper room of an inn, shrieked with laughter. And I remember also we crouched under the loose wall on the moors and the rain flew by in streams, and the wind came rushing through the chinks in the wall behind one's head, and we shouted songs and I imitated music-hall turns, whilst the other men crouched under the wall and I pranked in the rain on the turf in the gorse, and Koteliansky groaned Hebrew music – Ranani Sadekim Badanoi."[62]

The experience drew the four of them close together, and both Lewis and Horne feature prominently in the letters Lawrence sent to Koteliansky in the months following their adventure. The fact that it was on that fateful walk that the four of them learned that the war had broken out must have added further to their bond. In the first surviving letter (and probably the first actual letter) that Lawrence sent to Koteliansky on 5 August 1914, Lawrence complained that he was, indeed, "very miserable about the war."[63] That was the day England officially declared war on Germany. *The New York Times* on that day proclaimed that England was "Cool in Great Crisis" and "facing this … with calmness and courage." It also stated that "Liberal newspapers like The Westminster Gazette, The Daily Chronicle, and even The Daily News accept the situation as inevitable" and praised Premier Asquith's "Impressive Speech."[64] But neither Koteliansky, whose return to Russia was now cut off by the war, nor Lawrence, who feared the draft, faced the crisis in a particularly cool or calm manner. They were, there-fore, natural correspondents with each other on that particular subject.

Even with all that in mind, the intimacy Koteliansky quickly developed with Lawrence is nothing short of remarkable. Lawrence appears to have been imme-diately comfortable having Koteliansky do favours for him. It was important, however, that Lawrence never thought of these as "favours." "If you don't want to lose Lawrence's friendship," Koteliansky would confide in another friend later, "you must be very careful never to let him guess that you are doing anything for him."[65] It is not clear what Lawrence considered the kind of service Koteliansky was performing for him to be but back then it included typing the manuscript of *A Study of Thomas Hardy*, since Lawrence could not afford professional help (5 October 1914), and picking up a necklace for Frieda (31 October 1914),[66] whom Lawrence had officially wed just two weeks prior to the tour.

At the time Frieda was going through a very difficult period: her divorce from her first husband, Ernest Weekley, Lawrence's English professor at the Univer-sity of Nottingham, left her three children solely in his custody. She therefore had to rely on her former husband's kindness in order to see them, but, given that she had run away with his student, such kindness was in very short supply. She also had to rely on the kindness and patience of her friends, whom she con-stantly begged to pass her letters to her children on their way to and from school. Koteliansky had little sympathy for her dilemma. Frieda, he always maintained, just had to choose between her children and Lawrence, because she plainly could not have both.[67] Lawrence, who himself often expressed a similar sentiment, was nevertheless annoyed at his Russian friend's simplicity and naïveté. "You must-n't judge her lightly," he admonished Koteliansky on 3 December 1914. "There is another quality in woman that you do not know, so you can't estimate it. You don't know that a woman is not a man with different sex. She is a different world. You do not understand that enough. Your world is all of one hemisphere."[68]

Koteliansky was probably generally incapable of being sympathetic to Frieda's parental grief because, in his largely black-and-white worldview, only bad moth-ers abandoned their children, but here his disapproval was further aggravated by the fact that he did not like her as a person. There were two aspects of Frieda that immediately repulsed Koteliansky. One was her obvious pride in her sexual prowess and the power it held over Lawrence; the other was her anti-Semitism. The latter generally matched her husband's, but to Koteliansky her prejudice was much less forgivable because there was so little to redeem it. He also believed that it was Frieda who was behind Lawrence's worst anti-Semitic outbursts and that he was just parroting her when he became angry at his Jewish publishers or agents. One of Frieda's beloved sisters, Else, was actually married to a Jew. Else's husband, Edgar Jaffe, came from a rich Hamburg family of textile manufacturers, but he was an intellectual, not a merchant. He met Else at Heidelberg University, where he taught her Political Economy. Frieda's entire aristocratic German family had been initially scandalized by Else's choice but then saw nothing wrong with relying on her husband's significant wealth and good nature. By the time Frieda abandoned Professor Weekley, Else and Edgar were separated, yet he continued to bestow his generosity on the entire clan, including now the new man in Frieda's life. In 1912, while in Bavaria, Frieda and Lawrence stayed in Jaffe's luxurious newly built chalet, and he continued to support them financially until his death in 1921. Despite it all, both Lawrences treated Jaffe with a certain degree of contempt. To his friends, including Koteliansky, Lawrence usually referred to his brother-in-law as "a rich Jew" first and "Professor" second.[69]

Later in 1914, Lawrence introduced Koteliansky to John (Jack) Middleton Murry and Katherine Mansfield, who were often referred to as "The Murrys" even though they would not be officially married till 1918; Gordon and Beatrice Campbell (Lady Glenavy), and Mark Gertler.[70] He also took Bertrand Russell to Ruslabu to see Koteliansky and the rest of the gang, but Russell found the atmosphere, and the company, not to his liking: "He took me to see a Russian Jew, Koteliansky, and Murry and Mrs Murry – they were all sitting together in a bare office high up next door to the Holborn Restaurant, with the windows shut, smoking Russian cigarettes without a moment's intermission, idle and cynical. I thought Murry *beastly* and the whole atmosphere of the three dead and putrefying."[71]

Among his newer acquaintances, Koteliansky was particularly drawn to Mansfield. She, in turn, was predisposed to like him simply because he was a Russian. "My mind is like a Russian novel," Mansfield wrote in her journal when she was just nineteen.[72] The passion of her response to the Russian books appearing in translation in England was truly unbound. But it was not Tolstoy – whom she nevertheless adored – but Anton Chekhov who became her literary idol and role model, even though she realized that reading him in translation was short of the mark. Sometimes her affinity with Chekhov even veered toward plagiarism. In 1911 she published a story, "The-Child-Who-Was-Tired," which was an unmistakable free rendition of Chekhov's early story "Spat' khochetsia" ("Sleepyhead"). In both, an overworked young girl smothers a crying baby she is tending to, in order to be able to sleep. In Chekhov's case, the girl is a poor peasant orphan working for a merchant family; in Mansfield's story, she is a poor orphan working for a middle-class family. The parents in "The-Child-Who-Was-Tired" are German, but two of their older children bear surprisingly Russian names – Lena and Anton, the latter, of course, Mansfield's tongue-in-cheek acknowledgement of the inspiration behind the story. While she was alive, however, Mansfield never publicly revealed that Chekhov's "Sleepyhead" was the source for the "The-Child-Who-Was-Tired."[73] Koteliansky must have made the link right away, and they probably even talked about it, but his reaction remained unrecorded.

After she was diagnosed with tuberculosis in 1917, Mansfield's bond with Chekhov, who had died of the same disease thirteen years earlier, became almost mystical. "Ach, Tchekov!" she wrote in her diary in 1918. "Why are you dead! Why can't I talk to you – in a big, darkish room – at late evening – where the light is green from the waving trees outside. I'd like to write a series of *Heavens*: that would be one."[74] Koteliansky, whose personality had little in common with the mild-mannered and civil Chekhov, gradually even became a stand-in for the Russian writer in her mind: "I can truly say I think of ... Tchekhov, Koteliansky ... every day. They are part of my life."[75] He also became, according to Murry, who often resented their closeness, "Katherine's most understanding friend": "[I]t was a maxim with Koteliansky that Katherine could do no wrong. Since, as he once put it, she 'had a greater talent for being just a human being' than anyone else in the world, his attitude was that her talent should have all the scope it demanded ... Koteliansky delighted in her 'wickedness.'"[76]

In early 1920 Mansfield was only too happy to be helping Koteliansky translate Chekhov's letters, which did not appear till after Mansfield's death, first in 1923 in *The Adelphi*, the periodical Murry started editing in June of that year, and then as a separate volume in 1925.[77] In the course of the translation, Mansfield somehow managed to lose the copies that Koteliansky sent her. Virginia Woolf, who considered it "wanton cruelty on her part" and wondered "How could one lose 3 books lent one by a man who gets his bread by writing?" had to marvel at how Koteliansky, already known for his short temper, did not even get angry at Mansfield but "patiently set ... to work to write them out again."[78] And yet, from time to time, he could be harsh even with her. "All our friends hurt me," Katherine complained to Murry soon after they met Koteliansky, "Kot very deeply."[79]

Around the same time his name did, indeed, get truncated to "Kot," because his English pals had an awfully hard time coming to terms with its difficult transliterated spelling, which they more often than not got wrong. In their early letters to him, Lawrence and Mansfield referred to their new friend as "Kotiliansky" or "Kotilianski," while Mark Gertler wrote his name as "Kotilanski" one day and "Cotilanski" just two days later.[80] Not just his name but his appearance stood out as well. According to Murry, Kot "looked like some Assyrian king ... with an impressive hooked Semitic nose, a fine head of coarse black curly hair, and massive features: very dark eyes with pince-nez."[81] Dorothy Brett, a painter and a close friend of Mansfield's and Gertler's, who befriended Kot in the early 1920s (only to become his enemy soon after Mansfield's death), left a similar but much finer description of him. Kot was, according to her, "so broad shouldered that he looks short, his black hair brushed straight up 'en brosse,' his dark eyes set perhaps a trifle too close to his nose, the nose a delicate well-made arch, gold eye-glasses pinched onto it."[82] But the best verbal portrait may belong to Lawrence. In *Kangaroo*, Ben Cooley looks very much like Kot, who was, indeed, "forty or so" by the time the book came out in 1923:

> His face was long and lean and pendulous, with eyes set close together behind his pince-nez; and his body was stout but firm. He was a man of forty or so, hard to tell, swarthy, with short-cropped dark hair and a smallish head carried rather forward on his large but sensitive, almost shy body. He leaned forward in his walk, and seemed as if his hands didn't quite belong to him. But he shook hands with a firm grip. He was really tall, but his way of dropping his head, and his sloping shoulders, took away from his height … Kangaroo was really ugly: his pendulous Jewish face, his forward shoulders, his round stomach …[83]

The reaction of the Bloomsbury set to Koteliansky's appearance is probably best summarized by David Garnett, Constance Garnett's son, who first saw Kot in January 1915: "[T]here was a ring at the bell … Duncan [Grant] went down and returned with an uninvited figure – a dark Russian Jew called Koteliansky – who had come to pick up Lawrence and Frieda with whom he had arranged to spend the evening … Koteliansky sat black and silent."[84] "An uninvited … dark Russian Jew" probably captures it all. Lady Glenavy maintains that Koteliansky presented an odd figure also because of the way he dressed: "To make himself look like an Englishman he bought a Panama hat and white tennis shoes; he also wore a Russian blouse with embroidered neckband. When he went out into the street the girls of Tottenham Court Road became so helpless with laughter that he used to stay in his room during the day and only come out at night."[85] Ridiculous as it may have looked in England, the Russian blouse did have its symbolic meaning: Koteliansky's initial value to all his new friends (with the possible exception of Gertler) was definitely his Russianness, which in their minds made him immediately connected with everything that was so exciting about Russia, including, of course, Diaghilev's Ballets Russes.

Barbara Bagenal, Mark Gertler's fellow student at the Slade School of Art, fondly remembered the gatherings at the house of Ottoline and Philip Morrell –

whose mansion's interiors definitely bore the significant influence of the "First Russian Ballet Period" – following the Diaghilev's Ballet performances: "Many of us who went to these parties were greatly influenced by the Russian Ballet and we often went to Ottoline's house straight from Covent Garden. Philip Morrell played the piano for us and we all danced madly together – probably still influenced by the ballet. They were great gatherings."[86] Gertler, who attended many of these parties, liked to later ridicule them in front of Kot and Lady Glenavy, the latter reminiscing that Mark "would go out of the room and return as Lady Ottoline Morrell, then as one of the Stracheys or Sitwells or Maynard Keynes … making himself fat or tall, short or thin, while we … laughed helplessly." Kot, according to Glenavy, particularly enjoyed Gertler's performance: "Kot's laugh was like a small continuous cough. In those days he wore pince-nez, and he had to take them off to wipe the tears of laughter from his eyes."[87]

Kot enjoyed Gertler's satire so much precisely because, with his Jewish Pale background and very liberal political leanings, he had so little to do with – and often much loathed – the aristocratic Russian "ambiance" of which Lady Morrell and her set were in such admiration. As he once confessed to Esther Salaman, who he knew would immediately understand him, his feeling about "average Russians" was that "under certain circumstances every one of them could be a 'pogromshchik,'"[88] and he had no reason to make exceptions for the Ballets Russes dancers. Furthermore, back in Russia, severely limited in his travels, Kot had not even been privileged to visit St Petersburg or Moscow; there is little doubt, therefore, that he thought he would be seen by the visiting Russians as not only hopelessly Jewish but also hopelessly provincial. But while Kot's English friends were well aware of the class distinctions in their own country, Russia's were another matter.

To his new friends Kot probably appeared not that different from other – non-Jewish – Russians in Bloomsbury's orbit: the Ballets Russes ballerina Lydia Lopokova and the artist Boris Anrep. Nothing could be further from the truth. Anrep, whose full name was von Anrep, is a particularly noteworthy study in contrast here. A poet as well as a painter, he came from a noble Russian-German family. Three years younger than Kot, he studied law at St Petersburg University before choosing to study art in Paris. He settled in London the same year as Kot but got to the heart of Bloomsbury through its painters much sooner. A regular at Ottoline Morrell's gatherings before the war, he was a natural person to hobnob with the Ballets Russes crowd. Morrell remembered how after she met Nijinsky on her own several times, she asked Anrep to join them and "he stayed for hours talking about Russian myths and religion."[89] There is no evidence that Anrep and Kot ever socialized, despite the fact that they had come from the same country and knew some of the same people. Their social origins and upbringing were just too different. Koteliansky likewise had only a minimal contact with Lopokova, who, like Anrep (with whom she was very friendly), grew up in St Petersburg, even though in a less aristocratic family.⁹⁰ To Kot, any suggestion that their backgrounds were similar just because they all had come from Russia was preposterous. When one of his friends, A.S. Fulton, remarked that Kot looked "like a Russian prince" on a photograph of him as a young man, Kot, according to Fulton "was quite angry … scorning any such comparison."⁹¹

These social differences could at least partially explain an incident that occurred during one of the Ballet seasons and mystified all who knew Kot. Lady Glenavy witnessed it:

> A friend of Gertler's, Montague Shearman, picture-collector and connoisseur, had a large room in the Adelphi, comfortably furnished … He gave a key of this room to several of his intimate friends, including Gertler, so that they could use it when they liked. While the Russian Ballet was still having its season in London, Kot and Gertler, Gordon and I dined somewhere and afterward Gertler suggested going to Shearman's room, which we did. On opening the door, we were surprised to find the whole place arranged for a party … We guessed that Shearman was at the ballet with a party, and would be bringing them back, probably Lopokova, Diaghilev and half the company. For some extraordinary reason which has never been explained, Kot and Gertler seemed to go raving mad. It was really Kot who started it. They dashed at the bottles and the liqueurs, drinking everything and eating all the sandwiches…
>
> They threw the flowers and cushions all over the place and Kot took a painted wooden tray made by Roger Fry … and smashed it down with both hands over Gertler's head. I can still see Gertler's startled, delighted expression.⁹²

Kot's reaction may indeed be explained as his vigorous statement against snobbery and class prejudices, yet his behaviour here, which is somewhat reminiscent of the incident with the family dog and his mother's jewels, will still strike many as downright manic. It is probably not at all a coincidence, then, that he was also subject to dramatic mood swings, as Kot's close friends, including Lawrence, were quick to discover. "My dear Kot," Lawrence wrote on 11 November 1914, "But why this curtness? What ails you? Are you cross or offended, or have you got a 'bad mood' – which is it? Why can't you come down? Why are you so silly? Why don't you say what's amiss? Is it Slatkowsky, or Horne, or just yourself?"[93] Since Koteliansky's letters to Lawrence did not survive, we do not know how he replied in this particular case, but the theme of his "bad moods" or "black moods," as he often defined them, will dominate his correspondence with many of his friends for the rest of his life.

Kot was also rapidly gaining a reputation as an absolutist who judged people around him in harsh and uncompromising terms. It was becoming evident to all that he loved to hate as much as he loved to love, and his expressions of loathing were legendary. "Kot's hate was a terrible thing," writes Lady Glenavy. "For Kot people were either 'ordinary' or 'exceptional' and these two kinds were miles apart."[94] "There are pigs and people," he allegedly told May Sarton, who became one of the people who moved from one category to the other over the years.[95] When Katherine Mansfield found herself detesting a particular nurse at a sanatorium, she kept repeating to herself one of Kot's favourite sayings: "Let her be beaten – simply – but to death."[96] Others remembered the modifier as "plainly," rather than "simply." "If you are sad, we'll plainly beat you,'" Lawrence joked in an early letter,[97] and Murry recorded two examples of what he considered to be Kot's "strange locutions" as follows: "'She wants beating, *plainly*' – 'He is a bli-ghter, plainly.'"[98]

He liked to call people he hated "blighters." While the range of the "blighter" in common usage was anywhere from a mildly annoying pest to an absolute moron, in Kot's mouth it was always the latter. His anger, Kot told Gertler in 1917, was such that "it could scorch lots of noisy talkative blighters."[99] Once he designated people as "blighters," they were doomed to stay in this category until the end. The process of designing someone a blighter, as he explained to Ida Baker, was a quick one: "[I]f I dislike a person, – and that's nearly always on the first meeting, that person may possess all possible virtues, but to me he is just a good-for-nothing blighter for ever and ever."[100] Lawrence, who himself was not a stranger to fits of uncontrollable rage ("I ... know what it means suddenly to feel blazing mad"[101]) and rushes to judgment, still felt uncomfortable with Kot's fury and black-and-white dogmatism. "[D]on't avoid everybody, and annihilate him straight off," Lawrence pleaded with Kot a week after he wondered about his friend's bad mood. "You must give yourself to people more, & take them as they are."[102]

In addition to trying to soften his personality, Lawrence teased Kot – good-naturedly, it appeared – about his Jewishness: "I must call you – what is it – Shimiel – Schmuel – it ends in 'el' like all the Angels..."[103] To another Jewish friend, Barbara Low, a relative of David Eder, Lawrence jokingly characterized

Kot as "a very bossy and overbearing Jew" with whom Barbara should "quarrel … very much" in order to "save the race!" "If it ever comes to blows with Kot," Lawrence instructed her, "please beat him with the poker."[104] Kot did not seem to be particularly bothered by this ribbing. In December, he invited the Lawrences to celebrate a Jewish Sabbath with him, and Lawrence liked the red wine Kot served on the occasion so much that he asked him to bring some for the small Christmas party they were having later in the month: "[P]lease bring two flasks of Chianti … such as we had at your Jewish Cosher Supper."[105]

Kot, in the meantime, was discovering his new friend as a novelist. By the end of 1914 Lawrence had published three novels: *The White Peacock*, *The Trespasser*, and *Sons and Lovers*. *The White Peacock* came out the year Kot arrived in London but since his walking tour friends had to explain to him who the "writer chap" joining them was, it is obvious he had not read it, or the other two novels that followed, prior to forming a relationship with Lawrence. *The White Peacock* probably quite appealed to him. It was filled with smells and images of farm and country life which were not that different from his memories of Ostropol, especially since the book's locale was, like Ostropol, positioned between "the woods and water," in the words of Cyril, the largely autobiographical narrator, who also suggests that these "woods and … waters were distilled in the essence of our veins."[106] Lawrence's first published novel also contains casual Russian references. The characters discuss reading Maxim Gorky, possibly allude to Chekhov's *Wood Demon* (which Koteliansky would translate in 1925), and Cyril's sister Lettie even once calls her mother using the Russian endearing term "matouchka."[107] Lawrence also mentions Chekhov's "Spat' khochetsia," the very same story that Mansfield would later appropriate for her own means. While watching a tired maid handle a cranky baby, Cyril, we are told, "thought of the girl in Tchekov story who smothered her charge."[108]

A feature of the novel that may have intrigued Kot even more is how honestly the narrator talks about his physical attraction to strong manly men, in this case a farmer, George. After a swim together, Cyril is entranced by looking at the "well proportioned, and naturally of handsome physique, heavy limbed" George, whose body's "noble, white fruitfulness" is in stark contrast to Cyril's own skinniness. Then George, realizing that his young companion is so distracted as to have forgotten to dry himself, grabs his towel and starts drying him:

[H]e … began to rub me briskly, as if I were a child, or rather, a woman he loved … I felt myself quite limply in his hands … the sweetness of the touch of our naked bodies one against the other was superb. It satisfied in some measure the vague, indecipherable tearning of my soul; and it was the same with him. When he had rubbed me all warm, he let me go, and … our love was perfect for a moment, more perfect that any love I have known since, either for man or woman.[109]

Reading Lawrence's published works led to Koteliansky's early and unshakable determination that his new friend possessed true genius that had to be nourished and protected at all costs. Traditionally, it was of course largely the role of a genius' wife to do so, but in this case Kot became firmly convinced that Lawrence had to be protected *from* his wife if he were to develop his full potential as a writer. Kot's relationship with Frieda therefore was further doomed.

# YEAR 1915: KOT AS KANGAROO

It was in 1915 the old world ended ... The spirit of the old London
collapsed, the city, in some way, perished, perished from being a
heart of the world, and became a vortex of broken passions, lusts,
hopes, fears, and horrors. The integrity of London collapsed,
and genuine debasement began ...
~ D.H. Lawrence, *Kangaroo*

Koteliansky told Lady Glenavy that he "came for three months, and ... stayed for
ever."[1] A notation in his Russian passport stated that on 24 July 1914, several days
prior to the outbreak of the war (and the walking tour with Lawrence), Koteliansky visited the Russian Consulate in London "for the purpose of proceeding with
his passage to Russia, as circumstances permit."[2] Within a couple of weeks of this
visit, with the war raging on and showing no signs of abating, it must have
become obvious to Kot that circumstances would not permit his return and that,
for better or for worse, he was indefinitely stuck in London. Unfortunately, we
do not have any letters from Koteliansky prior to 1916. However, because of the
letters and journals of his literary and artistic friends – especially Lawrence,
Mansfield, and Gertler – 1915 is already a year in his life in England that is possible to partially reconstruct.

In January 1915 England's sense of security was shattered by German Zeppe-
lin raids on the island. During the same month poison gas was first used by the
Germans against the Allied Forces on the Eastern Front; the Western Front would
experience a chemical attack and horrendous casualties (three times as many as
in the German army) in April. In May, the Germans sank *Lusitania*, a British
cargo and passenger ship that sailed between England and the United States,
killing more than a thousand people.[3] The battle for Gallipoli, which started in
spring 1915 and lasted for almost ten months, resulted in 300,000 allied deaths,
including 120,000 British.

Throughout the year, talk of impending compulsory service was growing louder; it was constantly being debated on the pages of the leading journals and periodicals. The January issue of *The Nineteenth Century and After*, an influential British monthly literary journal,[4] featured a lengthy discussion of three possible kinds of service: voluntary, obligatory, and in-between ("compulsory minimum" that leads to "the voluntary maximum").[5] The so-called "Derby Scheme," named after its proponent Lord Derby, held that, although all men should be potentially eligible, bachelors were more eligible than others. Mark Gertler, a twenty-four-year-old bachelor, was very worried. "I expect I shall be dragged into this wretched war, before it's all over," he wrote to a friend in July 1915, "but I shall keep out of it as long as I possibly can. How hateful it all is. How shall I hate it if it spoils my life and prevents me from carrying on my work. How hateful it would be to lose one's life, or even be maimed for life, through a purpose in which one has no sort of belief."[6] Gertler's parents, who, unlike him, were not British subjects, began the process of changing their citizenship from "Austrian" to "Polish" in order to avoid being labelled "enemy aliens," but Frieda Lawrence had no such choice.

Yet, despite the war, life for Koteliansky appeared to go on much like the year before, except that there was new professional excitement since his first book of translations – Anton Chekhov's *The Bet and Other Stories* – came out both in England, published by Maunsel & Company, and in the United States. The volume, as with several others to follow in 1916, was done in collaboration with Jack Murry, but Koteliansky's name appeared first and, unlike later editions, there was yet no introduction from the better-known English member of the duo. Instead, it contained Kotelianky's very own "Translator's Note," where he explained to the readers that the Russian dishes mentioned in one of the stories ("A Tedious Story") "have no exact equivalents" and that "*schi* is a soup made out of sour cabbage."[7]

Koteliansky probably chose "The Bet" ("Pari") as the leading story because, at least on the surface, it expressed his own vehement anti-materialism, and, for that reason, the story is worth retelling here. Written by Chekhov in 1889, "The Bet" opens with an aging banker remembering a discussion among guests at his party fifteen years ago on what was more cruel: capital punishment or life imprisonment. Back then the debate lead to a bet between the banker, who thought execution was more humane, and a young lawyer, who proclaimed he would prefer any life to no life. Started as a joke, the bet became serious when money got involved: the lawyer agreed to a solitary confinement in the banker's garden house for the next fifteen years, with no opportunity to see people or even hear voices, on condition that, if he stuck it out, the banker would pay him two million roubles. The story then shifts back to the eve of the fateful day when the lawyer is supposed to be set free and pocket the money but the banker is now having much regret about the silly bet, since due to bad investments and the vagaries of the market he is no longer as wealthy as he was fifteen years ago. The banker is angry that the lawyer did not give up or die, and even contemplates rectifying the situation by killing his prisoner and throwing suspicion on the gardener.

It so happens that during his confinement the prisoner has read almost all the books in his jailer's substantial library and has learned several languages. There was a long period of time after ten years of his confinement, however, when he was reading nothing but the Bible. When the banker enters the little cottage in the middle of the night, he finds his prisoner asleep next to a note denouncing everything, including the promised two million dollars:

> I despise ... all worldly blessings and wisdom. Everything is void, frail, visionary and delusive like a mirage ... You take lie for truth and ugliness for beauty ... That I may show you in deed my contempt for that by which you live, I waive the two millions of which I once dreamed as of paradise and which I now despise.[8]

Chekhov, who, against everyone's advice, would visit the penal colony on Sakhakin Island two years after the publication of "The Bet" specifically because of his concerns about imprisonment, torture, and capital punishment, is obviously most interested in this particular aspect of the discussion. He takes the story in an ironic direction when the young lawyer who prefers life in prison to no life ends up losing his sense that life has any meaning whatsoever while still technically winning the bet. What his character suggests at the end about everything being void and delusive are largely clichés, and anyone who knows Chekhov as a writer is well trained not to attribute these sentiments to him. But it was, most likely, precisely this cliché that so appealed to Koteliansky in the story for it summarized perfectly his own sense that people around him often took "lie for truth and ugliness for beauty."

The peak years for the wartime love affair between England and Russia were 1915-1916. When a delegation of Russian writers, journalists, and politicians – among them Vladimir Nabokov's father, V.D. Nabokov – arrived in early spring 1916, they were lavishly received by the king and the English Parliament, as well as by H.G. Wells, who invited them for a visit at his family villa in Easton. Other admirers of Russian culture organized a "Russian Exhibition" in their honour in Piccadilly Circus.[9] Murry and Kot further capitalized on this interest in all things Russian by collaborating on three more translations: *Pages from the Journal of an*

*Author: Fyodor Dostoevsky,* Alexander Kuprin's *The River of Life and Other Stories,* and Leo Shestov's *Anton Tchekhov and Other Essays.* All three books came out in 1916 from the same publisher. Murry wrote introductions for all three, although in the case of Kuprin it was just a short "Introductory Note." Neither Kuprin, a popular but rather mediocre writer in Russia at the time, nor Leo Shestov, an influential Russian philosopher, were known in England, and that was undoubtedly a part of Koteliansky's strategy. Translating Chekhov, Dostoevsky, and Tolstoy he faced fierce competition – he needed his own authors to distinguish himself from the likes of Constance Garnett and the Maudes. While a legitimate tactic, banking on lesser-known writers carried very substantial risks since, lacking the name recognition, the books would be a harder sell unless they were very well advertised by the publishers or through word of mouth. Murry remembered this period of their collaboration in 1915 and 1916 with considerable nostalgia: "In the evenings Koteliansky would come round with a generous supply of Russian cigarettes and we would work together translating Tchehov and Kuprin – a speculative venture for we had no publisher."[10]

*Pages from the Journal of an Author,* the "little Dostoevsky book," as Lawrence called it, elicited a harsh comment from him: "I have only read Murry's Introduction, and Dostoevsky's 'Dream of a Queer Fellow.' Both stink in my nostrils."[11] Murry's introduction is, indeed, simultaneously pompous and simplistic. "An artist," he wrote, "great or small, works for the salvation of his own soul above all other things … If he is a novelist, he may write because he looks upon the world and sees that it is good, and his joy and acceptance are a perfect and complete philosophy." From there he proceeded to point out, with excessive verbosity, that Dostoevsky lacked "joy" but was "great not least, because he was a great Russian."[12]

Kot, very reluctantly, continued working at Ruslabu, and his new friends continued to visit. "A wet day," wrote Mansfield in her journal in the beginning of January. "Saw a cinema in the afternoon. Tea with Kot, at the Russian Law Bureau. He was quiet & unhappy. He cut his finger. There was something very desperate about him."[13] Toward the end of the month she writes: "Kot for lunch at the Dieppe café among the singing canaries … Had supper with Kot and went to Pavillion after."[14] And two days later: "Saw Koteliansky at the station. He was very nice. I rather cling to him. He brought me a skirt and some cigarettes & some chocolates."[15] Kot apparently also supplied her with some "ancestral" medical advice. "I am in bed," she wrote to him in March. "I am not at all well … All the same I am grateful to your Ancestral Grandfathers – for – for some curious reason I can work."[16] Sometimes she felt remorse that she did not express her sympathy and understanding more strongly: "I understood you that weekend at the Lawrences for I have been like that myself. It is a kind of paralysis that comes of living alone + to oneself and it is really painful. I was silly and unsympathetic for Lawrence could not understand it because he has never felt it and I should have been wiser."[17]

Mansfield was not the only one warming to Kot; so was Gertler: "I think of you ... sometimes in the evening, talking 'plainly,'" he wrote to Kot in July, lovingly using Kot's favourite word.[18] "How is it that you have not written to me yet?" Gertler asked in August after Kot apparently did not respond to his July letter. "Did you get my last letter? I wrote you a long one, about a fortnight ago. I hope you have not forgotten me, or [are] offended with me. I should be sorry to lose your friendship as it means a great deal to me."[19] He need not have worried. Like Lawrence and Mansfield, Gertler had made it into the essential core of the "accepted" ones to whom Kot would remain loyal, despite occasional squabbles, for the rest of his life.

What drew them to him once they went beyond his superficial exotic "Russianness," and what drew him to them is a fascinating and very complex matter. The easiest relationship to figure out, perhaps, is the one with Gertler. Eleven years younger than Kot, Gertler, it appears, sought Kot out because he was an ideal older brother for him – a man who shared his background and understood everything about his circumstances without any need for explanations. Unlike his real brothers, though, Kot inhabited the same "Goyish" literary and artistic circles. It is not clear whether Gertler and Kot ever spoke Yiddish to each other, but Kot was one of very few people on this other side who could, even though their dialects were a bit different. Kot was, therefore, a perfect antidote to the often unbearable cultural schizophrenia: the chasm between Whitechapel with Gertler's Yiddish-speaking parents and siblings on the one hand, and the new Bloomsbury environment, which often included members of English aristocracy, on the other. Gertler's value to Kot was probably similar. Never close to his own brothers, Kot appeared eager to take Gertler under his wing and, throughout his friend's life, displayed the kind of love and anxiety for him that are usually reserved for members of one's own family.

Mansfield was an entirely different matter. Leonard Woolf simplifies things quite a bit when he states: "He was perhaps the only person whom she trusted and respected completely. And of Katherine Kot always said: 'She is a real person.'"[20] Their bond would often be tested, at times severely. His loyalty and dedication to her, however, did weather it all in the end, in spite of his tendency to write people off for much lesser transgressions. Mansfield's letters to Kot during the initial months of their friendship are full of gratitude ("When I opened the parcel I found your presents ... Thank you very much indeed for them"; "I did not realize until I reached home how many cigarettes you have given me. Kotiliansky, it is my turn to give presents, I am beginning to feel"[21]), desire to see him ("Will you be at the Bureau next Monday afternoon at about 4?"; "I am coming to London on Friday, mon cher ami, and I will come then and see you a moment"[22]), genuine declarations of fondness ("I am extremely fond of you this afternoon. I wish you would walk into this café now ..." "Yes, Kotiliansky, you are really one of my people ..."[23]), and occasional requests for favours ("And will you buy a postal order for 2 francs 50 for me and put it in the letter ... – I will pay you when next we meet"; "I can't find the English address of the Smart Set – so would you look it up in a telephone book ... and send this story for me as soon as possible"[24]). When she was upset or in bad mood, it was, according to Murry, Koteliansky "to whom she always turned."[25]

There was much good-natured banter going on between them during these early months, some of it of a mildly sexual nature. "No, I won't come to any of your weddings," she wrote to him in March. "You will marry some woman who will show me the door – because I come and sing in the street you live ... and you dare to look out the window."[26] But was Kot really in love with her, as some mutual friends and subsequently biographers believed, on the assumption that Kot's vehement hostility toward Jack Murry was, in part, a lover's jealousy? John Carswell, whose mother, Catherine, knew both Kot and Mansfield well, suggested as much stating that Kot "never, so far as is known, made any ... gesture towards marriage or even attachment, unless we can so describe his abiding passion for Katherine."[27] Several of Mansfield's biographers, most notably Jeffrey Meyers and Nora Crone, make even stronger leaps, concluding that Kot – who once apparently told a Mansfield scholar that "If Kat'run ever wanted a greater relationship with me, she had only to indicate it" – definitely "fell in love with her."[28]

Kot himself called their relationship "our perhaps uncommon friendship,"[29] and he expressed his feelings for Mansfield most clearly in a 1921 letter to Dorothy Brett: "[I]f K. has a real friend, perhaps cruel at times – in the whole universe it is myself. Because inspite of [sic] all defects, she knows I am sincerely fond of her, – not sentimentally, not for her good qualities, but just for herself, for what she is, for that indeed for which all others might be frightened away from K. That K. is unique, perfectly unlike anybody else in existence, and not to be judged in the same way ..."[30] He was, most likely, to use the words of Mansfield early biographer Antony Alpers, "not ... a lover, but in an oddly paternal way ... a sort of father-figure, admirer-from-afar, and frowning disapprover."[31] He definitely did disapprove of Murry, and of Katherine's return to him after several of their breakups. In many cases when Kot disliked the spouses or partners of his friends – and as a rule he *did* dislike them – his jealousy indeed smacked of parental possessiveness. Like a proverbial Jewish mother, he seemed to believe that no one was ever good enough for those he loved.

His feelings for D.H. Lawrence, on the other hand, probably were more complicated. Kot was, Catherine Carswell tells us, "captivated by a kind of sensitive innocence in Lawrence which he had never before seen in an Englishman. It roused a jealously protective tenderness."[32] When, several years later she witnessed a drunken outburst during which Kot declared that "no … woman here or anywhere can understand anything about Lawrence or what kind of being he is," Carswell's immediate reaction was pity: "We women were silent. We felt, I think, very sympathetic to Kot. Anyhow I did. Sympathetic to his jealous, dark and over powering affection."[33] Dorothy Brett, herself in the early stages of being in love with Lawrence at the time, was another witness to the scene. Brett became Kot's confidante in the early 1920s, and they exchanged intensely personal letters before their friendship came to an abrupt end. In one of the letters, Brett added a curious postscript: "Are you still alone. I somehow feel that it is all wrong, that there is somewhere some man who would interest you and be worth your while."[34] The implication here seems to go hand in hand with Lawrence's own seemingly immediate certainty that Kot somehow did not know "that a woman is not a man with different sex," and that Kot's world was "all of one hemisphere." Frieda made a similar observation in 1923 when she wrote to Kot: "you [should] also know that man was meant to have a woman; I am supposed to be impressed by your chastities: I am not, it's male conceit."[35]

Frieda Lawrence also often referred to Kot as Lawrence's "slave."[36] "[H]e would like to separate us," she announced to Mabel Luhan years later when the Lawrences were already in New Mexico. "Well, I'd like to see *him* live with Lawrence a month – a week! He might be surprised."[37] "He did not like me but he loved Lawrence," Frieda told another New Mexico friend, Witter Bynner. "Yes, he loved Lawrence, Ja!"[38] Frieda by no means exaggerated Kot's antipathy toward her. "If she disappeared," Kot wrote to Gertler in 1916, "L. would be saved, because she is devouring him bit by bit … How I wish Frieda disappeared. Lawrence is most interesting and of the real few who matter."[39] Confronting Kot's hostility very early in their relationship, Frieda gave as good as she got. "You think I do not count besides Lawrence," she wrote in February 1915. "You do not think much of women, they are not human beings in your eyes – It's *your* fault, not mine – You will not have me for a friend…"[40] She also instructed Gertler to tell Kot "he is an old fraud, he always *pretends* he is a humble person, but in his heart he thinks he is very great."[41]

The fact that Koteliansky had little tolerance for Frieda should not obscure, however, how remarkably alike the two were in some crucial ways. Both were foreigners with thick accents who stuck out in the mostly homogeneous English cultural and intellectual elite; both were blunt and unsparing in their pronouncements and judgments; both felt unappreciated for who they were on their own and tended to draw their sense of self-worth from their closeness to Lawrence, who often verbally attacked them. Their reactions to such attacks were markedly different, though. While Kot retreated and sulked, Frieda counterattacked, once going so far as smashing a plate over Lawrence's head when he said that "women had no souls and couldn't love."[42] But then Frieda always did everything with zest; and her general and unquenchable zest for life is what Kot, who totally lacked one, seems to have not been able to forgive her.

In another contrast to him, Frieda showed not just resentment but also appreciation of how similar their situations were. Two years after Lawrence's death, she wrote a remarkable series of letters to Kot; they were simultaneously accusatory and understanding of his pain, which, she well knew, could only match her own. "And you, you have been a sinister influence in my life," she wrote on 1 July 1932. "Lawrence's philosophy you hate, because it's *me* – still you loved him in *your* way but the very pure flame in him meant nothing to you, you only loved him in a 'mortal' way." "No, I don't believe your nonacceptance of his views was precious to him," she replied to his response two days later, "it made him suffer and doubt himself; you loved him like a man loves a woman or a child – you thought him charming … Yes, of course, we could never be indifferent to each other, our love for him, different as it was, is a bond."[43] "Dear Kot," she wrote again, two weeks later, "How sad you must be never to have told him you loved him! But there, it's always too late – and he knew it – he knew everything."[44]

Kot was not the only man trying to separate Lawrence from Frieda in order to get closer to Lawrence – so was Jack Murry.[45] "Poor devil," Murry complained to Mansfield in 1915, "he is so lonely, with that bitch of a Frieda, always playing traitor, and hurting him in every secret and intimate part of his soul … But I think I shall ask him to come away with me for a fortnight's holiday during this summer to see if I can urge him to the point of leaving her. Not that I think I can do very much directly; but I have an idea that he might be happy were he away with me for a bit, because he would know that I was loving him."[46] Mansfield, it should be noted, was not amused: "Fancy GIVING YOURSELF to LOVING someone for a fortnight, as you say you will do for Lawrence in the summer. My strike!"[47] Whether as a consequence of her hurt feelings or not, two days later she wrote a particularly warm and urgent letter to Kot: "Kotiliansky, dear friend, I will not wait any longer for a letter from you … I had wanted a letter from you to say that you 'understood' – not to reassure me, you understand, but just because – I always want you to understand … Don't forget me – don't go far away. As I write I hear your voice … With this letter I send you big handfuls of very 'good' love."[48]

Lawrence's professed attitude toward open, demonstratively physical, homosexuality was often viscerally negative. In April 1915, his outrage against it was stirred anew when he visited Cambridge at the invitation of Bertrand Russell and went to see Maynard Keynes: "We went into his rooms at midday, and it was very sunny. He was not there, so Russell was writing a note. Then suddenly a door opened and K. was there, blinking from sleep, standing in his pyjamas. And as he stood there gradually a knowledge passed into me, which has been like a little madness to me ever since. And it was carried along with the most dreadful sense of repulsiveness – something like carrion – a vulture gives me the same feeling. I begin to feel mad as I think of it – insane."[49]

"These horrible little frowsty people," Lawrence wrote to Kot a day later, "men lovers of men, they give me such a sense of corruption, almost putrescence, that I dream of beetles. It's abominable."[50] David Garnett, who had visited the Lawrences with his male admirer in tow, was harshly lectured and urged to reform: "It is foolish of you to say that it doesn't matter either way – the men loving men. It doesn't matter in the public way. But it matters so much, David, to the man himself – at any rate to us northern nations … It is something unbearable to me. And not from any moral disapprobation … Never bring B[irrell] to see me any more. There is something nasty about him, like black-beetles. He is horrible and unclean … But you, my dear, you can be all right. You can come away, and grow whole, and love a woman, and marry her, and make life good, and be happy."[51] "When man and woman come together in love," Lawrence wrote to another friend in late November 1915, "that is the great *immediate* synthesis. When men come together, that is immediate reduction: those complex states, the finest product of generations of synthetic living, are *reduced* in homosexual love."[52]

And, yet, as the sensually homoerotic passage in *The White Peacock* declared from the start, Lawrence, to use Frieda's subtle formulation, "did not disbelieve in homosexuality."[53] In *Son of Woman: The Story of D.H. Lawrence* Murry, too, insists that Lawrence highly valued and sought out emotionally charged relationships with other men. In the prologue to *Women in Love*, which he chose not to publish when the novel came out in 1920, Lawrence included very provocative statements about the protagonist's attitude to men and women that further reinforced the sentiments expressed in *The White Peacock*:

> Birkin felt a passion of desire for Gerald Crich, for the clumsier, cruder intelligence … and for the striving, unlightened body of his friend … All

the time he recognized that although he was always drawn to women, feeling more at home with a woman than with a man, yet it was for men that he felt the hot, flushing, roused attraction which a man is supposed to feel for other sex … So he went on, month after month, year after year, divided against himself, striving for the day when the beauty of men should not be so acutely attractive to him, when the beauty of woman should move him instead.[54]

"You've got to take down the love-and-marriage idea from its pedestal," Rupert tells Gerald at one point. "We want something broader. I believe in the *additional* perfect relationship between man and man – additional to marriage.[55] Lawrence expressed a similar conviction in a letter to Katherine Mansfield: "I believe tremendously in friendship between man and man, a pledging of men to each other inviolably. But I have not ever met or formed such friendship."[56] He did try to form one with her husband. "Lawrence was really a new experience," Murry confessed in 1936. "I was quite unprepared for such an immediacy of contact … Lawrence believed … that the relationship between Katherine and me was false and deadly; and that the relationship between Frieda and himself was real and life-giving: but that this relation with Frieda needed to be completed by a new relation between himself and me."[57] If Kot hated Murry on account of Mansfield, he probably hated him even more on account of Lawrence. Did Lawrence attempt to establish a similar relationship with Kot, and did Kot scare him off with his intensity, or go too far in attempting to convince Lawrence that "false and deadly" equally applied to Lawrence's own marriage to Frieda? Or did Kot desperately want such a friendship but turned out to be, unlike Murry, not physically or spiritually acceptable for such a role? Lawrence's novel *Kangaroo* just may give us some answers.

Most critics suggest that while Lawrence endowed Ben Cooley of *Kangaroo* with Kot's "swarthy" Jewish features, in everything else Cooley was nothing like Kot.[58] That view is probably based on a lack of knowledge of – and even interest in – Koteliansky, who comes across in much of Lawrence scholarship as an odd, minor Russian character who just happened to have developed an inexplicably close relationship with Lawrence.[59] A notable exception was Lawrence biographer Harry T. Moore, for whom Frieda Lawrence was the primary source and who interviewed Koteliansky on a number of occasions. In *The Intelligent Heart: The Story of D.H. Lawrence*, he stated inequivocally, that "the Jewish lawyer Ben Cooley, was a projection of Koteliansky."[60]

As Virginia Woolf used to say, "a book makes everything into itself,"[61] and it would be inappropriate to suggest that Cooley/Kangaroo is a precise portrait of

Kot. Kot was obviously not an Australian, and not a leader of a big secret political organization (unless we consider his clandestine political activities in Russia). Kot's family may have been well off back in Russia prior to the revolution but, unlike Kangaroo, he was a total stranger to splendour by the time Lawrence came to know him. Furthermore, Lawrence himself may have suggested a crucial difference between the two when he had Richard Lovatt Somers, his alter ego in the novel, reflect on how he "had once had a Jewish friend with this wonderful, Jehovah-like kindliness, but alas, without the shrewd fiendish subtlety of will." From time to time, the narrator reminds us again of Somers's other Jewish friend, as if intentionally (for Kot's sake?) to separate the two: "A sardonic letter from a Jewish friend in London, amusing but a bit dreadful."[62]

And yet, there is an uncanny likeness between the two men. In addition to the traits mentioned earlier, there is the same well-pronounced belly and short legs that make them both look like a kangaroo, as well as the oft-observed yellowness of Kot's and Cooley's faces.[63] "Kangaroo smiled slowly," the narrator tells us,

> and when he smiled like that, there came an exceedingly sweet charm into his face, for a moment his face was like a flower. Yet he was quite ugly. And surely, thought Somers, it is Jewish blood. The very best that is in the Jewish blood: a faculty for pure disinteredness, and warm, physically warm love, that seems to make the corpuscles of the blood glow. And after the smile the face went stupid and kangaroo-like, pendulous, with the eyes close together above the long drooping nose. But the shape of the head was very beautiful, small, light, and fine … And he was almost purely *kind*, essential kindliness, embodied in an ancient, unscrupulous shrewdness. He was so shrewd, so clever. And with a rogue or a mean man, absolutely unscrupulous. But for any human being who showed himself sincere and vulnerable, his heart was pure in kindliness. An extraordinary man. This pure kindliness had something Jehovah-like in it.[64]

The reference to "Jehovah," which serves as a metaphor for the firmness of one's principles and convictions, is a constant in Lawrence's correspondence with Kot ("O dear, why are you so Jehovahish! … I'm weary of Jehovah, he's always so right"[65]). In the novel it keeps being reinforced. "You're a Jew," Somers tells Cooley at one point, "and you must be Jehovah or nothing."[66] Lawrence further elaborates on what he calls Cooley's "absoluteness, and his strange blind heroic obsession" by making Cooley declare, in a very Kot-like fashion: "Either you are with me, and I *feel* you with me: or you cease to exist for me."[67]

The fictional pair also appears to have arguments very similar to the ones

Lawrence had with Kot. One of these focused on Lawrence's notion of "chaos" as a necessary stage in changing old societies. "As for Russia, it must go through as it is going," Lawrence wrote to Kot soon after the Bolshevik revolution. "Nothing but a real smelting down is any good for her; no matter how horrible it seems. You who are an ultra-conscious Jew, can't bear the chaos. But chaos is necessary for Russia ..."[68] An almost identical discussion takes place between Kangaroo and Somers. When Somers declares that "[i]t's much easier to point to a wrecked house, if you want to build something new than to persuade people to pull the house down and build it up in a better style ... There has to be chaos occasionally," Kangaroo replies: "You are so hopelessly facile ... It is anarchy and unrule ... and that is what I, as an order-loving Jew ... do not want ... You are not such a fool ... that you can't see that once you break the last restraints on humanity today, it is the end. Once burst the flood-gates, and you'll never get the water back into control. Never."[69]

Later on, when the narrative point of view shifts from Somers to Kangaroo, the latter is seen thinking through all the dangers of popular upheavals in terms that sound very similar, as we will see, to Kot's own apprehensions about the course of the Russian revolution:

> In the end, it is a question with us today whether the masses will degenerate into mobs, or whether they will still keep a spark of direction. All great mass uprisings are really acts of vengeance against the dominant consciousness of the day.[70]

Given these similarities and echoes, one cannot help but wonder whether the fictional relationship between Cooley and Somers (who comes to Australia with the Frieda-like Mrs Somers) contains the nuances of the actual relationship between Lawrence and Kot. We learn, for example, that, despite his better judgment, Kangaroo is "hopelessly attracted" to Somers:

> There was a hostile silence from Kangaroo. He knew that this subtle, attractive Somers with the faint glow about him, like an aura, was venomous. And yet he was helplessly attracted to him ... It frightened the big man ... And yet, as an individual, he was attracted to the little fellow now, like a moth to a candle, a great lumbering moth to a small, but dangerous candle.[71]

Somers, on the other hand, is simultaneously drawn to and repulsed by Kangaroo. One of their heated discussions leads to a dramatic scene that reveals the complex feelings on both sides:

Kangaroo glowered like a massive cloud … Suddenly, with a great massive movement, Kangaroo caught the other man to his breast.

"Don't, Lovatt," he said, in a much moved voice, pressing the slight body of the lesser man against his own big breast and body … "Don't thwart me," pleaded Kangaroo. "Don't – or I shall have to break all connection with you, and I love you so. I love you so. Don't be perverse, and put yourself against me." […] "It is impertinence, that he says he loves me," [Somers] thought to himself. But he did not speak, out of regard for Kangaroo's emotion, which was massive and genuine, even if Somers felt it missed his own particular self completely … "He doesn't love *me*," he thought to himself. "He just turns a great general emotion on me like a tap. I feel as cold as steel, in his clasp – and as separate … Damn his love. He wants to *force* me."[72]

When Somers finally stops thinking to himself and actually addresses Kangaroo, the scene reaches its crescendo:

"I just hate it … Don't love me. Don't want to save mankind. You're so awfully *general*. And your love is so awfully general … Don't love me. Don't want me to love you. Let's be hard separate men. Let's understand one another deeper than love…" "Is any understanding deeper than love?" asked Kangaroo with a sneer. "Why yes, you know it is. At least between men." "I am afraid I don't know it. I know the understanding that is much *less* than love. If you want me to have a merely commonplace acquaintance with you, I refuse. That's all." […] Kangaroo's face had gone like an angry wax mask, with mortification … Richard had a moment of pure hate for him … He had become … hideous, with a long yellowish face and black eyes close together … For a moment Somers was afraid of him, as of some great ugly idol that might strike. He felt the intense hatred of the man coming at him in cold waves. He stood up in a kind of horror, in front of the great, close-eyed, horrible thing that was now Kangaroo. Yes, a thing, not a whole man. A great Thing, a horror.[73]

Cecil Gray, a composer and music critic who knew Lawrence and was not one of his fans, once remarked that "Lawrence was always inclined to treat his friends and acquaintances as if they were characters in one of his novels, and sought accordingly to mould their characters and direct their actions as he desired. When he failed in this – and he invariably did fail – he took revenge by putting the said friends and acquaintances, recognizably, into his books, and there worked his will upon them."[74] Kot must have known it was Lawrence's revenge on him.

According to Esther Salaman, he "resented this implication … that Kangaroo and Somers have a homosexual attachment." He thought it was outright "misleading" of Lawrence to suggest it in the novel, and Salaman herself was quite vehement in her interview with Lawrence scholar George Zytaruk about what she considered an unfair conclusion made by some people in their circle: "[I]t isn't right … Lawrence and Kot did not have this [i.e. "homosexual attachment"] either!"[75] She may have been right but then she was also probably not someone with whom Kot would ever discuss his true sexual feelings since she came from the same traditional Russian-Jewish community, where homosexuality was considered both unnatural and sinful. Given such background, if Kot was indeed attracted to Lawrence or other men, the sense of shame and guilt would be hard to overcome, making his black moods even blacker.

But *Kangaroo* was yet to come. Back in 1915, the relationships between Lawrence, Frieda, and Kot – and, for that matter, Kot, Mansfield, and Murry – were still evolving and just barely beginning to take their final shapes. In early January, Kot took it as a personal slight that Lawrence had not invited him to a party with the Murrys; Lawrence reassured him that he was indeed invited but the party had to be "postponed to an indefinite date."[76] Throughout that month and until the Lawrences moved to Sussex at the end of it, Lawrence and Kot met regularly and they sent each other letters several times a week. "Dear Kot," read a typical letter, "I was sorry you did not sleep when you got back to the Bureau. But we laughed at you in your letter nevertheless. What about *Rananim*? Oh, but we are going. We are going to found an *Order of the Knights of Rananim*. The motto is 'Fier' or the Latin equivalent. The badge is so: an eagle, or phoenix argent, rising from a flaming nest of scarlet, on a black background."[77] By now "Rananim" is of course legendary in Lawrence studies as his notion of an ideal "little colony," preferably on an island, and thus his version of Moore's *Utopia*.[78] "I want to gather together twenty souls," Lawrence wrote in January to another friend, "and sail away from this world of war and squalor and found a little colony where there shall be no money but a sort of communism as far as necessaries of life go, and some real decency."[79] Lawrence's "little colony" was his own idea but it owed its name to Kot.

The "piece of paper … on which a few bars of music had been written," to which Lady Glenavy referred in her book, still exists in Catherine Stoye's private archive. On it, in Kot's hand and English spelling, the words appear as follows: "Ran-na-ni Za-di-him Za-di-him b'a-do-noi," repeated four times. He supplied his own translation on the back: "Rejoice O Just One in God." This is the first line of Psalm 33, and the translation is, indeed, "Rejoice o just/righteous ones in God" but it can also be rendered as "Sing joyfully o just / righteous ones to

God."[80] This is the "Hebrew music" Lawrence referred to in his description of the 1914 walking tour to Lady Asquith. In a 6 February 1917 letter to Kot, which is now in the British Library, Frieda told him that at Christmas time they sang "Ranani/Tza-diekim," corrected in Kot's hand on her letter to "Ranani Tzadikim."[81] The Lawrences' spelling of this Hebrew line in English continued to vary throughout the years. By 1922 Lawrence transcribes it as "Ranane Sadihkim Sadihkim Badanoi,"[82] and after Lawrence's death Frieda reverted to his original transcription: in *Not I but the Wind* she states, "Koteliansky sang soulfully his Hebrew song: 'Ranani Sadekim Badanoi.'"[83]

One can only speculate as to why this particular psalm was such a favourite of Koteliansky's. It is possible that it was simply the one most often sung by his parents during their prayers, or the one drilled into him most effectively during his long hours at the heder. It could also be, however, that he preferred it to all the others because in the psalm God promotes equity and justice and frustrates nations and people in their plans. The psalm is, furthermore, quite instructive for times of war: it teaches that no king can be saved by his great army, and no warrior can be delivered by his great strength or be victorious through the might of his horse. These sentiments were, no doubt, music to Lawrence's ears as well and can explain why he chose to bestow the word associated with the opening of Psalm 33 on his dreamland. "Rananim" (perhaps more accurately transcribed as "Renanim") exists in Hebrew as an independent form as well: it is a plural noun meaning "songs." Interestingly enough, the word can also be found in one other language, Chuukese, where "Rananim" means "Hello."[84] It is unclear whether or not Lawrence was aware of this linguistic curiosity, but Chuukese is a language of islands – specifically the Micronesian islands, like Guam, in the Pacific – so the name goes quite well with Lawrence's original idea of where to found his utopian community.

In February, we learn from Lawrence's letters that Kot had plans to go to Glasgow (which, like most of his travel schemes, probably never materialized). He was asked to do more time-consuming favours for Lawrence (among them, buying and mailing to Sussex "flat shape" and "tall shape" wooden boxes, which Lawrence would then paint for his friends), while Lawrence – with the help of others – was further refining the notion of "Rananim": "Tomorrow Lady Ottoline is coming again and bringing Bertrand Russell … We are going to struggle with my Island idea – *Rananim*. But they say, the island shall be England, that we shall start our new community in the midst of the old one, as a seed falls among the roots of the parent. Only wait, and we will remove mountains & set them in the midst of the sea."[85]

Lawrence also continued to upbraid Kot for his behaviour toward Frieda: "You are a great donkey, & your letters to Frieda are ridiculous. – Why the hell do you make such a palaver to her? She was cross with me – at such times she is indignant with you for your imagined adoration (as she puts it) of me. You are an ass to make so many postures & humilities & so forth about it … And if you're going to come & see us, why for Heaven's sake don't you come – fidgeting & fuming & stirring & preparing & communing with yourself & reading the portents – it is preposterous. If you are coming, come, & have done. If you have anything to say, say it, & have done. But *don't* be so queasy & uneasy & important – oh damn. Plainly I do not like you."[86]

It is easy to see from this letter how ruthlessly honest and unsparing the two men often were with each other. This honesty, based on the belief that an honest slap was indeed much better than a false kiss, is probably the strongest attribute that they shared, and the one they most admired in each other. Frieda possessed it, too, but of course only one of them could ever admire it in her.

In March, Lawrence pleaded with Kot: "Don't be gloomy, neither defiant of all governments and all the Fates: prison, Siberia, and the hangman's noose."[87] In April he vehemently reproached Kot for his apathy and passivity: "But you positively *must not* be so inert. You are getting simply a monolith. You *must* rouse yourself. You *must* do something – anything. Really it is a disgrace to be as inert as you are. Really, it is unforgivable. Write for the papers, do anything, but don't continue in this negation … It is so terrible to be such a weight upon the face of the earth."[88] Kot's passivity was by then legendary. Lady Glenavy noted that there was "something Oblomov-like in his laziness about making the effort to write"[89] – but if that was the case, Kot was definitely Oblomov with insomnia; his inability to sleep haunted him his entire life and added to his overall sense of gloom and fatigue.

Kot did hope to leave his hated job at the Bureau and maybe pursue journalism again, so in these initial months of 1915, when he was not writing letters to Lawrence and Mansfield, running errands for them, or fuming at Frieda and Murry, he must have been following the new prominence that Russia, as one of Great Britain's major allies, was getting in the British press. *The Nineteenth Century and After* alone published six articles on Russia that year: "The Soul of Russia" (January); "Temperance Reform in Russia" (February); "Resiliency in Russia" (June); "A Russian View of Reprisal" (August), "Resolute Russia" (October), and "The Peasant Songs of Russia" (November).

This was fairly typical fare for what constituted analysis of Russian society and politics at the time in mainstream periodicals, all calling for a better awareness of what was going on there. As one author in *The Nineteenth Century and After* put it, "the British, as a rule, were very ignorant about Russia in spite of the marked development of her industrial life and her splendid contributions to literature and music…"[90] Another author, while lamenting that "the ignorance of Russia among Englishmen is … far greater than their ignorance of us," did not quite stop there but blamed Jews for overly publicizing pogroms and making the English see Russia as one "bloodstained Cossack."

While lamenting England's ignorance, the "experts" themselves were often significantly off the mark when it came to true understanding of what was going on in Russia. Thus the same author who blamed Jews for influencing the press coverage was quite dismissive about a potential of a "Russian revolutionary," whom he described as "apt to be passionately idealistic, to swallow whole the creed he has got from the West … still loyal to the death and a martyr, with that strange Russian instinct for suffering." At the same time, he was very naïve about the capabilities of the tsar: "Russia is a family as no other nation is; and the Tsar deserves his popular title of Little Father, because he is the head of a family."[91] Regardless of what the actual articles said and how much he disagreed with them, Koteliansky was undoubtedly encouraged by the fact that the interest in Russia was going beyond the British bohemians' love for the Ballets Russes and Tolstoy.

Around this time he started a close relationship and collaboration with Michael Farbman, a professional journalist who, like Koteliansky, had come from Russia. Farbman, whose birth name was Grigory – "Grisha" – Abramovich, was married to a sister of Zinovy Grzhebin, the force behind Maxim Gorky-sponsored publishing house "World Literature" (renamed by 1919 into "Grzhebin Publishing House"), first in Soviet Russia, and then, starting with 1921, in Berlin, where the cost of publication was cheaper. At Gorky's insistence, Grzhebin and his family were allowed to go to Berlin while still remaining Russian citizens. Farbman, even though he by then lived in London, was one of Grzhebin's employees both in Russia and later in Berlin, and therefore travelled freely to Petrograd and Moscow.[92] After the revolution he authored and edited several influential books on Russia – including *Russia and the Struggle for Peace* (1918), *Bolshevism in Retreat* (1923), and *After Lenin: The New Phase in Russia* (1924). He also wrote for major papers, among them *Daily Herald*, *the Observer*, and the *Manchester Guardian*, for which he interviewed Lenin in 1922.[93]

Farbman was originally from Odessa – hence Lawrence's joking nickname for him, "Grisha the Odessa villain"[94] – while his wife, Sonia Grzhebin Farbman, hailed from Kharkov, so both were, like Kot, Jews from Ukraine. Given that the two were the same age, Kot could have made friends with Farbman in Odessa during his early studies – or, as Esther Salaman suggested to George Zytaruk, they could have met already in England, either through Ruslabu or Fanny Step-niak.[95] This would prove to be a very lasting and important relationship in Kot's life, for by the end of 1915 and for many years to come, Grisha and Sonia Farb-man, as well as their daughter Ghita, would function as Kot's housemates and, in many ways, a surrogate family.

But while he was growing closer to Farbman, Koteliansky appears to have become, for a while, much more distant from Lawrence, who seemed to be in a particularly foul mood throughout the month of May. Earlier that month Kot must have complained to Lawrence that his eyes were hurting from all the typ-ing he was doing for him. Lawrence linked that ailment as well to Kot's overall "passivity": "I am sorry your eyes are bad. I think it is your liver, which is slug-gish." He did, however, release Kot from his secretarial duties: "And don't bother about the type-writing – I will get it done outside somewhere."[96] Having it done "outside somewhere" involved paying someone money, and money was a par-ticularly touchy subject at the time since on 10 May Lawrence was supposed to appear in court for having failed to pay roughly 150 pounds as part of Frieda's divorce proceedings from her husband. "I cannot tell you," he wrote to Bertrand Russell two weeks before his summons date, "how this reinforces in me my utter hatred of the whole establishment – the whole constitution of England."[97]

While in London for the court day, Lawrence probably saw Kot. On 19 May, he complained to Kot about Frieda's spending "her time thinking herself a wronged, injured and aggrieved person because of the children, and because she is a Ger-man." He also suggested that he and Frieda might separate, at least "for some time."[98] Lawrence elaborated on Frieda's unhappiness in a letter he sent the same day to Ottoline. "Isn't it a funny thing," he asked rhetorically, "if a woman has got her children, she does not care about them, and if she has a man, she does not care about him, she only wants her children ... Frieda only cares about her chil-dren now."[99] This observation, of course, echoes the very sentiments for which Kot had been earlier censured by Lawrence. Lawrence was touchy on the subject of husbands versus children. Based on his own experience with his mother, he suggested in *Sons and Lovers* that women turn to their children when they no longer sufficiently love their husbands: "At last Mrs Morel despised her husband. She turned to the child; she turned from the father."[100]

Lawrence and Frieda ended up not separating at all – instead, it was Kot and Lawrence who parted ways, probably because Kot pushed too hard for the sepa-ration. After 19 May, Kot did not receive another letter from Lawrence until 22 July, and even then it was just a short note: "Forgive my not having answered your letter sooner. Even now I don't know how to answer it. My feelings are con-fused and suffering under various sorts of shocks in one direction and another.

I hope you will not mind if we leave it for a while, this question of a relationship between us, until I am settled and dependable. Then I will answer your letter."[101] It took another month before they resumed their regular correspondence, but, if Lawrence ever fully addressed in another letter the question of "a relationship between us," that letter has not been preserved.

The next letter from Lawrence to Kot is dated 23 August 1915, by which point the Lawrences had relocated to Hampstead, London. The letter must be in response to Kot's request to be allowed to visit Lawrence and bring friends along in order to discuss a certain "scheme."[102] Lawrence assumed that it was about translating his *Rainbow*, which was coming out from Methuen the following month, into Russian. He was quite receptive to the idea: "Murry just mentioned something about the translating of my book into Russian. I should like it very much. Was that the scheme you meant? I should be very proud to see myself in Russian, & not to understand a single word." The letter also bore the instructions of how to get to the Lawrences' new place.[103] Kot and Lawrence probably did meet later that week (even though Lawrence had to change the date once because Frieda was "still in bed with her cold"[104]), but the visit was then followed by another month and a half of silence before the correspondence between the two resumed in earnest in early October.

In the meantime, Lawrence and Murry decided to publish a magazine called *The Signature*. It was to contain, according to Lawrence, Murry's "ideas of immediate, personal freedom," his own "ideas of the other, the impersonal freedom, the freedom of me in relation to all the world," and Katherine Mansfield's "satirical sketch[es]."[105] "We have found a little Jew in the Mile End Rd," he boasted to Lady Cynthia Asquith in September, "who will print us 250 copies of our little journal at £5 a time."[106] When Lawrence and Koteliansky resumed their relationship in early October, Kot was drafted to do what the Kiev Commercial Institute supposedly had prepared him for – serve as "business manager," which was a rather glorified title for a combination bookkeeper, errand boy, and mailing clerk. It most likely did not escape his notice that in this relationship, too, Murry and Lawrence were co-equals and major players while he was relegated to a non-intellectual, facilitating role – not unlike the "little Jew" printer from the East End, and, no doubt, an equally good bargain.[107] Among the commissions Kot was entrusted with were bringing coal for the fireplace to keep the editors warm during their meeting (10 October); taking the carpet and curtains out of the *Signature* office on Fisher Street and storing it at his Bureau (29 October), and then selling the furniture from the same office (6 November).

The first letter from Lawrence concerning Kot's tasks as business manager ("Will you send a copy of the *Signature* to each of the following ..."[108]) is dated

7 October, which also happened to be the date Katherine Mansfield's younger brother, Leslie, was killed in France. Leslie, who had come from New Zealand in August, stayed with his sister and Murry on Acacia Road prior to his departure for battlefields of France. On 11 October, she heard about his death in a grenade accident. Murry wrote in his diary that day: "Three minutes ago … a telegram to say her brother is dead … I cannot believe it yet, and she cannot … She did not cry. She was white and said 'I don't believe it, he was not the kind to die …'"[109] The very same evening they expected the Campbells and Kot for dinner. Kot apparently already knew about Leslie, but the Campbells did not. According to Lady Glenavy, "Kot and Murry had been very silent but Katherine had seemed exceptionally talkative and gay. She had been wearing her embroidered shawl, which gave her a party air. Evidently she had told Kot and Murry not to mention her brother's death to us. It was as if the knowledge of his death was too terrible and unbelievable a fact to share with other people."[110] That very same evening, Lawrence, who was in London, sent a note to Kot that underscored just how precarious their relationship still was: "Did you not stay … because you were busy, or too sorry about Katharine's brother, or because you were offended with me. If you are offended, that's foolish. But do as you like."[111]

Since the house on Acacia Road was associated with the last time Katherine saw her brother alive, and then with the telegram announcing his death, Mansfield came to realize that "Acacia Road and all that it implied is over – for ever."[112] Kot suggested the Murrys lease the house to the Farbmans. "Dear Mr Farbman," Mansfield wrote in a contract letter on 11 November 1915, "I agree to sublet to you the house and furniture contained therein at No 5 Acacia Road from November 18 at an inclusive monthly rental of seven pounds ten shillings. Such rental to be paid in advance in monthly installments as arranged. The terms of our agreement [are] for not less than half a year." She signed the letter "Katherine Murry."[113] Kot moved in with the Farbmans – and continued to reside at the house until his death. He was asked by Mansfield to be a safekeeper of her cherished items: "I left one of my brother's caps in a drawer upstairs in his room. Would you get it and keep it safely for me. Also, I meant to give you the *fur rug* in my sitting room – you know the one. I don't want the Farbmans to use it and I do want you to keep it for me. Put it on your bed. It is so warm and it looks and feels so lovely."[114]

Kot's relationship with Mark Gertler was on a much more even keel than his relationships with Lawrence or Mansfield. For one thing, there was no spouse yet to irritate him – and Kot dearly wanted to keep it this way. "I shan't rest until I have … a good wife and a comfortable house," Mark informed him in August 1915. "PLAINLY that is what I want. I don't care what *you* say."[115] Gertler was very much in love with his fellow student from Slade, Dora Carrington. Kot knew that Mark was intensely unhappy with how Carrington was treating him, and that did not endear her to Kot in the least. By January 1915 Gertler had left the East End behind and moved to his own place in Hampstead, supported in part by his other Slade friend, Dorothy Brett, and his benefactor Eddie Marsh, a classical scholar, prominent Tory, and collector of modern British art. Gertler was looking forward to being, as he put it, "free and detached … neither Jew nor Christian … just myself."[116] He was, he confessed, "both sad and immensely relieved at having to leave the East End and my parents." But the feeling of relief was greater than the feeling of sadness.[117] Throughout that year, as Gertler was getting closer to Kot, he was also becoming more attached to Lawrence, and by October Lawrence's visceral distaste for the war had infected Gertler to such an extent that he felt it his duty to discontinue his friendship with – and significant subsidy from – Marsh, who in 1915 still served as Winston Churchill's private secretary and was a most ardent war supporter.

Gertler was also becoming fast friends with Murry and Mansfield. Very good-looking and reputed to have an easy time conquering women's hearts, Gertler was encouraged by Kot to conquer Katherine's in order to drive her and Murry apart. "I like Katherine Mansfield," Gertler wrote to Carrington in January 1915, describing a party where Kot was also present and, most likely, trying to make Carrington feel jealous in the process. "Katherine and myself – both very drunk – made passionate love to each other in front of everybody! And everybody was drunk too. No one knew whether to take it as a joke or scandal … Seeing that Katherine's man and myself were just as friendly afterward, they *had* to take it as a joke. They were very disappointed to have to take it so."[118] Kot was, no doubt, very disappointed indeed.

The party took place in Cholesbury, Buckinghamshire, in a cottage that belonged to Mary and Gilbert Cannan. An author, critic, and translator from French and German, Gilbert Cannan was known by then for having published more than ten books of plays, fiction, and poetry, as well as critical studies. Mary, who had been married before to J.M. Barrie, the author of *Peter Pan*, was almost twenty years older than her second husband. She considered Gertler "too much of the back street Jew to be a wholly agreeable companion,"[119] but Gilbert found Mark's Jewish background and family fascinating enough to be featured in his next book. Throughout 1915 Gertler often stayed with the Cannans at Cholesbury, and, according to Gertler, he and Gilbert talked "all about where I came from and all about my people."[120] "Gilbert is a very good companion," Gertler assured Kot in August. "He is soothing. I like him immensely."[121] Gertler's great fondness for Cannan would undergo a serious test with the publication of *Mendel* the following year. It is likely that Kot, too, took the novel very personally since it was about an experience of an Eastern European Jew in London.

There can be little argument as to whether Cannan, in betraying his friend's confidences, did the all-too-talkative Gertler a grave disservice (he definitely did). And yet *Mendel* is a remarkable historical document, inasmuch as it allows us glimpses of how Gertler himself felt about being a Jew in England, and how Russian and Eastern European Jewish refugees were viewed there, circa 1915. The novel is an account of a Jewish family virtually identical to the Gertlers (here named the Kühlers), trying to adjust to life in London. The bulk of the novel, however, concerns itself with the plight of their youngest son to establish himself as an artist in the mainstream, non-Jewish world. *Mendel* probably owes its title to Mendel Beilis, who at the time Cannan was writing the novel was still very much in the news. The Beilis "affair" and trial are actually referred to in the novel, when a friend of Mendel's family reads out "how a Jew in Russia had been accused of killing a Christian boy for his blood, and how over a thousand Jews had been massacred on the instigation of the police."[122] The "massacre" alluded to here is largely fictional. While, as mentioned earlier, massacres were expected and caused many Jews, including Kot, to flee Kiev, nothing on such a large scale occurred immediately following the murder and Beilis's arrest.

When the book came out, many in Gertler's circle of friends were scandalized by how shamelessly Cannan exploited Gertler for his own purposes and by how gullible Mark was to believe that some of his revelations and confessions would be off the record. "If Gilbert had taken Gertler's story and *re-created* it into *art*, good," Lawrence fumed in a letter to Koteliansky when the book came out. "But to set down all these statements is vulgarizing of life itself … Oh, I *don't* like *Mendel*."[123] Lawrence had other reasons not to like it: he and Frieda were prominently, but not always flatteringly, featured in the novel as "Logan" and "Oliver." Mad not just at Cannan but also at Gertler, Lawrence declared that it was very "Jew-like" of Gertler to be such a blabbermouth[124] and that, in the long run, his sufferings and unease "serve him right" for having been so stupid.[125]

Cannan obviously meant no intentional harm. He prided himself on being quite a Judophile and even considered Gertler "extremely fortunate to live in the East End amongst *real* people."[126] "Real" or not, London's Jewish community was an uncomfortable terrain for most of Gertler's other friends. Ottoline Morrell remembered the street where Gertler's family lived as "mean, hot, stuffy, smelly," and Nina Hamnett, a fellow artist whom Gertler knew from Slade and who prided herself on being a true Bohemian, found it disconcerting to be in a place

"where hardly anyone spoke English."[127] Their poorly disguised aversion probably made Cannan's positive attitude even more remarkable to Gertler. Cannan
also held his Jewish friend personally in very high esteem; in a letter to Ottoline
Morrell he went as far as to suggest that Gertler was just like another Jewish
"genius" Cannan greatly admired – the poet Heinrich Heine – "only stronger."[128]
And yet even Cannan could not help slipping into obvious ethnic stereotyping.
"It takes a Jew to catch a Jew," his narrator tells us at one point, describing the
moment Mendel senses inferiority hang-ups in his rich Jewish benefactor.[129] At
another point, in order to "counteract the disturbing effect of [the] coolness" of
his friends who accused him of being "a Jew and uneducated," Mendel is said to
have become "very Jewish and hugged his success, gloating over it rather like a cat
over a stolen piece of fish."[130]

The other characters in the novel are of course even more prejudiced, and
Mendel encounters a classical array of anti-Jewish sentiments. "Jews don't stand
for anything but money," says his art teacher; "Jews can never produce art. They
can only produce infant prodigies," opines a critic at Mendel's exhibition, who is
then eagerly echoed by the Frieda-like Oliver.[131] The protagonist himself is quite
torn about his Jewishness. On the one hand, when the same art teacher does what
he thinks is a favour to Mendel by introducing him to the other students as
a Pole rather than a Jew ("You don't look it, and there's some swing about being
a Pole. There's no swing about being a Jew"), Mendel not only resents it but it becomes "his first intimation that there was, in the splendid free Christian world,
a prejudice against Jews."[132] On the other hand, Mendel himself strives not to be
seen as a Jew, dreaming that "because of his wonderful work, everybody would
forget that he was a Jew, and he would move freely and easily in that wonderful
England."[133] How "that England" can be all that "wonderful" and "the Christian
world" so "splendid" if in order to move in them "freely and easily" others had
to forget that he was Jewish is never quite resolved. Instead, Mendel is forever
vacillating between being proudly defiant about his origins ("It became his whole
object to beat the Christians … he would paint better than any of them") and
being deeply ashamed that he is "bearing the marks of the place he came from,
smelling of the gutter."[134] The shame is especially acute around the non-Jewish
girl he likes, who is dead ringer for Dora Carrington. It depresses him to no end
that people around him "think all the Jews are the same," and he declares: "I am
very lonely because I am a Jew."[135]

While the novel does not offer a happy resolution, it does offer a resolution of
sorts. Having decided that the "Jewish way was no longer his," the protagonist
leaves the safety of his Jewish home, where he feels that even the language, Yid-

dish, is "a barrier against the outer world, in which terrible things were always happening."[136] He is therefore poised at the end to face the world as, in Gertler's own words, "neither Jew nor Christian … just myself." Gertler would spend the rest of his life trying to figure out whether, in the England that he loved so much, being neither Jew nor Christian was truly an option. If he read the reviews of the novel, he would know that some considered it an impossible dream. "[H]e is a man without roots," declared one reviewer,

> the child of a race without a country, whose aspirations, shorn of that loyalty which we call patriotism, can find no outlet in the Ghetto and is yet unable to accept or understand the ideals which actuate the Christian people among whom he lives … [it is a] tragic portrait of a young Jew, for whom the law and the prophets are barren, but who cannot discover the fount of the waters of life.[137]

Ironically, it was in his pre-Mendel period, when Gertler was not yet even trying to transcend his Jewish background, that he may have come closest to the true "fount of the waters" of his artistic life, producing, in a quick succession, four very mature and hauntingly beautiful paintings: "The Apple Woman and Her Husband" (a portrait of Golda and Louis Gertler, 1912); "The Artist's Mother" (a portrait of Golda, 1913), "The Rabbi and His Grandchild" (1913), and "Rabbi and Rabbitzin" (1914). Not wanting to be forever branded as just "a Jewish painter," he then largely moved away from the subjects he knew so intimately – yet these early paintings continue to resonate today, while his later paintings, with the obvious exception of the "Merry-Go-Round" (1916), often fail to achieve similar impact and poignancy.[138]

For Koteliansky and his friends, 1915 ended on the same note it began: with deep anxiety about the war, one's identity, and personal relationships. "You can't think how many wonderful ideas I have for future work," Gertler wrote to Kot, "yet any moment I may be dragged away into this war. You can't think what a nightmare it is to me!"[139] In mid-December, Lawrence went to a recruitment station "to be attested and to get a military exemption." "I hated it so much after waiting nearly two hours," he wrote to Ottoline, "that I came away."[140]

For Christmas, Lawrence sent Kot a handkerchief, but whatever warm feeling Kot might have derived from the present was immediately chilled by Frieda's postscript: "I hope you like the hanky … *I* chose it."[141] By underlining "I" Frieda seemed to be virtually daring Kot to use it, and he most likely did not. Lawrence was also recommending Kot to his friends. "If you go to London," he wrote to

Ottoline Morrell, "ask Kotilianski [*sic*] to see you, will you? You will like him. S. Kotilianski, Russian Law Bureau, 212 High Holborn. He is on the telephone, Russian Law Bureau."[142]

"Is Kot my enemy now?" Katherine Mansfield asked Murry in a letter from France the same December. "I feel he is."[143] Several days later, after she finally got a letter from Kot, Mansfield was reassured enough to pour out her immense tenderness for him: "My extremely wicked and neglectful and utterly faithless friend! As last you have sent me a letter … You need not bother to write me letters if it is a trouble to you; it's enough if, *occasionally* you send me a little card and tell me you have not forgotten. For I shall not forget you. I often think of you. I wish you would come into my room now & smoke a cigarette with me … This is not a letter at all, darling – only a message – Take care of yourself. I do not know why but just this moment I see awfully clearly the elephant on your big inkstand."[144]

**4**

# REVOLUTIONS AND CATASTROPHES

Your elation over Russia, has it come back, or do you feel
still despondent?
~ Lawrence to Kot, 1 April 1917

Poor Kot. offers me his remaining ten pounds. He might
as well offer me his nose.
~ Lawrence to Gertler, 16 February 1918

In early spring 1916 Koteliansky apparently suggested that Lawrence should write a novel about a young Englishman. "I don't want to write the novel of the young Englishman," Lawrence replied, "he bores me ... Why don't you write your novel of a Jew: the truth, all of it. *That* would be interesting indeed; only save yourself from being sentimental."[1] The following summer Lawrence would formulate his own unsentimental conclusion about Jews in a letter to Kot: "Why humanity has hated Jews ... is that Jews have always taken religion ... and used it for their personal & private gratification, as if it were a thing administered to their own importance & well-being & conceit. This is the slave trick of the Jews – they use the great religious consciousness as a trick of personal conceit. This is abominable ... a Jew cringes before men, and takes God as a Christian takes whiskey, for his own self-indulgence." The letter astounds not because of what it expresses, since it is consistent with Lawrence's other pronouncements on Jews and their religion, but because he was addressing it directly to a Jewish friend of whom he was supposedly quite fond. "[D]on't be cross," Lawrence added at the end. "I am preaching at you, Kot, because you are 'near the mark.'"[2] "Near the mark" seems to imply that Kot was, mercifully, not too much of that kind of Jew. The same sense emerges from Lawrence's response in 1916 to one of the portraits Gertler painted of Kot: "You are here, the old old old *Jew*, who ought to hasten into oblivion. But there is a young & clumsy uncouth human being, not a Jew at all, a sort of heavy colt, which I should paint if *I* painted your portrait."[3]

Lawrence seemed to consider his feelings about Jews to be philosophical and theological in their nature rather than personal, and that may explain why he never tried harder to hide them from his Jewish friends and acquaintances. Around the same time, he asked a casual American correspondent if he was Jewish and then instructed him, in terms quite similar to the ones in his letter to Kot, that "The best of Jews is, that they *know* truth from untruth. The worst of them is, that they are rather slave-like ... they must cringe their legs and betray it."[4] When his correspondent responded with his own much more positive theory about Jews, Lawrence continued to be merciless: "So Judas was a Super-Christian! And Jews are super-christian lovers of mankind!.. It makes me dislike Judas and Jews very much."[5] Similarly, even while Lawrence was considering joining David Eder in Palestine in search of "Rananim," he exhorted the Zionist Eder to "cease to be a Jew, and let Jewry disappear." "Why," he asked Eder, "do you go with the Jews? They will only be a mill-stone round your neck."[6]

Behind his Jewish friends' backs Lawrence was even less diplomatic. Douglas Goldring, an acquaintance of Koteliansky's who met Lawrence through him, was shocked when Lawrence "dispensed with 'loyalty'" during their very first meeting and said in reference to Kot, who Goldring thought had devoted himself to Lawrence as if to a Messiah: "These Russian Jews are so *heavy*."[7] Lawrence also labelled Barbara Low – Eder's sister-in-law, a Freudian psychologist and another dedicated Lawrence devotee – "the Jewish magpie," whom he did not want to "settle chattering on my roof," that is, come for a visit.[8]

Lawrence's outbursts against Jews may have contributed to Koteliansky's more and more frequent "black moods." On 10 August 1916, Kot wrote to Gertler that he had embarked on "renewed revision of myself, of life, of everything. I am so tired of everything and chiefly of myself ... life seems old, antiquated, settled for ever, and so boring."[9] "[Y]our case seems beyond comprehension to me," Gertler responded several days later. "You hate the Bureau, yet you make no effort to get out of it. If you had a certain thing in view, you could then fight for it and the fight would mean a great deal to you. But no; apparently you want nothing."[10] "Kot is in an extremely depressed state," Gertler wrote to Carrington on 14 August. "His life and future outlook is certainly most dreary and there seems no way out for him, because it is not so much the circumstances of his life, but the way he is made. Some moments his life oppresses me terribly."[11]

Financial hardships were as serious as emotional ones. Thinking that his translations could earn him enough money if the negotiations with publishers were conducted properly, Koteliansky was eager to quit his day job. Murry, engaged in talks about a long-term contract for Kot and himself with Maunsel and Company, asked him to "linger at the Bureau" a bit longer. He also shot down Kot's idea that other publishers should be contacted, suggesting that they should stay loyal to the publisher who "seems prepared to offer us the kinds of terms you want."[12] Koteliansky hated Ruslabu ("I am in terrible rage now with my boss ... and the stinking hole called the Bureau," he wrote to Gertler around the same time[13]) but was understandably afraid of losing his only, meagre source of income. In August he encouraged Gertler – only half-jokingly, it seems – to find him "a very, very old but awfully rich woman": "I'll marry her, take her money, bury her, and then we should find a few more good men & women and live for a time so that we should never want to return to the old things."[14] Within a month Kot could linger no longer and quit the Bureau. Lawrence questioned his decision. "Why are you leaving the Bureau," he wrote from St Ives on 12 September, "and what are you going to do? Is it merely that you have had enough Slatkovsky, or is it something better?"[15] There was, alas, nothing better. No offer from Maunsel was forthcoming, and a "very, very old but awfully rich woman" had not materialized either.

Throughout the second half of 1916 Koteliansky was also very concerned that he may be forced into the army. The Military Service Act of 1916, enacted in January to confront the increasing shortage of volunteers, specifically exempted foreigners from serving in the British army. By May 1916, however, the War Office was announcing that, while not drafting "friendly aliens," it would allow them to volunteer. Since Russia was an ally, about 30,000 Russian Jewish men of the proper age (eighteen to forty-one) became primary targets of the drive.[16] When too few enlisted, the "invitation" was backed up by a threat of deportation. "Now about the conscription of friendly aliens," Koteliansky wrote to Gertler in July 1916, "it looks as if the government is seriously going to make me a Tommy."[17]

Lawrence, fresh from his exemption ("I spent last night in the barracks here, like a criminal. Today I have a complete exemption. But – fui!" he wrote to Koteliansky on 29 June[18]), offered some practical advice: "You must, if they are really going to 'compel' you militarily, get a job in an office. With your knowledge of English, and other languages, I am sure they would have every use for you." "Besides," he added, even though a similar sentiment had failed to console Lawrence himself while he was going through his own conscription-induced anxiety, "the war is not going to last much longer."[19] "You sound gloomy again in your letter," Lawrence wrote a week later. "I suppose it is the army. Don't bother, I feel sure they will give you a decent job, which you will like."[20] In another letter the same month, Lawrence exclaimed: "How queer, if they send you to Russia!"[21] By September, however, Lawrence sounded almost sure that Kot would not be forced into the military service or deported: "I don't believe they will conscript you, in the end. For some reason, I think they will leave alone the

Jews and the Russians. Surely they have got their mouths as full of conscripted England, as they can chew."[22]

Koteliansky would, indeed, never be conscripted, but Lawrence's optimism was still premature. After the Russian February Revolution of 1917, the British government made an even more serious attempt to either conscript Russian Jews or send them back to what they now considered a free, democratic country. In March 1917 the new government in Russia even co-signed the Anglo-Russian Convention of Military Service, which established "the reciprocal liability to military service of British subjects resident in Russia and Russian subjects resident in Great Britain."[23] The convention was ratified and went into effect in August of that year, but on 28 August Kot, much to his relief, was issued a certificate from the Russian Consulate General in London (where Konstantin Nabokov was now the acting head) stating that "Samuel Coteliansky," serial number "EQ 801," was "temporarily exempted from military service."[24] When he obtained it, Koteliansky probably uttered one of his favourite Jewish sayings: "Frighten me, Lord, but do not punish me."[25]

The Military Service Act of 1916, christened by some "The Bachelor's Bill," posed even more of a threat to Gertler. In February he was called to his local recruiting office, where he went "trembling in every limb," as he described it to Dorothy Brett.[26] For once, his parents' "enemy alien" status, which they still held at the time, actually helped, and, to his joy, Gertler was deemed unfit for conscription. Many of his other more personal issues remained unresolved, though, and he continued to seek advice from his older and wiser friend. At his rabbinical best, Kot saw two wars raging in Gertler's life at the time: one around him and one within him. The one within he considered to be not only Gertler's curse but also his blessing: "[I]ndividuals who have to endure their own state of war – with themselves, with things important and unimportant, even with shadows and ghosts, – must not desire the things and state of mind that the many possess. This is the price of *being*. You know quite well that all personal troubles … are, on the whole, reducible to whether one, notwithstanding all the great toll, wants to remain *being* himself, or one prefers quiet peace of mind, the love of his friends & neighbours and the other blessings of earth to negation, rejection of one's own being … Out of troubles and suffering for that which matters and which is incredibly difficult to attain, – is built the way of real being and creating."[27] Always striving toward peace of mind and personal happiness, Gertler definitely would have preferred if the price of being were a bit lower.

Kot was right, however, about "troubles and suffering" building "the way … of creating." Gertler's anxiety over the war and the possibility of being conscripted ended up aiding him in creating the painting he is best known for: "The Merry-

Go-Round," which he finished in September 1916. The seemingly endless and, to Gertler, meaningless nature of the war is portrayed in the painting through puppet-like male and female figures, their mouths open in constant readiness to echo the latest political sloganeering, forever riding a very unmerry merry-go-round. Of the three dominant colours in the painting – red, blue, and black – red, the colour of human blood, is most vivid. Now among the most prized possessions of the Tate Gallery, "The Merry-Go-Round" was very controversial at a time when the government was trying to enlist at least two million more British subjects to fight the war.

The canvas provoked a mixed reaction even among some of Gertler's friends and fellow pacifists. Lytton Strachey, who was officially a conscientious objector, confessed to Ottoline Morrell that, while he admired the painting, he did not really like it, "for liking it one might as well think of liking a machine gun."[28] Lawrence, who saw a photograph of the picture, was sufficiently impressed to alter the draft of *Women in Love* to include a sculpture that was very similar in theme to Gertler's painting.[29] Characteristically enough, though, he managed to see even "The Merry-Go-Round" through the prism of Gertler's Jewishness. "My dear Gertler," he wrote on 9 October 1916, "Your terrible and dreadful picture has just come … it is the best *modern* picture I have seen … But it is horrible and terrifying. I am not sure I wouldn't be too frightened to come and look at the original … It would take a Jew to paint this picture … you must, in your art, be mindless and in an ecstasy of destructive sensation … At last your race is at an end – these pictures are its death-cry. And it will be left for the Jews to utter the final and great death-cry."[30]

Equally puzzling at times was Lawrence's reaction to Kot's depression. "My dear Kot," he wrote somewhat unhelpfully in November, "I must tell you we laugh at you when you are in your bad moods … The world is quite as bad as you have ever seen it in your worst and most lucid moments, and *even worse*."[31] What continued to draw them together is a bit puzzling as well. Even aside from Lawrence's attitudes toward Jews, the two were, in many ways, direct opposites. Lawrence, though always surrounded by people ready to worship him, believed that one needed "to be alone. Always."[32] Kot, who felt that he was, indeed, always alone, was in no mood to celebrate or cherish solitude. While Lawrence was famously restless and could rarely stay at the same place or even in the same country for more than several months, Kot moved into the house on Acacia Road and stayed there until his death, hardly ever leaving it even to go several kilometres outside of London. Despite it all, their bond still appeared to be strong. "Kot wearies me to extinction," Lawrence wrote to Gordon Campbell early in 1917, "and yet I wouldn't forego him."[33]

Kot always looked forward to seeing Lawrence; he hated, however, when Frieda came along. "The idea of Frieda coming here … irritates me and gives me a kind of stubborn muddle-headed anger," Kot wrote to Gertler after one such visit. "We had a few more quarrels and she shed profused tears, but I think, she weeps only to benefit her digestion."[34] He was not alone in seeing Frieda as a bad influence on Lawrence both as a person and a writer. Mansfield soon did too. "The 'dear man' in him whom we all loved," she complained to Ottoline Morrell in spring 1916, "is hidden away, absorbed completely lost, like a little gold ring in that immense german christmas pudding which is Frieda. And with all the appetite in the world one cannot eat ones way through Frieda to find him. One simply looks and waits for someone to come with a knife and cut her up into the smallest pieces that L. may see the light and shine again."[35] Mansfield expressed similar sentiments about Frieda in her letters to Kot while showering "Catalina," as she sometimes liked to call him, with much warmth and affection: "You are so often in my thoughts […] Let us be happy when we see each other – if only for a minute of time."[36] In summer 1916, much to Kot's delight, she even confided to him that she was contemplating leaving Murry. After Katherine and Jack – quite predictably to all but Kot – reconciled, his disapproval and hostility toward Murry must have become uncomfortable to both Mansfield and Murry – not unlike the situation in spring 1915, when Kot was rooting for Lawrence to leave Frieda but ended up with a temporary breakup in his relationship with both of them.

The breakup with the Murrys seems to have moved Kot – at least for a short while – closer to Frieda, and she did her best to keep it that way. In London during the third week of September, Frieda told Kot that Jack Murry – with Katherine's seeming acquiescence – had been saying unkind things about him. Writing to him the next day, she begged him not to be "miserable" since neither she nor Lawrence "would believe such small things of you."[37] On 4 October, Frieda, back in St Ives, brought up the topic again: "I hope you and Katherine will be friends again – you see she really loves Murry and then also she plays other people against him … I knew that Murry was jealous of you that's why he told lies."[38] By 15 October, it became obvious to Frieda and Lawrence that Kot and the Murrys had already had their explanation, which, given Kot's intensity, must have been very heated. "As Katherine does not write to me," Frieda informed Kot, "I believe you must have told Jack what I said. I am *glad* if you have … It is time that Jack stopped the lies he tells about people to satisfy his own meanness."[39] Lawrence instructed Kot in an attachment to Frieda's letter not to "take any notice of the Murrys & what they say & do."[40] Lawrence's sage advice was, of course, absolutely contrary to Kot's nature and temperament, especially given how special his relationship with Mansfied had been prior to this incident. The breakup would last for two whole years.

Kot's feelings of betrayal ran so deep that when Gertler suggested in summer 1918 that the four of them should finally get together again, Kot angrily – and at times ungrammatically (his English often suffered when he got emotional) – protested: "I want to tell you, if I hadn't told it you before that it is simply impossible for me to meet the Murries until a time comes in me when I could completely forget the wrong attitude that they had towards me. You see I don't mind their false attitude to others, I could even excuse it, but I cannot notwithstanding all my self-persuading, excuse their attitude to me. I gave them friendship and they simply accepted it as something due to them, they took me as any one other of their hundreds of friends – to deceive. But perhaps this is not the chief point. If you only knew what sometimes means the desire to be, to talk, to commune with one, who understands, and how painful sometimes is loneliness … you would realize that it is not so easy to meet again those, who have been something to you and ceased, of their own individual fault to be."[41]

He also told Virginia Woolf that Mansfield's "lies & poses have proved too much for him."[42] Frieda, in the meantime, continued adding fuel to the fire by reporting to Kot what the Murrys were saying about him. "Katherine is very hostile to both of us," Kot would then update Gertler. "[I]n her letters to Frieda she calls us 'dirties' who should not be believed, as we are talking always against them."[43] Mansfield, however, sounded anything but hostile when, at the end of 1917, she wrote to Ottoline about how happy she was that at Ottoline's house Murry and Gertler came together: "He talked of Mark so much last night and wants to be a friend of his. I wish I could see him again. It is years since I have."[44]

For Christmas, Lawrence, who was still at St Ives, sent Kot "a tiny little paper-knife of blue agate."[45] Unlike the handkerchief the year before, this gift he chose himself.

When the February Revolution took place in Russia, Koteliansky, like many other expatriates, began to hope that his country, now a fledging democracy, was ready to embrace people like him. One can hear Koteliansky's excitement in a letter he sent to Mary Hutchinson in early April. Commenting on her husband's bout with influenza, he wrote: "He ought to get up instantly and make a trip to Russia … Revolutionary air is a splendid cure against all kinds of influenza." He also added a tongue-in-cheek reference to his parents back in Russia: "My parents are at the Mill at present. Do you not think that their cruelty in deserting their only begotten son is beyond grasp of mind or emotion? (I believe I've borrowed last phrase from today's newspaper)."[46] There are, of course, two playful inaccuracies in this statement: it was he who "deserted" his parents in 1911, and, as we know, he was definitely not their "only begotten son."

Unsurprisingly, then, early spring 1917 was one of the most joyful, active, and fulfilling periods in his stay in England. During that time, according to Lady Glenavy, "Kot and old Madame Stepniak … walked the streets of London all night till the dawn" because they "were so happy for Russia; it was as if their dreams had come true."[47] Koteliansky's one-time benefactor, Maxim Gorky, was now the editor of the resurrected *Novaia zhizn'* (The New Life). It was still the organ of the Russian Social Democratic Labour Party, and while its former editor, Maxim Litvinov, had earlier joined the Bolsheviks, Gorky was holding on to his old political views. As had been the case in the 1905 Revolution, *Novaia zhizn'* would not survive for very long; in July 1918 it became the last opposition paper to be banned by the Bolsheviks. Immediately after the February Revolution, however, it was still going strong; the Bolsheviks were not yet in power, and Gorky's paper represented the views of many liberal and democratic factions who supported the peaceful abolition of monarchy in Russia and the establishment of a Western-type liberal democracy.

In April (for a part of which Lawrence and Frieda were staying on Acacia Road[48]) and May 1917 Koteliansky was busily sending telegrams to Gorky and the editorial staff at *Novaia zhizn'* about his contacts with the British labour activists, writers, and intellectuals who were responding to his pleas to welcome the Russian revolution and contribute to Gorky's publication. As the records – most handwritten in Russian with occasional words in English – show, he kept a painstaking track of all the telegrams he sent for that purpose. One such document reads as follows:

29 April (Sunday). Having received a telegram from Grisha [Farbman] concerning [William] Anderson, [James] Ramsay MacDonald, [Philip] Snowden and others, I sent that same evening a telegram ("urgent," 60 words) to [Novaia] Zhizn' stating that I have secured the consent of Anderson, Miss [Mary] Macarthur, Snowden, [H.W.] Massingham, Ramsay Macdonald to participate in N. Zh. The same Sunday evening sent 4 congratulatory telegrams – all in all 260 words – to the editorial board of N. Zh. (And with the first telegram – 320 words.) Since [George] Bernard Shaw and [H.G.] Wells were out of town, I sent them, as well as Arnold Bennett, telegrams inviting them to participate in N. Zh. and asking them to immediately send congratulations and their consent to participate in N. Zh. directly to Gorky (I also promised to reimburse their expenses in sending telegrams).[49]

On 1 May, he again sent telegrams to "Wells and others. All in all 270 words," and more words ("May 12 – 130 words; 14 – 100 words; 21 – 150") followed. The responses were for most part very enthusiastic,[50] but some, like G.B. Shaw's, expressed caution. Shaw wrote that he already greeted the revolution in other Russian periodicals and was hoping Gorky would not "misunderstand my discretion."[51] Kot also sent a telegram on 1 May to Lawrence, who responded that he would be "only too glad to contribute anything I can" and went on to let his Rananim-inspired vision of new Russia soar: "I feel that our chiefest hope for the future is Russia. When I think of the young new country there, I love it inordinately. It is the place of hope ... *Nuova speranza – la Russia.*"[52]

Kot was now contemplating going to Russia and took some steps to get a visa but was persuaded to postpone the trip for reasons that he laid out in a letter to Gertler: "Last week, after a long series of depressing [*sic*], I got an 'inspiration' to go to Russia. I thought it the best under the circumstances and meant staying there for a couple of months and returning back here. But on seeing the man in the Foreign Office who could have helped me in getting a pass I was advised to postpone my journey for some time in view of the new circumstances taking place now in Russia. It has also been hinted to me that no passport would be granted me at present. Strangely enough I was so glad that I have not to go that my 'black mood' became pinkier."[43]

It is remarkable that, despite all his excitement over the winds of change blowing through Russia and the fact that he had been away from his family for six years, Kot was still reluctant to go back. Was he concerned, as he should have been, about being stuck there if political winds suddenly shifted? Was he afraid that his family would try to persuade him to stay? Or did he sense that his six years in England made him even further removed from the rhythms and culture of his birthplace? Probably all of the above. He also, no doubt, would have felt differently if he could have foreseen that this would be his last chance to see his parents alive.

While not enough to beckon him back, Russia's gradual political transformation in early 1917 did renew Koteliansky's desire to introduce Russians to a great English writer: D.H. Lawrence. This desire coincided with Lawrence's difficulties in finding a publisher for *Women in Love*, so the thought that the novel could instead be first published in Russia quite appealed to him. "I should be very glad," he wrote to his agent in January, "if you would make me a fair typed copy, at the same time as the one is being made for Koteliansky, for Russia."[54] "I should like the novel to be published in Russia," he told Kot on 9 February. "Certainly it won't come out here – certainly not as long as the war lasts: but I am just as well content."[55] Frieda was equally enthusiastic: "I think Russia would appreciate Lawrence."[56] By April, however, Lawrence was having second thoughts. "Don't hurry about Russia," he wrote to Kot then. "I always believe in giving things time."[57] Three months later he sounded even more reluctant: "How can I write for any Russian audience! – the contact is not established. How can the current flow when there is no connection?"[58] Russian *Women in Love* was, after all, not to be, and it took three more years for the first English edition of the novel to appear, and even then not in England but in the United States.[59]

Like most people in his old country at the time, throughout spring and early summer Kot was truly on an emotional rollercoaster. By mid-May his elation had given way to what Lawrence called "unfathomable depths of gloom," making him wonder whether Kot sensed that "the wrong things were happening in Russia."[60] They were: Lenin returned from abroad in April, the Bolsheviks were gaining strength, and the provisional government, which had come to power as a result of the February Revolution, was woefully ineffective in carrying out economic and political reforms. It did not help either that the government had chosen to support Russia's continued participation in World War I.

There were also unsettling developments in Ukraine. Even though Jews there had suffered grievously under the Russian authorities, one thing they always feared even more was Ukraine's independence. They assumed, with good reason, that the violence against them would only accelerate if Ukraine became an independent state. This anxiety was particularly acute because Jews were buoyed by the changes instituted by the Russian provisional government – like the lifting of restrictions on where Jews could live or study – and were finally looking forward to leaving their painful experiences and boundaries behind. They could now entertain a more realistic hope of a just and peaceful future for their children.

Esther Salaman was still in Zhitomir at the time of the February Revolution, and in her autobiographical novel, *The Fertile Plain*, she describes both the elation and the pressure to side with a variety of movements that were all trying hard to advance their political and ideological agendas, including independence:

There was a military band, and soldiers carrying red banners with the words: Liberty, Equality, Fraternity ... We were bespattered with mud, but the sun was shining. I heard for the first time the Marseillaise; it brought tears to my eyes. The crowd was learning to sing it ... People were coming out of the Catholic Cathedral, and joined the Polish contingent; on their flags was written in Polish and Russian 'A free Poland.' As we passed a column carrying a red flag someone tapped me on the shoulder: it was Lipman.

'Come and join the Mensheviks,' he said ... Close by was the Jewish *Bund* ... I stopped to say a word to my Zionist friends. 'Don't you join those bourgeois nationalists,' Lipman shouted from some distance to me ... I ... found myself near Anatol Victorovsky. 'Are you looking for the Ukrainian contingent?' he asked. 'No, why?' 'I thought, perhaps, you were a Ukrainian patriot. I am one myself' [...] Victorovsky picked up a little girl and sat her on his shoulders. A woman near me cried. There were shouts of 'Long live the revolution! Long live Russia! Long live freedom!' There was almost unbelievable happiness.[61]

The push for Ukrainian autonomy and eventual independence started days after the February Revolution with the formation of the Ukrainian "Central Rada" (Council). The council operated under the leadership of Mykhailo Hrushevskyi, a famous Ukrainian historian, and Symon Petliura, one of the founders of the Ukrainian Labour Party and a journalist; both proceeded to Petrograd to negotiate the terms with the Provisional Government. Kerensky and most other ministers in the new government were cool to the idea but by early August a compromise of sorts was reached, which made the Rada "the highest organ of the Provisional Government's local administration in Ukraine until such time as the All-Russian Constituent Assembly made the final decision on what would constitute the future regional administration."[62]

In July, Grisha Farbman, who had just come back from Petrograd, apparently brought back some "hopeful news."[63] Kot must have sounded very enthusiastic in his letter to Lawrence describing Farbman's impressions, since both Lawrence and Frieda remarked on his high spirits. "Indeed you are no longer dead!" Frieda exclaimed in one of her longer letters devoted to all things Russian. "I can imagine *how* good it must be for you when you had *almost* given up hope to find what you strove for from your boyhood in your Russian village has come – It is marvellous for everybody this new Russia that is a fact now and not only a dream."[64] Alas, the dream was not of a lasting nature, and one does wonder what was so hopeful about Farbman's news, since his own published comments were not rosy. Most importantly, while still in Russia, Farbman had reported in the *Daily Herald* that the country was facing "the growth in the power of the extremist socialists owing to mistrust of the war aims of the Allies,"[65] thus foreseeing the imminent triumph of the Bolsheviks.

Toward autumn, Koteliansky's letter exchanges with his major correspondents appear to have decreased significantly. It was partially for personal reasons. Lawrence's 3 July letter, which contained his diatribe against Jews on the grounds that they "cringe ... before men," proved too much even for Kot.[66] Lawrence made an attempt to restore the lines of communication in late September by suggesting to Kot that he "should never mind my onslaughts," but this feeble attempt at an apology fell short.[67] Kot was also continuing to fight Murry. Convinced that the slow pace of Murry's negotiation with Maunsel led to them not issuing a long-term contract for translations, Kot accused Murry of not having negotiated in good faith. Murry was incensed. "No, Kot," he wrote on 1 June 1917, "we have had good times together … but, right down at the bottom, I cannot understand you & I am just as certain that you can't understand me. So it is as well that we should go our separate ways for ever."[68] Even Gertler's letters became rare. There is a letter dated 29 August, in which Gertler talks about his own state of depression, occasioned by both Carrington's coolness toward him and a still-life which "came to nothing."[69] Then there is a letter from 20 October, in which Gertler makes excuses for going to Ottoline Morrell's estate at Garsington and mixing with a crowd Kot did not approve of.[70] After that, as in Lawrence's case, there is nothing until late December, even though several months earlier Gertler had reaffirmed to Carrington that Kot was one of his two "only friends."[71]

These autumn months were, of course, a period of catastrophic events in Russia. By capturing the majority in the Moscow and Petrograd Soviets in September, the Bolsheviks firmly established themselves as the dominant force in Russian politics. Emboldened by their success, they started aiming for the outright overthrow of the provisional government, which they succeeded in doing several weeks later, on 25 October Old Russian Style – 7 November everywhere else.[72] Chances are, Kot spent most of this time by himself, suffering from the blackest moods.

We do, finally, get a glimpse of Kot in mid-November, a week after the fateful events in Petrograd. It comes in a letter Carrington sent to Gertler: "I had dinner with Monty [Montague Shearman] … Lawrence and Koteliansky came in also later. Good old Kot! How charming he is."[73] This brief mention may be important for two reasons. On the one hand, it may provide evidence that Kot's and Lawrence's reconciliation had already occurred by then. On the other, if Kot felt like being social and even "charming" again, it may mean that he was slowly recovering from the shock of the Bolsheviks taking power in Russia. It is also possible that, like many émigrés at the time, he believed that the Bolsheviks would not last very long.

He also probably assumed that his friends could not understand his pain anyway, so it was best to hide it – and in that he was right. When he shared his apprehensions about the Bolshevik revolution at a dinner with the Woolfs in January 1918, Virginia sarcastically called it "a formal address upon Russia in broken English" and noted that he did not particularly care about Russia's fate: "He …

thinks Russia too little civilized to profit by revolution ... Russia scarcely interests him; he never means to go back; prophesies civil war in the spring, & no
advantage won by it. In 1905 they were burning houses & stabbing nobles too."[74]
Even Gertler would admit that he could not quite grasp Kot's anxiety: "I feel far
too detached to understand that feeling *for a people* as a whole, as you feel about
the Russians. It seems uninteresting to me as many other sentiments."[75] Lady
Glenavy, who prided herself on being able to lighten Kot's moods, was not of
much help either, as she herself admitted in her book: "There was murder, fighting and starvation. Kot did not speak of it, but this must have been a terrible
time for him. We carried on with our own lives and our own war without
paying much attention to his."[76]

"How is he?" Lawrence asked Gertler in June 1918. "Is he metamorphosing
into some sort of unnatural ichthyosaurus now – some black-crested lizard – in
his No. 5 isolation [?] The house is like a cave."[77] But that summer Kot actually
did something unusual: to take his mind off political upheavals and unrealized
dreams, he left London and ventured into Sussex. It was, he explained to Gertler,
just "for a fortnight to experience what it is to be in a seaside place." He quickly
decided, however, that the elements were against him and it was "not at all as romantic ... as it is reported to be."[78] And then the period of relative socialization
passed quickly and Kot indeed retreated back into his lonely angst over the
events taking place in Russia and Ukraine. By summer 1918, "murder, fighting
and starvation," as well as deadly epidemics, were indeed taking place there. It
did not bypass Ostropol, and would touch his family in the most immediate
and tragic way.

Living in Ukraine after the October Revolution was even more disorienting
and calamitous than living in Russia, especially if one happened to be a Jew. For
three years following the revolution, Ukraine lived through head-spinning se-
quences of one regime replacing another. From 1918 through 1920 Ukraine served
as the theatre of war for at least five armies: the Red Army fighting to maintain
the control over the territory; the White Army, under general Denikin (and
greatly aided by France and England), fighting to overthrow the Bolsheviks; the
German Army trying both to defeat the Bolsheviks and to keep England and
France at bay; the Ukrainian Army, under Symon Petliura (and at times reinforced by the Polish Army or aided by the German Army), fighting for the
Ukrainian independence; and the Polish Army trying to attach the western part
of Ukraine (which did not include Kot's Volhynia) to its own newly independent state.

The Rada used the occasion of the October Revolution to finally proclaim
Ukraine's independence from Russia. At first the new Russian government

appeared to look the other way but by February 1918 the Bolsheviks resolved not to let it stand and established their rule over Ukraine. The rule did not last very long, though: within a month the German Army came in at the invitation of the Rada and chased the Bolsheviks away, but instead of reinstating the Rada, whom the Germans considered too liberal and ineffective, they installed their own more conservative puppet regime under Paul Skoropadsky, who, in turn, was deposed by the slighted Rada in December 1918. The White – also known as "Volunteer" – Army was composed of Russians of different political persuasions (from monarchists to liberal democrats), and classes (from aristocracy to peasants), all united through their hatred for the Bolsheviks. It marched into Kiev soon thereafter and occupied Ukraine for the next nine months. The Bolsheviks again restored their rule in autumn 1919, but in May 1920 power was once more retaken by Petliura's Ukrainian Nationalist Army. Finally, less than a month later, the Bolsheviks were back, this time establishing a firm and long-lasting grip.[79]

While towns and villages went from one occupier to the next, one thing remained constant: the fate of the Jews. Jews were now hated not just for all the old reasons but for new ones as well: the Ukrainian nationalists resented their opposition to Ukraine's independence, while the Whites saw the Bolshevik revolution as largely a Jewish affair, since Jews were so prominent both in the Bolshevik movement and the new government. It is estimated that just in one year, 1919-1920, anywhere from 35,000 to 50,000 Jews perished in pogroms instigated by all sides. Most murderous were the White Army, the Petliura Army, and free-agent anarchist peasant bands (like the one led by Nestor Makhno), which abounded at the time in Ukraine.[80] Peter Kenez, a historian of that period, describes a typical pogrom by the White Army troops in 1919:

> Troops of the Volunteer Army, usually the Cossacks, entered a little town. They immediately divided themselves into small groups of five or ten, often including officers. These groups attacked Jews on the streets, beat them and sometimes stripped them. Then they entered Jewish houses, demanding money and other valuables. The frightened victims handed over everything they owned without the slightest resistance. The pogromists then searched and destroyed the interior of the house. The destruction was frequently followed by rape. Sometimes the Cossacks forced the women to follow them, killing those who did not obey. The local [non-Jewish] population usually … joined the looting once the violence had begun … Methods of murder varied greatly. Generally the Cossacks shot or bayoneted their victims, but hanging, burning, drowning in wells, and live burials also

occurred. There were recorded instances of people buried up to the necks in sand and then killed by horses driven over them.[81]

While in Zhitomir, Esther Salaman experienced the often lethal pogroms first-hand. In *Two Silver Roubles*, her 1932 novel, which chronologically follows *The Fertile Plain* but was written almost twenty five years prior to it (when memories were still both fresh and raw), she describes two of many incidents she witnessed or became aware of while she and her family expected every day to become next victims:

> On that day a Jew called Tobias was killed in our street. He sold forage for horses and was a poor man, but he never complained. He had eight daughters and still prayed to God, hoping for a son … On the eve of the pogrom he counted the money he saved during many years. It was eight hundred roubles – a big sum for him. He said to his wife: "I see it is our lot to give this money up to the robbers. Never mind. The Lord giveth, the Lord taketh away …" In the morning, when the Cossacks entered his house, he was standing, dressed as usual in his ragged, dirty, grey frock-coat with a silk cap on his head, unwinding the *Tphillin*, for he had just finished the morning prayer. Afraid to profane the *Tphillin*, he said one word in the holy tongue to his wife: "Give …" and pointed to the Cossacks. She rushed into the other room, while the Cossack raged: "You Jew, with your confounded language." The wife brought all the money, and Tobias, who had taken off the *Tphillin*, said in broken Russian: "Here is all I possess: take it." They took it, and dragged him out of the house and killed him.[82]

Based on the experience of others, Esther knew full well that if the Cossacks came to rob her family (and there were several very close calls), in addition to murdering her father and grandfather, they would probably also rape her.[83]

The relatives Koteliansky had left behind were also facing death and violence. Still in Ostropol at the time were, in addition to his parents, his two brothers, David and Moishel, two sisters, Yokhevet and Rokhl, and nephews and nieces, among them Eliahu, or Eli (his other nickname was "Lucy"), the son of Yokhevet and her husband Isaak Chernomorsky, and their daughter Perl (later Pauline or Polly). When Kot was leaving for London, Eli was two and Perl barely a week old.[84] In early 1920, the family suddenly got smaller: Kot's father and his sister Yokhevet succumbed to typhoid fever within a couple of days of each other.[85] Letters travelled very slowly, if at all, in the post-revolutionary chaos that was

Ukraine, and it would take months for Kot to learn anything about this tragedy. He continued to have vague plans to go back there at the first opportunity and was obviously still unaware of what had happened when in the spring of that year he mentioned to Lawrence in a casual way that he was again thinking of visiting his folks. Lawrence, in Sicily at the time, thought it was a superb idea: "I imagine you setting off for the Ukraina. God, what a grand excitement, after so long!"[86] By autumn Kot already knew that something was terribly wrong.

In late October, when Mark Gertler was in a sanatorium, having been just diagnosed with tuberculosis (at that time, three of Kot's closest friends in England suffered from the same dreadful disease), he received a letter from Kot, in which he revealed that his family in Ukraine was not doing well. He spared Gertler the details – or maybe he himself had been spared the details by Beila. He simply told Gertler that it was very difficult for him to talk about it but that he felt he had to go to Ostropol to help them cope. Gertler responded that he was "sorry about these worries over your people" and that he wished "you would tell me more about it; if it's not unpleasant to do so."[87] By December Gertler still knew very few details, and was genuinely wondering why his friend felt he had to go to Ostropol: "Why I wonder is it necessary to join your people at all? Would it not be sufficient if you sent them some money? Of if you do go out to them, wouldn't a short visit suffice? I only mention this because in your letter you say that if you go, you 'hope' only to come back to London."[88] Koteliansky did not go back home on this occasion either. Given the situation in Ukraine, it was probably virtually impossible for him to get there.

It was, apparently, Yokhevet's nine-year-old daughter, Perl, who first came down with typhoid fever, and the deaths of her mother and grandfather were not the last deaths in the family that young Perl had to witness and endure: in less than a year her father would be savagely killed in front of her. Perl later told her children that Isaak Chernomorsky was in bed when a group of Red Army commissars and soldiers, who just reoccupied the town, rushed in demanding that the family leave the house, which, as one of the largest houses in Ostropol, was to be used for their headquarters. Chernomorsky apparently objected and was then threatened with a gun while his young daughter begged for his life to be spared. Someone in the party told the grownups in the room, "If you don't take her away, we'll kill her too," and, as she was dragged out of the room, she heard a shot. She turned back and saw her father falling down and then lying in a pool of blood.[89]

Kot must have received the news about the killing of his brother-in-law by early spring 1921. "It certainly sounds most distressing about your people," Gertler commiserated with him in March. "It must be awful not to be able to help them."[90] "[T]he events … I mean what happened to my family in Russia," Kot wrote to Dorothy Brett in August, "were such, that not being a very active and energetic person, they weigh me down. My mere helplessness in alleviating their situation makes me miserable day and night." He added that he did not want to "infect" others with his misery and therefore preferred not to see anyone.[91]

Between the deaths of Yokhevet and Avrum-Shloima and the murder of Isaak Chernomorsky, something else of major importance took place within the Koteliansky family: Samuel's brother, Moishel Koteliansky, and his family left Ostropol in autumn 1920 and reached Canada the following spring.[92] 1920 was, in fact, the year several Jewish Ostropol families took advantage of the chaos in Ukraine and the new independence of Poland to cross the border by obtaining Polish travel passports. Ben Richman, by then already in North America, was one of the people dispatched by the anxious American and Canadian relatives of Ostropol Jews to Warsaw to accompany the refugees to Antwerp and then on a Canadian ship named "Sicilian" to Halifax. Like the Kotelianskys, many of them were heading for Sherbrooke, a city not far from Montreal, where Ostropol Jews had been settling since escaping the pogroms of the 1880s. It was an expensive proposition, for not only did the families have to pay for their passage, including bribes along the way, their relatives in Canada had to pay big sums to sponsor them.[93] Three days after their arrival, Moishel received twenty-five British pounds from Kot, and then it was followed with one hundred more in spring 1922.[94]

Perl and Eli, in the meantime, went to live with Beila and, when Beila felt she was too old to care for them, with their aunt, Rokhl. When Dorothy Brett, who was wealthy, offered material help to the orphans, Kot politely turned it down but went on to say: "Although if I personally, without any assistance, had a thousand pounds I could help my people perhaps radically – by getting them out of Russia and then arranging their going to my brother in Canada. But I haven't got the thousand pounds, and I am sure that, if I had them now, it would not change matters really very much. The chief evil has been done, and one, in a sober mood, is inclined to feel fatalistically."[95] It took four more years, and probably much pressure from Beila, for the decision to be made that the money had to be found for the children to be sent to Canada. Since his mother and sister no longer had any funds, Kot took the responsibility for paying for the children's passage while Moishel took care of the sponsorship fees.

Somewhere along the way Kot was apparently "duped," as he would inform his niece in 1948: "I had to spend nearly £200, that is a thousand dollars, to get you and Lucy (your brother) out of Russia ... I had at that time to deal through agents, who might have been dishonest, and robbed me; but the fact is that I spent on your getting to Canada two hundred pounds."[96] "I am sorry that you still have more bother with your relations in Russia," Gertler wrote in July 1925. "How depressing it must be for you – after all these efforts."[97] "The whole thing has been so much messed up by the Bolshevik authorities," Kot complained to a friend, Sydney Waterlow, in September that he had to be "at home constantly and attend to any new fact that may arise. Today, for instance, I had to go to the representative of the Canadian Government to ask him for an extension of time of the children's admission. I also had to cable home to that effect. I may have a cable from home in reply, and may have to go again to ask for extension of admission."[98]

When it all got worked out, it was arranged that on their way to Canada, Perl and Eli would stop in England and see their uncle, or "The Uncle," as Perl would always refer to him later.[99] Kot was, by all accounts, particularly impressed by Eli, who was sixteen years old at the time.[100] Since his opinion of the "New World" was never high, Kot probably wished he could offer them, and especially Eli, to stay with him in England, but he also no doubt felt that neither his financial circumstances nor his temperament were well suited to act as a surrogate father to teenagers. "I like children from the age of two till 12," he would tell a friend two years later. "After 12 they cease to be children and become very old people … not at all interesting."[101] Soon after they arrived in Sherbrooke, Eli was taking a bath at Moishel's house when the pilot light of the gas heater suddenly went out while gas was still coming in, and, by the time his sister and uncle began to wonder why his bath was taking so long, Eli was dead.[102]

There are some indications that this latest family tragedy was kept a secret from Kot for a while, or that the bad news was given to him gradually, to prepare him and soften the blow. Gertler seems to refer to it in his 22 December 1925 letter: "I only heard – today – from Waterlow about your troubles – I am very upset about it … you must be very worried – why I wonder did you not let me know when you were having all the apprehensions about the boy …"[103] The lack of candor from his Canadian relatives seems to have had unfortunate consequences for Perl, whom, even though she was only fourteen at the time, Kot held personally responsible for not telling him the truth. He also blamed his brother for not watching over their nephew better.[104] On that occasion, too, he retreated into his cave and would see no one, telling Dorothy Brett, who was genuinely concerned about him: "Everyone has his or her own troubles, and to add someone else's to those is really unpardonable. Especially remembering that real great troubles must be gone through, and no sympathy can alleviate them."[105] Soon thereafter Beila and Rokhl's family moved to Kiev, and the Ostropol chapter of the Kotelianskys' life was over.

# H.G. WELLS IN RUSSIA AND THE DEATH OF MANSFIELD

You are a most extraordinary man and I do not pretend to
understand many things about you but it would be very
difficult for you to make me anything but your very warm
and steadfast Friend.
~ H.G. Wells to Koteliansky, 18 November 1924

Yes, I love Koteliansky – no less.
~ Mansfield to Dorothy Brett, 26 February 1922

There was another Russian Jew living in London immediately before the Russian revolutions who, like Koteliansky, was waiting for the right moment to go back to Russia. His name by then was Maxim Litvinov, and he would become one of the most successful Soviet officials, serving at different points of his career as the USSR's Foreign minister and, during the Second World War, as Soviet ambassador to the United States. What makes his parallel existence fascinating is how much he had in common with Kot – childhood circumstances, the experience of living under a constant threat of pogroms, strong political beliefs, and, while already in London, sharing the same friends and acquaintances – and yet how very differently their lives were shaped by the Bolshevik revolution.

Litvinov was born in 1876 in Belostok (also spelled "Byelostok") and, like Koteliansky, belonged to a prosperous family of Jewish merchants. His original name was Meer Genokh Wallach-Finkelstein. Like Koteliansky, he received a traditional Jewish upbringing and education, but his revolutionary zeal was much stronger. It carried him all the way to membership in the underground Russian Social Democratic Labour Party and, by 1900, to the executive committee of the party's branch in Kiev. In 1903 he joined what then still was the Bolshevik faction of the Social Democratic Labour Party and two years later became the editor of the first legal paper published by his party, *Novaia zhizn'* (New Life), the very same organ that was resurrected under Gorky after the February Revolution and for which Koteliansky would then solicit contributions from the likes of George Bernard Shaw and H.G. Wells. By 1906, however, the paper was closed by the government, revolutionaries were being again arrested, and Litvinov fled back West, this time to London.

Whether Koteliansky and Litvinov met in London prior to 1916 is not clear, but it is quite possible since Litvinov likely kept company with Fanny Stepniak. During the war he also became a regular in what John Carswell calls "The Eder salon" in London. In addition to David Eder, his wife Edith, and their equally intellectual relatives, the gatherings were frequented by H.G. Wells, George Bernard Shaw, A.R. Orage, and many others.[1] That is where Litvinov met his future wife and Edith Eder's niece, Ivy Low, whom both Lawrence and Koteliansky knew well.

Litvinov and Ivy married in February 1916. Litvinov was forty at the time, Ivy fifteen years his junior, and the event was seen by Ivy's circle as an entertaining curiosity but of little consequence. "[I]t is well for her to be married," Lawrence opined to Catherine Carswell the same month, "then she can be unmarried when she likes again."[2] To another friend he wrote: "[O]ur dear Ivy has married a poor Russian revolutionary of forty – quite nice-looking, I believe, but of no account … Heaven knows how it will end …"[3] The Russian revolution a year later would, of course, provide a most unexpected end to that seemingly banal story: the "poor Russian revolutionary" would go from being "of no account" to becoming of immense account, while his wife would serve as a tenuous link between two worlds rapidly moving even further apart. For several years after the revolution Lawrence kept contemplating using the Litvinov connection to visit Russia: "As for Russia, I still think I should like to go, in spite of all the 'rulers.' Don't I remember Litvinov in a steam of washing and boiled cabbage? And isn't he, too, in the seats of the mighty?"[4]

While Lawrence hesitated, a person who was definitely going to Russia was H.G. Wells. Wells was always very interested in Russian politics and progress and first went there early in 1914, at which point he decided that "Russia is a big developing thing."[5] Upon returning to England he suggested to the headmaster of the school his sons attended that Russian should be taught there. The headmaster obliged.[6] As we have seen earlier, Wells's acquaintance with Koteliansky started between the two revolutions of 1917, back when Kot was recruiting English writers to contribute to Gorky's publication. They exchanged several brief notes then, after which their correspondence appears to have ceased. When the first volume of Wells's *The Outline of History* came out in 1919, Kot wrote to the publisher suggesting that since "H.G. Wells is the most favourite English writer in Russia," and a Russian translation was "certain to be a financial success," he would be willing to "undertake the translation of the 'Outline' into Russian and be generally useful with regard to the publication and sale of the 'Outline' in Russia."[7] Nothing came out of that idea but the letter was forwarded to H.G. Wells and probably resulted in Kot's receiving the following brief missive from Wells at the end of December:

Dear Mr Koteliansky,
Are you still in London? I want very much to secure two hours conversation a week in Russian for my eldest son (who can read and write Russian a little). Do you know of anyone who could give him conversation lessons?[8]

Kot offered himself: "To be of any service to you, I will consider as an honour and privilege."[9] So started the most long-lasting and rewarding relationship of Kot's entire English life. This very important relationship was not, strictly speaking, as much with H.G. Wells, even though Kot cherished their friendship, as with the family of his son, George Philip, or Gip, as he was known. Gip's future wife, Marjorie Wells, and their children, Catherine and Oliver, who lovingly called him "Koto," would replace the Farbmans as the closest thing he ever had to a family in England. He would experience serious nervous breakdowns and undergo electroshock treatments; there would also be an attempted suicide, but it is a testimony to their, and, in particular, Marjorie's, remarkable care that Kot lived to be almost seventy-five years old.

In August 1920 Kot – still mostly in his role as a Russian tutor and informant but already intimate enough with Wells to address him in his letters as "My very dear author"[10] – was summoned to come right away to the Wells's house because H.G. and Gip were going to Russia on 14 September and needed intensive lessons. Kot entertained hopes that he could come along if Wells "had the choice of the delegation,"[11] but Wells had no such choice. His wife, Catherine, with her characteristic kindness and thoughtfulness, tried to sweeten Kot's disappointment: "Gip left with H.G. yesterday … All went well with the passports and so on – and they are really off. They will have a most interesting time and very much its usefulness will be due to your having helped Gip to learn Russian as he has. In fact he could not have gone if that had not happened."[12]

Winston Churchill's cousin, sculptor Clare Frewen Sheridan, was also invited to come to Russia the same time as Wells. In Moscow, Sheridan, who would be allowed to sculpt Lenin's and Trotsky's heads, was in close contact with Litvinov and recorded meeting Ivy, whom she had not known in England: "At luncheon I met Mrs Litvinoff and was surprised to find that she is English, a friend of …

H.G. Wells. She has short black hair and is unconventional. She did not seem to be very political or revolutionary. The third baby is imminent."[13]

Wells spent most of his time in Russia in Petrograd, where he was staying with Maxim Gorky and a woman who would later become his own common-law wife: Gorky's secretary and mistress, Moura Budberg. It was she – and not Kot – who served as Wells's translator, and for that Wells must have been profoundly grateful. British Intelligence would in time build up a very large and curiously worded dossier on Moura Budberg, which read in part:

> Countess Budberg, Mistress of Bruce Lockhart, Maxim Gorky and H.G. Wells – suspected as a Soviet agent … Formely Countess Benckendorff, Marie married Baron Budberg in 1922. In 1923 she left Budberg and took a post as secretary to Maxim Gorky in Berlin, soon becoming his mistress … 'Gorky is the Bernard Shaw of Russia and about as futile' … [T]he [British] Embassy considered her a very dangerous woman, she was seen in the company of H.G. Wells and had met Stalin several times and brought an accordion … '[S]he can drink an amazing quantity, mostly gin, without it showing any apparent slow-up in her mental process. She drinks gin like one would drink vodka …'[14]

Russian émigré writer Nina Berberova, who knew Budberg well, left a somewhat less sensationalist description of the "Iron Woman," as she called her: "She was clever and tough and fully aware of her uncommon abilities. She had a sense of responsibility, not just in feminine ways but in general. Knowing very well what her own capacities were, she learned to rely on her physical health and energy, and on her considerable charm as a woman."[15]

Wells, seeing Moura with Gorky, was immediately conquered by her vitality and strength. Back then he probably did not even see any of the imperfections that he would eventually attribute to her – and, by extension to all her fellow Russians, including Koteliansky:

> She thinks like a Russian; copiously, windingly and with that flavour of philosophical pretentiousness of Russian discourse, beginning nowhere in particular and emerging at a foregone conclusion. I say she thinks like a Russian because I suspect that there is some weakness in the very structure of the Russian language and in the tradition of Russian literature that gives those who use it this disposition.[16]

In *Russia in the Shadows*, published upon his return, Wells saved the harshest criticism not for Russians in Russia but the Russian refugees in England, whom he called "politically contemptible": "They rehearse endless stories of 'Bolshevik outrages'; château-burnings by peasants, burglaries and murders by disbanded soldiers in the towns, back street crimes – they tell them all as acts of the Bolshevik Government."[17] Since the book was written shortly before a real "Bolshevik outrage" befell Kot's family, it can only be hoped that Wells re-evaluated his statement upon hearing about it.

*Russia in the Shadows* also featured a rather awkward discourse on the predominance of Jews among the Bolsheviks, the tenor of which was also probably jarring to Kot: "Many of them are Jews ... But few of them have any strong racial Jewish feeling. They are not out for Jewry but for a new world. So far from being in continuation of the Jewish tradition the Bolsheviks have put most of the Zionist leaders in Russia in prison, and they have prescribed the teaching of Hebrew as a 'reactionary' language. Several of the most interesting Bolsheviks I met were not Jews at all but Nordic men." Then he added, confidently yet quite erroneously: "Lenin, the beloved leader of all that is energetic in Russia to-day ... is certainly no Jew"; but Wells was not the only one at the time who did not know, since it was such a well-kept secret, that Lenin in fact had a Jewish grandfather.[18]

Wells was granted an audience with "the beloved leader," and, unlike Sheridan, was much more interested in picking the Soviet leader's brain than molding his head. He was pleasantly surprised. In one of the chapters of *Russia in the Shadows*, entitled "Dreamer in the Kremlin," Wells, much to the chagrin of the conservative press in England, described Lenin as pleasant and even charming, as well as very genuine: "[H]e talked quickly, very keen on his subject, without any posing or pretences or reservations, as a good type of scientific man will talk ... In him I realized that Communism could after all, in spite of Marx, be enormously creative."[19] If we are to believe Trostky, Lenin, on the other hand, deemed Wells to be "a bourgeois" and "a Philistine."[20]

Koteliansky's friend Grisha Farbman went to Russia a year later and also interviewed Lenin (for *The Observer and Manchester Guardian*). In the interview, Farbman referred to articles published in the "anti-Russian press in Britain," the same press that was attacking Wells a year earlier for his *Russia in Shadows*, and gave Lenin a chance to shoot their "accusations" and "rumours" down.[21] In 1923 Farbman published *Bolshevism in Retreat*, in which, like Wells before him, he emphasized the visionary, almost divine quality of Lenin and the huge gap that there existed between him and the rest of the Bolsheviks at the top: "In the upper regions there is Lenin, the thunder-maker. Then, till the very surface of the earth is reached, there is nothing."[22] Apparently, neither Wells nor Farbman succeeded in convincing even their friends that Lenin was not evil. "It is strange I fear Lenin, even personally, to such an extent," Mansfield wrote to Koteliansky in 1922, "that I am frightened to look at a picture of him ..."[23] Kot was definitely no fan of Lenin either.

Wells's and Farbman's books were among many works on Russia proliferating in England as a result of the revolution. For the most part Koteliansky was not amused. He was, as we will see from his unpublished review, particularly offended by Hugh Walpole's *The Secret City*, which came out in 1919. Walpole worked as a journalist in Russia before the First World War and then joined the Russian Red Cross. This Russian experience provided him with the material for two highly commercially successful novels which share the same, largely autobiographical, narrator: *The Dark Forest* (1916) and *The Secret City*.

In his introduction *The Secret City*, Walpole makes it clear that, despite spending several years in Russia, he in no way considers himself an expert: "of Russia and the Russians I know nothing but of the effect upon myself and my ideas of life that Russia and the Russians have made during these last three years I know something."[24] This, of course, did not stop English and American reviewers from proclaiming him to be one, with some even comparing him to Tolstoy.[25] While definitely not another Tolstoy (and probably influenced much more by Dostoevsky), Walpole did manage to write a rather engaging account of a Russian family and three Englishmen connected with experiencing the Russian revolutionary upheavals of 1917.[26]

Koteliansky hated it all, though. In a rather rambling handwritten piece, which he obviously meant for publication, he accused Walpole of exploiting his Russian experience for profit and of suggesting by his novel that "Russia, her revolution, men, women and children are rot, worse than rot." "Certainly Mr W. has a terrifically imposing air," Kot proclaimed, with obvious sarcasm:

> His equipment, erudition of matters Russian is stupendous?! Never mind that in his "Secret City" all the would-be Russian sentences are, without exception, wrong and mis-spelt, and, when deciphered, are in no possible way characteristic. Also if the Russian sentences were not given in an English translation on the spot, it would be just impossible to say in what language those sentences are written. But, it looks so new, original and piquant.[27]

It is hard not to see this sardonic denunciation as more revealing about Kot himself than about the book he was panning. After all, here he was, a true erudite of all matters Russian, yet no one was rushing to publish him or his trans-lations of genuine Russian classics, while Mr Walpole, with his imperfect Russian and superficial knowledge, was milking it all the way to being a bestselling author. There was, however, more to Kot's rage, for he was also genuinely offended by what he perceived as Walpole's anti-Semitism.

Walpole makes glancing references to Jews in the novel, and, for most part, they are definitely not of a complimentary kind. There is "a stout perspiring Jew," who manages the cinema where the protagonists go; "a very fat Jew" who is horrified at the riots he is witnessing; and, at a market, "the fat, huge-breasted Jewish women [who] screamed and shrieked and waived their arms like boughs in a storm."[28] But it is the name Walpole bestows on the market itself that truly got Koteliansky's goat: the "Jews' Market."[29] Koteliansky complained that Walpole's "description of Petrograd is a grand flight of imagination":

M.W., who learnt a bit of his neorealism from third rate Russian novelists … must needs call the Alexandrovsky market, in the neorealist manner, the Jewish [sic] market. *Modo artis* he gets into the very substance of reality at the most economic expense. Jewish instead of Alexandrovsky market – isn't in this association revealed the soul, the essence of the market place? Now, does not Mr W. beat the Russian neorealist most superbly?[30]

Apparently not satisfied with the first draft of the review, Koteliansky starts another, more metaphorical and ornate one:

Have you ever happened to walk aimlessly in obscure streets of a large city in a hot summer day? The shop windows display fly-beleaguered sweets, melting chocolate, sausages boiling in angry splitting gravy, martyred fish. You wonder who ever does eat these articles, the mere sight of which is nauseating. But at the same time you are aware that this stuff is being consumed daily, and more and more of it appears in the windows. The same is with certain books: habent sua fata libelli … Mr W's manufactured Russian sweets whet the appetites of his customers – the sweets being so piquant, exotic. The poor dears of the public (and reviewers) swallow those sweets "made in Russia" *ad majorem gloriam* of themselves and of their provider, their ideologue … His knowledge and insight of Russia is be-coming theirs. But is his hypocrisy that wishes to pass as honesty also theirs? And Mr W. is waiting, waiting on them holding his mirror and whispering to them that the monsters they see therein are not they themselves, but hor-rible "possessed" Russian monsters. What a happy and gay comforter! What a happy and gay lot of customers![31]

But even in this fancier version, no one appeared to have been interested in publishing Kot's review, unless he never even submitted it.

The translations were not forthcoming either. In 1917, having quarrelled with Murry and wanting to publish another volume of Chekhov stories, Kot turned to Gilbert Cannan, of *Mendel* fame, who wrote no introduction and functioned mostly as a proofreader for *The House with the Mezzanine and Other Stories*. The book came out in the United States (Charles Scribner's Sons) but, at the time, not in England. The fact that a whole three years then elapsed between the publication of *The House with the Mezzanine* and the subsequent translation volumes is a good indicator of how deflated Kot was in the post-revolutionary years. During much of this time he spent entire days either at home or in the immediate vicinity of it. The modest stucco house (which still exists) at 5 Acacia Road was near Wellington Road in St John's Wood, close to Regents Park, the trees of which could be seen from the backyard. It was also within a two-minute walk of St John's Wood High Street, where there were numerous small shops, which Kot patronized when running errands for Lawrence or buying food for occasional guests, and pubs, which he sometimes visited.

The house had three floors and, all in all, seven rooms. Kot occupied four rooms downstairs. His bedroom, which one friend called "monastic,"[32] was what used to be Mansfield's bedroom. Her blanket was on his bed; her chair was at his desk in the study; "a little blue-green bowl" she once gave him[33] occupied a place of honour on a small table in a sitting room. After Mansfield's death, her carved walking stick, which she bequeathed him because he liked it so much, found its special niche as well. "I leave the two upper floors untouched," he explained to his niece in the 1940s, long after the Farbmans ceased being his housemates, "except that I give them a cleaning a few times during the year. I only keep clean four rooms, and during the winter months I spend nearly all the time in the kitchen, it being the warmest room, as it has a kitchen range, using coal."[34]

Lady Glenavy quotes Kot as saying "a man's house is himself," and many of his friends and acquaintances liked to comment on how bare, meticulously organized, and clean his residence was. Virginia Woolf, upon visiting him in the 1920s, was struck by the house's three main attributes: "poverty-stricken, tidy, clean."[35] Kot's hatred for excess and materialism might have had roots in the Hasidic tradition to which he was exposed as a child, but Kot's obsessive cleanliness was definitely his own. "His house was scrubbed and polished and dusted," writes Glenavy, "with a special place for every cup, plate, book or piece of paper."[36] Similarly, May Sarton, who befriended Kot in the 1930s, remarked on "a minimum of furniture" of the "plainest" kind where "not the slightest disorder was permitted."[37] He laundered all towels, sheets, and even blankets weekly, and he polished the floors just as often. According to all who left accounts of his residence, Kot polished the floors in the traditional Russian way, with "dusters tied around his feet [while he] slid about on his hall – swishing from side to side in sort of a wild dance."[38] The floors were so slippery as a result that on the day of waxing his guests were afraid to step on them. To keep the floors clean longer Kot would do another Russian ritual: he asked his guests to take off their shoes and wear the slippers he provided, which, of course, made walking even more hazardous.

Most of his activities, including his work on translations, took place in the warm kitchen downstairs. Lady Glenavy, who stayed with Kot every time she came to London and was allowed by him to pay at least something for room and board, describes how "[o]n entering the little bit of front-garden you could see Kot sitting at his kitchen table through the half-basement window, then you made a sign that you were going round by the side-door which led into the scullery. There he would meet you and say, 'It is good that you have come.'"[39]The kitchen was "the center of his life," "a hearth in the most ancient sense of the word," and he would make sure that "so much Russian tea was drunk."[40] He also would feed his guests his own culinary concoctions. Dorothy Brett described one such dish as "a strange Russian mixture of sardines and mustard, pepper and God knows what [ground] into a paste."[41] Frieda Lawrence was in awe of his fried potatoes: "I used to say to Lawrence 'Is my Kartoffel frei as good as Kot's?'"[42] He also made them Jewish latkes and Russian borsht.[43] His one cooking regret was that he never learned how to bake.[44] But mostly they were treated to his conversation. "He would sit in the kitchen and people would come," remembers Catherine Stoye, "and it was talk, talk, talk all the time. He would talk about everything under the sun."[45] It was in some ways similar to what he himself may have experienced in the Ostropol Hasidic heder, except now he was the presiding rebbe, and people sitting around his kitchen table and eagerly asking him questions or exulting in his pronouncements were not pimply boys with long earlocks but adult men and women very far removed from any Jewish tradition.

Kot's friends were by turn delighted and exasperated by how Russian Kot remained despite his years in England. To Kot, for example, "[n]o English fruit [was] so good as Russian fruit" – English apples were "not so sweet and good as Russian apples," and he would not even touch English cherries because "Russian ones used to be twice the size and fifty times as good." He also maintained that English milk and butter were vastly inferior to their Russian counterparts, and the likes of the goosebury jam that his mother and sisters used to make were "never seen in England."[46] "The Russian in Kot was never very deeply submerged," May Sarton observed. "Just under the thin English surface, the Russian suffered and rejoiced, and led his natural passionate life."[47]

Kot suffered much more than he rejoiced, though, and when in the midst of his black moods – or, as he once put it to Frieda, when he felt "the law and order in myself *disordered*"[48] – he did not want to see anyone or even talk to anyone on the phone.[49] He retreated instead into his spartan house and stayed inside for days and even weeks, unable to exercise the same control and discipline over his mental chaos as he did over the slightest disorder at his home. During these dark periods, which were now more and more frequent, he was so "ill & forlorn in the Cave"[50] that his friends were genuinely concerned about his health and state of mind. "I'll … stay in the cave. I have no desire to move or undertake anything" was Kot's typical response to the well-wishers encouraging him to go out.[51] Lawrence called it Kot's "gangrened inertia"[52] and was vocal in his irritation: "You! – you irk me: hiding yourself at the bottom of that Cave at No. 5, without even risking one hair of your beard. What must I make of you? Even a toad goes out hunting: but you, crouching in the shelter of the cave don't do anything but croak. No, no! Life is ours to be spent, not to be saved."[53]

When Wells came back from Russia in the late autumn 1920, he wrote to Kot: "We are safely back and I have much to tell you. Will you come … and have dinner with me on Thursday next at 8. And can you find me a translator for these two scientific abstracts. Manuchin (?Manoukhin) is very eager for their publication in Europe."[54] Kot probably translated the abstracts himself, and the following day Wells thanked him: "for your kindness to myself and Manikin (? Manoukhin). I have sent the documents to Cambridge to Gip and they then shall be published."[55] The name was, indeed, Manoukhin, and Wells must have met him through Gorky, whose doctor Manoukhin had been for many years (Gorky, too, suffered from tuberculosis).[56] In April of the following year Manoukhin published a piece in the British medical journal *The Lancet* under the title "The Treatment of Infectious Disease by Leucocytolysis Produced by Rontgenisation of the Spleen." In it he claimed that he personally treated eight thousand cases of tuberculosis in Russia and was able to cure the disease by irradiating the spleen with X-rays.[57]

In the meantime Mansfield's health started to deteriorate further in late summer 1921, and she went to Switzerland in hope that the mountain air would help her. In September she wrote to Dorothy Brett from there: "Id [*sic*] like to send my love to Kot, if he wasn't my enemy."[58] But even though he refused to answer her letters and sent them back, he was by no means her enemy. Just a month earlier, Kot had written to Dorothy Brett that "if K. has a real friend – perhaps cruel at times – in the whole universe it is myself."[59] By October, Mansfield decided to make another attempt at reconciliation and asked Kot about Manoukhin: "Dear Koteliansky, my enemy, can you tell me anything about that Russian doctor?"

"Not a day passes," she continued, "but I think of you. It is sad that we are enemies. If only you would accept my love. It is *good* love – not the erotic bad kind
… Don't return the postcard. If you hate me too much – burn it in a candle."[60]
This time he did respond, and, from then on, perhaps because they both suspected that she did not have much time left, their friendship became even warmer
and closer than it had been prior to their estrangement. D.H. Lawrence, who was
in Italy at the time, was a bit slow realizing that the reconciliation had taken place.
In November he would still cruelly mock Mansfield to Kot as "the long-dying
blossom Katharine," no doubt making Kot cringe.[61]

Manoukhin by then was living and practicing in Paris. Kot sent Mansfield his
address and most likely told her that Gorky thought Manoukhin had cured him
of tuberculosis back in 1914.[62] "As I cannot go to Paris until the spring I shall not
write to the doctor until then," she informed Kot in early November. "But I am
very glad to have his address."[63] "Do you know where I can obtain any information about Doctor Manoukhine's treatment?" she asked two weeks later. "I mean
– has it appeared in any possible papers or journals that I can get hold of? … My
doctor here says he will very gladly consider any information I can get him about
this treatment and as he has a very good X-ray apparatus it could, if it is not the
'professional patent' of Doctor Manoukhine, be tried here, immediately."[64] In
December she wrote to Manoukhin, in French, telling him it was her Russian
friend Koteliansky who highly recommended him. She also wrote the same day
to Kot: "I have written to M. today. Whatever he advises that will I do. It is strange
– I have faith in him. I am sure he will not have the kind of face one walks away
from … Do you know I have not walked since November 1920? Not more than
to a carriage and back. Both my lungs are affected, there is a cavity in one and
the other is affected through. My heart is weak too. Can all this be cured. Ah,
Koteliansky – wish for me!"[65]

She waited for ten days and, when there was no response from Manoukhin,
she called his clinic in Paris. The doctor was not there, and the secretary did not
know when he would return. Mansfield was crushed. Then on 23 December she
heard from him, and it was "A good letter – *very*." Manoukhin suggested that she
should come to Paris as soon as she is "well enough to get up" for a fifteen-week
treatment.[66] She wrote to Brett: "I think of Manoukhin more than anyone can
imagine. I have as much faith in him as Koteliansky has."[67] Around the same time
she wrote in her journal: "I want to adopt a Russian baby, call him Anton, and
bring him up as mine, with K. for a godfather, and Mme. Tchehov for a god-
mother. Such is my dream."[68]

Ida Baker, her close friend and perhaps lover from college days in London,
was in Switzerland with Mansfield at the time. Ida liked Kot – Mansfield had sent

his name and address to her earlier, while Baker was in Rhodesia, "as a safe deposit" for Baker's letters, saying that she "could always rely on him."[69] Like Kot, Baker detested Murry, who was jealous of her continuing presence in Katherine's life. At the end of January, Baker accompanied Mansfield to Paris, where Mansfield intended just to discuss the possibility of the treatment with Manoukhin. According to Baker, Manoukhin, however, "advised starting straight away, while Katherine was already in Paris, to avoid the hazards of yet another journey."[70] In February Murry came to Paris, and Baker was immediately dispatched to Switzerland to rent a chalet there in preparation for the Murrys' return once the first part of Katherine's treatment was over.

Mansfield was full of apprehensions – and hope. Her first impression of Manoukhin was decidedly mixed: "M. had a lame girl there as interpreter. He said through her he could cure me completely. But I did not believe it. It all seemed suddenly unimportant and ugly … While I waited, voices came from another room very loud voices, M.'s over and above them: 'Da! Da!' and then an interrogatory 'Da?' I have the feeling that M. is really a good man. I have also a sneaking feeling … that he is a kind of unscrupulous impostor."[71] In letters to Kot, however, she was uniformly positive, probably because she knew how much he believed – or wanted to believe – in Manoukhin's healing powers. "I have seen Manoukine," she wrote to him on 1 February. "Yes, one has every confidence in such a man … While I was waiting at the clinic tonight the doors were all open and in the doctor's cabinet people were talking Russian. They talked all together. Doctor M.'s voice was above the other voices, but there was a continual *chorus* – all speaking. I cannot tell you how I love Russian. When I hear it spoken it makes me think of course always of Tchekhov."[72]

On 3 February she wrote again: "I wanted to tell you something very good that happened today … I was sitting alone in the waiting room of the clinique … when M. came in. He came quickly over to me, took my hand and said simply, 'Vous avez decidé de commencer avec la traitment. C'est très bien. Bonne santé,' and then he went as quickly out of the room saying 'tout de suite' (pronounced 'toot sweet' for he speaks very little French). But this coming in so quickly and gently was a beautiful act, never to be forgotten, the act of someone *very good*. Oh, how I love gentleness, Koteliansky, dear friend."[73] Yet in her diary she recorded the same incident with much more ambivalence: "I went to M. for a treatment. A curious impression remains. M.'s beautiful gesture coming into the room was perfect. But D. [Dr Donat, Manoukhin's French partner] shouted so, pushed his face into mine, asked me *indecent questions*. Ah, that's the horror of being ill."[74] "Manoukhine drew the picture of my heart," she noted a week later. "I wish he has not, I am haunted by the hideous picture, by the thought of my heart, like a heavy drop in my breast. But he is good."[75]

By late March she was exhausted and hugely disappointed both in the treatment and in Manoukhin. "The worst of it is," she informed Brett, "I am not one atom better so far. – Theres no talking to Manoukhin. He either does not listen or does not understand but shouts across one about his other cases to his partner." She still held out some hope, however, that "it may turn out better than one imagines. Perhaps this is that famous 'darkness before dawn'…"[76] And in May it looked to her like the "dawn" may have indeed arrived. "As far as can tell," she wrote to Ida, asking her to keep it confidential since she was afraid to jinx it, "this treatment has been (I hesitate to use this big word) completely successful. I hardly ever cough. I have gained 8 pounds. I have no rheumatism whatever … My voice has changed back. I take no medicine. The only thing that remains is that my heart is tired and weak. That means I get breathless and cannot walk yet…"[77] In a letter she wrote the same month to Koteliansky she bestowed on Manoukhin what amounted to her highest praise: "Tchekhov would have liked him very much."[78] By early June the first part of the treatment was over, and Murry and Mansfield went back to Switzerland.

"Koteliansky Would you care for a cat?" she queried him from there: "I have a cat who is at present in England and I cannot have him with me. It is too cruel to make cats travel. He is a beautiful animal, except for a scratch on his nose, one ear badly bitten and a small hole in his head. From the back view however he is lovely for he has a superb tail. In all his ways he can be trusted to behave like a gentleman. He is extremely independent and, of course, understands everything that is said to him … He has a fair knowledge of French."[79]

Kot, whose own truncated name meant "a cat" in Russian, did not adopt Katherine's "beautiful animal," probably because he already had his own, a dog. The dog, whose name was "Fox," officially belonged to the Farbmans, but, in reality, it was Kot, revealing his gentle and loving side, who most cared about the dog's well-being and, according to Lawrence, spoiled him rotten by overfeeding him ("starve Fox for one day, for my sake," Lawrence would plead with him[80]). Lawrence actually believed that Fox's personality perfectly fit Kot's for the dog liked to "howl … in soul-lacerating despair."[81] When Fox once ran away in autumn 1919, Lawrence knew right away what a blow it was for Kot: "if he doesn't come back, he'll be *your* tragedy more than anybody's."[82] The dog turned up several days later and remained at Kot's side till 1928.[83] Mansfield's cat, "Wingli," did end up travelling back and forth across the channel. "Awful to love that cat as one does," she told Ida.[84] Kot definitely understood.

In July, Mansfield wrote to Kot that she thought of him every time she made herself tea: "Every time I drop a piece of lemon into a glass of tea, I say 'Koteliansky.' Perhaps it is a kind of a grace."[85] In August she went to London, in part to see her English doctor and let him evaluate her lungs. She joked that she would serve as "an advertisement for Manoukhin."[86] She stayed with Brett but appeared in no hurry to see Kot: "I prefer to leave our meeting to chance. To know you are there is enough. If I knew I was going to die I should even ask you definitely to come and see me. For I should hate to die without one long, uninterrupted talk with *you*. But short of it – it does not greatly matter."[87] To Kot it obviously did matter, and he probably insisted, so on 30 August she wrote: "I am so unsettled this week that I would rather we did not meet until next week."[88] The following week she wrote again: "I could not ring you up. I was too tired. I had been out seeing the X-ray specialist and having my lungs photographed, and so on and so on. Please forgive me. Will you come here on Friday afternoon or evening? ... I *long* to see you."[89] According to the notations in her diary, she did see him four times after that – Saturday, 16 September ("Kot at 2"), Monday, 18 September ("Kot at 2"), 21 September ("Kot in afternoon"), and, finally, 23 September ("Kot at 3 p.m.").[90] We get a sense of their conversations in a letter Mansfield sent him in October, when she was back in France: "When we met in London and discussed 'ideas' I spoke as nearly one can the deepest truth I knew to you. But even while I spoke it I felt a pretender – for my knowledge of this truth is negative, not positive, as it were cold, and not warm with life ... The world as I know it is no joy to me and I am useless in it. I have to let you know for you mean much to me. I know you will never listen to whatever foolish things other people may say about me. Those other helpless people going round in their little whirlpool do not matter a straw to me."[91]

While in London, Mansfield helped Kot translate Gorky's *Reminiscences of Leonid Andreyev*, which would be published in the two issues of *The Adelphi*, edited by Murry, a year after her death.[92] She also worked on some Chekhov letters. On 19 September she wrote down: "Cough very troublesome"; on 15 October: "Orage goes to Paris."[93] Unconnected as these remarks seem to be, they were not. Before she met with Kot in London she did see A.R. Orage, whom she had known and liked for many years, ever since 1911, when she was given a job as a drama critic for the *New Age*, which he edited. Now Orage was keenly interested in the writings of the Russian mathematician and philosopher Petr Ouspensky, and through him he also got exposed to the teachings of George Gurdjieff. Having sold the *New Age*, in October 1922, Orage went to the newly created Gurdjieff Institute for the Harmonious Development of Man in France where Mansfield would spend her last days.

In order to understand the Gurdjieff phenomenon, one needs to appreciate the extent to which Russia at the turn of the twentieth century was a feeding ground for quasi-religious, metaphysical, and mystical movements, many of which would then be successfully transported abroad. Madame Blavatsky and her theosophy are probably the most famous example.[94] At the turn of the century, however, one of the most intriguing concepts which fascinated many Russian intellectuals – including the great Symbolist writer Andrey Bely – was that of the so-called "Fourth Dimension." It combined elements of Eastern religions and Freemasonry, and its main proponent was Ouspensky, who came to the whole notion of the Fourth Dimension through his professional field of geometry. The notion challenged the common belief that we live just in a three-dimensional physical space. The Fourth Dimension, not discernable by the human eye but attainable by the human spirit, was man's path to immortality. The early Ouspensky, while convinced of the Fourth Dimension's existence, was not quite clear about how to attain it. And that is where Gurdjieff came in. Gurdjieff's background was not science but movement and ballet, which he used in the exercises he prescribed for the harmonious development of one's inner self. Ouspensky became his pupil in St Petersburg in 1915 and collaborated with him by contributing his theory of the "Fourth Dimension," which was then renamed into "Fourth Way."

Orage met Ouspensky in London in 1914 and was impressed with his ideas. The two stayed in touch.[95] During the Russian civil war Ouspensky was with Denikin's White Army, and, when the White Army was defeated, he made his way across the Black Sea to Constantinople. There he briefly reunited with Gurdjieff but then went his separate way. In 1921 Ouspensky moved to London, where he established his own group and gave lectures attended, among others, by Orage. Gurdjieff, in the meantime, moved around, trying to establish centres in several European capitals. In February 1922 he came to London, and Ouspensky, while himself at this point moving further and further away from Gurdjieff and his methods, introduced him to Orage. That pretty much decided Orage's fate – and Mansfield's.

Mansfield came to think of her stay in London as a time of "spiritual crisis": "When I came to London from Switzerland … [f]or the first time in my life, everything bored me. Everything, and, worse, everybody seemed a compromise and so flat, so dull, so mechanical. If I had been well I should have rushed off to darkest Africa or the Indus or the Ganges."[96] Instead she rushed to Gurdjieff's Institute – but not before she gave Manoukhin another chance. At first, she appeared happy with that decision. "I saw Manoukhine today," she informed Kot on 5 October. "It was real happiness to meet even though we can't talk, hardly. It does not seem to matter. One talks as Natasha would say 'just so.'"[97]

Natasha was, of course, Tolstoy's Natasha Rostova, for Mansfield's mind was still "like a Russian novel." Four days later she was reading Dostoevsky's letters to his wife, which Kot had sent her. Kot had just translated them and was probably wondering if Katherine would be strong enough to improve the translation. She thought neither Mr nor Mrs Dostoevsky came across very well: "There's no expansion, no evidence of a *living* man, a *real* man. The glimpse one has of his relationship with Anya is somehow petty and stuffy, essentially a double bed relationship … Oh dear, oh dear, it would take an Anna Grigor'evna to be proud of such letters."[98] She was too sick to edit his translation, but in December she would learn that Kot approached Murry with the same request to which her husband readily agreed, relieved to be "quite simply … reconciled" with Kot.[99]

The "real happiness" of seeing Manoukhin did not last long for Mansfield. According to Ida Baker, who again accompanied her, "She … had several treatments. These gradually proved more and more exhausting and she would come back and lie down in a breathless condition, her heart beating furiously. This continued for two weeks, then she felt much worse and was really frightened, terrified by the thumping of her heart; she said she could not risk another session."[100] Baker thought the treatment was effective and Mansfield was making a mistake by discontinuing it, but she could not change her friend's mind. On 15 October, Mansfield wrote to Brett: "Manoukhin isn't a magician. He has cured some people – a great many – and some he hasn't cured. He made me fatter – that is quite true. But otherwise? I am exactly where I was before I started … it's all a sham. It amounts to nothing."[101] Two days later she joined Orage at Fountainebleau, where the Institute for the Harmonious Development of Man was located. In November she wrote to her father: "I got in touch with some other Russian (Russians seem to haunt me!) doctors, who claim to cure hearts of all kinds by means of a system of gentle exercises and movements."[102]

It is probably safe to assume that at this point of the rapid progession of Mansfield's disease nothing could have thwarted it or even slowed it down – yet many found her behaviour in the last days of her life foolhardy. "Katherine's attraction to Gurdjieff was the fatal culmination of her life-long passions for Russians," writes one of her biographers.[103] But it was, of course, her tuberculosis that was fatal, not her attraction. Despite her bravado, she had known she was dying already in August, even before she went to London, for it was back then that she made her will. For someone who loved all things Russian as much as she did, spending her last days in a company of Russians was probably therapeutic. Since the young Russian women caring for her spoke little French or English, she kept compiling lists of English phrases and their Russian equivalents, both practical requests and questions – "I am cold," "Light a fire," "what is the time" – and grammatical exercises: "I was, she was, we were," "he was not, you were not, they were not," "was he? was not she? we were not. were you not? was he not?"[104]

The last letter she wrote to Koteliansky was in October. In it she tried to justify her decision to throw her lot with Gurdjieff, using Gurdjieff's ideas (and terms) of how people who are not conscious of themselves are doomed to "live in sleep" instead of "waking": "This world to me is a dream and the people in it are sleepers. I have known just instances of waking but that is all. I want to find a world in which these instances are united. Shall I succeed? I do not know. I scarcely care. What is important is to try ..."[105]

She died on 9 January 1923, after a gush of blood poured from her mouth, suffocating her. Being an alien, Kot did not succeed in getting permission to leave the country to attend her funeral in France. "I loved her so much," he wrote to a friend several years later in one of his most poetic letters. "It is her being, what she was, the aroma of her being, that I love. She could do things that I disliked intensely, exaggerate and tell untruths, yet the way she did it was so admirable, unique, that I did not trouble at all about what she spoke, but only the way she spoke, it was just lovely ... Her 'divisions' and 'secret sorrow' I felt from the very beginning of my meeting her, but the extent of her suffering I realized only a few months before her death."[106]

Kot was fortunately spared Frieda's rather shallow take on Mansfield's last days. "Our poor Catherine [*sic*] Mansfield is buried near Paris," she wrote in February to Adele Seltzer, the wife of Lawrence's US publisher, "it was so sad and again so inevitable that she had to die – She chose a death road and dare not face reality!"[107] In that assessment she was probably echoing Murry, who never forgave Kot for what he judged to be Kot's encouraging Katherine's misguided trust in Russian doctors and spiritual healers. To Lady Glenavy he wrote: "Kot's influence upon her was quite pernicious. The one chance of saving (or prolonging) her life was in her staying quiet with me in Switzerland. He filled her with the dangerous dream of being completely cured by the Russian, Manoukhin, from the inevitable failure of which she reacted into the spiritual quackery of Gurdjieff – and death."[108]

Murry's vengeance came in the form of Mansfield's *Letters* to himself, which he published in 1951. Full of Mansfield's vehement declarations of love for Murry, accompanied by professed hatred for Ida Baker and virtually no mentions of Kot, these letters, according to those who were close to Kot at the time, "broke his heart."[109]

# TRANSLATING FOR THE HOGARTH PRESS

"The Gentleman from San Francisco": translated from the
Russian of S. [sic] Bunin by my friend S. Koteliansky, and by
me rubbed up into readable English …
~ Lawrence to Scofield Thayer, 30 July 1921

Kot's English, which I had to turn into my English, was usually
very strange, but it was also so vivid and individual that I was often
tempted to leave it untouched. For instance, he wrote: "She came
into the room carrying in her arms a peeled-off dog," and on
another occasion: "she wore a haggish look."
~ Leonard Woolf, *Beginning Again*

By spring 1919 Kot was ready to do translations again. Despite his legendary tidiness, during his intense work on translations, and especially when the Farbmans were away, the kitchen of 5 Acacia Road would be full of papers, dictionaries, and newspapers lying everywhere. "You will be glad to have Sonia back," Lawrence wrote to Kot during one such peak of activity. "I shudder to think of that cave, the flood of newspapers rising silently in a fog of cigarette smoke, and you swimming slowly and hopelessly, in the heavy ocean of printed slush, gasping to sink …"[1] The period between 1920 and 1923 was both the most intense and most successful in Koteliansky's career as a professional translator: he published eleven volumes of translations in these three years, many in collaboration with Leonard and Virginia Woolf.[2]

Yet this second wave of translations did not start all that well. The initial failures had a lot to do with Kot's renewed attempts to find his own authors to translate and thus establish a turf where he would not be challenged by the likes of Constance Garnett and the Maudes. Not yet ready to abandon the idea of popularizing Leo Shestov, Kot managed to convince Lawrence to give Shestov another try by helping him translate Shestov's philosophical treatise, *The Apoth-*

*eosis of Groundlessness: An Essay on Dogmatism*. Kot's affinity for Shestov may have stemmed from their shared background as Jews from Ukraine. Born Yehuda Leib Shwartzman in Kiev in 1866, young Shestov was deemed gifted enough to be allowed to attend Moscow University, where he specialized in physics and mathematics. He never finished his studies, though, and instead devoted most of his time to writing books on literature and philosophy, including *Dostoevsky and Nietzsche: The Philosophy of Tragedy* (1903). *The Apotheosis of Groundlessness* came out in 1905 and became the best known as well as the most controversial of Shestov's works.

*All Things Are Possible*, as the translation was entitled – "*Apotheosis of Ground-lessness* will never do," Lawrence decreed[3] – was also to feature Lawrence's foreword. It was truly a test of Lawrence's loyalty to Kot that he agreed to participate in the project, for he did it solely as a favour, in the hope that it would further establish his friend as a major translator from Russian. While performing all his functions diligently, Lawrence did not enjoy either the experience of translating with his often impatient and cranky collaborator, or dealing with Shestov's writings. "I have done a certain amount of ... 'Apotheosis,'" he wrote to Kot in August 1919, "but either Shestov writes atrociously – I believe he does – or you translate loosely ... he isn't anything wonderful, is he?"[4]

For the publishers, Lawrence's appraisal of Shestov's book was much more positive; he described it as "by no means a heavy work – nice and ironical and in snappy paragraphs."[5] He also felt obliged not only to champion the book, but, once the publisher agreed, to transmit Kot's grumblings about the terms offered:

Dear Secker,
Koteliansky is furious at your offer of £20. for all rights, and asks me to write to you ... These are his terms.
1. That the book be published before April 1st. 1920: that you pay 10% royalty, with settlement for the copies subscribed on publication day.
2. That you supply me with proofs within one month's time after signing agreement.
3. That we have the right to publish paragraphs from the book in periodicals, in the meantime, before you are ready for publication.[6]

Adding his own instruction, Lawrence asked Secker to make sure that they use Lawrence's corrected proofs rather than Kot's: "Koteliansky will miss a thousand things, particularly German misprints."[7]

When Lawrence finished the foreword, Kot hated it, fearing that it would be insulting to Shestov and Russians in general. "European culture is a rootless thing in the Russians," Lawrence declared there. "They have only been inoculated with the virus of European culture and ethic. The virus works in them like a disease. And the inflammation and irritation comes forth as literature."[8] "I got the proofs … and write at once," Kot informed Lawrence on 10 December 1919 and, while somewhat apologetic, proposed that the foreword should be scrapped unless Lawrence wanted to change it: "For my sake, if not for anything else, change the first two pages of it … Please do not say anything against Russian literature or about their having swallowed the virus of European culture. If you for some reason do not want to change it, then leave it without a Foreword. Cannot you make Secker publish Shestov's Preface? … It may be wrong of me to want your Foreword be changed but you know I would not trouble you for nothing. As it stands it is an accusation against Russian literature, a thing quite *impossible* in an Introduction to a Russian book."[9]

Ironically, Lawrence's sentiment was a precise echo of what Shestov himself said in *The Apotheosis*, which was one of the reasons why the work was so controversial:

> Scratch a Russian and you will find a Tartar … To us in Russia, civilization came suddenly, while we were still savages … In a short time we were swallowing in enormous doses those poisons which Europe had been gradually accustoming herself to … A Russian had only to catch a whiff of European atmosphere, and his head began to swim. He interpreted in his own way, savage-like, whatever he heard of western success.[10]

Peeved that he was being censored by someone whom he was doing a big favour, Lawrence was defiant: "I mean what I say in it: and as it would be my signed opinion, I don't see that it matters: not a bit."[11]

Kot was also touchy about his more famous friends, including Lawrence, getting a bigger billing than he did. "Secker should be told," he instructed Lawrence, "that the title page should have: '*Authorised* translation by S.S. Koteliansky.' Certainly I would like your name too as translator or editor."[12] Lawrence assured him that he would try to arrange for just that and, to appease him even further, softened his stand about the foreword: while he was not willing to rewrite it, he did not mind if the publisher would "leave it clean out."[13] He therefore wrote to Secker, while not hiding his frustration with Kot's demands, that he was "perfectly willing to have the 'Foreword' omitted altogether … Let Koteliansky know, will you, what you decide and please arrange the title page to suit him, will you. Ach, Ach! These little businesses! Every hen is occupied with her own tail-feathers."[14] Secker, of course, kept both Lawrence's foreword and his name on the title page, for these were the only reasons why the book was accepted for publication in the first place.

The problems did not stop when *All Things Possible* finally came out in England. First there was a mishap with the book's publication in the United States. Lawrence placed it with Huebsch, who then proceeded to publish parts of it in a periodical named *The Freeman*. Huebsch also offered £50 for the rights, which was more than twice as generous as what Secker had provided. Secker, however, had already sent the book to another US publisher. In the end it all just fell through, with the book not coming out in the United States at all, and with Kot not being paid even for the parts appearing in *The Freeman*.

Then there was the issue of "authorization" and copyrights. The English edition came out, as Kot requested, with the title page declaring that it was an "authorized" translation. "Koteliansky is the *authorised* translator of this work," Lawrence likewise assured Benjamin Huebsch. "He wants to sell the translation outright – not bother with copyrights."[15] There was a good reason why Kot did not want to bother with copyrights: something changed dramatically while the book was in process of being finalized and published. Shestov was no longer in Russia but in France, and loudly complaining that no one had asked for his approval. He did not, Shestov kept assuring Koteliansky and the publisher, begrudge his translator the money, but "in all fairness, both the author and the translator should get what they are entitled to." "In Germany," Shestov pointed out, "the author receives 10% of all sales while the translator just 5%." He was, therefore, hoping that the publisher would deem his demands modest and grant him fair compensation.[16] Martin Secker was sympathetic but explained that all money was paid to Koteliansky and that Shestov should therefore seek compensation directly from him. Shestov volunteered to forward Secker's letter to Kot for his further consideration,[17] but there are no subsequent letters in the archive, so we do not know if the dispute was ever resolved. It probably was not, but it hardly mattered for there was not much to share. Notwithstanding Lawrence's name and foreword, Shestov, once again, flopped in England. "As for Shestov, wait, he will start later. It is not all over," Lawrence tried to reassure Kot at the time,[18] but the book's sales continued to be anemic.

The next book was even more of a fiasco. Koteliansky chose to translate a 1914 play, *Zelenoe kol'tso* (The Green Ring), by Russian writer and poet Zinaida Gippius – or "Hippius," as her name appeared in the West. According to the title page, this translation again was "authorized." It was yet another attempt on Koteliansky's part to introduce a largely unknown author to the English public in hope that, if she managed to become popular as a result of his translation, he could add her to the stable of his personal authors. *The Green Ring* was never-theless an odd choice: it is truly hard to see why Koteliansky thought this insignificant play, which even he admitted was "not a superb thing," only "pass-able,"[19] could be of much interest to the English public, who by then expected translated Russian playwrights to be at least approaching Anton Chekhov in talent and execution. Furthermore, the play was written before the revolution and was full of naive hope that the younger generation was somehow wiser than their parents and would manage Russia's future better. And then there was Koteliansky's translation of it. He obviously decided it was high time for him to go solo and have the entire title page just for himself. As a result, he did not ask anyone to assist him in this project, except beseeching Lawrence to keep men-tioning the translation to his publishers.[20]

Kot once admitted to a friend that he did "not mind very much if the English is not excellent. The translation literally is correct, and that is all I care for."[21] The English in *The Green Ring* was definitely not excellent. It was, in fact, a linguistic case of "the Russian in Kot" being "never very deeply submerged," starting with a brief, one-page "Note" that was wooden and unidiomatic, blindly following Russian sentence structure and ways of expression:

Hippius ... represented the "new movement." They were nicknamed décadents, symbolists, æsthetes ... for their opposition to the strangling influences of "civic" motives ... Hippius and her group introduced new motives ... Thanks to them were translated into Russian the works of French decadents ...[22]

The play itself bore even more serious blemishes because of the word-for-word translation, where a maid, for example, was described as "a smart Petrograd maid with an air, dry, imposing, wearing a cap" in one place, and in another as having a nose which "is red with the frost" (Russian: "s moroza nos krasnyi").[23] Lawrence was quite charitable, though. "Have the *Green Ring* – and many thanks," he wrote to Kot in early 1921 in a postcard from Italy, "read it again and find something attractive in it as I did before."[24]

Frustrated by how little money and publicity his translation was earning, Kot then tried to find a publisher for the book in the United States, "on any terms," "on any conditions," "for a lump sum of £20 even."[25] There were no takers among US publishers, but the Neighborhood Playhouse of New York did decide to stage it, and agreed to pay Koteliansky, through his English publisher, C.W. Daniel, LTD, a total of $400 for four performances. And then, as with Shestov, it became clear that Hippius, who was also in France by then, felt that she was more than entitled to her share of the pie. Unlike Shestov, she was skillful enough to rectify the perceived unfairness by convincing the New York theatre group to pay the $400 to her instead. Koteliansky was incensed. "The situation is this," he wrote to Robert Mountsier, Lawrence's US literary agent, whom Lawrence had asked to assist Koteliansky, "Hippius has no right whatsoever to the English translation … Yet when Hippius arrived lately abroad and wrote to my publisher about the 'Ring' I asked the publisher to write to her and say that any money I may receive for the production of the play I shall share with her – half and half … But Hippius, who is a notorious swindler, somehow managed to get the money from the Neighborhood Playhouse and does not pay me anything. If you could see the people of the Neighborhood Playhouse and ask them why they don't pay me?.. If they paid m-me Hippius thinking that she had the right to the money, it is a gross mistake on their part … Hippius has embezzled the money, under false pretences, for it is me, the English translator of the play who is the rightful owner of it (particularly having in view that there is no copyright between Russia and other countries)."[26]

The statement in parenthesis about there being "no copyright between Russia and other countries" reveals Koteliansky's modus operandi when it came to translations from books published in Soviet Russia. Since the Bolshevik regime was not yet recognized as legitimate by the West, there was, indeed, no binding copyright agreement. And yet he was on a slippery ground here and he knew it, for otherwise he would have never offered Hippius half the earnings. As Shestov kept pointing out to him, in most European countries the author received twice as much money as the translator for the publication or production of his or her work. While it made legal sense when Hippius and Shestov were still in Russia that their permissions were not required, they both were no longer Russian citizens and their demands now carried more weight.

It was also further complicated because Shestov and Hippius were very recent refugees and therefore virtually penniless, so even a little bit of money for the publication of their works in the West became a desperate issue. W. Chapin Huntington, who interviewed prominent Russian émigré writers, including Hippius, noted that even as late as in the 1930s most of them still largely lived off "the royalties on their German, French, English, and occasionally other editions" for the simple reason that "Russia-out-of-Russia, with its scant million population, poor and scattered, would not afford them a sufficient market for their work."[27] It is worth mentioning that at the time Hippius was also complaining about Grzhebin, who, through Farbman, was the source of Kot's new Russian books. Calling his publishing business "semi-illegal under the wing of Gorky," she accused him of buying émigré writers' copyrights "just for a couple of slices of bread."[28] Kot, who was often strapped for funds himself, could have been more compassionate on that score from the start, but – maybe precisely because he badly needed money too – he was not.

Mansfield, being treated in Paris by Manoukhin at the time, met Hippius, who was friends with Manoukhin, through him and assured Kot that she immediately and intensely disliked her: "I have never felt a more complete physical repulsion for anyone. Everything about her is false – her cheeks, glowing softly with rouge. Even her breath – soft and sweet. She is a bad woman, and it is simply infernal that she should worry you." Kot urged Mansfield to present to Manoukhin his side of the story, and, after she obliged, Manoukhin, according to her, "understood only 'trop bien' as he said. He was disgusted with her. And he *begged* me … to tell you how extremely sorry he would be to think you did not know how he regretted all the trouble you had had with Hippius."[29]

Kot was no doubt grateful to have Mansfield's and Manoukhin's support, but he was understandibly experiencing serious legal angst about the statement on the title page claiming that his translation of Hippius was "authorized." Still hopeful that the play might eventually be picked up by a US publisher, he asked Mountsier to make sure the translation would be labelled differently there: "I should prefer that the title page should omit the word 'authorised' and simply say 'translated from the Russian by SS Koteliansky.'"[30] A less obstinate – or needy – person may have allowed Hippius to pocket all the money so that she would consider the case closed, but Koteliansky just soldiered on, trying both to recover the money from "the notorious swindler" Hippius and to procure a US publisher for the play that she never authorized him to translate.

"I have been anxiously expecting to hear from you with regard to the Green Ring," he wrote to Mountsier again in December 1922. "Did you see the Neighborhood people? What did they say? Is there any hope of recovering the money stolen by Hippius? … Tell me also if there is any prospect of having The Green Ring published in America on any conditions." He then repeated the same questions in several letters throughout January and early February: "I am anxiously awaiting your reply as regards the Green Ring"; "You never answered me if you considered it possible to place The Green Ring in America." Finally, by mid-February, Koteliansky appeared to be ready to throw in the towel yet not quite willing to accept the responsibility for the botched enterprise: "As regards 'The Green Ring' I understand it turned out a complete failure, and that now I may try myself to place it. What a pity that I can't do it successfully. Neither did I arrange matters with the Neighborhood Playhouse. It was all done by the London publisher Daniel and an American agent, called I believe Daniels. The publisher is bankrupt now – and the whole business is just one piece of fraud."[31]

After two publishing disasters in a row, the third time *was* the charm for Koteliansky in 1920, and the last translation that came out that year, Maxim Gorky's *Reminiscences of Leo Nicolayevitch Tolstoi,* was altogether a different story. "I do not remember how we first came to know S.S. Koteliansky," Leonard Woolf would write in his autobiography, "but I think it must have been through Katherine Mansfield and Murry. In 1919 he came to us with a copy of the *Reminiscences,* just published in Moscow, which Gorky had sent him, giving him the English translation rights. Kot suggested that he and I should translate it and The Hogarth Press publish it."[32] The Woolfs actually first met Kot in July 1917, around the time they were starting their Hogarth Press, mostly as a hobby. According to Virginia, Kot told them then, in his typically categorical manner, that starting a small press was a bad idea because "to write for a small public is damnation."[33] He obviously left enough of an impression on her for his opinion to be recorded in her diary, but several months later she was still not sure what his name was, calling him "Kabotinsky."[34]

By early 1918 Kot progressed to being an occasional guest at the Woolfs' dinners. Because of her own interest in Russian writers, Virginia was at first quite intrigued by him. There was, she thought, "a good deal to be said for Kot. He has some likeness to the Russians in literature. He will begin to explain his soul without preface."[35] In June 1918 Koteliansky brought Gertler along, and, according to Virginia, they "both described their Jewish families," probably mostly for Leonard's benefit. She found Gertler "unscrupulous" but continued to be fascinated by Kot, who "sat indulgently silent, professing scarcely to notice what was before his eyes." She compared him to "the solid lodging house furniture, but with an air of romance."[36] In July, Virginia noted in her diary that Kot was "a mysterious figure – not only in his occupations, but in his desire to be a friend of ours, though he seems without many friends."[37] She also wrote to Ottoline Morrell that "Koteliansky ... wanted us to come and meet Lawrence."[38]

Kot's professional collaboration with the Woolfs may have started with a letter he sent Virginia on 3 April 1919. In his best cursive handwriting Kot requested there that he should be allowed to see them without other guests or meals present. Both his letter and her response were quite formal in their addresses, which underscores how little familiarity there still was in their relationship at the time despite occasional get-togethers:

Dear Mrs Woolf,
I should very much like to see you, and as I like and respect both you and Mr Woolf, allow me to be quite frank: it somehow embarrasses me to eat in company, it spoils my pleasure of seeing and speaking with people.

(Please do not interpret it psycho-analytically; I know it is not true in my case). May I just come any afternoon or evening when you are free?[39]

The joke (or was it a joke?) about psychoanalysis probably brought a wicked smile to Virginia Woolf's face. Koteliansky was alluding, of course, to Freud's well-known linkage of feelings about eating to feelings about sex. Freud famously said that "Loss of appetite is in sexual terms loss of libido," and he also suggested that a loss of both led to "Melancholia."[40] Kot's primary purpose in including the parenthesis may have been to let the Woolfs know that he was well aware of their friendship with James Strachey (Lytton's kid brother) and Alex Sargant-Florence, who were not married yet but whose passion for Freud was already well known and whose annotated translation of Freud's works the Hogarth Press would publish in 1924.[41] Koteliansky probably underestimated how much the Woolfs gleaned from their conversations with him or knew from their mutual friends, like the Murrys, about his reputation for leading a very monastic, celibate existence, and also for suffering "black moods." It would have been hard for them, and especially for Virginia, with her keen sense of irony, not to feel that the man doth protest too much. But whatever her private thoughts were, she responded with respect and understanding, and even got his name right. "Dear Mr Koteliansky," Virginia wrote in reply. "We quite understand your feeling which we rather share ourselves – at least we would generally rather not dine with people. If you would come in after dinner on Sunday we should like it very much."[42]

It is unknown whether they did meet on that Sunday in April, but in early August it was all arranged – whether again or for the first time that year – for Kot to go down to Richmond for the weekend and see the Woolfs without the crowds. "If nothing extraordinary happens, and it won't rain on Saturday I will leave Victoria Station at 12," Kot assured the Woolfs. Something extraordinary did happen, and on Saturday he wrote to excuse himself "for my troublesome behaviour regarding my coming to you today. There are several little reasons, but the chief one is that a very black depression descended on me yesterday; I could not chase it off today, and it would be indecent of me to bring it to your house."[43]

The meeting eventually did take place and led to several years of close collaboration between Kot and both Woolfs. Before Koteliansky approached them with his proposal to publish Gorky, the Hogarth Press was by no means a serious professional enterprise. According to Leonard, on 23 March 1917, he and Virginia were just taking a walk when they happened to pass Excelsior Printing Supply Co., whose window display made them stop and look: "Nearly all the implements of printing were materially attractive and we stared through the window at them rather like two hungry children gazing at buns and cakes in a baker shop window.

I do not know which of us first suggested that we should go inside and see whether we could buy a machine and type and teach ourselves."[44] By spring 1919, they had printed and bound 5 "boutique" editions of no more than 300 copies: *Two Stories* by Virginia and Leonard Woolf (Leonard's contribution was "Three Jews"); Katherine Mansfield's *Prelude*; Virginia Woolf's *Kew Gardens*; T.S. Eliot's *Poems*, and J. Middleton Murry's *Critic in Judgment*.[45]

For Kot, Gorky was an inspired choice. On the one hand, he was infrequently translated into English, so he could be added to Koteliansky's very own authors. On the other hand, Gorky's memoirs were of Tolstoy, a subject of constant curiosity in England, and they were written in a very lively and even racy way. It helped that, like Lawrence, Leonard had always been interested in Gorky: among his books, which are now in the Manuscripts, Archives and Special Collections at Washington State University Libraries, there are two volumes of Gorky going back to 1905 and 1915.[46] The timing was also perfect. Leonard had decided at that point that "the Hogarth Press ... must either expand or explode or dwindle and die; it was too young and too vigorous to be able just to sit still and survive."[47] Virginia, too, loved the idea of translating the Gorky volume, even though she fretted now and then that "publishing Gorki ... marks some step over a precipice."[48] For once her angst was not justified. On the contrary, the Gorky publication, for which the Woolfs had to contract a commercial printing firm, started the transformation of the Hogarth Press into a much more serious and successful publisher.

Given Grisha Farbman's direct connection to Grzhebin Publishing House (at that time still in Petrograd), which published Gorky's reminiscences in 1919, there is little doubt that in this case Gorky had indeed bestowed the English translation rights on Kot. Kot used that fact to tell Leonard at one point that because of his "obligations to Gorky" he had to make sure that if Hogarth Press was not also interested in publishing Gorky's reminiscences of yet another writer, Leonid Andreyev, he "shall have to return Gorky his permission to me to translate it, as well as to free the Russian publisher of the exclusive right he gave me to translate and publish the book here and in America."[49] Leonard did not budge, and Kot of course never acted on his rather empty threat.

Leonard's legendary patience made him in many ways an ideal collaborator for Kot. Here is how he described the process of their translating together: "If he was in doubt about a word, he sometimes looked it up in the dictionary and put all the variants into his translation, occasionally with curious results, e.g. 'he looked in the glass at his mug, dial, face.' One learned to the full Kot's iron integrity and intensity only by collaborating with him in a Russian translation. After I had turned his English into my English, we went through it sentence by sentence. Kot had a sensitive understanding of and feeling for language and literature, and also a strong subtle mind. He would pass no sentence until he was completely convinced that it gave the exact shade of meaning and feeling of the original, and we would sometimes be a quarter of an hour arguing over a single word."[50]

Leonard's forbearance was helped by the fact that he loved Gorky's writing in *The Reminiscences*: "I do not think that I have ever got more aesthetic pleasure from anything than from doing this translation ... The writing is beautiful; every word and every sentence are perfect, and there is not one superfluous word or sentence in the book. I got immense pleasure from trying to translate this ravishing Russian into adequate English."[51] Leonard's sense of Gorky's Russian was greatly aided by the lessons in Russian that he started taking from Kot at the same time as they began collaborating on the translations.

*The Reminiscences* are based on the thirty-six lengthy notes Gorky took during 1901 and 1902 while Tolstoy was in Gaspra, Crimea. Gorky, who lived nearby because he had been exiled from Moscow and St Petersburg for his political activities, often visited him in Gaspra, as did Chekhov, who had moved to Yalta, next door to Gaspra, in 1898 because the dry and warm climate of the Black Sea and surrounding mountains were deemed beneficial to people with tuberculosis. Gorky apparently thought that the notes had been lost, but discovered them soon after the revolution, which led to the 1919 publication of the book in Russia.

Gorky was in his early thirties and Tolstoy in his early seventies at the time they had their conversations. The dynamic of their relationship was peculiar. Gorky, who was largely self-educated, wanted to discuss literature; Tolstoy did not, criticizing Gorky for being "very bookish, very."[52] Neither did Tolstoy hide from Gorky that he did not think much of him as a writer. Having decided some time ago that peasants possessed the simple but ultimate wisdom in questions of life, death, and meaning of one's existence, Tolstoy was, however, genuinely intrigued by Gorky's peasant background. Gorky, on the other hand, could not help but detect hypocrisy in how Tolstoy viewed peasants. "His interest in me is ethnological," Gorky wrote in his notes. "In his eyes I belong to a species not familiar to him – only that ... Perhaps peasant to him means merely – bad smell. He always feels it, and involuntarily has to talk of it ... Yesterday he said to me: 'I am more of a mouzhik than you are and I feel better in a mouzhik way.' God, he ought not to boast of it, he must not!" He also complained that Tolstoy was interested in just three subjects – which were of little interest to Gorky – and would therefore talk almost exclusively "of God, of peasants, and of woman."[53]

It was the latter topic – "of woman" – that provided the most sensationally revealing moments, which delighted the Hogarth Press readers. Constance

Garnett's or the Maudes' translations of Tolstoy never treated them to tasty morsels of this kind:

> Of women he talks readily and much, like a French novelist, but always with the coarseness of a Russian peasant ... To-day ... he asked Anton Tchekhov: "You whored a great deal when you were young?" Anton Pavlovitch ... muttered something inaudible, and Leo Nicolayevitch, looking at the sea, confessed: "I was an indefatigable ..." He said this penitently, using at the end of the sentence a salty peasant word. And I noticed for the first time how simply he used the word, as though he knew no more fitting one to use.

Once, seeing a large peasant woman working on the flower-bed in a park and "shaking her ten-pound breasts," Tolstoy remarked: "If the aristocracy had not from time to time mated with such horse-women as she, they would have died out long ago." "With her body woman is more sincere than man," Tolstoy decreed on a different occasion, "but with her mind she lies."[54]

The publication also included a letter that Gorky started writing in 1910 when he first heard that Tolstoy had disappeared from the family estate in Yasnaya Polyana. In it he explained that he had often come close to hating Tolstoy: "In Leo Nicolayevitch there is much which at times roused in me a feeling very like hatred, and this hatred fell upon my soul with crushing weight." Yet he loved Tolstoy much more than he hated him, and that became even more obvious to him once he heard of his death:

> It struck me to the heart: I cried with pain and anger and, now, half crazy, I imagine him as I know and saw him – I am tormented by a desire to speak with him ... I do not know whether I loved him; but does it matter, love of him or hatred? ... The old magician stands before me, alien to all, a solitary traveller through all the deserts of thought in search of an all-embracing truth which he has not found – I look at him and, though I feel sorrow for the loss, I feel pride at having seen the man, and that pride alleviates my pain and grief.[55]

The book was enormously successful. The Woolfs thought they "took the plunge" when they had the initial 1,000 copies printed, but these were almost immediately sold, and they had to print another 1,000 copies before the year's end.[56] That started the most intense "Russian" period for the Hogarth Press and for the collaboration between Koteliansky and the Woolfs. In a rapid succession they published *Reminiscences of Anton Chekhov by Maxim Gorky, Alexander Kuprin, and Ivan Bunin* (1921, translated by Koteliansky and Leonard Woolf); *Anton Chekhov's Note-books Together with Reminiscences of Tchekhov by Maxim Gorky* (1921, translated by Koteliansky and Leonard Woolf); F.M. Dostoevsky, *Stavrogin's Confessions and the Plan of the Life of a Great Sinner* (1922, translated by Koteliansky and Virginia Woolf); *Autobiography of Countess Tolstoy* (1922, translated by Koteliansky and Leonard Woolf); I.A. Bunin, *Gentleman from San Francisco and Other Stories* (1922, translated by Koteliansky, D.H. Lawrence, and Leonard Woolf), A.B. Goldenweiser, *Talks with Tolstoy* (1923, translated by Koteliansky and Virginia Woolf); and *Tolstoi's Love Letters* (1923, translated by Koteliansky and Virginia Woolf). The translation of *Anton Chekhov's Note-books Together with Reminiscences of Tchekhov by Maxim Gorky* was promptly acknowledged in 1923 in the first full-length study of the writer appearing in England, written by William Gerhardi, who had been born in an English industrialist family in St Petersburg, was fluent in Russian, and would later become a very fashionable English novelist.[57]

Kot's friends marvelled at his transformation. "I shall soon begin to agree with Beatrice [Glenavy] who says that you are a very social person!" Gertler exclaimed in February 1921, commenting on Kot's budding professional and social relationship with the Woolfs.[58] Virginia herself noted the change in him: "Kot … came to bring us Tchehov, & was so excited over it & other projects as to twang like a fiddle, instead of solemnly resounding as usual like a full barrel of beer."[59] Koteliansky had finally hit on just the right formula. Instead of introducing new Russian authors, always a gamble, most of the successful 1920–23 volumes focused on translating recent publications in Russia of autobiographical and biographical materials (including letters, notebooks, journals, and memoirs) that pertained to the three most popular Russian writers in England – Tolstoy, Chekhov, and Dostoevsky.[60] Eight of the eleven translations were of that nature, and by now easily identifiable as a definite trademark of both Koteliansky and the Hogarth Press.

And, yet, the second most popular and commercially successful book that the Hogarth Press printed in this period was a volume of stories by a yet another writer who was still not well known in England: Ivan Bunin.[61] In 1933 Bunin would become the first Russian writer to be awarded the Nobel Prize for Literature,[62] but back in 1921, when Kot and Lawrence first began their work on one of his more famous stories, "The Gentleman from San Francisco," translations of Bunin into English were virtually nonexistent. The story, published in Russia in 1915, had been translated in 1918 in the United States by Abraham Yarmolinsky, but no British publisher picked it up.[63] Lawrence was immeasurably more enthusiastic about Bunin than he had been about Shestov. He was in Baden-Baden when Kot, in early June, wrote to him, asking whether he would "'English' a translation he has made of a Russian story."[64] Less than two weeks later, Lawrence read the story and it made him "grin with joy": "in spite of its lugubriousness ... it is screamingly good of Naples & Capri: so comically like the reality."[65] Two months later the translation was complete and Kot liked the results.[66] It was, in many ways, a triumph of Koteliansky's method of translating because it brought together two great literary talents with similar sensibilities.[67] As a consequence, the Koteliansky-Lawrence English text represents Bunin accurately both linguistically and poetically.

Bunin, who was also a painter, a first-rate poet, and a musician, uses all his keen artistic senses in his prose. Lawrence, himself a painter and a poet, obviously recognized it in him, helping Kot to render strong pagan, anthropomorphic elements and bold colours in Bunin's descriptions of nature much better than the smooth but much more pedestrian translation by Yarmolinsky. Just to give one example, here is Lawrence and Koteliansky's nuanced version of a morning scene in the story:

> When the dawn grew white at the window of No. 43, and a damp wind began rustling the tattered fronds of the banana tree; as the blue sky of morning lifted and unfolded over Capri, and Monte Solaro, pure and distinct, grew golden, catching the sun which was rising beyond the far-off blue mountains of Italy; just as the labourers who were mending the paths of the islands for the tourists came out for work, a long box was carried into room No. 43.[68]

And here is Yarmolinsky:

> At dawn, when the window panes in Number Forty-three grew white, and a damp wind rustled in the leaves of the banana-tree, when the pale-blue morning sky rose and stretched over Capri, and the sun, rising from behind the distant mountains of Italy, touched into gold the pure, clearly outlined summit of Monte Solaro, when the masons, who mended the paths for the tourists on the island, went out to their work, – an oblong box was brought to room number forty-three.[69]

The happy synergy of Lawrence and Bunin was reflected upon in several reviews. The *Times* of London were particularly complimentary: "[T]he present translation, by D.H. Lawrence and S.S. Koteliansky, although it cannot reproduce precisely the style of the original, is a remarkably able piece of work. A better translation is hardly possible."[70] Lawrence liked the story so much that he wrote to Kot that he would not mind working with him on other Bunin stories, but by then Kot was already collaborating on the rest with Leonard Woolf.[71] The translation first appeared in *The Dial* and then was included with three other stories – "Gentle Breathing," "Kasimir Stanislavovitch," and "Son" – in the 1922 Hogarth Press volume. Woolf was full of praise for Lawrence's translation of "Gentleman," calling it "maginificent."[72] Lawrence, on the other hand, was not quite as generous with praise about Woolf's contributions. "Some of Wolf's [*sic*] sentences take a bit of reading," he complained to Kot.[73]

As the volume was being prepared for publication, there were again sensitive issues with the names on the title page and their order. Lawrence had asked *The Dial* to put just Koteliansky's name as the translator, but they ignored his request and not just listed Lawrence as one as well but also put his name first. "They are impudent people," Lawrence wrote apologetically to Kot after seeing the publication, "I had told them not to put my name. Of course they did it themselves."[74] When the Hogarth Press volume was printed, Lawrence's name, in accordance with his wishes, was omitted from the title page but Woolf's name was on it, second to Kot's. Then, at the last moment, it must have been decided that the omission was unwise since Lawrence's name had appeared in *The Dial* publication, so all first editions featured an attached erratum slip declaring that the first story in the book was "translated by D.H. Lawrence and S.S. Koteliansky" and that "[o]wing to a mistake Mr Lawrence's name has been omitted from the title page."[75] The US edition, which came out a year later (from Thomas Seltzer), restored Lawrence to the title page, and also put him first.[76]

Despite these minor hiccups, 1922 was the high mark for Kot's collaboration with the Woolfs, and he was apparently full of ideas and suggestions. When in 1922, T.S. Eliot, who had just started publishing *The Criterion*, a literary review, wrote to Leonard asking him for extracts from Hogarth's Russian translations, Leonard offered him "Stavrogin Confessions," which Kot was translating with Virginia (and which Eliot eventually published) and then enumerated other possibilities by quoting Kot: "If it is no good, Koteliansky has two other suggestions: (1) There is a book just published consisting of 12 letters exchanged between the best living Russian poet and the best living Russian critic who were in a Bolshevik kind of Convalescent Home. The letters discuss the influence of culture in the modern world and according to Koteliansky are very good. He says that one or two of them could be published alone if there were difficulty regarding length. (2) Kot. again says that there is a most interesting writer, Rosanov [*sic*], who died a little time ago, and wrote volumes of 'pensées.' He says they are very good and have never been translated."[77]

The letters Woolf was talking about were the ones between the Symbolist poet Viacheslav Ivanov and the critic Mikhail Gershenzon. They shared a room in a Moscow sanatorium in summer 1920, and the book, "Perepiska iz dvukh uglov" ("A Correspondence from Two Corners") came out in Russia in 1921. Koteliansky's sales pitch, if recorded accurately by Leonard, had a strong whiff of hyperbole. Among the still living turn-of-the-century poets, including Osip Mandelstam, Anna Akhmatova, and Andrei Bely, to say that Ivanov was "the best" was a stretch. To call Gershenzon the best living critic was even more of a stretch, and the book itself, with its heavy emphasis on religious and moral philosophy, would probably have been as unsuccessful as the Shestov volume had been earlier. Koteliansky did publish the second author in the list, Vasily Rozanov, after he and the Woolfs went their separate ways, but the two volumes, *Solitaria* (London: Wishart & Co, 1927) and *Fallen Leaves* (London: The Mandrake Press, 1929), were, likewise, commercial duds.

In late 1922 Koteliansky started translating with Virginia Woolf, who once complained that critics who had influenced the British perception of Russian writers "have never read a word of Russian, or seen Russia, or even heard the language spoken by the natives."[78] Hoping to be different, Virginia, like her husband, attempted to learn some Russian, partially, it seems, out of a sense of rivalry with him. "[A]m I to learn Russian with [Leonard] & Kot," she asked herself in January 1921. "If he can read it & solace his age with it I shall be furious."[79] "Russian from 12.15 to 12.45," she noted in her diary in February, "& from 5.30 to 6. From 9.30 to 10, & on the way to Waterloo and back again must have some result."[80] "We are taking Russian," she informed Kot in March 1921. "The aspects seem to me very interesting – that is not to say that I understand them at all."[81]

Virginia's interest in perfective and imperfective aspects of Russian verbs, one of the trickiest parts of Russian grammar, probably owed a lot to the 1915 publication of Jane Harrison's short monograph *Russia and the Russian Verb: A Contribution to the Psychology of the Russian People,* which was based on a lecture she had given at Cambridge the same year. Woolf greatly admired Harrison, a Greek scholar and lecturer in Classical Arhaeology at Newnham College, one of two Cambridge colleges for women at the time. Harrison, in fact, served as an inspiration for Woolf's *A Room of One's Own,* which had its origins in two lectures Woolf read at Newnham in October 1928, six months after Harrison's death.[82] In *Russia and Russian Verb,* Harrison postulated that the imperfective was "the aspect of intellect, of the thing thought rather than the thing lived; of the mental net, in which … our mechanizing minds and brains have caught the living universe." She then provocatively suggested that it was in the Russian national character to "cling … to the imperfective, at all costs" because "The Russian hungers for durée [duration]."[83] In a later version of her presentation, the 1919 monograph *Aspects, Aorists and the Classical Tripos*, Harrison declared that "aspects are in the very blood of the Slav. A Russian moujïk may blunder in his cases and his spelling … but in his aspects … he will blunder never; they are part of him … The Slav is not much interested in order … he *is* interested in … *quality* of action and in sympathy with action." To prove her point further, Harrison even quoted from Kot's and Murry's 1916 translation of Shestov's *Anton Chekhov and Other Essays,* where Shestov maintained that Russians "want not so much a science as an art of life" – but, probably much to Kot's disdain (and he would have been very likely to read Harrison's work), the reference to the Shestov volume came out quite garbled for it read "Anton Shestov and Other Essays."[84]

Woolf's interest in aspects notwithstanding, her study of Russian seems to have ended quite soon after it started. "[Y]ou will not find that I have learnt Russian," she wrote to Kot in June 1921.[85] She did, however, assure Kot that she was still interested in working on translations with him. Their first project was *Stavrogin's Confessions: Suppressed Chapters from* The Possessed, a translation of three chapters from the manuscript of Dostoevsky's 1871 novel, which had been omitted from the original publication of *The Possessed* and were published for the first time in Soviet Russia in 1921. The chapters featured the protagonist's gruesome confession to the rape of a fourteen-year-old girl, and Woolf, who herself may have been sexually molested by her stepbrother when she was a teenager,[86] must have found the topic both painful and poignant. While she did consider Tolstoy to be "the greatest of all novelists," it was, in fact, Dostoevsky who really got under her skin – often, as she pointed out, despite her attempts to withstand him: "The novels of Dostoevsky are seething whirlpools, gyrating sandstorms, watersprouts which hiss and boil and suck us in … Against our wills we are drawn in, whirled round, blinded, suffocated, and at the same time filled with giddy rapture."[87] She found Kot a tolerable informant on Dostoevsky, "stuffed with facts, & of course passionate severe & uncompromising,"[88] but Kot was also beginning to get on her nerves: "Kot persisting, enforcing, emphasizing, analyzing, rubbing in – how we are to publish Russian books – how L[eonard] is to give up the Contemporary – no, you misunderstand me – I did not say I consider your life to be worthless."[89]

When, in early 1923, she and Kot switched to translating Tolstoy, Woolf again assured her collaborator that she was "greatly interested" in the two volumes they were working on almost simultaneously: *Tolstoi's Love Letters* and Goldenweizer's *Talks with Tolstoi*; these were, according to her, "almost the best we've done."[90] The volume of Tolstoy's letters also included "A Study on the Autobiographical Elements in Tolstoi's Work," written by Paul Biryukov, a young Tolstoy disciple who spent time with him at Tolstoy's estate at Yasnaya Polyana. Biriukov published three thick volumes of Tolstoy's biography, based on the writer's letters, his conversations with Tolstoy, other materials in the archive (to which he was allowed access by Tolstoy himself), and Biriukov's own diary at the time. The first three volumes came out in the 1905-15 period. The fourth and final volume came out in 1922, and it was then that Biriukov also updated the first volume, adding Tolstoy's letters to his first fiancée, Valeriia Arsen'eva. In his preface, which was also translated in the Hogarth publication, Biriukov explained that Tolstoy's wife did not want to see those letters published while she was still alive but gave him permission to "do what you like" upon her death.[91]

The title page of *Tolstoi's Love Letters*, for a change, did not claim that the translation of Biriukov's part of the book was authorized. Koteliansky was now just honestly exploiting the lack of a copyright agreement with Soviet Russia. It is possible that he asked Virginia to write a foreword, like many of his other distinguished collaborators did, and that she refused – just like she would in 1933 when she declined to write an introduction for a reprint of *Stavrogin's Confession*, claiming that she did not have "anything interesting to say."[92] She may have also believed that Russian literature, like Koteliansky's soul, is most natural when revealed "without a preface."

Toward the very end of 1922 Kot appeared to have become more impatient in his dealings with Leonard. What was happening with his family back in Ukraine was, probably, a large contributor to his foul mood, but, whatever was the reason, Kot's correspondence with Leonard during this time reads like a fast-approaching train wreck. It started with Kot's request at the end of December 1922 that Woolf should instruct the US publisher to send Lawrence his share for "The Gentleman of San Francisco" in dollars and straight to New Mexico. Woolf thought it improper since the policy was for all transactions to go through the Hogarth Press. He also objected to Kot's suggestion that Kot and Lawrence should be getting 75 percent of the money for the US publication, instead of 50 percent. Since there was no prior written agreement, Woolf consented to doing it just "in this case" but not in the future, for he felt they were already "being generous … at our own expense."[93] That made Kot furious: "Now I don't know whether you intended your refusal to instruct Mountsier to pay Lawrence his share out of the next installment as a personal insult to me; and also whether you meant it as an insult to tell me that you were generous to me. If you want to insult me there is no need doing it in a round about way: we could put an end to our relations, if you want it, in a straightforward way, without any need at all to insult each other ... I repeat again, if, for some reason, you find that, as you once said it, we were incompatible, and therefore you want to put an end to our relations, [I] think you ought to say so straightaway."[94]

That the ever-so-patient Leonard had told Kot even prior to this incident that the two of them were "incompatible" as colleagues and collaborators fully reveals the amount of frustration that accumulated between them, but Leonard must have been soothing and reassuring in response to this particular outburst; by mid-January the storm was largely over, and they proceeded with other projects seemingly without another problem for a month. Then, in mid-February, Kot suggested to Leonard that Goldenweizer's memoirs of Tolstoy – which he initially wanted Leonard, not Virginia, to help him with – could be "condens[ed] ... to half its, Russian, size."[95] A week later, he expressed his further unhappiness about the part of the contract that left it to the publishers to make the final selections from Goldenweizer's memoirs. On that occasion Kot wrote to Leonard that he simply could not put himself "in a position of being dictated in such matters": "Not that I doubt Virginia's taste, not a bit of it ... [but] [t]he selections of what is to be included should be done ... by mutual agreement."[96] He was also irked that "Virginia had no time to see me to go through the Goldenweiser book."[97] Leonard, perhaps not wanting to endure another unpleasant ordeal, was obliging. *Talks with Tolstoi*, too, came out without Virginia's introduction.

While Leonard was at least trying to control his exasperation and be stoic, Virginia was nothing of the sort. As far as she was concerned, Kot was no longer someone who intrigued or amused her, and thus he was outstaying his welcome. As early as 1922 she was already telling friends that "Koteliansky is a fanatic about Russian literature, and rather inarticulate,"[98] and later she mocked his "seriousness, & concentration upon say 5 objects which he has been staring at these 40 years."[99] At times she was quite unabashedly anti-Semitic, once explaining to Clive Bell that, when chatting with friends during an intermission at a concert, she made sure she stayed in one place for fear that she would "run into Koteliansky that fervid Jew."[100]

She was more diplomatic in public. When, in 1932, she was asked by a potential biographer to explain her collaboration with Koteliansky, she chose not to go into details by downplaying her role: "With regard to the translations – I scarcely like to claim that I 'translated' the Russian books credited to me. I merely revised the English of a version made by S. Koteliansky."[101] Leonard, on the other hand, did not to mince words. To B.J. Kirkpatrick, who was working on Virginia Woolf's bibliography in the 1950s, he underscored the truly uneasy coexistence that his late wife and Koteliansky had as collaborators: "We taught ourselves a little Russian in order to understand Koteliansky's problems in translating. The procedure was that Koteliansky translated the Russian book into very bad English by double-spaced lines, so that Mrs Woolf went through the text with him, sentence by sentence, and then put the translation into good English."[102]

Virginia's discomfort with Koteliansky, bordering on outright hostility, as well as Leonard's growing impatience were the obvious reasons why 1923 was the last year of Koteliansky's collaboration with the Woolfs and the Hogarth Press. It did not help that in May of that year Kot requested a full account of "what 'profit' means ... the expenses in producing the books ... and the sales of copies"; and in August he complained that Leonard agreed to sell *Tolstoi's Letters* to a US publisher "on such beggarly terms."[103] In 1923, when the Woolfs wanted to publish Leonid Andreyev's story "The Dark,"[104] they already employed different translators: L.A. Magnus and K. Walter. After 1923, the Press would publish other translations from Russian, among them *The Life of Archpriest Avvakum by Himself* in 1924, translated by Jane Ellen Harrison and her friend and companion, Hope Mirrless. Spurred by the Nobel Prize, more of Bunin was translated and published: in 1933, *The Well of Days*, translated by Gleb Struve and Hamish Miles, and in 1935, *Grammar of Love*, translated by John Cournos. Koteliansky, too, would go on to translate more Russian works, but now he again had to spend much time and nervous energy looking for publishers since the Hogarth Press was no longer available to him. What started as a boon for both the translator and the publishers failed to end happily for one of the two parties involved.

Despite all their disagreements, Kot retained fondness for both Leonard and Virginia for the rest of his life. He told May Sarton, his young American friend who was about to visit the Woolfs in 1937, that when "V. is at peace, her face is lit up with great beauty."[105] He was absolutely devastated by her suicide in 1941. Leonard – perhaps, due to his empathy for a fellow Jew but also because, despite Kot being "not a comfortable man," he found a lot in him to admire – remained a helpful friend, assisting Kot with his application for citizenship in 1929 and being one of the very few people Kot wanted to see in the last days of his life.

# THE ADELPHI AFFAIR AND THE
# CAFÉ ROYAL

I wanted to chloroform you and take you to Mexico, and there
was a tremendous argument about it.
~ Dorothy Brett to Kot, 26 November 1923

They started a publishing house, like ours; which went smash,
or never started, which had killed Kot's hopes; & Lawrence, who
thought the whole of London would flock after him to Mexico,
has retired with Brett alone.
~ Virginia Woolf, Diary, 1 November 1924

In early autumn 1922, the Lawrences moved to Taos, New Mexico, at the invitation of Mabel Dodge Sterne (later Mabel Dodge Luhan), a rich US heiress who
was trying to create a vibrant artistic "cosmos"[1] there, not unlike Lawrence's
notion of "Rananim." Upon leaving Australia for the United States, Lawrence
labelled himself and Frieda "new Jews" who "shall wander on."[2] Though not
enchanted with the USA – and fully aware of how much his friend detested the
very notion of its materialistic culture – Lawrence wrote to Kot that he nevertheless admired the USA's "bigness, a sense of space, & a certain sense of rough
freedom" while abhorring England's "pettifogging narrowness" so much that he
would need a very good reason to settle in his native country ever again.[3] Kot –
who wanted Lawrence at the very least in Europe, if not in London – immediately
started working on what he thought would be a compelling reason for Lawrence
to want to return: the publication that would soon be called *The Adelphi*.

Koteliansky's crucial role in the creation of *The Adelphi* has been largely over-
looked by Lawrence and Murry scholars and biographers, who attribute the
initial idea for the new publication solely to Murry. Yet the initial push for *The
Adelphi* came from Kot. The journal, in Kot's plan, was to serve as a forum and
mouthpiece for Lawrence: it would glorify him as a writer by publishing his new

works, and it would also show off his editorial talents and his convictions as a social and literary critic. Kot knew, however, that before Lawrence would even consider getting involved, someone with experience editing similar publications had to lay the foundation by raising money and volunteering to shoulder the editing responsibilities. Murry, who had edited the *The Athenaeum* and *The Signature,* was the most logical person for the job. The problem was, of course, that in 1922 Kot was still not on speaking terms with Murry.

In his later accounts to friends, Kot liked to justify their eventual reconciliation as a gesture of posthumous tribute to Katherine Mansfield. Thus to H.G. Wells he wrote: "I thought that my friendship for Katherine obliged me to transfer my loyalty to Murry, after Katherine's death. That is why, after a complete breach with Murry during Katherine's lifetime, I renewed my friendship with him."[4] But, as we have seen earlier, it was in October 1922, while Mansfield was still alive, that Kot and Murry began to patch up their relationship. Murry wrote to Kot first: "I probably shouldn't be writing to you. But here I am … I feel that I have some sort of right to know why you so carefully avoid me and why (as I am told) you have such an extremely bad opinion of me."[5] On October 18, Murry wrote again: "Many thanks for your letter. It quite satisfies me. I understand as well as you do that we must leave our future relations to accident or destiny … I was merely distressed & worried that one whom I do like & respect should apparently hold a low opinion of me."[6] Given Kot's usually ferocious clinging to his grudges against people, the fact that he wrote a letter that "satisfied" his long-term nemesis was tantamount to extending an olive branch.

According to Murry, soon after Mansfield's death, Koteliansky arrived at his house "in a sort of tender anguish." "I see him now," Murry would reminisce years later, "with a piece of string in his hands, knotting and unknotting it, as he told me of his new-born faith." The professed faith was in Murry as a saviour of both Lawrence and English literature and in the future journal that Kot thought should be "as big as a telephone book."[7] The two of them arrived at a clear understanding that "the main purpose of the *Adelphi* [was] to make a place for Lawrence"[8] and that until Lawrence was ready, Murry would "act … 'simply' as Lawrence's lieutenant and *locum tenens* [place holder]."[9] Koteliansky was determined to position himself, to use Catherine Carswell's phrase, "sternly by [Murry's] elbow,"[10] making sure Lawrence was well served by the new publication. "Kot is the busy bee of the *Adelphi*, Murry the sort of queen bee," was Lawrence's summary of their arrangement.[11]

What seems to have helped persuade Murry to give it a try was the idea, also probably first formulated by Kot, that the initial issues of *The Adelphi* could honour Mansfield's memory – as well as feature "the essential chapters" of

Lawrence's *Fantasia of the Unconscious*, the US copy of which Murry and Kot had just received from Lawrence's publisher. Koteliansky and Murry then cabled Lawrence in New Mexico and received his blessing to have parts of *Fantasia* published in the first issue.[12] Lawrence, as the heir apparent, expressed muted encouragement to his old friends in London while voicing serious misgivings to his new friends in Taos.[13] As in the case of *The Signature*, Koteliansky, it was agreed, would have the title of "business manager."[14] The others involved in the new journal were J.W.N. Sullivan, a literary journalist and a popular science writer, whose idea it was to call it *The Adelphi*, Greek for "brothers," and H.M. Tomlinson, a well-known fiction and travel writer. They would be joined later by another "brother" – H.M. Tomlinson's real brother, Philip Tomlinson.

The first issue of *The Adelphi: A Shilling Monthly Magazine* was to come out in June 1923 but the subscription flyer went out several months earlier so that money could start pouring in. The new publication sounded not that different from *The Athenaeum*, which Murry had edited before, even though the brochure promised *The Adelphi* would "fill … a place apart among contemporary magazines." Like *The Athenaeum*, it was to feature contents that were not just "literary" but "literature" itself, and in addition plenty of science, philosophy, music, art, and drama was to be covered. "Finally," the flyer went on to proclaim, "THE ADELPHI will not be a high-brow magazine. It aims at being comprehensive and interesting to as many people as possible. But it will not be written down to suit the needs of an imaginary audience of the semi-educated and half-witted."[15] The inaugural issue featured as its frontispiece a previously unpublished portrait of Mansfield while Murry's editorial essay fearlessly, albeit rather simplistically, tackled the issues of life, death, and faith:

> Belief in life is not, strictly speaking, an idea at all. It is a faith.
>
> A moment comes in a man's life when suddenly all the hard things are made plain, when he knows quite simply that there is a good and a bad, that he must fight for the one and make war on the other.
>
> And the good things are the things which make for life, and the bad things are the things which make for decay … THE ADELPHI is nothing if it is not an act. It is not a business proposition, or a literary enterprise, or a nice little book in a pretty yellow cover; it is primarily and essentially an assertion of a faith … that life is important.[16]

Immediately following Murry's essay were Katherine Mansfield's story "The Samuel Josephs" and Lawrence's "Trees and Babies and Papas and Mamas," which was chapter 4 of his *Fantasia*. H.M. Tomlinson was next with "The Estuary," a long story that concluded in the next issue, and then came Koteliansky's translation of a letter Chekhov sent to a friend regarding a play he was planning to write, *The Wood Demon*, the early version of *Uncle Vanya*. Koteliansky's choice was rather odd, even though the timing for it was understandable: Constance Garnett's translation of Chekhov's major plays came out that year, and Kot's publication was obviously intended to supplement it. But the translated letter had just a brief outline of the proposed play and some discussion of the characters and their names. To an English reader it probably meant absolutely nothing.

Koteliansky was almost definitely responsible for one other item in the issue, even though it does not carry his name as a translator. In the "grab bag" section of the journal, called "Multum in Parvo," the first item, "Dostoevsky and Drapery," was a translation from the memoirs of Russian painter Karl Briullov, whose father apparently witnessed Dostoevsky's outburst on the subject of Raphael's Sistine Madonna being placed against tasteless drapery. At the end of the issue, where the editor made recommendations for "Books to Buy" and "Books to Borrow," Koteliansky and Murry's translation of *Dostoevsky: Letters and Reminiscences* was under the "Books to Buy." The entry, however, was stripped of the translators' names, most likely so it would not strike the readers as self-serving.[17]

In the next six months Koteliansky had five more translations, all, save for the November item, of Maxim Gorky, published by *The Adelphi*: "More Recollections of Tolstoy" in July; "Recollections of Tchehov" in August; "authorized translation" of "From My Diary" in October; "Letters from Tchehov to Gorky," in November, and his and Mansfield's "authorized" translation of "Reminiscences of Leonid Andreyev" in February and March. Lawrence, likewise, had a chapter from *Fantasia* appear in virtually every issue. While Kot liked *The Adelphi* for the opportunity it afforded him as a translator, his larger objective for its creation was not being met: the new publication failed to impress Lawrence. "*The Adelphi* ... came," he wrote to Kot after receiving the first issue, "and oh dear, I was badly disappointed. It seemed to me so weak, apologetic, knock-kneed, with really nothing to justify its existence ... No really! Is this the best possible in England?"[18] For a while it even appeared that rather than enticing Lawrence to come back to England, *The Adelphi* might cause him to cancel the visit that he had planned prior to its publication. "Murry's *Adelphi* came," he wrote to his US publisher in mid-June. "How feeble it is! Oh God, am I going back to Europe to that? ... I don't feel like supporting the knock-kneed *Adelphi*, Katherine Mansfield's ugly bits etc."[19] "I don't know what I should write to your *Adelphi*," he grumbled to Kot in September.[20]

The prospects of Lawrence coming to England were further endangered when he and Frieda seriously quarrelled, and in August she set out on the voyage to

Europe by herself, not even sure she ever wanted to reunite with her husband. "I will not stand his bad temper any more," she declared to Adele Seltzer. "He can go to blazes, I have had enough."²¹ Lawrence chose to explore the West Coast of the United States and Mexico instead, still undecided as to whether he would make his way to England before the end of the year. His feelings about *The Adelphi* did not improve when, in the third (August) issue, Murry paid a dubious compliment to Lawrence by stating that "he is become, since Katherine Mansfield's death, incomparably the most important English writer of his generation."²² Lawrence wrote to Murry in mid-August that he "liked this month's *Adelphi* best"; yet in October, in another letter to Murry, he fully showed his frustration with what he thought was Murry's gross exaggeration of his late wife's talents: "Poor Katherine, she is delicate and touching. – But not *Great*! Why say great?"²³ His irritation over Murry's aggrandizement of Mansfield appears to have further jaundiced Lawrence's assessment of her work as a whole. Sending her last collection, *The Dove's Nest and Other Stories*, to a friend in New York, Lawrence could not resist savaging it: "I posted Kath. Mansfield's last book. I think it's a downright cheek to ask the public to buy that waste-paper basket."²⁴

Back in England personal relationships in Kot's circles were spiralling into chaos. Dorothy Brett, guided, she thought, by the otherworldly spirit of Katherine Mansfield, was having an intimate relationship with Murry, which led to her erroneously or wistfully believing – twice – that she was pregnant with his baby. She was also overcome with grief every time Murry appeared less than ready to marry her. Still Brett's confidant at the time, Kot would receive exhaustive daily descriptions of the status of her dealings with Murry.²⁵ Frieda's appearance in London complicated things even further: determined to separate from Lawrence, Frieda felt free to pursue her own relationship with Murry, who soon accompanied her to Germany. Kot, by then, must have felt his red-hot rage rapidly rising against all three "blighters," but, for the sake of Lawrence's return, he kept it in check. And, with the same goal in mind, he did something else that was utterly unlike him. Instead of being happy that Frieda and Lawrence had split up, possibly for good, Kot urged Frieda to send a cable to Lawrence indicating that she missed him and wanted to see him in London.

Kot must have been exceedingly nice to Frieda while at it, so nice, in fact, that she praised him to a friend: "I had great discussions with Kot, who is really a very decent person."²⁶ She was still reluctant to ask Lawrence to come, but Kot appears to have convinced her that, without her, Lawrence would soon die. "Now you have made me telegraph to Lawrence," Frieda reproached him after the fact, "and I am not at all sure that he thinks I feel lovey-dovey; I don't; I am cross in my heart with all so-called 'men!'"²⁷ Kot's ploy worked. Lawrence informed Kot on 20 November that he had bought his ticket to England and would be "glad to see you & pick up again the old connections." To make sure that Kot's expectations would not soar, Lawrence added: "I've lost my faith in the old world."[28]

Lawrence's anti-England sentiments must have been very painful for Kot, not only because it made Lawrence's permanent return less likely, but also because Kot was a true fan of his adopted country. He once assured Juliette Huxley that the English were "the most innocent, the most decent, the best human beings on earth."[29] "No more patriotic refugee ever came to this nation," writes John Carswell, who also quotes Kot as saying that England was so "old, ordered, spiritually disciplined" that no violent revolutions could happen there – which to Kot, no longer a revolutionary of any kind, was a great thing.[30] The quote comes from Kot's letter to Sydney Waterlow in 1926 and is his response to the General Strike of that year. It was called by the General Council of the Trade Union in solidarity with English miners, whose wages were about to be reduced by their employers. Gratified by how peaceful the confrontation was, Kot – very naively, as we know now – suggested to Waterlow that England could become a powerful role model for the rest of Europe: "The experience of the general strike here was really a very valuable one, as it impressed me, a foreigner, seeing things in a different way than the native. It revealed to me an aspect of the English character which I wanted to believe to exist, yet did not believe it. And that crisis, – for it was tremendously serious, – showed me that an old, ordered, spiritually disciplined nation can really be, inspite of all the evidence to the contrary. [...] I believe that the people generally have learnt a great useful lesson, and the English example may help on to introduce order in Europe, instead of disorderly eruptions."[31]

He expressed a similar idea to Virginia Woolf soon after the October Revolution: she recorded in her diary that while Kot thought revolution would lead to nothing good in Russia because the country was so uncivilized and unstable, "here in England its bound to come with immense benefit because we've carpets & gas in our poorest houses."[32] As Lady Glenavy informs us, Kot's "love of England [even] included the Royal Family," despite his strong anti-monarchist feelings back in Russia, but, she adds, "there was a time when he disapproved of the Princesses going to dances and night-clubs 'just like any other girl on the Finchey Road – Princesses should be different.'"[33] And though he himself never revealed much sexual interest in women, Kot once wrote to May Sarton, who he knew preferred women to men, "When we meet I'll entertain you to a long discourse on the superiority of English women to all other European women. The theme of discourse: 'Even the best continental women are only parvenus as compared to the best English women.'"[34]

When Lawrence arrived in early December, Kot was there to greet him, as were Frieda and Murry, who was struck by how "positively ill" Lawrence looked and how "his face had a greenish pallor." Lawrence was definitely not thrilled to be back. "Almost the first words he spoke," wrote Murry, "were: 'I can't bear it.' He looked … as though the nightmare were upon him again."[35] That Lawrence was not interested in assuming the editorship of *The Adelphi* became obvious to Murry right there on the platform, but Kot continued to be in denial. He had worked too hard to allow his hopes to be dashed the moment Lawrence stepped onto English soil again.

For his part, Lawrence truly regretted having returned to England. "[L]oathe London – hate England," he wrote to his New York publisher, "feel like an animal in a trap … Taos is heaven in comparison."[36] His other letters to friends in the United States carried the same message day after day. To a friend back in New Mexico he complained: "Here I am. London – gloom – yellow air – bad cold – bed – old house – Morris wall-paper – visitors – English voices – tea in old cups – poor D.H.L. perfectly miserable, as if he was in his tomb."[37] Kot, in the meantime, was only getting more ambitious. "Koteliansky has a scheme," Lawrence informed his literary agent in January, "to become a small publisher of special books. He thinks that by May he should have some five or six books ready: The Adelphi Press: with Murry and myself and Kot and two others all partners in the company."[38] Soon it was apparent even to Kot, however, that Lawrence had no plans to edit *The Adelphi*, co-found a publishing house, or stay in London. Within days of his arrival, Lawrence, in fact, already seemed to have convinced Murry to drop *The Adelphi* and follow them to Taos. "Middleton Murry wants to come along," Lawrence informed Mabel Dodge Luhan on 19 December, "also, probably, Dorothy Brett, who paints, is deaf, forty, very nice and daughter of Viscount Esher."[39]

Some time in late December Lawrence took Kot, Murry, Gertler, and Brett to see *The Covered Wagon*, a 1923 Hollywood western that had just opened in England and was showing in the Hampstead Theatre on the Strand. The movie was made on a massive scale, with a cast of about 3,000, of whom one third were genuine American Indians. It told a story of American pioneers in the middle of the nineteenth century making their slow and often treacherous way from Missouri to Oregon in a long train of covered wagons. On their journey west they encounter both friendly and hostile Indians, the latter coming close to killing the heroine with their arrows. There is, of course, a love interest too, with two men competing for the young heroine's affection. *The Covered Wagon* was mostly filmed in Nevada and around Four Corners, where Utah, Colorado, Arizona, and New Mexico come together, so the terrain was quite familiar to Lawrence.

"I am sitting next to you," Brett would record in her memoir later, addressing herself to Lawrence, "in that long, dark movie house. You are tense with excitement, and we are all infected by your love for the West ... You seem to be greeting old friends, far off across that long, dark movie house ... You are watching it, as if you were part of it yourself. 'How like it is, how like it is,' you keep on saying."[40] Brett, of course, would follow Lawrence to New Mexico, and her cabin there would be just slightly larger than the covered wagons she was seeing on the screen that day. Gertler almost got infected, too: "I am feeling sick of things," he wrote to Kot soon after, "and ... I could go to Mexico myself! – But not with Brett or Murray [*sic*] because in their company Mexico would seem merely like the Hampstead Cinema!"[41]

Kot was unpersuadable, though. At one point in the film, a white trader and a guide for the party drink a toast "To the days that's gone when a friend could trust a friend!" – and that was perhaps the only notion in the entire movie that Kot was generally sympathetic to.[42] The movie overall must have produced a disconcerting impression on him. On the one hand, the long-bearded American pioneers in homespun clothes looked a lot like the poor Jews in his native Ostropol. On the other, both the high desert landscape and the Indians would definitely appear alien to him; as would the American English in the intertitles, which tried to imitate the settlers' idiomatic and often less than grammatical usage. The idea of this kind of "Rananim" across the ocean could not appeal to him, no matter how much he wanted to be near Lawrence. The American Wild West did have its colourful share of Jewish cowboys, but as a young man Kot had lived for far too long in a small place in the middle of nowhere to be tempted to trade London for a tiny log cabin in the hills and valleys of a distant American state.

Lawrence was determined "by early March ... to be in New York; and in New Mexico by the end of that month."[43] Kot's frustration with the failure of his plan to use *The Adelphi* to lure Lawrence back to London found its most manic manifestation at a dinner party at the Café Royal organized by the Lawrences for a small group of friends – among them Kot, Gertler, Murry, and Brett. What occurred in the gilded room of the Café Royal has been one of the most discussed events in the literature about Lawrence. Many focus primarily on the impact the gathering had on Lawrence's relationship with Murry, who had by then most likely become Frieda's lover.[44] Some, in fact, refer to it as the "Last Supper," where "Murry played Judas to Lawrence's Jesus."[45] But in Lawrence's mind there was, undoubtedly, more than one betrayal going on in that room. He after all had summoned his friends to urge them once again to follow him to New Mexico in order to help create the "Rananim" colony there. This was, in essence, Lawrence's last chance to convince them to believe both in his vision and in his leadership – and, as such, it largely failed. Likewise it was Kot's last – and even more futile – attempt to persuade Lawrence not to go away.

While there are several published accounts by people who were there, none gives the precise date, but Lawrence's biographer, David Ellis, believes that between Lawrence's spells of illness and his friends' Christmas family commitments, the Café Royal dinner could have only taken place between 21 and 24 December.[46] The most detailed description of this "charming dinner at the Café Royal," as Lawrence would sarcastically refer to it a year later,[47] comes from Catherine Carswell. Her husband, Donald, was there, too, and Kot managed to immediately conceive "a murderous dislike" for him: "Lawrence began to talk in Spanish (which he learned in Mexico). Donald, who prided himself on knowing a bit of Spanish … endeavoured to engage in Spanish conversation with Lawrence. This, for some reason, infuriated Kot to such a degree that he looked like taking the unwary Donald's life … Kot's idea seemed to be that Spanish language was Lawrence's special perquisite." Then Kot rose to his feet and delivered a long, Russian-style toast "in praise and love of Lawrence." It was, according to Carswell, "punctuated by his deliberate smashing of a wine-glass at the close of each period. As – 'Lawrence is a great man.' (Bang! Down came Kot's strong fist enclosing the stem of a glass, so that its bottom came in shivering contact with the table.) 'Nobody here realizes how great he is.' (Crash! Another good wine-glass gone.) 'Especially no woman here or anywhere can possibly realize the greatness of Lawrence.' (Smash and tinkle!)."[48]

Koteliansky himself gave an oral account of the dinner to Stephen Spender in 1952, which Spender then recorded in his diary: "Kot's version of this is that it was ruined by the fact that Lawrence, who was staying with Catherine Carswell and her husband, brought them to the dinner in the private room without having told the little group, Gertler, Kot … and Murry that he was going to do so. There was also Brett there. As soon as the party was assembled, Lawrence realized that he had done the wrong thing to bring his hosts. Out of a kind of defiance he started talking Italian,[49] though the only people who could understand him were the Carswells. Catherine Carswell's husband started also talking Italian, and Kot said to him that if he went on he would throw him out of the window. Carswell realized that K was serious and shut her husband up. Lawrence realized that the whole atmosphere was ruined and started drinking and getting excited – usually he did not drink at all – and vomited. He was terribly unhappy, Kot said, and kept on returning to the theme of Lawrence's terrible unhappiness … 'Frieda of course enjoyed the whole occasion very much, in the same way as she enjoyed everything always.'"[50]

Whether she truly enjoyed herself or not, Frieda actually happened to agree with Kot's assessement of Mr Carswell. "I see a lot of Cath. Carswell," she had informed Adele Seltzer three months prior to this fateful evening, "she is so nice but has a nasty child and a failure of a husband!"[51]

Soon after the party, Sarah Gertrude Millin, a South African writer who had met the Lawrences and Koteliansky several days earlier, invited the three of them for dinner. According to her, "The Lawrence party arrived very late, and without Mr Koteliansky. There had been, it appeared, a row with Mr Koteliansky about Tolstoi, and this row made them late, and it had prevented Mr Koteliansky from coming at all." The row may have been further exacerbated by Frieda choosing to wear "a white Russian blouse" for the occasion.[52] Instead of Koteliansky, the Lawrences brought along Brett, who was rapidly becoming another victim of Kot's "murderous dislike," as he – and others – were observing her nascent infatuation with Lawrence.

While Kot was tolerant of Brett's attachment to Murry, as long as he needed Murry to be a co-conspirator in luring Lawrence back, her love interest in Lawrence was too much for him to take. In an angry phone call in mid-January he, according to Brett, "pounce[d]" on her and made her feel "hurt," "uncomfortable," and confused as to the reason for his rage.[53] Finally Kot informed Brett that he could no longer be her friend. She tried to reassure him that she was not after Lawrence at all, that she still considered herself Murry's loyal lover, and that it was not in her character to be unfaithful ("[Murry] is free – but I am not – I keep myself clean"[54]) – but to no avail.

Whatever it was that Kot told her upon ending their relationship, it was powerful enough to deeply shock her. She had grown to consider Kot "family" to such an extent that it irritated her real family, whose attitude toward Jews was not as charitable as hers. "I am glad you find a Russian Jew more helpful than your brothers and relatives," her father, Reginald Brett, wrote to her once. "It used to be the fashion for young men to go to the Jews when they got into scrapes. I fully realise both the equality and similarity of the sexes in these days."[55] Now feeling betrayed, Brett kept appealing to Kot to reconsider: "I could not reconcile you with it. There has been a mistake … I believe more in my friends."[56] But there was no mistake. Brett was out of Kot's life forever and, from then on, firmly in the category of people he loved to hate. When she made an attempt to resume their friendship two years later, Kot would not hear of it. "Brett was here some time ago," he wrote to Ida Baker in December 1925. "She … had the impudence of wanting to come and see me. But she was warned not to."[57] Frieda, on the other hand, never stopped believing that Brett's attention toward Lawrence during that winter was instigated by Kot himself, now in order to split her and Lawrence up again. She thought Kot's anger actually stemmed from his frustration with Brett for making such a hash of his scheme. "How Lawrence would have hated him," she wrote to Brett in 1932, "for practically putting it into your head that Lawrence might marry you and I Murry – and then *hating you* for his tricks."[58]

At the end of January Lawrence and Frieda went to Paris and from there to Germany to visit Frieda's family. As planned, by early March they were back and ready to depart for New Mexico. Brett joined them. Murry promised to follow in April but never did. Koteliansky was not among the people who saw the party off. "I left Kot with a sore head," Lawrence wrote to Gertler from onboard the *R.M.S. Aquitania* sailing to New York, "but better that than a sore heart and spirit. It's no good, the Old Jehovah does *not* rule the world any more. He's quit."[59] Kot had indeed quit trying to rearrange Lawrence's life, but his other battles, including those surrounding *The Adelphi,* were far from over. There would also be plenty of "a sore heart and spirit" to come.

Lawrence's refusal to have anything to do with *The Adelphi* meant to Murry that he was no longer just a placeholder: it was now truly his journal. This change in attitude is well documented by *The Adelphi* issues for 1924. The January issue was dominated by Murry's homage to his wife occasioned by the anniversary of her death ("In Memory of Katherine Mansfield"); his long essay on "Religion and Christianity" (a topic near and dear to Murry's heart at the moment, since he was undergoing a religious revival); and "Extracts from Katherine Mansfield's Diaries." Koteliansky – again anonymously – contributed two paragraph-long bits of trivia: one about Einstein's proclamation that "Dostoevsky gives me more pleasure than any scientist," and the other dealing with Tolstoy's will, wherein the writer asked scholars analysing him to "dwell upon those passages in which I know the Divine power spoke through me."[60] The February issue also carried a translation from Koteliansky, but it was one he had worked on with Mansfield ("Reminiscences of Leonid Andreyev"), and, in an obvious slight to Kot, her name appeared first in the credits. The same issue contained a poem and another story by Mansfield ("Something Childish but Very Natural"), and a poem by a young woman, Violet Le Maistre, an uncanny Mansfield lookalike, who would soon become Murry's second wife. By the May 1924 issue there were no traces of Koteliansky even in the "Multum in Parvo" section.

In early October 1924, Kot wrote a letter to Murry in which he emphasized his disapproval of Murry's editorial practices and stated his opinion that *The Adelphi* should simultaneously expand and go back to its roots in order to become again what it had supposedly been conceived as by its founders: a magazine with "a life of its own, irrespective of the views, beliefs and convictions of anyone of its contributors."[61] In response, Murry suggested that his mind was at the moment "on other things" and that Kot, too, should have other interests: "You don't think about anything else than *The Adelphi*, I do. It would be a good thing if you thought about something else; then you wouldn't get depressed about *The A* ... the A. never will be A BIG MAGAZINE ..." Murry then unapologetically acknowledged that *The Adelphi* was indeed changing to suit him as the editor: "That isn't vanity at all. But I am convinced that I have a work to do, a function to perform, in the world: and the Adelphi is the instrument of that function. It is not, never has been, and never will be a thing in itself."[62]

The latter point was quite well taken by Murry. *The Adelphi*, indeed, was never planned to have "a life of its own" and be "a thing in itself." It was originally intended by both Kot and Murry as a mouthpiece for Lawrence, but Lawrence, as Murry pointed out to Kot several days later, "didn't care a rap about" *The Adelphi*,[63] so Kot's real objections were not as much to the nature of the journal as to whose mouthpiece it had become. But then Murry added something else to his letter, which would stun Kot to the core: "You and I have at bottom quite different attitudes to life. The mere fact that I do most sincerely believe in an absolute truth will convince you how different they are."[64]

It was not difficult for Kot to see that Murry was referring to the Christian version of the "absolute truth," which he, as a Jew, supposedly could not possibly grasp. Kot protested: "Here is my notion of truth: truth *per se*, with whatever adjective, is to me a plaything of the mind. Only truth *felt*, *seen* by great men, chiefly by writers, is truth, and such truth is always reticent and shy." Kot once again listed his objections to how *The Adelphi* was run, and to his diminishing role in it: "By your letter you destroy [the] original idea and introduce a perfectly new one, namely, of transforming the A. into your own instrument. Even if I kept silent you would know that I could not accept the new situation as too humiliating to my dignity as a man who does not like to deceive himself with words, however unpleasant the consequences of lack of self-delusion might be. Simply stated you offer me to become a sort of an errand boy in the A., for you know that once the original idea is gone, there could be no interest for me to be connected with the A. except the salary."[65]

Kot then offered to resign from *The Adelphi*. Murry, who, in the best of times, viewed Koteliansky as nothing more than a "pleasant piece of furniture,"[66] was now convinced that "either he must cease to be editor, or Koteliansky to be business editor."[67] And yet, perhaps in an attempt to be a humble and compassionate Christian, which he now believed he should be, in his 8 October letter he pulled his punches and sounded almost apologetic, suggesting that he was not really establishing "a new principle," and that Kot's role in *The Adelphi* "is just

the same as it ever was."[68] Several days later, instead of accepting Kot's resignation, Murry went even further in his exercise of humility and actually proposed
that Kot could take over *The Adelphi* entirely by himself while Murry would
"promise to write as well as I can for *your* magazine month by month without
payment until you are in a position to pay me."[69] Kot was no doubt puzzled by
the offer but cautiously accepted it, saying it was "perfectly fair."[70] But then Murry
just as suddenly changed his mind about contributing to *The Adelphi* under Kot's
stewardship: "If you take control of the A. it will be *impossible* for me to write in
it … The break must be absolute and entire. I am sorry that I did not realize this
when I wrote to you."[71]

What Kot meant to do when he accepted Murry's unexpected offer was to
agree to it provisionally, in hope that the rest of the founders were willing to go
along with the switch. He soon found out that they were not. Their understandable reluctance – which Murry must have clearly foreseen – was furthered by,
among other things, the ugliness of the side battle that Kot was waging with
Philip Tomlinson, by now a regular contributor and active in running the office.
It all started when Kot recruited Tomlinson to be his English helper in the translation of *The Life and Letters of Anton Tchekhov*, the project Kot had begun with
Katherine Mansfield several months before she died. With Lawrence away in the
USA, Mansfield dead, Murry too busy with *The Adelphi*, and the Woolfs, as well
as their press, no longer available, Kot had little choice but to settle on someone
of a lesser stature – something that Kot, with his usual insistence on an honest
slap being preferable to a false kiss, kept pointing out, again and again, to Philip
Tomlinson. Tomlinson, who would later become an influential literary critic,
writing for many years for *The Times Literary Supplement*, was, in the eyes of
those who knew him, "slight and sensitive, modest and mild-mannered, silent
in strident company … laconic … meditative."[72] Kot's version of stridency
when it came to both their translation and *The Adelphi*, made Tomlinson go far
beyond his characteristic silence and laconism.

As the book was being readied for publication in early summer 1924, Tomlinson, who by prior agreement had consented to receiving just a third of all profits
(whereas Lawrence, Mansfield, Murry, and the Woolfs had all received half), was
"nettled," as he put it, when Kot suddenly proposed to leave his name out as the
second translator. He objected in a letter that mixed poor attempts at light-
heartedness with outright indignation: "It's just as well to get things right at first.
It's better than brooding, as Tchehov said to his missus … there's a good old chap
… I am not afraid of comparing mine with the work of any of your collaborators." The letter ended with a plea that since "truth is essential between friends"
the two of them "must be perfectly straight."[73] Their relationship got only worse

once Kot began his negotiations with Murry over the editorship of *The Adelphi*. In October, several days after Murry suggested Kot should run the journal, Kot offered the editor's position to Tomlinson's elder brother, H.M. Tomlinson, who was considered the second most valuable contributor to the magazine after Murry. Philip Tomlinson felt slighted again, and the natural sibling rivalry with his better-known brother only fuelled the fire. "I resent editorship being offered Harry," he cabled to Kot on 27 October. "I have given much time & work to Adelphi and will not allow my interest to be bartered by you nor Murry nor Harry."[74]

H.M. Tomlinson refused the editorship anyway, and once it became clear that Koteliansky could not gain the support of the other founders, Murry withdrew his offer to Kot. By then Kot himself decided that without the support of most of the founders he was in no position to run the publication, and yet he felt incensed that he was deprived of an opportunity to step away with dignity: "In accepting your offer to take over the Adelphi I had in view only and exclusively to continue it on its original lines and by its original founders. Having failed in this I have made no other attempt to avail myself of your offer. So that now you are free of me and I leave the A. for good and ever. I only await your advice as to when I should hand over the key and the petty cash. I would rather hand it over personally to you or to H.M. Tomlinson."[75]

A telegram that impulsively followed the letter made it clear, however, that Kot was not quite ready to let it go: "In created situation my decision is final but there is one more way of reconstructing Adelphi and your immediate presence here is urgent."[76] Murry, who was in the countryside, was not amused: "Whether I had the right to offer it to you, or you to accept the offer, the situation as between me and you is clear. You cannot run the A. alone. Therefore it reverts to me." Murry added that he would still come if a full meeting of the founders could be arranged. Murry then sent copies of the letter to the full board.[77]

Two days later, Murry insisted that Kot should turn his key to the office over to Philip Tomlinson, who "must have complete charge of the Adelphi; and as it is impossible for him to do the necessary work unless he is alone at the office, I am assuming that for the time being you will not go to the office."[78] This was reinforced by Philip Tomlinson's wire the same day, which no longer contained any pretences of civility: "Situation unendurable. Refuse to attend office while you remain."[79] Unwilling to be unceremoniously evicted from the office and thus allow Philip Tomlinson to triumph, Kot suggested to Murry that he should "remain in the office of the A. for another few days so that no harm should come to the A. through any fault of mine." He also sarcastically referred to Tomlinson as "the fine fellow."[80] Murry, who was genuinely grateful to Tomlinson for his service, took umbrage at Kot's insulting him and requested again that Tomlinson should be allowed to work in peace: "If Phil. Tomlinson has the key and is alone in the office, the A. for December will appear without any trouble."[81] The next day, Tomlinson informed Kot in an angry three-page letter that it was he now who was resigning from *The Adelphi* because Kot was still in the picture. The letter also gives us a good – albeit unsympathetic – glimpse of what Kot's ideas were for "reconstructing" *The Adelphi*: "I understand that Murry has proposed a conference consisting of himself, you, Sullivan, H.M. and myself to settle it. Well, it must be settled without me … You object to Murry's editorship: his conduct … does not accord with the ideals and and principles – oh! these terrific words! – on which the 'Adelphi' was founded … Knowing your ideas (for I have heard them every day for the Lord knows how long: starting publishing business and weekly papers without capital; adding to the number of pages in the 'Adelphi' without, in some mysterious way, adding to the cost of production; more expensive contributors when we haven't enough money to pay the present ones decently) I object as strongly to your conception of the 'Adelphi' as you do to Murry's."[82]

On 10 November, Kot turned in both the keys and his final resignation: "Complying with the request contained in your letter … I placed the keys in an envelope with severing letter and took it down to the Savage Club … I declare again and finally that I have nothing more to do with the Adelphi in any way whatever, nor with you personally. Finis … I do not want anything of mine to appear in the Adelphi.[83]

The next day, Murry, in an apparent new burst of compassion and humility, had second thoughts. He admitted that there was "something all wrong about what is happening" and took part of the blame: "I think that I am wrong and that you are wrong." Murry also asked Kot not to make "any irreversible decisions" until he came back to London.[84] It was too late. The same day Kot wrote to H.G. Wells: "It finally came to an open quarrel with Murry, and I am out of the A." Kot then assured Wells that after having "argued, discussed, struggled, fought with Murry" in vain for seventeen long months to correct the direction *The Adelphi* was taking, he now felt "greatly relieved."[85] Kot expressed a different sentiment, however, to H.M. Tomlinson, to whom he indicated that he felt used and discarded by Murry – not unlike the young female typist in the office whom Murry had sacked, according to Kot, after the two had an affair. "[B]roken and weeping," Kot wrote to Tomlinson, the girl confided in him and regaled him with "a few facts of M's behaviour with regards to her." It seemed to Kot that "stripped of phrases, M's behaviour with regard to myself was of the same kind."[86]

Murry of course had a very different take on who the harasser and the victims were in this particular case. Sorting things out after Kot's death in a letter exchange with Beatrice Glenavy, who was fiercely defending Kot's reputation, he wrote: "[F]ortunately you never had to work with Kot in matters of practical business. He really was *too* difficult. He had the habit of treating people with whom he did not agree like dirt. The poor devil who put up money for *The Adelphi* he regarded as beneath contempt; his only function, in Kot's eyes, was to put up much more money than he did and ask no questions. Which was highly embarrassing for me."[87] In his published response to the *Times* obituary for Tomlinson, who, like Kot, died in 1955, Murry would pay a heartfelt tribute to the man who – unlike Kot – remained his good friend: "He was one of the most generous men I have ever known. At a time when I was having great difficulty, owing to illness, in carrying on the *Adelphi*, he took over all the hard work of editorship at a moment's notice, with scarcely any remuneration, simply in order to relieve me from worry."[88]

Kot's latest – and last – fight with Murry was finally over but the same could not be said of his battle with Philip Tomlinson. The two of them still had to work on the proofs of *The Life and Letters of Anton Chekhov*, and when H.M. Tomlinson rejected Kot's request to be the go-between for the warring parties, things got even more out of hand. "To state it in the plainest language," Kot wrote to Philip on 27 November, "it is humiliating for me to have anything further to do with you after your part in the affair of The Adelphi. But as I have a certain obligation to the publishers I have simply to compel myself to see the thing through." Moved by now by uncontrollable hatred and desire to hurt at all costs, he also indicated that he did not trust Philip Tomlinson's English and would therefore seek confirmation from a third party that it was acceptable.[89] Tomlinson, not surprisingly, found the letter "most insolent," and so, according to him, did H.M. Tomlinson, who advised his younger brother to seek "legal advice."[90] On 2 December, Philip Tomlinson apprised Kot that he was "legally advised to continue the work of seeing the Tchekhov book through the press in entire disregard of your letter of November 27."[91] Kot, in turn, accused Tomlinson of trying "to provoke me and bully me" and reiterated that he could no longer look on him "as on a gentleman."[92]

And so it went on and on, well into 1925, when things were finally settled, but not the way Kot was hoping they would. The book came out under both names, and the lawyer Philip Tomlinson hired made sure Tomlinson got a full half of the translators' share, rather than just one third.[93] Ironically, despite all the complications, the book was very well received. "The general level of the translation is exceedingly high," wrote a critic for the *Times* of London. "Mr Koteliansky and Mr Tomlinson merit nothing but praise for their careful, sympathetic labour."[94] The praise would be repeated thirty years later, when Kot's edition would be favourably compared to *The Selected Letters of Anton Chekhov*, edited by Lillian Hellman and released in 1955, several months after Kot's death.[95]

The other silver lining in the whole affair was that Kot had acquired a new friend and confidant: Sydney Waterlow, a son of London's one-time lord mayor and, as a young man, an unsuccessful suitor of Virginia Woolf. Kot and Waterlow, who was by then already a prominent diplomat, were mere acquaintances when, during *The Adelphi* squabbles, Waterlow wrote to Murry and took Kot's side, making Kot want "to shake your hand and to thank you for what, in your definite and clear attitude to M., I take, indirectly, to be also an act of friendship and support for myself."[96] Waterlow became a frequent visitor at "the Thursdays," weekly men-only gatherings, held at Kot's house or, until his marriage, at Gertler's apartment, where the participants discussed politics, literature, art, and, at times, just gossip.

The "salon," emulating Ottoline Morrell's more famous and less gender-exclusive "Thursdays" of the previous decade, was Kot's idea. In the 1930s, the meetings moved to Wednesdays and were then called, accordingly, "the Wednesdays." Sometimes they occurred over tea at the Twinings shop on Oxford Street, or over beer or dinner at several pubs, cafes, and restaurants, including "Ross's" – "the Jew's" or "The Wr-r-rotten Jews," as Gertler referred to it since the proprietor was Jewish[97] – near the Tottenham Court Road; Hans Appenrodt's Delicatessen on the Strand; Café Monico in Piccadilly, or a place called "Ridgeway's." Throughout the 1920s and early 1930s "the Thursdays" and "the Wednesdays" kept dying off and reviving again, but always with only a few regulars, despite Kot's best efforts. Chief among the regulars were: Gertler; Sullivan, Kot's only remaining friend from *The Adelphi*; W.J. Turner, a poet and a friend of Gertler's; Herbert Milne, a classicist and author on the staff of the British Museum; A.S. Fulton, Milne's colleague from the British Museum who was an orientalist; and, later, James Stephens. Sometimes they were joined by T.A. Levi, who taught jurisprudence at University College, and by John Mavrogordato, a poet and a Modern Greek scholar at King's College in London and later at Oxford, also a good friend of Gertler's.[98] When Waterlow was not around, Kot's letters informed him of who was there and what was discussed. It was very rare for the full cast to be present; frequently the meetings had no more than three or four people.

Lawrence watched the *Adelphi* turmoil from afar, glad, no doubt, that he did not have to participate or take sides. Once Lawrence left London, he and Kot in fact ceased communicating, and Kot relied on Gertler for any news of "the Mexican Troupe," as Gertler now labelled them.[99] "Kot and Murry have relapsed into disapproving silence – tant pis pour eux," Lawrence wrote to Gertler a month after the Lawrences went back to New Mexico where the two of them and Brett settled seventeen miles from Taos, in the cabins of a mountain ranch that used to belong to Mabel Luhan but now was officially Frieda's in exchange for the manuscript of *Sons and Lovers*.[100]

Kot's silence, however, was occasioned not just by his disapproval of Lawrence's departure. Around the same time he finally read and absorbed Lawrence's *Kangaroo*, which came out in September 1923. While in England, Frieda enjoyed spreading the notion that Ben Cooley in *Kangaroo* was, indeed, a fictional replica of Koteliansky. Lawrence's attempts at damage control were only half-hearted. "Kangaroo was never Kot. Frieda was on the wrong track," he wrote to Murry in October 1924. "And now Kot is sodden."[101] As to Kot and Murry's disagreements over *The Adelphi*, Lawrence once again chose to cast it in terms of Kot's Jewishness: "It is absurd, but here it is. The ultimate son of Moses pining for heavy tablets. I believe the old Moses wouldn't have valued the famous tablets if they hadn't been ponderous, and millstones round everybody's neck. It's just Hebraic."[102] In general, however, Lawrence took a plague-on-both-your-houses attitude. "Remember, you have betrayed everything and everybody up to now," Lawrence wrote to Murry in January 1925, now alluding to Judas rather than Moses. "It may have been your destiny. – But in Kot you met a more ancient Judas than yourself. There are degrees within degrees of initiation into the Judas trick … Kot is miles ahead of you."[103]

While away from Kot, Lawrence was not altogether deprived of the company of Russian Jews. One of them was Lawrence's US publisher, Thomas Seltzer, born in Poltava, Ukraine, and brought to the United States by his parents when he was a boy of twelve. The history of Seltzers' and his wife's association with the Lawrences is noteworthy because it sheds more light on Lawrence's ability to, on the one hand, have close Jewish friends while, on the other, seemingly never to forgive them the fact that they were Jews.

Thomas and Adele Seltzer visited the Lawrences in New Mexico in December 1922, and until autumn 1925, when the relationship, both personal and professional, abruptly ended, the Lawrences routinely stayed with them in New York every time they sailed to and from Europe.[104] Like Kot, Seltzer translated from Russian. "I know Russian well enough to have translated works by Gorky, Andreyev and other authors," he informed a prospective employer in 1933, after his publishing business ceased to exist.[105] In 1908, long before he became a publisher, Seltzer translated Gorky's novel *Mother* for B.W. Huebsch, and he, too, claimed to be Gorky's only "official translator and interpreter."[106]

The Seltzers were not just delighted but truly starstruck to have Lawrence as their author and friend. "[F]or once Fate seems kind," Adele gushed to her sister,

Henrietta, in 1921, "that she has granted to the little Russian Jew, Thomas Seltzer, to be the publisher of the works of a century marvel."[107] She expressed a similar sentiment in a letter to a friend two years later: "Lawrence is a Titan, and I go about with an ever-present sense of wonder that we, Thomas & I, little, little Jews, should be the publishers of the great English giant of this age."[108] Her husband, apparently, felt equally emotional about both his good fortune and Lawrence himself. "He carefully, most tidily, most scrupulously keeps L's letters in a locked drawer in the office," Adele wrote to Henrietta in 1922. "I have come upon him unawares when he has opened the drawer and is tenderly fingering the piles. He won't let me touch a letter unless I have just washed my hands."[109]

Lawrence's attitude toward the Seltzers was decidedly less romantic. "If Seltzer deals decently with me," he wrote to his agent in 1920, "then I don't mind if he is a Jew and a little nobody, I will stick to him. *I* don't really like Jews … Seltzer *may* do all well with me, and through me."[110] In autumn 1925, Lawrence decided that Seltzer, despite his bravery in publishing *Women in Love*, was not strong enough as a publisher or as Lawrence's champion, so he pragmatically chose to cast his lot with Knopf instead. This action devastated the Seltzers both financially and emotionally, but Lawrence was seemingly not moved much. "I did not care for New York," he complained to friends back in New Mexico in September. "I had to run about and see … the two little Seltzer's [*sic*] dangling by a single thread, over the verge of bankruptcy, and nobody a bit sorry for them … [T]he Seltzers had too many 'feelings.' Adele said dramatically to Frieda: 'All I want is to pay OUR debts and DIE.'"[111] To Kot he expressed himself even more brutally, albeit somewhat sympathetically: "Seltzer is hopeless, he ought to go bankrupt and have done with it … I wish he'd never existed, poor devil."[112]

Lawrence's resumed correspondence with Kot at the end of December 1925, when he informed him of Seltzer's dismal state of affairs, was preceded by more than a year and a half of total silence on both sides. For much of this time, however, going to Russia appears to have been frequently on Lawrence's mind, helped along, perhaps, by the presence in Taos of another Russian Jew, Leon Gaspard, a painter from Vitebsk (where he shared his teacher, Yehuda Pen, with Marc Chagall), who had joined Mabel Dodge Luhan's fast-growing community of artists in 1918. Gaspard left an account of a dinner at the Lawrences – whom he called "that tortured Englishman of genius … and his robust German wife" – where the couple started arguing, no food was served, and Mr and Mrs Gaspard just "crept quietly out."[113] Restless in New Mexico – as he was everywhere – and tired of his trips to Mexico, where during one winter he got so sick with what he came to believe was malaria that he thought he would die – Lawrence was both ready to sail back to Europe and seriously considering writing to Ivy Litvinov and paying her and her husband a visit in Moscow.

The Lawrences arrived in England on 30 September 1925. Lawrence immediately contacted Murry but not Kot; in fact, he specifically informed both Murry and Brett that he had no plans to seek Kot out.[114] Kot was, at the time, in the hectic midst of trying to get his niece and nephew over to Canada, but he still followed the news of the Lawrences' movements in England quite closely. "I am surprised to hear that there is a probability of Lawrence coming to London," Gertler wrote to Kot on 8 October, by which time Lawrence had already been in England for more than a week. Gertler further assured Kot that he had "no desire to see" Lawrence, would not "be sour if I miss him," and that, in general, "the kind of disturbance he creates is of the wrong sort – and does me only harm."[115] By 24 October, both Gertler and Kot already knew that Lawrence had contacted Murry, making Gertler exclaim: "So the friendship between Lawrence and Murry still persists. How awful that is! How glad I am to be out of it …"[116]

Between his health and personal life, Gertler had plenty of disturbances without Lawrence. Carrington, for whom he still deeply cared, had been living since 1918 in a complicated relationship with Lytton Strachey, the only man she truly loved despite their different sexual inclinations. Gertler was so incensed when he first learned about their cohabitation that, quite drunk after one of the parties the three of them attended, he followed Strachey and Carrington down a dark street and fiercely attacked Strachey with his fists. "Anything more cinematographic can hardly be imagined," Strachey told Clive Bell several days later, confessing that "it was at the time exceedingly painful."[117] In 1921 the situation became even more complex when Carrington married Ralph Partridge, a man deeply in love with her whom Strachey, in turn, passionately desired. The three of them would live together for the next eleven years. Gertler was so distressed by it all that he seriously contemplated buying a revolver and shooting himself, but the thoughts of what it would do to his mother stopped him.

"If I marry at all," he told his friends once, "it will only be to please my mother and then I must marry a Jewish girl."[118] Three years later, with Carrington no longer even a feasible dream and aware of how much it would please his mother, Gertler willed himself to fall in love with Phyllis Wilkinson, who was related to one of his brothers-in-law.[119] At the end of December the two secured permission from Phyllis's father for the marriage, and Gertler informed Kot he was engaged. He added that "my people are excited and pleased" and promised to "bring Phyllis along to Acacia Road."[120] The excitement did not last very long, however – at the end of January the engagement was called off. By then Gertler had realized that he was enticed not by Phyllis but by "the theory of marriage": "such ideals may be beautiful but they cannot be manufactured."[121]

When Gertler received the news of the Lawrences' coming to England in autumn 1925, he was back in a sanatorium because of a recent incident of pulmonary bleeding. The doctors were reassuring, saying that there was "no active trouble at all," but Gertler was understandably anxious.[122] To add to his troubles, his paintings were not selling well and his agent had just died. "My future seems dreadful to me," he complained to Kot on 24 September. "What with this pernicious disease hanging over me, and a still great uncertainty about money …"[123]

In November, Gertler's first-ever monograph, a small black-and-white catalogue of seventeen of his paintings, came out in the new series "British Artists of To-Day." Plate number three featured Gertler's 1921 portrait of Koteliansky (here spelled "Kotelianski"), where his melancholy-looking friend, wearing a dark three-piece suit, tie, and old-fashioned monocle in his left eye, is shown sitting in an armchair, with two large pillows propping his head. The latter is turned sideways, and his pensive eyes seem to glance at nothing in particular.[124] Even the appearance of the catalogue, however, did not manage to lift Gertler's spirits, especially since he was back in the sanatorium by then and experiencing "fit[s] of gloom" and "mood of super depression."[125] Kot tried to stay optimistic. "Gertler has been ill again, and only yesterday returned from a sanatorium," he wrote to Ida Baker in December. "I hope that his recovery now may be a permanent one, if he takes good care of himself."[126]

The Lawrences stayed in London until the end of October and then went to Baden-Baden to visit Frieda's mother. From there, Lawrence wrote to Brett, in response to her second inquiry about Koteliansky: "I did not see Kot: felt I couldn't stand any more."[127] Two weeks later the Lawrences were in Spotorno, on the Italian Riviera, and by then Lawrence was actively recruiting volunteers among friends and acquaintances to accompany him to Russia. Thus he invited Carl Seelig, a Swiss literary critic and translator (whom he had assured earlier that "Yes, the Russian novelists have meant a great deal to me"), to "pay us a visit, down here: and we can learn Russian, in preparation for the trip in the spring."[128] On 25 November, he reiterated to Brett that he had no interest in initiating contact with Koteliansky: "As for Kot, Murry … and the rest – well, I only saw Murry, and what was the good of that? Let the dead bury their dead."[129]

And yet, ten days later, Lawrence reached out to Kot. He needed Kot's advice about going to Russia but also had a convenient excuse for suddenly contacting him: the royalty cheque that Lawrence had (finally) received from Thomas Seltzer, by now his former US publisher, for his part in translating "The Gentleman from San Francisco." Lawrence proceeded to write to Kot in a matter-of-fact tone, as if nothing was ever seriously amiss in their relationship. Among other things, Lawrence asked Kot whether it was a good idea to go to Russia: "Should I, do you think? and could I? I have a feeling inside me, I should like to go to Russia."[130] Kot's response was clearly anything but immediately forgiving, as we can glean from Gertler's approval of the way Kot had handled the exchange: "I am surprised Lawrence wrote to you just now, because if he wanted to resume friendship I should have thought it would have been a good opportunity for him to have done so when he was in London recently – I think you were right to write to him as you did."[131] Consequently, on 18 December, Lawrence put aside the false casualness of his previous letter and almost begged Kot to let bygones be bygones: "Oh, but don't let's bother any more about people and lies. I am so weary of human complications. I expect I know you well enough, of myself, no matter what anybody says. In the end one's very heart gets tired. But somewhere, inside myself, I don't change: and I don't think you do."[132]

Earlier Kot had heard from Murry as well. Now remarried, Murry had his first child born in April 1925; soon after giving birth, his wife, Violet, developed health problems and, like Katherine Mansfield before her, was eventually diagnosed with tuberculosis. Wanting to spend more time taking care of Violet and the baby, Murry was again contemplating quitting the editorship of *The Adelphi*. Incredibly, he reoffered it to Koteliansky: "I have been thinking that it is only fair to offer it once more to you – on the conditions which, because of the bitterness I felt against you, I proposed and then withdrew a year ago – namely that I would continue to write for the Adelphi gratis, while dissociating myself completely from editing." Unlike Lawrence, Murry was not ready to resume even the semblance of a friendship with Kot, but he thought it should still not affect the transaction: "Personally I (and no doubt you also) am disinclined for a renewal of *personal* relations. But I think this is quite unnecessary. It is a business matter, & can be discussed in a businesslike way." If Kot was interested "in this proposition," he was instructed to look for Murry "during the morning & afternoon till 4 pm … in the British Museum Reading Room in sections A or B." If Kot was not interested, Murry urged him to send him a note "simply saying No, as soon as possible."[133] Perhaps not wanting to go through again what he had gone through in the closing months of 1924 – only to discover that others in *The Adelphi* still did not want him at the helm – Koteliansky declined Murry's offer. *The Adelphi* would, in fact, stay in Murry's hands for many years to come.

Kot did, however, decide to give Lawrence another chance. As a result, by early January, Lawrence and Kot were once again exchanging almost weekly letters. Lawrence was, as he informed Carl Seelig at the time, "still keep[ing] my idea of

Russia in the later spring.[134] He therefore asked Barbara Low to write to her sister, Ivy, "concerning my coming to Russia,"[135] even though he confessed to Brett that "Nobody encourages me in the idea."[136] It is not clear whether Kot was among those trying to talk Lawrence out of the trip, but he did oblige him with Farbman's 1924 study *After Lenin: The New Phase in Russia*.[137] He also sent him Russian grammar books because, like the Woolfs before him, Lawrence was now interested in learning Russian. (Lawrence even suggested that once he was back in England, Kot could give him "a few lessons."[138]) Having asked just for one text-book but receiving four, Lawrence jokingly complained that he felt "like a man who asked for a piece of bread, and was given a field of corn."[139] He also was about to order a copy of *Brothers Karamazov* since "the time has come to read Dostoevsky again: not as fiction, but as life."[140] This laid the foundation for Kot and Lawrence's last collaboration: Lawrence's introduction to Kot's translation of the "Grand Inquisitor" chapter of Dostoevsky's novel, which would become one of the best-known and most influential of the introductions he ever wrote for someone else's literary work.

As to Lawrence's dream of learning Russian and travelling to Russia, it was not to be. "Since I had influenza I abandoned my Russian Grammar in despair," Lawrence told Kot in March. By April he had made up his mind about his Russian trip as well: "I don't want to go to Russia now: I hear such dreary tales about it from people in Florence." "I feel the Bolshevists are loutish and common," he wrote in May. "I don't believe in them, except as disruptive and nihilistic agents. Boring!"[141]

# ROZANOV AND *LADY CHATTERLEY'S LOVER*: THE END OF AN ERA

Things don't get much brighter in the world, do they? That's why
one sticks to the Mediterranean, with its sun. But I hope you are well.
The thought of St John's Wood is gloomy to me.
~ Lawrence to Kot, 3 December 1928

Although I neither repent, nor regret my past, there is one thing
I am extremely sorry for, and that is that I have not manifested
sufficiently clearly my love to those whom I loved, and my affection
to those of whom I was fond.
~ Kot to Sydney Schiff, 14 December 1936

1923–26 was a very long stretch of darkness even for Koteliansky: the death of
Mansfield, his professional failures with the Hogarth Press and then *The Adelphi*,
the unsettling of his relationship with Lawrence, the humiliation of having to
borrow money – twice – in order to pay for his niece's and nephew's passage to
Canada. When Kot's orphaned nephew and niece came through England to visit
him at the end of 1925, it may have given Kot hope that at least the younger generation would be spared the grim fate of the family left in Ukraine, but then he
eventually learned of Eli's accidental death in Canada and was again plunged
into despair. In spring 1926 his application for naturalization in England was
rejected, which also upset him. All of it had taken a further toll on Koteliansky's
emotional well-being, and the notes of desperation and self-doubt were now
creeping more and more often into his correspondence.

"It gives me a great pleasure to be reminded that good and kind feelings exist,"
he wrote in summer 1926 to Sydney Schiff when Schiff, who was a wealthy man,
suggested that he would pay for Kot's vacation in Italy. "I cease at times to believe
that such a thing exists. I wonder whether it's because I am dried and shrunk up,
or life and circumstances are so unpleasantly complicated that whenever I meet

an unmistakable sign of friendship, – mixed with delight, I feel a sort of pang as though I don't deserve it or that I may forfeit it. I think that after all it must be a sign of badness for I know that good and kind people never experience such Hamletian feelings."[1]

Putting the blame on himself for failed friendships, however, did not lessen his anger toward others, including, paradoxically, the very same Sydney Schiff, who just half a year later was suddenly off Kot's list of good and kind friends. "Now here is another person who is finished to me – S. Schiff," Kot wrote to Waterlow in December. "He came here about five weeks ago – to a suite of rooms in the Savoy. From Switzerland he sent me several postcards, stating how young and happy he felt, completely free and without any cares. Perhaps out of perversity I could not stand that 'new happiness,' and did not reply to him … I have been in a 'black mood' for a considerable time before … I had to be at Schiff's at the Savoy at 9. I went to a pub. The whole affair seemed to me ridiculous – to make myself behave in a 'Christian way' toward Schiff, while I felt quite the opposite towards him. At 9 I was in the place … He began, – in his after dinner, good-for-digestion manner, – to argue that publishers were poor victims of lying journalists … He went on for a while, wanting me to confess now and then that I hated the capitalist system in general. By that time I was bored and ashamed of myself … When he finished I just rose up and said that, inspite of my dislike for romantic gestures, I must not see him again."[2]

This episode at Sydney Schiff's dinner is a true manifestation of Kot's emotional volatility at the time. Sydney Schiff, who wrote under the pen name "Stephen Hudson," was a minor novelist but a major patron of the arts in both England and France. In 1922, he and his second wife, Violet, had hosted a much talked-about party at the Majestic Hotel in Paris for Marcel Proust, for whom Schiff was a champion, a close friend, and later a translator. That was the party where Proust first met James Joyce, with the likes of Picasso, Diaghilev, and Stravinsky looking on. According to T.S. Eliot, Schiff was superb at running events of this kind because of his particular talent "of bringing very diverse people together and making them combine well."[3] As it turned out, however, making the combustive Kot mix smoothly with others at a much smaller dinner party was a bigger challenge.

Koteliansky's suggestion in the letter to Waterlow that he was trying to force himself to behave toward Schiff in a "Christian way" is particularly ironic because neither man was a Christian. Schiff's father, the son of a wealthy Trieste banker, was Jewish, and there is every indication that, despite his Christian mother, Schiff considered himself a Jew. Mrs Schiff was Jewish as well, and contemporaneous descriptions of the couple tended to emphasize their origins:

in one Sydney is depicted as "a jew with twisted yellow white moustache like an ex-colonel," while in another Violet is said to possess a "Biblical profile ... the feminine equivalent of some beautiful statue of Moses."[4]

Schiff's origins and self-identification as a Jew may have been, in fact, the main reason why, in the best Jewish tradition of "tzedakah" ("charity"), according to which Jews should help the less fortunate among them, Schiff chose to patronize not just famous writers, artists, and musicians but also Kot. Kot's feelings toward Schiff clearly ran the full gamut from sincerest gratitude to resentment for being treated like a poor relative. An anti-materialist, he also did not approve of Schiff's showing off his wealth. But it was the unwelcome feeling of being indebted to Schiff and therefore obligated to him in some way that seems to have triggered this outburst, as an undated letter to his niece makes clear: "You see, what is absolutely necessary is to be independent, particularly economically independent. The more you depend on others ... the more you dislike them, because one blames others for one's own insufficiency."[5]

Kot's rage in this instance and its consequences help us fully realize not only what a ticking emotional bomb he was at the time but also how the breakups he initiated often left the other party searching in vain for rational explanations. Schiff, understandably, was bewildered and deeply saddened. He had legitimate grounds to believe that he had been nothing but a kind and generous benefactor not just for Kot but his closest friends: he had bought several paintings from Gertler, and he and Violet had lavished Mansfield with warmth and hospitality when they were staying in Switzerland while Mansfield was undergoing her treatment there. The day after the dinner Schiff called on J.W.N. Sullivan, whom he also knew well, and described what had happened, calling it "tragedy." Kot and Sullivan met later the same evening and, according to Kot, "had some beer and a good laugh" over the whole incident as well as over Schiff's hurt feelings.[6] Violet Schiff's feelings were hurt, too; she never forgot that unfortunate event. Later, while acknowledging to their mutual friend Kot's "great wish to exercise a good influence on others" and his "fundamentally benevolent, kind and anxious to help" nature, she confessed that for her it was all overshadowed by his tendency "to hate most people he met," which she attributed to "the frustration of his personal aims and hopes."[7]

Kot's hatreds could be indeed inexplicable by any rational standards. Lady Glenavy remembered an incident when two women came by to see the pear tree that Mansfield had written about in her story "Bliss": "One was elderly and smartly dressed, carrying a little dog. The other was a young negress. Kot took a great dislike to the lady with the dog and ordered them out of the garden, saying it was private property ... When they were gone Kot was terribly sorry, because of the black girl; he wished he had been kind to them since she had come to see Katherine's pear tree."[8]

It is not clear whether friends like Sullivan or Gertler did not really mind Kot's explosive outbursts or just pretended not to for fear that otherwise they would also be on the receiving end of such "annihilations," as Lawrence called them. It is also not clear that anything or anyone could have helped. "You make yourself ill with hatred," Frieda Lawrence once told Kot.[9] Paradoxically, however, while in the long run his hatreds were destructive not just to those against whom they were directed but, as Frieda aptly pointed out, to his own inner core, in the short term they might have provided the essential adrenaline that kept him going. After all, he lived on strong emotions, but, away from his family, he was forced, at best, to share the tender attachment to people he loved – like Mansfield, Lawrence, and, later, James Stephens – with their spouses. Kot's hatreds, on the other hand, were largely his own, for very few people could match him in the intensity of this particular feeling.

His legendary compatriot, Hershel of Ostropol, warned that it was important for a fellow Jew to avoid the dangers of being "too bitter," for then the world would "spit you out."[10] Kot liked to pretend that he was the one spitting out the world instead, but deep inside he probably knew better and yet could not help himself. One can reasonably trace much of the bitterness to his growing up as a Jew in Russia, where lines were always drawn so starkly and where he himself felt so hated. The violence he had witnessed in his native land, the pogroms he had thought he was escaping when he fled Kiev at the start of the Beilis affair, and the tragic deaths of his family members after he had left could have all resulted in something akin to what we now refer to as post-traumatic stress disorder, with the accompanying depression, anxiety, and uncontrollable rage.

The burgeoning psychoanalysis movement in England in the 1920s,[11] spearheaded by Ernest Jones, a Welsh disciple of Freud, was just beginning to deal with what they called the "war shock" or "war neuroses." One of the earliest specialists in the field was Kot's and Lawrence's friend David Eder, who in 1917 wrote a study called *War-Shock: The Psycho-Neuroses in War - Psychology and Treatment*. The working definition of the term "psycho-neurosis" as used by Eder there was quite applicable to Kot: "any psychic shock or strain … provided it be of sufficient intensity relative to the nerve resistance of the individual." The preferred treatment right after the war was "suggestion under hypnosis," which, according to Eder, "cured" 70 percent of those he had treated.[12] However, as Jones pointed out three years later in "Traumatic Neuroses, Including War Shock," by 1920 "the passage over from the ranks of the hypnotists to those of the psycho-analysts has

… been very pronounced."[13] The traumatic shock of the war was soon recognized by politicians as well, and in 1922 the British War office Committee of Enquiry issued its "Report into 'Shell-Shock,'" which included testimonies from psychologists and a section entitled "Summary of Psychological Evidence."[14]

From Lawrence, we know that Kot read at least some Jung in 1918. "I send you the Jung book, borrowed from Kot, in the midst of his reading it," Lawrence wrote to Mansfield then.[15] And yet, Koteliansky, who prided himself on receiving confessions rather than giving them, was an unlikely analysand. Given Kot's general distrust of theoretical thinking of any kind – "I personally consider 'sophistication' the greatest obstacle to anything valuable," he once told Waterlow[16] – he no doubt agreed with Lawrence, who, in his 1921 *Psychoanalysis and the Unconscious*, accused psychoanalysts of being overreaching frauds who "have crept in among us as healers and physicians; growing bolder, they have asserted their authority as scientists; two more minutes and they will appear as apostles."[17] It would not be until 1936, and his first full-fledged breakdown, that Kot would allow psychiatrists anywhere near him.

Kot was also experiencing some health problems, which dated back to at least 1921. We do not know the exact nature of his medical complaints at the time but, judging from Gertler's relatively unconcerned response, Kot probably had made light of it. "I am sorry to hear about your disease," Gertler wrote in January 1921. "It sounds a very original ailment. Certainly I have never heard of it before." Neither, apparently, had Lady Glenavy who, according to Gertler, seemed "very interested and intrigued by your … ailment. She looked it up in a medical dictionary."[18]

Kot's financial well-being was even more in jeopardy than his physical condition following the breakup with the Hogarth Press and *The Adelphi*. In 1925–27 he did, however, manage to a large extent to replace *The Adelphi* as the home for his translations by publishing in *The Adelphi*'s rival, *The Calendar of Modern Letters*, one of whose editors, Edgell Rickword, was friendly with Lawrence. Soon after the first issue came out in March 1925, Koteliansky published his translations of Anna Dostoevsky's reminiscences of her husband, as well as Dostoevsky's 1867 letter to his mistress, Appolinaria (Pauline) Suslova, accompanied by an article by Leonid Grossman detailing the affair.[19] In the December 1925 and January 1926 issues Kot published his translation of Chekhov's *Wood Demon*. The same translation had appeared several months earlier in *The London Mercury*, another literary monthly to which Lawrence frequently contributed. A review in the *Times* justifiably called the play "interesting, if not important."[20] Subsequent installments in *The Calendar* featured selections from Vasily Rozanov's *Solitaria* (which

Kot would translate in its entirety later), and E. Gollerbach's article on Rozanov. Kot either did all the translations solo this time or he received some help from friends but chose to acknowledge or give credit to no one.[21]

He also hastened to produce the same translations as separate books. In 1926 *Dostoevsky Portrayed by His Wife: The Diary and Reminiscences of Mme Dostoevsky* came out from George Routledge & Sons. The book featured a lengthy "Prefatory Note" in which Kot explained the history of the diaries and their publication (they were not published in Russia until 1923). In addition to Anna Dostoevsky's diaries and Dostoevsky's letter to Pauline Suslova, both of which had appeared a year before in *The Calendar*, the volume contained newly translated letters relating to Dostoevsky's quarrel with Turgenev, Tolstoy's letters about Dostoevsky, and some writings from Dostoevsky's own notebooks. *Dostoevsky Portrayed by His Wife* did not sell well, and neither did a separate thin volume of Chekhov's *The Wood Demon*.[22] This and the sudden folding of *The Calendar* in summer 1927 led to Kot complaining to Waterlow in late 1927 that "it has become more and more difficult to make a living by translating."[23]

Kot then once again started thinking about becoming a publisher. Describing his decision to Waterlow, he confessed that in summer 1926 he "felt so depressed" that he "decided to look for a job": "I did a bit of looking, distressfully, and realized that it was just impossible, that I must do something which eventually may turn out useful in the way of giving me some sort of income. And I turned to my old idea – publishing." Yet, as he told Waterlow, this made his depression not better but worse: "Added to my usual 'black mood' there is also this unusual thing that I am trying to become a practical man, a publisher ... and the 'business worry' heightens the tint of blackness."[24] The renewed pursuit of a career in publishing also put him in need of Lawrence's help and advice once again.

The Lawrences came back to London – as it would turn out, for the last time as a couple – in September 1926. This time they did see Kot, who informed Waterlow of the details of the visit: "The few days [Lawrence] was in London he felt depressed and miserable and ill ... [H]e goes back to Italy next week. No longer Mexico and 'religion of death'; rather quiet; a sort of grumbling return to essentials; but not reconciled yet to various obvious things. He says that 'he is not going to write more novels for the swine' – the publishers and public ... We had no chance somehow of having a quiet talk; but if even he goes away without our talking about his present mood, there is somehow a silent recognition on his part of the change that is definitely taking place in him. I feel that the change is for the good."[25]

Kot was to be proven wrong on all three counts. Several months later Lawrence was still, in his own words, "tempted to go back to America." Europe, he thought, was "like a dying pig uttering a long, infinitely-conceited squeak," and America was "[a]t least [not] so depressing."[26] Lawrence was also writing another novel, the one for which he would become most notorious – *Lady Chatterley's Lover* – and Koteliansky would even play a substantial role in its genesis.[27] Neither was the change in Lawrence's mood "for the good" – he was, in fact, growing more and more depressed. "I feel a bit like you," he wrote to Kot in June 1927, "nothing nice ever happens, or ever will happen."[28] Having to deal with Kot's black moods again obviously did not help Lawrence's own state of mind, and he often sounded more impatient than sympathetic: "I had your little De Profundis: the worst of you is, there's never any *oro te* follows. Now what's the matter? Anything new, or just the continual accumulation of the same old badness? It seems to be a fight between you & time; whether Time will wear out your inertia, or your inertia will wear Time out. Caro, there's nothing to be said to you: one has long realized the futility."[29]

In autumn 1927, Lawrence found himself, once again, serving as a sounding board for Kot's idée fixe about starting a publishing company, except that now it had a bit of a new twist. While not availing himself of the therapeutic potential of psychoanalysis, Kot seems to have been prompted by its growing popularity in England to come up with the latest incarnation of his business "scheme," for he now began pitching to Lawrence the concept of an "Intimate Series," or confessional writings from famous writers, as a launching pad for the new enterprise.

In visualizing his latest project Kot was also perhaps influenced by the publication of the selections from Mansfield's *Journal* that Murry brought out that year. Almost too intimate for some – Dorothy Parker, for example, wrote in her review that she felt like apologizing to Mansfield for having read it[30] – *Journal of Katherine Mansfield* was a great commercial success in both England and the United States. At first Kot was just aghast at what he considered to be Murry's latest despicable act. Prior to the *Journal's* publication, Kot had tirelessly spread what would turn out to be a false rumour that Murry was bent on "dedicating Katherine's Journal to his second wife."[31] "I need to tell you, Ida," he complained to Baker after he read the book, "how disgusted I am by Murry … for a sheer profanation of K. How ashamed K would feel of having certain so strictly personal and intimate jottings made public and common."[32] He resented not only Murry's exploitation of his late wife for a monetary gain, he equally bristled at the fact that Murry had carefully excised any mention of Kot – as well as any negative comments about himself – from Katherine's entries. Yet, soon after the publication of the *Journal* Kot could also see quite clearly that confessional writings by famous writers did indeed sell very well.

What Kot had in mind for his new venture was a press along the lines of not just the early Hogarth Press, with its expensive limited editions, but also the Nonesuch Press, which had been founded in 1923 by Francis Meynell and Constance Garnett's son, David Garnett. Similarly to the Woolfs' press, which was undoubtedly an inspiration for Nonesuch, it used a small handpress to design books, and then had them printed by commercial printers. It was Nonesuch, in fact, that in 1926 published another collaborative production by Jane Ellen Harrison and Hope Mirrlees – *The Book of the Bear, Being Twenty-One Tales Newly Translated from the Russian*, a small volume, nicely decorated by Ray Garnett, David's then wife, featuring bear tales from Russian folklore, Pushkin, Tolstoy, and lesser-knowns like Vsevolod Garshin and Aleksei Remizov.[33] Harrison's and Mirrlees's translation could not fail to attract Kot's attention, especially since they had followed him as the Russian translators for Hogarth in 1924. Drawing on the example of Hogarth and Nonesuch, Kot now wanted to start by publishing the Intimate Series as "little books, 8,000 to 10,000 words each … limited edition of 400 copies maximum, at … £1."[34]

Lawrence had fresh memories of another Russian Jew, Thomas Seltzer, going bankrupt because, in Lawrence's mind, he should have never become a publisher, and he was justifiably skeptical about Kot's prospects: "You see no man today will risk himself in print, at least under his own name … Unless you could persuade a few people to do you an *anonymous* declaration: a *confessio* or an *apologia* in which he really said all he wanted to say – really let go."[35] "Myself, I feel it terribly difficult to write intimately," he continued two days later, "one feels colder and colder about unbosoming oneself. I'll give you anything I can give: but what in God's name am I to write *intimately*?"[36] Letting go was, of course, not in Kot's character, so Lawrence obligingly started writing "A Dream of Life," a fable about falling asleep in a quarry in Eastwood, his hometown, and waking up 1,000 years later. The "Dream" was clearly a version of his Rananim utopia:

> We climbed up towards the top of the town, and I felt I must be passing the very place where I was born, near where the Wesleyan Chapel stood. But now it was all softly lighted, golden-coloured porticoes, with people passing in green or blue or grey-and-scarlet cloaks. We came on top into a circular space, it must have been where our Congregational Chapel stood, and in the centre of the circle rose a tower shaped tapering rather like a lighthouse, and rosy-coloured in the lamplight.
>
> Away in the sky, at the club-shaped tip of the tower, glowed one big ball of light.[37]

He never finished the fable.

Another writer Kot approached was E.M. Forster, whose work he greatly admired and whom he must have originally met either through the Woolfs or through Lawrence. Kot and Forster started corresponding in 1924, with Kot mostly praising Forster's new publications and inviting him to come to their "Thursdays" (which Forster usually declined).[38] Forster's refusal to participate in the Intimate Series was apologetic but firm: "I have hunted well, both in my drawers and my heart, and can find nothing, nothing that will do. I am very sorry indeed. I realise so well it is no ordinary refusal – i.e. that you have (rightly or wrongly) this strong affection for my work and wanted to start your series with it, and that my inability to produce some definitely creates difficulty for you … [I]t does distress me that I should offer this duck."[39] His "drawers" by then contained a manuscript for *Maurice*, a novel about a character's awakening to his homosexuality. It could have not been any more "confessional," but while Forster's homosexuality was an open secret in Bloomsbury, *Maurice* was not for public view, even though Forster now and then did consider publishing it.[40] He showed the novel mostly to his homosexual friends, like Lytton Strachey and Christopher Isherwood. Kot was not close enough to Forster to know about *Maurice*, and, at any rate, it is highly doubtful that, no matter how sympathetic, he would have wanted Forster to use the Series to reveal his homosexuality.

Kot sought Wells's help too, asking in September whether Wells would allow him to come and see him "for a few minutes? … I would not trouble you, but I very much need your advice." The timing was all wrong, however. Unbeknownst to Kot at the time he was writing to Wells, Mrs Wells was dying of cancer. "I am so very sorry and distressed to hear of Mrs Wells' illness," he wrote to Wells three days later. "My troubles of which I wanted to speak to you and to be strengthened by your sympathy are as nothing to what you are going through now. From my heart and soul I offer you my love and devotion."[41] (Mrs Wells died on October 6.)

Being thus deprived of Wells's guidance, Kot put even more pressure on Lawrence, and Lawrence agreed to consult with Norman Douglas, a British writer living in virtual exile in Florence after he had been accused in England of indecent sexual assault and subsequently jumped bail. Douglas was associated with the Italian publisher and bookseller Pino Orioli, who often published English authors and would soon publish Lawrence's controversial *Lady Chatterley's Lover*. Having then heard back from Douglas, Lawrence, for reasons that were known only to him, chose to forward to Kot Douglas's original letter, in which Douglas wrote: "I wish I could do something for your little Jew, but it's quite impossible."[42] "[D]on't mind that he calls you a little Jew," Lawrence advised Kot, "it's merely Douglas."[43] What Lawrence left unsaid was that in his own letter to Douglas, asking for his advice, he had introduced Kot as a "friend of mine, Jew, but a poor one, [who] wants to become a publisher, on very little money: his peculiar paranoia."[44]

It appears Kot did not respond for almost a month after receiving Douglas's letter, since Lawrence's next letter was dated 22 November. In it he again behaved in a nonchalant manner, as if he was not aware that Kot's feelings could have been hurt by Douglas's "your little Jew" and his own casual reaction to it. He asked Kot how things were, and whether he had done "any more about your scheme." Lawrence then talked about publishing *Lady Chatterley's Lover* "here in Florence, myself privately," and ended the letter with "But tell me about the scheme, and what's to be done."[45] Kot did respond this time. By the end of December it was decided, at least by Lawrence, that the "scheme" "will have to wait a bit."[46] In January, Kot wrote to Waterlow that there was "still a scheme" but that his "first attempts to get manuscripts turned out a failure," and he had to abandon the Intimate Series idea: "I must change the original plan: perhaps, after all, I may succeed in becoming a publisher." He also assured Waterlow that he was feeling much better: "My 'blackness' is lighter now, for I have succeeded in selling a bit of 'old clothes' (translations) and shall be economically secure for a few months."[47] "Selling … old clothes" was a particularly Jewish metaphor that equally applied to the practices back in his old country and in England, where peddling used clothes was likewise becoming a typical occupation among recent Jewish immigrants from Eastern Europe. The translations that Kot sold to put food on his table were Anton Chekhov's *Literary and Theatrical Reminiscences*, and Vasily Rozanov's *Solitaria*, both of which came out in spring 1927.

*Literary and Theatrical Reminiscences* came out in March from Routledge & Kegan Paul. Without any introduction – in contrast to the earlier Routledge volume, *Dostoevsky Portrayed by His Wife* – or any explanation as to why all the disparate parts were put together in one volume, it was a veritable hodgepodge of reminiscences, diary entries, unfinished short stories, and one-act plays. It definitely contained a large share of "old clothes": some of the materials had already appeared in *The Life and Letters of Anton Tchekhov*, the volume Kot had produced, so eventfully, with Tomlinson for Cassell and Company in 1925; other parts came from *Reminiscences of Anton Chekhov* and *Anton Chekhov's Note-Books*, both of which Kot had translated with Leonard Woolf for the Hogarth Press. The new sections were reminiscences by not only writers but also Chekhov's relatives and friends, as well as directors (among them Stanislavsky) and actors of the Moscow Art Theatre, with which Chekhov worked most closely during the production of his plays. The last part contained several less-known short stories and one-act plays not previously translated into English.

Rozanov's monograph was the one Kot had tried to persuade the Woolfs to publish in 1923 (and the one Leonard Woolf brought to the attention of T.S. Eliot), the selections from which he then placed with *The Calendar of Modern Letters*. At first glance, Kot's desire to have Rozanov translated and introduced to English readers appears puzzling. After all, at the time Kot was fleeing Kiev to escape what many thought were impending pogroms, Rozanov was publishing articles in the reactionary press about how, like vampires, Jews craved Christian blood. He had no doubt that Beilis had indeed committed the ritual murder of the Christian boy, and that Jews fully deserved the pogroms they were subjected to. It is probably a testimony to how much intolerance Koteliansky had learned to put up with while in Russia that he would even consider spending so much time on translating a man who for most of his life held such radical views about Jews.

"As a man I dislike him, almost despise," Kot would confide in Ralph Hodgson, a poet and one-time small press publisher who became his good friend soon after Lawrence's death and to whom he sent a copy of *Solitaria* in 1930, "but he was a tortured soul and a born writer."[48] Coincidentally or not, Kot, according to Gertler, seemed even more depressed than usual that spring as he was working on Rozanov.[49] Yet in persevering despite his distaste for Rozanov's ideas, and by sharing his translation of Rozanov with Lawrence, Koteliansky probably made one of the most lasting contributions to literary history for, as we will see below, Rozanov, whose views on sex were no less radical than his views on Jews, influenced the very last novel that Lawrence was to write – *Lady Chatterley's Lover*.

When it came to Rozanov's anti-Semitism, Koteliansky, in his brief introduction to the volume, let him off the hook surprisingly gently by calling his positions simply expedient:

> Rozanov ... with considerable talent, though with utter cynicism ... dared to defend ideas and policies, which no reactionary journalist would have dreamt of supporting in the Press. Whether it was necessary for his paper to show that the Church acted nobly in excommunicating Leo Tolstoy; or to prove that Jews killed young Christian boys in order to use their blood for ritual purposes – Rozanov performed the task unblushingly, boldly, and most cynically.[50]

But there was nothing expedient in Rozanov's writings at the time: his screeds were too irrational even for most reactionary periodicals, and in 1913 he was expelled from Russia's very conservative Religious Philosophic Society. Furthermore, in 1914 Rozanov published *Olfactory and Tactile Attitude of Jews to Blood*, in which he further revealed himself not as a cynic but a true believer by elaborating on his theory that Jews carried ancient cells from the times when human sacrifice was a norm, and thus were programmed to find the smell and feel of human blood irresistible.

Rozanov's was, however, a love-hate relationship with Jews, and there was a strange tinge of appreciation for them even in the midst of the most vicious anti-Semitic diatribes. E. Gollerbach, whose abridged "Critico-Biographical Study" Koteliansky included in the volume in addition to his own "Note," echoed many Rozanov critics when he stated that Rozanov "[i]n the same breath ... cursed and blessed the Jews."[51] He envied Jews what he saw as their earthy attitude toward sex and physical joys; he admired their intellect and practical skills, and, at the same time, he feared that they were not just uncontrollable bloodsuckers but would soon take over Russia and turn Russian Christians into their servants. In 1917, with a large number of Jews participating in overthrowing the monarchy, Rozanov believed that his prediction had come true. Yet in 1918, just before he died in a Christian monastery near Moscow, he appeared to repent, requesting that all his anti-Jewish writings be burnt. He also offered to Russian Jews half the profits for the publications of his less incendiary works – provided that they use the other half to take good care of his wife and daughters. While some Jews in Russia were mollified by his gesture, others saw it simply as a ploy to make sure that revolutionary Jews would protect his family. This last-minute repentance, whether genuine or "expedient," as Kot would put it, probably made Kot's decision to translate him a bit easier.

Rozanov's controversial ideas about sex and physical love were somewhat connected to his ideas about Jews. His preoccupation with sex and bodily functions went so far that in press he was routinely called "a pornographer."[52] Like Otto Weininger, whom he undoubtedly read, Rozanov believed that all human beings contained both male and female natures and were essentially bisexual. He also maintained that same-sex love should not be criminalized but neither should it be encouraged, because it did not lead to procreation. In *Solitaria,* Rozanov's obsession with Jews and sex converge in the discussion of "mikvah," a Jewish ritual of cleansing the body in a pool of natural springs or rainwater in order to achieve or regain purity after menstruation or childbirth for women, and "emissions of semen" for men. In Russian synagogues there was always an area with a ritual bath either on the territory of the synagogue itself or, if there was not enough room, in a separate structure nearby. Women and men purified themselves separately, and a rabbi was usually on hand to pronounce the faithful "kosher." As Rozanov tells us, conversing with a young female Jewish visitor, "Rebecca N.N.," he, much to her embarrassment, "began talking to her about the *details ...* of the *mikvah*":

[A]fter a silence she remarked: "This *name* I pronounce *aloud for the first time.*"

"Mikvah?"

"But it is an *obscene word*, and among Jews it is not admissible to speak it aloud."

I grew agitated.

"But the mikvah, isn't it *sacred*?"

"Yes, it is *sacred* ... So we were told ... But the name is obscene, and isn't pronounced aloud or in the presence of others.

Rozanov then proceeds to argue that in Judaism, as opposed to Christianity, "the 'obscene' and the 'sacred' can be *compatible! coincident! one!!!*":

(1) With Christians everything "obscene," – and inasmuch as the "obscenity" grows – becomes "sin," "evil," "filth," "disgusting": so that without comments, evidence, and demonstrations, *without theory*, the sphere of sexual life and of the sexual organs – this domain of universal shyness, of universal reserve – has *sunk down into the infernal regions* of "Satanism," of "Devilry," and has for its foundation the "terrible, unbearable, abomination," "universal stench."

(2) But among Jews thought has been so *trained* that what is "obscene" (for the tongue, the eye, and the mind) does not at all appraise the inward properties of the object, does not say anything of its content; since there is one thing, always, "close at hand," familiar, the weekly ritual, which being "the height of obscenity" in name, never *pronounced aloud*, yet at the same time "sacred." It is not amplified, it is not pointed out; it simply *is*, and all *know* it.[53]

Given the complexity of Rozanov's views on Jews, and on sex, both of which quite mirrored Lawrence's own,[54] it is no wonder that Lawrence was so excited when he read the copy of *Solitaria* that Kot sent to him in April 1927: "I read Rozanov as soon as he came and wrote a criticism as soon as I'd read him: and send you the criticism so you will know what I think. Do you agree at all? ... I was very pleased to have Rozanov."[55]

Lawrence's short review of *Solitaria* appeared in the journal *Calendar of Modern Letters* in July. In *D.H. Lawrence: Dying Game*, a biography of Lawrence's last years, David Ellis surprisingly misses the point entirely when he suggests that Lawrence wrote the review solely as "a favour for a friend" and that he simply found Rozanov "another of those 'morbidly introspective Russians.'"[56] Nothing could be further from the truth. After first making fun of the rather disjointed, impressionistic, and very casual nature of the book – "fragmentary jottings of thoughts … scribbled down where they came, in a cab, in the train, in the W.C., on the sole of a bathing slipper … 'examining my coins'" – Lawrence turns very serious when he describes what he calls Rozanov's "phallic vision":

> The book is an attack on Christianity … Rozanov has more or less recovered the genuine pagan vision, the phallic vision, and with these eyes he looks, in amazement and consternation, on the mess of Christianity. For the first time, we get what we have got from no Russian, neither Tolstoy nor Dostoevsky nor any of them, a real, positive view on life … His background is the vast old pagan background, the phallic … He is the first Russian, as far as I am concerned, who has ever said anything to me. And his vision is full of passion, vivid, valid … [T]his book is extremely interesting, and really important … It is the voice of the new man … And it means a great deal.[57]

"He is the first Russian … who has ever said anything to me" is definitely not synonymous with Ellis's just "another of those … Russians." It was, overall, a glowing review, and his enthusiasm probably had everything to do with his own pursuits in *Lady Chatterley's Lover*. George Zytaruk was the first Lawrence scholar to assert that Rozanov's *Solitaria* had a substantial impact on the final version of Lawrence's novel, and there should be no doubt that this was indeed the case. By the time Lawrence read *Solitaria* and organized his thoughts about it in a review, he had finished the first and second drafts of *Lady Chatterley's Lover* but was not satisfied yet, especially with the parts that concerned the description of sexual acts. A day before he acknowledged to Kot that he had received *Solitaria*, Lawrence complained to his agent: "I'm in a quandary about my novel, *Lady Chatterley's Lover* … I always labour at the same thing, to make the sex relation valid and precious, instead of shameful."[58] As Zytaruk points out, soon after that "[s]omething seems to have convinced Lawrence that he must go even further than he had done," and this "something" was most likely Rozanov, who happened to arrive at just the right moment.[59] At the very least, it undoubtedly helped to reaffirm Lawrence's sense of the importance of being as truthful as he could be to his own "phallic vision" in *Lady Chatterley's Lover*.

As he was working on the second and third drafts of the novel, Lawrence in fact often described his goal to his friends in terms very similar to the ones he used to describe Rozanov's worldview. Thus in a letter to Kot in December he called his novel "a declaration of the phallic reality." To a typist who was appalled by what she had to type, he responded: "I consider mine is the truly moral and religious position. You suggest I have pandered to the pornographic taste: I think not." To Edward McDonald, a US scholar who had published a bibliography of Lawrence's works in 1925, he wrote: "Of course the book *isn't* improper: but it *is* phallic ... And the phallic reality is what one must fight for!"[60]

Lawrence finished the third and final version of the novel in January 1928. Two months later he acknowledged once again the commonality of his and Rozanov's "phallic vision" in a letter to Max Mohr, a German writer who had visited him in Italy several months earlier: "It is really a novel contrasting the mental consciousness with the phallic consciousness. Do you remember saying that Rosanov [*sic*] is wrong, making *sex* the new great liberator. But I think even Rosanov was trying to express the phallic urge and consciousness, not merely the sexual ... [T]he phallic reality is a free consciousness and a vital impulse, and is the great and saving reality."[61]

When in December 1927 Kot expressed interest in reading *Lady Chatterley's Lover* and maybe even publishing it in his future press, he was rebuffed by Lawrence as too prudish to enjoy the book: "my novel ... [is] so improper, you wouldn't dare to touch it. It's the most improper novel ever written: and as Jehovah you would probably find it sheer pornography."[62] Lawrence was right: once Kot read *Lady Chatterley's Lover*, he told Virginia Woolf he found it "DISGUSTING."[63] Lawrence's novel was not all about sex, however, and at least one part of it, the discussion of the Bolsheviks in Russia, was no doubt of some interest to Kot. It occurs during a conversation Clifford Chatterley and his three "highly mental" male friends have one afternoon, in which a character named Tommy Dukes is in possession of Lawrence's own views:

> "Bolshevism, it seems to me," said Charlie, "is just a superlative hatred of the thing they call the bourgeois; and what bourgeois is, isn't quite defined ... "Absolutely!" said Tommy. "But also, it seems to me a perfect description of the whole of the industrial ideal. It's the factory-owner's ideal in a nutshell; except that he would deny that the driving power was hate. Hate it is, all the same ... We're all Bolshevists, only we are hypocrites. The Russians are Bolshevists without hypocrisy ... Personally, I consider Bolshevism half-witted; but so do I consider our social life in the west half-witted. So I even consider our far-famed mental life half-witted. We are all as cold as crétins, we're all as passionless as idiots. We're all of us, Bolshevists, only we give it another name."[64]

Kot, while no fan of capitalism himself, undoubtedly did not approve of blurring the distinctions between the two regimes to such an extent, especially after what had befallen his family following the revolution.

As much as Kot disapproved of *Lady Chatterley's Lover*, he still felt compelled to help Lawrence sell it in England, essentially turning into his agent and distributor. Knowing that no censor in his right mind would allow the novel to be published by any mainstream press in England or the United States, Lawrence had 1,000 copies of the novel printed in Italy by Pino Orioli. It made the sales rather tricky, so Lawrence relied on subscription notices for interested parties to order the books directly from the publisher. He had 1,500 leaflets printed all in all, and sent numerous copies of them to friends in England and the United States asking them to spread the word. Kot got the lion's share of the notices and worked tirelessly on pressuring others to buy the book he himself found disgusting.

In April he contacted Ottoline Morrell, whom he did not know well at that point, and enclosed "five notices of D.H. Lawrence's novel in case you might like to give them to some of your friends willing to possess a copy."[65] In August she wrote to Gertler, whom she knew much better, who then forwarded her request for further notices to Kot, together with his own offer to help: "I have received a letter from Ottoline [Morrell] – she rather likes Lawrence's Book and would like you to send a notice of its existence to Augustus John – she thinks he would like one – so do as you think fit about it … Also – shall I try and sell some copies of the book if I find likely people?"[66] Lawrence's letters to Kot in spring and summer 1928 were full of instructions regarding the novel. A typical one read: "I'm glad you will keep 36 copies by you … Now Orioli says he has sent you some orders to distribute. Perhaps you have done it already … Did you send the two copies to Cornish Bros. of Birmingham? Orioli says he sent you their order for two copies, & then wrote to you they had *cancelled* it. – Dirty swine … I'm most awfully sorry to give you such a lot of trouble."[67] But Lawrence at times felt not quite as grateful or apologetic as he sounded in his letters to Kot. "Kot is such a fusser," he complained to one friend, while to Orioli he affirmed that the reason for problems with Kot's accounting was because "Kot is a very real Jew, as you say."[68]

In the middle of it all Kot took two weeks off for a vacation in Cornwall. It was most likely one of the organized "motoring" tours. For a man who hardly ever left his abode, this was obviously a big decision, and, in typical Kot fashion, he almost did not go. "I am sorry you're not going to the country," Lawrence wrote to him on 10 August, "it might have done you good. But perhaps you'll get your trip yet."[69] He did, and it was probably then that he discovered he liked long car rides. A year later, after a shorter motoring trip to visit Gertler at the Mundesley sanatorium in Norfolk, Kot would wistfully confide in Waterlow: "It would be nice to learn to drive a car and to possess one (having of course a secure income)."[70] Kot found Cornwall "curiously impressive" but complained to both Gertler and Lawrence that it was not cheap.[71] As far as we know, this was the last time Kot would leave the immediate vicinity of London for recreation purposes. Having virtually no income, he could not afford regular vacations, but one also gets a sense that the worldly pleasures of life that included travel, beautiful scenery, and meeting new people were not entirely his cup of tea, even though he professed enjoying reading the accounts secondhand when his widely travelled friends, like Lawrence or, later, Ottoline Morrell, embarked on their adventures.

Once back, Kot reimmersed himself in helping Lawrence sell his novel, as well as an unexpurgated edition of his equally controversial poems, *Pansies*, which Lawrence again published privately. While never a stickler for copyrights when it came to the authors he himself translated, Kot became so zealous about protecting Lawrence's work from being pirated – he believed there were many unauthorized copies of *Pansies* floating around – that he even got on the nerves of Lawrence's agents, one of whom wrote to her boss upon getting Kot's latest "alert": "Need I read Koteliansky? Don't much like that man!"[72] Since the edition was illegal in Britain, detectives from Scotland Yard visited several people involved in the distribution and Kot was apparently "rather in a funk" himself, "fearing they may call on him."[73]

Lawrence was getting weaker and sicker all through 1929 and therefore staying put in Bandol, near Toulon in southern France, but still dreaming of going back to New Mexico. "I feel once I got there, I should begin to be well again," he told Mabel Luhan. "Europe is killing me, I feel." He also informed her that he had a revised plan for his Rananim – "a sort of old school, like the Greek philosophers, talks in a garden … with a few young people, building up a new unit out there, a new concept of life … My being ill so long has made me realise perhaps I had better talk to the young and try to make a bit of a new thing with them, and not bother much more about my own personal life. Perhaps now I should submit, and be a teacher. I have fought so against it."[74] He still did not want to believe he had full-blown tuberculosis and blamed his condition on bronchial tubes rather than his lungs. Gertler and Kot thought otherwise, but both knew that their advice would fall on deaf ears unless Lawrence stopped pretending "that it is something else."[75] They also, of course, were quick to blame Frieda: "[I]t really seems almost as if it is she who is killing him … her influence is so great that nothing can be done."[76]

In 1929, Kot translated another volume by Rozanov, *Fallen Leaves*. He did it with the assistance of Sydney Waterlow, whose contribution is not acknowledged in the book. Despite a largely cavalier attitude toward stylistic excellence in his translations, Kot was not all that happy with Waterlow's proofreading job and even mildly reproached him for not giving "sufficient attention" to correcting his English. It is unlikely that Waterlow was ever asked again.[77] James Stephens wrote a short and rather pedestrian introduction to the volume, which made it clear that he was much less personally affected by reading Rozanov than Lawrence had been. Stephens merely noted that "When one has read this … one is better briefed on the Russness of Russia than one could be by much reading of many novelists."[78] As Kot told Waterlow, it was at the insistence of the publisher that he had asked Stephens to write a preface; as far as Kot was concerned, he did not feel it needed one.[79]

Lawrence helped, too, first by finding a willing publisher, the Mandrake Press, and then by writing another review in which, without going into too much detail, he proclaimed that Rozanov's "attitude to the Jews is extraordinary, and shows uncanny penetration."[80] Kot considered the publication a triumph. "I actually managed to sell the Rozanov for ready cash," he boasted to Waterlow, "formally for £100, in actual fact for £91, which to me is a godsend."[81] The Mandrake Press, however, published Rozanov mostly as a favour to Lawrence since they were about to bring out a limited edition of Lawrence's paintings, some of them "phallic" (of which neither Kot nor Gertler approved[82]). P.R. Stephensen, one of the partners in the press, while generous in his payment, was frank in his assessment of Fallen Leaves' potential: "Dear Old Kot. is hoping that somebody will read Rozanov. I am completely pessimistic, and don't suppose we shall sell fifty copies … I only published FALLEN LEAVES to do Kot. a service because I like him … the book will not sell, because Solitaria made hardly any headway at all."[83] Stephensen also liked Kot (and definitely Lawrence) enough to publish the same year a small book of New Dostoevsky Letters – just eight letters all in all, with no introduction or explanation as to why these particular letters had been selected. It was most likely "old clothes" again – something left over from Kot's previous translation efforts (probably for The Adelphi), and it must have sold even fewer than fifty copies.

Kot's next project was translating The Grand Inquisitor, the most celebrated chapter in Dostoevsky's The Brothers Karamazov, in which the skeptical Ivan Karamazov tells his idealistic younger brother, Alyosha, a parable about Jesus returning to Earth at the time of the Spanish Inquisition, only to be told that his return interferes with the mission of the church established in Jesus's name because freedom and happiness are incompatible. The most stunning part of the parable is the end, when Jesus, silent through the Grand Inquisitor's long soliloquy, does not argue or protest but humbly departs.

Translating *The Grand Inquisitor* put Koteliansky in direct competition with Constance Garnett, who had translated *The Brothers Karamazov* back in 1912. Without substantial help, translating a literary masterpiece, where it is never enough to be just literally correct, was a bold move on Kot's part. We do not know who helped him with his English; it was definitely not Lawrence, who in his letters appeared to be unaware of the project until Kot asked him to write an introduction.[84] It is also doubtful, as mentioned earlier, that Kot would have relied on Waterlow to help him again; and he could not have asked James Stephens, because Stephens was in the United States at the time. Whoever performed that service for Kot must have edited rather superficially, for the translation still suffers from being literal rather than literary. Unlike Garnett, who immediately transforms sentences that are peculiarly Russian, both in length and structure, into something much more appropriate for English usage, Koteliansky's word-for-word translation is often awkward and cumbersome. "Similar plays, chiefly from the Old Testament, were occasionally performed in Moscow too, up to the times of Peter the Great," reads Garnett's smooth rendition.[85] "With us, in Moscow ['U nas v Moskve']," reads Koteliansky's, "in the old days before Peter, almost identical dramatical performances, particularly such as were based on the Old Testament, used to be given from time to time."[86]

Kot had grand plans for this translation. Banking on Lawrence's introduction and the popularity of this particular Dostoevsky narrative, he decided to follow the example of *Lady Chatterley's Lover* and sell it by subscription. He had therefore a very limited first edition – 300 copies – printed at his own expense by a London publisher, Elkin Mathews and Marrot, which specialized in limited editions. The subscription notices then went to potential readers, who were exhorted to buy it at 3 guineas each. The sales went well – many undoubtedly felt they were buying it as a tribute to Lawrence since the edition came out soon after his death – and the same year another edition was published, from the same type, but this time by the "Aquila Press."[87] The next edition would be picked up and reset by Martin Secker five years later, primarily, again, because of Lawrence's excellent introduction, which by then had gained further poignancy as one of Lawrence's last pieces of writing.

In Lawrence's earlier review of Rozanov, who in the 1890s published his own study called "Dostoevsky and the Legend of the Grand Inquisitor," Lawrence was not complimentary to Dostoevsky:

One gets tired of being told that Dostoevsky's *Legend of the Grand Inquisitor* is "the most profound declaration which ever was made about man and life – " As far as I am concerned, in proportion as a man gets more profoundly and personally interested in himself, so does my interest in him wane. The more Dostoevsky gets worked up about the tragic nature of the human soul, the more I lose interest. I have read *Grand Inquisitor* three times, and never can remember what it's really about.[88]

The third time he read it was, supposedly, back in early 1926, when he told Kot that he had ordered a copy of *The Brothers Karamazov* to read it "not as fiction, but as life." In 1930, just weeks before his death, he read it for the fourth time, now in Kot's translation. Lawrence had just also reread the Bible in the 1924 James Moffatt translation and was writing *Apocalypse*, his commentary on the Book of Revelations. "I was just writing about the impossibility of fitting the Christian religion to the State," he told Kot in early January. "Send me *The Grand Inquisitor*, and I will see if I can do an introduction."[89]

Lawrence now saw Dostoevsky's work very differently, and in the opening paragraph of his introduction he intended to contrast his latest impression with his initial reaction to the parable of the Grand Inquisitor as follows: "It is a strange experience to examine one's reaction to a book over a period of years. I remember when I had just read *The Brothers Karamazov*, in 1913, how fascinated yet unconvinced it left me. And I remember Middleton Murry saying to me: 'Of course the whole clue to Dostoevsky is in the Grand Inquisitor story.' And I remember saying: 'Why? It seems to me just rubbish.'"[90] Interestingly enough, this is not how the opening paragraph appeared in Kot's volume, for Kot would not have Murry's name besmirching the first publication he was bringing out on his own, probably borrowed, penny. "Yes, you can leave out Murry's name," Lawrence humoured him on 9 February, in the last letter Kot would ever receive from him, "put Katharine's instead, if you like."[91] And so Kot did. The opening paragraph in the volume, which came out in July, more than three months after Lawrence's death, now read: "And I remember Katherine Mansfield saying to me …"[92]

In everything else Lawrence got his way. Originally, Kot asked him to write an introduction of no longer than 1,000 words, but Lawrence, refusing "to squash myself down to a thousand words,"[93] produced 4,000, which made his introduction almost one third of the entire volume. The introduction is, unsurprisingly, as much about Lawrence as it is about Dostoevsky. Other critics may argue whether Dostoevsky fully shared Ivan's and the Grand Inquisitor's pessimistic view of human nature; for Lawrence, who did share it, the answer was unequivocal:

[W]e cannot doubt that the Grand Inquisitor speaks Dostoevsky's own final opinion about Jesus. The opinion is, baldly, this: Jesus, you are inadequate. Men must correct you. And Jesus in the end gives the kiss of acquiescence to the Inquisitor ... We may agree with Dostoevsky or not, but we have to admit that his criticism of Jesus is the final criticism, based on the experience of two thousand years ... and on a profound insight into the nature of mankind. Man can but be true to his own nature. No inspiration whatsoever will ever get him permanently beyond his limits.[94]

While Lawrence was working on the introduction, Kot continued to be anxious about his friend's fast-deteriorating health. When Gertler's doctor from Mundesley, Andrew Morland, went to France to place his tubercular wife in a sanatorium there, Kot and Gertler convinced him to visit Lawrence and urged Lawrence to accept his visit. Morland saw Lawrence on 20 January and recommended "absolute rest"[95] for two months. He also advised Lawrence to spend those two months at a sanatorium in Vence, near Nice. Lawrence was hesitant, hoping that he would be able to forego the sanatorium, where other tubercular patients and strict rules would only further distress him. "Dr Morland said I must lie still and see no one and do not work," he informed Kot on 25 January, "the lung trouble active, but the bronchitis the worst, and I must get it down – they aggravate one another. So I am lying quite still, and already feel rather better."[96] Frieda was trying to be reassuring as well. "You will have heard," she wrote to Kot a day later, "that Dr Morland thought L. *very* ill. He must have perfect rest ... I have pulled L. through many times; he'll get better."[97] While reluctant until the very end, Lawrence did enter the sanatorium in Vence ten days later, facing the fact that despite his and Frieda's bravado he was not improving.

On 11 February, Kot received a letter from Andrew Morland in which Morland expressed his relief that Lawrence had made the right decision about checking himself into the sanatorium, where he would have "proper nursing and attention."[98] When Vence doctors contacted Morland about Lawrence's progress they told him the prognosis was "none too good": "Both lungs appear to be affected with moderate severity but it is his general condition which is causing the greatest amount of anxiety; his appetite is poor & he does not seem to be responding to treatment."[99] On 24 February, H.G. Wells, who was spending the winter in nearby Grasse, came to visit Lawrence and concluded that his illness was "chiefly a question of hysteria."[100] It is not known whether he reported his assessment to Koteliansky. Lawrence, who used to admire Wells, found him this time "a common temporary soul."[101]

Feeling that the sanatorium was only making him feel worse, Lawrence left it on 1 March, against the recommendation of his doctors. He died the next day. Morland was having second thoughts about having insisted on Lawrence's going to the sanatorium: "I wish now that I had never urged him to go to Vence as I am afraid my efforts only made his last weeks more unhappy."[102] Koteliansky who, like the rest of Lawrence's friends, did not expect the end to come so soon, asked Morland if there could have been another reason for Lawrence's sudden demise. Morland doubted "if any other disease was present."[103] Lawrence was buried on 4 March. Koteliansky, by now an English subject, could travel but the news reached him too late to arrange a trip to France. On 3 March, Gertler, too, was still unaware that Lawrence had died the day before. Writing to Marjorie Hodgkinson, who would soon become his wife, Gertler noted: "Lawrence really seems to be very ill. I believe it's serious."[104]

Frieda after Lawrence's death, New Mexico, 1937
(National Portrait Gallery, London).

Kot with Fanny Stepniak in the 1930s
(courtesy of Nadia Slow).

Kot among his friends who attended the "Wednesdays" and "Thursdays" in the 1930s. The reverse side of the picture, sent to his brother Moishel in Canada, identifies them. The Russian says "Standing, from left to right," and "Sitting, from ~~right~~ left." Number 7 says "I" in Russian. (Courtesy of Sonny Surkes.)

Стоя[ - е левой сторона к правой:
1/ Mark Gertler
2/ W. J. Turner
3/ Professor H. Levy
4/ J. H. M. Milne 606A

Сидят - е правой:
6) Ralph Hodgson
7/ Я
8) J. W. N. Sullivan

Lady Glenavy (Beatrice Campbell), with her daughter-in-law, Cherry Campbell, and granddaughter Bridget in front of her castle in Ireland in the late 1940s (courtesy of Hon. Bridget Campbell).

Kot's niece, Pauline Smith, in the early 1940s, when she was sending regular packages to Kot and he was pleading with her not to (courtesy of Marvin Smith).

Kot's 1931 postcard to Polly. She had just married Manuel Smith, and they were on their honeymoon in Florida (JFA).

H.G. Wells in the early 1930s, around the time Kot was lobbying
him to allow the Cresset Press to publish his *Autobiography*. Kot
thanked him for autographing the portrait. (CSA.)

Marjorie Wells, Kot's guardian angel in the last twenty
years of his life, in the 1940s (courtesy of Catherine Stoye).

Kot in 1930. The picture was taken by Lady Ottoline Morrell in her garden. (National Portrait Gallery, London.)

Kot with Mark Gertler and Philip Morrell in 1931, photographed by Lady Ottoline Morrell (National Portrait Gallery, London).

Kot and Ottoline in 1933 (National Portrait Gallery, London).

Kot and James Stephens in the Morrells' garden. 1933. Most likely, photographed by Ottoline Morrell. (National Portrait Gallery, London.)

In this 1934 picture taken by Ottoline, Kot is shown talking to Dilys Powell. (To the right of her is Philip Morrell; to the left, a man identified as "Dr Frankfort.") (National Portrait Gallery, London.)

Kot, James Stephens, and Ottoline in 1935, just months before his breakdown and unnecessary tooth-extraction (National Portrait Gallery, London).

May Sarton in the 1930s, around the time she first met Kot (NYPL).

Kot with Juliette Huxley, late 1930s. She is probably about to light one of the famous Kot-made cigarettes. (Courtesy of George Zytaruk.)

Kot in front of the pear tree made immortal by Mansfield's "Bliss." Late 1930s (CSA).

Kot just before the onset of the Second World War (CSA).

Above: Kot, in late 1946, in front of the grandfather's clock willed to him by H.G. Wells.

Left: The inscription on the back was written for Ralph Hodgson. "Catherine" is Catherine Stoye, Marjorie Wells's daughter. (Yale.)

Above: Kot in his kitchen with a statuette of Tolstoy, which had been given to H.G. Wells by Maxim Gorky bequeathed by Wells to Kot.

Right: the inscription on the back was for Ralph Hodgson. (Yale.)

In ( kitchen. By the kitchen range, with ( Tolstoy statuette on ( table.

Taken by Catherine

Kot in 1951 with Catherine Stoye's son, Jonathan (CSA).

Polly Smith showing Lawrence scholar George Zytaruk in 1967 the first editions of Lawrence's novels that she inherited from her uncle. The large bag in front of them holds Kot's letters to her. (Courtesy of George and JoAnn Zytaruk.)

# PART 2
# AFTER LAWRENCE
# 1931–1955

# MOURNINGS: OLD ENEMIES
# AND NEW FRIENDS

I feel such a "sadness," as Kot would say …
~ Lawrence to Murry, 13 August 1923

Kot came here the other day, just the same,
the same schemes and curses.
~ Virginia Woolf to Ottoline Morrell, 17 July 1935

In November 1929 Kot was finally made a naturalized British subject,[1] and in early December, as Kot was worrying about Lawrence's battle with tuberculosis, he received the news that his mother had died back in Ukraine. She was seventy-seven. It is not clear how much Beila ever knew of her son's life in England. He apparently wrote her very few letters. To Lady Glenavy he confessed that while he "knew what happiness a letter from him could give her and how she must have longed for news of him," he "had hardly written" to her. Glenavy attributed it to Kot being "almost incapable of writing letters,"[2] which is of course contradicted by the fact that he wrote letters almost daily to many of his friends. It was probably just that "the news of him" was never that good, and he knew how important it was for Beila to think that he was thriving. He was incapable of lying so he must have assumed that it would be better just to leave it mostly to her imagination, and let the motherly love take her in whatever comforting direction she desired.

As a tribute to her, in 1937 Kot would make his mother a published author by placing two of the stories she liked to tell him back at home in *London Mercury and Bookman*. In his short preface to the "Two Jewish Stories: Recorded by Beila Koteliansky (b. 1852; d. 1929)," Kot reminisced:

After the Russian Revolution, when postal communications were resumed between Russia and Great Britain, I wrote to my mother, asking her if she remembered the stories of Maimonides and the Ba'al-Shem, which she used to tell us when we were quite young children. I left home at a very early age, and throughout the years I remembered fragments of the two stories, but not connectedly. My mother wrote down the two stories, given here, in Yiddish – she knew no other literature except the Bible in Yiddish – and sent them to me by post. The beauty and mystery of the stories have been lost through their being written down, instead of being told by her. Yet they deserve to be known.[3]

The stories were "Maimonides and Aristotle" and "The Salvation of a Soul," the latter a tale about Ba'al Shem Tov, the famous rabbi who founded the Hasidic movement and hailed from Medzhibizh, not far from Ostropol.[4] Kot noted in his preface that "in 1926 or 1927" he sent his translation of the stories to Lawrence and asked him to improve on it. Lawrence, according to Kot, started polishing the short "Maimonides and Aristotle" but left even that unfinished. While in 1937 Kot would say that Lawrence "liked the stories very much," Lawrence's praise was much more subdued: "As they stand, they wouldn't sell, of course, though the kernel is interesting."[5]

"Maimonides and Aristotle" is an especially whimsical narrative, which probably said a lot about Beila's sensibility and colourful personality. In it, Moses Maimonides, a Jewish philosopher who was an admirer of Aristotle and even attempted to reconcile Aristotle's teachings with the Bible, made a pact with the Greek thinker that he would cut out and preserve his vein because, as the two of them had discovered, after "very many years of study and thinking," "if a certain tiny vein were cut out from a living human being, and put into a jar and kept among certain herbs, the little vein would begin to grow and grow until it became a man." Aristotle's little vein indeed was happily growing in a jar, but, instead of rejoicing, Maimonides now "felt terribly distressed": "Rabbi Moses Maimonides – blessed be his memory! – perceived that the man who was to grow up from the little vein and live eternally, would be made into a God by the people; that the people would abandon the living God and serve the eternal man, whom Aristotle and himself had created." Since Maimonides had given an oath to Aristotle "not to interfere with the growth of the man in the jar," he felt he had no right to "destroy the jar and thus prevent the little vein from becoming an eternal man."

What in the long run saved Judaism was that, in the best Jewish tradition, Maimonides was a bit of a "shlemiel": when he prayed he constantly walked around the room and fiercely waved his cloak, oblivious to what was around him. It so happened that at the moment of his most fervid prayer for the resolution of this difficult situation, all around him were the household's "chickens and cocks" with whom he for some reason shared his study. Frightened by the rapid movements, the poultry all "began to jump and fly about the room" until "a big cock jumped on the shelf where the jar stood, and upset the jar." Maimonides thus saved his "living God" – but at a personal price to himself, for "the tiny little creature" in the broken jar "pointed a tiny little finger to him as a sign that he had broken his oath to Aristotle." Far from being relieved therefore, Maimonides "wept bitterly, and all the rest of his life prayed for forgiveness."[6]

Beila Koteliansky may have liked the story because of its peculiarly Jewish combination of poignancy and everyday reality and humour, but its appeal to Kot was probably different: it perfectly reflected his grim worldview, where no matter what one did there was no possibility for reconciliation or comfort but plenty of room for eternal regret and remorse. And regret and remorse were most likely what he felt when he learned of his mother's death. While it is true that his British citizenship, which made it safer for him to travel to Russia, came too late – his mother died just five days later, on 3 December – deep in his heart he must have known that on several occasions when it was still fairly safe to travel to Russia he had failed to reconcile his inertia and fear of uncertainty with his desire to see his mother and, more importantly, her desire to behold him at least one more time before she died.

Kot's friend Gertler was also dealing with not meeting his Jewish mother's expectations. At the time of Lawrence's death, Gertler was about to get married, this time for real and, much to Golda's disappointment, his fiancée was not a nice Jewish girl. Gertler first met Marjorie Hodgkinson, a fellow artist, in 1925, when she was twenty-two and he thirty-three. Their relationship, however, did not start in earnest until several years later. In 1929, when Gertler was again in a sanatorium at Mundesley, Marjorie was already at his side helping him through the depressing experience.[7] In April 1930, upon realizing that Marjorie was pregnant, the two eloped to Paris. The families only found out about the fait accompli from the English press, which somehow had gotten wind of the event and surprised the newlyweds with their cameras.

"Well we've just been married," Gertler informed Kot on 3 April 1930. "It was quite simple and only took ¼ an hour … But … my people object strongly, just what I expected …"[8] Comforted by the thought of one day beholding Mark's children, Golda came around rather quickly, with Mark's siblings reluctantly following. A week later Gertler described to Kot the much improved situation with his family but the trouble brewing on Marjorie's side:

Apparently there was a division in my family – my brother Jack, his wife and my mother were on my side and Harry and the others against. But now they are all in agreement so that's all over. On the whole they have been quite nice. Marjorie has a very religious aunt that is causing a certain amount of worry – she wants us to get married in a Roman Catholic church! And is making herself quite ill over it. She writes that it can be done quite easily inspite of the fact that I am a Jew. She has made enquiries. I don't mind – so we shall [think?] it over – only my people must *never* know of it – or they would *never* forgive me. Then there is the question, whether the children *have* to be brought up as R Catholics – what do you think about this point?.. If the papers would get hold of it, I certainly wouldn't do it – as I couldn't hurt my mother to that extent. This aunt is absolutely devoted to Marjorie ...[9]

Gertler's biographer, Sarah MacDougall, believes that even if Gertler seriously considered going through the Catholic wedding, in the end his fears about his mother's reaction trumped all other considerations.[10] A year before Golda had had a bad fall, dislocated her hip, and was still suffering from the effects of incompetent medical care. Gertler had every reason to believe that her son's Catholic wedding would kill her. There is, consequently, no further mention of it in Gertler's letters to Kot, who most likely also disapproved of the idea since he detested it when people changed their principles – or faiths – out of expediency or for material gain.

Kot did, on the other hand, approve of Marjorie – surprisingly, given his long-standing tradition of hostility toward spouses of close friends. He sounded genuinely pleased when, later in April, he wrote to Ralph Hodgson: "Gertler and Marjorie Hodgkinson (you know her, she used to come to the Turners; and she is very nice) got married about a month ago in Paris ... Gertler finds it awfully difficult to get used to the new situation; but as he knows perfectly well what Marjorie is, he will overcome the difficulty; and the change of situation will do him good."[11] Kot also assured Ottoline Morrell – with whom he was just establishing a close bond that would prove to be the most important one for him in that decade – that while the newlyweds were not "feel[ing] grand just now," they would eventually "be better." "It is so terribly difficult," he told her, "to get used to a startlingly new situation."[12] It was indeed a tough transition for Gertler, and throughout their marriage he and Marjorie often led separate lives, going away without each other for lengthy periods of time.[13]

Marjorie's first pregnancy ended in a miscarriage. Their only son, Luke, was born two years later, on 16 August 1932. While it was a very happy and welcome event for Luke's father – albeit wrought with anxiety since Luke had low birth weight and had to undergo several surgeries[14] – that year would otherwise prove to be the worst in Mark Gertler's life. In February, Golda Gertler died, having never fully recovered from her fall and botched treatment in 1929, and just months before the birth of the grandchild she had so long awaited from Mark. Golda's death was followed, just one month later, by the death of the woman Gertler still probably loved most after his mother – Dora Carrington.

Gertler had reestablished a connection with Carrington in 1928 when she was lonely because both Strachey and Partridge were deeply involved with other people. When Gertler heard in January of 1932 that Strachey had died of stomach cancer, he wrote to Carrington to tell her "how deeply I felt for you over Lytton's death" and how shocked he was "that his end should have come as such an early age, but still more at the enormous blow I knew it would be to you."[15] The blow to Carrington was so enormous that on March 11, almost two months after Strachey's death, she put on his favourite yellow silk dressing gown and took her own life. Kot, who still resented Carrington because of the pain she had caused Gertler, was startled by what her action revealed about her character. "She never struck me as a person capable of very great love," he confessed to Ottoline Morrell.[16]

Two weeks prior to her suicide, Carrington sent Gertler and Marjorie a very belated wedding present and told Mark she had been reading some of his old letters, to which Gertler responded that he, too, "went through all yours a few months ago": "I was alone in the flat with a bad cold one day when one of your letters fluttered out of the bundle in a drawer where I was looking for a book. So it struck me I might pass the time by reading the whole bundle through. It certainly made most moving reading. It must have been a most extraordinary and painful time for both of us."[17] With both Golda and Carrington dead, Marjorie, despite her best efforts, appeared largely incapable of filling the gaping void in Gertler's heart. He again was contemplating killing himself.[18]

Kot spent the first two years after Lawrence's death in a fight over who should inherit Lawrence's estate. Lawrence left no will, and according to the Administration of Estates Act of 1925 relating to the property of those who died intestate, Frieda, as his widow, was entitled to all his personal belongings ("wife shall take the personal chattels absolutely"), a payment of £1,000 ("free of death duties and costs"), and half of his estate, plus interest from the "residuary estate." Since the marriage produced no children,[19] and Lawrence's parents had preceded him in death, Lawrence's siblings were to inherit the other half of the estate. According to this scenario, upon Frieda's death, her half would revert to Lawrence's siblings and their heirs.[20] Frieda was in no mood, however, to share the benefits of the estate, especially Lawrence's manuscripts, royalties, and copyright, which she knew would bring her substantial amounts of money. She was also not about to deprive her three children – even if they were not Lawrence's – of what she considered to be their rightful inheritance. She was, though, willing to pay a substantial sum – 25 percent of all manuscripts she would sell – to buy off Lawrence's siblings and avoid going to court.[21] The siblings were not a monolithic front. While George, Lawrence's oldest brother, and his sister Emily believed that Lawrence intentionally left no will, his other sister, Ada, though no fan of Frieda's, thought Lawrence would have wanted his widow to inherit it all. In the interim, in accordance with the intestate statute, Frieda and George Lawrence shared the administration of the estate.

Kot's antipathy toward Frieda had only increased following Lawrence's death, for which he considered her at least partially responsible. In a gesture of good will she offered him a manuscript of Lawrence's play *David*, the London production of which Kot had helped with back in 1926. *David* was not among Kot's favourite Lawrence works, though. He told Frieda to give him instead the manuscript of *The Rainbow*, "if you really want to give me something,"[22] but that manuscript was obviously worth considerably more money, and Frieda's olive branch was never intended to be that long. Things between them got much worse when Kot discovered that she and Murry had a passionate fling just days after the funeral. He likewise was aware that, while Lawrence was still alive, Frieda had acquired another lover, Captain Angelo Ravagli, the Lawrences' former Italian landlord in Spotorno.[23] A married man at the time, Ravagli would eventually divorce his wife and, in 1950, become Frieda's third – and last – husband. Kot also resented Frieda because he wanted to publish Lawrence's letters in his possession without having to go through her or her agents. All that made him determined to do everything in his power, including strengthening the backbone of Lawrence's siblings, to thwart Frieda's attempts to claim sole ownership of Lawrence's estate.

For some inexplicable reason, Frieda asked for Kot's advice early on, and she also inquired whether he remembered that Lawrence and Murry had created identical wills in 1914, in which they left everything to their respective wives (or wives-to-be, as was the case with Mansfield). Murry, she said, was ready to swear to it and was looking for a copy of his own 1914 will. Frieda further informed Lawrence's sister Ada that Lawrence's 1914 will might be back at their Kiowa Ranch in New Mexico and would eventually be found.[24] Kot advised his nemesis – "seeing the perfectly friendly and correct attitude of Lawrence's relations" toward her – "to give up the idea of finding the Murry will; but to resume the legal settlement of the estate as if there were no will at all." "Most probably," he concluded optimistically in relating his response to Ottoline Morrell, "after her several 'business' attempts have failed, she will do so."[25] When it became clear that Frieda – and Murry – considered his suggestions plain "silly"[26] and were going to persist, Kot grew enraged and feisty.

He first approached Aldous Huxley, who with his wife, Maria, had been in Bandol at the time of Lawrence's death and was now entrusted by Frieda to put together a volume of Lawrence's letters. When Gertler and Marjorie went to visit the Huxleys in Paris several days after getting married there, Gertler carried a message from Kot that begged Huxley to persuade Frieda to forego contesting the intestate settlement and agree to allow a distinguished committee, with Huxley at the head as executor, to collect Lawrence's letters and possible future publications. A draft of his proposal for such a committee stated:

> The consultative meeting of of L's friends (E.M. Forster, Aldous Huxley, Lady Ottoline Morrell, Lady Cynthia Asquith, Mrs Carswell, Miss B. Low, Miss Beveridge, M. Gertler, David Garnett, Doctor and Mrs Eder, Ada Clarke etc etc) to appoint an editorial committee consisting of three or four responsible editors. The first act of Editors to make a statement to English and American Press about the organization for collecting L.'s letters. To warn, in a statement, editors as to accepting memoirs, impressions by unknown persons dealing with L. Perhaps to issue an appeal in the press about collecting funds for the L. museum.[27]

"I have given your message to Aldous," Gertler assured Kot on 9 April, and then again on 22 April: "I gave your message about Frieda, etc. to Huxley."[28]

"We have been seeing Aldous Huxley," Catherine Carswell wrote to a friend from Paris that spring. "There has been a painful-comic *geschichte* [history] over the literary executorship of D.H. Lawrence. Great snakes – what business of intrigues and recriminations! Huxley is decent I think. Murry is *not*, but thinks he is …"[29] The "geschichte" was as follows: in early May, Murry, who was by then in Vence with Frieda, sent a letter to Laurence Pollinger, formerly Lawrence's agent and now Frieda's, and humbly offered his services as Lawrence's executor. "Pollinger showed me a long letter from Murry written from Vence about business affairs," Huxley wrote to Kot in early May. "The most significant sentence was this: 'The best thing would be if I were to be appointed literary executor, which I don't want to be. (!) But if it is necessary … etc.' So you see where the wind blows!"[30]

Kot definitely did see where the wind blew and redoubled his efforts to persuade Huxley to wrest Lawrence's legacy out of Frieda's control. Huxley, too, was exasperated with Frieda's fight to become the sole heir to Lawrence's estate.

"The stupid woman," he complained to a friend, "is embarking on enormously expensive legal proceedings against Lawrence's brother now – quite unnecessarily in my opinion, but she rushes in where angels fear to tread. Her diplomatic methods consist in calling everyone a liar, a swine, and a lousy swindler … Since L is no longer there to keep her in order, she plunges about in the most hopeless way." And yet, there was an essential difference between his attitude and Kot's. "I like her very much," he added in the same letter.[31] Liking her, despite disapproving of her actions and even finding her "quite impossible,"[32] Huxley was not about to join Frieda's sworn enemies. He therefore politely declined Kot's suggestion, explaining that "[a]ny attempt to deprive Frieda of what she feels are her legitimate rights in the matter will only lead … to the most violent and troublesome reaction on her part and might drive her into the arms of Murry and others of the same breed." "Yes, Frieda makes one rather desperate," he continued several days later. "The difficulty will be … I can't go & tell her the truth, which is: 'We mistrust your judgment so much & I think you are such a fool, that we want you to have nothing more to do with your husband's writings, & hand over the control to me.'"[33]

Instead, as David Ellis points out, Huxley "proved a loyal friend during all [Frieda's] legal difficulties"[34] and even may have let Frieda learn the exact language Kot was employing to argue that she should be prevented from inheriting everything, which she then freely quoted back to Kot: "Why should Frieda's future husbands profit by this money?"[35] Several years later, writing from New Mexico, where he was a guest of Frieda's, Huxley tried to disabuse Kot of the notion that Frieda – or her "future husbands" – were doing anything wrong with Lawrence's legacy: "We are spending the summer on Lawrence's ranch – very wild and beautiful. Frieda has mellowed with time and is really very nice. Also we find to our immense relief, that the Italian captain is an extremely honest, simple and decent man. The rumours that they are exploiting Lawrence … as a commercial proposition are fortunately absolutely unfounded."[36] The letter (perhaps written with Frieda's encouragement) no doubt failed to convince Kot.

Kot's next move was to contact Ada Clarke and George Lawrence. Since Ada was ready to allow Frieda to have everything for now (she did, however, want the estate to revert to her and her siblings' families following Frieda's death), while George and Emily did not want to settle for anything less than half of the estate, Kot chose to work on bringing Ada in line with the other two. He had first met Ada in December 1917, when Lawrence asked him to pick her up at a train station and help her change trains since she was not familiar with London. "She says to look for a tallish thin woman with dark furs," Lawrence instructed him then, "in a pale bluey-grey long coat … I described to her your villainous appearance."[37] The meeting took place, and ten days later, when the Lawrences were staying with Ada in Midlands, Lawrence wrote to Kot that Ada made them "laugh very much about your one eye-glass, your pseudo-monocle, and your serious outgaze, and the relief you evidenced in fleeing."[38]

Following Lawrence's death, Kot and Ada exchanged letters – and occasionally met – during the two years leading to the trial over the will in late autumn 1932. Ada was firm in her belief that "Bert" (the family's name for Lawrence) would have intended Frieda to have everything, even though she was sorry to disappoint Kot. "I don't really like her," she told a friend, "but the way she stuck to him was wonderful. He would drag her off on one of his sudden journeys without giving her time to pack … but on she would go, and, if only for this, I say whatever Bert left she is entitled to."[39] Frieda, in the meantime, was becoming less and less willing to give anything to the family, especially to George, whom she disliked immensely. Kot then suggested that Ada should persuade George to relinquish his co-administrator role to her, since she and Frieda seemed to get along better. George would not hear of it.[40]

Kot's egging the Lawrence siblings on not to settle may have led George and Emily into cementing their belief that they indeed stood to gain more than what Frieda was proposing. The final settlment, however, proved to be much less advantageous to them than the initial offer. During the 3 November 1932 hearing, Murry produced a copy of his 1914 will, and Frieda testified that, three days before Lawrence died, he asked her where his will was. The 4 November account in the *Times* of London, under the headline "Mr D.H. Lawrence's Lost Will," gave the rest of the story:

The plaintiff, Mrs Frieda Emma Johanna Maria Lawrence … propounded a will of November 9, 1914, under which she was sole beneficiary, and asked that letters of administration granted on June 5, 1930, to herself and Mr George Arthur Lawrence, a brother of Mr D.H. Lawrence, be revoked … The last time that she … saw the will was when they were on her ranch at Taos, New Mexico, in 1925, when they were packing up to return to Europe. Her husband put it among some papers. He was arranging some papers at that time to be sent to New York. She had not seen it since. He was reading a book a few days before his death and an incident in the book about a Chinese making a will caused him to ask about his own will. He was very ill, and she told him not to worry about it.

He said in any case she would have everything. Mr J. Middleton Murry … gave evidence of the execution of Mr Lawrence's will. The President said that the evidence was quite clear. He suspected that the will was in the papers intended to go to New York and was lost. The letters of administration already granted would be revoked, and he would pronounce for the will.[41]

"Revenge is the joy of the gods" was one of Frieda's favourite sayings,[42] and she probably never felt the truth of it as acutely as she did after the trial. "I cannot tell you *how* deeply triumphant I feel," she wrote to a friend back in Vence. "I wasn't sure of winning not till the case came on; a severe old judge, Lord Merivale; but I pulled all my force together in the witness box, just went ahead, felt I could convince crocodiles that Lawrence wanted me to have his inheritance – They say I *was* convincing – But the triumph was *Lorenzo's*: The judge said: 'This very distinguished man' and treated *me* with such respect – you see this old Merivale wanted to sort of pay respect to Lawrence after all the persecution – I still feel a bit *drunk* … So there's song of triumph for you."[43]

Lord Merivale also thought that the terms Frieda was offering the family – which consisted of giving the siblings £500 and two manuscripts each[44] – were "generous."[45] The terms, however, were not as generous as Frieda's first offer of 25 percent of all manuscript sales. More importantly, the hostility also made it impossible to negotiate what would happen after Frieda's death. While George and Emily, according to Ada, were willing to settle for "nothing during Frieda's life and only the copy-right at her death,"[46] Frieda would not budge. Kot's "future husbands" prediction therefore came to pass: after Frieda's death half of the estate went to her third husband, Angelo Ravagli; the other half went to Frieda's children.

When Ada, as she intended to all along, waived her claim to the settlement, Frieda offered her one of Lawrence's paintings, "The Holy Family," suggesting it was worth at least £500, but Ada again wanted to have nothing to do with Frieda's largesse. She wrote to a friend that she had told Frieda "the triumph was Frieda Lawrence's, not Bert's, and that she had better keep the picture, as she might need £500 more than I."[47] In a letter to Kot, written eleven days after the hearing, Ada also said she had informed Frieda that she had letters from Bert that could "open people's eyes" about his widow's true nature and that, unless she wanted "reckoning," Frieda should be very careful about badmouthing Lawrence's family.[48] But Frieda, having triumphed in her litigation, whether for her own sake or Lawrence's, was quite ready to leave her late husband's siblings – and England – permanently behind. As to Kot, she had her own warning about him badmouthing her. "[T]ell him," she instructed Catherine Carswell, "he'd better be careful or I'll come down on him like a ton of bricks."[49]

Accompanied now by Captain Ravagli – who took a leave of absence from the army, as well as from his wife, whom Frieda agreed to support financially[50] – she went back to New Mexico, where she would reside, with Ravagli, until her death in 1956, supported by a nice income from Lawrence's estate. She felt that having gone through what she had gone through, she was simply entitled to "Capitano Ravagli" and other pleasures of life: "We have been fond of each other for years and … an old bird like me is still capable of real passion and can inspire it too … especially after all the agony of Lawrence … I have a car and everybody says what a woman full of vitality I am!"[51] While some – Ottoline notably among them – somewhat grudgingly admired Frieda's "vitality,"[52] Kot believed it was all just about how much Frieda was willing to pay Ravagli and his abandoned wife. Before the two reached their final decision to go to New Mexico for good, Kot wrote to Ottoline that Frieda was "evidently waiting in London for the Capitano to make up his mind to go with her to the ranch. I should say it is only a question of money now: she probably wants to get the Capitano at a cheaper price than he considers his job is worth. Well, well!"[53]

Throughout Kot's frenetic but futile efforts to thwart Frieda, other things were happening as well. In spring 1930 he started having what Gertler described as "attacks of feeling ill."[54] We do not know what their nature was, except that around the same time Ottoline Morrell was encouraging Kot to give up smoking "for a time,"[55] and there were several references to his heart. The same year Gertler painted yet another portrait of Kot, in which he was placed next to a painting depicting a fleshy female nude. It was probably Gertler's choice for the background, not Kot's. A year later Kot most likely met Moura Budberg for the first time, or at least was given a chance to do so when Ottoline Morrell invited him in early December to come to tea and meet Moura, who, she said, had "just" been with the "very ill" Gorky and was looking forward to making Kot's acquaintance.[56]

Most importantly, in 1931 Kot finally attempted to get a "real" job. According to Esther Salaman, that year he submitted an application for a Russian lecturer position at Cambridge University but "A Miss Hale got the position he applied for."[57] In the continuing absence of a regular job Kot started buying tickets for the "Irish Sweep," the Irish Hospitals' Sweepstakes, as soon as they were legalized in Ireland and the United Kingdom in 1930.[58] Now and then he apparently won a modest sum, and then, according to Esther Salaman, "he would fill his cellars with wine [and] entertain his friends."[59] As in everything else, he dreamed big. "Hope rose and fell each year when the results of the Irish Sweep came out," May Sarton remembered from the later period in his life. "'If I win the Irish Sweep, I shall be your publisher and there will be no need to deal with the blighters.'"[60] "Tell me now what present I should get for you when I win the Irish Sweep," he queried Ida Baker. "A house in the country, or near London?"[61] "When I win the Irish Sweep" was a common refrain in his letters even when things he wanted to buy were much less expensive than publishing companies or country houses. "When I win the Irish Sweep," he once wrote to Dilys Powell, "I'll buy several albums for photographs."[62]

In 1931, William Heinemann brought out a limited – 750 copies – edition of Koteliansky and Mansfield's translation of Gorky's *Reminiscences of Leonid Andreyev*. It was noted there that the translation was made during Mansfield's "last stay in England … August-September, 1922," and immediately following the title page was another title page in Mansfield's fine handwriting, and there, unlike on the official title page, Kot's name came first. It is not clear how much money he made on the edition, of which he retained at least twenty copies for his close friends and Canadian relatives.[63]

But it was still Lawrence and protecting his legacy that seemed to be foremost on Kot's mind. Books about Lawrence started appearing months after his death, mostly dealing with how important their respective authors had been in the writer's life. First came Murry's *Son of Woman*, published in 1931 and containing salacious details about their turbulent but often intimate relationship. In 1932 Mabel Luhan published *Lorenzo in Taos*, where she claimed her share of Lawrence's affection and his susceptibility to her creative influence. A year later, Brett published *Lawrence and Brett*, dedicating it to Lawrence as her "potential lover." Not to be outdone, in 1934 Frieda published her book, *"Not I but the Wind": Memoirs of Her Husband*, which even some of her detractors, like Kot's close friend James Stephens, found appealing. "[N]ot bad, tho' scrappy. She does give a sense of herself & he," was Stephens's verdict.[64] Kot vehemently hated Murry's, Brett's, and Frieda's books, and he disliked Luhan's, except for one saving grace, remarked upon by Ada Clarke as well – that it was "not very flattering to Frieda."[65]

Huxley's edition of Lawrence's letters came out in 1932. None of Koteliansky's letters were in there – unlike Gertler, who was very obliging, Kot refused to have Lawrence's letters to him published under Frieda's auspices. He also no longer trusted Huxley. "I'm not going to give my letters to be messed about," he declared to Esther Salaman soon after they met in 1932. "I don't want Huxley to change this and that. I'll do the selecting."[66] While Huxley's attack on Murry's *Son of Woman* in the introduction to the volume must have been gratifying (Huxley called it "that curious essay in destructive hagiography"[67]), there were several letters that probably upset Kot, chief among them Lawrence's letter to a publisher in which

Lawrence showed his irritation with Kot's demands about the title page arrange-ments and Lawrence's foreword for the 1919 translation of Shestov: "*Ach, Ach!* These little businesses! Every hen is occupied with her own tail-feathers."[68] Murry allowed a big chunk of his Lawrence letters to be published as well, and in one of them, from 1925, Lawrence told Murry he did not want to see Kot.[69] Even some of the more sympathetic mentions of Kot often sounded patronizing. "Poor Kot," Lawrence wrote to Aldous Huxley in 1927, when trying unsuccessfully to help Kot with his publishing ambitions, "he'll be depressed about his 'scheme' … Poor Kot – I do what I can for him – but why should anybody want to be a pub-lisher?"[70] "[S]tick pins or something into Kot," he beseeched Gertler in spring 1918. "I believe he's getting into a state of gangrened inertia."[71]

By 1932 there were already, as well, serious critical biographies being researched and written. That year Harry T. Moore visited Lawrence's family in Nottingham to collect information about the writer's early life. He then paid Kot the ultimate compliment by telling Ada Clarke that he had met Frieda, Koteliansky, Cather-ine Carswell, and Murry in London but thought Koteliansky had "the brains of them all."[72] Kot, however, never contemplated writing his own reminiscences of Lawrence; he just wanted to publish Lawrence's letters to him in a separate volume without any censorship from Frieda, and also to influence other people's accounts wherever he could. By the time Moore visited Ada and her family, Ada had already published her memoir – *Young Lorenzo* – which first came out in 1931, in Florence, from G. Orioli in a limited edition of 740 copies, and was picked up by Martin Secker a year later. It was one of the three volumes of reminiscences Kot initially encouraged and cheered as a counterbalance to the books by Murry, Brett, Luhan, and Frieda. The other two were Carswell's *Savage Pilgrimage*, which came out in 1932, and a book written by Lawrence's one-time girlfriend (and the prototype for Miriam in *Sons and Lovers*), Jessie Chambers Wood – *D.H. Lawrence: A Personal Record*, which came out in 1935 under the penname of E.T.

Wood first heard from Kot in 1930, when he must have suggested she should publish her memoir. Writing to a friend in October of that year, Wood men-tioned that "Mr Koteliansky can scarcely hope to get a biography of 'verified facts' during his lifetime."[73] After Wood's *Personal Record* came out, Kot advised Dilys Powell, who wrote literary reviews for the *Times* of London, that she should "praise it unreservedly, particularly after the 'clever' and 'illuminating' books on L.," its main merit being, according to him, "the fact that she is such a 'provin-cial' and cannot disguise it (I think she would like to, but not being 'literary,' she does not know how to do it)."[74] He was not, however, totally satisfied with the book; he told Wood he thought "the first part of that book better than the rest."[75] Even though he did not deem her to be "literary," he now urged her to write a very literary book, a fictionalized sequel (under a "nom-de-plume" again, if she was afraid to offend the living), making Lawrence the centre of her narrative, and, through him, showing "a life of several groups of people *at a given historical moment in England*."[76] It was obviously the kind of a book about Lawrence Kot wished he could write himself. While Wood said she shared his concept for the book, she told Kot she was going to make not Lawrence but "my own consciousness the focus of the story"[77] – something that no doubt lessened Kot's enthusiasm. Wood gave it a serious try, sending or delivering in person several drafts of her manuscript for Kot to read, but her stroke in 1939 put an end to the project.[78] In the meantime, a US edition of *D.H. Lawrence: A Personal Record* came out in 1936, with the introduction by, of all people, Murry, which obviously sullied the only book about Lawrence that Kot had come close to liking.

But it was Kot's experience with Carswell's book that most crystallized his hopes and frustrations when it came to Lawrence's legacy. In September 1930 Carswell told Kot that she had almost 120 letters and postcards from Lawrence and wanted Kot to see them. She even suggested she and Kot should collaborate on a book about Lawrence and call it *Lawrence Was Right*.[79] He declined. When the book, with its devastating portrayal of Murry (the part Kot was looking forward to seeing in print) came out, Murry immediately moved to start legal proceedings to have the book withdrawn. Chatto and Windus obliged, after just about 1,500 copies were sold, and even apologized to Murry. Carswell was devastated. "Chatto … has withdrawn the book from publication," she complained to a friend in July 1932. "So that's that. They are about to issue a public apology! My chief immediate concern is to make sure that *I* am not implicated, as I was never further from apologizing in my life. We must wait and see what the American publishers will do. If they run away it is a grave loss to me. If they stand firm they might eventually risk taking over the English rights as well."[80] Harcourt, the US publisher, did stand firm; the book was published there with just minor revisions and then reissued in England by a different publisher, Martin Secker, the very same year.

What Carswell also did not expect was how vehement Kot's reaction would be to the book. While she thought that her portrayal of Kot during "the last supper" at Café Royal (smashing wine glasses because of his "jealous, dark and overpowering affection" for Lawrence) was largely sympathetic, Kot would have none of it. He accused her of letting him down and demanded changes in the revised edition.[81] Carswell's changes when it came to Kot were, however, merely cosmetic. In the Chatto and Windus edition each odd page had a running title on top, signifying, in capital letters, who or what the main topic of the narrative below was. The title read "КОТ," where Kot described to Carswell the prewar walk in the

Westmoreland hills during which he had to share a bed with Lawrence; and "кот's рæн," on top of the scene at Café Royal. In the Martin Secker edition these headings were taken out.[82]

Kot was likewise upset about the way Carswell portrayed Lawrence, accusing her of "reducing" him. That did not sit well. "It is easy to sit doing nothing & to criticize any effort made by other people, my dear Kot," she wrote at the close of 1932. "I know that I 'reduce' Lawrence in certain ways. But I believe he is big and strong enough to bear such reduction … I like you very much, Kot, though I do wilt a bit under your eternal disapproving Negative. You are Carlyle's *Everlasting Nay* personified." The letter went on to say that she did not want to argue against his decision: "It is yours & you will stick to it."[83] It was a reference, no doubt, to Kot ending their friendship, as he had done with numerous others, including Brett, before her.

By mid-1932, Kot was also offended by how Carswell portrayed Ottoline Morrell, now his dear friend – especially after Ottoline herself complained to him that Carswell's descriptions of her, her family, and friends were spiteful, unjust, and, in essence, quite Frieda-like.[84] The true beginning of Kot's friendship with Morrell can be traced back to a month or so after Lawrence's death. "I am glad you like Ottoline so much," Gertler wrote from Paris in early April.[85] "As I feel very friendly to you," Kot told Ottoline at the end of April, "may I … be allowed to address you as, my dear Ottoline?"[86] He was of course allowed to do so, and for the next eight years, until Ottoline's sudden death in 1938, the two would be extremely close.

On the surface, they were an odd couple. An aristocrat by birth, Lady Ottoline Violet Anne Cavendish-Bentinck Morrell was known for her outré clothes, eccentric ways, excessive love for beautiful things, and scandalous extramarital relationships, most notably with Bertrand Russell. Kot of course often expressed detestation of such qualities, tastes, and behaviour. At different points Ottoline had been very close to Kot's friends – to Mansfield, until a rumour of the Murrys' badmouthing of Ottoline reached her; to Lawrence, until he depicted her as "Hermione Roddice," a woman of "the new school," in *Women in Love*; and to Gertler, who was one of her favourites and, prior to his marriage, regularly stayed in a cottage at Garsington, the Morrells' opulent manor and farm in Oxfordshire. Gertler, for one, was always very apologetic when corresponding with Kot, about his staying in Garsington and socializing with the bohemian crowd Ottoline attracted and Kot detested.

It all mysteriously changed in early April 1930 when Kot became so enthusiastic about Ottoline that even Gertler felt he had to bring him back to earth: "I don't know that I altogether agree with you about her having good friends, etc.

I mean that it is a good deal her fault that she has not had many real ones – she does get rather bored with one – in a way – when one ceases to perform – as it were."[87] Kot was unwavering, though. They were drawn together, it would appear, in equal parts, by their shared loving memories of Mansfield ("I have reread all Katherine Mansfield Letters to me," she wrote to a friend in 1932, "& I am overcome by this. They are *adorable*. I wish & wish & wish I could talk to her now"[88]) and their mutual hatred of Frieda, Murry, and Brett, who used to be a regular at Garsington. 1930 was also already post-Garsington: Ottoline and her husband, Philip, had sold their estate in 1928 and moved to a much more modest dwelling on Gower Street in the Bloomsbury section of London. Ottoline's parties became more subdued, and one of the new regulars, James Stephens, whom Ottoline had befriended during her trip to Ireland in 1919, was also of course a close friend of Kot's. It is more than likely that it was Stephens, in fact, who asked Ottoline to invite Kot to Gower Street.

Once the two of them got to know each other better, they undoubtedly realized that they shared even more. Like Kot, Ottoline suffered from frequent depressions, except, in her case, instead of retreating into the "cave," as Kot inevitably did, she put on a brave facade and sought out people and entertainment. Unlike the rest of her aristocratic family, she was very liberal and, much to Kot's delight, untouched by the all too common aristocratic (and Bloomsburian) prejudice against Jews. In 1932, while in Germany, Ottoline even dropped the doctor treating her "because she was horrified by [his] anti-Semitism."[89]

Kot never quite became what Ottoline called a "New & Superb Intimate friend in my Life," but then, according to her, no one else did in the 1930s, and "dear Koteliansky," as she liked to refer to him in her letters to friends, at least came very close.[90] Beginning in 1931 Kot was included in virtually all of the Morrells' parties on Gower Street. Ottoline's daughter, Julian, witnessed one such occasion where, at Kot's request, T.S. Eliot was invited, too. This gave Kot a long-sought chance to confront the poet on the subject of religion:

Koteliansky … battling against what he believed to be the deadening orthodoxies of the past, wanted to meet T.S. Eliot. They had known each other well in earlier days but had not seen each other for years, partly because Koteliansky had been disgusted by Eliot's conversion to orthodox Anglicanism. Lately, however, he had asked Lady Ottoline if she would arrange for him to see Eliot again in order to give him a piece of his mind on the subject. She said yes: so dramatic and possibly illuminating a confrontation was just the kind of thing to appeal to her and she took care to stage it properly … After tea we settled down in the drawing room; excitedly and with Slav volubility, Koteliansky launched his attack. Eliot, he said, must have turned to Christianity from a cowardly desire for comfort. Eliot rose to the occasion; his reply was deeply impressive … Koteliansky was silenced.[91]

The nature of the "attack" can be best gleaned from a letter Kot wrote in 1931 to Juliette Huxley, another person with whom he was establishing a warm personal relationship after Lawrence's death. Earlier that year she and her husband, Julian, went to the Soviet Union and did Kot a favour by mailing a parcel and a letter to his sister Rokhl from Moscow. Juliette must have mentioned to Kot her reaction to the suppression of religion in Russia, for Kot in response gave a lengthy statement on how he felt about any religion, including the communist dogma, which he considered a religion as well: "Until our own time man tried to adapt and adjust himself to the conception, outside of himself, the conception of God, with all the implications inherent in this; that is, man, in the process of adjustment, suffered a great deal for the rare moments of joy (a joy approved by the God conception held). Where there is no God, as in Russia at present, the community, or the idea of the community, occupies the place of the former God, yet with all the old implications, inspite of the unrecognizably changed phraseology. That is, man again suffers, as well as has his joys, according to approved dogmas. But those of us who are tired of making Gods and too conscious that, ultimately, this leads nowhere, and knowing ourselves to be human, are trying to live a new personal life, without Gods and dogmas, and without the support and comfort, vouchsafed by them. That is, we too have to suffer. Our joys are our very own, not God-approved … Just because the happiness and joy are our own, we have to be ready at any moment to be deprived of them … We have to pay for moments of happiness with patient suffering."[92]

This was probably the essence of his argument against Eliot's conversion. Deeply religious in her own way, Ottoline must have recoiled at some of Kot's blunter pronouncements about religion as an artificial crutch for weak people. As Morrell's biographer, Miranda Seymour, points out, judging by Ottoline's unpublished diaries from the 1930s, her relationship with Kot in general was not an easy one:

Fond though Ottoline became of "dear old Kot," she often found him infuriating. He was, she wrote, used to being humoured and allowed to get away with parading bombast as sense; she was exasperated when she saw him lumber up to Tom Eliot, wring his hand and boom for all the room to hear of the pleasure he felt in being able to tell him that he couldn't stand any of his poetry. She knew how much he enjoyed posing as a philistine, but it was going too far, she thought, when she had taken him out for an evening to see *Così*, her favourite opera, only to be thanked with the observation that it had been quite pleasant. "Quite pleasant!" she repeated: "I could have hit him." But she had already learned that there was no point in quarrelling with Kot. "I cannot argue with a nice dear old charming bull who just rushes at anything one says like a red cloth …" At the times when he could not be persuaded to come, she wrote him long, charming letters about writers they both admired and people who she thought might interest him; without being flirtatious, she encouraged him to think that he occupied a privileged place in her life.[93]

Her letters were, indeed, long and charming, despite occasional difficulties, but his letters to her were even more remarkable because they were so uncharacteristically effusive and even adoring. When, for Christmas 1933, Ottoline, who loved to shower her friends with expensive presents, gave Kot a blue-and-black eiderdown quilt, the warmth of his gratitude matched that of the quilt. "My dear Ottoline," he wrote to her the following day, "When I came home last night … I unpacked my treasures and enjoyed looking at them, while making my supper in the kitchen. At ten I went to bed, put the eider-down on it; could not decide whether to have the eider-down on the rug, or vice-versa; compromised by having the rug over the eider-down … It was a very pleasant sensation. Waking about 1 o'clock I looked at the two sides, and decided that during the cold the black should be on the top, and when it gets warmer – the light blue, which is a lovely colour."

But it was Ottoline's respect for him as a Jew for which he was even more grateful – and it is revealing how, at least in this letter, Kot directly linked his Jewishness to his black moods and the sense of "burden": "Waking at four and switching on the light again, I suddenly felt quite gay, remembering our conversation last night. During the last few months, arriving at your house in a rather 'black mood,' there would happen during my stay an expected exchange of ideas, an understanding smile from you, and my oppression and black mood vanished. The time before last was, when you asked Philip to read out the chapter from Disraeli's book on the Jewish Question. Last night, – your smile in answer to my idea of settling down as an obscure rabbi. All the evening I had a feeling of lightness, of a burden lifted. It is good to understand and to be understood without having recourse to long explanations in words."[94]

Despite her deep respect for Kot's Jewishness, Ottoline was pushing Kot to attend services at St Paul's Cathedral, where she worshipped. It was a tribute to their friendship that Kot took it as well as he did, yet he was slow to oblige her. "It is not out of 'spirit of negation,'" he assured her, and promised that "[o]ne day in the spring you will take me to St Paul's: I shall feel safer with you and the spring; on a winter day, like this, music … in a church would make me cry."[95] He finally did go, and according to Lady Glenavy, was not as impressed by it all as Ottoline hoped he would be: "Kot once said jokingly, 'Ottoline wants to convert me.' He told me how she persuaded him to go to St Paul's Cathedral with her. She thought he would be impressed by the beauty of the music and the Church of England service. The only feeling he got from it was … [that] it was all so completely Jewish; every hymn and psalm and prayer or reading from the Bible was about Jehovah, Jerusalem, the Children of Israel, Zion and the Hebrew prophets."[96]

While Kot was establishing this remarkable new friendship, he was about to lose yet another of his old friends – Grisha Farbman. Farbman, even after the death of his brother-in-law in 1929, continued to go to Russia regularly to gather material for his books, establish or maintain business contacts, and visit family and friends – among them, most likely, the Litvinovs (Maxim was by now Soviet Russia's Foreign minister). Upon his return from Moscow in early 1933, Farbman became sick with a mysterious illness. The details of his ailment are sketchy, but Gertler referred to it as "that awful skin disease he got somehow … most painful and dreadful."[97] At least some – apparently including Farbman himself – believed that he had been intentionally poisoned while still in Russia.[98]

At some point in early spring there was, apparently, hope that Farbman was going to survive whatever it was that felled him. "Mr Farbman is doing better and the doctor expects him to recover," Kot assured Ottoline on 4 March.[99] By late May, however, Farbman was dead.[100] Probably the last person whose condolences Kot wanted to hear was Frieda. But hear from her he did. She assured Kot that she felt very sorry for Mrs Farbman and wished she could help her financially, because Sonia Farbman had been so nice to Lawrence – but, alas, despite being the sole owner of her late husband's estate, she simply was not rich enough …[101]

In the early 1930s Kot was also getting much more welcome letters than Frieda's from his sister, Rokhl, and her daughter, Lina, living now in Kiev, as well as from his Canadian niece, Polly. Two of the earliest surviving letters from Rokhl – written in Yiddish – are both from April 1931, around the time she had received the parcel and letter that Kot asked the Huxleys to send her from Moscow.

These letters must have been preceded by a falling out of sorts between her and Kot following Beila's death, for Rokhl suggested in one of them that "If Mother were alive she would say you were right, not me" and begged him to give her "your word that you are no longer angry with me … I have sinned against you."

Her only excuse for whatever sin she might have committed against Kot was the difficulty of her life in Russia: "you have not lived for twenty years under the clouds … you will never know how it feels." Clouds or not, Rokhl went on to declare that she would never "suffer" living, like their brother Moishel, in Canada. She may have added that mainly for the benefit of the Soviet censors who would be likely to read her letters abroad, but she also probably shared Kot's disdain for what he considered the overly materialistic values of the Sherbrooke branch of their family.

Rokhl's letters were very emotional. She kept telling Kot, whom she addressed as "My dear beloved brother" or "Dear Shmuel," that she was indebted to him "with my whole life" and that nobody had taken his place: "After mother, you are the only person I have such a feeling for – that I can't express." Rokhl also gathered, not from any details that Kot had provided but by the tone of his letters, that he had "had a tragedy" and suspected that it had something to do with a bitter love affair. In the letters she chided him for prematurely complaining about "aging" and urged him instead to follow the example of Fanny Stepniak, who, though much older, was still "united in spirit and body." Rokhl also sounded very concerned about Kot's health problems and his attitude toward doctors: "You write you are afraid of doctors and hospitals, this scares us."[105] Her own husband, Naum (Noyakh) Marshak, she told Kot, was so sick that his condition kept him from working.

By then the Marshaks had two daughters: Mary, who was twelve in 1931, and Lina, who was sixteen. "Lina," Rokhl informed Kot, "looks like me with light hair, blue eyes, light complexion, rosy cheeks. Mary looks like you. I prefer Mary. I wish you could be close to them." Lina, Rokhl thought, could especially use Kot's help and was much more likely to follow her uncle's advice than her mother's.[103] Kot must have then written to Lina with his concerns about her behaviour as reported by her mother, for in early May 1932 he received a letter in which Lina apologized for having frightened her family and her London uncle with her talk about getting married in order not to have to obey her parents anymore. It was, she wrote, just a silly joke, and she promised Kot that, even though her mother "considers me to be a fool," she would not do a foolish thing like getting married when she was not even eighteen. Lina also assured her uncle that she read a lot and constantly worked on improving herself so that she could be "a real person" and, as such, "useful to the society."[104]

It was Kot's other niece, Polly, four years Lina's senior, who was in fact getting married. Her fiancé had also come to Canada from Ostropol, where he used to work for Kot's parents, Polly's grandparents. According to Polly's daughters, Kot made it clear to Polly that he was not at all pleased with her choice, deeming

Manuel Smith (Manuel's original last name, Shpiegelborg, was changed to Smith upon his entry to Canada) her social inferior.[105] He also complained to the Wellses that Polly was marrying "beneath her" and that her husband-to-be was nothing but "a tradesman."[106] By the early 1930s, however, Manuel Smith, who was thirteen years older than Polly, was already a respected and successful businessman, while Polly was still living with Moishel and his family, where, fairly or not, she often felt like a barely tolerated poor relative. By the age of twenty-two Polly had witnessed the tragic deaths of both parents and her only sibling, and she wanted to fill the void as soon as possible with a family of her own.[107] Despite Kot's misgivings, Polly and Manuel were married in summer 1933, and in August she sent her uncle a letter from her honeymoon in Saratoga Springs. He responded with a tender, albeit brief, postcard. Addressed to "Mrs M. Smith," it read: "My dear Polly, awfully glad to have your letter of Aug 28 from Saratoga Springs. Hope you are having a good time. Shall expect longer letters from you when you return home. Love and best wishes to you and Manuel. Your uncle."[108]

# CRESSET PRESS: LOSING EQUILIBRIUM

When I said I needed a mother or a wife just at this moment,
I meant it only as having someone who, in the confusion of all the
friendly advice and best meant intentions, would "manage" me.
~ Kot to Ottoline Morrell, 27 July 1936

The anxieties, the torments, my inner problems that have brought
on my illness remain, unsolved and insoluble … I am not sorry
for myself: I am only so grieved for having mismanaged everything
and for having wasted everything. And there is no way out of all
this … I am a shuddering, pitiable creature.
~ Kot to Ottoline Morrell, 5 September 1936

In 1933, for only the second time in his life in England, Kot got a regular, paying
job. With his dreams of owning his own press appearing less and less achievable,
Kot decided to accept a job at a press run by someone else – namely Dennis
Cohen, the director of the Cresset Press Limited and a cousin of Esther Salaman's
husband. The Salamans, it appears, successfully convinced their rich relative that,
as a friend of many writers, among them H.G. Wells, Kot would bring at least
some of those authors into Cohen's publishing stable.

Wells was indeed among the very first people Kot contacted about his new
job. "My dear H.G.," he wrote to him on 23 July 1933, "I should like to have your
blessing on my attempt to become something in the way of a publisher. Not that
I have any desire of becoming an active person, but I want to create a situation,
which would force me to get out of my inertia. Can you spare a few minutes for
me to come and see you[?]"[1] "[S]omething in the way of a publisher" was Kot's
own conceptualization of his new position, not his employer's. In fact, it sounded
much too grandiose to Cohen and his solicitors, who thought they were hiring
"a reader-advisor" but found his proposed terms and job description more be-

fitting of "a sleeping partner."[2] Once again, as in the sad saga of *The Adelphi*, Kot had grossly overestimated his value to a commercial enterprise. Given how penniless Kot was, his insistence on extraordinary terms and influence undoubtedly struck Cohen, a fellow Jew, as an act of unmitigated chutzpah.

Dennis Cohen founded the Cresset Press in 1927. In the beginning it specialized in expensively illustrated limited editions of classical works, like Milton's *Paradise Lost*. Too "cut-throat" for some, including his own niece,[3] Cohen was a prominent figure in London's social circles, thanks both to his wealth and his marriage to a beautiful Hollywood actress, Kathryn Hamill, who had been one of the original Ziegfeld girls. Cohen met her on one of his visits to the States and brought her to London. Throughout the 1930s she acted on London stages, except for several years when she took a leave of her acting career to work as secretary to Aneurin Bevan, the prominent Welsh Labour MP. No ordinary starlet, she received a degree in genetics from Cambridge in the 1940s and became a professional psychiatrist as well as a co-director of her husband's press.

A thin, pocket-sized Cresset Press catalogue published in 1929 boasted that while the past decade as a whole was "undoubtedly going to take a notable place in the history of fine printing in England … the Cresset Press … may well be remembered when time comes to pick out the most memorable productions of these years."[4] The inaugural publications of 1927 and 1928 were all limited editions. They included richly illustrated folio volumes of Bacon's *Essays, and Coulers of Good and Evil* and Bunyan's *The Pilgrim's Progress*. Then came translations of Ovid and *The Iliad*, as well as books on English foxhunting, angling, and gardening. In 1929 the press continued with classics, including an edition of *Gulliver's Travels*, illustrated by John "Rex" Whistler, a former Slade student whose mural decorations were exhibited at the Tate Gallery.

That year Cresset also published their first Russian book, Gogol's *Diary of a Madman*, translated by D.S. Mirsky, or Prince Mirsky, as he was better known, a Russian émigré and distinguished professor at the University of London. (He would return to the Soviet Union in 1932 and subsequently perish in the Stalin purges of the late 1930s.) The volume was illustrated by Alexander Alexeieff, a designer for the Ballets Russes who would later emigrate to the United States and work in Hollywood as both a book illustrator and an animator. Since these were limited editions, the prices were steep. In the United States, *Gulliver's Travels* went for $140, unless it was printed on Roman vellum, which hiked the price to $1,240. Gogol was cheaper but still quite pricey by the standards of the day – the set-by-hand edition, which featured twenty original aquatints (only 167 copies were published for the United Kingdom, and 83 copies for the United States) sold for $25, while copies printed on handmade paper (30 all in all) cost $75.[5]

The year after Kot joined the Cresset Press, a new, much fancier catalogue came out covering the years 1927-1934. It was now the size of a paperback and looked very Constructivist: it had plastic pages with white print on them on top of black paper pages with red print. Superimposed, they formed a full entry. The cover likewise had a plastic page attached to it, with "Cresset Press" printed in red. The plastic pages contained the title and the author; the paper pages had brief descriptions, number of copies within the limited edition, the kind of paper the book was printed on, and how it was bound. One entry was for D.H. Lawrence's *Birds, Beasts & Flowers*, which Cresset published in 1930. These were Lawrence poems originally published in 1923, whose republication he negotiated with Cresset during the last six months of his life. "Don't push the Cresset Press too hard about *BirdsBeasts*," he pleaded with his agent in September 1929. "I particularly want them to do the job, for the sake of Blair Hughes-Stanton, who is doing the illustrations, and is a friend ... So do please accommodate the Cresset all you can, as far as I am concerned."[6] The edition, indeed, featured "ten full-page illustrations and two head and tail pieces by Blair Hughes-Stanton" and was limited "to 500 copies on mould-made paper bound in vellum" and "30 copies on Bachelor's hand-made paper, bound in natural pigskin."[7] Lawrence, however, did not live to see it.

The catalogue was printed for the exhibition of the Cresset Press publications, which opened in June 1934. The exhibition displayed not just books but original drawings as well. By 1934, however, Cohen already felt that "like many other publishers of luxury books, the press ... had to concentrate more on 'unlimited' editions."[8] That, he thought, was where Kot, with his reputation of knowing so many contemporary authors personally and his expertise in Russian literature, could prove helpful. Another selling point were the letters Lawrence wrote to Kot, which Kot offered Cohen for publication, assuring him that Frieda had given him the permission to publish them. Yet, it is likely that, if Cohen had known Kot's business sense and his views on publishing, no personal connections to great authors, letters from famous writers, or entreaties from relatives would have worked. "[P]ublishers are such horrible blighters," Kot would complain in 1935 to Dilys Powell, whose first book was being published by the Cresset Press. "Publishers exist to lose money on good books, otherwise there is no justification for their lives and existence."[9]

Even though H.G. Wells's recent books had not been great commercial successes and publishers like Collins and Heinemann began to balk at his exuberant demands and even to turn him down, Cohen was not averse to making him one of the Cresset Press authors. Kot, needless to say, was eager to seal the deal as soon as he joined Cresset. He knew that, at the time, Wells was working on his most confessional book to date, *Experiment in Autobiography*. "I should be most happy," Kot wrote in early January 1934, starting his intense sales pitch, "if you thought it possible to let the Cresset Press publish a limited edition of your 'Autobiography.' The Cresset Press, with a wide experience of limited editions, will produce and publish your book as well, if not better, as any publisher in London, and the Press, generally, is of a higher standard. May I call on you one day, when you are free, to have a talk about it?"[10]

Within two days, Kot had Wells's manuscript and assured his friend that he was filled with joy to be able "to play even the slightest part in the publication of your Autobiography." He then proceeded to describe the generous terms that the press was willing to offer: "750 copies at £3.3. a copy ... a royalty, on the whole edition, of 20%." There was one hitch, however, concerning the book's publication in the United States: "The Cresset Press will do its utmost, – without charge or commission – to dispose of the American limited edition rights, but can undertake no responsibility, or guarantee the publication of such edition in the USA, in view of the present state of affairs there."[11] Depression or not, given that his other publishers had always arranged for the simultaneous publication of his books in the United States, this was quite a sticking point for Wells. But given his recent troubles with advantageously placing his books, he was prepared to be courted by Kot and Kot's new employer.

Things got ugly three days later, however, when it became obvious that the overzealous Kot had jumped the gun. Cohen and his solicitors, who were well aware that other publishers had lost money on Wells's most recent books, were not yet ready to promise anything. "Before committing himself to the terms contained in my letter," Kot apologetically explained to Wells on 9 January, "the proprietor of the Cresset Press, Mr Dennis M. Cohen, would like to see the MS. I hope you will not regard this as lack of courtesy on his part."[12] Wells did regard it as gross lack of courtesy; in fact, it enraged him. He marked this paragraph of Kot's letter and placed a huge exclamation point next to it for emphasis. He then wrote stern instructions in fat pencil for his secretary and daughter-in-law Marjorie Craig Wells: "No. The MS must not go out ... K is getting on too fast. I don't want NEGOTIATIONS! I didn't want *offers* from the Cresset Press. I simply wanted K's advice & comments. If that bloody Yid cant take K's report on it, what good is K?"[13]

Fortunately for "K," he never saw Wells's comments. Wells once said that part of his secretary's job description (in addition to doing "a lot of typing," and having to "deal with callers ... protect me from intrusion ... be loyal and silent") was "to translate a pencilled 'No' into a polite refusal."[14] Marjorie Wells undoubtedly did just that. Had Kot seen Wells's enraged notes, it is not clear what would have been more hurtful – Wells's devastating "What good is K?" or his calling Cohen – and by extrapolation Kot – "that bloody Yid."

There followed a month-long silence in Kot's correspondence with Wells, but in early March Kot approached him again: "I should like to see you for a few minutes any time you are free to have a talk about the publication of your 'Autobiography,' in a limited edition by the 'Cresset Press,' and in a general edition by one of the big publishers here, with an excellent organization for distribution. The drawback about the publisher, who is keen to do the general edition and to offer as good terms as any other publisher here could, is that he wants to see the MS, – rather more from the technical side, – before saying definitely, how much he is prepared to pay in advance for royalties ... Myself I shall be delighted to be instrumental in the publication of your 'Autobiography.'"[15]

The other publisher was Victor Gollancz, also a relatively new firm, founded the same year as the Cresset Press. It was an unusual arrangement (repeated again – but with a different publisher – for Wells's friend, Dorothy Richardson), but then, it was an unusual book, and Cohen knew as well as Kot did that intimate writings by famous authors did sell. Soon Wells left on visits to the United States and the Soviet Union, in a quest to interview the two world leaders, Roosevelt and Stalin, and compare them in his *Autobiography*. In May, while Wells was still away, Kot sent Marjorie Wells a letter that was both businesslike and very personal: "I enclose The Cresset Press and Victor Gollancz's letters, containing the offer for H.G.'s 'Autobiography.' I hope and pray that the offer might find grace in the eyes of H.G. and that he accept it, thus putting to shame all possible enemies, and crowning my head with eternal glory."[16] The enemies in question by now also included Mr Cohen and his solicitors, who were growing increasingly skeptical of whether Kot would ever deliver.

Cohen's was apparently the best offer Wells obtained, and the book came out later in the year, as it turned out, both in England and the United States, where it was published by Macmillan. The chill in Kot and Wells's relationship, however, persisted. In late October, having received a copy of *The Experiment in Autobiography* with Wells's inscription in it, Kot dared to hope that he was regaining Wells's esteem: "Am I to take this as a sign that you are no longer cross with me? I cannot tell you how painful this sudden estrangement on your part has been to me."[17] Kot must have winced, however, when he read the following description of Stalin in Wells's new book: "I have never met a man more candid, fair and honest, and to these qualities it is, and to nothing occult and sinister, that he owes his tremendous undisputed ascendancy in Russia. I had thought before I saw him that he might be where he was because men were afraid of him, but I realize that he owes his position to the fact that no one is afraid of him and everybody trusts him."[18]

*The Experiment in Autobiography* sold very well, and that success became Kot's shield against future criticism of his poor performance at the press. "When soon after I began working for the Cresset Press I succeeded in getting H.G. Wells' 'Autobiography,'" he would write in 1937 to Esther's husband, Myer Salaman, who no doubt kept hearing complaints from Cohen about the man he had recommended, "the profit received by Dennis on that book alone was such that it covered all the moneys paid by him to me during all the years of my employment."[19] He needed that shield badly when his subsequent recruits – Dilys Powell and Dorothy Richardson – cost the press dearly.

Dilys Powell was a beginning author whom he brought to the attention of the Cresset Press in 1934. He had known her for a couple of years through Ottoline Morrell, who had befriended Powell after reading her essay on T.S. Eliot's poetry in the *Times* of London, in 1931. Both Powell and Morrell were great fans of Hollywood westerns and screwball comedies, and the two often went to movies together.[20] Even though Kot and Powell routinely met at Ottoline's prior to 1934, their relationship was not yet close when he started preparing her book *Descent from Parnassus* for publication by the Cresset Press. His initial letters to her were all rather formally addressed to "Dear Miss Powell."

Kot had generally a low opinion of women writers. Lady Glenavy remembered his dismissive remark directed at "a distinguished woman novelist": "Embroidery ... Literature is Holy Writ. If she wants to do embroidery, let her embroider her knickers."[21] The women writers whom he liked personally, however – Mansfield most of all but also Woolf – were excepted from his generic criticism. Kot's attitude toward Powell, who was in her early thirties when they met, was very caring and paternal from the beginning. Her book was a serious literary analysis of such contemporary poets as T.S. Eliot, Edith Sitwell, and Siegfried Sassoon. The study started, surprisingly for some, with the poetry of D.H. Lawrence, which Powell felt gave readers insight into Lawrence as a prose writer. Kot liked her high opinion of Lawrence, whom she considered "a great writer ... careless of perfection, capable of shoddiness and even grossness of style; but still by virtue of his vitality, his shattering command of language and the rare sharpness of his sensibilities, a great writer." He also enjoyed her criticism of Murry's approach to Lawrence as "betray[ing] an insensibility to style unparalleled in criticism," as well the respect with which she treated Lawrence's *Pansies* (which Kot had taken so much trouble to protect from being pirated).[22]

Convincing Cohen that he should publish Powell's book was not easy. "I must not tell secrets," Kot wrote to Powell in early April, "yet for your patient waiting I will this once tell you that Mr Cohen likes your work, but his experience and booksellers make him hesitate quite a lot about the publication of it."[23] The first book by a largely unknown author, dealing solely with poetry and written in a rather academic manner, was something most publishers would definitely hesitate quite a lot about. What finally convinced Cohen, it seems, was Kot's firm belief that Powell would one day be a sought-after author and "a real 'good' success,'" and that, when her "next two books become great successes, he will be able to sell the remaining copies of 'Parnassus' at a premium."[24]

Once the Cresset Press accepted *Descent from Parnassus*, Kot started to devise ways to sell it well. His idea was to ask someone established, like Desmond MacCarthy, to write a preface, because it would "undoubtedly have the effect of making the book more acceptable and even tempting to an American publisher."[25] More importantly still, he thought it would protect the beginning writer's fragile ego by serving "as a sort of amulet against reviewers … so that the reviewers of your book, seeing D. MacC's name introducing you, should have a little bit of a fear of God, and treat your book more cautiously."[26] Cohen, who already feared the sales of the book would be lacklustre, refused to pay anything extra to MacCarthy, and MacCarthy, invoking poor health and too much work, turned the request down. The book came out with no introduction, and it lost money.[27] Powell would, indeed, eventually become more sought-after – yet despite her unwavering loyalty to Kot until the day he died, her subsequent books would be published not by Cresset but by Hodder and Stoughton, an older and more established press. Her eventual fame, however, did affect the later sales of her first book; in that Kot was to be proven right.

There was one book that Kot really wanted Powell to write after *Descent of Parnassus* came out, and it was, again, the book – or even books – about Lawrence he would have probably liked to write himself. "If you ever feel anxious about the lack of themes," he advised her in summer 1935, "be comforted by my assurance that a book or books on D.H.L. is a task, to which one can devote a great part of one's life to perform it. And the task is one of the most interesting and fundamentally important not only for the immediate time, but for the future."[28] Powell, however, had other plans. Her next book would be about Greece, where she had been spending summers with her archaeologist husband, Humfry Payne, since 1929, when he was appointed director of the British School of Archaeology in Athens.

During 1934–35 Kot was helping not just new friends but old ones as well. He was instrumental in Fanny Stepniak's decision-making as to what to do with her late husband's papers, which were by then sought after by both the London School of Economics and the Soviets – Sergei Stepniak was being celebrated in the Soviet Russia as a true, even if somewhat politically not entirely correct, revolutionary. She ended up giving them to the Soviets, who, in addition to paying for the archive (and even Stepniak's writing desk), granted her an annual stipend until her death in 1945, making the deal particularly attractive.[29]

Kot also kept close track of Gertler, and, during summer 1934, was happy to get cheerful letters from Spain, where the family was vacationing, highlighting, among other things, Gertler's fatherly pride in Luke: "In the village he is a great favourite. We took him to an open-air dancing … he caused a great sensation. He ran about laughing and excited during the intervals and the people threw confetti at him. As he ran the confetti showered from his head like Golden Rain which caused great excitement among the audience. It was difficult to believe that exactly two years ago he was a tiny shrimp wrapped in cotton wool at King's College Hospital."[30]

"Kot is much more composed now," Gertler updated Hodgson in August 1934, "he is much recompensated by being employed in … the Cresset Press."[31] At the end of 1934 Kot even felt like being more social as well as a good company man and attended a cocktail party that Cresset was throwing. He had invited Powell and Ottoline Morrell to join him. Ottoline had other engagements,[32] but Powell accepted the invitation. Kot however overestimated his social endurance and left the party very soon after he arrived. "I hope you did not mind my sudden disappearance the other night," he apologized to Powell later, "the heat, the evening dress, the 'deliberately' lively ladies and gentlemen were too much for me. Is this a sign of prickliness?"[33] His employer by then had, no doubt, stronger words that "prickliness" to describe Kot's professional demeanour, and the subsequent Dorothy Richardson fiasco did not help the matters.

Kot started courting Richardson in 1933, soon after he joined Cresset. Richardson was the author of one of the earliest works of English Modernism, *Pilgrimage. Pointed Roofs, Pilgrimage*'s first book, came out in 1915 and featured the first sustained stream-of-consciousness narrative in English. Richardson was an old friend of H.G. Wells and his second wife, Catherine, who had been her schoolmate. At one point she was even briefly Wells's lover and miscarried his child.[34] When Kot approached her, Richardson was sixty years old, in poor health, and – because her books were not selling well – in need of money. She and her husband, illustrator Alan Odle, rented a house in St John's Wood not far from Kot, but for the sake of Odle, who suffered from tuberculosis, they spent most of their time in Cornwall.

By 1933 Richardson had published ten "chapter-volumes," as she called them, all with the same publishers: Duckworth in England and Alfred Knopf in the United States. None repeated the success of the first volume and the last seven lost significant amounts of money. In early 1920 Duckworth began complaining of the losses incurred by her books, and Knopf echoed those complaints in spring

1923.[35] In the early 1930s, the protests from the publishers grew even louder, with Knopf refusing outright to publish her tenth volume in the United States.[36] Wells may have apprised Kot of the situation, possibly when they had that meeting that Kot requested to discuss his new job in summer 1933. Kot also was aware that Richardson was in financial need and that she was an accomplished translator from German and occasionally French. He convinced Cohen to let Richardson translate Joseph Kastein's book, *Jews in Germany*, which the Cresset Press wanted to publish. She was also paid to proofread Wells's *Experiment in Autobiography*.

Given Richardson's recent record of book sales, getting Cohen to publish the eleventh "chapter-volume" of *Pilgrimage*, *Clear Horizon*, was not as easy a sell. Kot's plan, however, went far beyond publishing one novel. Kot envisioned eventually publishing the whole cycle in an "omnibus" edition, and for that the Cresset Press would have to buy out Duckworth. As in Wells's case, another press, J.M. Dent, was appealed to. They agreed to join in, and then Cohen acquiesced as well. Somewhere along the way the fact that *Clear Horizon* would not be the last volume in the cycle had been lost. Both publishers believed they were signing on to publishing one new novel and then the omnibus edition, which they believed could be a moneymaker. It is quite likely that Kot, in his desire to make them commit but believing they would reject an open-ended venture, was intentionally vague in describing the sequence of events to them. He did, after all, pride himself on the fact that, regardless of who was paying him, his loyalty was always to the writers, not the publisher, and in that he functioned more as the writers' agent than the publisher's advisor.

Richardson would describe Kot to a friend in 1934 as "a little overwhelming on account of his dogmatic intellectualism & his big booming voice. He leaves us feeling we have been passed several times through a powerful mangle." She was grateful to him, though, for all the efforts on her behalf, and, early on, she was quite impressed with his knowledge of the publishing scene, albeit somewhat surprised by his lack of business sense: "He … at the end of a few months, seems to know the publishing world from end to end. Knows, that is to say, the name & disposition, & moral value, & taste in hats of the second cousin of the junior partner's sister-in-law's half-sister, by marriage, in all the firms in England & America as well as their methods, bank-balances & future prospects, He evolves, bless him, every few weeks, a fresh scheme of an omnibus Pilgrimage. In vain I point out, specify, the number of publishers who have seriously considered such a scheme & have dropped it – the moment they glanced through my sales record."[37]

Their relationship, while overall much less turbulent than many others he had been involved in, was not without occasional complications. "Ever since your letter came in, dear Kot," she wrote to him in April 1934, "I have been racking my brains to discover what I have done to merit reproaches. Something very stupid, I have no doubt, considering my large share of British stupidity. The only thing, in the end, I can suppose, with eyebrows in the air in incredulity, is that you somehow include some aspect of yourself in something I said in regard to Russians."[38] She was probably off the mark. It was not the Russian in him but the Jew whom she must have offended when, disagreeing with him and Cohen on the need for a preface for Kastein's book in addition to her translator's foreword, she had written: "What can one poor little Christian do, surrounded by large Jews, in shawls, laying down laws?"[39] She obviously meant it as a joke; having translated a book on the agony of Jews in Hitler's Germany and having written to Kot on many occasions about how profoundly Kastein's narrative affected her, she must have felt she would not be misinterpreted. It was not a joke, however, that Kot had much taste for.

Even though Kastein's book was about Jews, its main audience was supposed to be gentiles, so Cohen, as a Jewish publisher, wanted to make sure that the preface would be written by a non-Jew. Kot plainly did not trust Richardson to write about the situation in Germany with the sensitivity the topic required. He suggested James Stephens instead. Richardson's "Translator's Foreword" was thus reduced to a single page while Stephens's preface ran for twelve. Kot, no doubt, played a big part in shaping Stephens's introduction, which paid more than just token respect to Jews:

Any moderate statement that is made about the Jew, his personal quality, his national history, his world influence, is in itself an immoderacy. The debt which the Christian world owes to the Jewish world is incalculable ...

The Jew should have been for us the most favoured and honoured race in the world ... Mr Kastein knows how the Jewish case stands, and – although the Jew is the world's greatest optimist – he has no longer illusion as to what has occurred and is occurring to his people: or as to the more which may happen in the difficult days now overshadowing us all.[40]

A Stephens biographer aptly calls this preface Stephens's personal act of "celebrat[ing] friendship with a Jew."[41]

*Clear Horizon*, which Richardson dedicated to Koteliansky despite their disagreements, came out from Dent and Cresset in autumn 1934, and, like Dilys Powell's volume, it was a financial failure. Still reeling from the realization that there was now at least one more novel coming before the omnibus edition could be printed, and "shocked by small sales, 500 odd up to Christmas," Dent and Cresset tried to persuade Richardson "to postpone a new edition."[42] "Needless to say," Richardson wrote to Kot, "though a severe shock, this upshot, given the circumstances, did not surprise me."[43] The publishers blamed Kot both for the confusion and poor sales. Richardson heard that Cohen "was furious with Koteliansky, who had argued him into the purchase," and even that Cohen had fired him.[44] Kot probably would have been fired had he not fallen sick in summer 1936. With Esther Salaman, among others, very concerned about Kot's well-being and even sanity at the time, Cohen must have received an earful warning him not to contribute to Kot's problems. Instead of outright firing him, Cohen wrote a stern letter suggesting that Kot could continue with them only if he would find more suitable books for Cresset to publish – by that Cohen said he meant not only the ones "that have literary merit but books for which there is a fair chance of success."[45] Kot was not fooled. "I have not been going to the office for months," he informed Ralph Hodgson at the end of 1936. "My boss does not want me to go back: he thinks he can do without me. Well, let him. But I am still paid for the time being, which won't last very long."[46]

Richardson likely blamed Kot too, yet in her letters she always rose above it by claiming it was no one's fault, just a case of unfortunate misunderstanding. Yet the misunderstanding still continued: Richardson had no intention of completing the cycle even with her twelfth volume. She felt, however, it was not the time to complicate her dealings with Dent and Cresset any further. Unlike Kot, who apparently urged her to hold their feet to the fire and make sure they do not go back on their word, regardless of the number of future volumes, she actually felt sympathy for the publishers: "The whole of their plans having been made on the basis of this erroneous supposition, it is not surprising that they should wish, now, to revise those plans. Merely to compel them to fulfill their contract against their own judgment will help nobody."[47] Kot, needless to say, found this sentiment ridiculous. He firmly believed that the books he procured for the press would, in the long run, "go on bringing in profits for ever and ever." He also blamed Cohen, not himself, for the losses since, in his opinion, "in the hands of the proper publishers these books would have brought in at least a four fold profit."[48]

Kot was most definitely having very rough time with it all. "I wish now more than ever to win the Irish Sweep," he wrote to Ottoline in January 1936, "and that I shall never have to meet stupid people but only those very few who are essential in one's life."[49] It did not help his state of mind that, for months after Farbman's death in 1933, Kot had lived in what Gertler called "a sad household," with the grieving widow and daughter, both of whom Kot had to support emotionally.[50] It became even sadder when Sonia and Ghita Farbman, no longer able to afford the rent, moved out, and Kot had to find new tenants. He called his new housemates "smells and noises" and tried to minimize his contact with them as much as possible.[51]

These new tenants were Percy and Barbara Muir, he a bookseller, she an aspiring writer. "As you can imagine," Barbara Muir would write to Lady Glenavy after *Today We Will Only Gossip* came out, "sharing the house with Kot presented some difficulties, for both parties. We moved in shortly after Mrs Farbman and her daughter moved out. At first Kot and I shared the kitchen – but of course that soon proved an impossible arrangement. I am not particularly tidy and Kot used to say to me: 'Barbara, when Mrs Farbman cooked her meals, the kitchen used to look like a laboratory' … He hated the smell of mutton fat … [W]hen I cooked lamb cutlets … he would say: 'Barbara, you are cooking *mutton*.' And he would put on his big black hat and stump off down the road. My cat proved a trial to him too. It was a Tom and now and then would spray the front door. The smell greatly upset poor Kot."

Muir likened Kot at the time to a volcano, "full of subterranean fires that always threatened."[52] He was missing not just Mrs Farbman's cooking but also the Farbmans' very presence. "Kot has been very seedy and very depressed – has been going through a very bad time altogether," Gertler had let Hodgson know in March 1935. "There are new people sharing his house with him now and he feels lonely."[53]

By 1936, Gertler himself was not doing so well either. "I really do feel terribly weak," Gertler wrote to Kot in early July.[54] Gertler was back at the sanatorium, running a very high fever and fearing the worst. Added to his anxieties over his now increasingly distant relationship with Marjorie, his son's still continuing health problems, and the difficulty in selling his pictures, the relapse proved to be the last drop. With Golda dead, and thus one fewer reason to stay alive, eleven days after Gertler was admitted to the sanatorium he slit his throat and cut his wrist. Bleeding profusely, he had a change of heart and rang for a nurse. A blood transfusion saved him, but he was more disappointed than happy not to have died.

Gertler's attempted suicide was not the only piece of dreadful news that Kot received that year from the people whom he considered his "essentials." In early May he had heard from Dilys Powell that, while excavating, her husband developed an infection from a cut in his knee. Kot did not think it was too serious, but he advised Dilys to bring Payne to England so that English doctors could look at it. He also used the occasion to maliciously joke to Powell that "Mr and Mrs Cohen" should be put to work digging so that all cuts and infections would plague them and not her husband.[55] It was far from a joking matter, though: four days later, Payne died from blood poisoning at the age of thirty-four. "Dilys, my dear," Kot wrote to her the same evening, "in your distress and great unhappiness please remember that you have friends who love you and share your great sorrow."[56] Around the same time, Kot wrote to Ottoline, who was in Italy at the time, that he was hoping that by the time she returned to London he would have "succeeded in driving away the evil powers that have been tormenting me."[57]

In that he did not succeed. Because of the new calamities befalling people he loved, and his own professional and personal problems, Kot's health, both physical and mental, was fast deteriorating. That summer, he went to see his regular doctor, John Ledingham, about abdominal pain and frayed nerves. Ledingham thought Kot's physical condition was "not serious" and probably caused by infection of the gall bladder, which a strict diet would help. He was much more concerned about Kot's state of mind, considering that the "main trouble" demanding Kot's most serious attention. The doctor did not, however, recommend any treatment.[58]

Ruth Mantz, a Mansfield scholar who went to interview Kot in the second half of July, was concerned about Kot's state of mind as well. She went as far as alerting Lady Glenavy that something was seriously wrong with Kot and that it could lead to insanity if nothing was done. She did not know Lady Glenavy's address, so she sent her letter to Ottoline Morrell with a note asking Morrell to forward it but not mentioning her anxiety about Kot to her. Ottoline, not knowing any better and not having Lady Glenavy's address handy, forwarded the letter to Kot and asked him to address it. Suspecting that it may be about him, Kot opened the letter instead. Even though Lady Glenavy never received the letter, which is now among Kot's materials in Catherine Stoye's private archive,[59] she knew enough about Kot's troubles to be deeply worried on her own. Writing to Ottoline that summer, she suggested that Kot needed a good "doctor of the soul" and even proposed, quite astutely, that it could be someone who specialized in "shell shock."[60]

Around the same time Fanny Stepniak was also growing anxious about Kot's well being, especially after a postcard she received from him that she described as "painfully sad to read." She implored Kot to let her see him and allow Sonia Farbman, who desperately wanted to take care of Kot, help him.[61] But Kot did not want to see – or write to – almost anyone. He was clinging to his belief – the one he had formulated very clearly in a letter to Juliette Huxley back in 1931 – that the best action for him was "not to give in to the feeling of unhappiness, however deep and painful it may be; not to create unnecessary difficulties and anxieties for those who are dear to one; but to go through one's pains and suffering, with all possible patience."[62] He did make a few exceptions, though, and allowed himself to rely on Ottoline, to whom he wrote almost daily, and on Dilys Powell, whom

Kot allowed to visit him regularly. When the two proved to be not enough, "at the worst moment in my illness," as Kot explained it to Ida Baker, he cabled Marjorie Wells in Switzerland and asked her to come back from her vacation. He was deeply embarrassed to have to do it. This was, he told Ida, "a most shameful thing of me to have done."[63]

Kot would later blame Ledingham for the length and seriousness of his illness that year. But Ledingham was not the only doctor who recommended the course of treatment that eventually included removing Kot's teeth as a likely source of abdominal infection. Kot also consulted Andrew Morland, the same doctor who was treating Gertler and whom Gertler had sent to help Lawrence, and Morland approved all Ledingham's recommendations. Tooth extraction was a common practice in those days – both in England and the United States. It was just about to be discredited but too late for Kot. In a 1937 article entitled "Dentists Attack Extraction 'Orgy,'" *The New York Times* reported that the annual convention of the American Dental Association that year in Atlantic City heard "two attacks on what speakers called the 'orgy' of tooth extraction as a remedy for general ills or infections in other parts of the body … They asserted that mouth infection might be a result rather than a cause of infection elsewhere and that there was no proof that teeth were in any case the cause of disturbances in other parts of the system."[64] Kot was highly skeptical of the procedure from the start. "I follow the advice of doctor Morland – to have my teeth extracted. But I have not got his belief the extraction will cure me," he wrote to Ottoline who egged him on by stating that she knew people, including her own husband, whom it had significantly helped.[65] For the sake of expediency, she advised Kot to have all his teeth pulled out at once and check into a hospital for several days to have a nurse around. Kot chose, however, to do it in several visits.

In early August, the extractions were interrupted by his stay at a nursing home when Kot agreed to follow his doctor's new recommendations and go there in an attempt to soothe his nerves and regain mental balance.[66] "Am going today to the nursing home," he informed Ottoline on 6 August. "Don't be cross with me for my being now completely different from my former self … it is my former self that responds to your 'moralizing.' For my present self, – when I think of you, – I feel disgust."[67] He did not phrase it well – his English did tend to slip when he was angry or deeply emotional – but Kot probably meant here that the disgust he felt was for his "present self," not for Ottoline.

The nursing home was not far from his house.[68] He stayed there for two weeks, now and then jokingly begging Ottoline – whom he did allow to visit him "whenever you like" – to come and spirit him away. He assured her that "[a]t moments when my mind is clear I think of you constantly, with a good and happy smile," and that his only regret was that he had not confided in her earlier: "Had I come to you a few months ago, when I could no longer bear my troubles myself, I might have been saved by your sane judgment. I let myself drift, and here is the result."[69] Marjorie Wells was at his side almost constantly. A week into his stay he declared that "if a doctor kept me here some time, I should go all wrong, physically. But having submitted, what can I do?"[70] By 20 August, however, he felt he had had enough. "I left the nursing home today," he told Ottoline. "I could not stand it any longer. Shall try to get better in my own way if possible."[71]

Once he came home, he resumed the extractions. "Am having my teeth out, and am doing what the doctor advises," Kot wrote to Ottoline Morrell in early September. "But, Ottoline," he appealed to her with more emotion than she had ever heard from him before, "what can I do to get out of this utter darkness and despair? The means that good men and women naturally possess to overcome such trial, seem to be barred to me." Ottoline, who herself would overcome depressions by the "stiff upper lip" technique, kept instructing Kot that he should simply snap out of it and be strong. "But I cannot see how it is to come about," Kot retorted. "If wanting alone could do it, then there would still be hope. But how am I to overcome my utter helplessness and weakness? I know that I ought not to write about it as it only torments you to see my degradation. But some-how I have a need to tell you what exactly is the matter with me."[72]

Kot wrote to Ottoline almost every day in September, as he was going deeper and deeper into self-analysis and self-castigation. His September letters to her are more philosophical, thoughtful, nuanced, and poignant than anything he had ever written previously. Kot – whose friends had known him as someone they could confide in and seek strength from and who, when he himself suffered, kept everyone at bay – now needed Ottoline as his mother-confessor. Ottoline tried to steer him toward more professional help, suggesting at one point that if Kot could not will himself to feel better he might want to go to Dublin and con-sult with a good psychologist there whom she just had met on her trip to Ireland. Kot saw no point in it: "To see a good man, as the one in Dublin you mention, would do me good for the time or hours I am with him, just as it does me good to be with a friend, – but I doubt I can be helped in a permanent kind of way. The anxieties, the torments, my inner problems that have brought on my illness remain, unsolved and insoluble. My physical condition is deteriorating every hour … And for the cure of my soul, a nerve specialist or psychologist can do nothing. Having allowed myself to deteriorate, I cannot stop it. I am not sorry for myself: I am only so grieved for having mismanaged everything and for having wasted everything. And there is no way out of all this ... I am a shuddering, pitiable creature."[73]

Kot's present self was indeed very different from his former self, for he even found it difficult to be judgmental: "At rare moments, when I am calm, I can still go on expressing an opinion or view. But when I lose control of myself, I am just incapable of anything, and absorbed by terrors. I try very hard to keep control of myself, to drive away my terrors, but fail miserably ... I wish to become strong again so as to bring some order into the chaos, created by my own failings."[74] When Ottoline suggested that Kot's present self was not truly him, Kot begged to differ: "I am and have been a highly strung person, nervous, obviously sensitive, etc. But managed all my life not to betray any trace of it: evidently quite successfully."[75] "Be patient with me," he pleaded with her again and again. "In my own, clumsy and queer, way I am trying hard to get out of my present state."[76]

"I wish I could get sufficient control of myself as not to write to you horrible letters any more," he apologized to her in another letter. To invoke better days – and days he could still be looking forward to once he got better – Ottoline had reminded him of annual photographs she was in habit of taking of James Stephens, Kot, and herself sitting in her garden. It worked: "I think now that it would be worth my getting well again for the sake of one more photograph in your garden ... Strange how those intangible and indefinable things can grip me! And this again reminds me that nearly a whole of my life was kept together and sustained by intangibles. And it may be that my illness is due to the kind of realization of having failed to transform part of the intangibles into stark reality."[77]

He also reached out to Sydney Waterlow, who was by then the British ambassador to Greece. Kot's letter apparently did not survive but Waterlow's long response did. Written on 25 September, it dealt specifically with Kot's illness and his state of mind. Himself subject to depressions, Waterlow doubted that the cause of the malaise – in his case or Kot's – was physical. Apologizing ahead of time if he was off the mark, Waterlow offered a "political" theory of Kot's ailment: Kot's troubles, according to Waterlow, began when he uprooted himself from Russia and cast his lot with the West. It was Kot's deep disillusionment with the state of Western civilization at the time (with Hitler in Germany and the Spanish Civil War starting in summer 1936) that, Waterlow felt, had led Kot to the current depression. Waterlow likened Kot's mental state to a storm that had been gathering for years. He suggested that Kot had managed to more or less successfully stave it off until now, but that the storm's force had only increased and Kot was presently feeling the full brunt of it. While Waterlow did not think medications or surgeries could positively affect the condition, he did have "practical" advice for Kot: to see W.J. Dunning, a mystic and practitioner of yoga, the only person who, Waterlow believed, had helped him overcome his own depressions.[78] With Kot's aversion to faith-healing and mysticism of any kind, it is doubtful that he ever availed himself of his friend's advice.

While he was sick Kot missed the opportunity of a lifetime: meeting James Joyce. Stephens, who was Joyce's good friend, wrote in early June from Paris that he and his wife had had dinner with the Joyces and that Mr and Mrs Joyce would be soon coming to London. "I should like you to meet them," Stephens suggested.[79] The dinner took place on 20 September, but Kot, who on top of everything else was still in the middle of his tooth extractions, was obviously in no shape to go. In his report to Kot about the dinner, Stephens presented Joyce as an excellent role model for all suffering from depressions: "There is a man who is almost happy! He bothers, that is, if bothers at all, about his own bother-ations, and, in so far as I can see it, he doesnt bother one smallest part of a demi-damn about the world and its waggings."[80]

The breakthrough – of sorts – came in September when Kot agreed to see a different doctor. He was very reluctant at first: he was as loyal to his doctors as he was to his friends, even if he often mistrusted their recommendations. He therefore asked Morland for advice about seeing another specialist. As Kot informed his friends, Morland was against it, suggesting that the only thing Kot needed was "to take myself in hand and to try to get over my nervous state." In addition, Kot was "afraid of the confusion a new doctor is bound to produce in me, – sufficiently confused and chaotic as I am."[81] It was only when Juliette Huxley joined Ottoline in insisting Kot should be seen by Dr Leo Rau, who was her doctor as well as Ottoline's, that Kot gave in. He wanted, however, to make sure that neither Dr Morland nor "especially Dr Ledingham … know that I have been to another doctor": "After hearing Dr Rau's opinion, and after considering whether I can follow his advice or not, I shall have to talk to Dr Ledingham, who has been very nice and kind to me all the time. It is only with his approval that I can change him for Dr Rau."[82] Dr Rau examined Kot and ordered more tests at the London Hospital. Kot asked Esther Salaman to drive him there and stay with him during the tests because, as he explained to Ottoline, he was "such a terrible fool when I go to a doctor … it would be better if some one were there to be present and explain to me what the doctor says."[83] Rau rendered the diagnosis several days later. "It was found," Kot told Ida Baker on 2 October, "that the cause of my illness was 'Coronary thrombosis,' whatever it may mean or involve (I really cannot explain). The nervous condition and all the rest was due to that thrombosis."[84] Rau also recommended heart surgery.

Whether Kot believed that all his symptoms, including his mental anguish, could be explained away by such a simple diagnosis is hard to say. He obviously wanted to believe it, as a very detailed summary of his entire illness in a letter to Ralph Hodgson in December makes clear. The same letter also reveals that Dr Ledingham was no longer seen by Kot as either nice or kind: "For five months my doctor tortured me, first by saying that I had gall stones, and subjecting me to a strict diet, and then, as I could not sleep at all for nearly three months, inspite of horrible drugs, the doctor decided that I was 'mad,' – he called it acute neurasthenia, or melancholia. But as the blood tests repeatedly showed the presence of white corpuscles (16 thousand instead of 7 or 8), the doctor decided that the infection must come from the teeth, – therefore I had to have all my teeth out, with the exception of three, which my dentist out of charity left in. But as, inspite of it all, I continued being ill and could not sleep, I decided to reconcile myself to my state of 'madness' but to stop taking drugs. After a time I began to sleep, – at first half an hour, and then more. At that time Juliette Huxley returned from her holiday, and insisted on my seeing her doctor, who turned out to be a very conscientious man, and a good doctor. As a result of his examination, and tests undergone at the London Hospital, it was established that I had a coronary thrombosis, and the attack had occurred about two months or ten weeks before (at the time when my first doctor declared that I was 'mad')."[85]

Deep inside, however, Kot must have had serious doubts, for, beginning to feel better, he decided against surgery, apparently figuring it was by no means a magic bullet. He said it was just a temporary delay but he also rejected his friends' attempts to raise money for his future operation by giving donations to a fund established in his name. As he explained to Ottoline, he considered charity of this kind "degrading" and did not "like people who give a 'donation' to clear their consciousness."[86] In the absence of surgery, Dr Rau advised "a regular sort of life, much food, and hours and hours of walking."[87] That suited Kot just fine. The doctor also instructed him to cut down on those strong Russian cigarettes that he rolled for himself and his friends, but that was a much harder challenge.

In autumn, Kot heard from Gertler, who had been on his mind the entire time despite Kot's own troubles. "I cannot think of Mark or Marjorie clearly or co-herently," Kot had told Ottoline back in late July, when Mark's suicide attempt was still very recent. "It is something that is gnawing at my spirit, and I have no indication what is the right thing that should be done."[88] "My dear Kot," Gertler wrote to him in mid-October. "I was glad to hear that something has been located in the form of a definite disease – all the same you will have [to] look after yourself, as I believe that 'coronary thrombosis' can be serious though it seems that in your case the worst has passed."[89] Gertler was still in the sanatorium, longing to see Luke and curious about a new house in Highgate that Marjorie had rented for them in the hope that it would signify a new beginning. Soon after his attempted suicide, Gertler resumed writing his autobiography, which was his way to go back to his Jewish roots and hopefully find a life-saving shelter there. It would remain unfinished at the time of his death three years later. "I get too tired and over excited if I write more than one hour at a stretch," he complained to Ottoline.[90]

Kot continued to be attended regularly by Marjorie Wells, Dilys Powell, and Juliette Huxley – "a bevy of lovely handmaidens," as Ottoline called them.[91] There were weeks when he saw no one but the three of them. He became so dependent on their presence in his life that he even wondered if he would "ever be able to live without them."[92] And soon they were to be joined by another young and vivacious woman, May Sarton, with whom Kot would develop one of his most intense and loving relationships, which would prove a great solace to him for more than a year, starting in summer 1937.

# MAY SARTON, OTTOLINE'S DEATH, AND GERTLER'S SUICIDE

Maylume! ... After a hot little cry we are no longer "homeless":
we come into our own, into our Sabbath, purified, and everything
is right again. And your poem is good.
~ Kot to May Sarton, 25 June 1937

In 1939 ... I was sent to a sanatorium at Davos, Switzerland. One
day the head of the establishment ... asked me to come into her
office. I thought that I had done something wrong ... but it was to
tell me of my father's death. "It was an accident," she told me. "He ...
turned on the gas but forgot to light it ..." It was 10 years later that
I learned the real truth of his suicide.
~ Luke Gertler, "Memories of My Father"

May Sarton was a twenty-five-year-old American woman, born of a Belgian
mother and an English father. By the time Kot met her, Sarton had published a
book of poems – *Encounter in April* – in the USA and was in a relationship with
Julian Huxley while being in love with his wife, Juliette. Mrs Huxley was well
aware of May's relationship with Julian and seemingly unperturbed by it. Julian,
in fact, had convinced Sarton to get involved with him by suggesting that Juliette,
who had her own lover at the time, would not at all mind.[1] It was through the
Huxleys that Kot met Sarton in summer 1937. They invited him to discuss
the prospect of the Cresset Press publishing Sarton's first novel and a new volume
of poems.

Sarton immediately liked him. In a letter to a friend she described Kot, whom
she erroneously believed to be "chief editor" of the Cresset Press, as "darling" and
"sweet," "a big Russian bear, a gentle Jewish bigness."[2] For Kot it was, in many
ways, love at first sight. Kot's initial infatuation with Sarton – and no lesser word
would quite do here – probably did not have a sexual component to it. Kot was,

of course, old enough to be her father (but then Julian was, too, being only seven years younger than Kot), and he did know that May, her relationship with Julian notwithstanding, was mostly attracted to women. And yet his early letters to her were downright gushing. Kot thought Sarton had great talent, an opinion confirmed by James Stephens, the ultimate authority for Kot when it came to poetry. He thought she was very beautiful, strong-minded, and free-spirited – "a pagan," he called her.[3] In his letters throughout summer and autumn 1937 he addressed her as "May, luminous and wild," or just "Maylume," where "lume" was "short for luminous."[4] Sometimes he used the Russian name he gave her, "Maya," or referred to her, in endearing Russian, as "Moudroye oushko" ("wise little ear").[5] His letters are peppered with declarations of "very good and tender love."[6] "I am most terribly fond of you just now," he wrote to her in early August, and then several days later: "I am so very fond of you that I should like to protect you against the ills of life … May my wish be a shield against all ill, and a strength to you."[7] He wrote to her almost daily, in fact, and demanded immediate responses from her when she was not in London. "If I don't get a letter from you in a day or two, I'll simply have to beat you," he coyly advised her in mid-July, barely a month after they met.[8]

Kot was, in fact, so self-conscious about his infatuation that again and again he asked Sarton to destroy his letters. "Maylume, please tear up my letters: I can't stand the idea of them being seen by some one else, but you," he beseeched her on 14 July, and then again the following day: "Tear up my letters, or I'll give you a terrible beating."[9] Having just met her, he already felt he could not live without her and, jokingly, asked her to convince Julian, who was at the time secretary of the Zoological Society of London, to put him, James Stephens, and herself in the same cage at the Zoo: "If you, and J.S. are in the cage with me, I shall no longer need or want anything."[10] "I wish you came back soon," he wrote to her on 13 July, when she was in Belgium, where she would be soon joined by Julian Huxley. "If you come to London, and snatch [only] ten minutes from the hairdresser to come to see me in order to rush off to Ireland, I shall either get a thrombosis, or sit and cry until you return from Ireland."[11]

May Sarton was, by all accounts, a strikingly dynamic and charismatic young woman. She had a flair for the dramatic, or even "demonic," as she herself liked to describe it – "I really have a *daemon* you know," she wrote to Kot that summer. She was irrepressible and insatiable: she flirted with women and men, old and young, aiming, as she told Kot in the same letter, to "reach everyone's *heart*."[12] She apparently succeeded more often than not, conquering hearts by "lighting bonfires," as Juliette Huxley once characterized it.[13] It also helped in her relationship with Kot that she loved Katherine Mansfield, whose journal she had read when she was eighteen. "Once in a while you come upon a person who seems to be grafted onto your soul," she recorded in her diary after she finished reading it.[14] Furthermore, she was very interested in Russian literature, especially in Chekhov and Dostoevsky, and in all things Russian. There is a picture of her sitting with her father in 1929 wearing a silky Russian peasant blouse, not unlike the one Kot wore when he had just come to London a year before May was born. With her dark hair, prominent nose, and olive skin she looked almost Jewish, no doubt making her even more appealing to Kot.

Yet, even given all that, Kot's powerful reaction to her is somewhat puzzling. She was, after all, only twenty five, and an American – something that he usually held against people. She never kept her affairs secret from him; on the contrary, she liked him precisely because she could always take him into her confidence, so he knew about her affair with Julian. Kot had taken pleasure before in other people's extramarital affairs when the victim was a spouse he detested, like Murry. But he liked Juliette very much, and he was grateful to her for all she had done for him during his illness and convalescence. As someone Juliette routinely shared her troubles with, Kot may have known that Juliette's indifference toward her husband's new affair was not real. In fact, when she heard from Julian about the first night he spent with May at a hotel, she wrote to him: "*Must* I be made miserable so you may be happy? … Your selfishness can be so cruel."[15] Kot also learned from Sarton's letters that she was interested in Juliette: "In a curious way I am almost more fond of her than of Julian. She is less *great* but she is more *special* … She comes closer to my world."[16] Normally, the whole situation would have struck his puritan heart as too messy and decadent.

And yet Kot was bewitched, and his almost manic state of mind probably had a lot to do with the health problems and the nervous breakdown he had experienced the previous year. He was glad to be alive. He had a new appreciation of friends, especially the three young women who had seen him through his crisis. He had gained an understanding of how much the "intangibles," as he called them in his letters to Ottoline – the ordinary, enjoyable conversations and informal gatherings with people he cared for – kept him afloat. May Sarton, in addition to all her other attractions, had not been a witness to the low point in his life. Unlike Marjorie Wells, Dilys Powell, Juliette Huxley, and, of course, Ottoline Morrell, she had not had to nurse him through his illness and depression of 1936, when he was at his most pitiable and vulnerable. With Sarton he could once again be strong and paternalistic, giving her advice and protecting her rather than the other way around.

He could, in short, reinvent himself as the old Kot, even if much of it was just a facade. He could be the one telling *her* not to feel lonely, sad, or depressed. "One is not lonely," he lectured Sarton that summer, "inspite of experiencing all the pains and travails of loneliness. And if one knows it, one becomes immune against the sordidness of everyday life."[17] "You must not be depressed," he urged her in August. "All will be well."[18] "You are very tired, my dear," he argued with her in early September. "Don't then mistake your fatigue for something that is not there."[19] When that did not help to lift her spirits, he became positively Ottoline-like in his insistence that she should just snap out of it: "I order and command you to drive away your black mood and depression. Everything will be all right."[20]

He was not being disingenuous. He firmly believed that, unlike him, she was full of vitality and talent, so everything would indeed be all right in her case. Nurturing and protecting not just Sarton but her artistic gift, and making sure that it was not wasted on literary trifles, became his new mission in life. Having convinced himself, with Stephens's help, that she was a poet of potential greatness, he was wary of her prose attempts, so even though he continued pushing Cohen to accept *The Single Hound*, he also tried to talk her out of rushing to publish it instead of focusing on her poems. He kept encouraging her – "Your poems are very good … What a very gifted Maylume you are!" – and beseeching her to work harder and stop chasing the immediate success at the expense of long-lasting value: "Yes, May dear, you must learn patience. Whatever happens, remember that you have tremendous obligation to your talent … should it happen that the publication of your novel has to be postponed, nothing of that nature matters … Had I known you before the publication of 'Encounter,' I would have advised to postpone publication … had you waited another year or two, your book would be so much finer."[21]

Kot's other close friends were apparently not as enamored of Sarton – or she of them. Sarton would later confess to her biographer that she "couldn't stand James Stephens" despite relying on his professional advice and aid. He was, according to her, "such a show-off, drinking gin and reciting his poems endlessly."[22] She also maintained that Lady Glenavy was jealous of her relationship with Kot because "Kot loved Beatrice Glenavy before he met me," and therefore she wanted "to separate me and Kot, because Kot did love me."[23] This may sound childish, but it does contain a certain grain of truth. An interesting testimony to how important Kot indeed was in Lady Glenavy's life by the 1930s can be found in a biography of her sister, Dorothy Kay (also a professional painter), written by Dorothy's daughter, Marjorie Reynolds. Dorothy, who had married a South African and lived in South Africa for most of her adult life, came on a rare visit to London in 1933 and was supposed to meet Beatrice – for the first time in many years – in Hyde Park. A couple of minutes after they hugged and kissed, Lady Glenavy informed her that she had to go because "she had an appointment with her friend Koteliansky, 'Kot'." Dorothy was, according to her daughter, "dumbfounded": "After years of separation she had come six thousand miles, and at a first reunion meeting her beloved elder sister had another engagement!" Reynolds believes that this Kot-related event was "a turning point" in the two sisters' relationship: "Dorothy's thirty years of homesickness was to be cured by this London meeting."[24]

Neither was it without a friction when Sarton stayed with Kot. He was so "fanatic about order," she complained: "Once I unpacked and some powder from my puff fell on his spotless kitchen table. A sacrilege! Kot told Beatrice I was dis-orderly…"[25] He was also cranky when she came back late: "Even when … I tried to be exactly on time, impatience sometimes made him irritable. He had been ex-pectant for hours, or so he made one feel."[26] And yet, to her, too, it was all worth it. She loved his stories about Russia of his youth, and she liked the effect he had on her: "In his presence, emotions, ideas, fell into place; self-intoxication became self-searching."[27] In 1976, in *A World of Light*, she reminisced:

> [A]s I think back to the warm tiny kitchen where we talked so often and so long, I realize that there is no room in the world where I have ever felt so absolutely at home if being at home means being comfortable spiritu-ally, being able to be completely myself without fear or embarrassment because I was sitting opposite an old man who was completely himself and who was not afraid of a rather high emotional temperature – in fact thrived on it.[28]

Kot was on such an emotional upswing that year that he even went back to translating. In autumn, Dent published Chekhov's *Plays and Stories* as part of their Everyman's Library. It included two major plays, *The Cherry Orchard* and *The Seagull*, that Koteliansky translated for this particular volume; three shorter plays, including *The Wood Demon*, that had all appeared before, and thirteen short stories, some of them older translations and some new. The book included no introduction but featured a brief "Autobiography," taken from a letter Chekhov wrote in 1899, and a chronological table. With the new publication came new ideas and schemes. Knowing that May Sarton had dabbled in theatre when she was younger and that she still had connections in Boston, Kot suggested that they might become rich if she found "some theatrical person in the USA to buy from me the American dramatic rights of 'The Cherry Orchard,' 'The Seagull,' and 'The Wood Demon.'" He also promised that he would translate more Chekhov plays if she located "an American millionaire, wishing to invest £1000."[29] A year later *The Wood Demon* in his translation was staged in England instead, at the Barn Theatre, in the Surrey village of Shere, and the review in the *Times* gave it a moderately strong endorsement: "Mr Koteliansky's translation is fairly good for the most part – good enough at any rate, to make us wish that this brave experiment could be repeated by those who earn their living in the theatre."[30]

Kot's new translations of *The Seagull* and *The Cherry Orchard* were even more daring feats, in which he was going head to head with the previous translations by Constance Garnett. Garnett's *The Cherry Orchard and Other Plays*, which also included *The Seagull*, had been published by Chatto and Windus in 1926 and was reprinted by the same publisher in 1935, just two years prior to Kot's translations. Almost all theatres in England – and the United States – used Garnett's versions of *Seagull* and *Cherry Orchard*. To supplant them with new translations, one had to make a truly convincing case, get spectacular reviews, and indeed find someone with money and zeal to push for it. Koteliansky's prospects were thus quite remote. While superior to his earlier translation of Hippius's play, these translations were not remarkable enough in any way to replace Garnett's.[31] They would, however, prove to be good enough for Penguin Books, which republished *The Cherry Orchard, The Seagull*, and *The Wood Demon* in a paperback entitled *Three Plays* in 1940.

In November 1937 the Habima Players ("Habima" means "stage," in Hebrew), a theatre troupe that by then was based in Palestine, came to London for a performance that had special significance to Kot. It was their second international tour. The first one had taken place seven years earlier, in 1930, when the Habima Players were still affiliated with the Stanislavsky Theatre in Moscow. Back then it was brought to London by Sidney Bernstein, a theatre and cinema entrepreneur who had seen the play in Moscow in 1925 and who was to befriend Mark Gertler and Kot soon after the first Habima performances.[32] Both in 1930 and 1937 the highlight of the tour was a play by S. Ansky called *The Dybbuk*. Kot had seen it in 1930 and was eager to see it again, suggesting to all his friends that they should not miss it. "Good acting is really as terrific as a good book," he wrote to Sarton in early November. "But I haven't seen good acting for ages, – except the Habima a few years ago."[33]

There was much more than just "good acting," however, that drew Kot to the Habima Players and this particular play. The initial title of Ansky's play was *Between Two Worlds*, meaning this world and the otherworld that was home to the "dybbuk," or a soul of a dead person that attaches itself to a living body. Kot's two worlds were both on Earth, but he was likewise forever "between" them. It was very important to him, therefore, that his "essential" people in England, like the Huxleys whom he convinced to accompany him to the performance, should appreciate and accept his previous incarnation as a Russian Jew from a small shtetl that is very much like the shtetl in *The Dybbuk*. It also allowed him to fully reimmerse himself in the lore and traditions of his early years.

S. Ansky, the author of the play, was born in 1863 in Chashniki, near Vitebsk, as Shloyme-Zanvl Rappoport. As a young man, he left his family and their faith behind to focus on social activism. At seventeen, he was helping other Jewish boys like himself who wanted to escape their parents and their studies at the Vitebsk Yeshiva by providing a haven for them at the outskirts of the town. In his late forties, Rappoport not only made peace with his heritage but gave in to his deep-seated interest in Yiddish folklore and Hasidic tales, as well as social issues that concerned the Jewish population in the Pale of Settlement.³⁴

Just as Kot was leaving the Ukraine in 1911, Rappoport, who was by then known as Semyon Ansky (or An-sky), was about to travel through the shtetls of Kot's native region of Volhynia and the neighbouring Podolia as a part of the Jewish ethnographic expedition sponsored and financed by a rich Kiev Jew, Baron Vladimir Guenzburg. According to Guenzburg, in autumn 1912, Ansky and those accompanying him visited "Ostrog – Zaslav – Miropol' – Ostropol' – Staro-Konstantinov – Kremenetz."³⁵ Soon after the end of the expedition, which had been interrupted by the First World War in 1914, Ansky wrote *The Dybbuk*, a play that takes place in two locales, one of them being Miropol, just about 40 kilometres (25 miles) from Ostropol. In the play, Miropol is the seat of a famous rabbi who is called upon to resolve a difficult situation resulting from an impending wedding. The wedding itself is to take place in a place called "Brinits" – in Russian "Brinitsa"³⁶ – for which it is hard to find a real-life equivalent in the area. Most likely, whereas Miropol had to be real since it was the actual seat of a famous "tsaddik" (a Hasidic rabbi) "Brinits," in Ansky's mind, was any shtetl in Volhynia, Podolia, or even Galicia, where he found himself while writing the play.

However, although fictional, the place may have been, in fact, modelled on Kot's very own Ostropol. The description of the shtetl fits Ostropol perfectly: "A square … Left, the old synagogue built of wood and of ancient architecture … A wide road leading down to a river … To the left a bridge over the river and a mill."³⁷ Ostropol indeed had a very old wooden synagogue on the market square, a wide road (which connected Ostropol with Starokonstantinov) right below it, and, further down, a river with a mill (the very one that probably belonged to Kot's father at the time Ansky was collecting materials there). The description of the synagogue in the 1915 variant of the play, which was recently unearthed at the St Peterburg Theatre Library, makes this conjecture even stronger: it mentions multiple roofs, something for which the Ostropol synagogue was famous (judging by the images that survived, it had at least seven of them): "a tall wooden synagogue, blackened with age, with an elaborate system of roofs, one atop another."[38] Ostropol would also work perfectly as the real-life model for Brinits because the relatively short distance between it and Miropol would make the movements in the play very plausible, and because other towns mentioned in the play as the nearby seats of famous rabbis – like Ruzhin, Ostrog, Zaslav, and Annopol (the town where Kot's mother was from) – were, like Miropol, in Ostropol's close vicinity.

During the expedition, Ansky and his companions would ask whether their interviewees knew of any stories "about a dead person being brought before a rabbinical court," or "about a dead person's soul that finds no rest and that turns into a dybbuk and enters a living person."[39] The Dybbuk is a story about both. Ansky himself described the play as "a realistic play about mystics."[40] It is a simple love tale complicated by strong supernatural powers employed for the purpose of justice and revenge. As such it reads more like a Greek tragedy than the typical early-twentieth-century Russian dramatic fare, except that here the supernatural is based not on pagan but Jewish kabbalistic beliefs. The name "Dybbuk" in Hebrew means "attachment," and in Kabbalah a soul attaches itself to a living person in order to right injustices. In the play the injustice is suffered by a young and poor yeshiva student, Khonen, who is more interested in the Kabbalah than the Talmud, and by his long-departed father, whose agreement with a friend has been betrayed.

The plot, which was well known to Kot but obviously new to the Huxleys, goes as follows: Khonen and Leah, the beautiful daughter of a rich man, fall in love without being aware that their fathers had bethrothed them to each other when they themselves were young and idealistic Hasidic yeshiva students. The bethrothal was conditional, though: their wives were just expecting children at the time, so the sex of either child was not yet revealed. Since Khonen's father died before he got to see his newborn son, Leah's father has no way of realizing that the young man who just recently arrived to their shtetl and was their lodger for a while is his best friend's son. The father is certain, however, that a poor student is not a suitable match for his daughter. A better match, a son from a wealthy family, is soon found, leading to Khonen's broken heart. As a result, he whips himself into a prayerful frenzy, then collapses and dies.

On the wedding day, Leah goes to the cemetery to visit the grave of her mother, who died in childbirth, and the sacred spot of the "holy bride and groom" who, according to a legend, had been cut down by anti-Semitic thugs during a seventeenth-century pogrom just as they were being led to a wedding canopy, or "chuppah."[41] Leah also stops at the grave of her beloved Khonen, and his soul transmigrates into her body. To get the dybbuk exorcized, the girl's father takes her to a rabbi in Miropol, who is made aware by another Miropol rabbi of the pact that had been solemnly sworn by the two fathers. Khonen's long-dead father is then summoned to the rabbinical court; his forgiveness is sought but not given. In the end, Leah breaks away from the rabbi and a protective circle he draws around her, and she joins her beloved Khonen in death.

When Ansky, who initially wrote the play in Russian, showed it to Stanislavsky, the director of the Moscow Art Theatre, Stanislavsky expressed interest in staging the play but also encouraged him to translate the play into Yiddish and have Jewish, Yiddish-speaking actors perform it. Ansky did not live long enough to see his play staged by anyone. In 1920, following his death, a Jewish theatre in Vilna performed the *The Dybbuk* in Yiddish in his memory. It was a rousing success. The play was then translated again, this time into Hebrew, and Stanislavsky disciple Evgeny Vakhtangov staged it in the typical avant-garde fashion of the early 1920s. He did it with the Habima Players, a Jewish theatre group that had formed in 1912, reorganized in Moscow in 1917, and was by then affiliated with the Stanislavsky Theatre. The play premiered in 1922 and became a sensation. When the Habima Players took it abroad in 1926, *Time* magazine described it as a production "notable for its frank theatricality": "Not the slightest regard is paid to ordinary, familiar realities. The players confess themselves actors of parts, paint their faces with unusual pigments in strange designs, interpret their mysterious emotions before impressionistic scenery."[42]

This was the production Kot had seen in 1930 and was about to see again on 15 November 1937 at the Savoy Theatre. A reviewer for the *Times* attended the same performance and wrote the following day that, while the Habima Players could have chosen to perform Shakespeare in Hebrew (which was in their repertoire) for the English audience, *The Dybbuk* was the right choice because "the legend is so simple that none can fail to understand it." It was the performance itself, rather than the story, that the reviewer thought was going to enthrall the audience:

[T]his play is not to be considered in terms of its narrative, but rather as a study in spiritual exaltation. Every force of the collective stage is used to enhance its effect and increase its impetus – make-up that has the emphasis of masks, scenery and furniture distorted with genius to take off the brake of naturalism, music and dance that are a scourge upon the mind, and acting that is not the acting of separated entities, but of a group faultlessly attuned. The result is an experience different in kind, because different in purpose from any to be had in the English theatre.

The bar of language becomes not a bar but a release. It is even possible that, if the words were understood, the range of the play might seem to decrease.[43]

Kot's experience of watching *The Dybbuk* was, of course, much more nuanced. In addition to the all too familiar location and general environment, there were other aspects of the play that must have resonated for him, chief among them the total breakdown of confidence that the Rabbi Azriel of Miropol undergoes as he is called upon to exorcise the dybbuk. When the rabbi is informed that the father has brought his daughter to him so that she can be helped, his response is

To me? … To me? … Why to me, when there *is* no me to come to? For I am myself no longer … What do they want of me? I am old and weak. My body has earned its rest – my soul longs for solitude. Yet still they come thronging to me, all the misery and sorrow of the world … No, I have no longer the strength … I cannot … [Suddenly breaking into tears.] I can't go … I can't … [He weeps.][44]

The rabbi does go on – mostly to honour the rabbinical tradition of his father and grandfather; he even succeeds in exorcizing the dybbuk before the girl escapes. We know, however, that the crack in his confidence remains – his "protective circle" failed to work, after all – and this crack will come back to haunt him again and again. It probably was not lost on Kot how similar their situations were. People came to him with their problems as well, assuming that he was wiser and more confident than he knew he was. He too had succeeded in exorcising the demons a year earlier, his own in his case, but the crack remained and could open wide again and swallow him at any time, despite the "protective circle" of the "essentials" on whom he was heavily relying.

Kot was not the only fan of the play among his friends – James Stephens recommended it warmly to at least one of his friends: "This note is to say that the Habima Players will be in London, & on the 15th they will be playing The Dybbuk … When I saw it a few years ago I thought it one of the most remarkable pieces of dramatic work that had ever come my way."[45] It was important to Kot that the Huxleys too – and especially Juliette – should like it. In that, he was disappointed. Kot reported to May Sarton that Juliette "shuddered at the sight of the beggars" – who appear in act 2, the morning of the planned wedding. Still, Kot took the Huxleys to a reception on the stage after the performance and believed "J. and J. enjoyed it all." He himself definitely enjoyed meeting the actors and proudly emphasized to Sarton how different they were from the stereotypes of physically weak and hopelessly provincial Russian Jews: "They are a good lot: some of the men strong and good looking, and speaking excellent Russian."[46]

Kot was not ready to give up on Juliette. "When I see them again," he wrote to Sarton, "I'll explain to them what the Hassid movement means; and with that information, they will appreciate the more the marvellous acting of the Habima players." By 24 November, Kot knew that notwithstanding his explanation of the Hasidic tradition, the play and therefore Kot's own heritage were too alien for Juliette Huxley. She declined to go and see another play being performed by the Habima Players, *Uriel Acosta*, based on the life of seventeenth-century Portuguese Jewish philosopher Uriel da Costa, because, as Kot explained to Sarton, she "actually disliked the 'Dybbuk,' and does not want to see other plays by the Habima."[47]

Kot's friend J.W.N. Sullivan was not among the theatregoers that November, for he had succumbed to multiple sclerosis in August.[48] That was not the only death in Kot's circle that year: Stephens's son – who Kot always thought "was not any good"[49] – was accidentally killed two days before Christmas, causing his father immeasurable agony. To add to Kot's anxiety, there were serious concerns about Ottoline's health, and the continuing unpleasantness with Dennis Cohen at the Cresset Press.

May Sarton might have naively thought that Kot was an important man at the Cresset Press, but matters there were not much better in 1937 than they had been in 1935 or 1936. In March, Kot "suddenly thought" that Myer Salaman, Dennis Cohen's cousin, "probably never saw the position as between me and Dennis in its correct light," so he felt a lengthy explanation was in order. Kot proceeded to enumerate all the successful books he had recommended for the Press and others that Cohen rejected that were immediately picked up by other publishers. He emphasized that the salary he was getting was never out of Cohen's pocket or at his direct expense but drawn from the profits that the books Kot worked on had brought and that, in the long run, he was even underpaid for all his labour and for all the important authors he had recruited. He ended by saying: "This letter, by the way, will help you to form an idea as to whether I am good at the job I have undertaken. It will also help you to see why I can no longer bear a certain type of person, and particularly if that type is a Jew."[50] Cohen, in short, was not just an employer who was mistreating an employee. He was not even just a Jew harming a fellow Jew. Cohen was guilty of worse: he was a Jew who gave other Jews a bad name, and, painful as it might be since they were cousins, Myer Salaman, in Kot's opinion, had to be made aware of it.

Ottoline's health had been deteriorating the entire year. In March, while visiting Sullivan in the hospital, she felt ill and, upon return home, suffered a stroke.

She spent three months in a clinic. By late May she assured Kot that she was slowly on the mend, "more in the land of living and improving," yet still unable to move much.[51] To entertain herself and to please Kot, she initiated a new round of gossip about Frieda and the rest of the Taos crew based on the letters she was getting from Brett. Occasionally she would even send Kot Brett's letters for him to appreciate every detail. They both wondered whether Brett would now "try and 'pinch'" Frieda's Capitano, the way she had tried to steal Lawrence, with Ottoline comparing Brett to Balzac's "Cousine Bette," a viciously scheming middle-aged spinster.[52]

In August, Ottoline thought she had finally recovered. "I have been *very* ill, so ill that I very nearly died, or was paralysed," she wrote to a friend in New Zealand, "but thank God who gave me a Solid Constitution & Courage, I have wonderfully recovered. It was a poisoning of the Central Nervous System."[53] She even felt well enough to go to Europe. While there she learned about Sullivan's death and fretted that Dr Rau, whom she had recommended to Sullivan just as she had to Kot and who was no longer her favourite, might have done Sullivan more harm than good.[54] She now had a new doctor, Dr A.J. Cameron, whom she credited with bringing her to recovery. Ottoline came back to London in October but by then she was so weak that she hardly went anywhere and therefore did not attend any performances of the Habima Players, or the "Jewish Players," as she called them.[55] On Christmas Day, Ottoline thanked Kot for the volume of his Chekhov translations and expressed hope that 1938 would find her in better health.[56]

It did not. Dr Cameron decided to treat her "poisoning of the Central Nervous System" (a fashionable diagnosis as dubious as the one Kot had received a year and a half earlier, which had led to the extraction of his teeth) with the relatively new antibacterial drug called "Prontosil." A letter in the the *Times* of London in June of that year would attribute ten deaths to the use of Prontosil. "It is most unfortunate," the letter concluded, "that Prontosil can be purchased without a medical prescription, since the indiscriminate and uncontrolled use of such remedies may lead to tragedy."[57] But in Ottoline's case it was the doctor she blindly trusted who championed "indiscriminate and uncontrolled use." Cameron was doubling the recommended dosage with his patients for greater effect and prolonging the treatment four times beyond what was allowed. He also thought that injecting it, rather than administering it orally, would speed up the healing.[58] As it turned out, he was wrong on all counts. While Ottoline was undergoing the treatment of daily injections in his clinic, other medical specialists began to question Cameron's methods after some of his patients got progressively worse.[59] In April, Cameron committed suicide, but his assistants continued injecting Prontosil in the dosages Cameron had prescribed. Ottoline died on 21 April during one such injection. The cause of death was ruled to be "heart failure."[60] Her obituary in the *Times* stated that she "died unexpectedly" and "had been thought to be making a good recovery."[61] Ottoline's last letter to Kot was written in early February, when she invited him to come and have tea with her and also warned him that "Cousine Brett" was in town.[62]

Kot did not attend Ottoline's funeral service, and neither would he attend a service for Gertler a year later. In both cases he was probably reluctant to share his very personal and profound grief with others. As hard as it was for him to be deprived of Ottoline, Gertler's suicide in summer 1939 must have been immeasurably more devastating. After all, Gertler was Kot's surrogate younger brother – or even, as Juliette Huxley believed, "a wayward, difficult but much loved son."[63]

In 1937 Gertler appeared to be on an upswing, painting again and trying to mend fences with Marjorie and Luke. Writing to his vacationing wife in August, Gertler told her he was looking forward to her "physical presence" again, which to him was "always exciting[,] always comforting and stimulating." He went as far as to declare that he never had any serious doubts about their relationship, and that she had "a way of becoming more attractive – more and more beautiful." "I can't help feeling that all my former loves were childs [*sic*] play in comparison," he assured her.[64] Luke had another operation that summer, and his father tried hard to be as helpful and patient as he could.

The relatively happy family interlude did not last. By the following summer Mark Gertler was complaining to Kot that while he was relieved to see Luke "perfectly well and happy," the child's demands for constant attention were often "tiring and irritating."[65] The complaint was probably largely based on his son's tantrum, which Luke Gertler would remember as "the most dramatic incident ... in connection with my father": "In 1938 we went on holiday to Cassis in the South of France ... Since his treatment for tuberculosis [father] always took a rest in the afternoon. On that particular afternoon while he rested, my mother had gone out and I wanted to go with her. She had told me ... I must stay at home. I retaliated in the way I knew best. I was very good at screaming and began one of my supreme performances ... This went on for some time, until my father could bear it no longer. Suddenly an agitated figure tore down the stairs ... seized me and rushed back into the bedroom, literally throwing me onto the bed. The shock of the whole manoeuvre ... had the desired effect: I was silent."[66] "We are neither of us, I am afraid, good parents," Gertler concluded in the same letter to Kot.[67]

Gertler did not have much time or patience for Luke that summer because he was so preoccupied with his own health. He very much feared that his inability to have peace and quiet just then would further aggravate his condition. In his pocket diary he took note again and again of "Coughing with sputum most of the time," "Awful headache all day and night," and "More or less continuous bouts of depression."[68] In September he and Marjorie agreed that given his mood and need not to be disturbed by their at times unruly child, "some kind of more sep arate life might be preferable." He still tried to sound optimistic, though: "We both know," he wrote to Thomas Balston, a publisher and art collector who became a very close friend of Gertler's in the 1930s, "that the trouble is not fundamental, as we do really love one another."[69]

Usually less political than Kot, by now Gertler was also deeply concerned about Hitler's treatment of Jews in Germany, and its implications for his own future. In autumn 1938, Hitler's speeches increasingly blamed Jews and England (in particular, Churchill) for all the world's ills. "We may all be blown to bits any moment," Gertler wrote down in his diary. "I heard the voice of the brute pour-ing poison into the hearts of his countrymen on the wireless – it was awful – like wild beasts."[70] At the school where he taught he was told that "in the event of war the school would be closed instantly – and no salaries."[71]

In October, Gertler decided to discontinue the "Wednesdays," which were still taking place at his house. "Nobody seems to turn up," he complained to Kot, who himself had been increasingly skipping the gatherings because of bad health. "[W]e hang about waiting and waiting and it becomes very tiresome …" Gertler did assure his friend, though, that he still would like to see him regularly and would try to come "for tea when you are not too busy."[72] In January, Marjorie and Luke left for Europe. Despite the migraines, fatigue, anxiety, and depression, Gertler was working hard to finish more paintings for a show that was to open at the Lefévre Galleries in spring. He hoped that together with a positive critical response the show would stabilize his family's financial situation. But his hopes were dashed. When his exhibition opened with twenty-nine new paintings in early May, it brought mixed critical response[73] and virtually no money, since he managed to sell only one of his paintings. "It is very disheartening," he lamented to Tom Balston. "That show represents two years' hard work and there is all the expense, frames, etc., attached to it."[74]

Later that month, when he went to see his wife and son in Paris, Marjorie informed him she was not coming back. Gertler also knew by now that she was seeing another man, Franz Kostenz, with whom she would spend the war years in Europe. Soon after Gertler returned from Paris, he tried to kill himself by gas poisoning, but, as in his previous attempt at the sanatorium, could not go through with it. He turned off the gas and called his doctor instead. Gertler later told Balston that he had been depressed because Marjorie was not coming back and further aggrieved because of "the failure of his Exhibition that May at the

Lefévre Gallery," but that "Dr Morland got him well in 2 days."[75] The "wellness," alas, was illusionary.

During these last months of his life, Gertler's frequent companion was Maria Donska, a twenty-seven-year-old Polish Jewish woman who was a very gifted pianist and a graduate of the Royal School of Music. She had first studied music in Berlin in the early 1930s but left as soon as Hitler's threat to Jews became apparent. In London, she lived in St John's Wood, not far from Kot. Donska was supposed to have dinner with Gertler on Friday, 23 June, but instead, upon arriving at his house, found him absent and his studio locked. She called Dr Morland, Morland's driver broke down the door, but this time Gertler had let the gas fulfill its lethal purpose. Earlier in the day Gertler had been visited by an estate agent, sent by Marjorie's father in order to value the house before putting it up for sale. Many assumed that it was the finality of his separation from Marjorie and the immediate prospect of losing his studio that sealed Gertler's fate that day.

An envelope from one of Gertler's letters on which Kot jotted the notes for his friend's obituary survives in Koteliansky's archive in the British Library. All the information is purely factual: that Gertler was born in London in 1892, "had to earn his living in working in stained glass firm ... Was discovered (when 16 years old) by William Rothenstein ... Left 'Slade' at the age of 19 & was that year elected member of the New English Art Club ... After his success, he began to feel disatisfied [sic] with mere realism and felt a necessity to express his abstract & inner feelings."[76] The narrative ends abruptly (after Gertler completes his first sculpture, "The Acrobats") and there is no mention whatsoever of Gertler's Jewishness. The anonymous obituary in the 26 June *Times*, on the other hand, was all about Gertler's Jewishness. Entitled "Mark Gertler. Jewish Painter," it immediately noted the "racial character" in Gertler's paintings, especially "in a liking for smooth gradations of colour, which seem to be a Jewish taste." The writer did, at the same time, commend Gertler for being slightly less Jewish than many of his other coreligionists: "in his later work, the colour was so finely contained in the design that he was not so markedly a Jewish painter as some of his contemporaries." The obituary ended on a personal note that somehow managed to sound very impersonal: "He was of middle height, with a shock of hair, softly spoken, and of most lovable personality."[77]

His friends were no doubt incensed by the pedestrian nature of the tribute, but the following day the *Times* published another anonymous obituary, this time written by someone obviously closer to – and fonder of – Gertler. Called "Mark Gertler: An Appreciation," it stated that "The East End Jewish boy was received as the friend and equal of men like D.H. Lawrence, Christopher Wood, and Gaudier-Brzeska." It also remarked on the positive reviews of his last exhibition in the Lefévre Galleries and concluded by informing readers that "Mrs Gertler returned to London from Paris yesterday."[78]

No contemporaneous records exist of Kot's thoughts about Gertler's death. The closest one gets to Kot's reaction is the account by Lady Glenavy: "Gertler's tragic death in 1939 was [a] source of great unhappiness for [Kot]. I remember Kot saying, 'Gertler, who loved life, how could he have killed himself?' … It was Kot who wrote to tell me of Gertler's death. He was to have gone to tea with Kot – he did not appear. Kot began to get anxious, for he knew Gertler had been suffering great depression, and went to his studio. 'He was lying as if asleep on a mattress beside the gas-fire.'"[79]

The letter to which Lady Glenavy refers apparently did not survive, and, as with much of her book, this account is most likely only partially reliable. To begin with, the words she attributes to Kot are highly unlikely. Kot was a realist and knew that, if Gertler had attempted suicide once, he easily could do so again. He also knew more about Mark's own "black moods" than almost anyone else around Gertler. "It is difficult to be happy, especially I think after thirty," Gertler had written to Kot back in 1927. "One's youth is spent unhappily through over-ardent seeking for happiness. But at least one is hopeful. When youth has gone, there comes to take its place gradually but surely, the ever-increasing horror of approaching old age and the realisation of that awful and inevitable final, death. So how can we be happy? No, there is no such thing as a true happiness."[80]

But Glenavy is particularly untrustworthy, it would appear, when she describes Kot as having been present at the scene of the suicide. On 28 June 1939, both Dr Morland and Maria Donska described their discovery of Gertler's body to the *Islington Gazette*. Neither mentioned Koteliansky, so it is highly unlikely that he was indeed present. While it is possible that Gertler was in fact expected to have tea with Kot after his date with Maria Donska, or even that the two of them were going to Kot together (although Donska never mentioned it in several interviews she gave after Gertler's death), the only other people on record as having seen the body were Dr Morland's wife Dorothy, who accompanied her husband to Gertler's residence; their chauffeur, who helped break down the door; and Gertler's model, Celia Dennis, who sat for him earlier in the day and was instructed to return later. As Dennis observed in several tabloid stories in the following days, she came back "just in time to see Gertler's body being carried out."[81]

John Carswell, who follows Glenavy's account, suggests that Gertler's studio was "not far away" from Kot, who easily could have walked there once he got worried,[82] but that was not the case. Gertler's studio was in Highgate (on Grove Terrace), and therefore almost three miles, mostly uphill, from St John's Wood. As mentioned earlier, in the late 1930s Kot, in fact, had been increasingly skipping "Wednesdays" in Gertler's house precisely because, given his health problems, it was a bit too far to walk.[83] The mythmaking about where Gertler was supposed to be that Friday night is further underscored by published reports that he had also been expected the same day at Sidney Bernstein's "Coppings," his farm in Kent.[84] If Kot was indeed waiting for Gertler, he of course would have been concerned and would have done something to find out about the whereabouts of his friend. But there is no documentary or other plausible reason to believe he made it to the studio while Gertler's body was still there.

We should have no doubt, however, that Kot blamed Marjorie for Mark's death. Her presence at the funeral could have been yet another justification for him not to attend it, as could have been the perceived injustice of the abbreviated religious service because Mark had taken his own life. Gertler's suicide also delivered a very serious blow to Kot's relationship with May Sarton. Sarton came to England on 20 June. Four days later, as she was waiting for Julian Huxley to take her to Cambridge, Juliette Huxley called to tell her about Gertler's suicide the night before and suggested she should immediately go and see Kot. Sarton hesitated, first allowing Julian to start driving her to Cambridge, then, halfway there, asking him to stop the car so that she could ring Kot and take a train back to London to see him. She promised Julian she would come to Cambridge the same day. But when she called Kot to tell him about her plans, Kot, according to Sarton, "savagely dismissed her concern as hysterical."[85] Sarton proceeded to Cambridge with Huxley, and her relationship with Kot would never be the same.

"June the 20th – a whole eternity!" Kot had written to her back in early May, impatient for her to arrive.[86] But in July, as she was leaving for Belgium, she heard something very different from him: "Kot said something to the effect that it was a pity I had come, that it was the wrong time, as if I had showed a lack of delicacy. I seemed to have come like an American on a holiday …"[87] In her journal she wrote that Kot told her she was "brutally tactless."[88] While they reconciled somewhat by the end of summer, and continued to exchange letters for several years afterward, Kot's tone changed very markedly: never again would Sarton be his "May, luminous and wild."

# WORLD WAR II AND ITS AFTERMATH

Then there was the mad Kot: all his hair brushed up; heavy, yellow, bloodshot … Has become opinionated & violent. But his madness was about the war. He seemed raving. He seemed almost drunk … All Germans are devils. We must kill every one … [S]omething gone queer – a screw loose. He gets up at 6 to listen to the BBC at 7. is obsessed – brooding alone at Acacia Road.
~ Virginia Woolf, Saturday, 25 May 1940

I am going on as usual, blessing silently those I like and cursing noisily those I detest…
~ Kot to Mervyn Lagden, 8 December 1948

Kot's depression, like Gertler's, was fuelled throughout the 1930s by the persecution of German Jews. Around the same time as he was arranging for the publication of Kastein's *Jews in Germany* at Cresset, he contacted Sidney Bernstein – by then the managing director of Gaumont-British, one of the earliest British film companies – about the possibility "of getting Gaumont or any other film producing company in England interested in the idea of making an English version" of a French film entitled *Jewish Reply to Hitlerism*. The film would be produced, with Baron d'Erlanger's money, by a Russian Jew whom Kot knew – S. Liberman. "My dear Kot," Bernstein responded. "I would like to meet Mr Liberman but his proposition is impossible because the British Board of Film Censors have already stated they will not pass any film dealing with the Hitler regime, at least showing Nazis in a bad light. Gaumont British producing unit submitted three scenarios to the Censor for his approval dealing with anti-Hitler propaganda in a mild form, but the Censor was adamant despite political pressure."[1]

When Stalin and Hitler signed the non-aggression pact in August 1939, Kot, according to Esther Salaman, knew right away that "[t]he Communist lie will end in disaster." After France collapsed the following year, he was, Salaman observed, "in great despair," thinking not just about his own fate but also that of his relatives and friends in Ukraine. Some of them had already been affected by Stalin's purges: Esther Salaman told George Zytaruk in the 1967 interview that both she and Kot "knew the names of people who were being sentenced to death."[2] But while Stalin and Hitler were, in Kot's book, equally evil monsters he, in his categorical way, had different feelings about the countries that produced them: "if Stalin and all his regime is a gang of murderers and an abomination, Russia is redeemed by Tolstoy and other writers. But Germany will never be redeemed, neither now nor ever after, for the spirit never dwelt there ..."[3]

Virginia Woolf probably was not exaggerating much when, in late May 1940, she found Kot to be "violent ... raving ... almost drunk" while spouting that "All Germans are devils. We must kill every one."[4] Their meeting was occasioned, Kot told Sarton, by his "great desire to see the Woolfs," so he just "went there and spent a few hours," and it was "a real comfort to see them again."[5] It helped, no doubt, that Leonard's angst about the Nazis' treatment of Jews matched Kot's own. "Jews were hunted down, beaten up, and humiliated everywhere publicly in the streets of towns," Leonard would record in his autobiography:

I saw a photograph of a Jew being dragged by storm troopers out of a shop in one of the main streets in Berlin; the fly-buttons of the man's trousers had been torn open to show that he was circumcised and therefore a Jew. On the man's face was the horrible look of blank suffering and despair ... In this photograph what was even more horrible was the look on the faces of respectable men and women, standing on the pavement, laughing at the victim.[6]

Leonard, in fact, was so anxious that he even started preparing himself and Virginia for an eventual suicide were Hitler to be successful in conquering Europe and invading Britain. Virginia, too, was soon convinced that as the wife of a Jew she would have no chance of survival. Their initial plan was to kill themselves in their garage with fumes from the car; later they procured a lethal dose of morphine from Virginia's younger brother Adrian. "[T]his morning we discussed suicide if Hitler lands," Virginia wrote in her diary ten days before they saw Kot. "Jews beaten up. What point in waiting? Better shut the garage doors." Three weeks later she added: "[C]apitulation will mean all Jews to be given up.

Concentration camps. So to our garage."[7] In September 1940 the Woolfs' London house was damaged by German bombs, and they moved to their countryside cottage, "Monk's House," in the Sussex village of Rodmell. It was there that on 28 March 1941 Virginia – fearing of yet another bout with madness setting in – chose to end her life without waiting for Leonard. She did not use morphine or car fumes; instead she put a large stone into the pocket of her coat and walked into the river Ouse not far from the house. Her body was found three weeks later. "Virginia's death is a great blow to me," Kot wrote to May Sarton in April. "She was one of the finest human beings, apart altogether from her uniqueness as a writer. And she, among other English men and women, is a victim of the war as made by the Germans. This is not an exaggeration, but a sober fact."[8]

In a letter to poet Mervyn Lagden, whom, like Dilys Powell and Dorothy Richardson, Kot had met and befriended through his work at Cresset and whom he was now trying to recruit as a lodger, we get a rare firsthand account of Kot's existence in London during the heavy air raids in the initial years of the war. "I hope you know how to treat an incendiary," he wrote to her on 13 November 1940. "About a fortnight ago, quite early in the evening, one fell on my garden, close to the wall. I at once began pouring basins of water, and then started working the garden hose. In about ten minutes time a crowd of people (ARP men) rushed into the garden and one impressive, gentlemanly voice … addressed me in these words: 'You bloody fool, do you want to be blown up? Don't you know that you must not use water?' And he took a lid of a dustbin, covered the incendiary, and then put sand and earth all over it and around it – and that was the end of the incendiary."[9]

Despite heavy bombings, Kot advised his friends not to leave London and definitely not to leave the country. "If I had children," he counseled Esther Salaman, who was thinking of sending hers across the ocean, "I would not send them out of the country. I would take them, in case of need, to a safe place inside the country, and be with them; but I would never let them go either to Canada or the United States."[10] Kot liked to make light of raids, even attributing certain "fructifying" effects to the bombs, since during the years of the heaviest air raids his pear tree bore many more fruits than usual.[11] "He felt," Salaman remembered, that by staying put "he was keeping the city intact."[12]

Marjorie Wells also stayed in London while her family went away – her husband was evacuated to Bangor with University College, where he taught at the time, and Catherine and Oliver were at boarding school. Like Kot, H.G. Wells refused to leave the city, so Marjorie, as his employee, had no choice but to remain at his side. Her work for Wells included not just his correspondence and typing but also running the house and looking after him. When her day there was over, she visited Kot to keep him company and to make sure he had all he needed. "Then," according to her daughter, "she would go home to the empty house … She wrote us cheerful letters at school, and it was only later that I realized what a difficult time it was for her and how marvellous she was."[13]

"Your uncle is bearing the air raids remarkably well," Marjorie Wells assured Polly in autumn 1940. "[I]n fact they seem to stimulate him. He has been in pretty good health for the last year, but he complains that he cannot take an active part in the war."[14] Later on bombs started to hit closer, however, and, according to Wells, on at least two occasions Kot lost all his windows: "The first time was in the middle of the night when an ordinary bomb fell. He could not put on the light, of course, because of the black out, and had to lie among the broken glass until the morning. That was in the depths of winter. The second time was fortunately in summer, when a flying bomb fell in Wellington Road on the YWCA Hostel … He was just sitting down to lunch – bacon and mashed potatoes – when the bang occurred. All his windows broke, but the glass luckily fell outward, and his meal was covered with soot and dirt."[15]

At the end of the war, when Kot did not have to put up a brave facade anymore, he did confess to Polly that bombings were a "great strain … as London was all the time in the front line, day and night, at all hours and continuously."[16] His friend Lady Glenavy tragically lost her daughter, "a young gifted chemist … working … in one of the Ministries," who perished with her husband when a bomb fell on their house in June 1944.[17]

Many of Kot's friends did leave the city despite his advice, and he sorely missed them – in particular James Stephens, who was by then, in the words of Juliette Huxley, "Kot's … twin brother, so tangible was their unspoken solicitous tenderness."[18] Stephens's wife, whom Kot now hated as much as he had hated Frieda when Lawrence was alive, was apparently so "terrified of bombs" that she made the very reluctant Stephens "clear out of London" and go to a "disused chapel in Gloucestershire."[19] Stephens missed Kot as well, and his letters to him were indeed full of tenderness and love. "I wish we were back in London," he wrote in December 1940. "I wish we had never left it, I wish I was getting the every night bombing that London, and you, is getting. I wish I could see you every Wednesday. I wish I could see you every day of the week. I wish that U and I, and D [Dilys Powell], and whatever other alphebeticals [sic] you would elect for, could be meeting together once a week, and lunching together once a day, and dining together every night, and that, thereon, we all went to bed together. How delicious t'would be, then, for us all to breakfast together; and thereon, to start getting ready to lunch, and dine, and bed and board with ourselves, and with none others whatever. As far as the world is concerned I am indifferent – but, I like my loves!"[20]

For most of the war Kot was also alone in the house. When Lagden decided not to relocate to 5 Acacia Road, other lodgers moved in – two young women who, according to Marjorie Wells, were "most satisfactory tenants as they only came to London for one week in four." They soon moved out: Kot "had a spell of ill health during one of their visits, and couldn't bear them, and … he frightened them away."[21] There was one communal experience that the reclusive Kot did appear to cherish: that of sharing the common anxiety and deprivation with fellow Londoners, whom he admired for their famed English fortitude.[22] He even resented his niece's attempts to make his life easier. She kept sending him money and parcels, and he kept refusing to accept money orders – and scolding her in all his letters for the parcels. "I asked you so many times, through your uncle, not to send me anything," he wrote in summer 1940. "I, like everyone here, have everything we need. Perhaps not plenty of everything, but quite enough. And I just feel ashamed of receiving parcels, when the majority of the population, not having relatives abroad, does not get parcels."[23]

Kot told her that the only thing he would approve was her sending chocolates for Christmas to Marjorie Wells and her children. She did send the chocolates to the Wellses but ignored his scolding about the parcels and money orders, making Kot sound more and more exasperated: "Thank you very much for your good intention. But I told you, and particularly your uncle on many occasions that I need no money, nor parcels, nothing at all."[24] Polly was, however, getting a different message from Marjorie Wells: "Your uncle … I think … is pleased by your 'stubbornness' in sending him things, though don't tell him I said so, as he always says he doesn't need anything."[25]

Kot was not entirely without hope in the early months of the war. "God may step in!" he once said to Salaman.[26] "Now we must win soon," he wrote to H.G. Wells in early January 1941, "and if only the USA were to make an alliance with Great Britain, an alliance for putting the world on sound foundation, we could feel really happy."[27] When Germany violated the non-aggression pact and invaded the Soviet Union five months later, Kot's optimism about the early triumphant end to the war began to wane, but even if he was imagining the worst when it came to his relatives and friends back in Ukraine, it was still probably not as grim as what was in fact about to happen to Jews in Kiev, Ostropol, and nearby Starokonstantinov.

The last time Kot heard from his sister Rokhl before the war was while she lived with her two daughters, Lina and Mary, in Konotop, about sixty-five miles northeast of Kiev. Germans overran most of Ukraine soon after they invaded the Soviet Union, and Starokonstantinov and Ostropol were in their firm grasp by mid-July 1941, while Kiev and Konotop fell in September. On 29 and 30 September, in Kiev's Babi Yar, near an old Jewish cemetery, close to 34,000 Jewish men, women, and children were machinegunned. Mercifully for Kot, the atrocities that had taken place at Babi Yar took a long time to become known in the West. Being well aware of what the Nazis were capable of, Kot was still obviously ridden with dark premonitions. "I have no news from Russia," Kot shared his alarm with Sarton in December 1941. "My sister and her two daughters, very young, one an engineer, the other a medical student, and both married, lived in Kiev. What happened to them, I do not know. Nor can I expect to hear from or about them until the Germans have been driven out of Russia."[28] He would not, in fact, hear from Rokhl until late spring 1943, at which point Kot would learn that, mercifully, Rokhl and her family had been evacuated at the beginning of the war to Cheliabinsk and then Tomsk, two towns behind the Urals in Western Siberia. Were it not for that, they most likely would have perished together with countless other Jews in and around Kiev.[29]

Starokonstantinov became for the Nazis a shining example of good organization and efficiency, as evidenced by one of the circulars from the office of the "Generalkomissar" of Volhynia and Podolia.[30] Immediately after the invasion, Jews from all nearby towns and villages, including Kot's Ostropol, were rounded up with the help of local Ukrainian police and confined in a ghetto in the outskirts of the town. Perceived activists and Bolshevik sympathizers were hanged right away and left on the gallows for all to see; the rest were used as slave labour. Minister of Eastern Territories Alfred Rosenberg would testify at the Nuremberg tribunal in 1946 that the German policy with the prisoners in Ukraine was "Those who do not work can die." Since the labour was cheap, there was, furthermore, "no need for health services" and "fertility was not to be desired – the more contraceptives and abortions the better."[31] In 1942, the office of "Generalkomissar" implemented a new policy according to which all ghettoes and Jews in them were to be liquidated immediately. According to some estimates, around ten thousand Jews, including no doubt Kot's remaining relatives and childhood friends who were not in the army, were shot in a nearby forest on 23 June and 29 December 1942. Some were buried while still alive, and the locals reported seeing movement in the earth hill that was their mass grave for days after the killings.[32]

A Soviet document entitled "Act on the Mass Extermination of Civilians and Soviet Prisoners of War in the Town of Starokonstantinov" and dated 24 March 1944, two weeks after Starokonstantinov was liberated by the Red Army, would be later added to the materials of the Nuremberg tribunal. It was based on eyewitness accounts, although it did not describe most victims as Jews, since the Soviets liked to emphasize that Jews were not the Nazis' only victims, and it probably undercounted the dead. It stated:

On December 29, 1942 the Germans assembled 4,000 men, women and children, old people and cripples. They herded those people in a column … and ordered them to strip. Then the doomed were led to the edge of the prepared pit and shot in groups of 100 to 150. That massacre was directed by Gestapo department chief Graf, notorious for his cruelty, his assistants and gendarmerie men. The victims were covered with a thin layer of earth and the next day those … who lived nearby could still hear screams of women and children coming from the grave. We have established many facts when wounded people were buried alive.[33]

A much more recent document, based on the reminiscences of the survivors and their families, submitted to Yad Vashem, an organization dedicated to research of the Holocaust, paints a more detailed picture of what happened to the Starokonstantinov and Ostropol Jews during the entire occupation:

In July 1941, an unknown number of Jews was brought to the Novogorodskiy Forest, near the Novogorodskiy "kolkhoz" two kilometers from Starokonstantinov, to the right of the road to Shepetovka. There they were humiliated, and then killed.

On August 3, 1941, 489 Jews (302 men and 187 women) were assembled by Germans and local policemen in the town square near the power plant.

They were divided into two columns, men and women, and then led to the murder site, where they were shot in anti-tank ditches. The murder operation carried out by two companies of Battalions 1 and 2 of the SS infantry regiment 8, with the participation of Police Battalion 320.

In August or on September 2, 1941 (according to German sources, at the end of September), 500-800 Jews were taken to the Novogorodskiy Forest by members of Police Battalion 304 and shot.

In the morning of June 23, 1942, some 3,000-4,000 Jews (according to other sources, 6,500 Jews) – men, women and children – residents of the Starokonstantinov ghetto, including Jews from Gritsev, Ostropol and Novaya Sinyava, were rounded up near the town's power station. Seven Jews were hanged for being partisans – arms were allegedly found in their homes. After separating a number of families of professionals, the Jews were transferred by the Sonderkommando, with the assistance of Ukrainian police, to the Novogorodskiy Forest, where they were undressed and shot.

On November (or December) 29, 1942, 4,000 Jews (men, women and children) were taken to the same murder site and shot dead. The action was commanded by the local security police commander, Graff.[34]

Ostropol was liberated on 5 March 1944. On 10 March, the *Times* of London, one of the papers that Marjorie Wells brought Kot every day, carried an update from the Eastern Front with the headline: "New Russian Successes in the Ukraine. Staro-Konstantinov Taken by Red Army."[35] We know for sure that Kot saw this article because the same day Wells wrote to Polly that her uncle "was interested that his village of Ostropol has been in the news during the last few days ... It appeared on the maps in the daily papers for several days ... Poor Ostropol! I don't expect there is much of it left."[36]

It was not, however, until the Nuremberg tribunal that the details of the Jewish massacres in Ukraine started to come out in the English press where Kot could read it. On 4 January 1946 another article in the *Times* featured a testimony of SS Major-General Ohlendorf, who in 1941-42 was the chief of special operations in the south of Ukraine, which included Kot's Volhynia. Ohlendorf confessed – "with the utmost candour," according to the reporter – that "the group under his command had been responsible for 90,000 executions in a year of campaigning in Russia." Ohlendorf hastened to add, though, that that figure was "'less' than that of the three other groups operating with the armies on this front." He also testified that he objected to some extreme measures, like "gas vans," while preferring "'the purely military method' of employing execution squads, as submission to military discipline relieved them of any feeling of individual responsibility."[37] In August of the same year the *Times* also detailed the Nazi's "scientific" gathering of the skulls of the "Jewish-Bolshevist Commissars, who represent the prototype of the repulsive." People in the field were instructed not to kill these red Jews right away but, for the sake of the purity of the specimen, turn them over alive to German scientists. If the Jewish commissars were to be killed, the instructions continued, care had to be taken "not to damage the head." Hangings were thus preferable to shootings.[38]

The effect of these shocking reports was immediately felt by English Jews. As Noel Annan points out, in England these revelations "altered the way the educated classes spoke and felt about the Jews": "Anti-semitism never dies ... But ... after 1945 it became bad form and was regarded as disgusting to talk in a derogatory way about Jews, still less discriminate in public against them ... Jews were now wholly accepted in public life."[39] While enjoying the benefits of this new attitude, Kot undoubtedly felt that it was too high a price to pay for more acceptance.

Kot lost more old friends during the war years and immediately after. Sydney Waterlow and Sydney Schiff died in 1944. Despite Kot's heated outburst against Schiff in 1926, the relationship was subsequently patched up, and in a letter to Myer Salaman, written several days after Schiff's death, Kot could still note that he and Schiff "have been friends for many years."[40] In 1945, Fanny Stepniak died at the age of ninety. "The other day an old friend of mine died," Kot informed Polly. "She was a very interesting woman. The last few years owing to her leaving London, because of the bombs, etc, and going to live in the country, I did not see her, but I used to get frequent letters from her, and wishing in each letter to come back to London."[41]

On 13 August 1946, H.G. Wells passed away. Wells and Kot were not particularly chummy after the Cresset fiasco, but since he was so close to Marjorie, Gip, and their children, he experienced the death of H.G. Wells more intimately than he would have otherwise. Earlier in summer, Marjorie, who was still Wells's personal secretary, had to cut her and her children's vacation in Switzerland one week short to rush back to London in order to take care of her ailing father-in-law. His death was not unexpected, since he had been ill for several years. Writing to Ralph Hodgson back in 1945 Kot had sarcastically remarked that Wells refused to "oblige the blighters," i.e., his doctors, who predicted that "he would die in a fortnight." Kot had known even then, though, that Wells's days were numbered: "[H]e has been ill all the time, and as he is 78, one cannot expect him to get well. I wish he would."[42]

Kot attended Wells's funeral, and was among those who "from the cremato-rium ... went back to H.G.W.'s house, and ... had tea there."[43] He admired the family's reserved and dignified way of dealing with their loss: "Inspite of HGW's long illness, his son Gip and Marjorie feel their loss very much. So does Cather-ine and Oliver. But they do not show it at all, being of the true English breed that forbids any outward manifestation of grief."[44] It was in stark contrast to Jewish funerals he had attended during his years in Ukraine, which were marked by loud laments and raw emotions. Kot was gratified to learn in December that, according to the memorandum that Wells left to his sons, he was to inherit a bronze statuette of Tolstoy that had been given to Wells by Gorky in 1920 and bore Gorky's inscription. He immediately made several photographs of himself sitting next to the statuette and sent them to many friends and relatives. He also included the text of the inscription: "To my greatest friend H.G. Wells. 5. X. 20. M. Gorky." "I am proud and happy to have such a souvenir from H.G. Wells," he wrote to Polly. "It is standing on the dresser in the kitchen, as that kitchen is warm, and the other rooms are not. But later on, when it gets warmer, I shall put it in my study."[45] The Wellses also gave Kot H.G.'s old grandfather's clock that Kot always admired when he visited the writer, probably because it reminded him of the one his parents had in Ostropol.

There was also a death in the family: his only remaining brother died in Canada. On 13 August 1942, Moishel – or Morris Kay, as he was known by then

– succumbed to a heart failure at the age of sixty-four. Almost all of Kot's letters to Moishel have been lost but one survived. It was written on 5 August 1942, just eight days before his brother's death, and was in response to Moishel's letter from 7 July. In it Kot complained (in Russian) that in the pictures Moishel had sent him, Polly's daughter Jackie looked too thin and should therefore eat more. Kot was in fact so suspicious about the state of Jackie's health that he reproached his brother for not telling him the truth. "There is nothing I can do about it," he lamented, "you have your own methods of not making people worry."[46]

Now Polly – in the same well-established family tradition that Kot both railed against and would, ironically, practice himself on more than one occasion during the last ten years of his life – thought it was best not to add to Kot's mental anguish at the time of the war by informing him of his brother's death. But Kot was worried anyway after he abruptly stopped receiving letters from Moishel, and "imagining every possible calamity," according to Marjorie Wells, who wrote to Polly in November 1942. "If anything is wrong," she pleaded with Polly, "I am sure it would be better to tell him the truth, for it can't be worse than his imagination."[47] When the family in Canada finally told him, six months after the fact, about Moishel's death, Kot sternly rebuked Polly – just as he did after he learned belatedly of Eli's death. "Only selfish and stupid people conceal the truth," he declared to her, leaving it up to Polly to choose which group he thought she belonged to.[48] Mindful of his own possibly hereditary heart troubles, he also demanded more specifics from his niece: "Next time when you write, tell me what the doctor called the disease; he must have given it a name, – a 'weak heart,' as you write, is not a name of an illness."[49]

If his criticism hurt her feelings, Polly did not allow it to slow her down in showering him with money and parcels. "She was always running to the post office," her daughter Jackie recalls.[50] She also sought his fatherly advice about how to raise her three children, who were likewise encouraged to write to their great-uncle. "Thank you for your tiny letter to me," Kot wrote to Jackie in 1944. "I am very pleased to hear that you are third in your grade. With a little effort you will probably be first before very long."[51] He instructed Polly to teach her children to love reading and suggested she should "ask Mrs Wells to send you a list of books for children to read."[52] Marjorie Wells sent Polly not just a list but actual books. Some of them were definitely not of the kind Kot had in mind, as she confessed to Polly in 1943: "Your uncle always wants me to send them really good books, but this year I sent them thrillers which Oliver adores."[53]

To Kot, Catherine and Oliver Wells were ideal children, and he never tired of describing their accomplishments and successes to his niece. Polly's children, on the other hand, despite all her efforts to impress Kot, were never quite in the same category. He was not even sure they, unlike Catherine and Oliver, needed to be university educated. "I would advise such an education only to those, boys and girls, who are terribly keen on it, and can pursue their studies without any great difficulty," he informed Polly, adding that "the economic consideration … should never be ignored."[54] He would become even more blunt in the early 1950s when Polly's two older children were seriously contemplating higher education: "Sending Marvin to a university (also Jackie) is a grave mistake. They are not of the student type, so the university will do them incalculable harm … [They] will, no doubt, regret in a couple of years, for having entered the university."[55] Polly's motherly pride was undoubtedly bruised.

Once the war was drawing to a close, Polly and her uncle began to discuss seeing each other in London. "Do consider the idea of you and Manuel coming on a visit to London when the war is over and when travel becomes possible," Kot wrote to her in spring 1944. "I should love to see you and to hear how you have been getting on all these years."[56] Polly would indeed come to London three years later, but under very different circumstances.

As in the previous summer, in June 1947 Marjorie Wells again had to cut her and her children's vacation short (they were staying with Dorothy Richardson in Cornwall) in order to rush to London, except now the ailing person in need of her constant care was Kot. This was eerily reminiscent of Kot's first serious nervous breakdown in 1936, when he cabled Marjorie asking her to interrupt her vacation in Switzerland because he needed her presence. This time he was probably in no shape to cable her himself; instead it was most likely Gip Wells who informed his wife that, on 7 June, Kot had attempted to cut his throat with a razor blade. The method was sadly reminiscent of what Gertler had done in his unsuccessful 1936 suicide attempt at the sanatorium. The blade turned out to be fairly dull, and as Marjorie Wells explained to several of their mutual friends, Kot's physical "wounds were superficial and healed in a week."[57] He had lodgers living at the house at the time, Mr and Mrs Dickinson, and they found him bleeding in the bathroom. The fact that they, of all people, witnessed his botched attempt to kill himself added insult to injury. Just weeks earlier he had complained to Juliette Huxley that he hated their presence in his house so much that he "could strangle them."[58]

From surviving letters just prior to 7 June, it is hard to determine precisely what prompted Kot to apply a razor blade to a carotid artery in his neck on that particular day. Ironically, a day earlier, Marjorie, writing to May Sarton from Cornwall, actually used the word "cheerful" to describe Kot's state of mind: "Kot writes cheerfully. He is providing Gip with lots of meals while I am away."[59] Kot's letters to Polly around the same time were not particularly cheerful, but they still appear, for most part, to be just garden-variety grumpy. All through May he complained about the weather, which was still unseasonably cold and gloomy. He continued to scold Polly for sending too many parcels, and in one letter objected to meeting Polly's Canadian friend visiting London, saying he did not "like meeting new people." He also fretted about not being able to send parcels to Rokhl and her family, who by now were back in Konotop and in need of everything.[60]

Only toward the very end of May was there a hint of something more ominous, for the closing paragraph of his 27 May letter to Polly reads almost like a goodbye note: "I oftentimes feel that I do not write you enough. You must forgive me, for I have got into bad habits when I simply cannot write than [sic] is absolutely necessary. But I always think of you and always wish you all a happy life."[61] The last pre-breakdown letter, dated 2 June, was very brief – just half a page – and again expressed a hope that Polly's family "will all be happy and well." It implored her to help Rokhl and her children "now and always" and not to worry about him. He did promise, however, to write to her "again soon."[62]

In a letter to Hodgson half a year after the suicide attempt, Kot attributed his desire to end his life to his heart trouble and his doctor's insistence that he check himself into a hospital: "Last summer, after not feeling well, and threatened by my German Jewish doctor that I shall have to go to a hospital, I, in a moment of madness, tried to commit suicide by cutting my throat."[63] While it is impossible to account for every factor that led to Kot's 1947 breakdown, it is safe to assume that bad health was not the entire story, if at all. The explanation contradicts, in fact, Kot's statement to Sarton back in May, summarizing his tests and examinations as good news, especially when it came to an apparent blockage – "the thing," as he called it – in his stomach: "the good and kind doctor Leo Rau said that the thing had not grown worse, so there is a chance of my getting well soon."[64]

More likely, the long-lasting impact of the war played an important, if not crucial, role in driving him to attempt to take his life. The "stiff-upper-lip" resolve that he had shared with his countrymen was gone by now, and so were the effects of the postwar victory euphoria, when all that mattered was "the defeat of the most horrible Germans."[65] What remained were the accumulated experience of London air raids and the grim revelations of the Nuremberg trials about the mass extermination of European and Soviet Jews. Marjorie Wells being away was also probably a contributing factor. Dependent on her daily visits for both his health and his sanity, Kot appears to have been at his most vulnerable when she was not in town, so it is no coincidence that both of his serious breakdowns happened while Marjorie was on vacation.

To many, Kot and Marjorie Wells's relationship was a mystery. In an unpublished part of the memoir that Lady Glenavy sent to George Zytaruk for possible publication, she called Marjorie Wells "the most unapproachable person" she had ever met. She seemed to her "armour-plated against other people" and, at the same time, perfectly eqipped "for taking care of elderly literary gentlemen in poor health": "When Kot began to have heart attacks and moods of great depression, I had said to him, 'I wish I could do something to help you.' He said, 'They all say that – it means nothing, the sort of help I need is someone who will come to me every day, to do the shopping, the house-keeping and the cleaning, someone like a wife or mother who will take care of me.' The next time I went to London, I found that Marjorie was doing just what he wanted. He said she was 'his tower of strength,' that she was the only one of his women friends who was 'a free human being' – I wondered how she managed to look after her own house and family as well as Kot, but she did it all quietly and efficiently."[66]

Marjorie Wells seems to have provided Kot with the kind of unconditional and limitless support that, given the complexity of marriages (including her own), cannot even be routinely expected in a wife. She found the relationship gratifying as well. According to her daughter Catherine, Marjorie was "as close to Kot as she was to anybody at that stage," even though there was nothing "physical or romantic" about their friendship.[67] While playing a traditionally female nursing role both for H.G. Wells and Kot, Marjorie was by no means a "traditional" female. She was a fierce intellectual and a freethinker. She considered her day job "slavery" and insisted that Catherine should not even learn how to type because she needed to aim much higher.[68] There is every evidence that Kot treated her as his intellectual equal, and that probably went a long way to cement their bond.

Wells knew that the situation had to be handled very carefully, not just with Kot but also with his doctors, who were not to be allowed to institutionalize him before Kot had sufficient time to recover within his own walls and among his friends. She rightfully feared that, given his suicide attempt and previous history of severe depression, Kot would be admitted to an asylum as an involuntary patient, with no informed consent right to object to radical procedures such as lobotomy, and with a possibility that he could be kept there until the end of his days. She enlisted others in helping her to succeed in her aims. In an undated letter to Dilys Powell, obviously written within a couple of days of 7 June, Marjorie asked Powell to "back me up in my attempts to keep Kot here for three or four weeks" and to help her persuade Dr Rau "that it is unreasonable to come to any decision about Kot's mental state while he is still being drugged." "If he is to be cured," Marjorie declared, "he will only be cured in this, his own house." She also begged Powell to assure Kot, "[i]f he says he is doing harm to me," that "this is not so: say you will help me in every way."[69]

Wells also thought that having his niece around would be of great solace to Kot, so she cabled Polly urging her to come at once because her uncle was very ill. She likewise – and with Kot's consent – summoned Ida Baker, but Baker was unable to travel. Wells then arranged for Kot's lease on the house to be extended by three years, and for his lodgers to depart immediately, thus alleviating at least some sources of Kot's anxiety and discontent. In case Kot would still need long-term care, she and Esther Salaman established a fund where Kot's friends could contribute money.

In the unpublished portion of her memoirs, Lady Glenavy detailed spending eight days with Marjorie and Kot during these early stages of his convalescence:

> About the middle of June 1947, I went to London to the wedding of my brother Philip's daughter. I never got to the wedding – when I arrived at my hotel, I rang up Kot's house, I knew Kot had been ill and I was worried about him. Marjorie Wells answered the phone; she said "Kot has tried to cut his throat with the blade of a safety razor. I have been with him for about a week, night and day. Can you come and take over so that I can get some sleep?" I went at once to 5 Acacia Road … Kot was seated in a chair in his dressing-gown, looking terribly pale and miserable, with bandages round his neck … [H]e held out his arms to me and said, "Beatrice, I have done the most stupid wrong thing" … [H]e kept on telling me that Marjorie had been "wonderful" … The wound was slight. They decided not to call the police. Kot said, "Marjorie now arranges everything, you must do exactly as she tells you" … When Marjorie told me about his attempted suicide in the bathroom, she added that she had taken away the rug that was there, and hidden it, so that he would not see blood on it and be reminded of his terrible act. One morning we were sitting in the garden when she came out of the house carrying a large dripping bundle, she proceeded to hang it on the clothes line … It was the rug from the bathroom. I saw Kot turn his head from side to side to avoid looking at it; then he got up and went back into the kitchen.[70]

Upon receiving Marjorie's cable, Polly, according to her daughter Jackie, dropped everything and took her very first airplane trip. It was, her daughter believes, "a gigantic step" on Polly's part to board a plane.[71] It helped that just a month before, on 1 May 1947, Trans-Canada Air Lines had instituted a new daily service between Montreal and London. The North Star airliners that performed transatlantic flights were still relatively small. They carried up to thirty-six passengers, so getting a last-minute ticket to such a popular destination during the summer was, in all probability, not very easy.[72] Lady Glenavy was already there when Polly arrived at her uncle's house, therefore it must have happened soon after 15 June.

Lady Glenavy's assessment of Kot's niece was less than complimentary: "She had the most unpleasant, harsh, speaking voice and an American accent ... She ... was horrified at the 'poverty' in which her uncle lived ... It was interesting that, when she went out to do shopping in the little shops where Kot was known and loved and respected, they said to Marjorie afterward, 'Mr Koteliansky's niece a Jewess?' They thought of him as 'a Russian.'"[73] There is plenty of evidence in Marjorie Wells's letters to friends that she and Polly did not click either, despite all attempts by Polly to be helpful. Soon after Polly's arrival Wells in fact decided that summoning her from Canada was "a mistake."[74] It would take almost six years, and Kot going through another severe bout of ill health and depression, for the two women to renew their friendship. "I am glad we are friends again, or seem to be," Marjorie would write to Polly in February 1953, "because it always worried me that we were not. Well, well, no need to go into all that, I hope."[75]

Back in 1947, Polly definitely felt out of place in London and her uncle's house, and very homesick. On 27 June she reproached her husband for not writing: "I sure was hoping to hear from you before this, it is really very funny that you haven't written. I shall like to hear from you. How is everything and how are the children?"[76] But Polly's letters home were apparently so confusing that both her husband and her cousin Rita complained that she made little sense. Rita still had no clue about the nature of Kot's illness, but she did gather that Polly was shut out of major decisions concerning their uncle's treatment: "Is it an ulcer or is it his nerves? ... As far as I can see you must demand to be allowed to see the doctor with them – or else call in several well known doctors for a consultation and insist on being present." Rita also expressed "the greatest sympathy" to Polly "in having to go through such an ordeal alone."[77] Polly left before 1 July, sooner than she had expected.[78]

Kot stayed in his house until the end of June. Marjorie wanted him to stay longer, but, as she complained to Juliette Huxley, "no one agreed with me, not even Kot himself." By then Kot indeed realized that he needed a more aggressive treatment, but, according to Marjorie, he was full of premonitions, "very miserable at going away, and said he would never come back." That frightened Marjorie. "As you know," she wrote to Juliette in the same letter, "I always believe what he says."[79] And yet a major victory had been achieved through Marjorie's heroic efforts to keep him at home for as long as possible: Kot now could go to an insane asylum – Holloway Sanatorium in Virginia Water, Surrey, thirty-five kilometres from London – as "a voluntary patient," rather than being forcibly committed. Kot would later credit Wells with saving him "from becoming a loony for ever and ever."[80]

Upon his arrival at the asylum, Kot told the doctor in charge that "although he did not want to live, he would cooperate in the treatment."[81] He stayed at the Holloway Sanatorium for a month and a half. During this time he underwent intensive electroshock therapy – or "electroconvulsive therapy," as it was officially called (it had been in practice for almost ten years by then) – and, for two weeks, he was under a "deep narcosis."[82] The electroshock sessions, as expected, wiped out most of his short-term memory, including that of his suicide attempt. Catherine Stoye remembers that her mother was not allowed to see Kot for three weeks "because he was violent and had a black eye while in the hospital and undergoing electric shock."[83] When Marjorie Wells was finally allowed to see him for the first time on 22 July, Kot apparently "began to cry and then he said, 'I thought you had come to take me home!' Then he asked, 'What happened? Why am I here?' And at first she put him off and then ... told him that he had tried to commit suicide. And he cried and said, 'Why did I do it?'"[84]

He also did not remember anything about Polly's visit. In a letter to her, written by very shaky hand in early August while he was still at Holloway, Kot was hopeful that one day he would remember her being in his house on Acacia Road and what she looked like, but in the meantime he was going to rely on Marjorie for details. He later assured Polly that Marjorie told him that his niece had been "a great help and support to me during those distressing weeks."[85] By then he must have known that it was not exactly true, but he and Marjorie no doubt agreed that Polly should be spared a more accurate assessment.

That was not the only white lie Kot was ready to indulge in. A champion of never hiding unpleasant facts from the loved ones, he was now instructing Polly not to tell Rokhl about his attempted suicide: "She has worries enough without that news."[86] Once he was back at home, Kot wrote to his sister that he "had been in hospital ill for a few weeks, with 'coronary thrombosis,' – an affection of the heart." "There's no need," he told Polly, "to tell her anything more about my illness: it will only distress her and make her unhappy." "Particularly as she has the greatest capacity for feeling unhappy," he added, making his sister sound very much like himself.[87] After all the scoldings Polly had received from her uncle about her attempts to shield him for as long as possible from learning about family tragedies, she no doubt appreciated the irony of such a request. Polly apparently kept his suicide attempt a secret not just from Rokhl but from the rest of her family.[88]

At the end Kot came to view his stay at Holloway as almost beneficial. He was, he commented to Sarton in August, "positively glad of my experience in meeting a great number of men 'in the raw,' with some of whom I have made good friends … When Dilys Powell came yesterday, and I told her of one of my friends at the Holl. San., Mr Brown, who had been in the Metropolitan Police for 18 years, and bombed, – house etc, – several times during the war, – the realest of the real cockneys, and a splendid man, tears stood in her eyes."[89]

It is ironic, of course, that the man who always professed he did not like meeting new people in his regular life, was so drawn to other patients at the mental institution, but he probably did feel that he had much more in common with them than with most "sane" people outside of Holloway, and had much less explaining to do. When he came home, while still physically weak, he considered himself largely cured of depression.[90] As a result, Kot believed he no longer needed the fund that Marjorie Wells and Esther Salaman had established for him, and he made sure that all the money was immediately returned to the generous contributors.

He continued to be taken care of by Marjorie and was visited frequently by Powell and James Stephens, as well as by Juliette Huxley and Beatrice Glenavy whenever they were in London. Huxley's son, Francis, remembers with fondness "one happy afternoon" when he too was invited to come to Kot's place: "This was a great kindness of Kot's, for around this time he was being treated for a nervous breakdown with the earliest form of ECT, a peculiarly hellish experience that he endured with bitter resignation along with Russian cigarettes." Stephens was also there that time and regaled Huxley "with unforgettable stories," which Kot undoubtedly had heard many times before but was probably content to hear again as a welcome sign of returned normalcy.[91]

Polly was not the only person sending Kot packages from across the ocean during the war; so was May Sarton, whom Kot also chided for doing so. In July 1947, Sarton was coming to London for the first time after the war and was hoping to spend time with Kot. When she learned about his attempted suicide, her reaction was both shock and a tinge of regret that Kot had not succeeded. "He is so old and ill and tired," she wrote to her parents, "I can't *bear* to think of it. Why couldn't he have died if that was what he wanted? He has no one …"[92] She wanted to see him at Holloway, but the doctors there were leery of allowing anyone but Marjorie to visit. She could stay in London longer than planned, until Kot was released from the asylum, but decided that Kot, while significant, was not "the very center of my life, enough to make it possible to break" other more central pursuits.[93] So instead she accompanied Marjorie to Kot's house on 23 July and wrote him a letter from there: "What happiness to sit in the little house on Acacia Road … What a blessing. Everything looks so neat and clean and as if you had just swept the floor and were downstairs making a cup of tea – it is all waiting for you to rejoice in your homecoming … My sweet Kot, my darling, I shall not see you but I am coming back in the spring, perhaps when the pear tree is in flower …"[94]

She did come back the following year – only to lose Kot forever as her friend. The final break had to do with her relationship with Juliette Huxley, which became sexual when Sarton visited her in April 1948 in Paris, where Julian Huxley was stationed as the director-general of UNESCO. The love triangle turned very messy a month later, when May returned to Paris from Belgium hoping to find Juliette alone and Julian absent on one of his lengthy UNESCO trips, only to discover that he was ill and at home. Much to Juliette's chagrin, Sarton ended up in Julian's bed.

In early August, Sarton was in London, staying with Kot. Though she swore to Juliette that she would not tell him anything about their affair, she soon broke her promise. "I think it made him terribly angry," she reported to Juliette. "He takes it for granted that it is one more of my literary adventures and *all* on my side and quite hopeless … I feel I am in his mind *beyond the pale*."[95] Neither Sarton nor Kot appeared to enjoy her visit this time. "We had some good talks," she told Juliette, "but I felt more than usual his sometimes lack of humanity, simplification of everything to an absolute black and white." According to Sarton, Kot was also upset that she left her bag and four dresses on hangers at his house while staying with other friends, whereas she could not understand why he would even care, given that he had a "whole empty house!"[96] Seeing the dresses themselves probably rubbed Kot the wrong way. "I like people, men and women, to dress well," Kot had written to his niece two years ealier, "that is in neat, good-quality clothes, well made. But I detest everything ostentatious, loud, 'unusual.' People, especially women, who make a show of themselves by not dressing simply, and naturally, and neatly are just an abomination."[97]

In September, Sarton accepted Lady Glenavy's invitation to spend time at their estate in Ireland. While there, she believed herself to have fallen in love with the hostess, dedicating poems to her and writing passionate letters. Lady Glenavy was not amused. By then Kot, still angry at Sarton for both her seduction of Juliette and her behaviour at his house, was already not responding to her letters. In October, Sarton heard that Kot had indeed decided to "cast [her] out." She beseeched him to reconsider: "For many years I have thought of you as the unchanging friend … Surely Kot this is not true? I cannot believe it is true."[98] It was true enough, and Kot's decision was only solidified when in November Lady Glenavy came to London and told Kot and Juliette about Sarton's ardent pursuit of her. Juliette, in turn, revealed to the two of them that May, desirous of her undivided love, had threatened in Paris to "tell all to Julian."[99] "What happened,"

Sarton wrote to a friend in December, "is that Kot, Juliette and Beatrice Glenavy met in London and talked about certain matters concerning me that were in a way true but which in another way were simply lies, and they all convinced themselves that I am untrustworthy, superficial, dangerous and god knows what. Juliette wrote me a letter telling me that the two others don't want anything to do with me. As far as she is concerned, she'll continue to write to me for the sake of the past, but asked me never to mention the word 'love' when referring to her."[100]

Sarton would blame Lady Glenavy for it all. She remained convinced for years to come that this "thoroughly neurotic or just plain wicked … Irish woman,"[101] driven by jealousy, was from the very start on a mission to "destroy my friendship with Kot."[102]

While Kot's relationship with May Sarton ceased, his friendship with Juliette Huxley grew stronger. He was her constant correspondent while she and Julian were in Paris. She told him stories of Julian going to death camps on behalf of UNESCO – "Visiting the camp of corpses was bearable, but not the hospital of dying bodies who clutched at him with desperation and hunger for life" – and making crucial decisions in airless rooms – "The poor delegates sit under the glittering candelabra of the Ball Room at the Hotel Majestic, without even as much as one electric fan, going through an agenda bristling with controversies and harassed by the shortness of time."[103] Kot's suggestion on how Julian, as an Englishman, should deal with the rest of the world was decidedly undiplomatic: he thought that Julian should "simply tell … everyone they are blighters and know nothing and must wait 200 years till they are wiser and meanwhile take orders."[104] As to the Soviet Russia, no longer a war ally, Kot had a blunt solution there as well: "My sole prayer in night and day is for American bombs to fall on the Kremlin, after which there will be peace and good will on earth …"[105]

He was much more philosophical and nuanced on the issues concerning Jews, the state of Israel, and the fear, expressed even after the Holocaust, that Jews, if well treated, would be encouraged to "dominate the world": "Those Jews, in every country, who belong to the professional classes – doctors, lawyers, engineers, etc, – identify themselves with the nation among whom they live. Even in Unesco you will find numbers of Jews, who call themselves Poles, Uzbekhs, Rumanians, etc, and if their faces don't cry to heaven proclaiming their origin, you may not know that they are Jews. Then there are the Jewish masses in every country, – that is about 90% or 95% of the Jews who are mostly tailors, shoemakers, cigarette makers, dressmakers etc, etc, – these masses have no idea of dominating the world, and perhaps have no ideas at all, except a desire to make their sons and daughters be doctors, lawyers, etc, etc … The small group of Zionists want

Palestine, but can't possibly even think of dominating the world. So the idea of Jews dominating the world comes straight from Hitler's propaganda."[106]

All through the war Kot continued to read manuscripts for Cresset. "He hasn't discovered any new genius yet," Marjorie Wells informed Polly in 1944, "most of the manuscripts are poor, he says."[107] He was not translating any longer, but during the 1940s several of his translations were republished. In 1940 and 1941 Penguin Books issued two thin editions, *Three Chekhov Plays* and *Russian Short Stories,* selected by S.S. Koteliansky. In addition to two stories by Kuprin, which Kot had translated early on with the help of Murry; four stories by Chekhov, for which Kot was listed as a sole translator; and his and Lawrence's rendition of Bunin's "Gentleman from San Francisco" – this 1941 edition also featured "Four Days" by Vsevolod Garshin, a pacifist story from the turn of the century, which was obviously very timely. James Stephens congratulated him on getting "Penguined": "I was ... especially interested to see how your English moved under a pen."[108]

In 1948, Lear Publishers in New York reissued Kot's and Leonard Woolf's translation of Chekhov's notebooks. "A number of my translations have been pirated (stolen by American publishers) without my previous knowledge," Kot had complained to his niece two years earlier; this might have been one such case.[109] *The Personal Papers of Anton Chekhov*, as the volume was called, also contained Chekhov's letters as translated by Constance Garnett, Kot's celebrated archrival, who had died two years earlier at the age of eighty-five. Her obituary in the *Times* stated that Garnett's translations of Russian classics were "as spirited and idiomatic as they are accurate."[110] Kot could not have agreed less.

13

# FULL CIRCLE

As I have a
bad memory,
I bought this
for Kot,
Hoping that he
Me
Has not forgot
~ James Stephens

You must always remember that I am difficult, perhaps strange …
Even what I write may sound strange to you but never mind.
~ Kot to Polly, 11 December 1952

Kot's final five years were like a condensed version of his entire life in England: the death of a very close friend, bad health, gnawing concerns about the well-being of his Russian relatives, squabbles with Frieda over Lawrence's letters, aggravation caused by Murry, and severe bouts of depression.

The friend was James Stephens. Kot was as close to him as to anyone in his life, including Lawrence. Unlike his relationship with Lawrence, however, this one was very harmonious – full of mutual deference and utterly devoid of quarrels and long periods of silence. Like Ottoline Morrell, Stephens had a public persona that was impish and gay, but it hid deep melancholia and frequent depressions. Kot knew it better than probably anyone else, including Ottoline; to her friendly suggestion that the short and odd-looking Stephens was a quintessential Irish leprechaun, Kot once heatedly replied, "Under that leprechaun façade is a real suffering human being."[1] Kot and Stephens were the same age and in similarly poor health, including frequent bouts of pneumonia and stomach ulcers, except

Stephens's ulcers were so severe that he often had to fast for days. In short, they were a well-matched couple – but also an odd couple, seen by most as "exotics."[2]

Kot particularly enjoyed it when in his kitchen, after several glasses of Kot's "special" martinis, "Stephens would shut his eyes and rock backward and forward, reciting his poems in a crooning voice."[3] Among his poems there was one addressed directly to Kot. Called "For the Lion of Judah," which was Stephens's moniker for his friend, the 1938 poem bemoaned the spread of Nazism, with the despair finding its crescendo in the last three stanzas:

– Mind does mind no more, nor care,
Minding is no more its will:
To murder is its main affair,
Treachery its main of skill!

And the heart, that said to Love
– Thou and I – says that no more,
Phoenix and the Turtle-Dove
Show each other to the door.

Only now the third, the wise,
On the sole Arabian tree,
Who singeth only as he dies,
Sings the final ecstasy.[4]

Kot was delighted when Stephens came back to London after the war ended; he was a bit apprehensive, though, as he wrote to Hodgson, that after five long years apart their "talking behaviour has not established itself yet with its wanted smoothness." Kot was sure, however, that it would for the simple reason that "the essential James is unchangeable, and at his best just lovable."[5] They had less time now for their teas, martinis, and conversation, since Stephens was busy broadcasting lectures on the BBC and, because of his tight schedule and poor physical condition, he relied more and more on his wife to drive him around and pick him up. Kot complained that Mrs Stephens did not allow her husband to spend more than twenty minutes with his friends before starting to honk her horn insistently outside. As in the case of the Lawrences, Kot wished he could separate the two but decided that it was not practical given that Stephens was "so awfully helpless, in the housewife's sense of the word."[6] While jealous of all the new people Stephens met at the BBC, Kot was very proud of his friend's performance: "He is extremely good over the radio: his voice and the way he speaks." He was also thrilled when in 1947 Stephens was given an honourary doctorate by Trinity College in Dublin.[7]

In 1949 Stephens unexplicably collapsed on a London street and was rushed to a hospital. He had, Kot informed Hodgson soon afterward, "a very serious operation … gastric ulcers. The doctors … doubted if he would survive the operation."[8] Stephens did survive this time but would be dead in slightly more than a year. He passed away on 26 December – St Stephen's Day – 1950. Given the state of Kot and Mrs Stephens's relationship, Kot had to learn about it in the cruelest fashion – from the news on the radio: "On Thursday before Christmas James and Fulton came to tea, as usual. James was as lively and talkative as ever. On Boxing Day, in the 9 o'clock news, I heard of James' death (during the Christmas night). I rang up his wife. From a very long and incoherent recital, I only understood that he had died during the night, for when she called him at 10 o'clock in the morning, and having had no response, she went up to his room, and found him dead on the floor. The autopsy, a few days later, showed … that he died from high blood pressure in the brain. So James is no more. I shall miss him very much, for in the course of these long years we have become very good friends. (And I think, I was his only friend, to whom he could speak frankly about himself, without suspicion or fear.)"[9]

"My best friend died two years ago," Kot would complain to Polly in 1952, "and I have very few left."[10] According to Lady Glenavy, shortly after Stephens's death, Cynthia Stephens swallowed her pride and came to see Kot, ostensibly for help with her late husband's papers: "Kot explained some legal point to her and gave her some advice. She then opened her handbag and pushed a piece of paper across the table towards him saying, 'See how much he loved me.' It was a short poem written to her by James when he was a young man, a lodger in her house in Dublin. I watched Kot as he read it. I saw he was deeply moved. In silence he handed it back to her … I felt she had a moment of triumph over Kot. When she was gone he went round throwing open windows and doors, and breathing heavily, he said, 'The very air is contaminated!' Kot's hates and prejudices were no ordinary emotions."[11]

Murry's publication in 1951 of Mansfield's letters was undoubtedly yet another reminder to Kot of why he so loathed the spouses of his best friends. One did not have to go far into the volume to recognize Murry's self-serving intent; it was spelled out in the blurb on the front cover of the dust jacket:

This new edition … contain[s] only the letters written by K.M. to her lover and husband. The editor has restored all the passages omitted from the letters on their first appearance – passages of passionate intimacy written by a woman in love … The result is one of the most remarkable series of unexpurgated love-letters ever printed.[12]

Many passages were indeed passionate: "Last night, before you got into bed, you stood, quite naked, bending forward a little, talking … I saw you – I loved you so, loved your body with such tenderness … Every inch of you is so precious to me – your soft shoulders – your creamy warm skin, your ears cold like shells are cold – your long legs and your feet that I love to clasp with my feet – the feeling of your belly – and your thin young back … I want nobody but you for my lover and my friend and to nobody but you shall I be faithful."[13]

As if these affectionate and very frequent declarations of Mansfield's love for the man Kot detested were not enough to make his blood boil, they often ran parallel to vehement expressions of hatred for Ida Baker ("L.M."), whom Kot once designated as "Katherine's sole and only friend."[14]

This was not the Katherine Mansfield Kot thought he knew or wanted to know, and, on top of that, there was hardly any mention of him in the letters, as if Kot was a very peripheral character in her life. When he was mentioned – on just five occasions – it was always something very trivial, as, in one instance, her asking Murry to send Kot the pages of the story she helped in translating.[15] Another time she complained to Murry that the Farbmans and Koteliansky, who moved into their Acacia Road house, were hiding the letters for her that still kept coming to that address. ("They were, of course, quite innocent of Katherine's not so serious charge," Murry assured the reader in a footnote.[16])

Twice Mansfield simply quoted Kot's colourful expressions. When commenting on the childishly conceived "list of friends" that Murry sent to her and in which Kot was not included, she wrote: "I love her [Anne Estelle Rice, an American painter and a close friend of Mansfield] as a 'being,' as Kot would say." While raging against Marcel Proust, whose reputation as "perhaps … the greatest novelist that ever has been!!!!!" offended her, she thought of Kot's way with words again: "In very truth … Koteliansky's saying: 'This man must be beaten plainly' is profound."[17] There was one exception from these pedestrian mentions, but even here Kot merely received the warmth reflected from her love for her cat Wingli, the very same cat whom she asked Kot to adopt in 1922. Kot saw Wingli at Murry's house and apparently complimented Mansfield on her beautiful pet. "I had such a nice letter from Kot," Mansfield then wrote to Murry. "Wing has charmed even him. 'Small and slender and quickwitted' he calls him. What a little *briseur de cœurs* he is!"[18]

It was no surprise to his friends that Kot described his reading the letters as "a shattering blow."[19] A year earlier it had come to Murry's attention "by a side-wind," as he put it, that Kot's name for him was "Smerdyakov." "You, not being a Dostoevsky fan won't get a full flavour of it," Murry wrote to Lady Glenavy then.[20] The full flavour was, of course, that there are few characters in all of world literature more loathsome than Dostoevsky's Smerdyakov. An illegitimate son of Fyodor Karamazov, Smerdyakov tortures stray cats as a child, lives in Fyodor's house as a lackey, and eventually commits patricide. His mere name, which is based on the word that means "a vile stink," reeks of contemptibility. Now Kot probably felt that even Smerdyakov had a better moral character than Murry.

For Murry, it was just a simple case of Kot not really knowing the real Mansfield: "Kot's view of our relation was quite superficial," he explained to Glenavy, "and his relation to her was quite false. It consisted in making her up and sometimes she liked it, and sometimes she reacted against it because she knew I was being made the scapegoat, and since in her heart of hearts she recongnized that was unfair, a kind of treachery, she couldn't accept the position he wanted to thrust upon her ... Katherine was lovely, much lovelier than Kot ever knew ... Kot fed what was false in her, and what she knew was false. Knowing what I know, it would have been impossible for Kot and me to be friends, without my telling him the truth. He *would never* have taken it. He didn't like truth. It was not his kind of meat."[21] What Kot read in Mansfield's letters to Murry was definitely "not his kind of meat." If Murry's publication of Mansfield's *Journal* in 1927 had made Kot feel "disgusted" about "a sheer profanation" of Mansfield's "strictly personal and intimate jottings," this was tenfold worse.

Hating Murry, Kot no doubt immediately entertained the thought that many of the passionate declarations of her love for Jack and scorn for Ida were not in the original epistles. Being Kot, he also immediately started devising plans to set the record straight, and in that Baker was an equally insulted and willing participant. "*[L]isten very attentively*," he instructed her soon after the book came out. "If you can bring yourself into the mood of typing K's letters to you, please do so, as soon as you can. I have an idea of what can be done with the typescript, but the explanation of the idea can wait until you manage to come to London."[22] We do not know the particulars of Kot's "idea," but Baker did use the letters when collaborating with Antony Alpers, who was writing a biography of Mansfield at the time. It was precisely because Kot "found him sincere and honest" and thought that Baker "should help him as much as possible with his book" that she offered her letters and assistance to Alpers. Yet, when the book came out in 1954, it greatly disappointed them both, for they felt it sided with Murry's version of Katherine's life, and not with Ida's and Kot's.[23] Baker then used the letters when in 1972 she published her own book, *Katherine Mansfield: The Memories of LM.*

Though it came out seventeen years after Kot had died, in the preface she made sure to note that it had been in many ways instigated by him.

In 1951 Kot was also anxious about Polly, for it was now her turn to have a nervous breakdown and Kot's turn to pester her for more details about her illness. The trigger for Polly's breakdown followed the birth – on 22 March 1951 – of Polly's and Manuel's second daughter and fourth child, Sharon. Sharon was a late and probably not planned child: Polly was already forty and Manuel fifty-three. Like her uncle (and Aunt Rokhl), Polly was a great worrier. Having another baby when the family's sole breadwinner was already in his fifties must have weighed heavily on her mind, and, at least according to her husband, contributed to her post-partum depression.[24] But there was, of course, more to the story. This was the same Polly who, as a young child and teenager, lost her entire immediate family to a merciless epidemic, a violent murder, and a freakish accident. The new family she lovingly created after she moved to Canada allowed her to keep this darkness at bay most of the time, but their protective circle failed her that year.

Kot, bewildered by Polly's silence soon after Sharon's birth, finally got a letter from his niece in late April, in which she informed him that she "became ill a week or so after childbirth." Kot asked if it was "puerperal fever."[25] Not satisfied with his niece's vague explanations and sensing that Polly's ailment was much more serious than just childbirth fever, he wrote to her husband: "After a few happy letters from Polly, and in the last of which she wrote that she was returning home from hospital, there had been silence for nearly three weeks. Yesterday I received ... a very distressing letter, in which she speaks of her illness. But she does not say anything of the nature of her illness, and I am terribly anxious about her, about you, and about the baby."[26] The following day, he received two more letters from Polly, telling him that she had suffered "from a nervous breakdown as a result of childbirth," that she was in a clinic being looked after by three nurses, and that, according to her doctors, it "will be over quite soon." Mindful of his own history, Kot envisioned Polly's doctor asking her as to whether mental instability was common among her relatives, in response to which he wanted her to be unequivocal: "In case your doctor asks you, if there has been insanity in the family, you can tell him most definitely that there was no insanity at all." He also urged her – like so many of his friends had done, unsuccessfully, with him throughout the years – to "be brave," to "not give in," and to remember that she was "needed" – in her case by her children and husband.[27]

By early May, it seemed as if Polly was "well again" and that "a ghastly time" was behind her and her loved ones. Kot even suspected, given his mistrust of doctors, that they had invented Polly's illness in the first place "so as to frighten" her and then "take the credit for the patient getting well."[28] This lull in anxiety was followed again by two weeks of complete silence from Canada, forcing Kot to write to Polly's husband that he was now sure that Polly was not better but "very ill indeed." As he had done on so many occasions with his niece, Kot was now pleading with her husband not to hide anything from him: "However bad her state is, I want to know; for to live in constant anxiety day and night is worse than any bad news."[29] A somewhat reassuring letter from Manuel came the following day but Kot, who knew firsthand what mental anguish was all about, did not feel much comfort. He did not like the fact that Polly was still in a clinic and suggested that Manuel should bring her home so that she could be "with the children, and in her accustomed position," as well as away from the doctors who "with very rare exceptions … are no good … and can do a lot of harm."[30]

On 23 May, Kot received a cable from Manuel telling him that Polly was finally home. "So very many years ago," Kot wrote to his niece the same day, "when I used to leave home, father used to say: 'Well, my son, be a man!' I now say the same to you: 'be a man,'[31] that is, look after yourself, after your family, take care of all those you are fond [sic], and drive out of your head all stupid and silly ideas."[32] A week later, believing, apparently, that Polly was now strong enough to hear what his honest diagnosis of her ailment was, Kot delivered it in the same unmincing manner to which his friends were so well accustomed. Guided by the information he had received from Manuel about Polly's financial concerns, he now attributed it all to his niece's excessive preoccupation with money: "I have formed an opinion … It seems to me that you are obsessed by money; and that that is your chief trouble … Money can become a most terrible obsession, almost a madness. And you ought to know it, and also to remember that you have no concern with money. The only concern and care should be about your husband and children. All the rest is Manuel's affair. You understand that I write you all this out of ardent desire to get you out of your present condition. Don't rely on doctors; rely only on yourself, on your sense of duty and obligation to your family."[33]

But Polly was not strong enough. Her return home did not produce positive results. Two months after Polly left the clinic Kot was now reversing his judgment of what was better for her and urging Manuel to seriously consider sending her back. He also belatedly discovered that his letters might not have been sufficiently therapeutic: "I just received Polly's letter … Today's letter distresses me so much that I must ask you to tell me exactly what Polly's state is, and what do the doctors advise … It would seem that, perhaps, if Polly were to undergo a proper treatment, away from home, in a hospital, or in a nursing home, she might recover in a few weeks. I know that you are doing everything possible for her.

But it seems that her return home did not help her to get out of her state. From her letters, it would seem that it has become aggravated. I need not tell you how deeply I feel for Polly, for you and the children, and what a terrible time these last few months have been for all of us … It's no good my writing to Polly. I kept on all the time telling her that she must take herself in hand, and thus to recover. But my letters seem to have no effect on her, and if anything, I think she has become worse the last fortnight."[34]

It is not clear whether by "a proper treatment" Kot meant electroshock, in which he now was a firm believer. Polly, in all likelihood, did not undergo that kind of treatment; her uncle's having forgotten that she had been in London in 1947 probably had set her against electroshock treatment for the rest of her life.

Polly did bounce back eventually, and by 1952 there were, again, many more conversations about Kot's deteriorating health than about hers. Now and then Polly suggested that she could telephone him from Canada, but he was vehemently against it: "Please, I beg you, *do not* do such things. It frightens me. I cannot hear very well; and also the idea of you telephoning me is terrible to me."[35] "The Great Smog of London" on 5 December 1952, when smoke-filled fog covered the frozen London streets for four days, may have contributed to a particulary irritated letter on 6 December: "And now listen very carefully: I am ill, and have been so for two months now, and I just cannot bear anything which agitates or troubles me … Please, I beg you, don't ever irritate me … Remember that I am old and ill."[36] Five days later he asked for her forgiveness: "if I sometimes write in irritation: it is old age that is to blame, and my mood at the moment. But I never want to be unkind."[37]

He was indeed getting older and sicker. "He was possessed by the fear of illness the last five years," Juliette Huxley remembered. "He was terrified – not so much of dying, of being helpless, being touched."[38] A new bout of depression occurred toward the end of 1952. It was, as always, accompanied by insomnia, but after his doctor prescribed him sleeping pills and insisted that Kot should take them every night, he began to feel even worse. By now he blamed not his doctors but himself for not being able to recover quickly: "If I were not such a difficult person, my cure would not last long [sic]. But I am what I am …"[39]

By early January 1953, Kot was ready to go back to Holloway Sanatorium for another treatment of his depression. "The last few weeks were a misery and a constant torment," he wrote to Esther and Myer Salaman, justifying his decision. "There is just no other way possible in my circumstances."[40] It fell to Marjorie Wells to explain Kot's hospital routine to Polly – "He will probably have a little shock treatment and perhaps a little narcosis" – and to assure her that "[h]is case is not nearly so serious as it was last time." She also let Polly know that, due to the new National Health Scheme, the "cost of staying in hospital is considerably reduced since 1947," and therefore Polly should not worry about Kot not having enough money to cover it.[41]

Kot stayed at Holloway for almost two months. Marjorie, her friendship with Polly now restored, kept updating her about his progress, electroshock sessions, and the state of his memory. She also reported that he had received a letter from Rokhl, who pleaded with him to "please do what the doctors say." As to Kot's constant irritability, by now even the saintly Marjorie was mildly complaining about it: "All his friends … try to help him in little ways and at the same time not to annoy him – you know how easily he is annoyed! It really is most difficult to help him; I expect you understand him sufficiently to know his queer ways!"[42] Once Kot was out of the hospital he assured Polly that he was on the mend and "bound to get well again." He apologized for being cranky and saying "harsh or unpleasant things," asking her to always remember that his intentions were of the best kind. And, a fierce enemy of falsehoods, he nevertheless implored her again to lie to Rokhl about the state of his health: "With her constant anxiety and worry, it is better to tell her that I am perfectly well, and she need not trouble."[43]

Apologies notwithstanding, Kot's irritability returned with vengeance in May, at which point he accused Polly of writing to him about "trivial things" – like "your bar-mitzvahs, your dinner parties … Jackie's travels … [that] have no meaning to me." He warned her that in response to such empty letters he could decide "not to write at all" and added even more viciously that he was sure Polly "will be quite happy without hearing from" him. The rest of Polly's family was not spared Kot's ire either. He sternly reprimanded Jackie for her flimsy reason for writing to him, which she had explained as "I am sitting near mother and see her writing to you so decided to join her." "Do you expect me to be flattered?" he queried her sarcastically. "Hardly so when you think of it. But should at any time a terrific impulse drive you to write to me, I shall expect to hear about your studies, and your interests."[44] When Polly informed him that Jackie had gone to New York to do some shopping, Kot grew even angrier: "A minute's consideration, and you will see how preposterous it is for a student to fly to New York to shop."[45]

He also did not approve of Manuel's desire to sell his successful store: "[I]t is a mistake to retire: one should go on working until one has the physical strength to do so. That's all I have to say in the matter. And I am sure Manuel knows that my opinion is the right one."[46] (Manuel knew nothing of the kind, and he did retire despite Kot's dire admonitions.) As 1953 was drawing to a close, Kot again reminded his niece that he did not want her to call him on the phone or pay him a visit: "I must warn you that you will have few chances of seeing me, as any talk in company lasting even a quarter of an hour is a very great strain on me. You know that I never go out anywhere, and haven't been to a cinema, theatre, or restaurant for nearly twenty years."[47] Marjorie continued to stoically bear the brunt of Kot's cantankerousness. "I can honestly say he is well again," she updated Polly in June, "although of course it is terribly easy to irritate him, and one has to be careful what one says or does. However this is his natural state!"[48] He was apparently indeed well enough – and peeved enough – to also pick up his final argument with Frieda over whether he had the right to publish the letters Lawrence had written him.

Kot's insistence that Frieda had given him the right to publish Lawrence's letters rested on two typed letters dated 1 July 1932 and 15 November 1932. The first one was informal, which began with "Yes, of course I give you permission to publish L's letters!" and then went on to discuss Kot's "sinister influence" in her life, and the "mortal" way in which she thought Kot loved Lawrence. The second letter was much more official. It was addressed "Dear Koteliansky" and stated that Frieda was giving him "permission to publish a limited edition of D.H. Lawrence's letters, written by him to you, all through the years of your friendship – from the autumn of 1914 to his death … If you bring out a limited edition of D.H. Lawrence's letters to you, any profit therefrom shall belong to you only."[49] Neither one was signed by hand.

In 1953, when he was approached by Stephen Spender, Kot finally agreed to have at least six letters published individually, in an issue of the *Encounter* that Spender was editing. Kot apparently told Spender that the right to publish the letters was his and his alone, but Spender decided to run it by Frieda anyway and to assure her that there was nothing personal in them. He also offered to send her the typescript so that she could see for herself that they were not offensive to her.[50] Frieda subsequently wrote to her agent, Laurence Pollinger, that she was inclined to allow Spender to publish the letters and for "miserable Kot" to have her share because "somebody told me he was sick and half blind."[51]

Pollinger proceeded to remind Kot that the copyright was Frieda's and that it was her generosity that would allow Kot to pocket the money. Frieda waited in vain for Kot to express his gratitude. "Aldous [Huxley] wrote Kot did not know where S.S. Koteliansky left off and God began!" she complained to Pollinger. "[I]t's small things that stay in one's mind. When Lawrence had spent a night at Koteliansky's, he had a heavy trunk, and Koteliansky let him carry it to the bus. That hefty Kot!" And yet, she assured her agent, she did feel sorry for Kot, and was ready to be magnanimous because he was "a poor devil now."[52] Frieda did not sound quite as magnanimous, though, in her letter to Murry: "Kot wants 75 per cent for himself – he has no right to anything, he might at least *ask*! He must be unbelievably sour!"[53]

Kot did not think he had to ask, and he also did not appreciate being scolded by Pollinger. He decided, instead, to press the issue anew. He therefore approached Cohen again, offering him Lawrence's letters for publication by the Cresset Press and showing him Frieda's letters as a proof that the rights were his. Cohen then wrote to Pollinger, to whom the existence of Frieda's letters came as an unpleasant surprise. In his effort to protect the turf, Pollinger pointed out to Cohen that Frieda's written promises had been superseded by her having granted William Heinemann and Viking Press "the publication rights in all of her late husband's letters of which she owns the copyright." He very much hoped, Pollinger reported to Frieda, that his letter to Cohen would succeed in stopping both Koteliansky – for whom, he reminded Frieda, he "never had much love" – and the owner of the Cresset Press in their tracks.[54]

Frieda was still worried, though, and also ready to disown the November 1932 letter, suggesting that it did not sound like a letter written by her: "I always called him 'Kot,' not Koteliansky ... And the phrase: 'Should you, however bring out an ordinary edition, you have to share with me any profit therefrom in equal parts,' that is not like me. I don't write that way." She also confessed to Pollinger that she was concerned about the nature of Lawrence's letters to Kot, since she believed Kot always encouraged Lawrence to criticize her: "I also do not like Kot. I wish he had not been a friend of L's. He could be so mean. I fear there are unkind things in those letters ... That pretentious Kot behaves as if those letters to him were the only ones L ever wrote."[55]

Unlike Kot, Cohen was a practical enough man to realize that without Frieda's signature and with her denying that the letter was written by her, they stood no chance of prevailing in any court were they to pursue it further. "Don't worry," Pollinger assured Frieda in late August 1954. "I think I have fully stopped him and that no publication here will be out ... I felt when I saw that copy of the letter ... that it was not written by you ... I think you can safely take it that Kot's letters will never be published."[56] "Never" was too strong a word, of course. Lawrence's letters to Kot would be, in fact, brought out in 1970 by Lawrence scholar George Zytaruk, and done so with the full consent of the very same Mr Pollinger.[57] But for Kot and Frieda it was, indeed, "never," since both of them would be dead within the the next two years. Kot's last Lawrence "scheme," therefore, went nowhere while earning him a reputation in certain circles of being not just a tiresome man but a forger to boot.

His reputation was also not enhanced by the publication in 1954 of Harry T. Moore's biography of Lawrence, *The Intelligent Heart: The Story of D.H. Lawrence*. According to Marjorie Wells, while Moore was writing his book, Kot "did not take a great liking to him, although he helped him with information at the time."[58] Moore, whose most trusted source for the biography was Frieda, obviously did not take a great liking to Kot either, despite earlier describing him to Ada Clarke as having "the brains of them all." In the book he labelled him "the pompous Koteliansky" and described his appearance as "swarthy." As was mentioned earlier, Moore also made it official that "the Jewish lawyer Ben Cooley [in *Kangaroo*], was a projection of Koteliansky."[59]

By August 1954 Kot, however, hardly cared what people other than his close friends thought of him – he was struggling to stay alive. If there had been any benefits from the previous year's electroshock treatment, they were no longer in evidence, and he was again subject to severe depression. In addition, his heart was very weak (many years of chain-smoking strong "Russian" cigarettes probably did not help), and he also had a much enlarged prostate. One worry was no longer there – a new doctor whom Kot consulted found he no longer had an ulcer and suspected it had never existed.

"I am extremely sorry to tell you," he wrote to his niece on 31 January 1954, "that I have not been well for several weeks. The usual case of a physical poor state, and of depression which the doctor thinks is the main cause of my poor state … Because of the state of my heart, the doctor is against my going to a sanatorium to have shock treatments."[60] A week later he was sending her some hints about his will, urging her "to behave sensibly and correctly" upon his death: "I have made certain dispositions with regard to my money, papers and belongings, and I beg you to accept my wishes, however strange they may seem to you, without causing any unpleasantness to any of my friends, and thus to avoid damaging my reputation … Marjorie Wells has seen me through all my illnesses since 1936, and without her help and support I would have been dead long ago. I wish you, therefore, to express to her your gratitude for all she has done for me, just as all my other friends are grateful to her. When the time comes, my lawyer will let you know the terms of my will, and I hope that you will accept them in the right spirit; and I sincerely believe you will do so."[61]

He did have "papers," including, of course, Lawrence's letters to him, and he did have some valuable belongings, which had come to him from the famous people he had known in his life. As to money, he was penniless, largely being sustained, especially during his last five years, by Polly's parcels and money orders, so the mention of that category undoubtedly struck his niece as odd. Nevertheless, she wrote him in response a letter that even hard-to-please Kot acknowledged as being "loving and understanding." "I am so glad to see," he wrote approvingly, "that at last you do understand me and my positions."[62]

By late February, Dr Rau relented and allowed Kot to have shock treatments. His rationale was most likely that Kot was not doing well no matter what, so even a slim chance of the shock treatments helping him was worth pursuing. Before he was admitted as an outpatient into London Hospital, Kot wrote to Polly that he might need money because "going to specialists … costs a lot."[63] Needless to say, Polly immediately sent a cheque. Through March and April, Marjorie assured her that he was in good hands, liked by all nurses and doctors, and getting the best possible treatment. She also told Polly that the atmosphere at the London Hospital was "much more pleasant than the specialized hospital he was in last year and in 1947."[64]

But Kot's doctor at the London Hospital was hesitant to perform another round of shock treatments on such a sick and feeble patient. In late March he sent Kot home, suggesting that "the depression will lift of itself … as the spring approaches."[65] It did not. "He is very much the same," Marjorie wrote to Polly on 1 April, Kot's official but fake birthday, "struggling very hard – it is very pathetic."[66] "I am terribly sorry to tell you that I am not getting better," Kot himself wrote ten days later. "Even the sun shining today and the warmer weather does not help."[67] Seeing that even after the spring set in the patient was making no progress, Kot's doctors agreed to try electroshock again.

By mid-May, Marjorie sounded decidedly more optimistic: "Well, I am delighted to say that your uncle is really very much better. He has had five treatments, and seems to have forgotten all his worries for the time being."[68] Kot, too, felt that he might have enough of a future to invest in some home improvements, namely the basement, where the kitchen was, and the staircase on the ground floor, which all badly needed fixing. Toward the end of July, however, he was complaining to Polly that the work in the house was taking too long, and that had he known such would be the case he would have not undertaken it despite "the most terribly shabby state" of the house: "The workmen have been in the house about three weeks, work that 20 years ago would have taken no more than 4 days. I am not going to have any more work done now: it is too expensive. I will wait for better times."[69]

Better times would never come. In August he blamed the weather for feeling worse: "rain, rain every day. So instead of my health improving, there has been lately a deterioration."[70] Mindful of the effect the sleeping pills had on him, Kot stopped taking them as soon as he was released from the hospital, but now he was feeling exhausted and weak due to the lack of sleep. In early October he informed Polly that he believed that "there is no use having shock treatment" and that it would be best to "let things take their own course."[71] A month later he could no longer move "even to go out into the garden," and asked her to send him more money for his medical and rental needs: "I am terribly ashamed of taking money from you, without any prospect of return. But my only comfort is that when I, in the past, could help ... I did so with pleasure."[72] His letters after that point become briefer and briefer. "I do not want to go into details," he wrote on 16 December, "as a friend of mine says that it's shameful to moan and to complain."[73]

In early December something akin to providence spared Kot a visit from Murry. After Murry came back from London from an annual William Blake dinner, he found a letter from Lady Glenavy, with whom he frequently corresponded and who had just returned to Ireland after visiting England and the ailing Kot. "If your letter had been forwarded," Murry suggested to her, "I should have taken a chance and tried to see him." He added that he knew his visit would have not had "the life-giving effect."[74] But then Glenavy's presence was not helpful either: "My visits did nothing to dispel his gloom. It was as if all his queer hate and intolerance of other people had become centred on himself. He could not even forgive himself for being old and ill. His bitterness and resentment seemed to come from a sense of guilt and failure."[75]

Majorie Wells's update for Polly on 30 December was uncharacteristically bleak: "I am very sorry to tell you that your uncle is ill, though at the moment he is carrying on in his usual way, which he prefers. Dr Rau gave him a thorough physical examination yesterday, and says his heart is very bad and his prostate gland very much enlarged. Dr Rau says an operation is undesirable, because of the general state of his health."[76] What Wells sparingly omitted from the letter was that Rau had told her that Kot "could only live for three months and might die at any moment."[77] Kot wrote to Polly the following day, possibly the last letter he ever wrote to her, and while begging her not to be "unduly anxious," he once again shot down the notion that she should come to London to take care of him: "the mere idea of you coming here to visit me is almost frightening to me for its effect on me."[78]

Knowing that Kot was dying, Marjorie tried to talk to him "about the eternal and spiritual world" but got nowhere, as she confessed to Lady Glenavy after his death: "he used to laugh and say 'You are just like Beatrice. You want to believe.' ... [H]e said he wished he could believe, but had made up his mind years ago and couldn't change it back again."[79] He spent most of January at home, "carrying on, doing all or most of the things he used to do but more slowly."[80] On 18 January he was visited by Leonard Woolf, who had heard from Dilys Powell that Kot was gravely ill and would like to see him. The desire to see Woolf at this tragic moment of his life was reminiscent of Kot seeking him out in the midst of grim reports about the fate of German and European Jews under the Nazis.

"I went yesterday to see Kot," Woolf reported to Powell a day after his visit. "He was so much exactly what he has always been as long as I have known him that one almost forgot the years and how ill he really is. I have never understood how Kot lived – I mean monetarily – and have never had the courage to talk to him about it. And I hadn't yesterday. Do you think there is anything that he is in want of that one could give him?"[81] Marjorie Wells wrote to Leonard that after he left Kot told her that "for a quarter of an hour the past came alive but now, alas, it is fading very quickly."[82] He was no longer "his old self," Kot told Wells, "although while Woolf was there he thought he was."[83] According to Woolf, Kot even "insisted upon coming upstairs with me to the front door," making Woolf fear that "my visit to Kot had tired him."[84]

Two days after this visit, Kot was hospitalized again. "I am sorry to tell you," Marjorie Wells wrote to Lady Glenavy on 21 January, "that Kot is in Hampstead General Hospital, following an attack (heart or something) on Wednesday, and another 'falling down' on Thursday (yesterday) morning since when he has been hardly conscious, partly as a result of injections."[85] Kot never truly regained his full consciousness and was not able to speak but still apparently managed to open his eyes when spoken to. He died late in the afternoon on 22 January 1955. Marjorie's telegram to Polly read: "DEEPLY SORRY INFORM YOU YOUR UNCLE DIED PEACEFULLY THIS AFTERNOON WRITING. WELLS."[86] The letter that followed gave further details: "Your uncle died about half past five … the end came very suddenly. I do not think he suffered any pain towards the end … He loved you all very much … Your uncle wished to be cremated, and to have no funeral service: so we will respect his wishes."[87]

Kot was indeed cremated. It happened on 26 January, four days after he died and therefore – undoubtedly much to his niece's sorrow since she was more religious than her uncle – in violation of the Jewish custom that the burial should be performed as soon as possible, ideally no later than twenty-four hours following the death. But then Jews were not supposed to be cremated either. Marjorie Wells informed Rokhl that a couple of days after the cremation she "went to see the ashes scattered in the garden of the crematorium. There will be no memorial stone, as he did not want this."[88] Kot's design for his death ritual mimicked H.G. Wells's – except H.G. Wells's ashes had been scattered from an aircraft flying over the Channel between the Isle of Wight and St Alban's Head.[89] Unlike Wells, however, Kot was not much of a traveller, so his ashes did not travel either.

Kot's friends decided to disobey one of Kot's wishes and did hold a funeral service prior to the cremation, with his body still in a casket; it was at one of the smaller chapels at Golders Green Crematorium. According to Marjorie Wells, there were "between twenty and thirty people … at the funeral and many of them weeping."[90] Marjorie's daughter Catherine, who had always been Kot's favourite, was sobbing beside her mother.[91] Admiring as Kot had been in his letter to Polly of Marjorie's and Catherine's stoic behaviour during H.G. Wells's funeral, it is highly doubtful that he would have disapproved of such outward manifestation of grief and love for him, even if it did make them a bit less of "the true English breed."

Among those present were two women Kot would have most likely not invited to his funeral: Marjorie Gertler and Cynthia Stephens.[92] Kot's long-time friend, Dr Fulton, gave an "address" (he and Marjorie Wells were careful not to call it a "eulogy," in order, perhaps, to make it sound as secular as possible). He spoke of Kot's magnetism, which attracted to him both eminent personalities and "relatively obscure folk like myself." He grounded Kot firmly in "the stark veracity of the Old Testament" and considered himself privileged to have been "admitted to his friendship," always feeling "not only wiser, but happier, cleaner, stronger and braver" after seeing Kot. He also suggested that while all his friends were "familiar with his fierce denunciation of those things which he hated with a deep and fervent hatred," it was all offset by "the glowing warmth of his affection for the things and people he loved." At the end of his address Dr Fulton lamented that it was still hard to believe "that never more can we go to Acacia Road and be welcomed by him in those simple rooms, rooms which he ever kept as clean and spotless as his own brave and faithful heart."[93]

As Kot lay dying with no fight left in him, Frieda was still in a feisty mode. "No, no sympathy for Kot," she declared to Murry earlier in January, and to Harry T. Moore she wrote around the same time: "That horrid Kot, I never liked him. Beatrice Campbell told Murry she had seen him and he was very old and miserable."[94] News from England travelled slowly to New Mexico and she kept raging against him until late April when Murry set the record straight: "Evidently you haven't seen the news of Koteliansky's death. It happened on January 22. He had been very ill with a weak heart for a long while … I can't help thinking of him affectionately: in those early days at the Russian Law Bureau with Slatkowsky – who dyed his beard – he was very sweet."[95]

The two dichotomic views of Kot as either a pillar of moral strength or a bitter and intolerant man were neatly summarized by Murry in a letter to Lady Glenavy, who definitely belonged to the first camp: "I suppose you romanticized him. So did Katherine. I rather feel that, for some reason, women were inclined to do this. But then I think of Bill Dunning's remark about him: 'You call Kot a great rock, I call him a bloody mule,' which always stuck in my mind. I always thought of him as terribly unhappy – on the simple principle that to *go on* hating people must make one terribly unhappy. It certainly would me."[96]

Kot's death certificate listed his occupation as "an Author (Retired)."[97] The first obituary that appeared in the *Times* on 24 January contained nine short lines and almost as many mistakes. It gave his first name as "Sergei," stated his age at the time of death as seventy-two, and declared that "He was born in Kiev and came to England as a boy."[98] Three days later a much fuller and more accurate obituary by Dilys Powell was printed in the same paper. It noted that he was "more English than the English" and yet retained "his proud Jewish sense of obligation."[99] The obituary Leonard Woolf wrote, which he called simply "Kot," appeared a week later in *The New Statesman and Nation*. It was by far the longest, unusual in its size for someone as relatively obscure as Kot. It zeroed in on his "spiritual grit" and "pure, undiluted, austere, fanatical passion." Kot was "not a comfortable man," Woolf declared, "but neither was Elijah nor Isaiah."[100]

And then there was Kot's will. It began with his niece, who was to receive "my silver cigarette case[,] the mirror in my bedroom given to me by her mother and such books as she may care to select." Kot's solicitor, Alan Edward Oliver, sounded rather apologetic when he assured Polly on 26 January of "how kindly your Uncle spoke of you and of the practical kindnesses that you had shown to him for many years. The small gifts that he made you … he said could only be a mere *token* of his affection."[101] The same week, Polly received a letter from Lady Glenavy, whom she had met in 1947 after Kot's attempted suicide. "I just want to send you all my sympathy in your loss," Glenavy wrote. "We will all miss him so much, he had a great talent for friendship – he was a unique and wonderful person." Written by hand, the letter revealed that the phrase "so much" was at first "as much," until Glenavy changed it. The corrected slip speaks volumes about Glenavy's sense of her place in Kot's heart – which, given her dislike of Polly, she must have considered equal, if not superior, to his niece's.[102]

Kot bequeathed his main treasure, Lawrence's and Mansfield's letters – "and any other of my letters that they are willing to accept (including letters from H.G. Wells[,] James Stephens[,] T.S. Eliot and others" – to the British Museum. The will noted that the bequest to the British Museum was "made as an acknowledgment of my affection for England and of the frienship that I have enjoyed with many of her writers and citizens for nearly half a century."[103] Before the two executors of the will, Marjorie Wells and Mr Oliver (who was a partner at Bircham & Co), could officially finalize the transfer of the letters, there came a last-minute plea for postponement from Dennis Cohen of the Cresset Press. He informed them, somewhat disingenuously, given the experience of the previous year, that there was "an understanding that we would have the first opportunity of publishing collections of letters that he possessed. As recently as June of last year we were in active negotiation for the publication of Lawrence's letters to him, and there is little doubt that we would have done so had we not encountered copyright difficulties ... I was wondering whether before they are lodged with the British Museum they could be examined, and whether we could see if there is any possibility of a suitable book being made out of them."[104]

The executors were quick to shoot Cohen's request down. Oliver, without knowing many details, responded to Cohen that "it might be hard to read a binding contract into your amicable general understanding with Kot."[105] Marjorie Wells's reaction was so clear-sighted and unambiguous that it makes one wonder why she had not succeeded earlier in persuading Kot not to engage in quixotic fights with Frieda: "Mr Cohen may ... wish to publish Lawrence and Katherine Mansfield letters. The copyright in these, however, belongs to Frieda Lawrence and Middleton Murry respectively: and they no doubt have obligations to publishers other than Mr Cohen."[106]

Cohen was not the only person with practical interest in the letters. After her obituary of Kot appeared in the *Times*, Dilys Powell received a letter from Percy Muir, Kot's former housemate who was by now the director of Elkin Mathews Ltd, a bookselling firm. Not knowing – yet – the nature of Kot's bequest, Muir wanted a shot at selling Katherine Mansfield's letters for the estate and also revealed that at some point Kot had employed him to shop them around: "There is probably at least one thing of value in his estate, namely the letters from Katherine Mansfield. If I mention these it is less from a commercial angle than to ensure that they are not sold too cheaply. I got him an excellent offer for these from the States some years ago, but he could not bring himself to part with them."[107]

Before he died, Kot also gave Marjorie instructions "to return letters written by living correspondents to their writers" but with two exceptions: he wanted the British Museum to accept Frieda Lawrence's and Dorothy Brett's letters, even though they were still alive, because of the light their letters could shed for scholars and biographers on Lawrence's life.[108] When Lady Glenavy received from Marjorie boxes full of her letters (there were many boxes, for she wrote to him at least once a week for many years), she "soaked them in turpentine and took them out to the garden and burnt them."[109] May Sarton, on the other hand, kept her letters to Kot, and many of them were published after her death.

Polly Smith also apparently destroyed hers. A year after Kot's death, Polly's daughter Jackie had a son, Stephen, whose Hebrew name was "Shmuel," in honour of Kot. Polly often called him "Shmilik."[110] Kot's sister Rokhl died in 1960.

After Kot's death, she confessed to Marjorie Wells that she had been seriously ill herself for eleven years, but, like her brother, strove to spare her favourite sibling from such a painful knowledge.[111] Polly outlived Kot by more than forty years and died in 1997, having, according to her daughters, kept her pride in him until the very end, talking of her remarkable uncle often – but never divulging, at least to her children, the real nature of his illness in 1947, when she flew across the ocean for the very first time to be with him.[112] Marjorie Wells, whom Kot frequently – and rightfully – credited with saving his sanity and his life, died in 1962, at the age of sixty-one.

# POST MORTEM

What does God think of money? Look who He gives it to.
~ Hershel of Ostropol

I haven't much doubt you are right in seeing Kot "as defeated by
his own high aspirations." The trouble was that he always blamed
other people for defeating them – at least I cannot remember
an instance where he blamed himself.
~ Murry to Lady Glenavy, 5 July 1955

Money and fame eluded Koteliansky during his lifetime – and, in all fairness, he never tried very hard to obtain either – but England's awareness of him did receive a modest posthumous bump, starting with the publication of Lady Glenavy's *Today We Will Only Gossip*. Before the book came out from Constable in 1964, several major publishers had turned it down because "no one would ever have heard of Kot, and there wasn't enough about Murry and Lawrence."[1] When the book came out, the reviewer in the *Times* particularly liked the account "of how that odd fish Koteliansky went berserk in Montague Shearman's room" when he and Gertler ate all the food prepared for the Ballets Russes stars and then vandalized the furniture for good measure. The reviewer concluded that the "way in which Koteliansky is painted – with sympathy and yet without smudging out faults – is one of the best things in this nicely done conversation piece."[2]

In 1970, George Zytaruk fulfilled Kot's fervent desire and published his letters from Lawrence in one volume, calling it *The Quest for Rananim: D.H. Lawrence's Letters to Koteliansky, 1914–1930*. Zytaruk's introduction to the book became the first, and most accurate, mini-biography of Koteliansky. That it was published not just in Canada, but in Montreal, where Polly Smith and her family lived, bore a certain symbolism. Eight years later, when Catherine Carswell's son, John, published his book, *Lives and Letters*, Koteliansky again made it into the subtitle, together with Orage, Mansfield, Beatrice Hastings, and Murry.

Koteliansky was also prominent in May Sarton's autobiographical writings. There is a chapter devoted to him in her 1976 book, *A World of Light: Portraits and Celebrations,* and he is equally present in her earlier memoir, *I Knew a Phoenix* (1959). When Juliette Huxley published her autobiography, *Leaves of the Tulip Tree*, in 1986, she included an entire section of Kot's letters to her and hers to him while she and Julian were in Paris in connection with his work for UNESCO. There were also tidbits on Koteliansky sprinkled throughout almost every volume of Leonard Woolf's *Autobiography* (1961–69).

"Odd fish" or not, Koteliansky had his champions among book reviewers as well. One of them was Sir William Haley, who, when he reviewed John Carswell's book in 1978 for the *Times*, described Kot as a very noble being – "loyal, disinterested, living on goodness knows what … constant." Haley had taken offense two years earlier when the second volume of Virginia Woolf's *Letters* came out and he discovered that her letters hardly mentioned Koteliansky: "Was it because Virginia Woolf found Koteliansky 'rather inarticulate' that he made so little impression on her? They collaborated in translating Dostoievsky and Goldenveizer, yet he is subjected to no comment. Maybe his integrity also commanded respect. He flits tantalizingly in the various records of those years without ever being seen fully in the round."[3]

But the fiercest defender of Koteliansky on the pages of the *Times* was Oliver Edwards, whose columns in the 1950s and 1960s were called Talking of Books.[4] He routinely ranked Koteliansky in the top echelon of translators from Russian, right below Garnett and the Maudes. In his 1964 column on Mansfield, Edwards called Kot "one of the clearest eyed people in her circle" and revealed that Kot once wrote to him that Mansfield was "the most worth-while person" in that group.[5] Edwards also turned an entire 1965 column into a veritable hymn to Koteliansky:

> That strange outlier of the D.H. Lawrence-Middleton Murry-Katherine Mansfield circle has never had his due paid to him. He had many friends outside that circle also, notably H.G. Wells and the Woolfs. But as the Lawrence circle was, and has stayed, most prominently in the news, and it has been the most written about, it is there that Koteliansky's name is most likely to be encountered. He was about the best and most disinterested friend Katherine Mansfield had … He always kept an ironic detachment from the circle. I remember a letter he wrote to me at the time Middleton Murry's autobiography, *Between Two Worlds*, was published.

It was devastating. Koteliansky came to London from Kiev about 1911 on a three months university grant. He stayed here for the remaining forty-four years of his life. Though he loved England and became thoroughly English, he never forgot his Russian roots. He interested his circle of English friends, almost all writers, in Russian literature. He induced Murry and Lawrence to collaborate with him in translations. He also worked on his own. He gave English readers tales by Dostoevsky and Chekhov, Gorky, and Rozanov, also Kuprin. Those years from 1915 onwards saw the real spread of Russian literature in England. Constance Garnett had been a forerunner; alongside her Herculean labours on the great Russian writers, Koteliansky's output was slight. But ... Koteliansky did as much by his influence as by his work.[6]

One can almost believe that a dybbuk of the restless Kot entered Edwards's body at the moment he was writing the column in order to right the wrong and set the record straight once and for all. Except, just nine years earlier, having learned of Frieda Lawrence's death, the same Edwards said nice things about Frieda, too, calling her "a noble, healthy, fertilizing influence" on Lawrence and "an essential part of his innermost life and therefore of his best work,"[7] so Kot's uncompromising dybbuk is probably wandering still. I do not think my book will put him to rest either.

Ostropol, where it all began, is called Starii Ostropil' now (Ukrainian for "Old Ostropol"). These days it is a small and very poor Ukrainian village, with just one Jew living there. The beautiful multi-tiered wooden synagogue was burned down soon after the revolution; on the site there is now a shabby wooden structure, which in Soviet times used to be a grocery store. The two Jewish cemeteries, "old" and "new," where Kot's, Rokhl's and Polly's ancestors and immediate family had been buried, were vandalized soon after the revolution as well, with most of the gravestones taken for personal construction needs. Anatoly Polonsky, the only remaining Jew in Ostropol when I visited in 2006,[8] collected the remaining gravestones and stored them in his backyard, creating a personal memorial for all the Ostropol Jews who died peacefully or violently throughout the ages.

In 1991, after the fall of the Soviet Union, a monument was erected at the spot of the 1942 Starokonstantinov massacres. It was created largely with money donated by the survivors, their children and grandchildren living abroad. The Ukrainian government at the time only allowed an inscription that mentioned "the remains of 5,200 citizens of Jewish nationality." Images of the Star of David and a Menora were added later. Another memorial – a granite slab engraved with

"In Memory of the Jewish Communities of Starokonstantinov and Ostropol" – was erected in Brooklyn. Every year in December elderly ex-Soviet Jews and their families with links to the two neighbouring Ukrainian communities gather there to commemorate yet another painful "yahrzeit."

Given the turbulance of the century Koteliansky inhabited, it could be considered a miracle that, as a Jew from Ukraine, he died a non-violent death. And yet he was still a victim. The darkness he had brought to England with him never lifted, and it was this darkness, more than anything, that may have defeated him in the end. It smothered not just his ambitions but also, at times, his will to live. But it did not smother his desire to be a true and truthful friend to those he liked and whose talents he appreciated. He survived for as long as he did precisely because there were people in his circle to whom he was fiercely loyal and loving; they paid back in kind and in kindness, sustaining him through his emotional turmoil and nervous breakdowns, and taking care of him when he became feeble.

Were Koteliansky to have a tombstone, it would be best graced by two statements from people whom he cherished and respected and who, while often exasperated with his dogmatic and inflexible ways, cherished and respected him in return: Leonard Woolf's "Kot was not a comfortable man," and Katherine Mansfield's "You are really one of my people." Such an epitaph may still not be enough to make peace with Kot's dybbuk, but it does capture the essence of the man who, despite being neither rich nor famous, was a very significant presence in the English cultural scene for half of the century and who, as a Jew, embodied much of the angst of his age.

# APPENDIX A

# S.S. KOTELIANSKY, 1880–1955
# A CHRONOLOGY

1880 Born 28 February in Ostropol, Ukraine, Russian Empire. One of five children of Avrum-Shloima and Beila Koteliansky.

1894–99 Studies in Zhitomir and Odessa.

1900 Sent back to Ostropol and put under house arrest for subversive political activities. Writes to Maxim Gorky and receives from him books for a local library.

1904 Allowed to enroll in the Kiev Commercial Institute, where he studies statistics, bookkeeping, law, as well as English, French, German, and Italian.

1910 Graduates from the Kiev Commercial Institute.

1911 Leaves Russia after the mutilated body of a twelve-year-old Christian boy is found in Kiev and Jews are blamed. Arrives in London in early July. The same month attends the First Universal Races Congress in London as an accredited journalist from Kiev. The Imperial Russian Ballet (the Ballets Russes) comes to England on tour and takes London by storm.

1912 Starts working at the Russian Law Bureau, or "Ruslabu," which is located on High Holborn, near Southampton Row.

1914 In July, meets D.H. Lawrence through an English colleague at Ruslabu. Joins him and two others in a walking tour in the Lake District. Lawrence introduces him to Katherine Mansfield, John Middleton Murry, Mark Gertler, and Beatrice and Gordon Campbell. Lawrence, Mansfield, and Gertler form a very close friendship with Koteliansky, who develops a definite antipathy toward Lawrence's wife, Frieda. World War I makes it impossible for him to visit his family in Ostropol.

1915 Moves to 5 Acacia Road, the house previously occupied by Katherine Mansfield and J.M. Murry. He will live there for the rest of his life. Publishes his first book of translations – Anton Chekhov, *The Bet and Other Stories* – in collaboration with Murry.

1916 Continues to collaborate with Murry and publishes three more books of translations: Fyodor Dostoevsky, *Pages from the Journal of an Author*; Alexander Kuprin, *The River of Life and Other Stories*; and Leo Shestov, *Anton Tchekhov and Other Essays*. Quits his job at Ruslabu.

1917 Welcomes the February Revolution in Russia and helps drum up support for Maxim Gorky's resurrected periodical *Novaia zhizn'* (New Life). Contacts, among others, H.G. Wells, who is very sympathetic to Gorky and his cause. Koteliansky's application for a passport in order to visit his family in Ostropol is turned down. In early June, severs his relationship with Murry. In July, meets Virginia and Leonard Woolf. In August, is exempted from military service by the Russian Consulate General in London. The October Revolution in Russia horrifies him.

1918 His relationship with Mansfield is strained because of Murry. Suffers from severe depressions.

1919 Starts his collaboration with the Woolfs and their Hogarth Press, which will last till 1923 and will be the most productive period of Koteliansky's translating career.

1920 Back in Ostropol, his father and one of his two sisters succumb to typhoid fever. Hogarth Press publishes Maxim Gorky's *Reminiscences of Leo Nicolayevitch Tolstoi* in a translation by Koteliansky and Leonard Woolf. The book becomes an immediate sensation and bestseller. Koteliansky's brother, Moishel, and his family leave Ostropol for Canada and settle in Sherbrooke, not far from Montreal.

1921 Starts tutoring H.G. Wells's son Gip in Russian. Rekindles his close friendship with Mansfield. His brother-in-law is killed by Bolsheviks in Ostropol. Hogarth Press publishes two more books translated by Koteliansky and Leonard Woolf: *Reminiscences of Anton Chekhov*, by Maxim Gorky, Alexander Kuprin, and Ivan Bunin, and *Anton Chekhov's Note-books Together with Reminiscences of Tchekhov*, by Maxim Gorky.

1922 Controversy over his "authorized" translations of two authors now living in Paris. *Gentleman from San Francisco and Other Stories* comes out, with the title story by Ivan Bunin having been translated by Koteliansky and D.H. Lawrence. Koteliansky reconciles with Murry.

1923 Mansfield, in Paris, succumbs to tuberculosis in early January. Koteliansky does not attend her funeral because he cannot secure a passport to travel abroad. He and Hogarth Press part company. He talks Murry into starting a new magazine to serve as a mouthpiece for D.H. Lawrence. The first issue of *The Adelphi* comes out in June with his translations in it. Lawrence comes to London but is not interested in editing *The Adelphi*. Infamous dinner with the Lawrences at Café Royal.

1924 Argues with Murry and Philip Tomlinson at *The Adelphi*. Breaks up with Murry and leaves *The Adelphi*. Tries to secure passage of his orphaned nephew and niece from Ostropol to Canada. Is duped into paying for their papers twice.

1925 His nephew and niece, Eli and Polly, visit him in London on their way to Canada. Several weeks later Eli dies in an accident at Moishel Koteliansky's house in Sherbrooke.

1926–27 His application for naturalization is rejected. Publishes translations in *The London Mercury* and *Calendar*. During a severe bout of depression decides to shake up his life and pursue more seriously a career in publishing. Conceives the idea of "Intimate Series" to start his publishing business. Tries to solicit material from writers he knows but is unsuccessful. Advised by Lawrence to give it up. Translates Vasily Rozanov's *Solitaria*, which Lawrence reviews in *Calendar of Modern Letters*.

1928–29 Vacations in Cornwall. Is very concerned about Lawrence's worsening tuberculosis. Helps Lawrence sell copies of *Lady Chatterley's Lover* published in Italy. His mother dies in Kiev.

1930 In January, Lawrence writes an introduction for his translation of Dostoevsky's "Grand Inquisitor." Koteliansky obtains British citizenship. Develops a very close friendship with James Stephens. Lawrence dies in early March. Koteliansky begs Aldous Huxley to prevent Frieda Lawrence from being in charge of Lawrence's literary estate.

1931  Applies for a position as a Russian Lecturer at Cambridge University but is turned down. Re-establishes a connection with his only remaining sister Rokhl in Kiev. Becomes friends with Ottoline Morrell. Meets Dilys Powell at Morrell's gatherings.

1932  Meets Esther Polianowsky Salaman, a former student of Einstein and an early Zionist. Her book *Two Silver Roubles*, which comes out that year and is based on her childhood in Zhitomir, reminds him of his own early years. Trial over Lawrence's will in which Frieda Lawrence prevails. Seeks Frieda Lawrence's permission to publish all Lawrence's letters to him.

1933  Through the help of Esther and her husband Myer Salaman, starts working as a reader for the Cresset Press. Is intrumental in securing H.G. Wells's *Autobiography*. Recruits Dilys Powell and Dorothy Richardson.

1934–35  Koteliansky's relationship with his employer deteriorates. He is seen as not a company man and as not effective in attracting profitable prospects. The Salamans intervene and prevent his outright firing but he is no longer a full-time employee of the Press.

1936  In June, suffers a severe nervous and physical breakdown. Has almost all his teeth extracted on the advice of his doctor. Gertler attempts suicide. Stays in a nursing home for two weeks. Relies on Ottoline for strength and moral support. Is finally diagnosed with "coronary thrombosis." Refuses to have heart surgery and is cared for at home by Marjorie Wells, Juliette Huxley, and Dilys Powell.

1937  Beila Koteliansky's "Two Jewish Stories" are published. Meets May Sarton. Translates Chekhov plays. In November, takes his friends to see *The Dybbuk* when Habima Theatre comes to London.

1938  Grows increasingly despondent about the fate of Jews in Germany and the possibility of World War II. Approaches Sidney Bernstein, the managing director of Gaumont-British, about producing a documentary about Jewish response to Hitler. Bernstein tells him the censors would not allow anything negative about Hitler's regime. Ottoline Morrell dies in April.

1939  In June, Mark Gertler kills himself. May Sarton's inadequate reaction to Koteliansky's grief almost extinguishes their friendship.

1940–41 Stays in London when the air raids begin, while many of his friends, including James Stephens, go to the country. Several times his windows are shattered. Marjorie Wells visits him every day. His niece sends him parcels and money orders from Canada. Koteliansky is anxious about the fate of his sister and her family in occupied Kiev. Does not know yet that in September nearly 35,000 Jews were killed in Babi Yar by the Nazis. Penguin issues his translations of Chekhov's plays and Russian short stories.

1942  The massacres of Jews in Starokonstantinov claim more than 10,000 lives. Among those murdered are Jews from Ostropol. His brother Moishel unexpectedly dies in Canada.

1943  Hears from his sister that she and her family left Kiev before the Babi Yar massacre and are now safely in the Urals.

1944  Follows the *Times* of London's daily updates from the Eastern Front. Ostropol is liberated.

1946  Attends the H.G. Wells's funeral. Wells wills him a statue of Tolstoy that Wells received as a gift from Gorky. Reads about concentration camps and German atrocities in the British press.

1947  In June, attempts to kill himself by cutting his throat with a razor blade. Marjorie Wells moves into the house and takes care of him around the clock. His niece flies in from Canada. Goes to a psychiatric hospital and undergoes electroshock treatment. Loses most of his short-term memory. Does not remember that Polly came from Canada to be with him.

1948  Breaks up with May Sarton over her behaviour toward Juliette Huxley, with whom he now frequently corresponds.

1951  After the birth of her fourth child, Polly experiences a serious nervous breakdown of her own. Koteliansky, concerned, bombards her and her husband with letters and cables. Mansfield's letters to Murry are published, where Koteliansky is hardly mentioned.

1952  Is interviewed by Stephen Spender about the Café Royal dinner in 1923. Battles severe bouts of depression.

1953  Goes back to the psychiatric hospital for more electroshock treatments. Stays in the hospital for two months. Renews his attempts to publish Lawrence's letters to him. Claims that he had permission from Frieda back in 1932 and produces her typed letters to him. Frieda Lawrence believes they are fakes.

1954  More bouts of depression and more electroshock treatment, despite concerns that he is too feeble to receive them. By October he cannot walk even as far as the garden. His doctor tells Marjorie Wells that her friend may now die at any moment.

1955  Dies 22 January. Wills his letters from Lawrence, Mansfield, and others to the British Museum.

# WHO'S WHO IN KOTELIANSKY'S LIFE IN ENGLAND

BAKER, IDA (1888–1978). A friend of Katherine Mansfield from New Zealand, Baker shared Kot's antipathy toward Mansfield's husband, J. Middleton Murry. Author of *Katherine Mansfield: The Memories of L.M.* Kot corresponded with her until his death. Knowing his fondness for her, Marjorie Wells asked Baker to come to London in 1947 after Kot's attempted suicide, but she was not able to travel.

BERNSTEIN, SIDNEY (1899–1993). A friend of both Gertler and Kot; a capitalist with definite socialist leanings, which made it possible for Kot to relate to him. A theatre and cinema entrepreneur, he was instrumental in bringing Jewish Theatre "Habima" to London. Before WWII he served as the managing director of Gaumont-British, in which capacity in 1938 he was lobbied by Kot to produce a documentary about the Jewish response to Hitler. Bernstein told Kot British censors at the time did not allow any criticism of Hitler's regime.

BRETT, DOROTHY (1883–1977). A painter and friend of Mark Gertler from Slade School of Art. Kot's correspondence with her was intense in 1921–23, but the relationship abruptly ended in 1924, when Kot accused her of being "after Lawrence." She followed the Lawrences to New Mexico that year and became a significant painter of Ameican Indian mythology and rituals. Kot refused to see her when she came to London for visits. She became a US citizen in 1938 and died in Taos. Author of *Lawrence and Brett: A Friendship.*

CAMPBELL, BEATRICE (Lady Glenavy, née Elvery) (1881–1970). An Irish painter, children's book illustrator, and stained glass artist. She was among the earliest friends Kot made in England; together with Mansfield, Murry, and Gertler, she and her husband Gordon were introduced to Kot by Lawrence in 1914. She wrote letters to Kot every week and stayed with him whenever she came from Dublin to London. She insisted on paying for room and board while living at Kot's house, which came to be known as "the Campbell arrangement." Her propensity to gossip created a new verb in her circle of friends – "to campbell." Author of

*Tomorrow We Will Only Gossip.* Her description of the days immediately following Kot's attempted suicide, not published until now, can be found in appendix C.

CARSWELL, CATHERINE (1879–1946). A close friend of the Lawrences, who stayed with her in London when they were not staying with Kot. A journalist and an author. On friendly terms with Kot until 1932, when her depiction of him in *The Savage Pilgrimage* ended their relationship. Her son, John Carswell, presented a very sympathetic portrait of Koteliansky in *Lives and Letters: A.R. Orage, Katherine Mansfield, Beatrice Hastings, John Middleton Murry, S.S. Koteliansky, 1906–1957.*

CLARKE, ADA (née Lawrence) (1887–1948). D.H. Lawrence's younger sister, who was in frequent contact with Kot following her brother's death and the subsequent intestate trial to settle the rights to Lawrence's estate. Unlike her siblings George and Emily, Ada, while also no fan of Frieda's, believed that Lawrence would have liked his widow to inherit virtually everything. Kot tried to disabuse her of that notion but did not succeed.

COHEN, DENNIS (1891–1970). A cousin of Kot's friend Myer Salaman, Cohen founded the Cresset Press in 1927 and, on the Salamans' recommendation, employed Kot as a "reader" there in 1933. It proved to be a very difficult professional relationship for both, and, while not officially fired, Kot saw his duties and influence at the press substantially reduced by 1935. He was, however, still evaluating occasional books for them throughout the war.

FARBMAN, MICHAEL ("Grisha") (1880–1933). A Jew from Ukraine, like Kot, Farbman was one of Kot's closest friends in London, and with his wife, Sonia, and daughter, Ghita, shared Kot's house at 5 Acacia Road. A journalist and author of many books on Russia, Farbman was affiliated with Gorky's publishing house, World Literature, which was run, first in Soviet Russia and then in Berlin, by his brother-in-law, Zinovy Grzhebin. Most of the new books Kot received for translation in the 1920s, both for the Hogarth Press and elsewhere, came from Grzhebin through Farbman. Farbman contracted a mysterious disease while on his trip to Moscow in 1933 and died soon upon his return to London.

GERTLER, MARK (1891–1939). A painter and, because of their similar backgrounds, a very close and cherished friend. Unusually for Kot, in the twenty-five years of their friendship, there seem to have been no serious quarrels or long periods of silence. Gertler was, for all intents and purposes, Kot's younger brother.

He painted several portraits of Kot. Since Kot was used to seeing Gertler at least once a week for most of these twenty-five years, and since his love for him was never marred by complications, Gertler's suicide was probably even more devastating to him than the deaths of D.H. Lawrence and Katherine Mansfield.

HODGSON, RALPH (1871–1962). An English poet whom Kot befriended soon after Lawrence's death in 1930. The two frequently corresponded while Hodgson first taught in Japan and then lived in Minerva, Ohio. They saw each other when Ralph and his wife Aurelia visited London.

HUXLEY, JULIETTE (1896–1994). Wife of Julian Huxley and sister-in-law of Aldous Huxley. While Kot was friendly with both Julian and Aldous, his fondness of Juliette went much deeper, deep enough for him to break up his relationship with May Sarton in 1948 because he felt she had mistreated Juliette. Juliette was one of three female friends who took care of Kot after his nervous breakdown in 1936. In her autobiography, *Leaves of the Tulip Tree*, she reproduces letters that Kot wrote to her while she was in Paris after WWII, when Julian served as director-general of UNESCO.

LAWRENCE, D.H. (1885–1930). A major English novelist with whom Kot developed the most complicated but also the most rewarding relationship while in England. Lawrence was the one who, having met Kot virtually by chance while on a walk around the Lake District in July 1914, introduced him to the literary and artistic society in London that otherwise would not have been Kot's natural social habitat. Kot admired Lawrence as a writer, even though he did not approve of all his work. He was especially critical of *Lady Chatterley's Lover*, and he resented being portrayed as Ben Cooley in *Kangaroo*. Kot's jealousy when it came to Frieda may suggest that his love for Lawrence had a sexual component, which also found its way into the character of Ben Cooley. Lawrence, in his own way, was more often than not a loyal and very patient friend, never quite able to walk away from Kot for good, despite how much Kot exasperated him at times.

LAWRENCE, FRIEDA (1879–1956). Lawrence's wife Frieda was the person Kot most loved to hate. Virtually everything in Frieda was detestable to him, including her zest for life and her influence over Lawrence, which he blamed for Lawrence's anti-Semitism. Before the Lawrences went to Taos, Kot seriously considered "schemes" to separate them. Frieda's attitude toward Kot was a bit more nuanced. She resented his attitude toward her and rightfully considered him the enemy of their marriage, but she also occasionally expressed understanding, sorrow, and regret over their relationship, as two letters from 1932 published here for the first time (appendix E) reveal.

MANSFIELD, KATHERINE (1888–1923). New Zealand-born short-story writer, whose love for Chekhov and all things Russian was instrumental in her initial enthusiastic reaction to Kot. Their relationship, however, grew to be based on much more than that. She did trust him and his opinion more than almost anyone else's, and she felt she could be herself with him, despite several long periods of estrangement. As with Lawrence, he tried to encourage her separation from the spouse he loathed, J. Middleton Murry, and some believed he may have been in love with her. Her letters to him are full of tenderness. He moved into the house that she vacated after the death of her brother during WWI and cherished it as a shrine to her. She helped him with several translations.

MORRELL, OTTOLINE (1873–1938). Perhaps one of Kot's most surprising friendships was with Lady Ottoline Morrell, among the most colourful personalities of the Bloomsbury set. It developed in the early 1930s, after she had sold her estate at Garsington and had stopped giving the lavish parties for which she was so famous and which Kot liked to ridicule. Because she died in 1938, their relationship was relatively short but very intense. During his nervous breakdown in 1936, it was Ottoline on whom he relied for strength and support, and to whom he bared it all.

MURRY, J. MIDDLETON (JACK) (1889–1957). Author, essayist, and editor of several influential English literary journals as well as Mansfield's second husband. Before they became enemies, Murry was the first literary figure to help Kot with his translations and to ensure their publication in 1915. Kot's issues with him arose not just because of Mansfield but also because of Lawrence, to whom Murry at some point was very close. While they reconciled briefly just prior to Mansfield's death in 1923, the disagreement about *The Adelphi* in 1924 put a definite end to any appearance of comity in their relationship.

POWELL, DILYS (1901–1995). A literary and film critic. Kot met Powell through Ottoline Morrell in the early 1930s and championed her book of essays, *Descent from Parnassus*, convincing the Cresset Press to publish it. His letters to her were tender and playful. She was a very loyal friend who helped nurse him back to health in 1936, following his nervous breakdown, and wrote a very touching obituary in the *Times* of London following his death.

RICHARDSON, DOROTHY (1873–1957). A writer. Kot probably met Richardson through the Wells family prior to helping her publish the later volumes of her groundbreaking *Pilgrimage* with the Cresset Press. The confusion about this project and the seemingly misleading information Kot gave to his bosses about it greatly damaged Kot's standing at the press. Richardson dedicated *Clear Horizon*, published by the Cresset Press in 1934, to Kot. The correspondence between them continued through the war but was infrequent.

SALAMAN, ESTHER POLIANOWSKY (1900–1995). Russian-born scientist, novelist, and early Zionist. Kot met her soon after her book *Two Silver Roubles* was published in 1932. Their very similar backgrounds of growing up in the Volhynia Province in Ukraine helped cement the bond. Salaman and her husband, Myer, helped Kot obtain a position at Cresset Press, and were always there for him in other ways, especially in times of his medical and financial needs. In 1936, Esther Salaman drove Kot to doctor's appointments and, by his request, stayed with him during consultations. When heart surgery was recommended, she and Marjorie Wells started a fund for him to pay for it – which Kot later demanded be liquidated.

SARTON, MAY (1912–1995). An American poet and writer whom Kot met through his work at the Cresset Press in 1937. Kot developed very strong feelings for Sarton, leading some, including her, to conclude that he was in love with her. Their relationship cooled after she chose, on one of her visits to London, not to rush to Kot's side following the news of Gertler's suicide. She became a lover of both Julian and Juliette Huxley, and the messiness of this relationship and what Kot perceived as her poor treatment of Juliette led to their final breakup in 1948. May Sarton wrote about Kot extensively in *I Knew a Phoenix* and *A World of Light*. She also saved his letters to her, which are now in the New York Public Library.

SCHIFF, SYDNEY ("Stephen Hudson") (1868–1944). A writer and translator, and with his wife, Violet, a major patron of the arts. Kot appreciated the Schiffs' interest in him and readiness to help financially not just him but his friends, like Mansfield and Gerter. On the other hand, he resented Sydney Schiff's pride in his wealth and his extolment of capitalism. The resentment came to a boiling point at a dinner at the Schiffs in 1926. Even though the relationship was somewhat patched up afterward, it never went back to the warmth and cordiality of the earlier years.

SMITH, PAULINE (1911–1997). Kot's niece. By 1925, when she was just fourteen, Pauline had witnessed the death of her mother and grandfather of typhoid fever, the murder of her father, and an accidental death of her only sibling, an older brother. Kot helped her relocate to Canada, and she worshipped him as a father figure. Their correspondence was, for most of Kot's life, at least bi-weekly. During the war, she sent him packages and money orders. In 1947 she flew from Montreal to be with him following his suicide attempt. The visit was frustrating for her: she did not get along with Marjorie Wells, with whom she had corresponded frequently and had been on very friendly terms prior to coming to London. She felt excluded from all deliberations about Kot's treatment and left earlier than she had planned. Things got even sadder when Kot informed her that, due to his electroshock treatment, he did not remember her being in London at all.

STEPHENS, JAMES (1882–1950). An Irish storyteller, novelist, and poet, Stephens became Kot's closest friend and ally following the deaths of Mansfield and Lawrence. As was the case with Gertler, this was a relationship that never experienced any breakups or other negative upheavals. In the 1930s, the two were inseparable and frequent guests at Ottoline Morrell's house in London, where they were often referred to as "twins." As was routine with other spouses of people he deeply cared for, Kot could not stand Stephens's wife, Cynthia. Stephens's impracticality and helplessness in domestic matters were the only reasons Kot did not try harder to separate the two. His death in 1950 was devastating to Kot.

STEPNIAK, FANNY (1855–1945). Widow of Sergei Stepniak, anarchist and revolutionary. Kot helped her sell the archive of her late husband to the Soviets in the 1920s, as a result of which she got a pension from them for the rest of her life. Stepniak and Kot stayed in close touch for all the years leading to WWII, at which point she left London for the country but they continued to correspond regularly.

SULLIVAN, J.W.N. (1886–1937). A popular science writer and biographer, Sullivan was one of the co-founders of The Adelphi and a frequent attendee of Kot's "Thursdays" and "Wednesdays." His wife, Vere, was also a friend of Kot.

TOMLINSON, PHILIP (1882–1955). A contributor to The Adelphi and Kot's one-time co-translator with whom he had a spectacular fight, both about The Adelphi and the translations, in 1924. Tomlinson later became an influential literary critic, writing for many years for The Times Literary Supplement.

WATERLOW, SYDNEY (1878–1944). A son of London's one-time lord mayor, a diplomat, and an unsuccessful suitor of Virginia Woolf. Kot and Waterlow grew close when Waterlow protested, in a letter to Murry, Murry's treatment of Kot during *The Adelphi* argument. He was a recipient of many letters from Koteliansky throughout the 1920s, and in the 1930s, when Waterlow served as British minister (ambassador) in Greece. The letters are kept in The Alexander Turnbull Library, Wellington, New Zealand.

WELLS, H.G. (1866–1946). A very prolific writer of fiction and nonfiction who had a keen interest in Russia. Kot developed a friendship with Wells when in 1920 he started tutoring Wells's son Gip (G.P. Wells) in Russian. Whenever Kot needed professional advice or professional contacts, he could rely on Wells for both. In 1933, Kot was instrumental in persuading Wells to publish his *Autobiography* with the Cresset Press, but tensions and complications between Wells and Dennis Cohen affected Kot's relationship with Wells as well, which greatly saddened him. There was never a definite breakup, however, and they continued to meet and correspond throughout the war. Kot was delighted when Wells willed him a statuette of Tolstoy that had been presented to Wells by Gorky in the 1920s.

WELLS, MARJORIE (1901–1962). H.G. Wells's secretary and Gip's wife. She played the most crucial role in Kot's life starting with the 1930s as his friend, confidante, and, often, nurse. It was Marjorie whom he cabled in 1936 during his nervous breakdown, asking her to come back to London from a vacation. During the war she visited him every day, and she almost singlehandedly took care of him and made all the necessary arrangements following his suicide attempt in 1947. Her family virtually adopted Kot, who spent most of the holidays with them and took enormous pride in the successes of Marjorie's and Gip's children, Catherine and Oliver. After Kot's death, she served as the executor of his estate. Her daughter, Catherine Stoye, who is now in charge of the estate, has many of Kot's private documents and personal items in her private archive in Oxford.

WOOLF, LEONARD (1880–1969). An author and publisher. Husband of Virginia Woolf. Kot's collaboration with Leonard on translations that were published by Hogarth Press began in 1919 and ended in 1923, but their friendship lasted until Kot's death. Kot felt a special connection to Woolf as a fellow Jew and sought him out in the prewar years when both were experiencing extreme anxiety over what was happening to Jews in Germany. Days before his death in 1955, Kot expressed a desire to see Leonard, who thus became one of the last people to see him alive.

WOOLF, VIRGINIA (1882–1941). A major English novelist as well as essayist and publisher for whom Kot had much respect both as a person and a writer. They collaborated on several translations for Hogarth but her feelings for – and patience with – Kot did not match her husband's. Kot intrigued her at first, and she readily joined in the occasional Russian lessons that Kot was giving to Leonard, but soon she grew disenchanted with him. Her remarks about Kot to friends or in her diaries often carried an anti-Semitic tint to them. Kot was shocked and distressed when she killed herself in 1941.

# LADY GLENAVY, "MORE MEMORIES OF KOT" (1969)[1]

Marjorie Wells played a very important part in the later years of Kot's life. To me she was a complete mystery. I had often met her at his house in the years before the last war and several times I went with her to the Wells' house, somewhere near Swiss Cottage. She and I were very polite to each other but somehow I found her the most unapproachable person that I had ever met. She seemed to be armour-plated against other people, perhaps it was only against me, she appeared to be on friendly terms with Kot's other women friends. Kot must have noticed the strain between us and several times he said to me, "Beatrice, do be 'nice' to Marjorie" – I was not conscious of not being nice to her, I just could not find any method of approach, any effort I made met with no response.

Marjorie Wells had been H.G. Wells's secretary before she married his son, Gip Wells – when H.G. was ill, she had also been his nurse; I felt she had a genius for taking care of elderly literary gentlemen in poor health. When Kot began to have heart-attacks and moods of great depression, I had said to him, "I wish I could do something to help you." He said, "They all say that – it means nothing, the sort of help I need is someone who will come to me every day, to do the shopping, the house-cleaning and the cleaning, someone like a wife or mother who will take care of me." The next time I went to London, I found that Marjorie was doing just what he wanted. He said she was "his tower of strength," that she was the only one of his women friends who was "a free human being" – I wonder how she managed to look after her own house and family as well as Kot, but she did it all quietly and efficiently.

Marjorie had what Kot would call "a nice face," her hair was grey and cut short like a man's; she did not seem to have any interest in clothes, she wore rather shapeless tweeds and jerseys. Her one beauty was her lovely peaches-and-cream schoolgirl's complexion.

I remember going to see Violet Schiff one day; she said, "I want to talk about Marjorie Wells, I cannot make her out," so we talked and talked but did not come to any conclusion.

I have lately come across some letters that Marjorie wrote to me in Ireland during Kot's last illness – they seem so simple and friendly that I can't help wondering how there could have been any strain between us, but it certainly did exist all the time I knew her.

About the middle of June 1947, I went to London to the wedding of my brother Philip's daughter. I never got to the wedding – when I arrived at my hotel, I rang up Kot's house, I knew Kot had been ill and I was worried about him. Marjorie Wells answered the phone; she said, "Kot has tried to cut his throat with the blade of a safety razor. I have been with him for about a week, night and day. Can you come at once and take over so that I can get some sleep?" I went at once to 5 Acacia Road. Marjorie opened the hall door; we went into the sitting room off the hall. Marjorie said a nurse was in Kot's bedroom getting him ready to receive me, he had insisted on getting up so that he would be sitting in a chair when I arrived. On the table was "Kot's tray," covered with medicine bottles. I was shocked and suddenly very angry. "Kot's tray" had been painted for him by Ruth Pitter, a poet, who was a great friend of Kot's and whose poetry he greatly admired. The painting was beautiful, Victorian, rather stylized flowers with a suggestion of sky and some landscape behind them, and a small inscription to Kot and the date. He valued this gift from his friend very much. I took all the bottles off the tray and tried to clean away something which had been spilt on it. I then put the tray back on the shelf where Kot kept it, and said firmly that it was not to be used like that. Marjorie said nothing, but looked on as I fussed about the tray, with a remote, cold, uninterested expression on her face.[2]

Then the nurse appeared and we both went with her into the next room. The nurse was an elderly woman in a not very clean white coat. Kot was seated in a chair in his dressing-gown, looking terribly pale and miserable, with bandages round his neck. Marjorie and the nurse left the room as he held out his arms to me and said, "Beatrice, I have done the most stupid wrong thing."

I went and knelt beside him and we held to each other. I said, "Such nonsense, you have done nothing wrong. You are ill. Now it is over, you must get well again." There was nothing more to be said. Marjorie and the nurse came back and said he must go back to bed.

Later on, I was alone with him again and he kept on telling me that Marjorie had been "wonderful." He had rung her up when he did the awful deed; she came and got a doctor.[3] The wound was slight. They decided not to call the police.

Kot said, "Marjorie now arranges everything, you must do exactly as she tells you." I promised that I would do so. He seemed quite like himself except for the terrible depression, the Black Mood. Later that evening, Marjorie's husband, Gip Wells, arrived, carrying a huge chaise-longue made of cane, which folded up. He opened it out and placed it in Kot's bedroom, it took up nearly the whole room. This contraption was for me to lie on, so that I could keep an eye on Kot during the night while Marjorie was getting some sleep in the little room at the top of the house where Katherine Mansfield used to write. Marjorie explained that the day nurse would go off duty about nine o'clock and a night nurse, Irish, would then take over. She added that Kot did not like the night nurse. My impression was that he could hardly bear the presence of the day nurse either. Marjorie said that I was to stay awake till four o'clock on the following morning and then go upstairs and awake her, and she would take my place on the day-bed and I could sleep. She spoke as if the two nurses did not exist, but Kot had given me his instructions about doing anything she ordered, so I kept silent.

The day nurse departed and a younger woman arrived, looking even less like a nurse. She made some joking remarks to Kot about all the women. He did not answer, he just looked at her with loathing.

Marjorie retired to the attic, having explained to the night nurse that I was to spend the night on the chaise-longue. The young woman was full of curiosity and amusement. Kot watched us from his bed with his dark eyes in his bead-white face, a mixture of resignation and fury, especially when the nurse closed the window, turned on the electric fire and the two electric lights. Marjorie had put an armchair for the nurse in front of the fire; she seated herself and began to read a book that she had brought with her. I lay down on the creaking day-bed and so we proceeded to pass the long night.

Very soon the nurse was fast asleep. When she began to snore, I looked across at Kot and tried to smile, but he was not amused. I made signs to him suggesting that I should open the window and turn off the lights and the stove, but he shook his head fiercely, so we both remained quietly watching the sleeping nurse. Never for a moment did he close an eye in sleep.

Later on in the night, the nurse woke up and went to the kitchen to get tea or supper for herself. Again I suggested that we should turn off the glaring light and the awful heat, but it seemed to distress Kot so much that I should go against Marjorie's "plans" that I gave up.

The night seemed to go on for years. I looked at my watch and saw it was almost four o'clock, so I made signs to Kot that I was going upstairs to wake Marjorie. The nurse was again sleeping soundly. When I opened the door of her room, I could see her dimly, lying on a mattress on the floor; she too was sleeping soundly and I felt it would be cruel to wake her. I went back and told Kot. He nodded his head. A short time after this, Marjorie suddenly appeared, she was annoyed that I had not awakened her. I found a bed somewhere and slept till I was awakened by the sound of angry voices. I listened; it was Marjorie and the day nurse, who had just arrived. Marjorie was saying that Mr Koteliansky had had a very bad night and no one was to go near him or disturb him – the nurse was shouting that never before, in her nursing career, had she been kept away from her patient and she could not understand what was going on in the house: she thought she was supposed to be in charge.

When I went down to the kitchen to make my breakfast, she also was preparing hers. She complained bitterly to me about her treatment by Mrs Wells and tried to enlist my sympathies. I tried to explain that Mr Koteliansky was a very exceptional person and Mrs Wells understood him, and we were to do as she wished. Later on that morning, I could not help telling Marjorie what I thought about it all. I suggested that we should get rid of the nurses, who were driving Kot mad. She agreed, and had another row with the day nurse who then left for good. (Kot almost smiled when we told him she was gone.) When the night nurse appeared, she too was paid off and sent home. Violet Schiff rang up to ask how Kot was – when he heard of her phone call, he said that I must go to her and tell her all about him, and the nurses. So I went and told my story to Violet.

Violet was horrified as I described the night with two women in Kot's bedroom and the window shut, the lights on and the place like an oven with the electric stove. I cannot quite remember how the days went on. We moved the chaise-longue into the sitting room, and either Marjorie or I lay on it at night with the door open so that we could hear any sound from Kot's room next door. Some days his mind seemed to wander. One morning, he said to me, very seriously, "The police will be coming for Marjorie soon." I tried to make a joke of it but he did not smile. Some days he appeared to be much better and would get up and dress himself, and we would sit in the garden. It was lovely sunny weather but that only seemed to make his Black Mood blacker.

When Marjorie told me about his attempted suicide in the bathroom, she added that she had taken away the rug that was there, and hidden it, so that he would not see the blood on it and be reminded of his terrible act. One morning we were sitting in the garden when she came out of the house carrying a large dripping bundle, she proceeded to hang it on the clothes line which was stretched between two poles right in front of where we were sitting. It was the rug from the bathroom. I saw Kot turn his head from side to side to avoid looking at it; then he got up and went back into the kitchen. Kot had a charlady, Mrs Hawkens, who came about once a week, she was devoted to him. She called him "Mr X" as she could not get round to "Koteliansky." A doctor also called several times. Mrs Hawkens remarked to me, "'E don't look like a Doctor, 'e don't look like a gentleman neither." Marjorie had private discussions with the doctor, who was trying to get a room for Kot in a place which took such cases in Virginia Water.

The first time that Mrs Hawkens came after Kot's act, he and I were reading the morning papers in his sitting room. Marjorie came in and said to Kot, "If you don't want to see Mrs Hawkens, I will talk to her, and she need not see you if you sit there." She placed a chair where Kot could not be seen by anyone coming to the house. Kot was saying, "Yes, Marjorie" very humbly and obediently. He seemed terribly ashamed of what he had done; he sat in the chair looking very unhappy. We could hear Mrs Hawkens and Marjorie talking in the hall. I looked around the corner of my newspaper and said, with mock solemnity, "Are you a man or a mouse?" Kot knew at once what I was at and said, "What am I to do? Help me." I said "Go out to the hall and see Mrs Hawkens and speak to her." He got up quickly and hurried out of the room. I heard her saying, "An Mister X, wot an awful thing you done! You must never do that again." She said it so kindly; he replied humbly, "Yes, it was very wrong. I will never do it again." He came back into the room where I was, with an eager look on his face, like a child wanting to be praised. I said, "Splendid! No one could have done it better!" Marjorie never said a word about my treachery. I liked her for that.

Several times I went to Violet Schiff to report. She was even more interested in what I told her about Marjorie than in Kot's condition, which had improved so much that his friends were coming to him, and his Thursday teas had started again. One morning the sun was shining, Kot and I were reading the newspapers in the little front room; Marjorie, as usual, was working hard on the house, and shaking rugs and mats in the garden. I always did my own room. Suddenly Kot and I noticed the man and his wife from next door passing the house looking magnificent, grey topper, race-glasses,[4] big flowery hat, summer dress and long gloves. We were astonished to see them so grand so early in the day. I quickly looked again at my newspaper and said, "Ascot!" I read all about the Queen arriving at the course, etc., etc. Kot seemed very interested. He liked the Donovans very much; they were Irish; they had a farm somewhere in Ireland and used to bring him butter and other things during the war. He also found their teen-age children very attractive: he spoke of their "Irish charm" and their "innocent Irish faces." I was going out to see some Art Exhibition that morning. I said we must have a bet on the Big Race, so we studied the names of the horses and their form and the odds. There was a horse with a Russian name, meaning 'darling,' but Kot said he must have an English name so he chose something else. I did not know that there were no betting shops at that time in London and that it was almost impossible or illegal to make a bet, unless you knew how. When I went out to go to my Art Exhibition, I asked some men working on the road, but they seemed very suspicious and disclaimed any knowledge of such things – but then directed me to a Commissionaire standing outside the door of a big hotel. He seemed even more embarrassed by my request as to how one could back a horse in London – so I gave it up. On the way back to 5 Acacia Road, I bought a newspaper at the Tube Station to see the racing results and was delighted to see that Kot's horse had won. When I arrived at Kot's house, I found Kot's kitchen full of people having Russian tea very quietly: Marjorie, James Stephens, Dr Fulton and, I think, Dilys Powell. Kot looked up eagerly and said "What won?" It was lovely to be able to say "Your horse," it was sad to have to explain that we had had no bet on it – but Kot seemed very pleased and James Stephens was delighted that Kot had taken to backing horses! I felt the rest of the party thought we had gone mad; we had to explain that it was the magnificent appearance of Mr and Mrs Donovan which had led to our downfall.

Kot had a niece from Kiev whom he had helped to get to America with others of his family during the war.[5] (Marjorie had cabled for her to come to her uncle who was "seriously ill," before my arrival.) I was with Kot when she arrived, Marjorie met her in the hall. She had the most unpleasant, harsh, speaking voice and an American accent. Kot looked horrified, saying, "What a terrible voice!" She in her turn was horrified at the "poverty" in which her uncle lived. She had married someone with money in New York[6] and told us about her "apartments," one room as big as Kot's back garden, with every comfort, modern gadget and convenience. She couldn't bear the thought of any of her relations living in such squalor as she saw in Kot's kitchen and scullery! She stayed a few days and tried to be helpful, but no one could bear her! Marjorie had to arrange a return journey for her as soon as possible. It was interesting that, when she went out to do shopping in the little shops where Kot was known and loved and respected, they said to Marjorie afterward, "Mr Koteliansky's niece a Jewess?" They all thought of him as "a Russian." It was a sad time for her and for Kot – she simply could not understand how Kot could be so proud of his scrubbed kitchen table and his back garden with "Katherine's pear tree." To her it was all terribly degrading.

There were other times when the inscrutability of Marjorie was a puzzle to me. I think her entire lack of any sense of the ridiculous was the greatest difference between us. I must have gone back to Ireland soon after all these happenings.[7] Marjorie used to write to me to tell me how Kot was; she and Sophie Jacobs,[8] who drove her own car, had taken him to the place in Virginia Water. Next time I was in London, he seemed much better. He was back again sitting at his kitchen table in Acacia Road. He talked with much interest about the shock treatment that he had had, and how much he liked some of the other patients, and how pleasant and well-run the place was. He loved the garden and there was one woman doctor whom he especially praised for her sympathy and understanding.[9] As time went on, he got back to his Black Moods. He went back to Virginia Water for more treatment, but things did not improve.

The last time I saw him was in a hospital in Whitechapel, where he was in the care of some special doctor. When I arrived, Marjorie was sitting beside his bed, tying up a large parcel. I gathered it was a present to Kot. The ward sister had told him that he must have a bed-jacket, so Marjorie had gone to Jaegers to get one. When she had finished making up her parcel, she got up and walked away down the ward, carrying it sadly. I said something to Kot about it being very ungrateful of him not to have accepted her present, he said: "But Beatrice, it was *Red*!"[10]

We then talked of Antony Alpers's[11] book on Katherine Mansfield, which had just been published. I was so glad that Kot had felt well enough to read the book. When Alpers first came to London, from New Zealand, he had gone to Kot for help. Kot took one look at him and decided that that young man could never write a book about Katherine – he now was surprised that it was so much better than he expected. I suggested that it was Alpers's wife who had written it, she had been Sarah Campion and had written a very good book which Kot at some distant time had recommended to me: it was called *My Father*. Kot was amused at this idea and agreed with me. Kot also spoke of the kindness of the nurses and staff of the hospital. Whenever our talk became silent, his mind seemed to wander and he would say softly, almost to himself, "It won't be long now." I don't think that people who talk about their deaths to their friends can know how cruel they are being. I know Kot was quite unconscious of the effect of his saying "It won't be long now" was having on me. Anyhow we had talked happily together. I had a feeling when I left him that I would never see him again. I never did.

# KOTELIANSKY TO STEPHEN SPENDER, CHRISTMAS DAY (1952); STEPHEN SPENDER, "KOTELIANSKY AND THE CAFÉ ROYAL."[1]

CHRISTMAS DAY (1952)

> 5, Acacia Road
> St John's Wood, NW 8
> Christmas day

My dear Stephen,

Thank you so very much for your letter this morning. The best X present is your news that you are starting a magazine.[2] It is a topic I had meant for a long time to talk to you. A literary magazine is an absolute necessity, in this most terrible and fateful time. And I wish you great success.

I am ill and cannot write about D.H.L. But when I am better, I think the best way would be for you to ask me all sorts of questions about him. And as I believe you to be a real writer, of the important ones (and this belief I had since I first read your first book (about D.H.L., Henry James etc),[3] I am sure you will do most valuable work.

When I am better I should love to meet Isaiah Berlin.[4] So let us wait.

If it is no trouble to you to speak to an ill person, do ring me up (Primrose 1947) and come.

> Yours ever Kot.

KOTELIANSKY AND THE CAFÉ ROYAL

From Stephen Spender's Journal: 26 December 1952

On Boxing day I went to see Kot again. He was very excited and pleased about the idea that I should edit a magazine; this is very much under discussion at the moment. I suggested to him that a feature I would like if I did so, was his memoirs. He said he could not bring himself to write these, but that perhaps I might ask him questions and then note down my impressions. He continued to talk about Lawrence; first of all describing how he had been going on a walking tour with Lawrence in August 1914, during which time they saw no newspapers, and arrived at one place to discover the headlines that war was about to be declared. He said that Lawrence was the man in all England the least prepared for the idea of war, the most innocent of power politics. To him the war between England [and] Germany – with his German wife – was the profoundest of shocks. All the things one reads about how he and Frieda were persecuted in Cornwall are of no importance; what is important is that Lawrence never accepted the idea of the war. Then he went into the question of the famous Café Royal dinner (in 1926?[5]) which has been described by Murry and others – quite wrongly, according to Kot. Kot's version of this is that it was ruined by the fact that Lawrence, who was staying with Catherine Carswell and her husband, brought them to the dinner in the private room without having told the little group, Gertler, Kot, Katherine Mansfield[6] and Murry that he was going to do so. There was also Brett there. As soon as the party was assembled, Lawrence realized that he had done the wrong thing to bring his hosts. Out of a kind of defiance he started talking Italian,[7] though the only people who could understand him were the Carswells. Catherine Carswell's husband started also talking Italian, and Kot said to him that if he went on he would throw him out of the window. Carswell realized that K was serious and shut her husband up. Lawrence realized that the whole atmosphere was ruined and started drinking and getting excited – usually he did not drink at all – and vomited. He was terribly unhappy, Kot said, and kept on returning to the theme of Lawrence's terrible unhappiness, which really began with the war. "Frieda of course enjoyed the whole occasion very much, in the same way as she enjoyed everything always."

Kot is so obsessed with every detail about Lawrence, that I began to feel it would be difficult to go over this material again which has been discussed so often before, and which doesn't seem very important. But Kot does confirm some impressions I had already come to myself: that Lawrence took Brett with him to Mexico,[8] for instance, in order to protect himself from Frieda: and that his relations with women were an elaborate defence system in which one was being used to neutralize the other or others. Until finally at Taos, he left a kind of self-perpetuating system of women loving and hating one another, and revolving round his memory, in a minor hell of their and his making, like Sartre's *Huit Clos*.[9]

# APPENDIX E

# TWO LETTERS FROM FRIEDA LAWRENCE TO KOTELIANSKY (1932)[1]

29 St Peter's Square
Hammersmith
Sunday [3 July 1932]

Dear Kot,

Yes, it's awful what is done with Lawrence, here I have a German book: Der Pessimismus von D.H.L.[2] and people using him as a *weapon* for their own ends. Where is the real Lorenzo? Perhaps you ought to write with your real feeling for him for the future.

No, I don't believe your nonacceptance of his views was precious to him, it made him suffer and doubt himself; you loved him like a man loves a woman or a child. You thought him charming. He told me: "you make me feel sure of myself" – that's what he needed. No, I don't feel humble. I feel proud, proud as Lucifer, when I think, that he told me, "nothing has mattered but you." And I dream of him so vividly and he says: "Don't worry, I love you forever now," and I really cant bear it and try not to think of his work and all this other Lawrence. I wish he had never written a line and my name were Faith Smith. I don't want to be his widow. He *was* very great and I shall never get over the wonder of him – but I don't want to *think* about him.

Yes, of course we could never be indifferent to each other, our love for him, different as it was, is a bond.

Ever yours,
F

But no, Kot, you cant [*sic*] get away with it so easily! Your not believing in the *prophet* L. was *bitter* to him and seperated [*sic*] him from you – don't you know it, even *now*, what he was?

10 Hammersmith Terrace
London W 6
Saturday [16 July 1932]

Dear Kot,

How sad you must be never to have told him you loved him! But there, it's always too late – and he knew it – he knew everything. I know *how* it is at times, I am haunted by his feet, that I loved so much, if I would only, only hold them once more – But he is inside me so strongly, thank God, active and alive. Don't think I have any friends – I am quite alone and know it. As for Murry I have'nt seen him for 2 years! I don't like the hysteria about Lawrence just now – but it will pass. And I love living, *he* left me that. And you shouldn't be sad and "have done." There's the spark he left us. I am fighting over the will. What had that beastly family got to do with him? Even Ada – took from his always and *gave nothing*. I meet lots of young who *do* understand him.

Yours ever
F

I suppose you dont remember anything he said to you about a will? Or about my being provided for? or anything like that? He didn't want George and the sisters to have money. He said they have husbands.

I will show [you] "his last months" that I wrote down, if you would like to know how his end was, so splendid!

# ABBREVIATIONS FOR ARCHIVES
# AND COLLECTIONS

ATL/KM  Katherine Mansfield Collection. The Alexander Turnbull Library, Wellington, New Zealand.

ATL/SW  Sydney Waterlow Papers. The Alexander Turnbull Library, Wellington, New Zealand.

BCA  Honourable Bridget Campbell's private archive, Ibiza, Spain.

BL/Kot  S.S. Koteliansky Papers. Manuscript Collections and Archives, British Library.

BL/SS  Sydney Schiff Papers. Manuscript Collections and Archives, British Library.

CSA  Catherine Stoye's private archive.

GZA  George Zytaruk's private archive.

HRC/DB  Dorothy Brett Collection. Harry Ransom Humanities Research Center, The University of Texas at Austin.

HRC/DHL  D.H. Lawrence Collection. Harry Ransom Humanities Research Center, The University of Texas at Austin.

HRC/MH  Mary Hutchinson Papers. Harry Ransom Humanities Research Center, The University of Texas at Austin.

HRC/OM  Lady Ottoline Morrell Collection. Harry Ransom Humanities Research Center, The University of Texas at Austin.

IPA  Ivor Powell's private archive.

JFA  Jackie Freedman's private archive.

JNUL  Beila Koteliansky Papers. Archive of the Jewish National and University Library at The Hebrew University of Jerusalem.

LGA  Luke Gertler's private archive.

Nottingham/CC  Catherine Carswell Collection. Manuscript and Special Collections, University of Nottingham.

Nottingham/DHL  D.H. Lawrence Collection. Manuscript and Special Collections, University of Nottingham.

NWA  Nina Wedderburn's private archive.

NYPL  May Sarton Papers, 1920–1995. Henry W. and Albert A. Berg Collection of English and American Literature, The New York Public Library.

Reading  Hogarth Press Files. Special Collections, University of Reading Library.

ssa  Sonny Surkes's private archive.

Sussex  Leonard Woolf Papers. Special Collections, The University of Sussex
Library.

ui  H.G. Wells Collection. Rare Book and Special Collections Library, University
of Illinois at Urbana-Champaign.

Yale  Ralph Hodgson Papers. General Collection, Beinecke Rare Book and
Manuscript Library, Yale University.

# NOTES

INTRODUCTION

1 Quoted in John Carswell, *Lives and Letters: A.R. Orage, Katherine Mansfield, Beatrice Hastings, John Middleton Murry, S.S. Koteliansky, 1906–1957*, 268. See also, Hilary Pyle, *James Stephens: His Work and an Account of His Life*, where the quote is slightly different: "[T]he greatest book on literature that has never been written is by Koteliansky" (118).

2 Constantin Nabokoff, *The Ordeal of a Diplomat*, 41.

3 Quoted in Virginia Nicholson, *Among the Bohemians: Experiments in Living 1900–1939*, 227.

4 Quoted in Nicholson, *Among the Bohemians*, 106, 108. For more on the influence of the Ballets Russes on interior designs, see the entire chapter in the book, "Dwelling with Beauty," 99–127.

5 Leonard Woolf, *Beginning Again: Autobiography of the Years 1911 to 1918*, 37, 48–9. For more on Ballets Russes London seasons, see Lynn Garafola, *Diaghilev's Ballets Russes*, 300–29.

6 Quoted in Evelyn Haller, "Her Quill Drawn from the Firebird: Virginia Woolf and the Russian Dancers," in Diane F. Gillespie, *The Multiple Muses of Virginia Woolf*, 187.

7 Something that D.H. Lawrence keenly satirized in *Women in Love:* "'There is a most beautiful thing in my book,' suddenly piped the little Italian woman. 'It says the man came to the door and threw his eyes down the street.' There was a general laugh in the company ... 'Bazarov came to the door and threw his eyes hurriedly down the street,' she read.... 'What's the book?' asked Alexander promptly. "'Fathers and Sons,' by Turgenev,' said the little foreigner.... 'An old American edition,' said Birkin. 'Ha! – of course – translated from the French,' said Alexander, with a fine declamatory voice. 'Bazarov ouvra la porte et jeta les yeux dans la rue.'" (D.H. Lawrence, *Women in Love*, 86–7). In the novel, Ursula and Gudrun also create "a little ballet, in the style of the Russian Ballet of Pavlova and Nijinsky" (91).

8 Virginia Woolf, *Common Reader*, 185–6.

9 Virginia Woolf to Philippa Woolf, 29 September 1939, *The Letters of Virginia Woolf*, vol. 6, 361. "Always the same reality," she wrote about Tolstoy in her

diary in 1940, "like touching an exposed electric wire … his rugged short cut mind – to me the most, not sympathetic, but inspiring, rousing genius in the raw. Thus more disturbing, more 'shocking,' more of a thunderclap, even on art, even on literature, than any other writer" (Virginia Woolf, 21 March 1940, *The Diary of Virginia Woolf,* vol. 5, 273). For an excellent study of Woolf's reaction to Russian writers, including her "Reading Notes" on Dostoevsky, Chekhov, Tolstoy, and Turgenev, see Roberta Rubenstein, *Virginia Woolf and the Russian Point of View.*

10 In Ottoline Morrell, *Ottoline at Garsington: Memoirs of Lady Ottoline Morrell 1915–1918,* 186.

11 Mansfield to Constance Garnett, 8 February 1921, *The Collected Letters,* vol. 4, 176.

12 Koteliansky to May Sarton, 28 February 1940, NYPL. This and all subsequent documents and letters of Samuel Koteliansky are quoted here with the permission of Catherine (Wells) Stoye, who is in charge of his estate.

13 Kennedy, Richard. *A Boy at the Hogarth Press,* 42.

14 In general, while among themselves Pale of Settlement Jews routinely differentiated between "Ukrainian Jews," "Lithuanian Jews," or "Belarusian Jews," it was mostly to emphasize different dialects of their spoken Yiddish, not their cultural identity.

15 May Sarton, *I Knew a Phoenix: Sketches for an Autobiography,* 212.

16 Leonard Woolf, *Beginning Again,* 249.

17 Virginia Woolf, 5 May 1920, *Diary,* vol. 2, 34.

18 See, for example his letter to Dorothy Brett, 22 August 1921, HRC/DB.

19 Koteliansky to Esther Salaman, 14 May (no year; 1930s), NWA. I am grateful to Esther Salaman's family, and, in particular, her daughter Nina Wedderburn, for sending me the originals of Koteliansky's letters to Mrs Salaman, which were in their possession.

20 Koteliansky to Morrell, 16 September 1936, HRC/OM.

21 Virginia Woolf, 18 December 1921, *Diary,* vol. 2, 150.

22 Lady Juliette Huxley, interview with George Zytaruk, London, 5 June 1972. Quoted with the permission of Victoria Huxley, Juliette Huxley's granddaughter. I am greatly indebted to Dr Zytaruk for sharing with me these and other unpublished materials relating to Koteliansky, which he had collected in the 1960s and 1970s while intending to write his biography of Koteliansky and while several very important people in Koteliansky's life were still alive.

23 Quoted in Beatrice Campbell (Lady Glenavy), *Today We Will Only Gossip,* 192.

24 According to Lady Glenavy, he did consider the Old Testament "great literature" as well and spoke of it with "a great pride" (Campbell, *Today We Will Only Gossip,* 183).

25 Virginia Woolf, 25 May 1940, *Diary,* vol. 5, 287.

26 Koteliansky to Morrell, 26 December 1933, HRC/OM.

CHAPTER ONE

1 Leonard Woolf, "Kot," obituary, 171.

2 Simon Dubnov, *Istoriia evreiskago soldata. Ispoved' odnogo iz mnogikh* ("History of a Jewish Soldier. A Confession of One of Many"), 4. There is no English translation available, and the Russian original is now accessible only in microfilm. There is a French edition, however: *Histoire d'un soldat Juif (1881–1915)*. The piece first appeared in *Evreiskaia nedelia* (Jewish Week) in 1916 (nos. 11 and 14) but was severely censored. Unless otherwise specified, all translations from Russian and Ukrainian are mine.

3 See, for example, Mikola Evtushok, *Ostropil': Kraeznavchii naris* (Ostropol: A Study of the Region), 3.

4 By contrast, the neighbouring Liubar was at least half Jewish, and in smaller villages nearby 90–100 percent of the population were Jews. The 1897 census results are reprinted in *Evreiskaia entsiklopediia: svod znanii o evreistve i ego kulture v proshlom i nastoiashchem* (Jewish Encyclopedia: A Code of Knowledge about Jews, Their Past and Present Culture). For the tables, including the ones from the *EE*, see also:
www.jewishgen.org/Ukraine/Volhynia/towns/populations.htm.

5 Thus the surviving nineteenth-century records from the town of Zaslav (now Iziaslav), 70 or so kilometres further north, feature such names as "Slavutsky," "Krasilovsky," "Shepetovsky," "Ostrogsky," and "Mezhobozhsky," derived from the nearby towns of Slavuta, Krasilov, Shepetovka, Ostrog, and Medzhibizh, all within 50–100 kilometres of Ostropol. Zaslav records are available on a database maintained by Daniel Kazez, Professor of Music at Wittenberg University.

6 N.I. Teodorovich in *Gorod Starokonstantinov Volynskoi gubernii* (The City of Starokonstantinov of Volhynia District). Quoted here from Victoriia Martiniuk, *Skromnye obeliski* (Modest Gravestones), 5. A more balanced and quite thoughtful earlier nineteenth-century description of the Jewish population in Ukraine can be found in a book by a St Petersburg Naval Ministry official: A. Afanas'ev-Chuzhvinsky, *Poezdka v iuzhnuiu Rossiiu* (Travel to the Southern Russia). Sent to Ukraine to research the "maritime and fishing activities as well as the general life of the rural population living along the Dnieper and Dniester rivers" (vol. 1, 1), the author ended up spending a very significant chunk of his two volumes describing the lives and habits of the local Jews, who more often sold fish than caught it and largely preferred to stay on dry land. Although Afanas'ev-Chuzhvinsky makes a point out of not calling them "yids," there is still plenty of stereotyping here about Jews: like the notions that they are extraordinary "breeders" and, for most part, cowardly, and the tribute to their work ethic, drive to succeed, and intelligence, saying, at one point, that "the energetic activity of the Jews is capable of breathing life into the saddest and most apathetic territories" (vol. 2, 176).

The work also includes a lengthy and passionate plea for the abolishment of the Pale of Settlement as the only way to solve "the Jewish Question" (vol. 2, 300–7).

7  Interview with Martin Packman, Washington, DC, 7 November 2003; Packman email to the author, 31 March 2004.

8  Unpublished interview by Natalie Wexler, 6 September 1991; Natalie Wexler email to the author, 6 April 2004 (quoted here with her permission).

9  Campbell, *Today We Will Only Gossip*, 159–60.

10  Interview with Jackie Freedman, Montreal, 26 April 2004.

11  Isaak Vainshel'bom, *Starokontantinovskie novelly* (Starokonstantinov Novels), 66.

12  Abe Koosis, *Child of War and Revolution: The Memoirs of Abe Koosis*, 5.

13  May Sarton, *I Knew a Phoenix*, 213.

14  Ben Richman, "Ostropol Map and Description," www.rosenblattgallery.com/ben/ostropol.shtml. This and all subsequent quotes from Ben Richman are given here with the permission of Suzanne Rosenblatt, his niece.

15  Eric A. Kimmel, *The Adventures of Hershel of Ostropol*, 63–4.

16  Virginia Woolf, 5 May 1920; *Diary*, vol. 2, 34.

17  Leonard Woolf, *Beginning Again*, 251.

18  Kimmel, *The Adventures of Hershel of Ostropol*, 63. As we will see, Koteliansky himself did not always follow it, though, especially when hiding the state of his health from his sister Rokhl.

19  Koteliansky to Pauline Smith, 28 May 1952 and 10 May 1953, JFA. Pauline spoke Yiddish but probably could not write it when she left, and she was illiterate in Russian, so she and her uncle communicated in English.

20  Marjorie Wells to Dr Bentwich, 3 December 1955, CSA. All quotes from Marjorie Wells's unpublished letters are used here with the permission of her daughter, Catherine Stoye.

21  Pauline Smith told George J. Zytaruk, who was about to publish D.H. Lawrence's letters to Koteliansky, that "the family owned a flour mill" – in *The Quest for Rananim: D.H. Lawrence Letters to S.S. Koteliansky, 1914 to 1930*, xv. Koteliansky also refers to the mill in a letter to Mary Hutchinson, 10 April 1917: "My parents are at the Mill at present" (HRC/MH), and Marjorie Wells refers to it in the lines quoted at the top of this chapter: "He often talked of … the flour mill" (Wells to Rokhl Marshak, 28 April 1955, CSA).

22  Interview with Jackie Freedman and Sharon Smith, Montreal, 26 April 2004.

23  In *Vsia Rossiia: Russkaia kniga promyshlennosti, torgovli, selskogo khoziaistva i administratsii* (The All-Russian Book of Industry, Trade, Agriculture, and Administration), no pp., columns 170 and 179 of Volhynia Region. The 1895 directory listed two Kotelianskys, of them one, with no first name, from Ostropol. His occupation was listed as "Fabric." This Koteliansky is obviously Samuel's father, and the entry points to the very business ran by Beila

Koteliansky but, as was the custom, registered in her husband's name instead. (Even though the entry does not have a first name, Beila's last name would have appeared differently, as "Kotelianskaia," which is the female version of it, if the business was registered to her.)

24 Unpublished. The autobiography is in JNUL, together with other documents in Yiddish, all sent by Marjorie Wells upon Koteliansky's death. Translated from Yiddish by Janie Respitz Ben-Shach. Quoted here with the permission of Jackie Freedman. "Khad Gadya" is the last song in most Hagaddahs. Written in Aramaic, it is most "children-friendly" because it allegorically uses animals to describe grim events in Jewish history. See, for example, Rabbi Dr Michael Shire, *The Illuminated Haggadah: Featuring Medieval Illuminations from the Hagaddah Collection of the British Library*, 58.

25 Ben Richman, "Second Letter to Joshua" (19 March 1977), www.rosenblatt gallery.com/ben/letters/letter_2.shtml.

26 Ben Richman, "Ostropol Map and Description," www.rosenblattgallery. com/ben/ostropol.shtml.

27 Interview with Jackie Freedman, 26 April 2004.

28 A note in Koteliansky's hand in CSA states (in Russian and with Hebrew names for the months): "Mother was born on the 7th of Adar 1852 … Father was born on the 10th of Sivan 1853." His Yiddish nickname "Shmilik" came up in several interviews with Koteliansky's relatives, including interview with Sonny Surkes (Koteliansky's grandnephew and his brother's Moishel's grandson), Montreal, 27 April 2004.

29 Koteliansky to Pauline Smith, 23 May 1951 and 6 March 1953, JFA.

30 The recollection belongs to Ruth Pitter; quoted in Pyle, *James Stephens*, 117. His friends were quite intrigued by the mystery of his birth date. See John Carswell: "Even the exact date of his birth is unknown – a blank which he filled in with one of the few flashes of humour ever recorded of him, by entering on all forms against the relevant question 1 April" (*Lives and Letters*, 268).

31 Koteliansky to Pauline Smith, 9 November 1953 and 24 July 1944, JFA. For more on Yom-Tov Lipmann Heller, see Joseph Davis, *Yom-Tov Lipmann Heller: Portrait of a Seventeenth-Century Rabbi*. Some caution may be in order here. Isaac Asimov, who was also born in the Pale of Settlement before his family moved to New York, was right to be overall rather skeptical of claims of this kind: "many Jewish people talk about their ancestors in [E]astern Europe, and one and all of them … were descended from a long and unbroken line of great scholars. I'm sorry, but I can't believe it" (*In Memory Yet Green*, 13). "Great scholars" were, indeed, Eastern European Jewry's substitute for aristocracy. They formed the foundation for what, in Yiddish, was called "yikhes," or belonging to an illustrious intellectual and spiritual lineage. It hardly matters, however, how close or genuine the link

really was in Koteliansky's case; what matters is that he and his whole family firmly believed it to be there.

32 Among those murdered was another Ostropol dignitary, the well-known Kabbalist Rabbi Shimshon, who is famous for his Passover writings and who is mentioned even today in some Haggadahs, where he is often identified as "Rabbi Samson." In the present-day Ukraine, Ostropol is located in the so-called "Khmelnitsky" region, named so after Bogdan Khmelnitsky, the leader of the Ukrainian peasants and Cossacks in the seventeenth-century rebellion against Poland. Khmelnitsky presided over a horrendous wave of massacres of Jews. Mercifully, in Koteliansky's time the town of Khmelnitsky, which now gives its name to the entire region, was still called "Proskurov."

33 "Outrages upon Jews in Russia," *The Jewish Chronicle* (London), 6 May 1881, 11.

34 "Jewish Massacre Denounced," *The New York Times*, 28 April 1903, 6.

35 See A. Linden (Leo Motzkin), "Prototyp des Pogroms in den achtzer Jahren," *Die Judenpogrome in Rußland*, vol. 1, 187–92. Motzkin states that altogether 725 pogroms took place.

36 See Shlomo Lambroza, "The Pogroms of 1903–1906," John D. Klier and Shlomo Lambroza, *Pogroms: Anti-Jewish Violence in Modern Russian History*, 228, 230. For an interesting discussion of some of the stated reasons for the violence against Jews and the social makeup of the attackers, see also the "Policing the Riotous City" chapter of Daniel R. Brower's *The Russian City between Tradition and Modernity, 1850–1900*, 188–221.

37 Ivan Bunin, *Russian Requiem 1885–1920: A Portrait from Letters, Diaries, and Fiction*, 95–6. The pogroms of 1881–82 and 1903–05 led to a very significant pickup in the Jewish exodus: between 1881 and 1914 about 2,000,000 Jews left the Russian Empire for Europe, Palestine, and the United States.

38 Campbell, *Today We Will Only Gossip*, 59.

39 Ben Richman, "Second Letter to Joshua."

40 Marjorie Wells to Dr Bentwich, 3 December 1955, CSA.

41 Quoted in Steven J. Zipperstein, *Imagining Russian Jewry: Memory, History, Identity*, 42.

42 Abraham Cahan, *The Rise of David Levinsky*, 16–7.

43 Campbell, *Today We Will Only Gossip*, 160. Like all members of her very musical family, Beatrice Campbell had a beautiful voice and could sing very well. The "piece of paper" is now in CSA. Ben Richman ("Ostropol Map and Description") recalled how, on Friday afternoons in Ostropol, "Shahmes [the synagogue's caretaker] would come out … and give warning 'time to close – for the Sabbath' in a very imperious loud voice."

44 May Sarton, *A World of Light: Portraits and Celebration*, 184.

45 Interview with Jackie Freedman, 26 April 2004.

46 Koteliansky to Pauline Smith, 4 June 1951, JFA.

47 He wrote to his niece that Zhitomir was "the first town I went to study, when

I was young" (Koteliansky to Pauline Smith, 9 February 1945, JFA). Marjorie Wells remembered that he told her he "went to study at Ghitomir when he was fourteen or fifteen" – cited in Richardson, *Windows on Modernism*, 185.

48 Esther Salaman, *A Collection of Moments: A Study of Involuntary Memories*, 91.

49 For a very poignant description of what it took for a Jewish student to get into a good gymnasium (as well as for a very vivid description of a pogrom), see one of Isaac Babel's best autobiographical stories, "The Story of My Dovecot" (*The Complete Works of Isaac Babel*, 601–11).

50 Unpublished interview by Natalie Wexler, 6 September 1991.

51 According to Troinitskii, *Pervaia vseobshchaia perepis' naseleniia Rossiiskoi imperii, 1897 g.* (The First All-Russian Census of the Population of the Russian Empire, Year 1897). For this particular table in English, see "Beyond the Pale: The History of Jews in Russia," www.friends-partners.org/partners/beyond-the-pale/eng_captions/31-11.html.

52 Anton Chekhov, "Ionych," *Lady with the Little Dog and Other Stories, 1896–1914*, 120.

53 Cited in Richardson, *Windows on Modernism*, 185. Martin Packman also cited Koteliansky's "police-enforced stays back in Ostropol" (Martin Packman, email to the author, 31 March 2004).

54 "Mr S.S. Koteliansky. Obituary," in *Times* (London), 27 January 1955, 10. Powell wrote: "As a student at Odessa he had been involved, like so many intellectuals of his time, in revolutionary discussion, and though he was never an active revolutionary he was obliged to live from 1900 to 1906 under police surveillance and at his birthplace."

55 Maxim Gorky, *Fragments from My Diary*, 163.

56 Koteliansky to Pauline Smith, 21 July 1944, JFA.

57 Leonard Woolf, *Beginning Again*, 252–3.

58 Carswell, *Lives and Letters*, 259.

59 Campbell, *Today We Will Only Gossip*, 160–1.

60 Unpublished interview that George Zytaruk conducted with Esther Salaman on 22 June 1967, GZA.

61 For an excellent study of Jews in higher education at the turn of the twentieth century, see Benjamin Nathan, *Beyond the Pale: The Jewish Encounter with Late Imperial Russia*.

62 In CSA.

63 For more information, see, for example, Albert S. Lindermann, *The Jews Accused*, 176.

64 Campbell, *Today We Will Only Gossip*, 59–60.

65 Unpublished interview by Natalie Wexler, 6 September 1991. Harry Wexler also stated there that Volodarsky was their tenant.

66 For more on Volodarsky, see Anatoly Lunacharsky, "Comrade Volodarsky," *Revolutionary Silhouettes*, 114.

67 From Pauline Smith's notes on her uncle. They follow, for most part, the published materials about Koteliansky, with direct quotes from some, like Leonard Woolf's obituary, from where Pauline Smith seems to have borrowed the incorrect year for her uncle's birth – 1882 (JFA; Pauline Smith's letters, notes, and unpublished interviews are quoted here with Jackie Freedman's permission).

68 May Sarton to Margaret Foote Hawley, 12 January 1949 (*Selected Letters, 1916–1954*, 297).

69 Unpublished 1967 Interview with Zytaruk.

70 Esther Salaman, *A Collection of Moments*, 32.

71 For more on BUND, see, for example, Henry J. Tobias, *The Jewish BUND in Russia from Its Origins to 1905*.

72 On how this deed was perceived by his friends in England, see Richard Garnett, *Constance Garnett*, 86.

73 [Sergei] Stepniak, *Underground Russia: Revolutionary Profiles and Sketches from Life*, 39–40.

74 Fanny obtained her residency in St Petersburg by studying medicine during the relatively tolerant period of Alexander II's rule. It was probably there that she met her future husband.

75 In M.E. Ermasheva, *S.M. Stepniak-Kravchinskii v londonskoi emigratsii* (S.M. Stepniak-Kravchinskii in London Emigration), 430.

76 Koteliansky's family in Ostropol probably knew Fanny Stepniak back in Russia since his sister, Rokhl, always referred to Fanny in her letters in very familiar terms. If that was the case, she would have been one of the few people he knew in London when he came in 1911.

77 For a copy of a leaflet, see www.friends-partners.org/partners/beyond-the-pale/eng_captions/37-2.html.

78 Koosis, *Child of War and Revolution*, 9.

79 George Zytaruk, *D.H. Lawrence's Response to Russian Literature*, 42.

80 *Rech'* (Speech) 244, 6 September 1911, 1.


CHAPTER TWO

1 C. Russell and H.S. Lewis, *Jew in London: A Study of Racial Character and Present-Day Conditions*, xvii–xviii.

2 Quoted in Ezekiel Leiken, *The Beilis Transcripts: The Anti-Semitic Trial That Shook the World*, xvi.

3 These numbers can be found in *London's Museum of Jewish Life: An Illustrated Guide*, 7, 10.

4 See Geoffrey Alderman, *London Jewry and London Politics, 1889–1986*, 2–4.

5 Robert Winder, *Bloody Foreigners: The Story of Immigration to Britain*, 131.

6 Winder, *Bloody Foreigners*, 131.

7 Leonard Woolf, *Beginning Again*, 74.

8 John Carswell, *The Exile: A Life of Ivy Litvinov*, 39.

9 Virginia Woolf, "Jews," *Carlyle House and Other Sketches*, 14.

10 The entry is from 4 January 1915: Virginia Woolf, *The Diary*, vol. 1, 6.

11 Virginia Woolf to Ethel Smyth, 2 August 1939, Virginia Woolf, *The Letters*, vol. 4, 195.

12 Quentin Bell, *Bloomsbury Recalled*, 118.

13 Alexander, *Leonard and Virginia Woolf*, 6.

14 Ibid. Strachey's emphasis. See also *Letters of Leonard Woolf*, 470.

15 Alexander, *Leonard and Virginia Woolf*, 6. For an excellent chapter on Leonard's Jewishness vis-à-vis his marriage to Virginia, see also Cynthia Ozick, "Mrs Virginia Woolf: A Madwoman and Her Nurse," *Art & Ardor: Essays*, 27–54.

16 Leonard Woolf, *Sowing: An Autobiography of the Years 1880 to 1904*, 213.

17 Ibid., 17, 21.

18 Ibid., 17, 28.

19 Leonard Woolf, "Three Jews," 5–6. His emphasis.

20 The phrase belongs to a Conservative politician Hope Kyd; quoted in Alderman, *The Jewish Community in British Politics*, 75.

21 Ibid., 71–4. The two Jewish candidates who supported the bill were Harry Lawson and Betram Straus.

22 In Mark Gertler, *Selected Letters*, 23.

23 Sarah MacDougall, *Mark Gertler*, 12–3.

24 John Woodeson, *Mark Gertler: Biography of a Painter, 1891–1939*, 12.

25 Ibid., 13.

26 Arnold Haultain, "England's Plight: A Returned Exile's Impressions," 386, 388.

27 Jane Ellen Harrison, *Reminiscences of a Student's Life*, 32.

28 H.G. Wells, *H.G. Wells in Love: Postscript to an Experiment in Autobiography*, 115. On H.G. Wells and anti-Semitism, see also: Bryant Cheyette, *Constructions of "the Jew" in English Literature and Society: Racial Representations, 1875–1945*, especially his chapter on George Bernard Shaw and H.G. Wells, 94–149.

29 Lawrence to Blanche Jennings, 9 October 1908, *The Letters* of *D.H. Lawrence*, eds James T. Boulton et al., vol. 1, 81.

30 The immediate reason for this outburst was the case of Daisy Lord, who murdered her out-of-wedlock child and in July 1908, amid the protests of UK suffragists, was sentenced to death. A month later the verdict was commuted to life in prison.

31 Lawrence to Edward Garnett, 8 July and 22 August 1912, *Letters* (Boulton), vol. 1, 424, 442.

32 Lawrence to Katharine Clayton, 13 July 1913, and to Edward Garnett, 14 July 1913, *Letters* (Boulton), vol. 2, 37, 39.

33 Brenda Maddox, *D.H. Lawrence: The Story of a Marriage*, 165.

34 Lawrence to Robert Mountsier, 3 March 1921, *Letters* (Boulton), vol. 3, 678.

35 Pauline Smith interview with George Zytaruk, 10 August 1968, GZA.

36 Interview with Catherine Stoye, Oxford, 4 July 2003.

37 In his early London address book, Koteliansky referred to it, most likely without any irony since it was a straightforward recording of someone's address, as "Nothing Hill Gate." This and all the subsequent documents cited here are in CSA.

38 In Spiller, *Papers on Inter-Racial Problems Communicated to the First Universal Races Congress Held at The University of London, July 26–29, 1911*, v.

39 In 1913, not surprisingly, given what we know of the generally liberal bend in his politics, he also attended the "No Conscription International Socialist and Labour Demonstration" held in Kingsway Hall.

40 In Spiller, *Papers on Inter-Racial Problems*, 279, his emphasis. For more on Zangwill, see Meri-Jane Rochelson, *A Jew in the Public Arena: The Career of Israel Zangwill*.

41 Koteliansky to Pauline Smith, 4 March 1947, JFA.

42 *Parliamentary Borough of Kensington in the Administrative Country of London Index to the Several Polling Districts in the North Division, 1911–12*, 442, 479, 518; *Kelly's Kensington, Notting Hill, Brompton & Knightsbridge Directory ("Buff Book" for 1911)*, 275, 377. The house still exists.

43 *Post Office London Directory* (London: Kelly's Directories, 1909–1913), 1012 (1909), 44 (1913).

44 Koteliansky to May Sarton, 19 August 1947, NYPL.

45 In *Electoral Roll for Islington, 1904–1911*. This information is found in three lists: "Division 1 List of Persons entitled to vote as Parliamentary Electors and County Electors," "List of Lodgers," and "List of Persons Entitled to Vote as County Electors and Parochial Electors."

46 Alexandra Kollontai, *The Autobiography of a Sexually Emancipated Communist Woman*, 21.

47 In Lindermann, *The Jews Accused*, 192.

48 Mendel Beilis, *Scapegoat on Trial*, 232.

49 This is according to Harry Wexler, who left Ostropol in 1914. He told his niece that Koteliansky "migrated to London, and without any knowledge of English he learned enough English to become assistant editor of the London Times." Unpublished interview by Natalie Wexler, 6 September 1991.

50 *Post Office London Directory for 1914*, 1256; *Electoral Roll for Holborn, 1913–1914*, 428.

51 Campbell, *Today We Will Only Gossip*, 75.

52 Mansfield to Koteliansky, 19 February 1921, *Collected Letters*, vol. 4, 183.

53 Mansfield to Koteliansky, 17 May 1915, *Collected Letters*, vol. 1, 193.

54 In Campbell, *Today We Will Only Gossip*, 75.

55 In Witter Bynner, *Journey with Genius: Recollections and Reflections Concerning the D.H. Lawrences*, 201.

56 Lawrence to Koteliansky, 18 December 1925 and 7 July 1916, *The Quest for Rananim*, 274, 87 (*Letters*, vol. 4, 355; vol. 2, 623). Zytaruk's edition of D.H. Lawrence's letters to Koteliansky has been superseded by the eight volume Cambridge edition of Lawrence's letters. For my purposes, however, I still found it more helpful to use *The Quest for Rananim* for Lawrence's correspondence with Koteliansky, therefore the quoted letters will refer to that edition – as *Rananim* – first, while pages from the Cambridge edition of Lawrence's letters will be given in parenthesis.

57 Lawrence to Koteliansky, 1 December 1916, *Rananim*, 100 (*Letters*, vol. 3, 43). His emphasis.

58 Lawrence to Koteliansky, 16 February 1918, *Rananim*, 130 (*Letters*, vol. 3, 208).

59 Horne probably knew Lawrence through Gordon Campbell, another barrister and the husband of Lady Glenavy.

60 Catherine Carswell, *The Savage Pilgrimage: A Narrative of D.H. Lawrence*, 23 (unless otherwise specified, all citation are from the 1951 edition).

61 Lawrence to Koteliansky, 18 December 1925, *Rananim*, 274 (*Letters*, vol. 5, 354–5).

62 Lawrence to Lady Asquith, 30 January 1915, *Letters*, vol. 2, 268.

63 Lawrence to Koteliansky, 5 August 1914, *Rananim*, 1 (*Letters*, vol. 2, 205).

64 *The New York Times*, 5 August 1914, 1.

65 Douglas Goldring, "The Lawrences at Home," *D.H. Lawrence: Interviews and Recollections*, ed. Norman Page, vol. 1, 149.

66 Lawrence to Koteliansky, 5 and 31 October 1914, *Rananim*, 5, 10 (*Letters*, vol. 2, 220, 228). *A Study of Thomas Hardy* was not published in Lawrence's lifetime.

67 Leonard Woolf remembered in the obituary how Koteliansky told him about Frieda constantly "lamenting how much she missed her children," to which Kot would say "Frieda, you have left your children to marry Lawrence. You must choose either your children or Lawrence – and if you choose Lawrence, you must stop complaining about children" ("Kot," 172).

68 Lawrence to Koteliansky, 3 December 1914, *Rananim*, 16 (*Letters*, vol. 2, 238).

69 See for example, Lawrence to Koteliansky, 1 January 1919: "My brother in law … a rich Jew & Professor" (*Rananim*, 155 [*Letters*, vol. 3, 316]). Frieda Lawrence's statements in her letters to her family and friends were often so full of anti-Semitic sentiments that Harry T. Moore and Dale B. Montague, the editors of *Frieda Lawrence and Her Circle: Letters from, to, and about Frieda Lawrence*, felt it was necessary to apologize to their readers: "The present editors deplore Frieda's occasional outbursts of anti-Semitism in these letters, which were uncharacteristic of her conversation" (137).

70 "How did you get on with Kotiliansky [*sic*]?" Lawrence asked Gordon Campbell soon after Campbell and Koteliansky met, and then he proceeded to mimic Koteliansky: "He says of you 'He is quite simple, really a simple man. When he is cynical, it is nothing. He knows – he knows'" (2 February 1915, *Letters*, vol. 2, 274).

71 Bertrand Russell to Ottoline Morrell, no day or month, 1915; in Ottoline, *Ottoline at Garsington*, 57, his emphasis. The "Russian cigarettes," for which Kot was so famous, were the ones he rolled himself, using a very strong tobacco that he bought – or, more likely, asked Gertler to buy – in a shop in the Jewish East End. According to Francis Huxley, who visited Koteliansky in the 1940s, he made these cigarettes "with the help of an ingenious device and a boxful of rice- and card- paper tubes some four inches long … Putting one of these in the device, he would then work a small piston to ram an inch or so of tobacco down its muzzle, and out would come a shapely cigarette complete with the holder" (letter to the author, 15 January 2011; quoted here with his permission).

72 Katherine Mansfield, 29 June 1907, *The Katherine Mansfield Notebooks: Complete Edition*, vol. 2, 104.

73 It was not, in fact, till 1935 that a Mansfield scholar, Elizabeth Schneider, made the connection between the two. See Elisabeth Schneider, "Katherine Mansfield and Chekhov," 394–7.

74 Mansfield, 5 July 1918, *Notebooks*, vol. 2, 141. Her emphasis.

75 Mansfield, 20 January 1922, *Notebooks*, vol. 2, 318.

76 John Middleton Murry, *Between Two Worlds: The Autobiography*, 322.

77 See Katherine Mansfield's entry in her journal from 5 January 1920, where she writes: "Worked on Tchehov all day" (*Journal*, 140). The book – *The Life and Letters of Anton Tchekhov*, translated and edited by S.S. Koteliansky and Philip Tomlinson – bore an acknowledgment of Mansfield's contribution to the translation of two of the letters.

78 Virginia Woolf, 13 March 1921, *Diary*, vol. 2, 99–100.

79 Mansfield to Murry, 16 December 1915, Mansfield, *Letters between Katherine Mansfield and John Middleton Murry*, 66.

80 Lawrence to Koteliansky, 5 and 9 August 1914, *Rananim*, 1–2 (*Letters*, vol. 2, 205, 206); Mansfield to Samuel Koteliansky, 1 and 5 February 1915, Mansfield, *Collected Letters*, vol. 1, 147; Gertler to Koteliansky, 15 and 17 August 1915 (Gertler's letters are in BL/Kot; all unpublished letters by Mark Gertler are quoted here with the permission of his son, Luke Gertler).

81 Quoted in Jeffrey Meyers, *Katherine Mansfield: A Biography*, 129.

82 Dorothy Brett, *Lawrence and Brett: A Friendship*, 17.

83 D.H. Lawrence, *Kangaroo*, 108, 114.

84 In Edward Nehls, *D.H. Lawrence: A Composite Biography*, vol 1, 267. Also reprinted in Page, *D.H. Lawrence: Interviews and Recollections*, vol. 1, 111.

85 Campbell, *Today We Will Only Gossip*, 59.

86 Quoted in Noble, *Recollections of Virginia Woolf*, 145.

87 Campbell, *Today We Will Only Gossip*, 173.

88 Koteliansky to Esther Salaman, Tuesday (no date), NWA. He also added: "It is a bit embarrassing for me to admit it, but that's how I really feel." The letter

is in Russian. "Pogromshchik" means a person who is actively involved in bloody violence against Jews, or pogroms.

89 Ottoline Morrell, *Memoirs of Lady Ottoline Morrell: A Study in Friendship, 1873–1915*, 231.

90 The only recorded and very brief contact occurred in 1936, when Lopokova sent Kot two tickets to Ibsen's "Master Builder," at the Arts Theatre of Cambridge, with which she and Keynes were involved at the time. Kot had apparently tried earlier to interest them in staging Chekhov's *Seagull* or *Wood Demon*. They were not interested but assured Kot that they "read [Wood Demon] out loud between themselves." Three brief letters, two from Lopokova and one from Keynes (March–June 1936) are all in English and quite formal, with Lopokova addressing him as "Dear Mr Koteliansky," while Keynes is slightly more chummy with "Dear Koteliansky." On 11 June, Keynes invited Kot to lunch but by then Kot was experiencing a serious breakdown and declined. The letters are in BL/Kot, unpublished. For more on this correspondence, see Andrei Rogatchevski, "Samuel Koteliansky and the Bloomsbury Circle," 370–2. For more on Lopokova, see also Judith Mackrell, *The Bloomsbury Ballerina: Lydia Lopokova, Imperial Dancer and Mrs John Maynard Keynes*.

91 A.S. Fulton to George Zytaruk, 22 June 1972, GZA.

92 Campbell, *Today We Will Only Gossip*, 102.

93 Lawrence to Kotel" Kotel" Lawrence to Kotel иansky, 11 November 1914, *Rananim*, 12 (*Letters*, vol. 2, 231).

94 Campbell, *Today We Will Only Gossip*, 102, 159.

95 Sarton, *I Knew a Phoenix*, 211. See also, for example, John Carswell, "He could be touchy and quarrelsome, and was given to dark fits of depression, but his sympathy and loyalty to his friends were unquestioned. His shoulder was always there to be leant upon, though his critical opinions were at no man's bidding" (*Lives and Letters*, 89), or Ida Baker, "To him an enemy was always an enemy, but nothing could shake his faith once his friendship was truly given" (*Katherine Mansfield*, 92).

96 Mansfield to Baker, 13 March 1921, *Collected Letters*, vol. 4, 190.

97 Lawrence to Koteliansky, 17 December 1914, *Rananim*, 19 (*Letters*, vol. 2, 242). Around the same time, Lawrence wrote to Amy Lowell, telling her that "the critics will plainly beat me, as a Russian friend says" for the book he was writing on Thomas Hardy (*Letters*, vol. 2, 243).

98 Quoted in Campbell, *Today We Will Only Gossip*, 191. His emphasis.

99 Koteliansky to Gertler, undated but since it is the same letter where he discusses his "'inspiration' to go to Russia," most likely summer 1917 (LGA).

100 Koteliansky to Baker, 3 July 1952, ATL/KM.

101 Lawrence to Alfred Decker Hawk, 4 May 1925, *Letters*, vol. 5, 205.

102 Lawrence to Koteliansky, 18 November 1914, *Rananim*, 14 (*Letters*, vol. 2, 233).

103 Lawrence to Koteliansky, 17 December 1914, *Rananim*, 19 (*Letters*, vol. 2, 242).

104 Lawrence to Barbara Low, 10 March 1915, *Letters*, vol. 2, 305, 306.

105 Lawrence to Koteliansky, 21 December 1914, *Rananim*, 20, 21 (*Letters*, vol. 2, 250–1).

106 D.H. Lawrence, *The White Peacock*, 44, 237.

107 Ibid., 108, 146, 173. The suggestion that "devil of the wood" (146) may be a reference to Chekhov's play can be found in the editor's note on p. 378. It is plausible, although I am not sure *The Wood Demon*, unlike its later version, *Uncle Vanya*, was all that well known in England even to those who, like Lawrence, followed Russian literature very closely. "Matouchka" (173) – or, more precisely, "matochka" – is one of the diminutives for Russian "mat'" (mother). Another possibility is that it is an awkward transliteration of another diminutive for the same word – "matushka."

108 Lawrence, *The White Peacock*, 274.

109 Ibid., 222–3. Lawrence's *Rainbow*, which he finished in 1915, contains a similarly homoerotic bathing scene, but it involves two women – Ursula and Winifred. The full scene has been cut from many editions; for the unabridged version see, for example, D.H. Lawrence, *The Rainbow* (unabridged), 344.

CHAPTER THREE

1 Campbell, *Today We Will Only Gossip*, 59.

2 CSA.

3 Among them was Charles Frohman, an American Jew who had produced J.M. Barrie's *Peter Pan* both in London and New York. Acclaimed as "the world's greatest *entrepreneur*," Frohman was one of the successful "cosmopolitan" Jews whom Israel Zangwill had cited as an example of Jewish viability during the First Universal Races Congress, which Kot had attended in July 1911 (*Papers on Inter-Racial Problems*, 274). For more on Frohman, see Isaac F. Marcosson and Daniel Frohman, *Charles Frohman: Manager and Man*.

4 It was founded by another James Knowles, unrelated, as far as I know, to the James Knowles with whom Kot was apparently staying in 1911. For more on this Knowles, see Priscilla Metcalf, *James Knowles: Victorian Editor and Architect*.

5 G.G. Coulton, "Voluntary or Compulsory Service," 1–28.

6 Gertler to Carrington, 1 July 1915, Gertler, *Selected Letters*, 96–7.

7 Anton Chekhov, *The Bet and Other Stories*, v.

8 Ibid., 10–11.

9 For the reminiscences of V.D. Nabokov, Kornei Chukovsky, and Aleksei Tolstoy, who were a part of the delegation, see O.A. Kaznina and A.N. Nikoliukin, eds, *"Ia bereg pokidal tumannyi Al'biona": Russkie pisateli ob Anglii. 1646–1945* ("I Was Leaving the Foggy Shore of Albion": Russian Writers on England. 1646–1945), 362–89.

10  Murry, *Between Two Worlds*, 344

11  Lawrence to Koteliansky, 15 December 1916, *Rananim*, 192 (*Letters*, vol. 3, 53).

12  Dostoevsky, *Pages from the Journal of An Author: Fyodor Dostoevsky*, viii, xiv. Murry was incensed by this reaction: "[H]e jumped on my Dostoevsky book … He did not trouble to read it … Since there was a good deal of hero-worship of Dostoevsky in the book, he had me fairly on the raw … It is much easier to accept an insult to oneself than one's hero" (*Between Two Worlds*, 424).

13  Mansfield, 7 January 1915, *Notebooks*, vol. 2, 3.

14  Mansfield, 27 January 1915, *Notebooks*, vol. 2, 7.

15  Mansfield, 29 January 1915, *Notebooks*, vol. 2, 8.

16  Mansfield to Koteliansky, 8 March 1915, *Collected Letters*, vol. 1, 152–3.

17  Mansfield to Koteliansky, 22 March 1915, *Collected Letters*, vol. 1, 163.

18  Quoted in Woodeson, *Mark Gertler*, 177. The letter is not in the British Library.

19  Gertler to Koteliansky, 15 August 1915, BL/Kot.

20  Woolf, *Beginning Again*, 252.

21  Mansfield to Koteliansky, 1 and 26 February 1915, *Collected Letters*, vol. 1, 147, 151.

22  Mansfield to Koteliansky, 4 February and 10 March 1915, *Collected Letters*, vol. 1, 147, 153.

23  Mansfield to Koteliansky, 29 March 1915, *Collected Letters*, vol. 1, 173–4.

24  Mansfield to Koteliansky, 1 and early March 1915, *Collected Letters*, vol. 1, 151–2.

25  Murry, *Between Two Worlds*, 404.

26  Mansfield to Koteliansky, 29 March 1915, *Collected Letters*, vol. 1, 173.

27  Carswell, *Lives and Letters*, 259. His suspicion was apparently further confirmed by seeing an early letter from Mansfield that did not make it to the British Library Archive: "'Koteliansky,' she wrote, 'it is my turn to give. Tell me what shall I give? One thing if you want it is yours to keep.' Whether this hint or a later one was the occasion, it later had to be withdrawn … There is one undated letter … that was not even included in the papers … bequeathed to the British Museum. It runs thus: 'No dear Koteliansky, my letter did not 'mean that'" (*Lives and Letters*, 101–2). Since the second, unpublished, letter is undated, it is of course quite a leap to assume it was in response to that particular offer that, in turn, could have been as trivial as an object, like a walking stick, that Kot liked.

28  Meyers, *Katherine Mansfield: A Biography*, 109, and Nora Crone, *A Portrait of Katherine Mansfield*, where she writes: "Kot fell in love with Katherine" (143). The scholar in question was Ruth Mantz: see Ruth Mantz, "In Consequence: Katherine and Kot," 107. The full quote is: "He also said once, inconsequently, 'If Kat'run ever wanted a greater relationship with me, she had only to indicate it.' After a silence, he added, 'Everything she did she did as a writer. She knew that with a strong man, she would not become a writer.'" Mantz's essay,

however, is so fictionalized (she imagines Mansfield's thoughts and quotes Mansfield and Koteliansky's conversation verbatim, as if she had been there and took it all down) that one tends to take her description of what Koteliansky told her with a healthy dosage of skepticism. A totally fictional account, based on Mansfield's life, by Linda Lappin presents an even more preposterous picture of Kot in love, with long gazes, sighs, and "I am yours forever" declarations – see *Katherine's Wish*, 92. Fictional portrayals of Mansfield's life appear to be a small industry these days – see also C. K. Stead, *Mansfield: A Novel*.

29 Koteliansky to Mansfield, 26 September 1919. The letter is published in full in Geraldine L. Conroy, "Our Perhaps Uncommon Friendship," 365.

30 Koteliansky to Brett, 10 August 1921, HRC/DB. Koteliansky habitually spells "in spite of" as "inspite of," as will become obvious in his subsequent letters, and so does Mark Gertler, who is, in general, a rather poor speller.

31 Antony Alpers, *The Life of Katherine Mansfield*, 168.

32 Catherine Carswell, *The Savage Pilgrimage*, 23.

33 Ibid., 219.

34 Brett to Koteliansky, 3 August 1921. The letter is published in George J. Zytaruk, "Dorothy Brett's Letters to S.S. Koteliansky," 245. The exact wording of the postcript is somewhat in question, though. A typed copy of the letter can be found in CSA. In that copy it reads "there is somewhere some men," which, of course, does not make any grammatical sense yet the typo here could be either "is" or "men." Kot, in his response, seems to justify the reading of "men": "At the end of your letter you say that it is wrong my being alone, that there are people who would interest me, etc. It is quite correct. I am sure that there are very nice people, whom it would be a joy to meet and be friendly with … But what can I in the mood I have been in for the last 8–9 months, give anyone, except a feeling of awkwardness" (22 August 1921, HRC/DB). George Zytaruk believes that he saw the originals in CSA in the early 1970s when he was working on the publication of "Dorothy Brett's Letters to S.S. Koteliansky" (email to the author, 17 September 2007). When Koteliansky died, his will specified that letters should be sent back to their addressees if they were still alive – with the exception of Frieda Lawrence and Dorothy Brett, since their letters could shed light on Lawrence's life and therefore, according to Koteliansky, belonged to the British Museum. Marjorie Wells was probably reluctant to do so, but Frieda's death following a year after Koteliansky's made that decision easy, and her letters did find their way to the British Museum. What happened to Brett's letters is not clear. By the time I examined CSA, the originals were no longer there, but they are also neither among Koteliansky's materials in the British Library nor among Dorothy Brett's papers at the University of New Mexico. The copies I saw

must have been made within the seven years that separated Koteliansky's death from Marjorie Wells's.

35 Frieda Lawrence to Koteliansky, Wednesday (no date) 1923, Frieda Lawrence, *Memoirs and Correspondence*, 222.

36 Koteliansky's legs were somewhat disproportionately short for his torso, so Frieda apparently liked to refer to them as "little slave legs," Carswell, *Lives and Letters*, 268.

37 Mabel Dodge Luhan, *Lorenzo in Taos*, 50. Her emphasis.

38 Bynner, *Journey with Genius*, 201.

39 Koteliansky to Gertler, 26 August 1916, LGA.

40 Frieda Lawrence to Koteliansky, 19 February 1915, D.H. Lawrence, *Letters*, vol. 2, 290. Can also be found in Frieda Lawrence, *The Memoirs and Correspondence*, 195, where it is misdated as "February 9, 1915." Her emphasis.

41 The letter is from March 1916; quoted in Harry T. Moore, *The Intelligent Heart: The Story of D.H. Lawrence*, 213. Her emphasis.

42 Frieda Lawrence to Harry T. Moore, 14 January 1955, *The Memoirs and Correspondence*, 390. The scene was apparently witnessed by Catherine Carswell, who was visiting them in Cornwell in 1916 – see *Savage Pilgrimage*, 76.

43 Frieda Lawrence to Koteliansky, 1 and 3 July 1932, BL/Kot. Her emphasis. Reproduced by permission of Pollinger Limited and The Estate of Frieda Lawrence Ravagli. See appendix E for the full 3 July letter.

44 Frieda Lawrence to Koteliansky, undated [stamp on the envelope: 17 July 1932], BL/Kot. Reproduced by permission of Pollinger Limited and The Estate of Frieda Lawrence Ravagli. See appendix E for the full letter.

45 Murry was drawn even more strongly to Gordon Campbell, who, in turn, felt very uncomfortable with the intensity and nature of Murry's attachment. In *Today We Will Only Gossip*, Campbell included a letter Murry wrote to her husband on 1 February 1915, in which he said: "I can hear Lawrence say that it [love] would only be possible between a man and a woman. I don't think so. It was possible for us, had you been other than you are" (66). In connection with that, Lawrence wrote to Gordon on 3 March 1915: "I was not hostile to you with Murry. I told him I thought you were very sound and healthy not to want his close love" (*Letters*, vol. 2, 301).

46 Murry to Mansfield, 11 May 1915, quoted in Mansfield, *Collected Letters*, vol. 1, 187.

47 Mansfield to Murry, 14 May 1915, *Collected Letters*, vol. 1, 187.

48 Mansfield to Koteliansky, *Collected Letters*, vol. 1, 191, 193.

49 Lawrence to David Garnett, 19 April 1915, *Letters*, vol. 2, 320–1.

50 Lawrence to Koteliansky, 20 April 1915, *Rananim*, 39 (*Letters*, vol. 2, 323).

51 Lawrence to David Garnett, *Letters*, vol. 2, 320–1. For Garnett's bristling response to Lawrence's letter see Nehls, *D.H. Lawrence: A Composite Biography*:

"Lawrence's letter made me angry. He seemed to me to be mad and determined to interfere in my life ... In retrospect the most astonishing thing was Lawrence's dislike of Frankie [Birrell]. Everyone else who ever knew him, of whatever age or sex, nationality or class, was charmed and delighted by him" (vol. 1, 302).

52  Lawrence to Philip Heseltine, 22 November 1915, *Letters*, vol. 2, 448. His emphasis.

53  Frieda Lawrence to Edward Gilbert, 17 September 1944, *Memoirs and Correspondence*, 295.

54  Lawrence, *Women in Love*, 503, 511, 514.

55  Ibid., 352. His emphasis. For a lengthy discussion of Lawrence's views on homosexuality, see Jeffrey Meyers, "D.H. Lawrence and Homosexuality," in Stephen Spender, *D.H. Lawrence: Novelist, Poet Prophet*, 135–46.

56  Lawrence to Mansfield, 5 December 1918, *Letters*, vol. 3, 301.

57  *Between Two Worlds*, 262, 413.

58  See for example, Jeffrey Meyers, *D.H. Lawrence: A Biography*: "Lawrence modeled the physical description (but not the personality) of Ben Cooley ... on Kot" (129).

59  Typical here is the following uninformed and inaccurate description of who Koteliansky was: "He was a Pole, knew Hebrew, and gave the island the name of Rananim." It can be found in Hugh Kingsmill, *The Life of D.H. Lawrence*, 108. Since the biography was written in 1938, Kingsmill – just like Harry T. Moore did later – could have easily interviewed Koteliansky to learn more about him. Inaccurate descriptions of Koteliansky persist to this day. See, for example, Janet Byrne, *A Genius for Living: The Life of Frieda Lawrence*: "Koteliansky [was] a morose, hopelessly romantic political refugee and translator ... on an economics scholarship from Kiev University. Lawrence liked his orderliness, impeccable manners, love of ceremony over tea, white shirts with colourfully embroidered neckbands, and frizzy hair ... Kot ... had a sturdy ego and an aptitude for difficult people" (160); "impeccable manners," "love of ceremony," and "sturdy ego" are the direct opposites of what Kot really was.

60  Moore, *Intelligent Heart*, 292. Moore also suggested that Maxim Libidnikov in *Women in Love* "may have been partly a portrait of Koteliansky" (239), which I find less convincing since Maxim's description as a "suave" and "prim young Russian with smooth warm-coloured face and black, oiled hair" is hardly a good match for Kot.

61  Virginia Woolf to Jacques-Émile Blanche, 20 August 1927, *Letters*, vol. 6, 517.

62  Lawrence, *Kangaroo*, 111, 151. His emphasis.

63  See, for example, Virginia Woolf's comment in on 18 March 1936: "Kot ... the same as ever: rather heavier, yellower ..." (*Diary*, vol. 5, 18).

64 Lawrence, *Kangaroo*, 110–11. His emphasis.

65 Lawrence to Koteliansky, 23 December 1927, *Rananim*, 334 (*Letters*, vol. 6, 247).

66 Lawrence, *Kangaroo*, 210.

67 Ibid., 209. His emphasis.

68 Lawrence to Koteliansky, 18 September 1918, *Rananim*, 150 (*Letters*, vol. 3, 284–5).

69 Lawrence, *Kangaroo*, 207.

70 Ibid., 301.

71 Ibid., 205, 206.

72 Ibid., 208. His emphasis.

73 Ibid., 209–11. His emphasis.

74 Cecil Gray, in Nehls, *D.H. Lawrence: A Composite Biography*, vol. 1, 352. Gray was unapologetic about not being a Lawrence fan: "Not many people … can have had so many and such good friends as I have had; but Lawrence was not one of them, and the fault was not mine … Friendship with Lawrence was essentially a one-way traffic. One was expected to give everything without a question. In return you received the scintillations and coruscations of his remarkable mind and sensibility…" (Cecil Gray, *Musical Chairs or Between Two Stools*, 136–7).

75 Unpublished 1967 interview with Zytaruk.

76 Lawrence to Koteliansky, 7 January 1915, *Rananim*, 23 (*Letters*, vol. 2, 256).

77 Lawrence to Koteliansky, 3 January 1915; *Rananim*, 22 (*Letters*, vol. 2, 252).

78 "The promised land has had many names," writes K.W. Gransden, a Lawrence scholar, who first described the collection of Lawrence's letters to Koteliansky bequeathed to the British Museum and Library. "Lawrence's name for it was *Rananim*. This is difficult to explain, but it seems probable that Kot may have bestowed it. It may have had something to do with the Hebrew root meaning 'rejoice'" ("Rananim: D.H. Lawrence's Letters to S.S. Koteliansky," 23).

79 Lawrence to William Hopkin, 18 January 1915, *Letters*, vol. 2, 259.

80 I am grateful to my UW colleague, Naomi Sokoloff, for helping me with Hebrew.

81 Frieda Lawrence to Koteliansky, 6 February 1917, *Memoirs and Reminiscences*, 209 (with a slight correction based on the original letter, which is among Koteliansky's Papers in the British Library).

82 Lawrence to Koteliansky, 14 January 1922, *Rananim*, 232 (*Letters*, vol. 4, 165).

83 Frieda Lawrence, *"Not I, But the Wind …": Memoirs of Her Husband*, 81.

84 In August 2004 a typhoon named "Rananim" swept across China.

85 Lawrence to Koteliansky, 5 February 1915, *Rananim*, 28 (*Letters*, vol. 2, 276–7).

86 Lawrence to Koteliansky, 22 February 1915, *Rananim*, 30 (*Letters*, vol. 2, 290). His emphasis.

87 Lawrence to Koteliansky, 10 March 1915, *Rananim*, 32 (*Letters*, vol. 2, 305).

88 Lawrence to Koteliansky, 8 April 1915, *Rananim*, 36 (*Letters*, vol. 2, 313). His emphasis.

89 Campbell, *Today We Will Only Gossip*, 191. Oblomov is the protagonist in Ivan Goncharov's 1856 novel *Oblomov*, who is famous for spending most of his life sleeping.

90 Robert Machray, "The Resiliency of Russia," 1277.

91 Percy Dearmer, "The Soul of Russia," 81, 72, 73, 75.

92 Esther Salaman told George Zytaruk in 1967 that "Farbman was connected with a publishing house in Berlin and … Kot got all his Russian books from there" (unpublished 1967 interview with Zytaruk).

93 Michael S. Farbman, *Russia and the Struggle for Peace*; and *After Lenin: The New Phase in Russia*. The interview even made it (corrected by Lenin) into Lenin, *Collected Works*, 383–9.

94 Lawrence to Koteliansky, 20 January 1918, *Rananim*, 129 (*Letters*, vol. 3, 198).

95 Unpublished 1967 interview with Zytaruk.

96 Lawrence to Koteliansky, 3 May 1915, *Rananim*, 42 (*Letters*, vol. 2, 333).

97 Lawrence to Bertrand Russell, 29 April 1915, *Letters*, vol. 2, 328.

98 Lawrence to Koteliansky, 19 May 1915, *Rananim*, 44 (*Letters*, vol. 2, 343).

99 Lawrence to Ottoline Morrell, 19 May 1915, *Letters*, vol. 2, 345.

100 D.H. Lawrence, *Sons and Lovers*, 14.

101 Lawrence to Koteliansky, 22 July 1915, *Rananim*, 45 (*Letters*, vol. 2, 369).

102 At least one of the friends was probably Farbman, who was trying to secure Russian translations of Lawrence for Grzhebin Publishing House.

103 Lawrence to Koteliansky, 23 August 1915, *Rananim*, 46 (*Letters*, vol. 2, 382).

104 Ibid.

105 Lawrence to Ottoline Morrell, 9 September 1915, *Letters*, vol. 2, 389.

106 Lawrence to Lady Asquith, 20 September 1915, *Letters*, vol. 2, 397.

107 In his recollections, Murry was modest about his role and generous about Koteliansky's: "I should be only too pleased to take all the credit for the venture if it belonged to me; but the credit belonged to us all, and not least to Koteliansky. We were all implicated" (*Reminiscences of D.H. Lawrence*, 70).

108 Lawrence to Koteliansky, 7 October 1915, *Rananim*, 47 (*Letters*, vol. 2, 407).

109 CSA. The diary has entries for 1914 and 1915. This entry, dated "October 11, 1915," is the last one in it. Murry probably left it on Acacia Road, and that is how it came to be among Koteliansky's possessions. The entry was previously published by John Carswell in *Lives and Letters*, 111.

110 Campbell, *Today We Will Only Gossip*, 83. Glenavy mistakenly remembered that the dinner was at their place instead. The "shawl" was probably a dress – the embroidered Russian peasant dress that Kot had given her. "You cannot think how much I like it," she had told him in February, when he gave it to her. "It is very lovely and there is something almost fairy about it" (Mansfield to Koteliansky, 26 February 1915, *Collected Letters*, vol. 1, 151).

111 Lawrence to Koteliansky, 11 October 1915, *Rananim*, 51 (*Letters*, vol. 2, 409). The question mark is missing in the letter.

112 Mansfield to Koteliansky, 19 November 1915, *Collected Letters*, vol. 1, 199.

113 Mansfield to Michael Farbman, 11 November 1915, CSA. Well into the 1930s and beyond, Kot, according to Esther Salaman, still paid "only 84 pounds a year" for the entire house (1967 interview with Zytaruk).

114 Mansfield to Koteliansky, 19 November 1915, *Collected Letters*, vol. 1, 199. Her emphasis.

115 Gertler to Koteliansky, August 19 1915, *Selected Letters*, 89. His emphasis.

116 Gertler to Carrington, ? January 1915, *Selected Letters*, 81.

117 Gertler to Lytton Strachey, 27 January 1915, *Selected Letters*, 109.

118 Gertler to Carrington, ? January 1915, *Selected Letters*, 79. His emphasis.

119 Quoted in MacDougall, *Mark Gertler*, 95.

120 Gertler to Brett, ? January 1914, *Selected Letters*, 63.

121 Gertler to Koteliansky, [August 1915], *Selected Letters*, 89; revised here to include the word "very," which is in the original letter, as well as to add the date which in the book is listed as "? 1915" since the letter is undated. The envelope in which the letter came is, however, postmarked 19 August 1915 (BL/Kot).

122 Gilbert Cannan, *Mendel*, 285. "Mendel" is not the only nonfictional name in the novel, so is "Golda," the name of the protagonist's, and Gertler's own, mother.

123 Lawrence to Koteliansky, 20 November 1916, *Rananim*, 96 (*Letters*, vol. 3, 35). His emphasis.

124 Lawrence to Catherine Carswell, 2 December 1916, *Letters*, vol. 3, 44.

125 Lawrence to Barbara Low, 11 December 1916, *Letters*, vol. 3, 50.

126 Gertler to Brett, ? January 1914, *Selected Letters*, 63. His emphasis.

127 Quoted in MacDougall, *Mark Gertler*, 96–7.

128 Quoted in ibid, 93.

129 Cannan, *Mendel*, 78.

130 Ibid., 136, 146.

131 Ibid., 53, 319.

132 Ibid., 53.

133 Ibid., 89.

134 Ibid., 53, 124.

135 Ibid., 350.

136 Ibid., 362, 391.

137 The review appeared in *New Witness*. Quoted in Woodeson, *Mark Gertler*, 238.

138 A review of Gertler's posthumous show that took place in 1941 was too dismissive of Gertler's non-Jewish art, but it did carry at least a kernel of truth when it stated: "What he seemed to lack was delicacy of understanding – except in his interpretations of his own Jewish people – though he could achieve a very high degree of smooth finish" (*Times* [London], 16 May 1941, 6).

139 Gertler to Koteliansky, 3 February 1916, *Selected Letters*, 108. Revised according to the original in BL/Kot. The published version reads: "What a nightmare it is to me!"

140 Lawrence to Ottoline Morrell, 12 December 1915, *Letters*, vol. 2, 474.

141 D.H. and Frieda Lawrence to Koteliansky, 23 December 1915, *Rananim*, 60 (*Letters*, vol. 2, 483). Frieda's emphasis.

142 Lawrence to Ottoline Morrell, 25 February 1916, *Letters*, vol. 2, 557. Ottoline Morrell would, indeed, like Koteliansky very much – but their close friendship did not begin until already after Lawrence's death.

143 Mansfield to Murry, 23 December 1915, *Collected Letters*, vol. 1, 225.

144 Mansfield to Koteliansky, [late December 1915], *Collected Letters*, vol. 1, 238–9. Her emphasis.

CHAPTER FOUR

1 Lawrence to Koteliansky, 2 March 1916, *Rananim*, 73 (*Letters*, vol. 2, 73). His emphasis.

2 Lawrence to Koteliansky, 3 July 1917, *Rananim*, 120–1 (*Letters*, vol. 3, 136–7).

3 Lawrence to Koteliansky, 1 December 1916, *Rananim*, 100 (*Letters*, vol. 3, 100). His emphasis. The whereabouts of this portrait are unknown, and it is feared to have been lost. There are, likewise, no reproductions. Both Woodeson and editors of Gertler's *Selected Letters* erroneously identify a later, 1921, portrait as the one Lawrence was commenting on.

4 Lawrence to Waldo Frank, 27 July 1917, *Letters*, vol. 3, 144. His emphasis.

5 Lawrence to Waldo Frank, 15 September 1917, *Letters*, vol. 3, 160.

6 Lawrence to David Eder, 24 August 1917, *Letters*, vol. 3, 150.

7 Douglas Goldring, *Life Interests*, 84. His emphasis.

8 Lawrence to Katherine Mansfield, 10 December 1918, *Letters*, vol. 3, 307.

9 Koteliansky to Gertler, 10 August 1916, LGA.

10 Gertler to Koteliansky, 16 August 1916, *Selected Letters*, 119.

11 Gertler to Carrington, 14 August 1916, *Selected Letters*, 117.

12 Murry to Koteliansky, 19 May 1916, CSA. Reproduced with the permission of The Society of Authors as the Literary Representative of the Estate of John Middleton Murry.

13 Koteliansky to Gertler. The letter is undated, but other topics in it suggest that it too was written in summer 1916. LGA.

14 Koteliansky to Gertler, 10 August 1916, LGA.

15 Lawrence to Koteliansky, 12 September 1916, *Rananim*, 93 (*Letters*, vol. 2, 654–5).

16 See Colin Holmes, *Anti-Semitism in British Society*, 126.

17 Koteliansky to Gertler, 16 July 1916, LGA.

18 Lawrence to Koteliansky, 29 June 1916, *Rananim*, 83 (*Letters*, vol. 2, 618).

19 Lawrence to Koteliansky, 4 July 1916, *Rananim*, 84 (*Letters*, vol. 2, 622).

20 Lawrence to Koteliansky, 10 July 1916, *Rananim*, 87 (*Letters*, vol. 2, 628).

21 Lawrence to Koteliansky, 7 July 1916, *Rananim*, 86 (*Letters*, vol. 2, 622).

22 Lawrence to Koteliansky, 4 September 1916, *Rananim*, 91 (*Letters*, vol. 2, 650).

23 The language of the Convention can be found in David Englander, *A Documentary History of Jewish Immigrants in Britain 1840–1920*, 327–9.

24 In CSA. The document is entitled "Anglo-Russian Convention: Military Service (Convention with Allied States Act), 1917."

25 He used it, for example, in one of his letters to Gertler (Wednesday; otherwise undated, probably 1918, LGA)

26 Gertler to Brett, 10 February 1916, quoted in MacDougall, *Mark Gertler*, 126.

27 Koteliansky to Gertler, undated, except for "Monday," probably March 1919, judging by Gertler's response that month (LGA). Also reproduced in Gertler, *Selected Letters*, 170. His emphasis.

28 Quoted in MacDougall, *Mark Gertler*, 139.

29 See Lawrence to Gertler, 5 December 1916, *Letters* vol. 2, 46. Gertler was talking at the time about making a sculpture based on the painting as well. In the novel, the sculptor named Loerke makes a granite frieze on top of a factory, which is a scene from a fair where the masses enjoy "whirling ridiculously in roundabouts" (Lawrence, *Women in Love*, 423).

30 Lawrence to Gertler, 9 October 1916, *Letters*, vol. 2, 660–1. His emphasis. While Lawrence assured Gertler in the 5 December letter that the sculptor in the novel "is not you" (*Letters*, vol. 2, 46), Loerke is also supposed to be "a Jew – or part Jewish" (*Women in Love*, 428).

31 7 November 1916, *Rananim*, 95 (*Letters*, vol. 3, 23). His emphasis.

32 Quoted in Luhan, *Lorenzo in Taos*, 78.

33 Lawrence to Gordon Campbell, 25 January 1917, *Letters*, vol. 3, 82.

34 Koteliansky to Gertler, 26 August 1918, LGA. Reproduced in Gertler, *Selected Letters*, 162.

35 Mansfield to Ottoline Morrell, 17 May 1916, *Collected Letters*, vol. 1, 267.

36 Mansfield to Koteliansky, 11 May, 24 June, and 27 June 1916, *Collected Letters*, vol. 1, 262–3, 269.

37 Frieda Lawrence to Koteliansky, 20 September 1916, *Memoirs and Correspondence*, 203.

38 Frieda Lawrence to Koteliansky, 4 October 1916, *Memoirs and Correspondence*, 205.

39 Frieda Lawrence to Koteliansky, 15 October 1916, *Memoirs and Correspondence*, 205. Her emphasis.

40 Lawrence to Koteliansky, 15 October 1916, *Rananim*, 94 (*Letters*, vol. 2, 667).

41 Koteliansky to Gertler. "Tuesday," but otherwise undated. LGA. Gertler's 19 July 1918 letter, to which this is a response, can be found in *Selected Letters*, 161. (Koteliansky's letter is reproduced there as well.)

42 Virginia Woolf, 18 January 1918, *Diary*, vol. 1, 108.

43 Koteliansky to Gertler. "Tuesday" but otherwise undated. Since in the same letter Koteliansky describes seeing the Ballets Russes' *Petroushka*, the letter is from autumn 1918 (LGA).

44 Mansfield to Ottoline Morrell, 28 December 1917, *Collected Letters*, vol. 1, 363.

45 Lawrence to Koteliansky, 23 December 1916, *Rananim*, 105 (*Letters*, vol. 3, 62).

46 Koteliansky to Mary Hutchinson, 10 April 1917, HRC/MH.

47 Campbell, *Today We Will Only Gossip*, 103. Kot's English friends got to know Stepniak quite well, with Lawrence being particularly impressed by her: "I find in her a beauty infinitely lovelier than the beauty of the young women I know. She has lived, and suffered, and taken her place in the realities. Now, neither riches, nor rank nor violence matter to her, she *knows* what life consists in, and she never fails her knowledge" (Lawrence to Sallie Hopkin, 22 April 1917, *Letters*, vol. 3, 116; his emphasis).

48 See, for example, Lawrence, letter to Robert Nichols, 21 April 1917, where Lawrence gives Nichols Kot's address and says: "I am here until Monday or Tuesday" (*Letters*, vol. 3, 23).

49 In Russian with occasional words in English. His emphasis. Farbman was a logical conduit for messages from Gorky since Gorky and Farbman's brother-in-law, Grzhebin, were close friends and collaborators at the time.

50 Especially enthusiastic responses came from the leaders of the Independent Labour Party, Macdonald and Snowden – see BL/Kot.

51 G.B. Shaw to Koteliansky, 30 April 1917. BL/Kot

52 Lawrence to Koteliansky, 1 May 1917, *Rananim*, 117 (*Letters*, vol. 3, 121).

53 Koteliansky to Gertler, undated but most likely April or early May 1917, LGA.

54 Lawrence to J.B. Pinker, 20 January 1917, *Letters*, vol. 3, 79.

55 Lawrence to Koteliansky, 9 February 1917, *Rananim*, 109 (*Letters*, vol. 3, 90).

56 Frieda Lawrence to Koteliansky, 6 February 1917, *Memoirs and Correspondence*, 209–11. In the same letter she asked Kot to try to catch a glimpse of her children and then report to her alone, since Lawrence would be angry if he found out that Frieda was still sending their friends on spying missions of this kind.

57 Lawrence to Koteliansky, 1 April 1917, *Rananim*, 112 (*Letters*, vol. 3, 108).

58 Lawrence to Koteliansky, 3 July 1917, *Rananim*, 120 (*Letters*, vol. 3, 136–7).

59 It was published in New York by Thomas Seltzer.

60 Lawrence to Koteliansky, 11 May 1917, *Rananim*, 118 (*Letters*, vol. 3, 124).

61 Esther Salaman, *The Fertile Plain*, 342–3.

62 Wolodymyr Stojko, "Ukrainian National Aspirations and the Russian Provisional Government," Taras Hunczak, *The Ukraine, 1917–1921: A Study in Revolution*, 23. The All-Russian Constituent Assembly never took place under the auspices of the Provisional Government. It was held, instead, in January 1918, already after the October Revolution, and then the Assembly was promptly dissolved by the Bolsheviks.

63  Lawrence to Koteliansky, 3 July 1917, *Rananim*, 120 (*Letters*, vol. 3, 120).

64  Frieda Lawrence to Koteliansky, June 1917, *Memoirs and Correspondence*, 211. Her emphasis.

65  Quoted in Martin Gilbert, *The First World War: A Complete History*, 343. Farbman's article was published on 28 June 1917.

66  This particular diatribe has already been cited earlier – "a Jew cringes before men, and takes God as a Christian takes whiskey" (3 July 1917, *Rananim*, 120 [*Letters*, vol. 3, 137]).

67  Lawrence to Koteliansky, 23 September 1917, *Rananim*, 122 (*Letters*, vol. 3, 162).

68  Murry to Koteliansky, 1 June 1917, CSA. Reproduced with the permission of The Society of Authors as the Literary Representative of the Estate of John Middleton Murry. Koteliansky and Murry could not, however, avoid the linkage of their names later that year when five of the Chekhov stories they translated together for *The Bet* appeared in The Modern Library of the World's Best Books series published in the United States by Boni and Liveright.

69  Gertler to Koteliansky, 29 August 1917, *Selected Letters*, 148.

70  Gertler to Koteliansky, 20 October 1917, BL/Kot.

71  Gertler to Carrington, 18 April 1917, *Selected Letters*, 142. The other one was "Monty" – Montague Shearman.

72  After the Soviets switched to the Gregorian calendar early in 1918, the October Revolution, while not renamed, was celebrated on 7 November. Similarly, the February Revolution actually took place in March (8–11) according to the Gregorian calendar.

73  Carrington to Gertler [November 1917], *Carrington: Letters and Extracts from Her Diaries*, 84. The letter is marked as "Thursday" but is otherwise undated. The editor felt confident it was written in November, and, by looking at Lawrence's published letters, it is safe to assume further that the precise date was 15 November since he wrote to Montague Shearman on Sunday, 11 November: "I am sorry we couldn't come on Friday evening … Shall we keep Thursday or Friday open?" (*Letters*, vol. 3, 181).

74  Virginia Woolf, 18 January 1918, *Diary*, vol. 1, 108.

75  Gertler to Koteliansky, June 1918, *Selected Letters*, 159. His emphasis.

76  Campbell, *Tomorrow We Will Only Gossip*, 104.

77  Lawrence to Gertler, 14 June 1918, *Letters*, vol. 3, 250.

78  Koteliansky to Gertler, undated but, given everything else discussed in the letter, it is safe to conclude that it was summer 1918 (LGA).

79  For an excellent and comprehensive discussion of this complicated period, see Hunczak, *The Ukraine, 1917–1921: A Study in Revolution*. The Russian-Polish War did not end as successfully for the Bolsheviks, however; in accordance with the 1921 "Treaty of Riga" the new Russian government had to relinquish a big chunk of Western Ukraine. Two remarkable Russian writers,

Mikhail Bulgakov and Isaac Babel, left their fictional accounts of the events taking place in Ukraine at the time based on their firsthand experience. Bulgakov, who was in Kiev for most of this period, describes the chaos of powers changing and bloodshed it occasioned in *White Guard* ("Belaia gvardiia," 1926), while Babel, who accompanied the Red Army as they were fighting the Polish Army on the territory of Western Ukraine, alludes to pogroms and the treatment of the Jews in his masterpiece, *Red Cavalry* ("Konarmiia," 1923). He is even more frank in his *1920 Diary* (published posthumously in 1995), where he reveals that both armies were responsible for the massacres (*The Complete Works*, 197–333, 377–472).

80 These numbers are cited in Orest Subtelny, *Ukraine: A History*, 363. They are based on several sources, including Salo W. Baron's *The Russian Jews under the Tsars and the Soviets* where the figure is 50,000 (184).

81 Peter Kenetz, "Pogroms and White Ideology," Klier and Lambroza, *Pogroms: Anti-Jewish Violence in Modern Russian History*, 298–9.

82 Esther Salaman, *Two Silver Roubles*, 137–8. "Tphillin" are two small black leather boxes that contain passages from the scripture that religious Jews tie to their forehead and left arm before the weekday morning prayer.

83 Upon meeting Salaman in June 1932, after her book came out, Kot apparently introduced himself by saying, "I've read your book and the town in it … is my town" (1967 Zytaruk interview with Salaman). Zhitomir appeared in *Two Silver Roubles* under a fictional name, "Vladimirsk," so it is possible that Kot would have assumed it could be Ostropol or Starokonstantinov. He also, of course, knew Zhitomir itself quite well since he studied there.

84 She was born on 12 June; he left Russia on 23 June.

85 Lina Marshak (Kot's niece) to Pauline Smith, 15 January 1985, JFA. Quoted with the permission of Jackie Freedman. 1920 was the peak year for pandemic of typhoid fever in Russia and Ukraine. It is spread by water and food infected by the salmonella bacteria, which thrives in poor sanitary environment, such as Ostropol's at the time.

86 Lawrence to Koteliansky, 9 March 1920, *Rananim*, 205 (*Letters*, vol. 3, 482). Lawrence is using the Russian name for Ukraine here – "Ukraina."

87 Gertler to Koteliansky, 22 November 1920, BL/Kot.

88 Gertler to Koteliansky, 12 December 1920, BL/Kot. Gertler was still mostly concerned about his own illness and upset that once he left the sanatorium and came back to London, "there won't be a soul left there to see so that it will be almost like leaving one sanatorium only to enter another" (ibid.).

89 Interview with Jackie Freedman, 26 April 2004. She also remembers being told that the Chernomorsky house eventually became Ostropol's City Hall. Like most of Ostropol's pre-WWII architecture, the house no longer exists. Perl's cousin and Rokhl's daughter, Lina, later suggested that Isaak Chernomorsky had been killed during a pogrom by Ukrainian nationalists or the

White Army (Lina Marshak to Pauline Smith, 15 January 1985, JFA. Since Lina was writing from the Soviet Union, where letters abroad were often opened and read by the authorities, it would have been unwise for her to suggest that Perl's father had been killed by Bolsheviks. Quoted with the permission of Jackie Freedman.

90  Gertler to Koteliansky, 12 March 1921, BL/Kot.

91  Koteliansky to Brett, 10 August 1921, HRC/DB.

92  A stamp in Moishel wife's, Sheindel's, passport shows that they were in Poland in October 1920, SSA.

93  All this information comes from two sources: Myron Echenberg and Ruth Tannenbaum, "The Echenberg of Ostropol and Sherbrooke: A Tale of Two Shtetls" (written for the Echenberg family reunion, 22–24 August 1986; Montreal), unpublished and used here with the permission of the authors; and Sonny Surkes, "My Mother, Rita Kay Surkes" (written on the occasion of Moishel and Sheindel's daughter's, Rita Surkes's, death in January 2003), unpublished and used with his permission.

94  Koteliansky to Pauline Smith, 13 September 1945, JFA. He gave his niece a full account of all the money he sent to Moishel from 1921 to 1937 because he was peeved that some of that money, sent specifically for Polly, appeared never to have reached her.

95  Koteliansky to Brett, 22 August 1921, HRC/DB.

96  Koteliansky to Pauline Smith, 11 November 1948, JFA. "Lucy" was another nickname for Eli.

97  Gertler to Koteliansky, 22 July 1925, BL/Kot.

98  Koteliansky to Waterlow, 3 September 1925, ATL/SW.

99  Interview with Jackie Freedman, 28 April 2004.

100 Interviews with Catherine Stoye, 4 July 2003, and with Jackie Freedman, 28 April 2004.

101 Koteliansky to Margery Waterlow, ? September 1927, ATL/SW.

102 Interviews with Jackie Freedman, 26 April 2004, and Sonny Surkes, 27 April 2004.

103 Gertler to Koteliansky, 22 December 1925, BL/Kot.

104 Interview with Catherine Stoye, 4 July 2003.

105 Koteliansky to Brett, 22 August 1921, HRC/DB

CHAPTER FIVE

1  John Carswell, *The Exile: A Life of Ivy Litvinov*, 77.

2  Lawrence to Catherine Carswell, 11 February 1916, *Letters*, vol. 2, 532.

3  Lawrence to Thomas Dunlop, 12 July 1916, *Letters*, vol. 2, 629.

4  Lawrence to Koteliansky, 18 December 1925, *Rananim*, 274 (*Letters*, vol. 5, 355).

5  A June 1914 letter to Frederick Macmillan; quoted in David C. Smith, *H.G. Wells: Desperately Mortal*, 233.

6  See Smith, *H.G. Wells: Desperately Mortal*, 246.

7  Koteliansky to Messrs [*sic*] George Newness, 20 November 1919, UI.

8  H.G. Wells to Koteliansky, 30 December 1919, UI. Reproduced with the permission of The Literary Executors of the Estate of H.G. Wells.

9  Koteliansky to H.G. Wells, 30 December 1919, UI.

10  See his letters to Wells dated 28 August and 23 October 1920, UI.

11  Catherine Wells to Koteliansky, ? August 1920, and Koteliansky to H.G. Wells, 28 August 1920, UI. Reproduced with the permission of The Literary Executors of the Estate of H.G. Wells.

12  Catherine Wells to Koteliansky, Friday, no date, UI. Reproduced with the permission of The Literary Executors of the Estate of H.G. Wells.

13  Clare Sheridan, *Mayfair to Moscow*, 56. For more on the rather sensational aspects of Sheridan's trip to Moscow, see Elizabeth Kehoe, *Three American Sisters and the English Aristocratic World into Which They Married*, and Anita Leslie, *Clare Sheridan: Her Tempestuous Life with Jennie Churchill, Mussoloni, Lenin, Charlie Chaplin, Trotsky, Winston Churchill, and Others*.

14  Security Service Release, 25–26 November 2002, KV 2/979–981. See www.nationalarchives.gov.uk/documents/nov2002.pdf.

15  Nina Berberova, *Moura: The Dangerous Life of the Baroness Budberg*, 5–6. Much of the biographical information about Budberg comes from this source as well. The Russian title of the book is "Zheleznaia zhenshchina," or "Iron Woman."

16  Wells, *H.G. Wells in Love*, 165. Budberg became the bane of Wells's grandchildren's existence. Catherine Stoye recalls that, when she and her brother Oliver would meet Moura on the staircase leading to their grandfather's office, they each tried to hide behind the other to avoid her often expansive – and to them seemingly insincere – embraces and other expressions of tenderness. Interview with Catherine Stoye, 4 July 2003.

17  H.G. Wells, *Russia in the Shadows*, 107–8.

18  Ibid., 88. Lenin's maternal grandfather, Alexander Blank, was actually born in Starokonstantinov, near Ostropol.

19  Ibid., 155, 161.

20  In *Lenin*, which Trotsky published in 1924, the year of Lenin's death, he wrote: "In one of the many books devoted to Lenin, I came upon an article by the English author Wells under the title of 'The Visionary of the Kremlin.' There is an editorial note that explains: 'Even such progressive men as Wells had not understood the proletarian revolution going on in Russia.' One would think this was not a sufficient reason to put Wells's article in a book devoted to the leader of this revolution. But it is not worth while criticizing; I personally at least have read some pages of Wells not without interest, for which to be sure the author, as is evident from what follows, is quite innocent. I have vividly before my eyes the time that Wells visited Moscow. It was

the hungry and cold winter of 1920–21. There was a restless foreboding in the air of the difficulties that the spring was to bring. Starving Moscow lay buried deep in snow. Our policy was on the eve of a sharp change. I remember very well the impression Vladimir Ilyich carried away from his conversation with Wells. 'What a bourgeois he is! He is a Philistine!' he repeated, and raised both hands above the table, laughed and sighed, as was characteristic of him when he felt a kind of inner shame for another man. 'Ah, what a Philistine,' he began the conversation anew. Our conversation took place before the opening of the session of the Political Bureau and was limited essentially to this repeated short characterization of Wells." Trotsky goes on to characterize Wells as "a stock conservative Englishman of imperialistic mold [who] was completely obsessed with the conviction that he was conferring great honour upon this barbaric land and its ruler by his visit" (172–4).

21  See V.I. Lenin, *Collected Works*, vol. 33, 389. It was also published in *Pravda*, 27 October 1922, after it was "corrected" by Lenin.

22  Michael Farbman, *Bolshevism in Retreat*, 50. The so-called "Retreat of Bolshevism," and namely the introduction of the New Economic Policy (NEP) in which private enterprise was allowed in order to restore the economy, was short-lived however. By the time Stalin consolidated his power in 1927, both NEP and many of those who took advantage of it were close to total extinction.

23  Mansfield to Koteliansky, 15 March 1922, *Collected Letters*, vol. 5, 110.

24  Hugh Walpole, *The Secret City*, 13.

25  Thus in *Hugh Walpole: An Appreciation* (also published by George H. Doran Company and released the same year) Joseph Hergesheimer wrote: "Mr Walpole makes Petrograd as memorable a city as does Tolstoy his Moscow, with Napoleon gazing upon its rounded domes." The *Appreciation* also carried a quote from the *New York Times* that declared that was Walpole's best novel to date and that it allowed the reader to "get the sense of the strange and alien forces lying beneath the somewhat Europeanized surface of Petrograd" (Joseph Hergesheimer, *Hugh Walpole: An Appreciation*, 35–6).

26  It has its somewhat ridiculous points, especially a sudden but mercifully brief appearance of Lenin ringing the bell to the apartment of one of the Russian characters, the so-called "internationalist Socialist" (Walpole, *Secret City*, 32). There are some howlers as well, like Moscow's "Red Square" appearing in Petrograd (22). Also whenever Russian is used it is at best phonetic rather than grammatical (see, for example, 94). Yet, overall, the author reveals a refreshingly decent knowledge of Russian history, as well as of major Russian writers and artists. One of the English protagonists' names happens to be "Lawrence."

27  CSA.

28  Walpole, *The Secret City*, 64, 207, 126.

29 Ibid., 36, 124–6.

30 CSA. His emphasis.

31 Ibid. His emphasis.

32 May Sarton, *A World of Light*, 178.

33 See ibid.

34 Koteliansky to Pauline Smith, 25 June 1944, JFA.

35 Woolf, 4 January 1919, *Diary*, vol. 3, 217.

36 Campbell, *Today We Will Only Gossip*, 161.

37 Sarton, *A World of Light*, 177; *I Knew a Phoenix*, 210.

38 Campbell, *Today We Will Only Gossip*, 161.

39 Ibid.

40 Sarton, *A World of Light*, 178; Sarton, *I Knew a Phoenix*, 210; Campbell, *Today We Will Only Gossip*, 161.

41 Brett, *Lawrence and Brett: A Friendship*, 25.

42 Frieda Lawrence to Koteliansky, Thursday, no date [March–April 1930], BL/Kot. Reproduced by permission of Pollinger Limited and The Estate of Frieda Lawrence Ravagli.

43 Interview with Catherine Stoye, 4 July 2003.

44 Koteliansky to Pauline Smith, 19 December 1945, JFA.

45 Interview with Catherine Stoye, 4 July 2003.

46 Marjorie Wells to Pauline Smith, 20 July 1943, 14 Februry 1942, and 18 December 1943, JFA.

47 Sarton, *A World of Light*, 183.

48 Frieda Lawrence to Koteliansky, 4 December 1923, *Memoirs and Correspondence*, 222. Her emphasis. The full quote is: "You said it, when you told the fact that you didn't like the law and order in yourself *disordered*. And that's just what I like to do: upset people's applecarts! They get such a surprise about themselves. And then they can make a new order!"

49 Kot's phone number back then was "Hampstead 6534." See Lawrence to Martin Secker, 26 September 1919, *Letters*, vol. 3, 398.

50 Lawrence to Koteliansky, 18 September 1922, *Rananim*, 247 (*Letters*, vol. 4, 296).

51 Koteliansky to Gertler, 26 August 1918, LGA. Partially published in Gertler, *Selected Letters*, 162, where "the cave" is for some reason capitalized while it is not in the original.

52 Lawrence to Gertler, 28 April 1918, *Letters*, vol. 3, 240.

53 Lawrence to Koteliansky, 2 February 1922, *Rananim*, 236–7 (*Letters*, vol. 4, 184–5). This part of the letter is in Italian. Kot, as was already mentioned, did study Italian during his last year at the Kiev Commercial Institute, although by 1922 it must have been rusty, unless he kept it up. As far as we know, unlike Lawrence, Kot never had a beard, which may have even been his rebellion against the Jewish orthodoxy. Therefore Lawrence uses this expression here figuratively.

54 Wells to Koteliansky, no date, postmark: 5 November 1920. UI. Reproduced with the permission of The Literary Executors of the Estate of H.G. Wells.

55 Wells to Koteliansky, 5 November 1920, UI. Reproduced with the permission of The Literary Executors of the Estate of H.G. Wells.

56 More details about Manoukhin can be found in a 1993 article by T.I. Ul'iankina published in a Russian journal on natural sciences and technology, "Etot neizvestnyi izvestnyi Ivan Manukhin," 45–62. In 1958, the year he died, his memoirs came out in New York's émigré publication *Novyi zhurnal* (New Journal) 54 (1958).

57 Ivan Manoukhin, "The Treatment of Infectious Disease by Leucocytolysis Produced by Rontgenisation of the Spleen," 685–7.

58 Mansfield to Brett, 12 September 1921, *Collected Letters*, vol. 4, 279. Mansfield and Kot had reconciled in late 1918 but by 1921 were on the outs again, mostly because of Murry's continuing presence in Mansfield's life.

59 Koteliansky to Brett, 10 August 1921, HRC/DB.

60 Mansfield to Koteliansky, 18 October 1921, *Collected Letters*, vol. 4, 299. Her emphasis.

61 Lawrence to Koteliansky, 10 November 1921, *Rananim*, 229 (*Letters*, vol. 4, 114).

62 *The New York Times* (6 April 1914) carried the article "Gorky Is Well Again: Novelist Says Roentgen Rays Cured Him of Tuberculosis." By 1920, however, Gorky's tuberculosis was back.

63 Mansfield to Koteliansky, 4 November 1921, *Collected Letters*, vol. 4, 312.

64 Mansfield to Koteliansky, 29 November 1921, *Collected Letters*, vol. 4, 326.

65 Mansfield to Koteliansky, 4 December 1921, *Collected Letters*, vol. 4, 332. As is common in Mansfield's letters, a question mark is missing here at the end of "Can all this be cured."

66 Mansfield to Koteliansky, 23 December 1921, *Collected Letters*, vol. 4, 347. Her emphasis.

67 Mansfield to Brett, 9 January 1922, *Collected Letters*, vol. 5, 9.

68 Mansfield, 11 January 1922, *Journal*, 218. "Mme Tchehov" was Anton Chekhov's wife, Olga Knipper.

69 Baker, *Katherine Mansfield: The Memories of LM*, 93.

70 Ibid., 175.

71 Mansfield, 31 January and 1 February 1922, *Journal*, 228–9.

72 Mansfield to Koteliansky, 1 February 1922, *Collected Letters*, vol. 5, 37–8. Her emphasis.

73 Mansfield to Koteliansky, 3 February 1922, *Collected Letters*, vol. 5, 41. The sentences in French read: "You have decided to start the treatment. That's very good. Good health!" "Tout de suite" means "immediately." Her emphasis.

74 Mansfield, 3 February 1922, *Journal*, 229. Her emphasis.

75 Mansfield, 10 February 1922, *Notebooks*, vol. 2, 325.

76 Mansfield to Brett, 30 March 1922, *Collected Letters*, vol. 5, 136–7.

77 Mansfield to Baker, 10 May 1922, *Collected Letters*, vol. 5, 171.

78 Mansfield to Koteliansky, 29 May 1922, *Collected Letters*, vol. 5, 185.

79 Mansfield to Koteliansky, 17 June 1922, *Collected Letters*, vol. 5, 208.

80 Lawrence to Koteliansky, 9 July 1922, *Rananim*, 244 (*Letters*, vol. 4, 275).

81 Lawrence to Gertler, 9 October 1916, *Letters*, vol. 2, 660.

82 Lawrence to Koteliansky, 4 October 1919, *Rananim*, 194 (*Letters*, vol. 3, 275). His emphasis.

83 The news of Fox's death reached Lawrence in Florence. "Sad to think of Fox gone," he wrote. "I can't believe he is no more in the Cave" (Lawrence to Koteliansky, 3 April 1928, *Rananim*, 340 [*Letters*, vol. 6, 356]). "He died like a man," Kot supposedly told Lady Glenavy (Campbell, *Today We Will Only Gossip*, 89). When Virginia Woolf visited Kot early in 1929, she wrote down in her diary: "His dog (a pure Jewish dog) is dead" (4 January 1929, *Diary*, vol. 3, 218).

84 Mansfield to Baker, 29 May 1922, Baker, *Katherine Mansfield: The Memories of LM*, 195.

85 Mansfield to Koteliansky, 17 July 1922, *Collected Letters*, vol. 5, 225.

86 Mansfield to Koteliansky, 31 May 1922, *Collected Letters*, vol. 5, 187.

87 Mansfield to Koteliansky, 2 August 1922, *Collected Letters*, vol. 5, 232. Her emphasis.

88 Mansfield to Koteliansky, 30 August 1922, *Collected Letters*, vol. 5, 262.

89 Mansfield to Koteliansky, 6 September 1922, *Collected Letters*, vol. 5, 265. Her emphasis.

90 Mansfield, 16 September 1922, *Notebooks*, vol. 2, 327–8.

91 Mansfield to Koteliansky, 19 October 1922, *Collected Letters*, vol. 5, 303–4.

92 It also came as a separate volume in 1931, bearing the following note: "This translation … was made by Katherine Mansfield and S.S. Koteliansky during the last stay of the former in England, August–September, 1922" (Maxim Gorky, *Reminiscences of Leonid Andreyev*, 5).

93 Mansfield, 19 September and 14 October 1922, *Notebooks*, vol. 2, 328.

94 Among Kot's friends, James Stephens was a definite Blavatsky fan and at times follower. For more on that, see Pyle, *James Stephens*, 56–76.

95 For more on Orage and Ouspensky, see Carswell, *Lives and Letters*, where Orage is the central figure of the narrative. For an excellent summary of Gurdjieff's and Ouspensky's theories and techniques, as well as Mansfield's last days, see Antony Alpers, *The Life of Katherine Mansfield*, 367–85. See also Paul Beekman Taylor, *Gurdjieff and Orage: Brothers in Elysium*, and James Moore, *Gurdjieff and Mansfield*. The latter has an obvious "pro-Gurdjieff" bias, which is not surprising since James Moore is a disciple of Gurdjieff and the author of his "official" biography: *Gurdjieff: A Biography*.

96 Mansfield to Elizabeth, Countess Russell, 31 December 1922, *Collected Letters*, vol. 5, 346.

97 Mansfield to Koteliansky, 4 October 1922, *Collected Letters*, vol. 5, 286.

98 Mansfield to Koteliansky, 9 October 1922. *Collected Letters*, vol. 5, 291. Her emphasis.

99 Murry to Mansfield, 17 December 1922, Mansfield, *Letters between Katherine Mansfield and John Middleton Murry*, 397.

100 Baker, *Katherine Mansfield: The Memories of LM*, 212.

101 Mansfield to Brett, 15 October 1922, *Collected Letters*, vol. 5, 301.

102 In Harold Beauchamp, *Reminiscences and Recollections*, 209.

103 Jeffrey Meyers, *Katherine Mansfield*, 242.

104 Mansfield, *Notebooks*, vol. 2, 343–4.

105 Mansfield to Koteliansky, 19 October 1922, *Collected Letters*, vol. 5, 303–4.

106 Koteliansky to Waterlow, 27 June 1927 and 12 December 1928, ATL/SW.

107 Frieda Lawrence to Adele Seltzer, 10 February 1923, D.H. Lawrence, *Letters to Thomas and Adele Seltzer*, 69.

108 Murry to Lady Glenavy; quoted in Campbell, *Today We Will Only Gossip*, 192.

109 Based on interviews with Catherine Stoye and Dilys Powell, in John Carswell, *Lives and Letters*, 267.

CHAPTER SIX

1 Lawrence to Koteliansky, 20 January 1922, *Rananim*, 324 (*Letters*, vol. 4, 171).

2 Around this time he met Roger Fry, probably through the Woolfs, and got him interested in a project that would never be realized – a book on Russian art. Among the Koteliansky papers at the British Library (probably because he never used it) is Fry's undated introduction letter to the art editor at Chatto and Windus, Geoffrey Whitworth, urging him to "kindly discuss with Mr Kotylianskj [*sic*] … his projects for a history of Russian art in English." Kot was a dubious art critic, but he might have had not himself but Grisha Farbman in mind. When ten years later Farbman edited *Masterpieces of Russian Painting*, the volume had an article by Fry on Russian icons as seen by Westerners. For more on Koteliansky and Fry, see Andrei Rogatchevski, "Samuel Koteliansky and the Bloomsbury Circle," 368–9.

3 Lawrence to Koteliansky, 2? August 1919, *Rananim*, 184 (*Letters*, vol. 3, 380).

4 Ibid.

5 Lawrence to Martin Secker, 2 September 1919, *Letters*, vol. 3, 388.

6 Lawrence to Martin Secker, 2 October 1919, *Letters*, vol. 3, 402.

7 Lawrence to Martin Secker, 20 December 1919, *Letters*, vol. 3, 437.

8 Leo Shestov, *All Things Are Possible*, 7.

9 Koteliansky to Lawrence, 10 December 1919, Nottingham/DHL. His emphasis. This is a rare letter of Koteliansky to Lawrence that actually survived and found its way into an archive.

10 Shestov, *All Things Are Possible*, 39.

11 Lawrence to Koteliansky, 17 December 1919, *Rananim*, 201 (*Letters*, vol. 3, 433).

12 Koteliansky to Lawrence, 10 December 1919, Nottingham/DHL. His emphasis.

13 Lawrence to Koteliansky, 17 December 1919, *Rananim*, 201 (*Letters*, vol. 3, 433).

14 Lawrence to Martin Secker, 17 December 1919, *Letters*, vol. 3, 434.

15 Lawrence to Benjamin Huebsch, 15 January 1920; *Letters*, vol. 3, 454. His emphasis.

16 Shestov to Koteliansky, 17 November 1928 (in Russian), CSA.

17 Shestov to Koteliansky, 2 December 1928 (in Russian), CSA.

18 Lawrence to Koteliansky, 17 July 1920, *Rananim*, 213 (*Letters*, vol. 3, 570).

19 Koteliansky to Robert Mountsier, 10 April 1922, HRC/DHL.

20 Which Lawrence did, with little success. "A friend of mine," he wrote to Benjamin Huebsch, his US publisher, "has done a translation of a play *The Green Ring*, by Merizkowsky's wife. It made a stir in Russia. He wants to know if you would like to consider it" (Lawrence to Benjamin Huebsch, 3 December 1919, *Letters*, vol. 3, 426). Dmitry Merezhkovsky, Hippius' husband, was a poet and prominent Symbolist thinker; together, they were a very influential couple in pre-Soviet, and later émigré, Russian culture.

21 Koteliansky to Waterlow, 3 August 1929, ATL/SW.

22 Zinaida Hippius, *The Green Ring: A Play in Four Acts*, 5.

23 Hippius, *The Green Ring*, 9, 42. For the original text, see Zinaida Hippius, *Sobranie sochineniia*, vol. 4, 473. In the first instance, the translation of Russian adjective "sukhoi" as "dry" works for weather but not for a person. A better translation here should have been "reserved" or "impassionate."

24 Lawrence to Koteliansky, 31 January 1921, *Rananim*, 215 (*Letters*, vol. 3, 658).

25 Koteliansky to Robert Mountsier, 9 December 1921 and 7 January 1922, HRC/DHL.

26 Koteliansky to Robert Mountsier, 4 October 1922. HRC/DHL. There was no copyright agreement because England had yet to recognize the new regime.

27 W. Chapin Huntington, *The Homesick Million: Russia-out-of-Russia*, 218.

28 See Hippius's diary, *Sobranie sochinenii*, vol. 9, 34.

29 Mansfield to Koteliansky, 29 and 31 May 1922, *Collected Letters*, vol. 5, 185–6. Her emphasis.

30 Koteliansky to Robert Mountsier, 4 October 1922. HRC/DHL.

31 Koteliansky to Robert Mountsier, 23 and 29 December 1922, 9 and 12 February 1923. HRC/DHL. It was probably not solely the poor sales of *The Green Ring* that led to the publisher's bankruptcy, but having another flop on their hands no doubt did not help. Before the publisher went belly up, however, Kot persuaded C.W. Daniel to publish the translation of Chekhov stories he had produced with the help of Cannan, which was published in the United States in 1917. The volume was identical, but, probably, again, to avoid copyright issues, it now carried the title *My Life and Other Stories*, instead of *The House with the Mezzanine and Other Stories*.

32 Leonard Woolf, *Beginning Again*, 247

33 Virginia Woolf to David Garnett, 26 July 1917, *Letters*, vol. 2, 167.

34 Virginia Woolf to Dora Carrington, 5 October 1917, *Letters*, vol. 2, 185. This version of the name probably deliberately echoes the last name of a famous Russian Zionist Vladimir Zhabotinsky (1880–1940).

35 Virginia Woolf, 18 January 1918, *Diary*, vol. 1, 108.

36 Virginia Woolf, 24 June 1918, *Diary*, vol. 1, 159.

37 Virginia Woolf, 31 July 1918, *Diary*, vol. 1, 177.

38 Virginia Woolf to Ottoline Morrell, 1? August 1918, *Letters*, vol. 2, 264.

39 Koteliansky to Virginia Woolf, 3 April 1919, Sussex.

40 See Sigmund Freud, "Melancholia from Extracts from the Fliess Papers," *The Standard Edition of the Complete Psychological Works of Sigmund Freud*, vol. 1, 200–6. Freud's 1905 monograph, *Three Essays on the Theory of Sexuality*, came out in English in 1910.

41 For more on the Stracheys, including their correspondence with each other, see Meisel and Kendrick, *Bloomsbury/Freud: The Letters of James and Alix Strachey*.

42 Virginia Woolf to Koteliansky, 4 April 1919, *Letters*, vol. 2, 344.

43 Koteliansky to Leonard Woolf. The dates of the two letters are just "Aug 3" and "Saturday," but the discussion of the Bolsheviks' poor handing of famine, and reference to specific articles in two Russian newspapers at the time – *Pravda* and *Ekonomicheskaia gazeta* – make it virtually certain that the year is 1919 (Sussex).

44 Leonard Woolf, *Beginning Again*, 234, 241.

45 For more on the history of the press, see J.H. Willis Jr, *Leonard and Virginia Woolf as Publishers: The Hogarth Press 1917–1941*, 80–101.

46 The volumes are *The Man Who Was Afraid* (1905) and *Comrades* (1915), presented to Leonard by Margaret Llewelyn Davies.

47 Leonard Woolf, *Downhill*, 67–8.

48 Virginia Woolf, 5 May 1920, *Diary*, vol. 2, 34.

49 Koteliansky to Leonard Woolf, 26 December 1922. Reading.

50 Leonard Woolf, *Beginning Again*, 248.

51 Leonard Woolf, *Downhill*, 67. As already mentioned, Leonard himself was a semi-serious student of Russian: his books at Washington State University Libraries include *Russian Grammar* and *Third Russian Book: Extracts from Aksakov, Grigorovich, Herzen, Saltykov*, both by Nevill Forbes. He also owned a dictionary with a very long title: *New English-Russian and Russian-English Dictionary, Containing the Whole Vocabulary in General Use, with Copious Selections of Scientific Technical and Commercial Terms and Others Lately Brought into Use, with their Pronunciations Figured* (Paris: Garnier Freres, 1924). For more on the collection, the circumstances of the acquisition, as well as the other titles, see www.wsulibs.wsu.edu/masc/woolflibrary.htm.

52 Maxim Gorky, *Reminiscences of Leo Nicolayevitch Tolstoi*, 32.

53 Ibid., 14, 23, 27, 20.

54  Ibid., 17, 16, 21.

55  Ibid., 43, 46, 48, 56.

56  Leonard Woolf, *Downhill*, 67.

57  William Gerhardi, *Anton Chehov: A Critical Study*, 9. Gerhardi would later attach an "e" at the end of his name.

58  Gertler to Koteliansky, 4? February 1921, BL/Kot.

59  Virginia Woolf, 18 October 1920, *Diary*, vol. 2, 71–2.

60  During the same four years Kot also found time, as was already mentioned, to collaborate with Katherine Mansfield on Gorky's *Reminiscences of Leonid Andreyev*, which was not published by William Heinemann till 1931. Leonard Woolf included it in the 1934 expanded Hogarth Press edition of Maxim Gorky's *Reminiscences*, which featured, in addition to Gorky's reminiscences of Tolstoy, Gorky's reminiscences of Chekhov and Andreyev. In 1923 Koteliansky and Murry brought out *Dostoevsky: Letters and Reminiscences*, published not by the Hogarth Press but by T. and A. Constable. These were Dostoevsky's letters to his wife as well as Mrs Dostoevsky's journals, which Kot had sent to Katherine Mansfield in autumn 1922 before approaching Murry.

61  As late as 1942, both Gorky's *Reminiscences* and Bunin were still selling well, unlike other translations Kot did with the Hogarth Press. "From the last royalty account received the other day," Kot wrote to Leonard Woolf then, "I see that there are only two translations selling: 1) Gorky's 'Reminiscences,' and 2) Bunin's stories" (Koteliansky to Leonard Woolf, 31 August 1942. Sussex).

62  In 1933 Leonard Woolf would send Bunin a letter congratulating him and mentioning that he and Virginia "began to admire your work when … we saw the translation of *The Gentleman from San Francisco*" (21 November 1933, *Letters of Leonard Woolf*, 319).

63  Leonid Andreyev and Ivan Bunin, *Lazarus and The Gentleman from San Francisco*.

64  Lawrence to Koteliansky, 4 June 1921, *Rananim*, 198 (*Letters*, vol. 4, 23); Lawrence to Robert Mountsier, 4 June 1921, *Letters*, vol. 4, 24.

65  Lawrence to Koteliansky, 16 June 1921, *Rananim*, 224 (*Letters*, vol. 4, 37).

66  See Lawrence to Koteliansky, 14 January 1922: "I am glad you liked the *Gent* when he was done" (*Rananim*, 232 [*Letters*, vol. 4, 165]).

67  As a writer, Bunin also had a lot in common with Katherine Mansfield: Chekhov was an idol for both of them, and like Mansfield (and Chekhov, of course) Bunin experimented with longer narratives, or novellas – in particular, *The Village* ("Derevnia," 1910) and "Sukhodol" (Dry Valley) (1912) (*Collected Stories*, 18–73) – which evoked his childhood, and which helped establish him as a major writer. Mansfield did not live long enough to read enough of Bunin to truly appreciate him, but she did like "The Gentleman from San Francisco," albeit with some reservations: "Bunin has an immense talent. That is certain. All the same – there's a limitation in this story, so it

seems to me. There is something hard, inflexible, separate in him which he exults in … He just stops short of being a great writer because of it … He lacks tenderness – and *in spite of everything*, tenderness there must be" (Mansfield to Koteliansky, 13 January 1922, *Collected Letters*, vol. 5, 13, her emphasis).

68 Ivan Bunin, *The Gentleman from San Francisco and Other Stories*, 32 (unless otherwise specified, the citations are from the 1922 edition).

69 Andreyev and Bunin, *Lazarus and The Gentleman from San Francisco*, 54.

70 "Ivan Bunin," *Times* (London), 17 May 1922, 16. When the volume came out in the United States, *The New York Times* noted: "'The Gentleman from San Francisco' called for the aid of D.H. Lawrence, and there are moments when the reader will realize it" ("Latest Works of Fiction," *The New York Times Review of Books*, 28 January 1923, 14).

71 See Lawrence to Koteliansky, 10 November 1921: "What are you doing about the rest of the Bunin book? … If it isn't very long, I'll do it if you wish me to" (*Rananim*, 228 [*Letters*, vol. 4, 114]).

72 Woolf, *Beginning Again*, 248.

73 Lawrence to Koteliansky, 9 July 1922, *Rananim*, 244 (*Letters*, vol. 4, 275).

74 Lawrence to Koteliansky, 14 January 1922, *Rananim*, 232 (*Letters*, vol. 4, 165).

75 *The Gentleman from San Francisco and Other Stories*, between two title pages. It is worth mentioning that even in this note Lawrence's name preceded Kot's. Interestingly enough, the copy of the book, which is in the Woolfs' library at the Washington State University, bears a bookplate that reads "From the Library of S.S. Koteliansky, Translator and Critic, 1880–1955." There is a date on the title page (most likely in Leonard's handwriting) – "XII72."

76 Bunin, *The Gentleman from San Francisco and Other Stories* (1923): in addition to the names of the translators on a separate page following the title page, the US edition also had another title page just for the eponymous story itself, which likewise stated that it was "Translated by D.H. Lawrence and S.S. Koteliansky" (2).

77 Leonard Woolf to T.S. Eliot, 25 May 1922, *Letters*, 283.

78 Virginia Woolf, *Common Reader*, 178.

79 Virginia Woolf, 31 January 1921, *Diary*, vol. 2, 88.

80 Virginia Woolf, 16 February 1921, *Diary*, vol. 2, 90.

81 Virginia Woolf to Koteliansky, ? March 1921, *Letters*, vol. 2, 459.

82 For more on Woolf and Harrison, see Natalya Reinhold, "Virginia Woolf's Russian Voyage Out," 16–9.

83 Jane Ellen Harrison, *Russia and the Russian Verb: A Contribution to the Psychology of the Russian People*, 8, 10.

84 Jane Ellen Harrison, *Aspects, Aorists and the Classical Tripos*, 7, 23, 33. Her emphasis. In 1925, in *Reminiscences of a Student's Life*, published by the Woolfs' Hogarth Press, Harrison once again reaffirmed her love for Russian,

which by then had even replaced Greek as her favourite subject: "If I could have my life over again, I would devote it not to art of literature, but to [Russian] language" (78), For more on Harrison and her passion for all things Russian, see D.S. Mirsky, *Jane Ellen Harrison and Russia*; Annabel Robinson, *The Life and Work of Jane Ellen Harrison*; and Jessie Stewart, *Jane Ellen Harrison: A Portrait from Letters*.

85 Virginia Woolf to Koteliansky, 25 June 1921, *Letters*, vol. 2, 476.

86 For a discussion of that, see Louise DeSalvo, *Virginia Woolf: The Impact of Childhood Sexual Abuse on Her Life and Work*. It should be noted that one of Woolf's biographers, Hermione Lee, strongly disagrees with DeSalvo's belief that these incidents played a crucial role in Woolf's later life – see Hermione Lee, *Virginia Woolf*, 124–6. For a broader analysis of incest within the Bloomsbury set, see Adam Kuper, *Incest & Influence: The Private Life of Bourgeois England*, 199–242.

87 Virginia Woolf, *Common Reader*, 182.

88 Virginia Woolf, 26 November 1921, *Diary*, vol. 2, 145. For Woolf's reading notes on *The Possessed*, see Rubenstein, *Virginia Woolf and the Russian Point of View*, 165–73.

89 Virginia Woolf, 19 December 1921, *Diary*, vol. 2, 152.

90 Virginia Woolf to Koteliansky, 9 March 1923, *Letters*, vol. 3, 19.

91 Leo Tolstoy and Paul Biriukov, *Tolstoi's Love Letters: With a Study on the Autobiographical Elements in Tolstoi's Work*, xiii.

92 Virginia Woolf to Koteliansky, 10 July 1933, *Letters*, vol. 5, 203. The book Koteliansky had planned came out fourteen years later, in 1947, and, in lieu of introduction, featured two articles, one of which was Freud's "Dostoevsky and Parricide."

93 Leonard Woolf to Koteliansky, 30 December 1922 and 3 January 1923. Reading. Reproduced with the permission of The University of Sussex and The Society of Authors as the Literary Representative of the Estate of Leonard Woolf.

94 Koteliansky to Leonard Woolf, 4 January 1923. Reading.

95 Koteliansky to Leonard Woolf, 14 February 1923. Reading.

96 Koteliansky to Leonard Woolf, 23 February 1923. Reading.

97 Koteliansky to Leonard Woolf, Monday evening, no date [1923]. Reading.

98 Virginia Woolf to T.S. Eliot, 14 April 1922, *Letters*, vol. 2, 521.

99 Virginia Woolf, 4 January 1929, *Diary*, vol. 3, 217–8.

100 Virginia Woolf, 7 February 1931, *Letters*, vol. 4, 289.

101 Virginia Woolf to Harmon H. Goldstone, 16 August 1932, *Letters*, vol. 5, 91.

102 B.J. Kirkpatrick, *A Bibliography of Virginia Woolf*, 120.

103 Koteliansky to Leonard Woolf, 22 May and 25 August 1923. Reading.

104 The Russian title of the story is "T'ma"; it is usually translated as "Darkness."

105 Koteliansky to Sarton, 25 June [1937], NYPL.

CHAPTER SEVEN

1 "Cosmos" is the word she used. See, for example, Lois Palken Rudnick, *Mabel Dodge Luhan: New Woman, New Worlds*, xi.

2 Lawrence to Baroness Anna Von Richthofen, 15 May 1922. The letter is in German (Lawrence always wrote to his mother-in-law in German), and the line reads: "So, die neuen Juden sollen weiter wandern" (*Letters*, vol. 4, 237–8).

3 Lawrence to Koteliansky, 18 September 1922, *Rananim*, 247 (*Letters*, vol. 4, 296).

4 Koteliansky to H.G. Wells, 11 November 1924. UI.

5 Murry to Koteliansky, no date but most likely second week of October 1922. CSA. Reproduced with the permission of The Society of Authors as the Literary Representative of the Estate of John Middleton Murry.

6 Murry to Koteliansky, 18 October 1922. CSA. Reproduced with the permission of The Society of Authors as the Literary Representative of the Estate of John Middleton Murry.

7 Quoted in F.A. Lea, *The Life of John Middleton Murry*, 105. The entries are from unpublished 1936 reminiscences and 1955 journal that Lea, as Murry's friend and authorized biographer, was allowed to see and quote from.

8 Murry, *Reminiscences of D.H. Lawrence*, 111.

9 Carswell, *The Savage Pilgrimage*, 245.

10 Ibid., 197. The fuller quote is: "In the third issue of the *Adelphi*, [Murry] (with Koteliansky sternly by his elbow) … made the utmost stand for Lawrence of which he was capable."

11 Lawrence to Frederick Carter, 11 January 1924, *Letters*, vol. 4, 556.

12 Lawrence to Robert Mountsier, 31 October 1921, *Letters*, vol. 4, 107.

13 In *Journey with Genius*, Witter Bynner relates Lawrence's reaction to Murry's letter, which he asked Bynner to read: "I did [read the letter]. It was highly overwrought – several closely written pages of adulation and of contrition concerning something he had done to alienate Lawrence. He begged at eloquent length for reconciliation … I felt a letter moving and worth a sympathetic answer … 'Don't be a fool,' he said. 'I know Murry. He's a shit-head … he drove [Mansfield] sick, neglected her, wandered away from her till she died, and then he prowled back like a hyena to make a meal of her! He'll do the same to me!'" (149–50).

14 Lea, *The Life of John Middleton Murry*, 113.

15 An *Adelphi* announcement flyer, with a form for subscribing. CSA.

16 *Adelphi* 1 (June 1923): 6, 8. The cover was, indeed, yellow but hardly pretty, since one half of it was taken by an ad for the "Remington Portable" typewriter, which was celebrating its fiftieth anniversary.

17 Ibid., 82. Other recommended translations, like Constance Garnett's volume of Chekhov's plays, did bear the translators' names, so the omission here was obviously deliberate.

18 Lawrence to Koteliansky, 22 June 1923, *Rananim*, 255 (*Letters*, vol. 4, 462).

19  Lawrence to Thomas Seltzer, 15 June 1923, *Letters*, vol. 4, 458.
20  Lawrence to Koteliansky, 25 September 1923, *Letters*, vol. 8, 86 (not in *Rananim*).
21  Frieda Lawrence to Adele Seltzer, 26 August 1923, D.H. Lawrence, *Letters to Thomas and Adele Seltzer*, 106.
22  *The Adelphi* 3 (August 1923): 183.
23  Lawrence to Murry, 14 August and 25 October 1923, *Letters*, vol. 4, 482, 521. His emphasis.
24  Lawrence to Adele Seltzer, 24 September 1923, *Letters*, vol. 4, 502.
25  Their correspondence was published by George Zytaruk in "Dorothy Brett's Letters to S.S. Koteliansky," 241–74. See also Sean Hignett, *Brett: From Bloomsbury to New Mexico*, 133–49. Brett's archive at the University of New Mexico contains an unpublished narrative, "Katherine Mansfield and Myself," written as letters to the late Mansfield, which Brett started on Valentine's Day in 1923 and which chronicles her relationship with Murry. In it she expresses her belief that Mansfield wanted the two of them to get married so that Brett could take care of Murry.
26  Frieda Lawrence to Thomas Seltzer, 9 December 1923, D.H. Lawrence, *Letters to Thomas and Adele Seltzer*, 121.
27  Frieda Lawrence to Koteliansky, Wednesday, (no month) 1923, *Memoirs and Correspondence*, 222.
28  Lawrence to Koteliansky, 20 November 1923, *Rananim*, 262 (*Letters*, vol. 4, 539).
29  Koteliansky to Juliette Huxley, 9 February 1948, GZA. I am grateful to George Zytaruk for sharing the materials – including this letter – that he obtained while interviewing Lady Huxley in 1972. The full letter is unpublished, but this part is also quoted in Juliette Huxley, *Leaves of the Tulip Tree*, 218, where the date is given as "February 1948."
30  John Carswell, *Lives and Letters*, 259.
31  Koteliansky to Waterlow, 20 June 1926, ATL/SW.
32  Virginia Woolf, 18 January 1918, *Diary*, vol. 1, 108.
33  Campbell, *Today We Will Only Gossip*, 187.
34  Koteliansky to Sarton, 30 November 1937, NYPL.
35  Murry, *Reminiscences of Lawrence*, 110.
36  Lawrence to Thomas Seltzer, 14 December 1923, *Letters*, vol. 4, 542.
37  Lawrence to Witter Bynner, 17 December 1923, *Letters*, vol. 4, 546.
38  Lawrence to Frederick Carter, 11 January 1924, *Letters*, vol. 4, 556.
39  Lawrence to Mabel Dodge Luhan, 19 December 1923, *Letters*, vol. 4, 546.
40  Brett, *Lawrence and Brett*, 26–7.
41  Gertler to Koteliansky, 11 January 1924, BL/Kot.
42  *The Covered Wagon*, dir. James Cruze (from the novel by Emerson Hough), Adolph Zukor and Jesse L. Lasky Studios, 1923.
43  Lawrence to Mabel Dodge Luhan, 22 January 1924, *Letters*, vol. 4, 560.

44 Murry claimed the physical consummation of their relation had not happened then: "I felt free to take Frieda, or thought I did; but when it came to the point, I didn't … [A]t the very moment when the decision lay wholly with me, I said to F. 'No, my darling, I mustn't let Lorenzo down – I can't'" (quoted in Lea, *John Middleton Murry*, 118).

45 Meyers, *D.H. Lawrence*, 306.

46 David Ellis, *D.H. Lawrence: Dying Game*, 148.

47 Lawrence to Murry, 28 January 1925, *Letters*, vol. 5, 205.

48 Carswell, *Savage Pilgrimage*, 218–9.

49 Lawrence spoke both some Italian and some Spanish by then. Kot, who studied Italian in Kiev, would know the difference between Spanish and Italian, and Mrs Carswell would definitely know which language her husband spoke to Lawrence that evening. Either Spender is not remembering correctly here what Kot said during the interview – or Kot might have forgotten this particular detail by 1952, which is less likely.

50 Stephen Spender, 26 December 1952, unpublished journals. Reprinted by kind permission of the Estate of Stephen Spender. Spender sent a copy of this entry to George Zytaruk, who shared it with me. For full text, see Appendix D.

51 Frieda Lawrence to Adele Seltzer, September 1923, D.H. Lawrence, *Letters to Thomas and Adele Seltzer*, 109.

52 Sarah Gertrude Millin, *The Night Is Long*, 157.

53 Brett to Koteliansky, 15 January 1924, Zytaruk, "Dorothy Brett's Letters to S.S. Koteliansky," 269.

54 Brett to Koteliansky, 25 February 1924, ibid., 270.

55 In Hignett, *Brett*, 117. The letter is dated 23 December 1920.

56 Brett to Koteliansky, 25 February 1924, Zytaruk, "Dorothy Brett's Letters to S.S. Koteliansky," 269–70.

57 Koteliansky to Baker, 30 December 1925, ATL/KM.

58 Frieda Lawrence to Brett, 14 March 1932, quoted in Hignett, *Brett*, 147. Her emphasis.

59 Lawrence to Gertler, 10–11 March 1924, *Letters*, vol. 4, 599. His emphasis.

60 *The Adelphi* 8 (January 1924): 674, 734.

61 Koteliansky to Murry, 4? October 1924, quoted in Lea, *John Middleton Murry*, 133, with an erroneous date (7 October). Koteliansky's letter was written prior to Murry's 5 October response.

62 Murry to Koteliansky, 5 October 1924, CSA. Reproduced with the permission of The Society of Authors as the Literary Representative of the Estate of John Middleton Murry.

63 Murry to Koteliansky, 8 October 1924, CSA. Reproduced with the permission of The Society of Authors as the Literary Representative of the Estate of John Middleton Murry.

64 Murry to Koteliansky, 5 October 1924, CSA. Reproduced with the permission of The Society of Authors as the Literary Representative of the Estate of John Middleton Murry.

65 Koteliansky to Murry [6 October? 1924], undated draft, CSA. His emphasis.

66 Murry to Mansfield, 19 May 1921, quoted in Lea, *The Life*, 136.

67 In ibid., 133.

68 Murry to Koteliansky, Wednesday [8 October 1924], CSA. Reproduced with the permission of The Society of Authors as the Literary Representative of the Estate of John Middleton Murry.

69 Murry to Koteliansky, 18 October 1924, CSA. His emphasis. Reproduced with the permission of The Society of Authors as the Literary Representative of the Estate of John Middleton Murry.

70 Koteliansky to Murry, 21 October 1924, quoted in Lea, *The Life*, 133.

71 Murry to Koteliansky, 24 October 1924, CSA. His emphasis. Reproduced with the permission of The Society of Authors as the Literary Representative of the Estate of John Middleton Murry.

72 "Mr Philip Tomlinson. A Sensitive Critic. Obituary," in *Times* (London), 3 March 1955, 10.

73 Philip Tomlinson to Koteliansky, 25 June 1924, CSA.

74 Philip Tomlinson to Koteliansky, telegram, 27 October 1924, CSA.

75 Koteliansky to Murry, 3 November 1924, CSA.

76 Koteliansky to Murry; an undated draft entitled "Wire to Murry" (4? November 1924), CSA.

77 Murry to Koteliansky, 4 November 1924, CSA. Reproduced with the permission of The Society of Authors as the Literary Representative of the Estate of John Middleton Murry.

78 Murry to Koteliansky, 6 November 1924, CSA. Reproduced with the permission of The Society of Authors as the Literary Representative of the Estate of John Middleton Murry.

79 Philip Tomlinson to Koteliansky, telegram, 6 November 1924, CSA.

80 Koteliansky to Murry, 7 November 1924, CSA.

81 Murry to Koteliansky, Saturday (8 November 1924), CSA. Reproduced with the permission of The Society of Authors as the Literary Representative of the Estate of John Middleton Murry.

82 Philip Tomlinson to Koteliansky, 9 November 1924, CSA.

83 Koteliansky to Murry, Monday, 10 November 1924 (copy), CSA.

84 Murry to Koteliansky, Tuesday [11 November 1924], CSA. Reproduced with the permission of The Society of Authors as the Literary Representative of the Estate of John Middleton Murry.

85 Koteliansky to H.G. Wells, 11 November 1924, UI. It was probably another thing that Murry was trying to avoid by making his last-minute appeal, for

he obviously was not looking forward to Kot's badmouthing him again to people with influence.

86  Koteliansky to H.M. Tomlinson, draft, no date, CSA.

87  Murry to Beatrice Glenavy, 4 March 1955, Nottingham/DHL. His emphasis. Reproduced with the permission of The Society of Authors as the Literary Representative of the Estate of John Middleton Murry.

88  *Times* (London), 10 March 1955, 10.

89  Koteliansky to Philip Tomlinson. Draft. 27 November [1924], CSA.

90  Philip Tomlinson to Koteliansky, 28 November 1924, CSA.

91  Philip Tomlinson to Koteliansky, 2 December 1924, CSA.

92  Koteliansky to Philip Tomlinson, draft, no date, CSA.

93  Two letters in CSA, one from the publisher, another from Philip Tomlinson, establish that Cassell and Company were ready to pay the translators £100 for the copyright to the work but needed the signatures of both parties (22 January 1925) and that Philip Tomlinson, in order "to be done with you," had no objection to the settlement "providing you pay me a sum of £50 for my rights in the work (2 February 1925).

94  *Times* (London), 13 February 1925, 17.

95  "Anton Chekhov: The Man of Letters," *Times* (London), 14 July 1955, 11. Ms Hellman was credited, however, with including Chekhov's letters from the Sakhalin Island, which Kot had, for some reason, omitted altogether.

96  Koteliansky to Waterlow, 28 November [1924], ATL/SW

97  See Gertler to Marjorie Gertler, 15 May 1931, *Selected Letters*, 234, and Campbell, *Today We Will Only Gossip*, 161.

98  For the description of "the Thursdays," see also Carswell, *Lives and Letters*, 263.

99  Gertler to Koteliansky, 22 April 1924, BL/Kot. The translation of French is "so much worse for them."

100  Lawrence to Mark Gertler, 23 April 1924, *Letters*, vol. 5, 36. The place was called "Kiowa Ranch."

101  Lawrence to Murry, 3 October 1924, *Letters*, vol. 5, 143. Lawrence probably now imagined the sodden Kot the way he described the sodden Cooley: "hideous, with a long yellowish face and black eyes close together … [a] great ugly idol that might strike" (*Kangaroo*, 210–11).

102  Lawrence to Murry, 3 October 1924, *Letters*, vol. 5, 143.

103  Lawrence to Murry, 28 January 1925, *Letters*, vol. 5, 205.

104  In October 1923 they stayed in New Jersey, in a cottage the Seltzers rented for them and paid for.

105  Quoted in Gerald M. Lacy's "Introduction" to Lawrence, *Letters to Thomas and Adele Seltzer*, x.

106  Alexandra Lee Levin and Lawrence L. Levin, "The Seltzers and D.H. Lawrence: Biographical Narrative," in Lawrence, *Letters to Thomas and Adele*

*Seltzer*, 171. It is possible that this was the translation of Gorky's *Mother* that Lawrence read as a young man, since we know he was devouring Gorky at the time. Gorky's work shares several major themes with *Sons and Lovers*: the central role of the mother, a very close emotional bond between the mother and her son, an alcoholic and often violent husband, the son raising a hand at his father to stop him from physically threatening the mother. To me, the influence of Gorky's 1906 novel on *Sons and Lovers* is, in fact, quite palpable.

107 Quoted in "Biographical Narrative," in Lawrence, *Letters to Thomas and Adele Seltzer*, 178. Her emphasis.
108 Adele Seltzer to Dorothy Hoskins, 15 January 1923, ibid., 254.
109 Quoted in "Biographical Narrative," ibid., 186.
110 Lawrence to Robert Mountsier, 7 June 1920, *Letters*, vol. 3, 547. His emphasis. He also calls Seltzer in this letter "a risky little Jew."
111 Lawrence to William and Rachel Hawk, 27 September 1925, *Letters*, vol. 5, 306.
112 Lawrence to Koteliansky, 6 December 1925, *Rananim*, 273 (*Letters*, vol.5, 347).
113 Frank Waters, *Leon Gaspard*, 102.
114 See Lawrence to Murry, 6 October 1925: "no more of the old crowd – not Kot"; and Lawrence to Brett, 8 October 1925: "Kot I've heard nothing of" (*Letters*, vol. 5, 311, 313).
115 Gertler to Koteliansky, 8 October 1925, BL/Kot. Published in Gertler, *Selected Letters*, where, erroneously, the last part reads "it does one only harm" (218).
116 Gertler to Koteliansky, 24 October 1925, BL/Kot.
117 Lytton Strachey to Clive Bell, 18 February 1918, quoted in Michael Holroyd, *Lytton Strachey: A Critical Biography*, 254.
118 Quoted in Woodeson, *Mark Gertler*, 293.
119 See ibid., 294
120 Gertler to Koteliansky, 30 December 1924, *Selected Letters*, 212.
121 Gertler to Koteliansky, undated 1925 and 28 January 1925, ibid., 213.
122 Gertler to Koteliansky, 11 September 1925, ibid., 216.
123 Gertler to Koteliansky, undated 1925 and 24 September 1925, ibid., 214, 216.
124 See *Mark Gertler* (*British Artists of To-Day*, no. 1). The monocle was legendary. Lawrence called it "your one eye-glass, your pseudo-monocle" (Lawrence to Koteliansky, 29 December 1917, *Rananim*, 127 [*Letters*, vol. 3, 193]).
125 Gertler to Koteliansky, 30 November 1925, *Selected Letters*, 219. Corrected here by comparing with the original letter in the British Library to read "of gloom" rather than "of the glooms."
126 Koteliansky to Baker, 30 December 1925, ATL/KM.
127 Lawrence to Brett, 4 November 1925, *Letters*, vol. 5, 332.
128 Lawrence to Carl Seelig, 9 October and 19 November 1925, *Letters*, vol. 5, 314, 339.

129 Lawrence to Brett, 25 November 1925, *Letters*, vol. 5, 344.

130 Lawrence to Koteliansky, 6 December 1925, *Rananim*, 273 (*Letters*, vol. 5, 347). In acknowledging the cheque to Adele Seltzer, Lawrence also wrote of his desire to go to Russia: "My imagination veers towards Russia, if only I can afford it" (28 December 1925, *Letters*, vol. 5, 364).

131 Gertler to Koteliansky, 22 December 1925, BL/Kot. (Also quoted in Ellis, *D.H. Lawrence: Dying Game*, 278.)

132 Lawrence to Koteliansky, 18 December 1925, *Rananim*, 274 (*Letters*, vol. 5, 354).

133 Murry to Koteliansky, Sunday, but no other date (his emphasis), CSA. Reproduced with the permission of The Society of Authors as the Literary Representative of the Estate of John Middleton Murry. The address on the letter, "1a The Gables, Hampstead," means, however, that it had to have been written after April 1925, for it was after their daughter, Weg, was born that the Murrys moved to that address (see Lea, *The Life*, 142).

134 Lawrence to Seelig, 7 January 1926, *Letters*, vol. 5, 371.

135 Lawrence to Koteliansky, 11 January 1926, *Rananim*, 278 (*Letters*, vol. 5, 374).

136 Lawrence to Brett, 29 December 1925, *Letters*, vol. 5, 365.

137 Lawrence did like what Farbman had to say in his book. "One friend, Michael Farbman, wrote quite a good book about Russia up to 1924," he told Carl Seelig. "Have you read it? … I can send it to you." (7 January 1926, *Letters*, vol. 5, 371).

138 Lawrence to Koteliansky, 4 January 1926, *Rananim*, 276 (*Letters*, vol. 5, 367).

139 Lawrence to Koteliansky, 15 January 1926, *Rananim*, 273 (*Letters*, vol. 5, 376–7).

140 Lawrence to Koteliansky, 11 January 1926, *Rananim*, 273 (*Letters*, vol. 5, 374).

141 Lawrence to Koteliansky, 17 March, 10 April, and 17 May 1926, *Rananim*, 283, 284, 286 (*Letters*, vol. 5, 404, 418, 455).

CHAPTER EIGHT

1 Koteliansky to Schiff, 15 June 1926, BL/SS. Like Leonard Woolf, Schiff had written a letter in support of Kot's unsuccessful naturalization application.

2 Koteliansky to Waterlow, 16 December 1926, ATL/SW.

3 Quoted in Richard Davenport-Hines, *A Night at the Majestic*, 4.

4 Novelist Stella Benson in her diary, and Julian Fane in *Memoir in the Middle of the Journey*, quoted in Davenport-Hines, *A Night at the Majestic*, 3–4.

5 Koteliansky to Pauline Smith, undated, JFA. Since in the letter Kot is telling Polly how important it is for her to learn "a trade," it must have been written prior to her marriage in 1933.

6 Koteliansky to Waterlow, 16 December 1926, ATL/SW. It is also true that Schiff tended to make somewhat exaggerated declarations of hurt feelings to his friends. When, for example, he did not hear from Proust for what he thought was too long, he wrote: "I feel very far away from you and I don't

know how much you really love me. Your last letter greatly saddened me, and I've written to you twice since then without getting a response. And I'm suffering, really very depressed" (quoted in Davenport-Hines, *A Night at the Majestic*, 288).

7  In a letter to Lady Glenavy, after Kot's death. Quoted in Campbell, *Today We Will Only Gossip*, 193.

8  Campbell, *Today We Will Only Gossip*, 159. In the story, the tree is described as "tall, slender … in fullest richest bloom … becalmed against the jade-green sky." It serves as a symbol of the female protagonist's seemingly very happy life and her bliss, until she catches her husband being intimate with another woman. The temporary euphoria is associated not only with the pear tree but also with Chekhov. The protagonist longs to tell the company they are having over for dinner (her husband's mistress, as is would turn out later, among them) just "how delightful they were, and what a decorative group they made, how they seemed to set one another off and how they reminded her of a play by Chekhov!" (Katherine Mansfield, "Bliss," in *Stories*, 149, 153–4).

9  Frieda Lawrence to Koteliansky, 25 February 1932, BL/Kot. Reproduced by permission of Pollinger Limited and The Estate of Frieda Lawrence Ravagli.

10 Kimmel, *The Adventures of Hershel of Ostropol*, 64.

11 For an informative brief summary of English psychoanalysis at the time, see Meisel, *Bloomsbury/Freud*, 39–41.

12 M.D. Eder, *War-Shock: The Psycho-Neuroses in War*, 5, 128.

13 Ernest Jones, *Treatment of the Neuroses: Psychotherapy from Rest Cure to Psychoanalysis*, 209.

14 For an excellent analysis of the Report, see Ted Bogacz, "War Neurosis and Cultural Change in England, 1914–22: The Work of the War Office Committee of Enquiry into 'Shell-Shock,'" 227–56.

15 Lawrence to Mansfield, 5 December 1918, *Letters*, vol. 3, 301.

16 Koteliansky to Waterlow, 21 September 1926, ATL/SW.

17 D.H. Lawrence, *Psychoanalysis and the Unconscious*, 10–11.

18 Gertler to Koteliansky, 16 January 1921, BL/Kot.

19 Suslova later became the wife of Vasily Rozanov, one of the authors Kot translated.

20 "The 'London Mercury,'" *Times* (London), 8 October 1925, 12. Even though Chekhov did not want to see *Wood Demon* staged after he finished *Uncle Vanya*, it has occasionally appeared in theatres in Russia and elsewhere.

21 See Rickword and Garman, *The Calendar of Modern Letters*. Koteliansky's Russian translations were not the only ones that *The Calendar* published. The September 1925 issue, for example, contained – probably much to Kot's chagrin since she was a definite competitor – a translation by Lydia Jiburtovitch of Leonid Leonov's "Three Tales."

22 This was again the same translation as the one that first appeared in *The London Mercury* and *The Calendar* but it had an additional letter, from Chekhov to Suvorin, outlining the play – the same letter that had first appeared in the *The Adelphi*.

23 Koteliansky to Waterlow, 20 November 1927, ATL/SW.

24 Ibid.

25 Koteliansky to Waterlow, 21 September 1926. ATL/SW.

26 Lawrence to Koteliansky, 13 June 1927, *Rananim*, 316 (*Letters*, vol. 6, 82).

27 In another letter to Waterlow, Kot admitted that he was wrong: "I had a letter from him … saying he is writing a new novel. The news to me was not pleasant, for I do not think that L. has the peace needed for a novel. And without that peace in himself I don't believe he will do justice to himself" (Koteliansky to Waterlow, 28 February 1927. ATL/SW).

28 Lawrence to Koteliansky, 13 June 1927, *Rananim*, 316 (*Letters*, vol. 6, 82).

29 Lawrence to Koteliansky, 26 September 1927, *Rananim*, 321 (*Letters*, vol. 6, 159). "Oro te" means "I beseech thee"; "Caro" is "dear" in Italian.

30 Dorothy Parker, "The Private Papers of the Dead: Katherine Mansfield's Journal," *Portable Dorothy Parker*, 451–2.

31 Koteliansky to Waterlow, 20 November 1927, ATL/SW.

32 Koteliansky to Baker, 26 October 1927, ATL/KM.

33 Ellen Jane Harrison and Hope Mirrless, *The Book of the Bear, Being Twenty-One Tales Newly Translated from the Russian.*

34 Lawrence to Douglas, 26 October 1927, *Letters*, vol. 6, 198.

35 Lawrence to Koteliansky, 8 October 1927, *Rananim*, 324 (*Letters*, vol. 6, 173). His emphasis.

36 Lawrence to Koteliansky, 10 October 1927, *Rananim*, 326 (*Letters*, vol. 6, 181). His emphasis.

37 Quoted in Ellis, *D.H. Lawrence: Dying Game*, 381.

38 He came to one, but, according to Koteliansky, was an awkward presence: "One night at Appenrodt's … Forster came in. He joined our table, ate his food nervously, hurried to get away from our 'solid commonness.'" (Koteliansky to Waterlow, 12 December 1928, ATL/SW).

39 E.M. Forster to Koteliansky, 19 November 1927, BL/Kot. Published in full in Rogatchevski, "Samuel Koteliansky and the Bloomsbury Circle," 377.

40 *Maurice* was published posthumously, in 1971.

41 Koteliansky to H.G. Wells, 11 and 14 September 1927, UI.

42 Norman Douglas to Lawrence, 29 October 1927, BL/Kot. Published in D.H. Lawrence, *Letters*, vol. 6, 203n2.

43 Lawrence to Koteliansky, 31 October 1927, *Rananim*, 329 (*Letters*, vol. 6, 203).

44 Lawrence to Douglas, 26 October 1927, *Letters*, vol. 6, 198.

45 Lawrence to Koteliansky, 22 November 1927, *Rananim*, 330 (*Letters*, vol. 6, 203).

46 Lawrence to Koteliansky, 23 December 1927, *Rananim*, 334 (*Letters*, vol. 6, 247).

47 Koteliansky to Waterlow, 22 January 1928, ATL/SW.

48 Koteliansky to Hodgson, 29 April 1930, Yale.

49 Gertler to Koteliansky: "You seemed depressed of late, are you still? Are there any special reasons?" (29 April 1927, BL/Kot; published in Gertler, *Selected Letters*, 223, but with the sentence "Are there any special reasons?" left out.)

50 "A Note on V.V. Rozanov," in Rozanov, *Solitaria*, viii.

51 Rozanov, *Solitaria*, 41. For another instance of Jews viewing Rozanov in complex and ambiguous ways, see the reaction to him of Avraam Uri Kovner, a Russian-Jewish journalist and novelist, in Harriet Murav, "A Jewish Casanova: Letters to Rozanov," *Identity Theft: The Jew in Imperial Russia and the Case of Avraam Uri Kovner*, 156–71. Kovner, who served a long term in prison and Siberia for bank fraud, also wrote letters to Dostoevsky, discussing Dostoevsky's anti-Semitic views. Kovner later converted to Russian Orthodoxy.

52 Defending Rozanov, Gollerbach suggested in his introduction that "those accusations came from people to whom sexual life and the cult of sex appeared nasty and evil. To Rozanov, on the contrary, sexual life breathes of the fragrance of religion, and shines as brightly as the sun" (*Solitaria*, 20).

53 Rozanov, *Solitaria*, 74–5. His emphasis.

54 In his introduction to Rozanov's *Fallen Leaves*, discussed later in this chapter, Lawrence states that Rozanov's "attitude to the Jews … shows uncanny penetration."

55 Lawrence to Koteliansky, 27 April 1927, *Rananim*, 310 (*Letters*, vol. 6, 41). Kot also sent him the Chekhov volume, but, unlike the rest of the crowd, and especially Mansfield, Lawrence never cared much for him – Chekhov's fans, he told Kot, were so "Murryish" (Lawrence to Koteliansky, 27 April 1927, *Rananim*, 310 [*Letters*, vol. 6, 41]). He also informed William Gerhardie in 1923 that "the cells of Chekhov's writing were disintegrating cells, emitting, as they burst, a doleful twang which remained with us" (William Gerhardie, *Memoirs of a Polyglot: The Autobiography of William Gerhardie*, 281). Even in that Lawrence was similar to Rozanov, who, too, saw "nothing particular" in Chekhov (*Solitaria*, 37).

56 Ellis, *D.H. Lawrence: Dying Game*, 363.

57 D.H. Lawrence, "Review of *Solitaria*," *Introductions and Reviews*, 317, 318.

58 Lawrence to Nancy Pearn, 12 April 1927, *Letters*, vol. 6, 29.

59 George Zytaruk, *D.H. Lawrence's Response to Russian Literature*, 157. See also his article, "The Phallic Vision: D.H. Lawrence and V.V. Rozanov," 283–97. Zytaruk analyzes there as well the influence of Rozanov's *Solitaria* on *The Man Who Died* (*The Escaped Cock*), a novella Lawrence was writing simultaneously with *Lady Chatterley's Lover*.

60 Lawrence to Koteliansky, 23 December 1927, *Rananim*, 334 (*Letters*, vol. 6, 247); Lawrence to Nellie Morrison, 8 January 1928, and Lawrence to Edward McDonald, 9 March 1928, *Letters*, vol. 6, 260, 314–5. His emphasis.

61 Lawrence to Mohr, 22–31 March 1928, *Letters*, vol. 6, 338. His emphasis.
62 Lawrence to Koteliansky, 23 December 1927, *Rananim*, 334 (*Letters*, vol. 6, 247).
63 Virginia Woolf: "[Kot] Still talking about Lawrence; a very good writer but his last book DISGUSTING" (4 January 1929, *Diary*, vol. 3, 217).
64 D.H. Lawrence, *Lady Chatterley's Lover*, 33, 36–7.
65 Koteliansky to Ottoline Morrell, 2 April 1928, HRC/OM.
66 Gertler to Koteliansky, 4 August 1928, BL/Kot.
67 Lawrence to Koteliansky, 8 August 1928, *Rananim*, 352 (*Letters*, vol. 6, 495–6). His emphasis.
68 Lawrence to Enid Hilton, 28 August 1928, and Lawrence to Orioli, 17 August 1928, *Letters*, vol. 6, 528, 514.
69 Lawrence to Koteliansky, 10 August 1928, *Rananim*, 353 (*Letters*, vol. 6, 500).
70 Koteliansky to Waterlow, 3 August 1929, ATL/SW.
71 Quoted by Gertler in his letter to Koteliansky, 22 August 1928. Gertler, on the other hand, found Cornwall "rather bleak and unsympathetic." BL/Kot.
72 The comment belongs to Nancy Pearn. Quoted in D.H. Lawrence, *Letters*, vol. 6, 593n1.
73 Lawrence to Orioli, 24 January 1929, *Letters*, vol. 7, 151.
74 Lawrence to Mabel Luhan, 6 January 1930, *Letters*, vol. 7, 616.
75 Gertler to Koteliansky, 16 August 1927. BL/Kot.
76 Gertler to Koteliansky, 11 April 1929, *Selected Letters*, 228.
77 Koteliansky to Waterlow, 3 August 1929, ATL/SW.
78 V.V. Rozanov, *Fallen Leaves*, v. It does say "Russness," as opposed to "Russian-ness," and as such is probably based on the old word for Russia – "Rus'," or, in English, "Rus."
79 Koteliansky to Waterlow, 3 August 1929, ATL/SW.
80 D.H. Lawrence, *Introductions and Reviews*, 350.
81 Koteliansky to Waterlow, 24 August 1929, ATL/SW.
82 See Lawrence to Enid Hilton, 12 September 1928: "I suppose you saw Kot and heard all his alarms. He is like that. He thinks because Gertler and a few like that will say nasty things about my pictures, it means all the world. It doesn't" (*Letters*, vol 6, 558).
83 P.R. Stephensen to Lawrence, 31 October 1929, in Lawrence, *Letters*, vol. 7, 556n3.
84 See Lawrence to Koteliansky, 9 January 1930, *Rananim*, 395 (*Letters*, vol. 7, 618).
85 Fyodor Dostoevsky, *Brothers Karamazov*, 227.
86 Fyodor Dostoevsky, *The Grand Inquisitor*, 27.
87 See Warren Roberts, *A Bibliography of D.H. Lawrence*, 215–6. Roberts suggests – erroneously – that Lawrence helped Koteliansky with the translation.
88 D.H. Lawrence, *Introductions and Reviews*, 315.
89 Lawrence to Koteliansky, 9 January 1930, *Rananim*, 395 (*Letters*, vol. 7, 618).
90 D.H. Lawrence, *Introductions and Reviews*, 127.
91 Lawrence to Koteliansky, 9 February 1930, *Rananim*, 398 (*Letters*, vol. 7, 643).

92 Dostoevsky, *The Grand Inquisitor*, 5. The substitution was of course ridiculous. Dostoevsky was Murry's favourite writer, not Mansfield's.

93 Lawrence to Koteliansky, 15 January 1930, *Rananim*, 396 (*Letters*, vol. 7, 620).

94 Dostoevsky, *The Grand Inquisitor*, 6–7.

95 Lawrence to Edward Titus, 23 January 1930, *Letters*, vol. 7, 626.

96 Lawrence to Koteliansky, 25 January 1930, *Rananim*, 397 (*Letters*, vol. 7, 629).

97 Frieda Lawrence to Koteliansky, 26 January 1930, *Memoirs and Correspondence*, 234. Her emphasis.

98 Morland to Koteliansky, 11 February 1930, in Lawrence, *Rananim*, 402.

99 Morland to Gertler, 25 February 1930, in ibid., 403.

100 Quoted in Ellis, *D.H. Lawrence: Dying Game*, 529.

101 Lawrence to Earl Brewster, 27 February 1930, *Letters*, vol. 7, 653.

102 Morland to Koteliansky, 4 March 1930, in Lawrence, *Rananim*, 404.

103 Morland to Koteliansky, 9 March 1930 in ibid., 405. Knowing how irrational Kot was when it came to Frieda, one almost suspects that he believed she could have poisoned Lawrence to hasten his death.

104 Gertler to Marjorie Hodgkinson, 3 March 1930, *Selected Letters*, 232.

CHAPTER NINE

1 Kot's naturalization certificate is in CSA. It is dated 27 November 1929. Under "Trade or occupation," Kot listed "Translator and Journalist." His Oath of Allegiance, a copy of which is also in the archive, was issued the following day.

2 Campbell, *Today We Will Only Gossip*, 194.

3 Beila Koteliansky, "Two Jewish Stories," 362. Since Kot was already thirty when he left Ukraine, "I left home at a very early age" is obviously inaccurate, unless he meant the years he studied away from Ostropol, in Zhitomir, Odessa, and Kiev. For an excellent discussion of Beila's stories, see Andrei Rogatchevski, "Iz istorii Rossiisko-evreiskoi emigratsii v Velikobritanii: Novye dannye o B.I. El'kine I S.S. Kotelianskom," 125–37.

4 His tomb and headstone are still in a crypt in an old Jewish cemetery in Medzhibizh.

5 As George Zytaruk first pointed out, it was most likely in early October 1927 that Lawrence received these particular stories and promised to "see what I can make of them." Lawrence does not name the stories he received from Kot, but it is a virtual certainty that they were indeed these two (Zytaruk, in Lawrence, *Rananim*, xxviii; Lawrence to Koteliansky, 6 October 1927, *Rananim*, 322 [*Letters*, vol. 6, 169]).

6 Beila Koteliansky, "Two Jewish Stories," 362–3.

7 Kot approvingly mentioned her presence in a letter to Waterlow that described the car trip to the sanatorium: "We arrived about 3 in the afternoon straight to the Sanatorium, and all of us (including Marjorie Hodgkinson) went to a place called Sheringham and had tea there" (Koteliansky to Waterlow, 3 August 1926, ATL/SW).

8 Gertler to Koteliansky, 3 April 1930, *Selected Letters*, 232–3. (The version here is slightly different from the published letter for it follows the original in the British Library.)

9 Gertler to Koteliansky, 9 April 1930, BL/Kot. An incomplete and, for some reason, somewhat rewritten version of the letter was published in *Selected Letters*, 233.

10 MacDougall, *Mark Gertler*, 266.

11 Koteliansky to Hodgson, 29 April 1930, Yale.

12 Koteliansky to Morrell, 30 April 1930, HRC/OM.

13 During one such separation in 1931, Gertler wrote to Marjorie that he particularly enjoyed "drinking tea with Kot at Acacia Road and resting on the sofa you sold them. Heavens! What a pity it was! It is a *most* comfortable sofa" (15 May 1931, *Selected Letters*, 234). His emphasis. The sale of extra furniture obviously occurred when the two were moving in together.

14 Gertler told Beatrice Campbell at the time: "It was awful! Marjorie nearly died, the baby nearly died, and I nearly died" (Campbell, *Today We Will Only Gossip*, 166). For more on Luke's birth and health problems, see MacDougall, *Mark Gertler*, 279, 295–8.

15 Gertler to Carrington, 20 February 1932, *Selected Letters*, 234.

16 Koteliansky to Morrell, 14 March 1932, HRC/OM.

17 Gertler to Carrington, 1 March 1932, *Selected Letters*, 235.

18 For more on his thoughts about suicide following Carrington's death, see his diary entries during this period, quoted in Woodeson, *Mark Gertler*, 291–2, and MacDougall, *Mark Gertler*, 261.

19 Lawrence very much wanted to be a father, and he and Frieda did try to have children. Brenda Maddox in *D.H. Lawrence: The Story of a Marriage* suggests that while many, including Lawrence himself, believed that "the failure was his … the trouble could equally well have been hers," either due to complications from her previous childbirths or effects from a possible venereal disease since she had multiple lovers (138). This is very speculative, of course, but the fact remains that Lawrence desperately desired children and, rightly or wrongly, blamed solely himself for their inability to have them.

20 See Administration of Estates Act 1925 (c. 23), Part IV (Distribution of Residuary Estate), and, in particular, "Succession to real and personal estate on intestacy" (www.statutelaw.gov.uk).

21 See Frieda Lawrence to Koteliansky, [2?] May 1931. BL/Kot. Reproduced by permission of Pollinger Limited and The Estate of Frieda Lawrence Ravagli.

22 Zytaruk, interview with Esther Salaman, 22 June 1967.

23 Lawrence knew of the affair, which started in 1926, and the situation between the husband, wife, and a working-class lover in *Lady Chatterley's Lover* was partially inspired by it.

24 See Ada Clarke to Koteliansky, 13 April 1930, BL/Kot.

25 Koteliansky to Morrell, 30 April 1930, HRC/OM.

26 See Frieda Lawrence to Koteliansky, no date [spring 1930?], BL/Kot. Reproduced by permission of Pollinger Limited and The Estate of Frieda Lawrence Ravagli.

27 Undated [1930], CSA.

28 Gertler to Koteliansky, 9 and 22 April 1930, BL/Kot.

29 Catherine Carswell to F. Marian McNeill [? May 1930], Carswell, *Lying Awake: An Unfinished Autobiography and Other Poshumous Papers*, 208. Her emphasis.

30 Aldous Huxley to Koteliansky, 8 May 1930, *Selected Letters of Aldous Huxley*, 229.

31 Aldous Huxley to Mrs Flora Strousse, 15 October 1932, *Letters of Aldous Huxley*, 364.

32 Aldous Huxley to Mrs Flora Strousse, 15 October 1932, *Letters*, 364.

33 Aldous Huxley to Koteliansky, 30 June and 6 July 1930, *Selected Letters*, 235, 237.

34 Ellis, *D.H. Lawrence: Dying Game*, 534. See also Nicholas Murray, *Aldous Huxley: An English Intellectual*, 225–43.

35 Frieda Lawrence to Koteliansky, no date [spring 1930?], BL/Kot. Reproduced by permission of Pollinger Limited and The Estate of Frieda Lawrence Ravagli.

36 Aldous Huxley to Koteliansky, 25 July 1937, *Selected Letters*, 341. Not only Huxley but also his wife Maria genuinely liked Frieda. While visiting her in New Mexico, Maria was horrified by sharing dishes with Frieda's domestic animals but was full of admiration for their hostess: "Meanwhile there she sits, talking of Montaigne or Buddha or Mabel Dodge and making us feel happy and at home" (quoted in Byrne, *A Genius for Living*, 377).

37 Lawrence to Koteliansky, 20 December 1917, *Rananim*, 125 (*Letters*, vol. 3, 192).

38 Lawrence to Koteliansky, 29 December 1917, *Rananim*, 127 (*Letters*, vol. 3, 193).

39 Quoted in Byrne, *A Genius for Living*, 351. See also Ada Clarke to Koteliansky, 21 October 1930, BL/Kot.

40 See Koteliansky's 1930–32 correspondence with Frieda, Ada Clarke, and George Lawrence, BL/Kot.

41 "High Court of Justice: Probate, Divorce, and Admiralty Division. Mr D.H. Lawrence's Lost Will, Lawrence v. Lawrence and Others," *Times* (London), 4 November 1932, 4.

42 See, for example, Frieda Lawrence to Adele Seltzer, 10 June 1923, in D.H. Lawrence, *Letters to Thomas and Adele Seltzer*, 97.

43 Frieda Lawrence to Martha Gordon Crotch, 7 November 1932, in Moore and Montague, *Frieda Lawrence and Her Circle*, 62. Her emphasis.

44 See Ada Clarke to Martha Gordon Crotch, 7 September 1932, in Moore and Montague, *Frieda Lawrence and Her Circle*, 59, and Ada Clarke to Koteliansky, 6 November 1932, BL/Kot.

45  *Times* (London), 4 November 1932, 4.

46  Ada Clarke to Martha Gordon Crotch, 7 September 1932, in Moore and Montague, *Frieda Lawrence and Her Circle*, 59.

47  Ada Clarke to Martha Gordon Crotch, 12 November 1932, in Moore and Montague, *Frieda Lawrence and Her Circle*, 64.

48  Ada Clarke to Koteliansky, 15 November 1932, BL/Kot.

49  Frieda Lawrence to Catherine Carswell, undated, but most likely late 1932/early 1933. Nottingham/CC. Reproduced by permission of Pollinger Limited and The Estate of Frieda Lawrence Ravagli.

50  Upon Frieda's death, Ravagli went back to his Italian wife. As a Lawrence biographer Jeffrey Meyers points out, since half of the estate went to Ravagli upon Frieda's death, "by a strange irony, fifty percent of Lawrence's royalties continue to go to the children of the man who cuckolded him in his lifetime" (*D.H. Lawrence*, 431n6). This is, of course, precisely the scenario that Kot anticipated and feared.

51  Frieda Lawrence to Martha Gordon Crotch, 22 July 1931, in Moore and Montague, *Frieda Lawrence and Her Circle*, 50.

52  Ottoline reportedly said, "I wish I had her vitality" (Quoted in Sandra Jobson Darroch, *Ottoline: The Life of Lady Ottoline Morrell*, 275).

53  Koteliansky to Morrell, 4 March 1933, HRC/OM.

54  Gertler to Koteliansky, 8 August 1930: "I hope you have had no more attacks of feeling ill" (BL/Kot).

55  Morrell to Koteliansky, 29 April 1930, BL/Kot.

56  Morrell to Koteliansky, 9 December 1931, BL/Kot.

57  Esther Salaman interview with George Zytaruk, 22 June 1967. "A Miss Hale" was probably Dr Elizabeth Hill. See Archives of the Department of Slavonic Studies (GBR/0265/SLAV) at Cambridge University, and "Obituary: Professor Dame Elizabeth Hill," *The Independent*, 6 January 1997.

58  For more on the Irish Sweepstakes, see F.E. Dowrick, "The Irish Sweep and Irish Law," 505–15.

59  Salaman, 1967 interview with Zytaruk.

60  Sarton, *A World of Light*, 184. Kot's letter, from which she is quoting verbatim – except that Kot's version has just "blighters," not "the blighters" – is dated 2 September 1937 and is among Sarton's papers in the Berg Collection of the New York Public Library.

61  Koteliansky to Baker, 20 January [1937?], ATL/SW.

62  Koteliansky to Powell, 24 April, no year [1935 or 1936], IPA.

63  Maxim Gorky, *Reminiscences of Leonid Andreyev*.

64  James Stephens to Koteliansky, 17 October 1934, *Letters of James Stephens*, 383.

65  Ada Clarke to Martha Gordon Crotch, 11 June 1932, in Moore and Montague, *Frieda Lawrence and Her Circle*, 56.

66  Zytaruk interview with Salaman, 22 June 1967.

67 D.H. Lawrence, *The Letters of D.H. Lawrence* (Huxley), x. Huxley's criticism was much more devastating in a letter to a friend: "Murry's vindictive hagiography was pretty slimy – the slug's eye view of poor L: and if you knew the intimate history of his relations with L and Mrs L, you'd really shudder. One day it really ought to be published. Some of the details are quite fantastically ghoulish and foul" (quoted in Meyers, *D.H. Lawrence*, 383).

68 Lawrence to Martin Secker, 17 December 1919, *The Letters* (1932), 487 (*Letters*, vol. 3, 434). His emphasis.

69 Lawrence to Murry, 6 October 1925, *The Letters* (1932), 639 (*Letters*, vol. 5, 311).

70 Lawrence to Aldous and Maria Huxley, 30 October 1927, *The Letters* (1932), 690–1 (*Letters*, vol. 6, 202).

71 Lawrence to Gertler, 28 April 1918, *The Letters* (1932), 440 (*Letters*, vol. 3, 240).

72 Ada Clarke to Martha Gordon Crotch, 16 July 1932, in Moore and Montague, *Frieda Lawrence and Her Circle*, 57. Koteliansky, as we will see later, was not equally complimentary about Moore.

73 Jessie Wood to Helen Corke, 6 October 1930, in Zytaruk, "The Collected Letters of Jessie Chambers," 52. The letter is in the D.H. Lawrence Collection at the University of Nottingham.

74 Koteliansky to Powell, 8 June 1935, IPA.

75 Jessie Wood to Koteliansky, 3 December 1936, in Zytaruk, "The Collected Letters of Jessie Chambers," 140. He repeated the same evaluation to Powell: "The E.T. book on Lawrence is very good, especially the first two chapters … (The later chapters, where she tries to be literary, are not so good)" (8 June 1835, IPA).

76 Jessie Wood to Koteliansky, 19 and 13 November 1936, in Zytaruk, "The Collected Letters of Jessie Chambers," 135. Her emphasis. Jessie and Jack Wood's letters to Koteliansky published by Zytaruk are kept in BL/Kot.

77 Jessie Wood to Koteliansky, 13 November 1936, in Zytaruk, "The Collected Letters of Jessie Chambers," 135.

78 See Zytaruk, "The Collected Letters of Jessie Chambers," 134–87. Kot was generally positive about the drafts he read, but, judging from Wood's responses, his praise was rather lukewarm and she continued to wonder whether he really liked it or was just being polite.

79 Carswell to Koteliansky, 11 September 1930, Saturday (no date; September 1930?), and 14 January 1931, BL/Kot.

80 Carswell to F. Marian McNeill [? May 1930], in Catherine Carswell, *Lying Awake*, 218. Her emphasis.

81 See Carswell to Koteliansky, 26 December [1932], BL/Kot.

82 Compare Catherine Carswell, *The Savage Pilgrimage: A Narrative of D.H. Lawrence*, Chatto and Windus (1932), 20–1, 209, and Martin Secker (1932), 23, 219. The subsequent 1951 Secker and Warburg edition follows the 1932 Martin Secker edition, and features no headings.

83  Carswell to Koteliansky, 29 December [1932], BL/Kot. Her emphasis.

84  See Morrell to Koteliansky, 25 June 1932, BL/Kot.

85  Gertler to Koteliansky, 3 April 1930, BL/Kot.

86  Koteliansky to Morrell, 30 April 1930, HRC/OM.

87  Gertler to Koteliansky, 3 April 1930, BL/Kot.

88  Ottoline Morrell to D'Arcy Cresswell, 11 June 1932, *Dear Lady Ginger: An Exchange of Letters between Lady Ottoline Morrell and D'Arcy Cresswell*, 40. Her emphasis.

89  Miranda Seymour, *Ottoline Morrell: Life on the Grand Scale*, 449.

90  Ottoline Morrell to D'Arcy Cresswell, 11 June 1932, *Dear Lady Ginger*, 40. The full quote reads: "There hasn't arisen any New & Superb Intimate friend in my Life. James Stephens whom you thought so wicked – I think so good, but so elusive – remains, & dear Koteliansky…"

91  Julian Vinogradoff, *Lady Ottoline's Album*, 13.

92  Koteliansky to Juliette Huxley, 22 August 1931, GZA.

93  Seymour, *Ottoline Morrell*, 509–10. The diary entry is from May 1931.

94  Koteliansky to Morrell, 26 December 1933, HRC/OM. The letter touched Morrell, who told Kot she cried when she read it – see Morrell to Koteliansky, 27 December 1933, BL/Kot.

95  Koteliansky to Morrell, 29 December 1932, HRC/OM.

96  Campbell, *Today We Will Only Gossip*, 183.

97  Gertler to Hodgson, 8 December 1933, Yale.

98  According to my interview with Nadia Slow, London, 27 July 2003. Her parents were close friends of the Farbman family (as well as with Fanny Stepniak), and, though still a child at the time, she remembers Farbman's illness well.

99  Koteliansky to Morrell, 4 March 1933, HRC/OM.

100  See Carswell to Koteliansky, 28 May 1933, expressing her sorrow upon hearing the sad news (BL/Kot).

101  See Frieda Lawrence to Koteliansky, Christmas Day 1933, BL/Kot.

102  Rokhl Marshak to Koteliansky, 21 and 23 April 1931. Rokhl's letters are in JNUL. Translated from Yiddish by Janie Respitz Ben-Shach. Quoted with the permission of Jackie Freedman.

103  Rokhl Marshak to Koteliansky, 22 March [1932?] and 23 April 1931, JNUL.

104  Lina Marshak to Koteliansky, 4 May 1932, JNUL. Quoted with the permission of Jackie Freedman.

105  Interview with Jackie Freedman and Sharon Smith, 26 April 2004.

106  Interview with Catherine Stoye, Oxford, 4 July 2003.

107  Interview with Jackie Freedman and Sharon Smith, 26 April 2004.

108  Koteliansky to Pauline Smith, 6 September 1933, JFA.

CHAPTER TEN

1 Koteliansky to H.G. Wells, 23 June 1933, UI.
2 Dennis Cohen to Koteliansky, 10 July 1933, CSA. Quoted with the permission of The Random House Group Ltd. Kot's letter that elicited this response did not survive, but, given his previous ideas about the publishing and Cohen's response, one can easily surmise how ambitious his proposed terms were.
3 Interview with Nina Wedderburn, London, 26 July 2003.
4 The Cresset Press, *A Catalogue of Books Published by The Cresset Press, 1929*, 3–4.
5 The Cresset Press, *Catalogue, 1929*, 19, 33. All prices in the catalogue are given in US dollars.
6 Lawrence to Laurence Pollinger, 29 September 1929, *Letters*, vol. 7, 503.
7 The Cresset Press, *Cresset Press Catalogue, 1927–1934*, 13.
8 "Modern Fine Printing: Publications of the Cresset Press," *Times* (London), 27 June 1937, 14. The exhibit took place at 12, Bedford Square, WC.
9 Koteliansky to Powell, 6 July 1935, IPA.
10 Koteliansky to H.G. Wells, 4 January 1934, UI.
11 Koteliansky to H.G. Wells, 6 January 1934, UI.
12 Koteliansky to H.G. Wells, 9 January 1934, UI.
13 In Wells's hand in pencil on Kot's letter of 9 January 1934, UI. His emphasis. Reproduced with the permission of The Literary Executors of the Estate of H.G. Wells.
14 Quoted in Smith, *H.G. Wells: Desperately Mortal*, 388–9.
15 Koteliansky to H.G. Wells, 3 March 1934, UI.
16 Koteliansky to Marjorie Wells, 8 May 1934, UI.
17 Koteliansky to H.G. Wells, 30 October 1934, UI.
18 H.G. Wells, *Experiment in Autobiography*, 689.
19 Koteliansky to Myer Salaman, 4 March 1937, NWA.
20 See Darroch, *Ottoline*, 281, and Seymour, *Ottoline Morrell*, 537–8. Powell would eventually become one of the most influential and prolific film critics of the twentieth century.
21 Campbell, *Today We Will Only Gossip*, 181.
22 Dilys Powell, *Descent from Parnassus*, 54, 48.
23 Koteliansky to Powell, 6 April 1934, IPA.
24 Koteliansky to Powell, 9 April 1934 and 6 July 1935, IPA.
25 Koteliansky to Powell, 30 April 1934, IPA.
26 Koteliansky to Powell, 3 June 1934 and 25 May [1934], IPA.
27 The US edition (Macmillan) did come out, however, even without an introduction by MacCarthy, but neither Cresset nor Powell were paid for it.
28 Koteliansky to Powell, 8 June 1935, IPA.
29 See Fanny Stepniak's letters to Koteliansky: 21 September, 5 December 1934; 25 January, 22 March, 24 April, 7, 11, 13, 17, 26 November, 2, 21 December 1935; 1 January, 17 July 1936 (in Russian), BL/Kot.

30  Gertler to Koteliansky, 29 August 1934, BL/Kot. Partially published in Gertler, *Selected Letters*, 238.

31  Gertler to Hodgson, 28 August 1934, Yale.

32  See Morrell to Koteliansky, 20 November 1934, BL/Kot.

33  Koteliansky to Powell, Saturday, no date [most likely 24 November 1934], IPA.

34  For more on that, see Gloria G. Fromm, *Dorothy Richardson*, 36–55.

35  See ibid., 142, 154.

36  See Richardson to Koteliansky, 16 April 1934, *Windows on Modernism*, 263.

37  Richardson to John Cowper Powys, [?] September 1934, ibid., 271.

38  Richardson to Koteliansky, 3 April 1934, ibid., 262. Koteliansky's letters to Richardson apparently did not survive.

39  Richardson to Koteliansky, 20 March 1934, ibid., 260.

40  Josef Kastein, *Jews in Germany*, x–xi.

41  Pyle, *James Stephens*, 142.

42  Richardson to Bryher, 15 April 1936, *Windows on Modernism*, 309.

43  Richardson to Koteliansky, 14 April 1936, ibid., 308.

44  Fromm, *Dorothy Richardson*, 306.

45  Cohen to Koteliansky, 17 June 1936, CSA. Quoted with the permission of The Random House Group Ltd.

46  Koteliansky to Hodgson, 8 December 1936, Yale.

47  Richardson to Koteliansky, 18 April 1936, *Windows on Modernism*, 311.

48  Koteliansky to Esther Salaman, 4 March 1937, NWA.

49  Koteliansky to Morrell, 22 January 1936, HRC/OM.

50  Gertler to Hodgson, 28 August 1934, Yale.

51  See, for example, Koteliansky to Sarton, 15 and 20 September 1937, NYPL.

52  Barbara Muir to Beatrice Glenavy, 18 November 1964, BCA. Her emphasis. Muir, however, did not find him "formidable in the unpleasant sense." She assured Glenavy that he was "fundamentally kind" and "sweet with children."

53  Gertler to Hodgson, 8 March 1935, Yale.

54  Gertler to Koteliansky, 4 July 1936, BL/Kot.

55  Koteliansky to Powell, 5 May 1936, IPA.

56  Koteliansky to Powell, Saturday evening [9 May 1936], IPA.

57  Koteliansky to Morrell, 20 May 1936, HRC/OM.

58  The letter from John Ledingham, dated 13 July [1936] (the letter erroneously dates it as 1937 but the envelope is stamped "13 July, 1936"). CSA.

59  Ruth Mantz to Lady Glenavy and Ottoline Morrell, 23 July 1936, CSA. A note from Ottoline Morrell asking Kot to forward the letter to Lady Glenavy ("Could you address this as I don't know her address") is also in CSA.

60  Lady Glenavy to Ottoline Morrell, 22 August 1936, HRC/OM. Reproduced here with the permission of Honourable Bridget Campbell, Lady Glenavy's granddaughter who is in charge of her estate. My thanks for all their help also go to Ian Smyth, an executor of Michael Campbell/William Harold Holden Estate, and to Dr Nicola Gordon Bowe, professor of Visual Culture

at Dublin's National College of Art and Design and the author of a rare article on Lady Glenavy as an artist, "The Art of Beatrice Elvery, Lady Glenavy (1883–1970)" (*Irish Arts Review* 11 [1995]: 168–75).

61 Stepniak to Koteliansky, 27 and 29 July 1936 (these are two parts of the same letter; she told Kot she "feared to send it"), in Russian, BL/Kot.

62 Koteliansky to Juliette Huxley, 22 August 1931, GZA.

63 Koteliansky to Baker, 8 September 1936, ATL/KM.

64 *The New York Times*, 15 July 1937, 20.

65 Koteliansky to Morrell, Saturday [most likely, 24 July 1936], HRC/OM. Kot was not the only skeptical one. When Vere Sullivan, the wife of Kot's friend J.W.N. Sullivan (who himself was slowly dying of multiple sclerosis), heard about Kot's teeth extraction, she declared it "damnable" and suggested that Kot should sue his doctor and "get heavy damages" (Vere Sullivan to Koteliansky, 2 November 1936, CSA. Quoted here with the permission of Beatrice Sullivan, Vere Sullivan's daughter-in-law).

66 See Morrell to Koteliansky, 22 and 26 July 1936, BL/Kot.

67 Koteliansky to Morrell, Thursday [6 August 1936], HRC/OM.

68 The address was "Miss Muir, 12 Menton Road (Swiss College) NW 3. Tel. Primrose 2086" – see Koteliansky to Morrell, Thursday [6 August 1936], HRC/OM.

69 Koteliansky to Morrell, Monday [10 August 1936], HRC/OM. See also Morrell to Koteliansky, 9 August 1936, where she proposes to bring a complete disguise, her own silk dress, a long black cape, and a large flowery hat for the escape (BL/Kot).

70 Koteliansky to Morrell, Saturday [15 August 1936], HRC/OM.

71 Koteliansky to Morrell, Thursday [20 August 1936], HRC/OM.

72 Koteliansky to Morrell, Friday [4 September 1936], HRC/OM. For Ottoline Morrell's letters during that period, when she responded to almost daily anguished letters from Kot with sometimes stern and sometimes soothing words, see BL/Kot.

73 Koteliansky to Morrell, Saturday morning [5 September 1936], HRC/OM.

74 Koteliansky to Morrell, 11 September [1936], HRC/OM.

75 Koteliansky to Morrell, 18 September [1936], HRC/OM.

76 Koteliansky to Morrell, 16 September [1936], HRC/OM.

77 Koteliansky to Morrell, Tuesday [8 September 1936], HRC/OM.

78 See Waterlow to Koteliansky, 26 September 1936, CSA.

79 Stephens to Koteliansky, 12 June 1936, *Letters*, 390.

80 Stephens to Koteliansky, 23 September 1936, ibid., 390.

81 Koteliansky to Morrell, 31 August [1936], HRC/OM.

82 Koteliansky to Morrell, 17 September 1936, HRC/OM.

83 Koteliansky to Morrell, 19 September [1936]. HRC/OM.

84 Koteliansky to Baker, 2 October [1936], ATL/KM.

85  Koteliansky to Hodgson, 8 December 1936, Yale.
86  Koteliansky to Morrell, 6 October 1936, HRC/OM.
87  Koteliansky to Morrell, 26 September [1936], HRC/OM.
88  Koteliansky to Morrell, Monday, 27 [July 1936], HRC/OM.
89  Gertler to Koteliansky, 13 October 1936, BL/Kot.
90  Quoted in MacDougall, *Mark Gertler*, 305.
91  See Morrell to Koteliansky, 15 September 1936, BL/Kot.
92  Koteliansky to Morrell, 16 October [1936], HRC/OM.

CHAPTER ELEVEN

 1  For more, see Margot Peters, *May Sarton: A Biography*, 96–129.
 2  May Sarton to Polly Thayer Starr, 26 May 1937, and to Edith Forbes Kennedy, 17 June 1937, *Selected Letters, 1916–1954*, 117, 121.
 3  See, for example, Koteliansky to Sarton, 17 June and 12 July 1937, NYPL.
 4  Koteliansky to Sarton, 5 October and 25 June 1937, NYPL.
 5  See, for example, Koteliansky to Sarton, 1 September 1937, NYPL.
 6  Koteliansky to Sarton, 13 July 1937, NYPL.
 7  Koteliansky to Sarton, 9 and 13 August 1937, NYPL.
 8  Koteliansky to Sarton, 12 July 1937, NYPL.
 9  Koteliansky to Sarton, 14 and 15 July 1937, NYPL.
10  Koteliansky to Sarton, 12 July 1937, NYPL.
11  Koteliansky to Sarton, 13 July 1937, NYPL.
12  Sarton to Koteliansky, 16 July 1937, quoted in Peters, *May Sarton*, 111. Her emphasis.
13  Peters, *May Sarton*, 111. Sarton quotes Huxley here.
14  Peters, *May Sarton*, 55.
15  Juliette Huxley to Julian Huxley, [15 or 16? April 1937], quoted in Peters, *May Sarton*, 105. Her emphasis.
16  Sarton to Koteliansky, 11 July 1937, quoted in Peters, *May Sarton*, 111. Her emphasis.
17  Koteliansky to Sarton, 25 June 1937, NYPL.
18  Koteliansky to Sarton, 13 August 1937, NYPL.
19  Koteliansky to Sarton, 1 September 1937, NYPL.
20  Koteliansky to Sarton, 2 September 1937, NYPL.
21  Koteliansky to Sarton, 1 September 1937, NYPL.
22  Peters, *May Sarton*, 394.
23  Ibid.
24  Marjorie Reynolds, *"Everything You Do Is a Portrait of Yourself"*: A Biography of Dorothy Kay*, 81–2.
25  Ibid., 394–5.
26  Sarton, *I Knew a Phoenix*, 209.
27  Ibid.

28 Sarton, *A World of Light*, 118.

29 Koteliansky to Sarton, 27 October 1937, NYPL.

30 "The Barn Theatre, Shere: 'The Wood Demon,'" *Times* (London), 21 July 1938, 12.

31 In many ways Kot's translations were, in fact, very similar to Garnett's but a bit wordier. Compare Anton Tchekhov, *Plays and Stories*, trans. S.S. Koteliansky (Dent, 1937), 3–101, and Anton Tchehov, *The Cherry Orchard and Other Plays*, trans. Constance Garnett (Chatto & Windus, 1926), 2–78, 152–230.

32 In a letter dated 3 January 1930, Gertler suggests that Kot and Bernstein just met: "I hope you got on alright with Bernstein" (BL/Kot). For more on Bernstein, see Caroline Moorehead, *Sidney Bernstein: A Biography*.

33 Koteliansky to Sarton, 2 November 1937, NYPL.

34 For an excellent new biography of Ansky, see Gabriella Safran, *Wandering Soul: The Dybbuk's Creator, S. An-sky*.

35 From a letter to Baron Vladimir Guenzburg. Quoted in Irina Sergeeva, "Etnograficheskie ekspeditsii Semena An-skogo v dokumentakh" (Ethnographic Expeditions of Semen An-sky in Documents), 10.

36 S An-skii, *Mezh dvukh mirov. "Dibuk"* (Between Two Worlds. "Dibuk"), 23.

37 S. Ansky, *The Dybbuk*, 68. This is a reprint of the first English translation of the play, which came out in 1926 to coincide with the theatre's first tour in England.

38 "Between Two Worlds (The Dybbuk): Censored Variant," in Safran and Zipperstein, *The Worlds of S. An-sky: A Russian Jewish Intellectual at the Turn of the Century*, 398. See www.museumoffamilyhistory.com/mf-syn-ukr-ostropol-1.jpg and www.museumoffamilyhistory.com/mf-syn-ukr-ostropol-2.jpg for a picture and a drawing of Ostropol's synagogue. Eva Hoffman, in *Shtetl: The Life and Death of a Small Town and the World of Polish Jews*, includes a drawing of a very similar synagogue in Zabludow, Poland, as an example of a design influenced by Polish folk art (insert between pp. 48 and 49). *Wooden Synagogues*, a 1959 book by Polish authors Maria and Kazimierz Piechotka, so impressed Frank Stella when he discovered it in 1970 that it spurred him to create the "Polish Village Series" of painted collages and mixed-media constructions. Among them were "Ostropol I" and "Ostropol II." See Frank Stella, *Polish Wooden Synagogues: Constructions from the 1970s*, and Sidney Guberman, *Frank Stella: An Illustrated Biography*, 136–41. For an image of "Ostropol II," see www.henkel.de/de/content_images/Frank_Stella_OstropolIII_pboxx-pixelboxx-118928_300dpi_1772H_1772W.jpg.

39 Quoted in S. Ansky, *The Dybbuk and Other Writings*, xxv, and Joachim Neugroschel, *The Dybbuk and the Yiddish Imagination: A Haunted Reader*, 56.

40 From a letter to Khaim Zhilovsky [no date], in Neugroschel, *The Dybbuk and the Yiddish Imagination*, 1.

41 According to Ansky, many places where he travelled had similar graves of the holy bride and groom: "In over fifteen or sixteen shtetls I was shown a small headstone near the synagogue and always told the same story about the couple" (in Neugroschel, *The Dybbuk and the Yiddish Imagination*, 99).

42 *Time*, Monday, 27 December 1926. Unlike the case in Europe, the play was not a commercial success in the States. Sol Hurok, himself a product of the Pale in Ukraine, served as their impresario and apparently lost $55,000 on the engagement – See Harlow Robinson, *The Last Impresario: The Life, Times, and Legacy of Sol Hurok*, 116–7.

43 "Savoy Theater, The Dybbuk," *Times* (London), 16 November 1937, 14.

44 Ansky, *The Dybbuk*, 102–3. His emphasis.

45 James Stephens to Lord Dunsany, 6 November 1937, *Letters*, 396.

46 Koteliansky to Sarton, 18 November 1937, NYPL.

47 Koteliansky to Sarton, 18 and 24 November 1937, NYPL. *Uriel Acosta* was written in 1848 by German writer and playwright Karl Gutzkow. It was translated into Yiddish in 1881 and became a staple of Jewish theatres in the Pale of Settlement. The Habima Players performed it in Hebrew. Other plays on that year's tour were "The Golem's Dream" and "The Wandering Jew" – see "The Habima Players," *Times* (London), 7 December 1937, 14. "The Golem's Dream" was written by Halper Leivick and also based on kabbalistic legends, in this case about a Prague rabbi in the sixteenth century. "The Wandering Jew" had preceded "The Dybbuk" in the Habima Players' repertoire. It was written by David Pinsky in Yiddish in 1906 and first staged (in Hebrew) by the Habima Players in 1918.

48 I am grateful to Barbara Sullivan, the widow of Sullivan's son Navin, for clarifying the disease that killed her father-in-law as "disseminated," or multiple, sclerosis.

49 Koteliansky to Sarton, 30 December 1937, NYPL. Kot also suggested in this letter that James Naoise Stephens "was killed somewhat mysteriously." Since he did not like the young man for having caused his friend much anxiety while he was alive, Kot naively underestimated the effect the death would have on Stephens: "The death of the son is a blow to J.S. and to his wife, but I hope not a terrible one" (Koteliansky to Sarton, 6 January 1938, NYPL.). Stephens was, in fact, devastated by the loss of his only biological child. In the years following his son's death he suffered severe depressions as a result of which he published virtually nothing.

50 Koteliansky to Myer Salaman, 4 March 1937, NWA.

51 Morrell to Koteliansky, 28 May 1937, BL/Kot, quoted in Seymour, *Ottoline Morrell*, 551.

52 See Morrell to Koteliansky, 25 June and 20 July 1937, BL/Kot.

53 Morrell to D'Arcy Cresswell, 18 August 1937, *Dear Lady Ginger*, 101. Her emphasis.

54 See Morrell to Koteliansky, 17 August 1937, BL/Kot.

55 See Morrell to Koteliansky, Christmas Day, 1937. BL/Kot.

56 Ibid.

57 Comyns Berkeley, "Prontosil and Its Derivatives," *Times* (London), 21 June 1938, 12.

58 A year earlier, Prontosil injections administered to Franklin D. Roosevelt's son, Franklin Jr, appeared to have cured him of infection in his sinuses. Prontosil was therefore widely publicized everywhere as a very promising new drug. See, for example, an article on Prontosil in *Time*, 28 December 1936.

59 See Seymour, *Ottoline Morrell*, 555, and Darroch, *Ottoline*, 289.

60 Philip Morrell to D'Arcy Cresswell, 28 May 1938, *Dear Lady Ginger*, 114.

61 "Lady Ottoline Morrell. Intellectual Gifts," *Times* (London), 22 April 1938, 16.

62 See Morrell to Koteliansky, 8 February 1938, BL/Kot.

63 Huxley, *Leaves of the Tulip Tree*, 147.

64 Mark Gertler to Marjorie Gertler, 13 and 23 August 1937, quoted in Mac-Dougall, *Mark Gertler*, 309.

65 Gertler to Koteliansky, 20 July 1938, *Selected Letters*, 245.

66 Luke Gertler, "Memories of My Father," *Mark Gertler: The Early and the Late Years*, 11.

67 Gertler to Koteliansky, 20 July 1938, *Selected Letters*, 245.

68 15 August, 17 November, 14 August 1938, quoted in Woodeson, *Mark Gertler*, 323.

69 Gertler to Thomas Balston, 27 September 1938, *Selected Letters*, 247. For more on Balston and their relationship, see MacDougall, *Mark Gertler*, 275–6.

70 Quoted in Woodeson, *Mark Gertler*, 326–7.

71 Gertler to Thomas Balston, 10 October 1938, *Selected Letters*, 247.

72 Gertler to Koteliansky, 30 October 1938, BL/Kot.

73 Virginia Woolf noted in her diary that both her sister Vanessa and Vanessa's lover Duncan Grant, usually stern critics, thought Gertler's new paintings were "a great advance & very remarkable" (*Diary*, vol. 5, 221). The general response, however, was less enthusiastic.

74 Gertler to Edward Marsh, 8 May 1939, *Selected Letters*, 247.

75 Balston's note is quoted in MacDougall, *Mark Gertler*, 325.

76 BL/Kot. The purpose of his notes is unclear, but he probably contemplated publishing it in one of the London papers.

77 *Times* (London), 26 June 1939, 9.

78 Ibid., 27 June 1939, 16.

79 Campbell, *Today We Will Only Gossip*, 166–7.

80 Gertler to Koteliansky, 29 April 1927, *Selected Letters*, 223.

81 MacDougall, *Mark Gertler*, 326.

82 Carswell writes: "[Gertler] was to have come to tea at Acacia Road and when

he failed to arrive Kot went to seek him in his studio not far away: he was dead beside the gas fire with his head on a pillow" (*Lives and Letters*, 267).

83 See Gertler to Koteliansky, 30 October 1938, BL/Kot.

84 See Moorehead, *Sidney Bernstein*, 109.

85 In Peters, *May Sarton*, 127.

86 Koteliansky to Sarton, 1 May 1939, NYPL.

87 Sarton to Juliette Huxley, 12 August 1939, *Dear Juliette: Letters of May Sarton to Juliette Huxley*, 79.

88 Peters, *May Sarton*, 128.

CHAPTER TWELVE

1 Quoted in Moorehead, *Sidney Bernstein*, 86–7.

2 Salaman interview with Zytaruk, 22 June 1967.

3 Koteliansky to Sarton, 7 May 1940, NYPL.

4 Virginia Woolf, 25 May 1940, *Diary*, vol. 5, 287.

5 Koteliansky to Sarton, 3 June 1940, NYPL.

6 Leonard Woolf, *The Journey Not the Arrival Matters*, 14.

7 Virginia Woolf, 15 May and 9 June 1940, *Diary*, vol. 5, 284, 292–3.

8 Koteliansky to Sarton, 28 April 1941, NYPL.

9 Koteliansky to Mervyn Lagden, 13 November 1940, BL/SS. "ARP" stood for "Air Raid Precaution Plans," which the British government had created in 1935 in case of the war. The plans were revised in 1939 to include, among other things, instructions for effective blackouts at night and learning how to put out incendiary bombs (by using sand or earth).

10 Koteliansky to Esther Salaman, 14 June 1940, NWA.

11 Koteliansky to Hodgson, 21 November 1945, Yale. Koteliansky himself did not care for pears, as with all English (as opposed to Russian) fruits, so he gave them to his friends – See Marjorie Wells to Pauline Smith, 20 July 1943: "Oliver and my husband climb the two trees and shake them down. Then they are distributed between all Samuel's friends. He himself says he does not like pears very much" (JFA).

12 Zytaruk interview with Salaman, 22 June 1967.

13 Catherine Stoye, "My Mother – Marjorie Craig Wells," 16–7.

14 Marjorie Wells to Pauline Smith, 16 September 1940, JFA.

15 Marjorie Wells to Ralph Hodgson, 30 July 1945, Yale.

16 Koteliansky to Pauline Smith, 30 May 1945, JFA.

17 Koteliansky to Pauline Smith, 18 November 1945, JFA.

18 Huxley, *Leaves of the Tulip Tree*, 147.

19 Koteliansky to Hodgson, 21 November 1945, Yale.

20 Stephens to Koteliansky, 15 December 1940, *Letters*, 407.

21 Marjorie Wells to Ralph Hodgson, 30 July 1945, Yale.

22 In early 1943, many Londoners found solace in the BBC's radio production

of *War and Peace*. As Marjorie Wells wrote to Polly, even when their listening pleasure was interrupted by an air raid, her son Oliver, who was with her at the time, "made me tell him all I could remember of the story." Kot refused to share that particular experience, though, complaining that "all the Russian names are Anglicised and the whole thing vulgarized" (Marjorie Wells to Pauline Smith, 21 January 1943, JFA.).

23 Koteliansky to Pauline Smith, 5 August 1940, JFA.

24 Koteliansky to Pauline Smith, 24 March 1941, JFA.

25 Marjorie Wells to Pauline Smith, 28 September 1943, JFA.

26 Esther Salaman interview with Zytaruk, 22 June 1967.

27 Koteliansky to H.G. Wells, 10 January 1941, UI.

28 Koteliansky to Sarton, 7 December 1941, NYPL.

29 Among other early massacres in the territories Kot knew were the ones in Esther Salaman's town of Zhitomir, where more than 3,000 Jews were gunned down in mid-September, and nearby Berdichev, where 12,000 Jews had been shot four days earlier.

30 The circular read: "The 'Aktionen' ... are to be organized in such a manner that, similarly to the areas of Brest-Litovsk, Pinsk, Starokonstantinov and Kamenets-Podolsk, they would be completed within five weeks." Quoted in Shmuel Spector, *The Holocaust of Volhynian Jews, 1941–1944*, 172.

31 "Work or Death in Ukraine. Evidence at Trial of Rosenberg," *Times* (London), 18 April 1946, 4.

32 Interview with Anatoly Polonsky, Ostropol, 2–3 July 2006.

33 In G.I. Changuli et al., *Nazi Crimes in Ukraine, 1941–1944: Documents and Materials*, 136. See also: Father Patrick Desbois, *The Holocaust by Bullets: A Priest's Journey to Uncover the Truth behind the Murder of 1.5 Million Jews*; Ray Brandon and Wendy Lower, eds, *The Shoah in Ukraine: History, Testimony, Memorialization*; and Wendy Lower, *Nazi Empire-Building and the Holocaust in Ukraine*. There were cases of Starokonstantinov Christians hiding Jews. See www1.yadvashem.org/untoldstories/starokonstantinov/righteous.html.

34 See www1.yadvashem.org/untoldstories/starokonstantinov/novogorodskii_forest.html.

35 "New Russian Successes in the Ukraine. Big Break-Through towards Nikolaev. Street Fighting in Tarnopol. Staro-Konstantinov Taken by Red Army," *Times* (London), 10 March 1944, 4.

36 Marjorie Wells to Pauline Smith, 10 March 1944, JFA. In an earlier letter (9 February 1944), Marjorie told Polly that her uncle "reads the newspapers a great deal and is remarkably correct in his political forecasts. He always seems to be able to read between the lines in the newspapers and weeklies" (JFA).

37 "Nazi Crimes in Russia. Admissions by Police Chief. 90,000 Jews Killed," *Times* (London), 4 January 1946, 4.

NOTES TO PAGES 271–6 · 399

38  "Nazi Collection of Skulls. Experiments on Jews. Doctor's Instructions," *Times* (London), 9 August 1946, 4.

39  Noel Annan, *Our Age: English Intellectuals between the World Wars, a Group Portrait*, 208–9.

40  Koteliansky to Myer Salaman, 3 November 1944, NWA.

41  Koteliansky to Pauline Smith, 5 May 1945, JFA.

42  Koteliansky to Hodgson, 21 November 1945, Yale.

43  Koteliansky to Pauline Smith, 5 May 1945, JFA. Koteliansky is listed as one of the attendees at the funeral in a brief notice in *Times* (London), 17 August 1946, 7.

44  Koteliansky to Pauline Smith, 18 August 1946, JFA.

45  Koteliansky to Pauline Smith, 21 December 1946, JFA. The pictures were taken by Catherine Stoye, in whose house in Oxford the statuette now resides.

46  Koteliansky to Moishel Koteliansky, 5 August (1942), JFA.

47  Marjorie Wells to Pauline Smith, 19 November 1942, JFA.

48  Koteliansky to Pauline Smith, 22 January 1943, JFA.

49  Koteliansky to Pauline Smith, 23 February 1943, JFA.

50  Interview with Jackie Freedman, 26 April 2004.

51  Koteliansky to Jackie Smith [Freedman], 14 January 1944, JFA.

52  Koteliansky to Pauline Smith, 28 March 1944, JFA.

53  Marjorie Wells to Pauline Smith, 18 December 1943, JFA.

54  Koteliansky to Pauline Smith, 25 June 1944, JFA.

55  Koteliansky to Pauline Smith, 12 October 1953, JFA. All four Smith children, two sons and two daughters, attended university, received post-graduate degrees, and became successful professionals.

56  Koteliansky to Pauline Smith, 13 May 1944, JFA.

57  Marjorie Wells to Sarton, 1 July 1947, NYPL. See also Marjorie Wells to Juliette Huxley, 1 July 1947, where she repeats it verbatim (GZA).

58  Koteliansky to Juliette Huxley, 17 February 1947, GZA. See also Koteliansky to Hodgson, 5 January 1948, where he calls the lodgers "semi-intellectual, simple lifers" whom he "could not stand" (Yale).

59  Marjorie Wells to May Sarton, 6 June 1947, NYPL.

60  Koteliansky to Pauline Smith, 5, 6, 19, 21, 23 May 1947, JFA.

61  Koteliansky to Pauline Smith, 27 May 1947, JFA.

62  Koteliansky to Pauline Smith, 2 June 1947, JFA.

63  Koteliansky to Hodgson, 5 January 1948, Yale.

64  Koteliansky to Sarton, 16 May 1945, NYPL.

65  Koteliansky to Pauline Smith, 30 May 1945, JFA.

66  The document consists of thirteen typed pages and is entitled "More Memories of Kot." It is dated "March 7th 1969." In a letter attached to it, Lady Glenavy wrote to Zytaruk that it was the part she did not include in her book and that Zytaruk should feel free to consider publishing it in *The D.H. Lawrence Review* or elsewhere if he felt it was not too offensive to Catherine

Stoye or Pauline Smith. Zytaruk assured Glenavy that her manuscript was very important and could be eventually published in the *Review*, but that it would be better to wait until his *Quest for Rananim: D.H. Lawrence's Letters to S.S. Koteliansky* came out and made Koteliansky better known (Zytaruk to Glenavy, 14 March 1969, GZA). For full text, see appendix C.

67  Interview with Catherine Stoye, 4 July 2003.

68  Catherine Stoye, "My Mother – Marjorie Craig Wells," 15.

69  Marjorie Wells to Dilys Powell, undated, IPA.

70  Glenavy, "More Memories of Kot," GZA. Reproduced here with the permission of Honourable Bridget Campbell. The narrative appears in full in appendix C.

71  Interview with Jackie Freedman, 26 April 2004.

72  See "London to Montreal. Start of New Daily Air Service," *Times* (London), 2 May 1947, 2.

73  Glenavy, "More Memories of Kot" (see appendix C). Glenavy mistakenly thought that Polly was American rather than Canadian.

74  Marjorie Wells to Dilys Powell, 23 June 1947, IPA.

75  Marjorie Wells to Pauline Smith, 14 February 1953, JFA.

76  Pauline Smith to Manuel Smith, 27 June 1947, JFA.

77  Rita Kay to Pauline Smith, undated [June 1947], JFA.

78  See Marjorie Wells to Juliette Huxley, 1 July 1947: "I stayed at 5 Acacia Road … with the help of Beatrice Glenavy, who stayed for eight days, and of Kot's niece, who flew over from Canada & has now flown back again" (GZA).

79  Marjorie Wells to Juliette Huxley, 1 July 1947, GZA.

80  Koteliansky to Juliette Huxley, 27 August 1947, GZA.

81  Marjorie Wells to Dilys Powell, 2 July 1947, GZA.

82  Koteliansky to Juliette Huxley, 5 August 1947, GZA.

83  Interview with Catherine Stoye, 4 July 2003.

84  Sarton to Juliette Huxley, 23 July 1947, *Dear Juliette*, 165–6.

85  Koteliansky to Pauline Smith, 19 August 1947, JFA.

86  Koteliansky to Pauline Smith, 6 or 7 August 1947, JFA.

87  Koteliansky to Pauline Smith, 19 August 1947, JFA.

88  When I interviewed members of Polly's and Moishel's families in Montreal it came to them as a surprise that Kot had attempted to kill himself.

89  Koteliansky to Sarton, 19 August 1947, NYPL.

90  See Koteliansky to Hodgson, 5 January 1948, Yale.

91  Francis Huxley, letter to the author, 20 August 2010. Quoted here with his permission.

92  Sarton to George and Mabel Sarton, 4 July 1947, *Selected Letters, 1916–1954*, 268. Her emphasis.

93  Sarton to Juliette Huxley, 23 July 1947, *Dear Juliette*, 167.

94  Sarton to Koteliansky, 23 July 1947, *Selected Letters*, 269.

95  Sarton to Juliette Huxley, 4 September 1948, *Dear Juliette*, 276. Her emphasis.

96  Sarton to Juliette Huxley, 14 August 1948, *Dear Juliette*, 253.

97  Koteliansky to Pauline Smith, 23 August 1946, JFA. One would expect him to have expressed similar objections about Ottoline Morrell, who was famous for her extravagant clothes, but, if he had done so, it would have been prior to his and Ottoline becoming friends, at which point he would never allow himself to consider her "an abomination."

98  Sarton to Koteliansky, 4 October 1948, *Selected Letters, 1916–1954*, 292.

99  Quoted in Peters, *May Sarton*, 175.

100  Sarton to Marie Cosset, 5 December 1948, *Selected Letters, 1916–1954*, 294.

101  Sarton to Margaret Foote Hawley, 12 January 1949, *Selected Letters, 1916–1954*, 297.

102  Sarton to Juliette Huxley, 8 August 1987, *Dear Juliette*, 331.

103  Huxley, *Leaves of the Tulip Tree*, 207, 213.

104  Quoted in Sarton, letter to Juliette Huxley, 16 April 1948, *Dear Juliette*, 211.

105  Koteliansky to Juliette Huxley, 22 February 1948, in Huxley, *Leaves of the Tulip Tree*, 218.

106  Koteliansky to Juliette Huxley, 9 February 1948, GZA.

107  Marjorie Wells to Pauline Smith, 29 February 1944, JFA.

108  Quoted in Pyle, *James Stephens*, 171.

109  Koteliansky to Pauline Smith, undated but definitely early summer 1946 since the letter discusses how ill H.G. Wells was, and how his children and grandchildren, home for the summer vacation, were at his house the whole time (JFA).

110  H.S. Brailsford, "Mrs Constance Garnett," *Times* (London), 19 December 1946, 7.

CHAPTER THIRTEEN

1  Quoted in Pyle, *James Stephens*, 116.

2  According to Ruth Pitter. Quoted in Pyle, *James Stephens*, 117.

3  Pyle, *James Stephens*, 117. The martinis had special herbs added to them; Kot was famous for them – almost as much as he was for his rolled cigarettes.

4  James Stephens, *Kings and the Moon*, 33–4.

5  Koteliansky to Hodgson, 21 November 1945, Yale.

6  Koteliansky to Hodgson, 22 December 1945, Yale.

7  Koteliansky to Hodgson, 5 January 1948, Yale. Uncannily, it was also during Christmas that Stephen's son was killed thirteen years earlier.

8  Koteliansky to Hodgson, 5 February 1950, Yale.

9  Koteliansky to Hodgson, 14 January 1951, Yale.

10  Koteliansky to Pauline Smith, 6 December 1952, JFA.

11 Campbell, *Today We Will Only Gossip*, 181–2.

12 Katherine Mansfield, *Katherine Mansfield's Letters to John Middleton Murry: 1913–1922*, n.p.

13 19 May 1917, Mansfield, *Katherine Mansfield's Letters to John Middleton Murry: 1913–1922*, 92–3.

14 From a letter Koteliansky wrote to her in 1926. Baker quotes it in her preface to *Katherine Mansfield: The Memories of LM*, 20

15 20 January 1920, Mansfield, *Katherine Mansfield's Letters to John Middleton Murry: 1913–1922*, 451.

16 23 December 1915, Mansfield, *Katherine Mansfield's Letters to John Middleton Murry: 1913–1922*, 66.

17 22 April and 1 December 1920, Mansfield, *Katherine Mansfield's Letters to John Middleton Murry: 1913–1922*, 529, 608–9. "Must be beaten plainly" has a very Russian ring to it: "Nado prosto pobit.'" In 1918 Anne Estelle Rice painted a remarkable portrait of Mansfield wearing a red dress, which is now kept in the Te Papa Tongarewa Museum of New Zealand. The same museum also owns the painting Lady Glenavy made for Kot, which rested on his mantle until his death. It depicts Mansfield and Kot sitting in deck chairs in the garden and conversing. For more on the latter, see Penelope Jackson, "Double Portrait: *Katherine Mansfield and S.S. Koteliansky in the Garden*," 188–95.

18 7 December 1919, Mansfield, *Katherine Mansfield's Letters to John Middleton Murry: 1913–1922*, 436.

19 Quoted in Carswell, *Lives and Letters*, 267.

20 Murry to Beatrice Glenavy, 12 August 1950, Nottingham/DHL. Reproduced with the permission of The Society of Authors as the Literary Representative of the Estate of John Middleton Murry. Lawrence occasionally used that nickname for Murry as well – see, for example, Lawrence to Koteliansky, 11 January 1926, *Rananim*, 279 (*Letters*, vol. 5, 374).

21 Murry to Beatrice Glenavy, 9 August 1955, Nottingham/DHL. His emphasis. The letter was published in Campbell, *Today We Will Only Gossip*, 192.

22 Koteliansky to Baker, 3 July 1952, ATL/KM. His emphasis.

23 Baker, *Katherine Mansfield: The Memories of LM*, 19–20.

24 Manuel Smith must have written to Kot that there had been friction between him and his wife about how much money they were spending, and that Polly was "a saver," for Kot responded on 19 May: "I will certainly write to Polly … that you, all of you, have a perfect right to enjoy life, and not turn it into a misery, just because it is pleasant to have a big bank account. Had I known that Polly was such a 'saver,' I would have certainly told her my mind" (JFA).

25 Koteliansky to Pauline Smith, 25 April 1951, JFA.

26 Koteliansky to Manuel Smith, 26 April 1951, JFA.

27 Koteliansky to Pauline Smith, 27 April 1951, JFA.

28 Koteliansky to Manuel Smith, 3 May 1951, JFA.

29  Koteliansky to Manuel Smith, 18 May 1951, JFA.

30  Koteliansky to Manuel Smith, 19 May 1951, JFA.

31  Kot's father spoke Yiddish and therefore used the Yiddish word "mensch." Even though "mensch" does mean "man," "be a mensch!" can be addressed to women, whereas Kot's "be a man," as applied to Polly, is awkward.

32  Koteliansky to Pauline Smith, 23 May 1951, JFA.

33  Koteliansky to Pauline Smith, 4 June 1951, JFA.

34  Koteliansky to Manuel Smith, 20 July 1951, JFA.

35  Koteliansky to Pauline Smith, 15 October 1952, JFA. His emphasis.

36  Koteliansky to Pauline Smith, 6 December 1952, JFA.

37  Koteliansky to Pauline Smith, 11 December 1952, JFA.

38  Juliette Huxley, interview with George Zytaruk, London, 5 June 1972. Quoted here with the permission of Victoria Huxley, Juliette Huxley's granddaughter.

39  Koteliansky to Pauline Smith, 29 December 1952, JFA. It is an awkward sentence, influenced by Russian usage. He means by it either that his treatment would not last long, i.e., be quick, or that "he would be cured soon."

40  Koteliansky to Esther and Myer Salaman, Tuesday [6 January 1953?], NWA.

41  Marjorie Wells to Pauline Smith, 7 January [1953; the letter is erroneously dated 1952], JFA.

42  Marjorie Wells to Pauline Smith, 5 and 23 February 1953, JFA.

43  Koteliansky to Pauline Smith, 6 and 17 March 1953, JFA.

44  Koteliansky to Pauline and Jackie Smith, 7 July 1953, JFA.

45  Koteliansky to Pauline Smith, 12 October 1953, JFA.

46  Koteliansky to Pauline Smith, 25 October 1953, JFA. "Until" here is another Russianism. He obviously means "as long as."

47  Koteliansky to Pauline Smith, 30 November 1953, JFA.

48  Marjorie Wells to Pauline Smith, 18 June 1953, JFA.

49  Frieda Lawrence to Koteliansky, 1 July 1932; Frieda Lawrence [?] to Koteliansky, 15 November 1932, BL/Kot. The 1 July 1932 letter is reproduced by permission of Pollinger Limited and The Estate of Frieda Lawrence Ravagli. Frieda denied the authorship of the 15 November letter.

50  See Stephen Spender to Frieda Lawrence, 4 August 1953, Nottingham/DHL.

51  Frieda Lawrence to Laurence Pollinger, 26 August 1953, Nottingham/DHL. Reproduced by permission of Pollinger Limited and The Estate of Frieda Lawrence Ravagli.

52  Frieda Lawrence to Laurence Pollinger, 21 September and 3 November 1953, Nottingham/DHL. Reproduced by permission of Pollinger Limited and The Estate of Frieda Lawrence Ravagli.

53  Frieda Lawrence to Murry, undated [probably August 1953], *Memoirs and Correspondence*, 355. Her emphasis.

54  Pollinger to Frieda Lawrence, 21 July 1954, Nottingham/DHL. Reproduced by permission of Pollinger Limited and The Estate of Frieda Lawrence Ravagli.

55  Frieda Lawrence to Laurence Pollinger, 21 September and 3 November 1953,

Nottingham/DHL. Reproduced by permission of Pollinger Limited and The Estate of Frieda Lawrence Ravagli.

56 Pollinger to Frieda Lawrence, 20 August 1954, Nottingham/DHL. Reproduced by permission of Pollinger Limited and The Estate of Frieda Lawrence Ravagli.

57 It should be noted that that publication was not entirely easy either. Having first appeared to acquiesce to the idea, in May 1966 Pollinger, expressing "surprise and shock" at Zytaruk's understanding that he indeed had the necessary permission, sent him a telegram stating that no such permission had been in fact granted or would be given. Pollinger, however, relented a month later and even apologized for the confusion. I am grateful to George Zytaruk for sharing with me his correspondence with Pollinger.

58 Marjorie Wells to Pauline Smith, 26 January 1956, JFA.

59 Moore, *Intelligent Heart*, 323, 167, 292.

60 Koteliansky to Pauline Smith, 31 January 1954, JFA.

61 Koteliansky to Pauline Smith, 8 February 1954, JFA.

62 Koteliansky to Pauline Smith, 18 February 1954, JFA.

63 Koteliansky to Pauline Smith, 27 February 1954, JFA.

64 Marjorie Wells to Pauline Smith, 11 March 1954, JFA.

65 Marjorie Wells to Pauline Smith, 22 March 1954, JFA.

66 Marjorie Wells to Pauline Smith, 1 April 1954, JFA.

67 Koteliansky to Pauline Smith, 10 April 1954, JFA.

68 Marjorie Wells to Pauline Smith, 12 May 1954, JFA.

69 Koteliansky to Pauline Smith, 23 June and 21 July 1954, JFA.

70 Koteliansky to Pauline Smith, 12 August 1954, JFA.

71 Koteliansky to Pauline Smith, 4 October 1954, JFA.

72 Koteliansky to Pauline Smith, 8 and 29 November 1954, JFA.

73 Koteliansky to Pauline Smith, 16 December 1954, JFA. "A friend of mine" is most likely Lady Glenavy, who was there at the time and who liked to tell him that it was always important to stay positive.

74 Murry to Beatrice Glenavy, 2 December 1954, Nottingham/DHL. Reproduced with the permission of The Society of Authors as the Literary Representative of the Estate of John Middleton Murry. The "Blake dinner" was attended by, among others, Anthony Blunt, who would a year later, following Guy Burgess's defection to the Soviet Union, be interrogated by MI5 and subsequently unmasked as a Soviet spy. Murry described him in the same letter to Glenavy as "something very important in the art world but I didn't – and don't – know what."

75 Campbell, *Today We Will Only Gossip*, 190.

76 Marjorie Wells to Pauline Smith, 30 December 1954, JFA. Dr Rau wrote to Polly five days after Kot's death that by the time he saw him "there was no chance for him to benefit from any medical treatment, as he had developed very serious heart trouble, for which unfortunately there was no cure" (JFA).

77  Marjorie Wells to Beatrice Glenavy, 22 January 1955, GZA.

78  Koteliansky to Pauline Smith, 31 December 1954, JFA.

79  Marjorie Wells to Beatrice Glenavy, 24 January 1955, GZA.

80  Wells to Pauline Smith, 16 January 1955, JFA.

81  Leonard Woolf to Dilys Powell, 19 January 1955, IPA. Reproduced with the permission of The University of Sussex and The Society of Authors as the Literary Representative of the Estate of Leonard Woolf.

82  Marjorie Wells to Leonard Woolf, 21 January 1955, quoted in Carswell, *Lives and Letters*, 267. See also Marjorie Wells to Beatrice Glenavy, 24 January 1954: "Kot said just afterwards … that for a quarter of an hour the past had become alive again. Then he grew sad and said alas! It was fading, he was not his old self, although while Woolf was there he thought he was" (GZA).

83  Marjorie Wells to Beatrice Glenavy, 24 January 1954, GZA.

84  Leonard Woolf to Dilys Powell, 26 January 1955, IPA. Reproduced with the permission of The University of Sussex and The Society of Authors as the Literary Representative of the Estate of Leonard Woolf.

85  Marjorie Wells to Beatrice Glenavy, 21 January 1955, GZA.

86  The telegram is on "A Canadian Pacific" form, dated "1955 Jan 22 PM 3:37" (JFA).

87  Marjorie Wells to Pauline Smith, 22 January 1955, JFA.

88  Marjorie Wells to Rachel Marshak, 28 April 1955. A typed copy of the letter is in CSA.

89  See Smith, *H.G. Wells: Desperately Mortal*, 479.

90  Marjorie Wells to Pauline Smith, 27 January 1955, JFA.

91  See Marjorie Wells to Beatrice Glenavy, 26 January 1955, BCA.

92  Wells specified those in attendance in a letter to Lady Glenavy: "The Huxleys and the Salamans and Sophie [Jacobs] and her daughter-in-law and the Donovans and Mrs Samson from No. 5 [Acacia Road], and Dennis Cohen and Mavrogordato and Dilys and Dr Batten and Dr Rau, were all there. And Marjorie Gertler, whom it was nice to see again. Mrs James Stephens was also there." Interestingly, both Marjorie Gertler and Mrs Stephens were added to the otherwise typed letter by hand – thus somehow separating them from the other, less surprising, attendees (Wells to Beatrice Glenavy, 26 January 1955, BCA).

93  The document entitled "Dr Fulton's Funeral Address" is in IPA (Fulton sent it to Dilys Powell on 29 January 1955, as per her request).

94  Frieda Lawrence to Murry, January 1955, and to Harry T. Moore, 14 January 1955, *Memoirs and Correspondence*, 387–8.

95  Murry to Frieda Lawrence, 21 April 1955, Lawrence, *Memoirs and Correspondence*, 396.

96  Murry to Beatrice Glenavy, 5 July 1955, Nottingham/DHL. His emphasis. Reproduced with the permission of The Society of Authors as the Literary Representative of the Estate of John Middleton Murry.

97  "Entry of Death," no. 226 (Registrar of Births and Deaths for the Sub-district of Hampstead North, in the Metropolitan Borough of Hampstead), issued on 24 January 1955, CSA.

98  *Times* (London), 24 January 1955, 10. The death certificate also listed his age incorrectly – as seventy-three.

99  D.P. [Dilys Powell], "Mr S.S. Koteliansky. Obituary," *Times* (London), 27 January 1955, 10.

100  Leonard Woolf, "Kot," 170–2.

101  On behalf of Alan Edward Oliver to Pauline Smith, 26 January 1955, JFA. His emphasis.

102  Lady Glenavy to Pauline Smith, 27 December 1955, JFA. Reproduced here with the permission of the Hon. Bridget Campbell.

103  "In the High Court of Justice, The Principal Probate Registry," dated 6 February 1954. A typewritten copy is in CSA. George Zytaruk also forwarded me the original "office copy," which bears the seal of the High Court of Justice and which he obtained while collecting materials for the Koteliansky biography. The will is witnessed by Koteliansky's two nextdoor neighbours, the Donovans, who lived on 6 Acacia Road and whom Lady Glenavy describes briefly in appendix C.

104  Dennis Cohen to A.E. Oliver, 28 January 1955, CSA. Quoted with the permission of The Random House Group Ltd.

105  A.E. Oliver to Dennis Cohen, 4 February 1955, CSA.

106  Marjorie Wells to A.E. Oliver, 5 February 1955, CSA.

107  Percy Muir to Dilys Powell, 24 January 1955, IPA.

108  Marjorie Wells to A.E. Oliver, 5 February 1955, CSA.

109  Campbell, *Today We Will Only Gossip*, 194. The rumour had it – as several people I interviewed in London, including Catherine Stoye, told me – that many of her letters to Kot, especially in later years, remained unopened. Whether she burnt them all immediately upon getting them back or kept them for a while stored in a small room in her castle is also somewhat of a mystery, since Lady Glenavy's granddaughter remembers "discovering a secret room above the garage at my grandparents' house in Dublin which could only be seen from my grandfather's bathroom window. Beattie said it was Kot's hidey-hole. No idea if that was true but it was very exciting to have discovered it!! Strange that no one ever went in" (Honourable Bridget Campbell, email to the author, 18 December 2010, quoted here with her permission).

110  Jackie Freedman, email to the author, 2 September 2009.

111  Rachel [Rokhl] Marshak to Marjorie Wells, [February] 1955, and Marjorie Wells to Pauline Smith, 28 April 1955, CSA.

112  Interview with Jackie Freedman and Sharon Smith, 26 April 2004.

POST MORTEM

1 Lady Glenavy to Mary Hutchinson, 4 December 1958, HRC/MH. Reproduced here with the permission of Hon. Bridget Campbell. The publisher in question was Methuen. The book was brought out six years later by Constable.

2 Anonymous, "Two-Stringed Bow," *Times* (London), 23 April 1964, 17.

3 Sir William Haley, "Group Portrait" and "Personal Touch," *Times* (London), 23 February 1978, 13, and 23 September 1976, 11.

4 In 1957 a collection of his columns came out in a book form – *Talking Books*.

5 Oliver Edwards, "Out of Russia" and "At Isola Bella," *Times* (London), 9 October 1958, 13, and 26 November 1964, 16.

6 Oliver Edwards, "The Captain's Doll," *Times* (London), 13 May 1965, 15.

7 Oliver Edwards, "Frieda Lawrence," *Times* (London), 16 May 1956, 9.

8 He survived the massacre because he ran away as the Germans were approaching and then joined the Soviet Army.

APPENDIX C

1 From GZA. Reproduced here with the permission of the Hon. Bridget Campbell and published for the first time. It is dated "March 7th 1969." Beatrice Campbell died the following year, at the age of eighty-nine. In an accompanying letter to Dr Zytaruk, bearing the same date, she wrote: "I am sending you some more memories of Kot, which I did not include in my book about our 'gossip' [i.e., *Today We Will Only Gossip*] … perhaps you might think of using this stuff … if you felt that Mrs Stoye or Kot's niece, Mrs Pauline Smith, might not be offended about things I have written about her or Mrs Stoye's mother" (Lady Glenavy to Geoge Zytaruk, 7 March 1969, GZA).

2 Kot met and befriended Ruth Pitter through his work at the Cresset Press, which started publishing her books of poetry in 1934. In 1955, the year of Kot's death, Pitter became the first woman to receive the Queen's Gold Medal for Poetry. This treatment of a painted tray probably reminded Lady Glenavy of the much earlier incident, which she described in *Today We Will Only Gossip*, when Kot smashed a wooden tray painted by Roger Fry in Montague Shearman's flat, which was set up for a Russian Ballet party.

3 Since Marjorie Wells was away when Kot attempted to take his life, this particular account is not accurate.

4 A pair of glasses with a magnifying effect that was used at horseraces; a variation of binoculars. The Donovans were going to Ascot Racecourse, which was not far from Windsor Castle and was, therefore, frequented by the Royal Family.

5 Totally inaccurate since he had helped Polly and her brother Eli (and not the rest of the family) leave Ukraine fifteen years before WWII started. They also went to Canada, not the USA.

6 Continuation of the US-Canada confusion. Polly of course had married her husband in Sherbrooke, not New York, and that is where they still lived.

7 According to Wells, Glenavy stayed with Kot for eight days – see her letter to Juliette Huxley, 1 July 1947, GZA.

8 Sophie Jacobs was a good friend of Koteliansky; she was an Irish Jew, whom Lady Glenavy had known since Jacobs's Dublin years (See Campbell, *Today We Will Only Gossip*, 190). But Glenavy is probably wrong here, and it was Esther Salaman instead, since she was the one who usually drove Kot to his medical appointments.

9 The last name of the female doctor was Mackay. See Marjorie Wells to Dilys Powell, 2 July 1947: "Yesterday I saw Dr Mackay, the woman doctor in charge of him, and liked her very much" (IPA).

10 Jaegers is a London department store. Her emphasis.

11 Alpers's biography of Mansfield was published in 1954. Her take on Kot's reaction to the book contradicts Ida Baker's, who stated that both Kot and she were disappointed in it – see Baker, *Katherine Mansfield: The Memories of LM*, 19–20. Glenavy's speculation about Alpers's wife having written the book is of course baseless.

APPENDIX D

1 Both documents are from GZA. Spender's journal entry is reprinted here by kind permission of the Estate of Stephen Spender.

2 The magazine in question was *Encounter*, which Spender founded in 1953 and edited for thirteen years.

3 *The Destructive Element: A Study of Modern Writers and Beliefs* (1935).

4 This suggests that prior to 1952 Kot had not met Berlin. Berlin, by then already a famous philosopher who also had spend several years in the 1940s working for the British Embassy in Moscow, was, like Kot, a Russian Jew. He was born in Riga in 1909 and came to England with his family in 1921. It would have been natural for people who knew them both to try to bring Berlin and Koteliansky together; it is somewhat surprising, therefore, that the meeting probably never took place.

5 The dinner took place in December 1923.

6 Mansfield died earlier that year. Must be Spender's confusion, definitely not Kot's.

7 Catherine Carswell in *Savage Pilgrimage* states that it was Spanish, not Italian (218). Confusion, again, must be Spender's, not Kot's.

8 Spender seems to confuse New Mexico with Mexico here.

9 Sartre's famous 1944 play; the English title is *No Exit*.

APPENDIX E

1 Both are among the Koteliansky Papers in the British Library – see: Add.48975, f.21–21v, f.22, f.23–23v., f.24 – and published here for the first time. While the second letter is undated, other than "Saturday," the postal stamp on the envelope is dated 17 July 1932, so Saturday would have been 16 July. The date on the first letter – "July 3, 1932" – is in Kot's handwriting. Frieda just dates it as "Sunday." The date on the envelope is "4 July, 1932." All emphases are hers. Reproduced by permission of Pollinger Limited and The Estate of Frieda Lawrence Ravagli.

2 Frieda is referring here to Werner Wesslau's book *Der Pessimismus bei D.H. Lawrence*, which came out in 1931.

# BIBLIOGRAPHY

Afanas'ev-Chuzhvinsky, *Poezdka v iuzhnuiu Rossiiu* (Travel to the Southern Russia). St Petersburg: A.F. Bazunov Booksellers, 1863.

Alderman Geoffrey. *The Jewish Community in British Politics.* New York: Oxford University Press, 1983.

– *London Jewry and London Politics, 1889–1986.* London: Routledge, 1989.

Aldington, Richard. *D.H. Lawrence: Portrait of a Genius But ...* New York: Collier Books, 1961.

Alexander, Peter F. *Leonard and Virginia Woolf: A Literary Partnership.* New York: Harvester Wheatsheaf, 1992.

Alpers, Antony. *The Life of Katherine Mansfield.* New York: Penguin, 1982.

Andreyev, Leonid, and Ivan Bunin. *Lazarus and The Gentleman from San Francisco.* Trans. Abraham Yarmolinsky. Boston: Stratford Company, 1918.

Annan, Noel. *Our Age: English Intellectuals between the World Wars, a Group Portrait.* New York: Random House, 1990.

An-skii, S. *Mezh dvukh mirov. "Dibuk"* (Between Two Worlds. Dibuk). Trans. from Yiddish by Georg. Leonidov. Kharbin: Tipografiia Frenkelia, 1929.

Ansky, S. *The Dybbuk.* Trans. Henry G. Alsberg and Winifred Katzin. New York: Liveright, 1971.

– *The Dybbuk and Other Writings.* Ed. David G. Roskies. New York: Schochen, 1992.

Asimov, Isaac. *In Memory Yet Green: The Autobiography of Isaac Asimov, 1920–1954.* New York: Avon Books, 1979.

Babel, Isaac. *The Complete Works of Isaac Babel.* Ed. Nathalie Babel. Trans. Peter Constantine. New York: Norton, 2002.

Baker, Ida ("LM"). *Katherine Mansfield: The Memories of LM.* New York: Taplinger, 1972.

Baron, Salo W. *The Russian Jews under the Tsars and the Soviets.* New York: Macmillan, 1964.

Beauchamp, Harold. *Reminiscences and Recollections.* New Plymouth: Thomas Avery, 1937.

Beilis, Mendel. *Scapegoat on Trial: The Story of Mendel Beilis, the Autobiography of Mendel Beilis, the Defendant in the Notorious 1912 Blood Libel in Kiev.* Ed. Shari Schwartz. New York: CIS Publishers, 1992.

Bell, Clive. *Civilization and Old Friends.* Chicago: The University of Chicago Press, 1973.

Bell, Quentin. *Bloomsbury Recalled.* New York: Columbia University Press, 1995.

– *Virginia Woolf: A Biography*. New York: Harcourt, 1972.

Berberova, Nina. *Moura: The Dangerous Life of the Baroness Budberg*. Trans. Marian
 Schwartz and Richard D. Sylvester. New York: The New York Review of Books, 2005.

Berkeley, Comyns. "Prontosil and Its Derivatives." *Times* (London), 21 June 1938.

Bishop, Edward. *A Virginia Woolf Chronology*. London: Macmillan, 1989.

Bogacz, Ted. "War Neurosis and Cultural Change in England, 1914–22: The Work of the
 War Office Committee of Enquiry into 'Shell-Shock.'" *Journal of Contemporary History* 2
 (April 1989).

Bowe, Nicola Gordon. "The Art of Beatrice Elvery, Lady Glenavy (1883–1970)." *Irish Arts
 Review* 11 (1995).

Brandon, Ray and Wendy Lower, eds. *The Shoah in Ukraine: History, Testimony, Memorialization*. Bloomington: Indiana University Press, 2008.

Brett, Dorothy. *Lawrence and Brett: A Friendship*. Philadelphia: Lippincott, 1933.

Brome, Vincent. *H.G. Wells: A Biography*. London: Spottiswoode, Ballantyne & Co, 1952.

Brower, Daniel R. *The Russian City between Tradition and Modernity, 1850–1900*. Berkeley:
 University of California Press, 1990.

Bryant, Louise. *Mirrors of Moscow*. New York: Thomas Seltzer, 1923.

Bulgakov, Mikhail. *White Guard*. Trans. Marian Schwartz. New Haven: Yale University
 Press, 2009.

Bunin, Ivan. *Collected Stories*. Trans. Graham Hettlinger. Chicago: Ivan R. Dee, 2007.

– *The Gentleman from San Francisco and Other Stories*. Trans. [D.H. Lawrence], S.S.
 Koteliansky and Leonard Woolf. London: The Hogarth Press, 1922.

– *The Gentleman from San Francisco and Other Stories*. Trans. D.H. Lawrence, S.S.
 Koteliansky, Leonard Woolf. New York: Thomas Seltzer, 1923.

– *Russian Requiem 1885–1920: A Portrait from Letters, Diaries, and Fiction*. Ed. Thomas
 Gaiton Marullo. Chicago: Ivan R. Dee, 1993.

– *The Village*. Trans. Hugh Aplin. London: Oneworld Classics, 2010.

Bynner, Witter. *Journey with Genius: Recollections and Reflections Concerning the D.H.
 Lawrences*. New York: The John Day Company, 1951.

Byrne, Janet. *A Genius for Living: The Life of Frieda Lawrence*. New York: HarperCollins,
 1995.

Cahan, Abraham. *The Rise of David Levinsky*. New York: Modern Library, 2001.

Callow, Philip. *Son and Lover: The Young D.H. Lawrence*. London: Allison and Butsby, 1975.

Campbell, Beatrice (Lady Glenavy). *Today We Will Only Gossip*. London:
 Constable, 1964.

Cannan, Gilbert. *Mendel*. London: T. Fisher Unwin, 1916.

Carrington, Dora. *Carrington: Letters and Extracts from Her Diaries*. Ed. David Garnett.
 Oxford: Oxford University Press, 1970.

Cassavant, Sharron Greer. *John Middleton Murry: The Critic as Moralist*. Birmingham:
 University of Alabama Press, 1982.

Carswell, Catherine. *Lying Awake: An Unfinished Autobiography and Other Posthumous
 Papers*. Ed. John Carswell. Edinburgh: Canongate Classic, 1997.

– *The Savage Pilgrimage: A Narrative of D.H. Lawrence.* London: Secker & Warburg, 1951.

– *The Savage Pilgrimage: A Narrative of D.H. Lawrence.* London: Chatto and Windus, 1932.

– *The Savage Pilgrimage: A Narrative of D.H. Lawrence.* London: Martin Secker, 1932.

Carswell, John. *The Exile: A Life of Ivy Litvinov.* London: Faber and Faber, 1983.

– *Lives and Letters: A.R. Orage, Katherine Mansfield, Beatrice Hastings, John Middleton Murry, S.S. Koteliansky, 1906–1957.* New York: New Directions, 1978.

Changuli, G.I., et al., eds. *Nazi Crimes in Ukraine, 1941–1944: Documents and Materials.* Trans. from Russian, V.I. Biley, S.I. Kaznady, A.E. Sologubenko. Kiev: Naukova Dumka Publishers, 1987.

Chekhov [Chehov; Tchekhov], Anton. *Anton Tchekhov: Literary and Theatrical Reminiscences.* Trans. and ed. S.S. Koteliansky. New York: George H. Doran, 1927.

– *The Bet and Other Stories.* Trans. S. Koteliansky and J.M. Murry. Boston: John W. Luce, 1915.

– *The Cherry Orchard and Other Plays.* Trans. Constance Garnett. London: Chatto & Windus, 1926.

– *The House with the Mezzanine and Other Stories.* Trans. S.S. Koteliansky and Gilbert Cannan. New York: Charles Scribner's Sons, 1917.

– *My Life and Other Stories.* Trans. S.S. Koteliansky and Gilbert Cannan. London: C. W. Daniel, 1920.

– *Lady with the Little Dog and Other Stories. 1896–1914.* Trans. Ronald Wilks. London: Penguin, 2002.

– *The Lady with the Toy Dog and Gooseberries.* Trans. S.S. Koteliansky. London: Todd Publishing (Polybooks), 1943.

– *The Life and Letters of Anton Tchekhov.* Trans. and ed. S.S. Koteliansky and Philip Tomlinson. London: Casell and Co, 1925.

_–*The Note-books of Anton Tchekhov Together with Reminiscences of Tchekhov by Maxim Gorky.* Trans. S.S. Koteliansky and Leonard Woolf. London: The Hogarth Press, 1921.

– *Plays and Stories.* Trans. S.S. Koteliansky. London: Dent, 1937.

– *Rothschild's Fiddle and Other Stories.* (Various translators, including Koteliansky and J.M. Murry). New York: Boni and Liveright, 1917.

– *Sobranie sochinenii* (Collected Works). 12 vols. Moscow: Gosudarstvennoe izdatel'stvo khudozhestvennoi literatury, 1962.

– *Three Plays.* Trans. S.S. Koteliansky. London: Penguin, 1940.

– *The Wood Demon: A Comedy in Four Acts.* Trans. S.S. Koteliansky. New York: Macmillan, 1926.

Cheyette, Bryan. *Constructions of "the Jew" in English Literature and Society: Racial Representations, 1875–1945.* Cambridge: Cambridge University Press, 1993.

Conroy, Geraldine L. "Our Perhaps Uncommon Friendship." *Modern Fiction Studies* 3 (Autumn 1978).

Coulton, G.G. "Voluntary or Compulsory Service." *The Nineteenth Century and After* (January 1915).

*The Covered Wagon.* Dir. James Cruze. Adolph Zukor and Jesse L. Lasky Studios, 1923.

The Cresset Press. *A Catalogue of Books Published by The Cresset Press, 1929*. London: The Cresset Press, 1929.

– *Cresset Press Catalogue, 1927–1934*. London: The Cresset Press, 1934.

Crone, Nora. *A Portrait of Katherine Mansfield*. Ilfracombe, Devon: Arthur H. Stockwell, 1985.

Darroch, Sandra Jobson. *Ottoline: The Life of Lady Ottoline Morrell*. London: Cassell, 1976.

Davenport-Hines, Richard. *A Night at the Majestic: Proust & the Great Modernist Dinner Party of 1922*. London: Faber and Faber, 2006.

Davis, Joseph. *Yom-Tov Lipmann Heller: Portrait of a Seventeenth-Century Rabbi*. Oxford: The Littman Library of Jewish Civilization, 2004.

Dearmer, Percy. "The Soul of Russia." *The Nineteenth Century and After* (January 1915).

DeSalvo, Louise. *Virginia Woolf: The Impact of Childhood Sexual Abuse on Her Life and Work*. Boston: Beacon Press, 1989.

Desbois, Father Patrick. *The Holocaust by Bullets: A Priest's Journey to Uncover the Truth behind the Murder of 1.5 Million Jews*. New York: Palgrave MacMillan, 2008.

Dickson, Lovat. *H.G. Wells: His Turbulent Life and Times*. New York: Atheneum, 1971.

Dostoevsky, Anna. *Dostoevsky Portrayed by His Wife: The Diary and Reminiscences of Mme. Dostoevsky*. Trans.S.S. Koteliansky. London: Routledge, 1926.

Dostoevsky, Fyodor. *Brothers Karamazov*. Trans. Constance Garnett. New York: Norton, 1976.

– *Dostoevsky: Letters and Reminiscences*. Trans. S.S. Koteliansky and J. Middleton Murry. London: Chatto and Windus, 1923.

– *The Grand Inquisitor*. Trans. S.S. Koteliansky. London: Martin Secker, 1935.

– *New Dostoevsky Letters*. Trans. S.S. Koteliansky. London: Mandrake Press, 1929.

– *Pages from the Journal of an Author*. Trans. S. Koteliansky and J. Middleton Murry. Boston: John W. Luce and Co, 1916.

– *Stavrogin Confessions*. Trans. S.S. Koteliansky and Virginia Woolf. London: The Hogarth Press, 1922.

Dowling, David. *Bloomsbury Aesthetics and the Novels of Forster and Woolf*. London: Macmillan, 1985.

Dowrick, F.E. "The Irish Sweep and Irish Law." *The American Journal of Comparative Law* 4 (Autumn 1953).

Dubnov-Erlich, Sophie. *The Life and Works of S.M. Dubnow: Diaspora Nationalism and Jewish History*. Bloomington: Indiana University Press, 1991.

Dubnow, Simon. *Histoire d'un soldat juif. 1881–1915*. Paris: Les Éditions du Cerf, 1988.

– *History of the Jews in Russia and Poland: From the Earliest Times until Present Day*. Trans. I. Friedlaender. Philadelphia: Jewish Publication Society of America, 1920.

Eder, David. *Memoirs of a Modern Pioneer*. Ed. J.B. Hobman. London: Victor Gollancz, 1945.

– *War-Shock: The Psycho-Neuroses in War – Psychology and Treatment*. London: William Heinemann, 1917.

Edwards, Oliver. "At Isola Bella." *Times* (London), 26 November 1964.

– "The Captain's Doll." *Times* (London), 13 May 1965.

– "Frieda Lawrence." *Times* (London), 16 May 1956.

– *Talking Books.* London: Heinemann, 1957.

– "Out of Russia." *Times* (London), 9 October 1958.

*Electoral Roll for Holborn, 1913–1914.*

*Electoral Roll for Islington, 1904–1911.*

Ellis, David. *D.H. Lawrence: Dying Game, 1922–1930.* Cambridge: Cambridge University Press, 1998.

Englander, David, ed. *A Documentary History of Jewish Immigrants in Britain 1840–1920.* Leicester: Leicester University Press, 1994.

Ermasheva, M.E., ed. *S.M. Stepniak-Kravchinskii v londonskoi emigratsii.* (S.M. Stepniak-Kravchinskii in London Emigration). Moscow: Nauka, 1968.

E.T. (Jessie Chambers Wood). *D.H. Lawrence: A Personal Record.* Second Edition. London: Frank Cass & Co, 1936.

E.T. (Jessie Chambers Wood). *D.H. Lawrence: A Personal Record.* New York: Knight Publications, 1936.

*Evreiskaia entsiklopediia: svod znanii o evreistve i ego kulture v proshlom i nastoiashchem.* (Jewish Encyclopedia: A Code of Knowledge about Jews, Their Past and Present Culture). Sankt Peterburg: Obshchestvo dlia nauchnykh evreiskikh izdanii i izd-vo Brokgauz-Efron, 1906.

Evtushok, Mikola. *Ostropil': Kraeznavchii naris* (Ostropol: Study of the Region). Zhitomir: Lenok, 1992.

Farbman, Michael S. *After Lenin: The New Phase in Russia* (London: Leonard Parsons, 1924.

– *Bolshevism in Retreat.* London: W. Collins Sons and Co, 1923.

– *Russia and the Struggle for Peace.* London: George Allen & Unwin, 1918.

Feinstein, Elaine. *Lawrence and the Women: The Intimate Life of D.H. Lawrence.* New York, Harper Collins, 1993.

Finestein, Israel. *Anglo-Jewry in Changing Times.* London: Valentin Mitchell, 1999.

Forbes, Nevill. *Russian Grammar.* Oxford: Clarendon Press, 1917.

– *Third Russian Book: Extracts from Aksakov, Grigorovich, Herzen, Saltykov.* Oxford: Clarendon Press, 1917.

Foster, Joseph. *D.H. Lawrence in Taos.* Albuquerque: University of New Mexico, 1972.

Freud, Sigmund. *The Standard Edition of the Complete Psychological Works of Sigmund Freud, Vol. I (1886–1899: Pre-Psycho-Analytic Publications and Unpublished Drafts).* Trans. and ed. James Strachey. London: The Hogarth Press, 1953.

– *Three Essays on the Theory of Sexuality.* Trans. and ed. James Strachey. London: Chatto and Windus, 1974.

Fromm, Gloria G. *Dorothy Richardson.* Chicago: University Press of Illinois, 1977.

Garafola, Lynn. *Diaghilev's Ballets Russes.* New York: Oxford University Press, 1989.

Garnett, Richard. *Constance Garnett: A Heroic Life.* London: Sinclair-Stevenson, 1991.

Gerhardi, William. *Anton Chehov: A Critical Study.* London: Richard Cobden-Sanderson, 1923.

Gerhardie, William. *Memoirs of a Polyglot: The Autobiography of William Gerhardie*. New York: St Martin's Press, 1973.

Gertler, Luke. "Memories of My Father." *Mark Gertler: The Early and the Late Years*. London: Ben Uri Art Gallery, 1982.

Gertler, Mark. *Mark Gertler. British Artists of To-Day*. No 1. London: The Fleuron, 1925.

– *A New Perspective*. Catalogue of an exhibit. The London Jewish Museum of Art and Ben Uri Gallery. 2002.

– *Selected Letters*. Ed. Noel Carrington. London: Rupert Hart-Davis, 1965.

Gilbert, Martin. *The First World War: A Complete History*. New York: Henry Holt, 1994.

Gillespie, Diane F., ed. *The Multiple Muses of Virginia Woolf*. Columbia: University of Missouri Press, 1993.

Goldenveizer, A.B. *Talks with Tolstoi*. Trans. S.S. Koteliansky and Virginia Woolf. London: The Hogarth Press, 1923.

Goldring, Douglas. *Life Interests*. London: MacDonald, 1948.

Gorky [Gorki], Maxim. *Fragments from My Diary*. Trans. Moura Budberg. Harmondsworth: Penguin, 1975.

– *Reminiscences of Anton Chekhov*. Trans. S.S. Koteliansky and Leonard Woolf. New York: B. W. Huebsch, 1921.

– *Reminiscences of Leo Nicolayevich Tolstoi*. Trans. S.S. Koteliansky and Leonard Woolf. London: The Hogarth Press, 1920.

– *Reminiscences of Leonid Andreyev*. Trans. S.S. Koteliansky and Katherine Mansfield. London: William Heinemann, 1931.

– *Reminiscences of Tolstoi, Chekhov, and Andreev*. Trans. S.S. Koteliansky and Leonard Woolf. London: The Hogarth Press, 1934.

Gransden, K. W. "Rananim: D.H. Lawrence's Letters to S.S. Koteliansky." *Twentieth Century* CLIX (January 1956).

Gray, Cecil. *Musical Chairs or Between Two Stools*. London: The Hogarth Press, 1985.

Guberman, Sidney. *Frank Stella: An Illustrated Biography*. New York: Rizzoli, 1995.

Harrison, Jane Ellen. *Aspects, Aorists and the Classical Tripos*. Cambridge: Cambridge University Press, 1919.

– and Hope Mirrless, *The Book of the Bear, Being Twenty-One Tales Newly Translated from the Russian*. London: Nonesuch Press, 1926.

– *Reminiscences of a Student's Life*. London: The Hogarth Press, 1925.

– *Russia and the Russian Verb: A Contribution to the Psychology of the Russian People*. Cambridge: W. Heffer and Sons, 1915.

Haultain, Arnold. "England's Plight: A Returned Exile's Impressions." *The Nineteenth Century and After* (August 1911).

Hergesheimer, Joseph. *Hugh Walpole: An Appreciation*. New York: George H. Doran Company, 1919.

Hignett, Sean. *Brett: From Bloomsbury to New Mexico, a Biography*. New York: Franklin Watts, 1983.

Hippius [Gippius], Zinaida. *The Green Ring: A Play in Four Acts*. Trans. S.S. Koteliansky. London: C.W. Daniel, Ltd, 1920.

– *Sobranie sochinenii* (Collected Works). 9 vols. Moscow: Russkaia kniga, 2001.

Hoffman, Eva. *Shtetl: The Life and Death of a Small Town and the World of Polish Jews*. Boston: Houghton Mifflin Company, 1997.

Holmes, Colin. *Anti-Semitism in British Society, 1876–1939*. London: Edward Arnold, 1979.

Holroyd, Michael. *Lytton Strachey, a Critical Biography: The Years of Achievement, 1910–1932*. New York: Holt, Rinehart and Winston, 1968.

Hunczak, Taras, ed. *The Ukraine, 1917–1921: A Study in Revolution*. Cambridge, MA: Harvard University Press, 1977.

Huntington, Chapin W. *The Homesick Million: Russia-out-of-Russia*. Boston: The Stratford Company, 1933.

Huxley, Aldous. *Letters of Aldous Huxley*. Ed. Grover Smith. London: Chatto and Windus, 1969.

– *Selected Letters of Aldous Huxley*. Ed. James Sexton. Chicago: Ivan R. Dee, 2007.

Huxley, Julian. *Memories*. Middlesex: Penguin, 1972.

Huxley, Juliette. *Leaves of the Tulip Tree: Autobiography*. Oxford: Oxford University Press, 1987.

Jackson, Penelope. "Double Portrait: *Katherine Mansfield and S.S. Koteliansky in the Garden*." *Katherine Mansfield Studies* 2 (2010).

Jones, Ernest. *Treatment of the Neuroses: Psychotherapy from Rest Cure to Psychoanalysis*. London: Bailliere, Tindall and Cox, 1920. Reprinted: New York: Schocken Books, 1963.

Kastein, Josef. *Jews in Germany*. Trans. Dorothy Richardson. London: The Cresset Press, 1934.

Kaznina, O.A., and A.N. Nikoliukin, eds. *"Ia bereg pokidal tumannyi Al'biona": Russkie pisateli ob Anglii. 1646–1945* ("I Was Leaving the Foggy Shore of Albion": Russian Writers on England. 1646–1945). Moscow: ROSSPEN, 2001.

Kaznina, Olga. "S.S. Kotelianskii i angliiskie pisateli" (S.S. Koteliansky and English Writers). *Russkie v Anglii: russkaia emigratsiia v kontekste russko-angliiskikh literaturnykh sviazei v pervoi polovine XX veka* (Russians in England: Russian emigration in the context of Russian-English connections in the First Half of the 20th Century). Moscow: Nasledie, 1997.

*Kelly's Kensington, Notting Hill, Brompton & Knightsbridge Directory ("Buff Book" for 1911)*. London: Kelly's Directories, 1911.

Kennedy, Richard. *A Boy at the Hogarth Press*. Harmondsworth: Penguin, 1972.

Kehoe, Elizabeth. *Three American Sisters and the English Aristocratic World into Which They Married*. New York: Atlantic Monthly Press, 2004.

Keynes, John Maynard, and Lydia Lopokova. *Lydia and Maynard: The Letters of John Maynard Keynes and Lydia Lopokova*. Ed. Polly Hill and Richard Keynes. New York: Charles Scribner, 1989.

Kimmel, Eric A. *The Adventures of Hershel of Ostropol*. New York: Holiday House, 1981.

Kingsmill, Hugh. *The Life of D.H. Lawrence.* New York: Dodge, 1938.

Kirkpatrick, B.J. *A Bibliography of Virginia Woolf.* Oxford: Clarendon Press, 1980.

Klier, John D. and Shlomo Lmabroza, eds. *Pogroms: Anti-Jewish Violence in Modern Russian History.* Cambridge: Cambridge University Press, 1992.

Kollontai, Alexandra. *The Autobiography of a Sexually Emancipated Communist Woman.* Trans. Salvator Attanasio. Ed. Iring Fetscher. New York: Heder and Heder, 1971.

Koosis, Abe. *Child of War and Revolution: The Memoirs of Abe Koosis.* Oakland, CA: Sea Urchin Press, 1984.

Koteliansky, Beila. "Two Jewish Stories." *London Mercury and Bookman* 208 (February 1937).

Kuper, Adam. *Incest & Influence: The Private Life of Bourgeois England.* Cambridge, MA: Harvard University Press, 2009.

Kuprin Alexander. *The River of Life and Other Stories.* Trans. S. Koteliansky and J.M. Murry. New York: Freeport, 1916.

Lappin, Linda. *Katherine's Wish.* La Grande, Oregon: Wordcraft of Oregon, 2008.

Lawrence, Ada, and G. Stuart Gelder. *Early Life of D.H. Lawrence.* London: Martin Secker, 1932.

Lawrence, D.H. *Apocalypse.* London: Penguin, 1976.

– *The Complete Short Stories.* Harmondsworth: Penguin, 1976.

– *The Fox.* London: Hesperus Press, 2002.

– *Introductions and Reviews.* Eds N.H. Reeve and John Worthen. Cambridge: Cambridge University Press, 2005.

– *Kangaroo.* London: Penguin Books, 1997.

– *Lady Chatterley's Lover.* New York: Signet, 1959.

– *The Letters of D.H. Lawrence.* Eds James T. Boulton et al. 8 vols. Cambridge: Cambridge University Press, 1979–2000.

– *The Letters of D.H. Lawrence.* Ed. Aldous Huxley. London: William Heinemann, 1932.

– *Letters to Thomas and Adele Seltzer.* Ed. Gerald M. Lacy. Santa Barbara: Black Sparrow Press, 1976.

– *The Rainbow.* New York: Viking, 1961.

– *The Rainbow.* Harmondsworth: Penguin, 1949. (Unabridged).

– *Sons and Lovers.* New York: Penguin, 1976.

– *Paintings.* London: Chaucer Press, 2003.

– *Psychoanalysis and the Unconscious.* New York: Thomas Seltzer, 1921.

– *The Quest for Rananim: D.H. Lawrence's Letters to S.S. Koteliansky, 1914 to 1930.* Ed. George J. Zytaruk. Montreal: McGill-Queen's University Press, 1970.

– *The White Peacock.* Ed. Andrew Robertson. Cambridge: Cambridge University Press, 1987.

– *Women in Love.* Eds David Farmer, Lindeth Vasey, and John Worthen London: Penguin, 1995.

Lawrence, Frieda. *The Memoirs and Correspondence.* Ed. E.W. Tedlock, Jr. New York: Alfred Knopf, 1964.

– *"Not I, But the Wind…": Memoirs of Her Husband.* Toronto: The Macmillan Company, 1934.

Lea, F.A. *The Life of John Middleton Murry.* London: Methuen, 1959.

Lee, Hermione. *Virginia Woolf.* New York: Vintage, 1999.

Leiken, Ezekiel. *The Beilis Transcripts: The Anti-Semitic Trial That Shook the World.* Northvale, NJ: Jason Aronson, 1993.

Lenin, V.I. *Collected Works.* Trans. David Skvirsky and George Hanna. Moscow: Progress, 1963.

Leslie, Anita. *Clare Sheridan: Her Tempestuous Life with Jennie Churchill, Mussoloni, Lenin, Charlie Chaplin, Trotsky, Winston Churchill, and Others.* New York: Doubleday, 1977.

Linden, A. "Prototyp des Pogroms in den achtizer Jahren." *Die Judenpogrome in Rußland.* 2 vols. Cologne and Leipzig: Jüdishe Verlag G.M.B.H., 1910.

Lindermann, Albert S. *The Jews Accused: Three Anti-Semitic Affairs (Dreyfus, Beilis, Frank), 1894–1915.* Cambridge: Cambridge University Press, 1991.

*London's Museum of Jewish Life: An Illustrated Guide.* London: The Jewish Museum, 2002.

Lower, Wendy. *Nazi Empire-Building and the Holocaust in Ukraine.* Chapel Hill: University of North Carolina Press, 2005.

Lucas, Robert. *Frieda Lawrence: The Story of Frieda von Richthofen and D.H. Lawrence.* New York: Viking, 1973.

Luhan, Mabel Dodge. *Lorenzo in Taos.* New York: Alfred Knopf, 1932.

– *Taos and Its Artists.* New York: Duell, Sloan and Pearce, 1947.

Lunacharsky, Anatoly. *Revolutionary Silhouettes.* Trans. and ed. Michael Glenny. New York: Hill and Wang, 1968.

Lynn, Andrea. *Shadow Lovers: The Last Affairs of H.G. Wells.* Boulder, CO: Westview Press, 2001.

MacDougall, Sarah. *Mark Gertler.* London: John Murray, 2002.

Machray, Robert. "The Resiliency of Russia." *The Nineteenth Century and After* (June 1915).

Mackrell, Judith. *The Bloomsbury Ballerina: Lydia Lopokova, Imperial Dancer and Mrs John Maynard Keynes.* London: Weidenfeld & Nicolson, 2008.

Maddox, Brenda. *D.H. Lawrence: The Story of a Marriage.* New York: Norton, 1996.

Manoukhin, Ivan. "The Treatment of Infectious Disease by Leucocytolysis Produced by Rontgenisation of the Spleen." *Lancet,* 2 April 1921.

– "Vospominaniia" (Memoirs). *Novyi zhurnal* 54 (1958).

Mansfield, Katherine. *The Collected Letters of Katherine Mansfield.* Eds Vincent O'Sullivan and Margaret Scott. 5 vols. Oxford: Clarendon Press, 1984–1996.

– *Journal of Katherine Mansfield.* Ed. J. Middleton Murry. New York: Alfred Knopf, 1933.

– *In a German Pension.* London: Hesperus Press, 2003.

– *The Katherine Mansfield Notebooks: Complete Edition.* Ed. Margaret Scott. 2 vols. Minneapolis: University of Minnesota Press, 2002.

– *The Letters of Katherine Mansfield.* Ed. John Middleton Murry. 2 vols. New York: Alfred Knopf, 1930.

– *Letters between Katherine Mansfield and John Middleton Murry.* Ed. Cherry A. Hankin. New York: New Amsterdam Books, 1991.

– *Katherine Mansfield's Letters to John Middleton Murry: 1913–1922.* Ed. John Middleton Murry. London: Constable & Co, 1951.

– *New Zealand Stories*. Selected by Vincent O'Sullivan. Oxford: Oxford University Press, 1997.

– *Stories*. Selected by Elizabeth Bowen. New York: Alfred Knopf, 1956.

Mantz, Ruth Elvish. "In Consequence: Katherine and Kot." *Adam International Review* 370–375 (1972–73).

– and J. Middleton Murry. *The Life of Katherine Mansfield*. New York: Haskell House, 1975.

Marcosson, Isaac F., and Daniel Frohman. *Charles Frohman: Manager and Man*. New York and London: Harper & Brothers, 1916.

Martiniuk, Victoriia. *Skromnye obeliski* (Modest Gravestones). Starokonstantinov: Drugii Vseukrainskii konkurs uchniv'skikh naukovikh robit "Slidami istorii" (Second All-Ukrainian Competiton of Students' Research Papers on "Tracing History"), 2000

Meisel, Perry and Walter Kendrick, eds. *Bloomsbury/Freud: The Letters of James and Alix Strachey, 1924–1925*. New York: Norton, 1990.

Metcalf, Priscilla. *James Knowles: Victorian Editor and Architect*. Oxford: Clarendon Press, 1980.

Meyers, Jeffrey. *D.H. Lawrence: A Biography*. New York: Vintage, 1992.

– *Katherine Mansfield: A Biography*. New York: New Directions, 1978.

Merrild, Knud. *A Poet and Two Painters: A Memoir of D.H. Lawrence*. New York: Viking, 1939.

Millin, Sarah Gertrude. *The Night Is Long*. London: Faber and Faber, 1941.

Mirsky, D.S. *Jane Ellen Harrison and Russia*. Cambridge: Heffer and Sons, 1930.

Moore, Harry T. *The Intelligent Heart: The Story of D.H. Lawrence*. New York: Farrar, Straus and Young, 1954.

– and Dale B. Montague. *Frieda Lawrence and Her Circle: Letters from, to, and about Frieda Lawrence*. London: MacMillan, 1981.

Moore, James. *Gurdjieff: A Biography*. Shaftesbury, Dorset: Element Books, 1999.

– *Gurdjieff and Mansfield*. London: Routledge & Kegan, 1980.

Moorehead, Caroline. *Sidney Bernstein, A Biography*. London: Jonathan Cape, 1984.

Morrell, Ottoline, *Dear Lady Ginger: An Exchange of Letters Between Lady Ottoline Morrell and D'Arcy Cresswell (Together with Ottoline Morrell's Essay on Katherine Mansfield)*. Ed. Helen Shaw. London: Century Publishing, 1983.

– *Memoirs of Lady Ottoline Morrell: A Study in Friendship, 1873–1915*. Ed. Robert Gathorne-Hardy. New York: Alfred Knopf, 1964.

– *Ottoline at Garsington: Memoirs of Lady Ottoline Morrell 1915–1918*. Ed. Robert Gathorne-Hardy. London: Faber and Faber, 1974.

Murav, Harriet. *Identity Theft: The Jew in Imperial Russia and the Case of Avraam Uri Kovner*. Stanford: Stanford University Press, 2003.

Murray, Nicholas. *Aldous Huxley: An English Intellectual*. London: Little, Brown, 2002.

Murry, John Middleton. *Between Two Worlds: The Autobiography*. New York: J. Messner, 1936.

– *D.H. Lawrence: Son of Woman*. London: Jonathan Cape, 1931.

– *Reminiscences of D.H. Lawrence*. London: Jonathan Cape, 1933.

Nabokoff, Constantin. *The Ordeal of a Diplomat.* London: Duckworth and Company, 1921.

Nathan, Benjamin. *Beyond the Pale: The Jewish Encounter with Late Imperial Russia.* Berkeley: University of California Press, 2002.

Nehls, Edward. *D.H. Lawrence: A Composite Biography.* 2 vols. Madison: The University of Wisconsin Press, 1957.

Neugroschel, Joachim. *The Dybbuk and the Yiddish Imagination: A Haunted Reader.* Syracuse: Syracuse University Press, 2000.

Nevinson, C.R.W. *Paint and Prejudice.* London: Methuen, 1937.

Nicholson, Virginia. *Among the Bohemians: Experiments in Living 1900–1939.* London: William Morrow, 2002.

Noble, Joan Russell, ed. *Recollections of Virginia Woolf.* London: Peter Owen, 1972.

Ozick, Cynthia. *Art & Ardor: Essays.* New York: Alfred Knopf, 1983.

Page, Norman, ed. *D.H. Lawrence: Interviews and Recollections.* 2 vols. Totowa, NJ: Barnes and Noble, 1981.

Parker, Dorothy. *Portable Dorothy Parker.* New York: Penguin Books, 1944.

*Parliamentary Borough of Kensington in the Administrative Country of London Index to the Several Polling Districts in the North Division, 1911–12.*

Peters, Margot. *May Sarton: A Biography.* New York: Alfred Knopf, 1997.

Piechotka, Maria and Kazimierz. *Wooden Synagogues.* Warsaw: Arkady, 1959.

Pope, Arthur Upham. *Maxim Litvinoff.* New York: L.B. Fischer, 1943.

*Post Office London Directory.* London: Kelly's Directories, 1909–1913.

*Post Office London Directory for 1914.* London: Kelly's Directories, 1914.

Powell, Dilys. *Descent from Parnassus.* London: The Cresset Press, 1934.

– "Mr S.S. Koteliansky. Obituary." *Times* (London), 27 January, 1955.

Pyle, Hilary. *James Stephens: His Work and an Account of His Life.* London: Routledge and Kegan Paul, 1965.

Reinhold, Natalya. "Virginia Woolf's Russian Voyage Out." *Woolf Studies Annual* 9 (2003).

Reynolds, Marjorie. *"Everything You Do Is a Portrait of Yourself": A Biography of Dorothy Kay.* Privately published by Alec Marjorie Reynolds, Rosebank, South Africa, 1989.

Richardson, Dorothy. *Clear Horizon.* London: J.M. Dent & Sons and The Cresset Press, 1935.

Richardson, Dorothy. *Windows on Modernism: Selected Letters of Dorothy Richardson.* Ed. Gloria G. Fromm. Athens: The University of Georgia Press, 1995.

Rickword, Edgell and Douglas Garman, eds. *The Calendar of Modern Letters* (March 1925–July 1927). London: Frank Cass & Co., 1966.

Roberts, Warren. *A Bibliography of D.H. Lawrence.* London: Hart Davis, 1963.

Robinson, Annabel. *The Life and Work of Jane Ellen Harrison.* Oxford: Oxford University Press, 2002.

Robinson, Harlow. *The Last Impresario: The Life, Times, and Legacy of Sol Hurok.* New York: Viking, 1994.

Rochelson, Meri-Jane. *A Jew in the Public Arena: The Career of Israel Zangwill.* Detroit: Wayne State University Press, 2008.

Rogatchevski, Andrei. "Iz istorii Rossiisko-evreiskoi emigratsii v Velikobritanii: Novye dannye o B.I. El'kine i S.S. Kotelianskom" (From the History of the Russian-Jewish Emigration in Great Britain: New Information about B.I. Elkin and S.S. Koteliansky), *The Russian Emigration: Literature, History, Chronicle of Films – Materials from the International Conference (Talinn, September 12–14, 2002)*. Eds V. Khazan, I. Belobrovtseva, S. Dotsenko. Jerusalem and Tallinn: The Hebrew University of Jerusalem and the Tallinn Pedagogical University, 2002.

– "Samuel Koteliansky and the Bloomsbury Circle (Roger Fry, E.M. Forster, Mr and Mrs John Maynard Keynes and the Woolfs)." *Forum for Modern Language Studies* 4 (October 2000).

Romain, Jonathan A. *The Jews of England: A Portrait of Anglo-Jewry through Original Sources and Illustrations.* London: Jewish Chronicle Publications, 1988.

Rozanov, V.V. *Fallen Leaves*. Trans. S.S. Koteliansky. London: Mandrake Press, 1929.

– *Solitaria*. Trans. S.S. Koteliansky. London: Wishart, 1927.

Rubenstein, Roberta. *Virginia Woolf and the Russian Point of View*. New York: Palgrave Macmillan, 2009.

Rudnick, Lois Palken. *Mabel Dodge Luhan: New Woman, New Worlds*. Albuquerque: University of New Mexico, 1984.

Rudnytsky, Ivan L., ed. *Rethinking Ukrainian History*. Edmonton: The Canadian Institute of Ukrainian Studies. University of Alberta, 1981.

Russell, Bertrand. *The Autobiography*. Boston: Little Brown, 1967.

Russell, C., and H.S. Lewis. *Jew in London: A Study of Racial Character and Present-Day Conditions*. New York: Thomas Y. Crowell & Co, 1901.

*Russian Short Stories*. Selected and trans. S.S. Koteliansky. London: Penguin, 1941.

Safran, Gabriella. *Rewriting the Jew: Assimilation Narratives in the Russian Empire*. Stanford: Stanford University Press, 2000.

– *Wandering Soul: The Dybbuk's Creator, S. An-sky*. Cambridge, MA: Harvard University Press, 2010.

– and Steven J. Zipperstein, eds. *The Worlds of S. An-sky: A Russian Jewish Intellectual at the Turn of the Century*. Stanford: Stanford University Press, 2006.

Sagar, Keith. *The Life of D.H. Lawrence*. New York: Pantheon Books, 1980.

Salaman, Esther. *A Collection of Moments: A Study of Involuntary Memories*. London: Longman, 1970.

– *The Fertile Plain*. New York: Abelard-Schuman, 1956.

– *Two Silver Roubles*. London: Macmillan, 1932.

Sarton, May. *Dear Juliette: Letters of May Sarton to Juliette Huxley*. Ed. Susan Sherman. New York: Norton, 1999.

– *I Knew a Phoenix: Sketches for an Autobiography*. New York: Norton, 1954.

– *Selected Letters, 1916–1954*. Ed. Susan Sherman. New York: Norton, 1997.

– *Selected Letters, 1955–1995*. Ed. Susan Sherman. New York: Norton, 2002.

– *A World of Light: Portraits and Celebration*. New York: Norton, 1988.

Schneider, Elisabeth. "Katherine Mansfield and Chekhov." *Modern Language Notes* (June 1935).

Sergeeva, Irina. "Etnograficheskie ekspeditsii Semena An-skogo v dokumentakh" (Ethno-graphic Expeditions of Semen An-sky in Documents). *Skidnu svit* 3 (2003).

Seymour, Miranda. *Ottoline Morrell: Life on the Grand Scale.* London: Hodder and Stoughton, 1993.

Sheridan, Clare. *Mayfair to Moscow: Clare Sheridan's Diary.* New York, Boni and Liveright, 1921.

– *Naked Truth.* New York: Harper and Brothers, 1928.

Shestov, Leo. *All Things Are Possible.* Trans. S.S. Koteliansky. New York: Robert M. McBride & Co, 1920.

– *Anton Tchekhov and Other Essays.* Trans. S.S. Koteliansky. London: Mauncel, 1916.

Shire, Michael Rabbi Dr, ed. *The Illuminated Haggadah: Featuring Medieval Illuminations from the Hagaddah Collection of the British Library.* London: Frances Lincoln, 1997.

Singer, Isidor, ed. *The Jewish Encyclopedia.* New York: Funk and Wagnalls, 1901–06.

Smith, David C. *H.G. Wells: Desperately Mortal, a Biography.* New Haven: Yale University Press, 1986.

Sohn, David. *The Activities of the Bialystoker Community in America : A Historical Outline.* New York: Bialystoker Center, 1934.

Spector, Shmuel. *The Holocaust of Volhynian Jews, 1941–1944.* Jerusalem: Yad Vashem, 1990.

Spender, Stephen. *The Destructive Element: A Study of Modern Writers and Beliefs.* London: Jonathan Cape, 1935.

– ed. *D.H. Lawrence: Novelist, Poet Prophet.* New York: Harper & Row, 1973.

– *Journals 1939–1983.* Ed. John Goldsmith. London: Faber and Faber, 1985.

Spiller G[ustav], ed. *Papers on Inter-Racial Problems Communicated to the First Universal Races Congress Held at The University of London, July 26–29, 1911.* London: P.S. King & Son, 1911.

Stead, S.K. *Mansfield: A Novel.* London: Haevill Press, 2004.

Stella, Frank. *Polish Wooden Synagogues: Constructions from the 1970s.* New York: The Jewish Museum, 1983.

Stephens, James. *Collected Poems.* London: Macmillan, 1954.

– *Kings and the Moon.* New York: Macmillan, 1938.

– *Letters of James Stephens.* Ed. Richard J. Finneran. New York: Macmillan, 1974.

Stepniak, Sergei. *The Career of a Nihilist.* New York: Harpers, 1889.

– *Underground Russia: Revolutionary Profiles and Sketches from Life.* New York: Charles Scribner's Son, 1883.

Stewart, Jessie. *Jane Ellen Harrison: A Portrait from Letters.* London: The Merlin Press, 1959.

Stoye, Catherine. "My Mother – Marjorie Craig Wells." *The Wellsian* 21 (Winter 1998).

Subtelny, Orest. *Ukraine: A History.* Toronto: University of Toronto Press, 1994.

Taylor, Paul Beekman. *Gurdjieff and Orage: Brothers in Elysium.* York Beach, ME: Weiser Books, 2001.

Teodorovich, N.I. *Gorod Starokonstantinov Volynskoi gubernii* (The City of Starokonstanti-nov of Volhynia District). Pochev, 1890.

Tobias, Henry J. *The Jewish BUND in Russia from Its Origins to 1905.* Stanford: Stanford University Press, 1972.

Tolstaya, Sofiya. *The Autobiography of Countess Tolstoy*. Trans. S.S. Koteliansky and Leonard Woolf. New York: Huebsch, 1922.

Tolstoy [Tolstoi], Leo. *Notes of a Madman and Other Stories*. Trans. S.S. Koteliansky. London: Todd Publishing (Polybooks), 1943.

– and Paul Biriukov, *Tolstoi's Love Letters: With a Study on the Autobiographical Elements in Tolstoi's Work*. Trans. S.S. Koteliansky and Virginia Woolf. London: The Hogarth Press, 1923.

Tomalin, Claire. *Katherine Mansfield: A Secret Life*. New York: St Martin's, 1987.

Troinitskii, N.A., ed. *Pervaia vseobshchaia perepis' naseleniia Rossiiskoi imperii, 1897 g.* (The First Comprehensive Census of the Russian Empire, 1897). St Petersburg: Izd. Tsentralnago statisticheskago komiteta Ministerstva Vnutrennikh Del (Ministry of Internal Affairs), 1899–1905.

Trotsky, Leon. *Lenin*. New York: Garden City Books, 1959.

Ul'ankina, T.I. "Etot neizvestnyi izvestnyi Manukhin" (That Unknown but Famous Manukhin). *Voprosy istorii, estestvoznania i tekhniki* 3 (1993).

Vainshel'bom, Isaak. *Starokontantinovskie novelly* (Starokonstantinov Tales). Kamenetsk-Podolskii: Abetka Nova, 2002.

Vallentin, Antonina. *H.G. Wells: Prophet of Our Day*. New York: The John Day Company, 1950.

Vinogradoff, Julian. *Lady Ottoline's Album: Snapshots and Portraits of Her Famous Contemporaries (and of Herself), Photographed for the Most Part by Lady Ottoline Morrell*. New York: Alfred Knopf, 1976.

*Vsia Rossiia: Russkaia kniga promyshlennosti, torgovli, selskogo khoziaistva i administratsii* (All-Russia's Book of Industry, Trade, Agriculture, and Administration). St Petersburg: Izd. A.S. Suvorina, 1895.

Walpole, Hugh. *The Dark Forest*. New York: George H. Doran Company, 1916.

– *The Secret City: A Novel in Three Parts*. New York: George H. Doran Company, 1919.

Waters, Frank. *Leon Gaspard*. Revised edition. Fenn Galleries. Flagstaff: Northland Press, 1981.

Wells, H.G. *Experiment in Autobiography: Discoveries and Conclusions of a Very Ordinary Brain (since 1866)*. New York: Macmillan, 1934.

– *H.G. Wells in Love: Postscript to An Experiment in Autobiography*. Ed. G.P. Wells. Boston: Little, Brown and Company, 1984.

– *The Outline of History: Being a Plain History of Life and Mankind*. New York: Doubleday, 1961.

– *Russia in the Shadows*. New York: George H. Doran, 1921.

Wesslau, Werner. *Der Pessimismus bei D.H. Lawrence*. Greifswald: Universitäts Greifswald, 1931.

West, Anthony. *H.G. Wells*. London: Hitchinson, 1984.

West, Rebecca. *D.H. Lawrence*. London: Martin Secker, 1930.

Willis J.H. Jr. *Leonard and Virginia Woolf as Publishers: The Hogarth Press 1917–1941*. Charlottesville: University of Virginia, 1992.

Winder, Robert. *Bloody Foreigners: The Story of Immigration to Britain.* London: Little Brown, 2004.

Woodeson, John. *Mark Gertler: Biography of a Painter, 1891–1939.* London: Sidgwick & Jackson, 1972.

Woolf, Leonard. *Beginning Again: Autobiography of the Years 1911 to 1918.* New York: Harcourt Brace Jovanovich, 1963.

– *Downhill All the Way: Autobiography of the Years 1919 to 1939.* New York: Harcourt Brace Jovanovich, 1967.

– *The Journey Not the Arrival Matters: Autobiography of the Years 1939–1969.* New York: Harcourt Brace Jovanovich, 1969.

– "Kot." *The New Statesman and Nation,* 5 February, 1955.

– *Letters of Leonard Woolf.* Ed. Frederick Spotts. New York: Harcourt Brace Jovanovich, 1989.

– *Sowing: An Autobiography of the Years 1880 to 1904.* New York: Harcourt, Brace & Company, 1960.

– "Three Jews." *Virginia Woolf Bulletin* 5 (September 2000).

Woolf, Virginia. *The Captain's Death Bed and Other Essays.* New York: Harcourt, 1950.

– *Carlyle House and Other Sketches.* London: Hesperus Press, 2003.

– *Common Reader.* New York: Harcourt Brace Jovanovich, 1925.

– *The Death of the Moth and Other Essays.* New York: Harcourt, 1970.

– *The Diary of Virginia Woolf.* Ed. Anne Olivier Bell. 5 vols. New York: Harcourt Brace Jovanovich, 1977–1984.

– *The Letters of Virginia Woolf.* Eds Nigel Nicolson and Joanne Trautmann. 6 vols. New York: Harcourt Brace Jovanovich, 1975–1980.

Zipperstein Steven J., *Imagining Russian Jewry: Memory, History, Identity.* Seattle: University of Washington Press, 1999.

Zytaruk, George. "The Collected Letters of Jessie Chambers." *The D.H. Lawrence Review* 1 and 2 (Spring and Summer 1979).

– *D.H. Lawrence's Response to Russian Literature.* The Hague: Mouton, 1971.

– "Dorothy Brett's Letters to S.S. Koteliansky." *The D.H. Lawrence Review* 3 (Fall 1974).

– "The Phallic Vision: D.H. Lawrence and V.V. Rozanov." *Comparative Literature Studies* 3 (1967).

## LIBRARY ARCHIVES

Dorothy Brett Collection. Harry Ransom Humanities Research Center, The University of Texas at Austin.

Dorothy Brett Papers, 1939–1986. General Library, Center for Southwest Research, The University of New Mexico.

Catherine Carswell Collection. Manuscript and Special Collections, University of Nottingham.

Ralph Hodgson Papers. General Collection, Beinecke Rare Book and Manuscript Library, Yale University.

Hogarth Press Files. Special Collections, University of Reading Library.

Mary Hutchinson Papers. Harry Ransom Humanities Research Center, The University of Texas at Austin.

Beila Koteliansky Papers. Archive of the Jewish National and University Library at The Hebrew University of Jerusalem.

S.S. Koteliansky Papers. Manuscript Collections and Archives, British Library.

D.H. Lawrence Collection. Harry Ransom Humanities Research Center, The University of Texas at Austin.

D.H. Lawrence Collection. Manuscript and Special Collections, University of Nottingham.

Katherine Mansfield Collection. The Alexander Turnbull Library, Wellington, New Zealand.

Lady Ottoline Morrell Collection. Harry Ransom Humanities Research Center, The University of Texas at Austin.

May Sarton Papers, 1920–1995. Henry W. and Albert A. Berg Collection of English and American Literature, The New York Public Library.

Sydney Schiff Papers. Manuscript Collections and Archives, British Library.

Sydney Waterlow Papers. The Alexander Turnbull Library, Wellington, New Zealand.

H.G. Wells Collection. Rare Book and Special Collections Library, University of Illinois at Urbana-Champaign.

Leonard Woolf Papers. Special Collections, The University of Sussex Library.

Leonard and Virginia Woolf Library. Rare Books, Manuscripts, Archives and Special Collections, Washington State University Libraries.

PRIVATE ARCHIVES

Honourable Bridget Campbell (Lady Glenavy's granddaughter), Ibiza, Spain
Jackie Freedman (Polly Smith's daughter), Montreal, Canada
Luke Gertler (Mark Gertler's son), London, UK
Ivor Powell (Dilys Powell's nephew), London, UK
Catherine Stoye (Marjorie Wells's daughter), Oxford, UK
Sonny Surkes (Moishel Koteliansky's grandson), Montreal, Canada
Dr Nina Wedderburn (Esther Salaman's daughter), London, UK
Dr George Zytaruk, North Bay, Canada.

INTERVIEWS

Jackie Freedman, Montreal – 24, 26, 28 April 2004
Luke Gertler, London – 14 July 2003

Juliette Huxley, London (George Zytaruk) – 5 June 1972
Martin Packman, Washington, D.C. – 7 November 2003
Anatoly Polonsky, Ostropol – 2, 3 July 2006
Esther Salaman, London (George Zytaruk) – 22 June 1967
Nadia Slow, London – 26, 27 July 2003
Pauline Smith, Montreal (George Zytaruk) – 10 August 1968
Sharon Smith, Montreal – 24, 28 April 2004
Catherine Stoye, Oxford – 4 July 2003
Sonny Surkes, Montreal – 27 April 2004
Nina Wedderburn, London – 26 July 2003
Harry Wexler, Philadelphia (Natalie Wexler) – 6 September 1991.

# INDEX

*The Adelphi*, 55, 118, 163, 165, 169, 182, 229, 309, 316, 318; Kot's role in creation of, 142–4; Lawrence's reaction to, 145–6, 148, 158–9; Murry's editorship of, 142–6, 152–7; Philip Tomlinson's argument with Kot over, 152–8

Akhmatova, Anna, 137

Alexander, Peter F., 44

Alexeieff, Alexander, 209

Alpers, Antony, 67, 288, 327

Anderson, William, 94

Andreyev, Leonid, 118, 131, 141, 145, 152, 159, 218

Annan, (Sir) Noel, 271

Anrep, Boris, 57–8

Ansky, S., 252–5; *The Dybbuk*, 252, 254–6, 310. *See also* Habima Players

anti-Semitism: "Beilis Affair," 39–40, 50, 83, 168, 175; blood libel 39, 41–2, 175–6; among Bloomsbury, 42–5, 56; in England, 41–9, 78, 151, 261, 271; Eder's experience with, 43; Gertler's experience with, 45–6, 82–5, 210, 246, 261; D.H. Lawrence and, 6, 47, 53–4, 59–60, 83, 87–8, 91, 97–8, 159–60, 173–4, 180; Frieda Lawrence and, 53–4, 345n69; Rozanov and, 175–8; in Russia and Ukraine, 27, 32–40, 100–1, 168, 268–71, 337n6, 340n32; Schiff's experience with, 166–7; Seltzer's experience with, 159–60; Lytton Strachey and, 43–4; Walpole and, 111; H.G. Wells and, 47, 109, 231–2; Leonard Woolf's experience with, 42–5;

Virginia Woolf and, 43–4, 140. *See also* Jews

Asimov, Isaac, 339n31

Asquith, (Lady) Cynthia, 52, 76, 80, 213

Babel, Isaac, 38, 341n49, 359n79

Bagenal, Barbara, 56

Baker, Ida, 115–17, 120–1, 277, 313; Koteliansky's letters to, 59, 151, 162, 171, 218, 241, 244, 287, 288

Ballets Russes, 4–6, 56–8, 78, 229, 303, 307, 335n7. *See also* Diaghilev

Balston, Thomas, 260

Balzac, 258

Bell, Clive, 140, 161

Bell, Quentin, 43

Bell, Vanessa (née Stephen), 43, 396n73

Bely, Andrei, 137

Bennett, Arnold, 94

Berberova, Nina, 108

Berlin, (Sir) Isaiah, 328, 408n4

Bernstein, Sidney, 6, 252, 263, 264, 310, 313

Biryukov, Paul, 139

Blavatsky, Helena, 118–19

Bloomsbury: and Ballets Russes, 4–6, 56–8, 78; and Jews, 6–7, 43–4, 56, 66; and Russian literature in translation 4–6, 78, 132–4

Blunt, Anthony, 404n74

Boas, Franz, 48

Brett, Dorothy, 51, 67, 113, 114, 148, 150, 161–2, 164, 301, 313, 329, 330; friendship with Gertler, 82, 90; intimacy with Murry, 146,